Martin Sixsmith was born in Cheshire and educated at Oxford, Harvard, in Leningrad and at the Sorbonne. From 1980 to 1997 he worked for the BBC, as the Corporation's correspondent in Moscow, Washington, Brussels, Geneva and Warsaw. From 1997 to 2002 he worked for the British government as director of communications. His previous factual books are *Putin's Oil: The Yukos Affair and the Struggle for Russia*, *The Litvinenko File* and *Moscow Coup: The Death of the Soviet System*. His novels include *The Lost Child of Philomena Lee*, *I Heard Lenin Laugh* and *Spin*.

RUSSIA

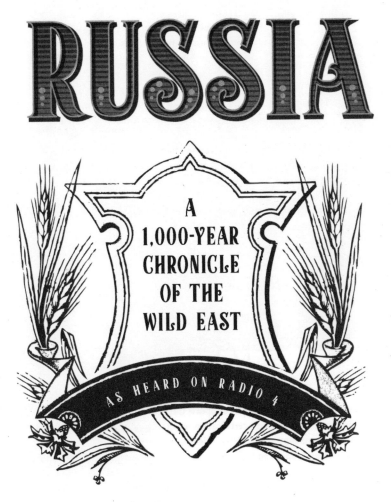

A
1,000-YEAR
CHRONICLE
OF THE
WILD EAST

AS HEARD ON RADIO 4

MARTIN SIXSMITH

BBC
BOOKS

This book is published to accompany the series entitled *Russia*,
first broadcast on BBCC Radio 4 in 2011.

Executive Producer: Jane Ellison

3 5 7 9 10 8 6 4 2

Published in 2011 by BBC Books, an imprint of Ebury Publishing.
A Random House Group Company

The Random House Group Limited Reg. No. 954009

Addresses for companies within the Random House Group can be found at
www.randomhouse.co.uk

A CIP catalogue record for this book is available from the British Library.

ISBN 978 1 84 990072 0

MIX

rom
sources
16897

Forest Stewardship Council® (FSC®),
nisation. All our titles that are printed
er carry the FSC® logo. Our paper
andomhouse.co.uk/environment

lbert DePetrillo
e McArthur
/e Tribe
Picture researcher: Sarah Hopper
Maps: Encompass Graphics
Production: Antony Heller

Designed and set by seagulls.net
Colour origination by: White Quill Press, Ltd
Printed and bound in the UK by Clays of St Ives PLC

To buy books by your favourite authors and register for offers, visit www.randomhouse.co.uk

CONTENTS

PREFACE AND ACKNOWLEDGEMENTS

'Russia is no longer to be gazed at as a distant, glimmering star,' George Macartney wrote in 1767, 'but as a great planet that has obtruded itself into our system, whose motions must powerfully affect those of every other orb.' Russia has that effect. A lifetime studying, working in and writing about the great planet has dragged me into her orbit.

I am grateful to the production team who worked with me on the BBC series *Russia: The Wild East* – Adam and Anna Fowler, Richard Bannerman and Neil Gardner. I wish to thank Geoffrey Hosking for reading the manuscript, and Don Murray for curbing the worst infelicities of my writing. I am indebted to my indefatigable and brilliant researcher, who also happens to be my son, Daniel Sixsmith. And I thank my wife Mary for putting up with a husband who has been annoyingly absent (mainly in the fifteenth century).

Thanks are due to Continuum for permission to quote from my book *Putin's Oil*, to Macmillan for the use of material from *The Litvinenko File* and to Simon & Schuster for the passages from *Moscow Coup*.

London, March 2011

INTRODUCTION

In the wake of one of Russia's most turbulent upheavals, the Decembrist Revolt of 1825, the poet Fedor Tyutchev wrote:

> ... Bless'd is he who visited this world
> In its moments of unruly destiny!
> For he was summoned by the gods
> To partake in their revels;
> A witness to their mighty deeds,
> Admitted to their inmost thoughts,
> He drinks immortal life
> From heaven's very chalice!

On the morning of Monday 19 August 1991 I felt I knew what he meant.

As BBC Television's Moscow Correspondent for the preceding three years, I had sensed something was in the offing, but the news that woke me that morning took my breath away. State radio and television were broadcasting Neanderthal Communist propaganda that hadn't been heard in Moscow for several years, accusing Soviet president Mikhail Gorbachev's reformist regime of undermining the Soviet Union and exercising power in the service of 'interests hostile to the Soviet people'. It was time, said the announcer, 'to restore the pride and might of the USSR'. The broadcast concluded: 'For reasons of ill health, Mikhail Gorbachev is unable to continue his duties ... a State Emergency committee has taken over.'

A hardline coup against the reforming Soviet president Gorbachev was under way. I remember speeding through the streets and seeing columns of tanks descending the broad avenues towards the Kremlin. They had been sent by the men who had put Gorbachev under arrest and were now running the country. It was an unsettling scene.

But in the days that followed ordinary Russians stood in the way of the tanks; some of them were shot or crushed to death for their determination to defend democracy. I was there when the Russian president Boris Yeltsin, liberalism's last champion now Gorbachev was in captivity, climbed on the back of a tank to dramatise his defiance of the coup. For two days and nights, Yeltsin waited in the Russian White House for the attack to begin. The dramatic events of those August days resolved the confrontation between the forces of reform and hardline autocracy in the Soviet Union. In the face of vociferous public opposition, the hardliners lost their nerve, the coup collapsed and its leaders were arrested.

I was convinced – and said in my reports – that the downfall of the Communist dinosaurs who had mounted the coup, together with the dissolution of the Communist Party after 70 years in power, meant that autocracy was dead in Russia, that centuries of repression would be thrown off and replaced with freedom and democracy. But I was wrong. For the next decade, Russia tried to turn itself into a Western-style market democracy but slid instead into runaway inflation, ethnic violence and chaos. The following years, from 2000 onwards, saw that process largely reversed. The country became stable and relatively prosperous, but democracy and freedom again took second place to the demands of the state. The spectre of autocracy was again haunting Russia.

Back in 1991, I should probably have known better. In the grip of Moscow's euphoria, I'd forgotten the lesson of history that in Russia attempts at reform are followed by a return to autocracy – unchecked power concentrated in the hands of a single unaccountable authority. It had happened so often in the past that it was improbable things would be different this time.

It was one thing for me to be wrong, but much more serious was the fact that the leaders of Europe and America were wrong too. They sent clever economists from Harvard to oversee Russia's transition to the market, rejoiced at the defeat of Communism and assumed the problem was solved: from now on, they triumphantly declared, Russia would be like us. If only the West had learned the lessons of history, it might have avoided some of the terrible mistakes it was about to make, mistakes that would darken East–West relations, squander billions of dollars and contribute indirectly to the failure of Russia's liberal experiment.

If we want to understand the processes at work in the last two decades, we need a proper awareness of Russia's thousand-year history. Russia has never really been 'like us', if by that we mean a liberal, market-oriented democracy where the wielders of power are there at the sufferance of the people and can be replaced through a law-governed process.* The Russian model, with the exception of brief, recurrent periods of radical experimentation, has always been the opposite: autocracy places the wielders of power above the law; they rule by divine right, or 'by the dictatorship of the people', but almost always by brute force.

Those who regard Russia as a proto-European nation miss the point. Russia looks both ways: to the democratic, law-governed traditions of the West, but at the same time – and with more of this inherited DNA in her make-up – to the Asiatic forms of governance she imbibed in the early years of her history, what Russians refer to as the *silnaya ruka*, the iron fist of centralised power.**

There is a school of Russian history, labelled path determinism, which says Russia is forever bound to be ruled by the fist of autocracy; that it's in her nature, and Western-style democracy will never work for her. It was a view commonly held by British and American conservatives during the Cold War years and has recently enjoyed a resurgence. That diagnosis is perhaps too categorical, too redolent of the discredited 'historical inevitability' of Hegel and Marx. But I can't help noticing how often it has been articulated over the course of Russian history. From the earliest rulers, Rurik and Oleg, to Ivan the Terrible and Peter the Great, the argument was

---

* I take as given, of course, that democracy as defined here could scarcely be said to exist anywhere in the world between the decline of Athens after 146BC and its shaky re-emergence in seventeenth century Europe.

** If proof were needed of Russians' ingrained identification with the autocratic model, the *Levada Public Opinion Research Center* in Moscow has for the past 20 years carried out an annual poll. To the question 'Does Russia need to be ruled by a *silnaya ruka*?' the average of positive responses has been between 40 and 45 per cent, with an additional 20–30 per cent agreeing that 'there are times at which Russia needs all power concentrated in a single set of hands'.

advanced that Russia was too big and too disorderly ever to be suited to devolved power; only the *silnaya ruka* of centralised autocracy could hold together her centripetal empire and maintain order among her disparate people. The same rationale would be used by the eighteenth- and nineteenth-century tsars, by the Communist regime in the twentieth century and – *mutatis mutandis* – by Vladimir Putin in the twenty-first.

Winston Churchill's exasperated quip about 'a riddle wrapped in a mystery inside an enigma' set the tone for a lazy Western assumption that Russians are too complex even to try to understand. But if we can grasp Russia's history, we can uncover the roots of her sometimes puzzling behaviour. She is a jarring combination of East and West that would trouble her artists, writers, politicians and thinkers for many centuries.

The poet Alexander Blok's agonised questions 'Are we Scythians? – are we Asiatics?' speak of a Russia striving to protect Western cultural values, but rejected by Europe because of her barbarian Eastern nature:

> Oh, yes – we are Scythians! Yes – we are Asiatics,
> With slanting, rapacious eyes!
> … Like obedient slaves,
> We held up a shield between two enemy races –
> The Mongols and Europe!
> Rejoicing, grieving, and drenched in blood,
> Russia is a sphinx that gazes at you
> With hatred and with love.
> We can recall the streets of Paris
> And shady Venice,
> The aroma of lemon groves
> And the hazy monuments of Cologne.
> … But now through the woods and thickets
> We'll stand aside
> Before the comeliness of Europe –
> And turn on you with our Asiatic faces …

The historical intermingling of East and West is made flesh in the Eurasian faces of many Russians. (Look at photographs of Vladimir Lenin, for example, and you can see something of the East in his narrow eyes.) The question of whether Russia should be 'European', or whether she should embrace her 'Asiatic' heritage, including the autocratic system of governance acquired from the Mongols, is deeply felt. And the sense that Russia is in Europe but not of it endures today. The Kremlin wavers between authoritarian repression of political opposition and a lingering desire to convince the West that it respects human rights.

My aim in this book has been to put the events I witnessed in 1991 into their historical context, to highlight the previous turning points in Russia's history, those 'moments of unruly destiny' when she could have gone either way – down the path of reform that might have made her a liberal democracy, or down the continuing path of autocracy, at times totalitarian, repressive and dictatorial.

I have not sought to make value judgements. I did not automatically assume that one path was better or more suited to the Russian condition. But I wanted to know why one path was taken and the other not, to weigh up what would have been needed to send this mighty nation down a totally different route, and to judge how close she came to doing so. Instead of today's renascent authoritarianism, could Russia have become a Western market democracy like ours?

LIST OF MAPS

PART ONE

KIEV AND PROTO-DEMOCRACY

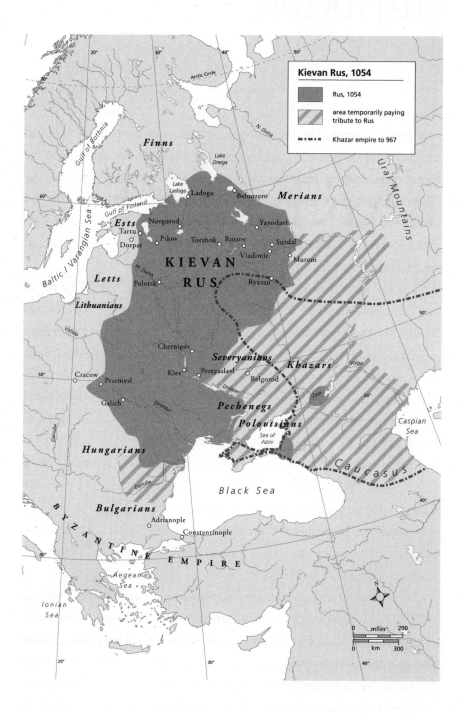

Kievan Rus, 1054

Rus, 1054

area temporarily paying tribute to Rus

Khazar empire to 967

CHAPTER ONE

I arrived in Novgorod before sunrise. I had slept for the first five hours of the overnight sleeper as it travelled north on the high-speed tracks of the Moscow–Petersburg mainline. But as soon as it turned off onto the Novgorod spur, the vibrations from the under-maintained branch line had shaken me awake. I was dressed long before the *dezhurnaya* arrived with my cup of black Russian tea. At 6 a.m. I walked out of Novgorod station into the crisp morning air.

The town was sleeping, so I asked the driver to take me to the far side of the Volkhov River. The city's ancient trading district, the Yaroslavovo Dvorische, where generations of merchants had bartered then gathered to pray in the white-walled, blue-domed church, was silent and cold. My breath rose in the darkness. Across the water, the full moon floated above the walls of the Novgorod kremlin in one of Europe's most perfect, unspoiled vistas – red medieval battlements planted on green riverbanks and, rising above them, the high golden dome of St Sophia's Cathedral.

In the middle of the ninth century, before the name Russia had ever been spoken, Novgorod was a staging post on the trade route from the Baltic Sea in the north to the Byzantine Empire in the south. The area was populated by Slavic tribes, who vied for supremacy. But, just as fratricidal war seemed inevitable, the tribal leaders sought a negotiated settlement. In an era dominated by military aggression, it was a remarkable event.

'There was no law among them,' the Russian *Primary Chronicle* tells us, 'and tribe rose against tribe. Discord ensued and they began to make war, one against the other. But they said unto themselves, "Let us seek a prince who may rule over us, and judge us according to the law."' The chronicler's record of events in ninth-century Novgorod gives an early hint of the conciliatory, law-based character the city would display in the centuries to come. Instead of civil war, the population chose to unite under the leadership of a neutral ruler summoned from outside:

> So they went overseas to the Vikings who were known as the Rus, just as others were called Swedes and Normans and Angles, for thus were they named. The tribes of the Slavs and others said unto the Rus, 'Our land is great and rich, but there is no order in it. Come reign as princes. Rule over us.' Three brothers were selected and the oldest, Rurik of Rus, located himself in Novgorod. From him, the Russian land – Rus – received its name.

It is a great story. Russians were brought up on it. But as so often in Russian history, there's disagreement over the details. The *Primary Chronicle* is the only source for the arrival of Prince Rurik and, indeed, for the whole period. It is part of a series of chronicles that were written considerably later by a succession of monks and, while they are evocative and poetic, their reliability is questionable. Rurik may have been real, or he may have been a mythical figure, possibly a composite of the Viking princes who went on to rule the Russian lands.

But Russian history is never just about the facts. Real history intertwines with romanticised history to form the myths had have shaped national identity. Like the rest of us, Russians have a pretty sketchy knowledge of their own past; even highly educated friends of mine struggle to name many key dates. But one they do all know is 862, the date Rurik allegedly arrived here to found the Rus-ian nation.*

Seven a.m. struck on the Novgorod clocks.

I could see the kremlin was stirring into life, so I took the footbridge over the river and strolled up the path to its tall wooden gates. Inside the

---

* Rus would be formed from an assemblage of individual princely fiefdoms with its centre in Kiev. These were the lands that later became the countries we know as Russia and Ukraine. Russians and Ukrainians still dispute which of their countries is the true inheritor of early Rus. It would undoubtedly be wrong to refer at this early stage to Russia, Russians, or a Russian identity. The adjective 'Rus-ian' is artificial and clumsy, but it is the best way of indicating the entity to which we are referring.

walls, an immaculate ensemble of historic structures encircles the splendid eleventh-century cathedral, and in the centre of a grassy lawn is Novgorod's Millennium Monument. Erected in 1862, another time of great change for Russia (see pp. 144–6), it is dominated by the bronze statue of a knight in armour with a Nordic-style helmet and the date 862. For centuries, school-children have learned that this was what Rurik the Viking looked like. My unscientific poll of passers-by revealed that all those willing to talk believed that his arrival in Novgorod was the moment their nation was born.

'I think that Rurik is a very important person in our history. He is the founder of the first Russian dynasty, the first monarchy of the tsars,' said Svet-lana, a languages student. 'Yes, of course he was a very important figure, because he was the one who united the country, who was the founder of our country,' agreed Alexei. 'There were just some tribes before him, but after him there was a country!' Masha went further: 'Rurik created our state, our Russia. He laid the foundations of our whole system … He was the first of the dynasty that ruled in Rus for a long time. So he's not just a ruler, he's a symbol for us.'

Such claims are a perfect example of romantic history getting ahead of the facts. By no stretch of the imagination could the lands ruled by Rurik (if he existed) and his heirs be said to resemble a nation or a state. They remained little more than one grouping of clans among many, and they would stay that way for several centuries to come. But, fact or fiction, the invitation to Rurik to rule over the warring tribes with a *silnaya ruka* hints at a craving for strong centralised power to bring order and unity to a turbu-lent land. It's a mindset that over the centuries would become ingrained in the Russian psyche. The very word for 'state', *gosudarstvo*, has different connotations from its English equivalent: it suggests not an impartial, repre-sentative government run by consent, with guaranteed rights and the rule of law, but something closer to a kingdom – literally, a 'lord-dom', dependent solely on the whim of its autocratic ruler. And it can be argued that it was this mindset that did, many years later, result in the birth of Russia.

As early as 862, we can already discern in embryo two tendencies that would compete for dominance over the next 11 centuries: on the one hand, the yearning for order through autocracy; on the other, the consultation and voluntary submission to a selected ruler and an impulse towards participatory compromise, a whiff of the democratic ethos that was to find expression in a quite astounding form in the Novgorod (but not Moscow) of later years.

As the only record of the times is contained in the ancient *Chronicles*, I travelled to the Russian National Library in St Petersburg, where the earliest surviving copies are now kept. I found the place had changed little from when I first went there as a student 30 years earlier, but this was the first time I had been given access to these precious documents normally kept under lock and key. The *Chronicles* are the life's work of usually anonymous monks, one after another down the centuries, toiling in their silent candle-lit cells to inscribe the history of their land. A librarian in white gloves showed me pages of illuminated manuscript from the *Novgorod Chronicle*, another of the prized sources of information that, together with the *Primary Chronicle*, make up our knowledge of the early years.

I read how the Viking incomers, Varangians as the chronicler calls them, stayed and ruled and intermarried with the Slavs. Rurik's descendants adopted Russian names – I found Olegs, Igors, Sviatoslavs – but they evidently didn't lose the Viking penchant for military conquest. On Rus's southern border lay the Byzantine Empire, Greek-speaking and Christian, with its capital in Constantinople, today's Istanbul. The chronicler says two of Rurik's men, Askold and Dir, led an expedition to lay siege to the city and 'upon arriving in the Bosporus strait, the Rus killed many Christians'.

In a later section of the manuscript, I saw exactly why the Rus acquired such a reputation for great ferocity. 'Of the prisoners they captured,' it reads, 'some they beheaded, some they tortured, some they shot and still others they drowned in the sea.' In a throwaway remark, it concludes that, 'The Rus inflicted many woes upon the Greeks *in the usual manner of their soldiers*.'

But, according to the chronicler, the pagan Rus failed to reckon with the one force that could deprive them of victory:

> For lo, the Byzantine Emperor prayed all night at the Church of the Holy Virgin, sang hymns and carried the sacred vestment of the Virgin and dipped its hem into the sea. The weather had been still and the sea calm, but suddenly a windstorm arose and great waves scattered the boats of the

pagan Rus. The storm dashed them upon the shore and broke them in pieces. Very few of them escaped the destruction.

By the late ninth century, two leitmotifs of Russian history were beginning to emerge – the tendency towards autocracy, and the urge for aggressive military expansionism. But the divinely aided defeat at Constantinople introduced a third. From initially trying to pillage Constantinople, the Rus-ians were exposed to its religion, and they were intrigued by it, an event that would ultimately have far-reaching implications.

A final consequence of Askold and Dir's expedition from Novgorod to Byzantium was that it led them to discover en route the city that would soon become the capital of the Rus-ian lands:

> They sailed along the Dnieper river, and in the course of their journey they saw a small burg on a hill. They asked, 'Whose town is this?' The inhabi-tants answered, 'There were three brothers, Kii, Shchek and Khoriv, who built this city, but they have since died. We who are their descendants dwell here and pay tribute to the tribe of the Khazars.' Askold and Dir remained in this city, and after gathering together many Varangians, they established their dominion over the area …

That 'small burg' was Kiev, possibly taking its name from the above-mentioned Kii. And while the story of its foundation may have been as mythical as the legend of England's King Alfred burning his cakes just a few years later, its strategic location on the Dnieper at the heart of the north–south trade routes persuaded the Rus-ians to make it their headquarters. In 882, Grand Prince Oleg, the heir of Rurik, seized the city and declared it would henceforth be his capital, an event that has inspired composers and writers down the centuries. Russian schoolchildren learn their classics by heart – their ability to recite screeds of great poetry puts us to shame – and Pushkin's 'Song of Oleg the Wise' is one of the works they can recite with unnerving assurance:*

---

* As Vladimir Putin did, to great effect, in a press conference shortly after he became prime minister in 2008.

So then did Oleg the Wise ride out,

At the head of his troops, on his charger true.

Oh warrior bold, honour and happiness wait on you!

… Forth Oleg rode with his Court and his friends,

High on the hill, where the river bank bends,

Where the rains on them beat, where the dust rises high,

Where ripples the sand when the storm passes by.

And recalling shared dangers of days long gone

They spoke of the battles they'd fought and won …

I have climbed 'the hill where the river bank bends' and it's easy to see why Oleg the Wise chose Kiev. The Berestov Mount is now crowned with a towering Soviet memorial to the soldiers of the Second World War, but it's not hard to imagine Oleg's thoughts as he rode up it. Looking down on the wooded banks of the stately Dnieper, the site's geographical advantages are clear: an easily defended location with good visibility on all sides, endless acres of fertile soil, forests to provide timber for houses and boats, and, most importantly, direct access to the Dnieper and its tributaries, which spread like a network of highways across the land.

For its first four centuries it was Kiev, now in Ukraine, and not Moscow that stood at the centre of the lands of Rus, and in many respects it was a golden age. Prince Oleg moved his court and retinue down from Novgorod. He fortified Kiev and sent military expeditions to neutralise the potentially dangerous nomadic tribes that surrounded it.

Then, in 911, Oleg set off with, according to later accounts, 80,000 men in 2,000 boats, to sail down the Dnieper and besiege Constantinople once again. This time the result was more successful. Terrified by the arrival of the Rus-ian hordes, the Greeks offered to negotiate. Oleg demanded the payment of tribute, not only to himself but to all the princes who had accompanied him, and to all *their* followers. When the Greeks meekly agreed, Oleg sealed his victory by nailing his shield to the wooden walls of the city. The impertinent Rus-ians agreed to leave only in return for an extremely favourable trade treaty, including a provision for Kievan merchants to reside in Constantinople for six months of every year.

Trade rather than conquest was almost certainly Oleg's aim all along, and the treaty laid the foundations of Kiev's future prosperity. From then on, a vast flotilla of Kievan boats sailed south every June, bearing furs and wax, honey and slaves, as a later Byzantine emperor recorded with a mixture of awe and bemusement:

> In the month of June the Russians gather in their dugout boats, each hewn from a mighty tree trunk, to descend the river from Kiev. They must cross the seething cataracts where great rocks bar their way and the water wells up and dashes down with a mighty din. But the Russians disembark and carry their boats around the falls, taking up the goods they have brought with them and leading the slaves in chains for six miles until the rapids are passed. This is where the Pecheneg tribesmen come to attack them. So their voyage is fraught with travail and terror, difficulty and danger. At the island called St Gregory, the Russians perform their pagan ceremonies around a giant oak which they call sacred, sacrificing live cockerels and casting lots to see how best to appease their gods.

On the return journey, the Rus-ians would bring back manufactured goods, such as wine, silks, jewellery and glassware. It is a seemingly idyllic picture of an entrepreneurial nation trading peacefully with its neighbours. But there are hints of more disturbing aspects in their life: the attacks by the Pechenegs and other nomadic tribes were a constant danger for a state surrounded by the wild steppes, with no natural defences against hostile incursions; the slaves the Rus-ians brought to sell in Constantinople would most likely be prisoners captured in these skirmishes, and it's safe to assume that equal numbers of Rus-ians were also captured or killed. Their exotic paganism, too, implies the threat of natural disaster and reliance on the bounty of nature, prompting the worship of sacred trees, and a compulsive need to placate the mysterious Dazhbog and Stribog, gods of sun and wind, and Perun, god of thunder. Rus-ian society existed in unsettled, potentially dangerous times but, remarkably, it survived and thrived.

With its merchants travelling the world and its warriors seeking out new territory to conquer, Kiev was at the origin of what would centuries later become the greatest contiguous empire on Earth, stretching from the Baltic Sea in the west, to the Pacific in the east, to oases of Central Asia in the south and the Arctic Ocean in the north. Today, even after the collapse of the Soviet Union, Russia still spans nine time zones and is home to a hundred nationalities speaking 150 languages.

But for most of its history, Russia has been an unwieldy giant threatened by invasion from abroad and divisions at home. From the very early days of Kievan Rus, the struggle for the unity of the Rus-ian lands and the forging of competing fiefdoms into a new single authority would be the most essential task if the state were to survive.

CHAPTER TWO

Russian history has long been the plaything of the propagandists. The tradition of rewriting the past to bolster current political priorities did not begin with Josef Stalin, but dates back to the very earliest times. The problem when sources are a millennium old is that checking their integrity isn't easy.

The only source available for the earliest years of Russian history is the *Primary Chronicle* and it was produced centuries after some of the events it describes. 'This is the tale of bygone years (the *Povest' Vremmenykh Let*),' it says, 'the tale of the origins of the Russian land, of who first ruled in Kiev and from which origins the Russian land had its beginning.' But if I was going to trust the *Primary Chronicle*, I wanted to find out a bit more about its shadowy author. The identity of most of the ancient chroniclers has been lost in the mists of time. For even the chief among them, our knowledge is limited to a title, some approximate dates and a place of work …

I arrived at the Monastery of the Caves in Kiev with little more than a name, Nestor the Chronicler, but the old lady at the gate was unfazed. 'Nestor,' she said. 'Yes, he's in the Near Caves, the Blizhnie Pechery. Go past the cathedral, take the road down the side of the hill and you'll see a white building. Ask again when you get there.' Considering that Nestor died in 1114, people around here seemed remarkably familiar with him. I walked through the monastery grounds, past a collection of golden-domed churches dominated by an ornate eighteenth-century bell tower and down a steeply descending path. The Monastery of the Caves has been one of the holiest places of Eastern Orthodoxy since it was founded over a thousand years ago. Back then it really was just a cave – or a series of caves – that Greek Byzantine monks had colonised in the hope of bringing Christianity to their pagan neighbours. Over the centuries it has expanded into an architectural ensemble that has recently been named a UNESCO World Heritage Site.

At the designated white building I was ushered into a small doorway leading down some steps and into what looked like a narrow tunnel. Just before I entered, another old lady said, 'Here. You'll need this,' and thrust a lighted wax candle into my hand. She was right. At the bottom of the steps I found myself in a rabbit warren of tunnels, just wide enough for my shoulders to scrape the wall on either side, and high enough for me to feel a constant urge to duck. There was no light of any sort and the tunnels were deathly silent. The realisation that the guttering wax taper in my hand was the only means of finding my way was worrying. I advanced with tentative steps. From time to time I came to lateral tunnels in which similar flickering candles, held by invisible hands, were advancing and retreating. I had noticed stone niches carved into the walls and bent down to glance inside one. Within a glass-topped coffin lay the body of a monk draped in a green satin cloth with a mummified hand protruding from it. Every few yards another niche revealed another glass-topped coffin, another dead monk. I was just getting used to the strangeness of it all when a flicker of light swept towards me, lighting up the cave walls. Somewhere behind the light a low voice mumbled over and over '*Gospodi pomilui, gospodi pomilui! Gospodi I vladyko zhivota moego …*' ('Lord have mercy! Lord God and master of my life …') and I made out the figure of a diminutive old lady, bent nearly double yet constantly bowing lower. In her hand was a cloth with which she rushed from one niche to another, wiping the coffin tops, then reverentially kissing the glass that covered the holy relics. As fast as she had appeared, she disappeared off down the corridor. Just as suddenly, another light rushed up, another hectic mumbled prayer, another old woman bending, bowing, kissing. The spectacle of fervent Christian devotion was shockingly unfamiliar to my blasé Anglican eyes. There was something medieval about it, a sort of living relic of the time when these caves had first been occupied.

At an intersection of four tunnels I found an Orthodox priest and asked him where I could find Nestor the Chronicler. He nodded down one of the corridors: 'Nestor is at the end, on the left.'

I found the man I had come here to see and peered into his coffin. His remains differed little from those of all the other monks – 123 of them – preserved in the eternal gloom of the Near Caves. But it was quite something to see at first hand the man to whom we owe our knowledge of the most mysterious periods of Russian history. Without his record, fragmentary and tendentious as it is, we would indeed be in the dark. We will never know the personal history of Nestor, his experiences, emotions and motivations. But I had the feeling that my visit had brought me closer to his spirit and to the spirit of the times he lived in. Most dramatically, it had put me in contact with the intense, anxious fanaticism that had marked the Christianity of those centuries, when offering the right prayers, atonements and bows were matters of life and death – when the wrong words or obeisances could bring eternal damnation.

Hurrying a little too quickly, I managed to extinguish my candle. With a slight feeling of panic, I latched on to one of the mumbling women and followed her closely in the hope that she was heading out. Thankfully, she was.

It was in such an atmosphere of Christian piety, apocalyptic fear and national claustrophobia that Nestor wrote, or at least compiled the text of the *Chronicle*. He was working 200 years after the arrival of Rurik at a time when Kievan Rus had expanded considerably. Through a mixture of trade and military aggression, its territories now stretched to the Black Sea in the south, the Volga in the east and the kingdoms of Poland and Lithuania in the west. But the Rus-ian lands were still an uneasy confederation of Slavic tribes, tenuously held together by the descendants of the first Viking overlords. Rus was divided, fearful and surrounded by enemies. Its survival was far from certain. To exist at all, it had to unite.

And this is where the element of propaganda creeps into the *Primary Chronicle*. Nestor and the other monks working on it knew their interests were inextricably linked with the interests of the princes of Rus. Christianity was still vying with the old pagan gods – with sacred oak trees and the spirits of earth, wind and thunder. So there is a real sense that the *Chronicle*'s version of history has been shaped to promote the supremacy of the state, to support the rule of the Grand Princes of Kiev and to present Christianity as a stabilising, unifying force.

Nestor's account of the advent of Christianity in 988, just 70 years before his own birth, credits the then Grand Prince of Rus, Vladimir, with taking the first crucial steps towards the creation of a unified nation and a princely state. The adoption of Greek Orthodoxy as its official religion would set Kievan Rus on a course that has shaped Russia's national identity right down to the present day. But according to the *Primary Chronicle*, things could have been very different.

Vladimir was something of a pragmatist who saw the political advantages of adopting a new state religion. He appears to have set up a sort of bidding war, sending envoys to canvass offers from the Islamic Ottoman Empire, the Jewish Khazars and the Western Christian Church in German, as well as that of the Eastern Greeks. The *Chronicle* explains Vladimir's choice as a spiritual awakening:

> When the envoys returned they made their report and said: 'We saw men worship in a temple that is called a mosque, where they sit and bow and look like men possessed; but there is no happiness among them, only sorrow and a dreadful stench. And we went among the Germans and saw their ceremonies, but we beheld no glory there. But when we entered the edifices of the Greeks we knew not whether we were on Earth or in Heaven. For on Earth there is no such splendour or such beauty and we knew not how to describe it. God doth truly dwell among men and there we saw beauty that we can never forget.'

Nestor's account is undoubtedly romanticised and partial. Quite apart from the beauty of their religion, it was almost certainly the Greeks' offer of gifts and trade privileges that convinced Vladimir to opt for Christianity. Islam he rejected because of its ban on alcohol, declaring, some might say prophetically: 'Drinking is the joy of the Russians. We cannot live without that pleasure!'

So Rus became the easternmost bastion of Orthodoxy, on the front line with the forces of Islam, and it would have long-term consequences for her future. If Vladimir had chosen differently, Russia today could conceivably be part of the Islamic world. But Christianity was to prove a powerful binding element, and it brought with it something else that helped unite the nation.

In the centre of Kiev, outside St Michael's Monastery, a white marble monument commemorates two Greek monks, later beatified as Saints Cyril and Methodius. They were two brothers, born in the Greek city of Thessaloniki in the early ninth century, and in mid life they came to Eastern Europe as missionaries for Christianity. But as well as religion, Cyril and Methodius brought with them an alphabet. If they wanted to introduce the Slavs to the Bible, they knew they had to create a standardised written language for the various dialects that had hitherto lacked a written tradition. Even today, if you look at Russian script – it's known as Cyrillic, after the man who invented it – you can see striking similarities with the Greek letters Cyril and Methodius based it on. The new alphabet was initially used for Old Slavonic, the language of the Church and scholarship. Later it was adapted for vernacular Russian, the language of the people, and – from the time of Pushkin in the early nineteenth century – of Russia's magnificent literature.

It is hard to overstate the importance of the Russian language in the development of a unified national identity. Over the centuries, Russians came to regard it, and the literature it produced, as the very essence of Russianness. When the Bolsheviks drove millions into exile after 1917, the consolation for many was that while they could be deprived of their native land, they could not be deprived of their native tongue. The poet Vladislav Khodasevich wrote on his departure from Russia in 1922 that he was taking with him the eight-volume set of Pushkin's collected works. 'All I possess are eight slim tomes, but they contain my native land.'

With its new religion and new written language, Kievan Rus found a voice in the world, and a belief that it had joined the community of pious Christian kingdoms. In 988, Vladimir married a Byzantine princess to seal the sacred union, but he insisted on the Russian Church retaining a large measure of independence from the mother Church in Constantinople. It was a state of affairs that would endure for many centuries and imbue Russia with a sense of its individual Christian mission. A crusading zeal became an important element in the nation's character. It would intensify after the fall of Byzantium in 1453 and take on many forms over the years. But all of its manifestations have their roots in the conviction that Russia is the spiritual inheritor of something unique – be it Christianity, peasant collectivism or Communism – that destiny has decreed it must teach to other nations.

In 988, turning towards the Christian world meant shuffling off, at least temporarily, the Asiatic influences that jostled on Rus's eastern borders. As we'll discover, Russia's attempts to embrace the West would rarely run smoothly, but, for the moment, Vladimir succeeded in strengthening contacts with Europe and introducing new societal values. The *Chronicle* is positively gushing about his civilising influence:

> So Vladimir did ordain that churches should be built where pagan idols once had stood … And there was rejoicing in Heaven to see the salvation of so many souls, while the Devil said, 'Woe is me, for I am cast out of the land!' Then the Prince invited every beggar and pauper to come to his palace to receive whatever he needed – food and drink and money – and to those who could not come, he sent out wagons with supplies of bread and meat, fish and mead, and kvas …

Even allowing for the chronicler's hyperbole, it seems that Christian Kiev took on a more humane style of governance – if not democratic, then at least more open and even-handed. Trade with the West blossomed. Merchants travelled abroad and traders came in from Germany, Denmark, Armenia and Greece. Vladimir reduced military aggression against his neighbours, and at home there was a new emphasis on the rule of law:

> For Vladimir now dwelled in the fear of God and did not execute bandits and robbers, for he feared the sin he might commit in doing so. But the bandits multiplied in number, and only when the bishops assured him that he was anointed by God to administer justice … did the Prince set out to punish the wrongdoers and execute them … But always did he insist on following the due process of the law.

The reference to the 'due process of law' is tantalising. It hints at a putative weakening in the absolute power of the monarch, a recognition of legal principles that even the greatest princes must respect.

The tenth century was a time of autocrats and despots, when rulers ruled by coercion and military might. Nowhere, not even in the most advanced nations, was anything approaching what we know as democracy remotely on the cards. But Kievan Rus offers an unexpected glimpse of embryonic princely rule based on the tenets of 'due process of law'. Such episodes would be the exception rather than the rule in the subsequent history of Russian governance.

Revered in folk legend as the nation's *Krasnoe Solnyshko* (Beautiful Sunshine), Vladimir was made a saint after his death in 1015. Rather unwisely, though, he had appointed his 12 sons to rule as equals in the city states that made up the Rus-ian lands, and arguments over precedence and rules of succession had led to violent conflicts. Two of Vladimir's sons, Boris and Gleb, were the victims of this power struggle in 1019. They have long been the most venerated of the early Russian martyrs because they offered no resistance to their murderers. According to the account of Nestor the Chronicler, Boris and Gleb learned that their brother Svyatopolk had sent soldiers to kill them, but refused to respond with violence lest it lead to civil war:

> Svyatopolk secretly summoned his men and commanded them to go and kill his brother Boris. The sainted Boris was singing vespers, for it was known to him that they intended to take his life. When he saw how men were come to kill him, he arose and began to chant, 'Lord, help me to endure my passion. For I accept it from the hand of my own brother.' …
> He lay down upon his couch and they fell upon him like wild beasts, piercing him with lances. Thus shall the blessed Boris join the choirs of martyrs and be numbered with the prophets and the saints. And Gleb too was offered up as a sacrifice to God, and he too received the crown of glory … Rejoice for our martyrs and intercessors! Now beseech the Lord God that our Princes may live in concord, free from internecine war among them!

The self-sacrifice of Boris and Gleb was an act of Christian humility and – even more important to Nestor – a symbol of the nobility of suffering in the cause of Rus-ian unity. 'Now may our Princes live in concord,' he says; 'may they learn from Boris and Gleb' to put the good of Rus before their own interests. The moral of the story was a useful piece of propaganda for Nestor, because he was writing nearly 70 years after Boris and Gleb's demise, at a time when Rus was descending into internal strife. It established the idea that the good of the state justified the ultimate self-sacrifice, an outlook that would endure in one form or another throughout Russia's history.

Nestor's account of events was loaded with vested interest and political spin. He promoted, possibly even created, the Boris and Gleb legend to place their deaths in a very Russian tradition of redemption through suffering, with the aim of promoting the unity of Rus's ruling dynasty as the paramount good. Their legend served a bigger purpose – to give this new state a history of its own and to establish it as one ordained by God.

In the short term, however, their sacrifice was in vain: the fratricidal war they'd sought to avert soon became a reality. It was to be divisive and destructive, and it would ultimately lead to the downfall of the Kievan state.

CHAPTER THREE

When the 'high place', or capital city, of the Rus-ian lands was transferred from Novgorod to Kiev in 882, it shifted power from the north to the south. The Kievan ruler assumed the title of Grand Prince to distinguish himself from the lesser princes in the realm's component city states. He was entitled to receive tribute, as a formal acknowledgement of his supremacy, from the princes of Ryazan, Suzdal, Rostov, Yaroslavl, Murom, Chernigov, Pskov, Vladimir, Polotsk, Galich, Belgorod and Novgorod. It was a delicate arrangement because it took only one prince with a grudge, a sense of injustice or exaggerated ambition to trigger conflicts like the one that put paid to poor Boris and Gleb. In the end it would be the consequences of such recurrent crises and internal divisions that would weaken and ultimately destroy Rus in the thirteenth century. But the 200 years after the death of Vladimir the Bringer of Christianity, roughly the eleventh and twelfth centuries, saw the development of a remarkably cultured and, by the standards of the day, liberal society.

Despite the looming political fragmentation, the middle years of Kievan Rus were one of those remarkable periods in Russian history when autocracy was tempered with a measure of democratic participation. The city state of Novgorod, in particular, had developed procedures of governance so far in advance of the rest of Europe at that time that I set out to look for evidence of it.

In the Novgorod kremlin, I located the site next to St Sophia's Cathedral where citizens were regularly summoned to public consultations to discuss the running of the city. And over the river, in the trading district of Yaroslavovo Dvorishche, I found the spot where the merchant classes held their own meetings next to St Nicholas's Church. Both sets of meetings were known as *veches*, from the ancient Russian verb 'to speak out', and they were announced by the ringing of the city's *veche* bell, with a distinctive note and ringing pattern used for that purpose alone.

I was eager to find the *veche* bell and was tremendously encouraged when a complex, decorative carillon struck up in the belfry of St Sophia's. Looking up, I could see that the myriad bells, small and large, were being rung in ever more dazzling combinations by a bell-ringer who walked back and forth between the belfry's high, open-sided arches, tugging ropes and flicking clappers with astounding dexterity. Bells were clearly an important part of Novgorodian culture, and I found a kremlin official who looked as though he could explain it to me. My guide took me to the side of the belfry where a row of ancient bells, each of them taller than a man, stood clapperless, waiting – he claimed – to be hoisted back skywards and rehung. I asked how long they had been waiting. 'Since 1437,' he smiled, and took me inside to see the ancient Plague Bell, now also decommissioned (luckily, the last plague warning was in the time of Ivan the Terrible).

But nowhere could I find the *veche* bell. My guide looked serious: 'You know what happened? Moscow came and stole our *veche* bell. They didn't like the democracy we had here. They wanted to rule with a *silnaya ruka* and they thought the bell was a symbol of freedom. They took it away. They've always been the same.'

I smiled, but he was deadly serious.

'You know all the rights our citizens enjoyed back then [before the rule of Moscow]?' he asked. 'They could decide for themselves how Novgorod was run, and who ran it! The people had the power to elect city officials and they even had the power to elect and fire the prince!'

I tried to point out that the only people who could do all these things were male heads of households, so it was no good if you were a woman or you didn't own property, but he was dismissive.

'If you look at the records,' he said, 'you'll see that many of the *veche* meetings included representatives from all social classes. We have documents to show that the archbishop took part, the *posadniki* [magistrates], the *tysiatskiis* [representatives elected on the basis of one per thousand citizens], the *boyars* [noblemen], the *zhitye liudi* [middle-class citizens], the merchants and even the *chernye liudi* [literally the 'black folk', meaning lower-class, taxpaying citizens]. Don't you think that's a fantastic achievement? It's so far ahead of anywhere else at that time. We were a model of democracy. The *veche* ratified treaties, declared war and peace, set taxes, conducted foreign relations and served as a court to settle public disputes. It also elected officials and invited the city prince [to govern]. Did you know that when our citizens got fed up with Prince Vsevolod Mstislavich in 1136, they got together and decided to give him the boot? What do you think about that? And afterwards they were equal partners in the way power was wielded. From then on, they elected the prince and they told him he couldn't live inside the city walls. He had to live out at Rurikovo Gorodishche, south of here, as a sign that he was subservient to the will of the people!'

I nodded. My guide was undoubtedly exaggerating the extent of democracy in Novgorod, but the essence of what he said was true. Similar institutions existed in Kiev and Pskov.

'And by the way,' he offered as a parting shot, 'you should go over to the State Museum have a look at our birch barks.'

In the early 1950s, when the foundations of a new housing estate were being dug on the outskirts of Novgorod, workmen made a fascinating discovery. A hoard of ancient documents written on strips of bark cut from silver birch trees dating back to the eleventh century had been immaculately preserved in the peaty subsoil of the East European Plain. Archaeologists took over the site and eventually dug up hundreds of birch barks spanning a period of 400 years.

In the State Museum's collection I was shown a selection of them. They ranged from official notices to merchants' bills to simple accounts of daily life in Novgorod between the eleventh and fifteenth centuries. And they provide startling evidence of widespread literacy and impressive cultural development. I read love letters exchanged between teenagers and crib sheets prepared for school exams. 'I love you and you love me,' writes one woman. 'So why don't we get married?' 'You owe me money – please send it with your servant … ' warns another. And my own favourite: a line drawing from the 1240s by a young boy showing a man raising his hands in the air – each of them has six fingers and the text surrounding the drawing is full of spelling mistakes. The seven-year-old author's name is Onfim, and from what the experts can decipher, he appears to be asking his friend Dmitry for a loan.

Visitors to Novgorod in the eleventh century describe women being equal to men and prominent in the affairs of the city. The city had a sewage system and reinforced wooden pavements on the streets – 200 years earlier than the pavements in Paris, my guide proudly told me, and 500 years earlier than London.

The birch barks reveal that there was a well-developed judicial system with juries and mediation procedures. The courts relied on fines rather than corporal punishment, and fragments of Kievan legal practice that have come down to us do sound remarkably modern. If, for example, a merchant hired a worker and then changed his mind, the contract was regarded as binding and the employer was obliged to pay; if he hired him through an intermediary who failed to give the man his wages, the employer was held liable. Of course, it was a far cry from our idea of a modern democracy, but Novgorod offers a startling glimpse of the *pravovoe gosudarstvo*, the law-governed state that Russia might have become.

The period of Kievan Rus was a potential turning point, the first of several in Russian history, at which the country could have gone either way. If the Kievan model had been allowed to develop, if the forces of autocracy had not ultimately gained the upper hand, Russia today might be a very different place. But Kievan Rus was not given the chance to perpetuate its model of society. Even at the height of its success, Rus was divided at home and threatened from abroad.

Although the Grand Prince in Kiev was nominally the country's supreme ruler, the city states – Novgorod among them – were led by individual princes with their own armies. Their power was not absolute and there was an absence of coordination, civil or military, between the various principalities. That lack of centralised government made Rus vulnerable. Her semi-independent fiefdoms had been locked in decades of feuds and dissension and potential enemies were well aware of her weakness.

In 1241, the Teutonic Knights – a highly militarised order of Prussian crusaders – launched a blitzkrieg attack on Rus's northwest border. It was a shock of immense proportions that would mark the Russian psyche for centuries to come. The Teutonic Knights were universally feared for their ferocious determination to spread the Catholic faith, and the Orthodox Rus-ians feared both political and religious domination. Led by Prince Bishop Hermann of Dorpat, the Knights advanced swiftly and seized the city of Pskov. In early 1242, they defeated a Novgorodian force at the battle of Tartu and began to march on Novgorod itself. The city's prince, the 20-year-old Alexander Nevsky, rode out to meet the invaders near the series of lakes that lie to the west of Novgorod. The fate of Novgorodian civilisation hung in the balance.

Centuries later, Sergei Eisenstein's film *Alexander Nevsky* (1938) would capture the horror and dismay of the invasion: the serried ranks of Russian soldiers are shown suffering appalling casualties but standing firm against the overwhelmingly superior German forces. We see the young Nevsky rallying his troops and turning back the enemy hordes, then luring them onto the thin ice of the Chudskoe lake. Eisenstein depicts the success of Nevsky's tactics as their horses and heavy armour sent the Knights plunging to their deaths in the chilly waters, a possibly legendary event that the director took directly from the account of the Russian *Primary Chronicle*:

> And Prince Alexander's men were filled with the lust for battle, for they had hearts like lions and said, 'Oh mighty Prince, today shall we lay down our lives for you!' And when the sun did rise, the armies clashed and the Germans fought their way into our ranks. Chudskoe lake was covered by their masses. In fierce battle came the crash of breaking lances and the ringing of sword on sword, until the ice turned red with the blood of men, and then the frozen lake did seem to give way … and in the sky appeared God's hosts of heavenly troops, aiding our Prince to victory … I know this is true, for an eyewitness hath told me so …

The Chronicler's delightful reassurance about God being on our side because 'an eyewitness hath told me so' shows how Russia has long used its history and associated myths to shape its present and its future, a practice that has continued well into our own times.*

---

* *Alexander Nevsky* is a case in point. The film was made in 1938, when Moscow had not yet signed its non-aggression pact with Nazi Germany and Hitler was still regarded as a future enemy. So the movie is charged with anti-German sentiment and rousing Russian patriotism. Eisenstein – and Sergei Prokofiev, who wrote the marvellous score – were hurried by Stalin to finish it, and prints were rushed into the cinemas. After a hiatus of two years, *Alexander Nevsky* was re-released when the Germans eventually invaded in 1941, becoming a potent symbol of resistance.

Far from securing Russia's survival, however, Nevsky's exploits in 1242 were in reality a minor victory, the last glorious swansong of Kievan Rus before an even greater enemy overwhelmed it from the south.

By the twelfth century, the nomadic tribes in the steppes on Russia's southern frontier had grown in strength and ambition. From sporadic border raids, they were now threatening the Rus-ian heartland. Vast swathes of the population lived in terror of the savage Pechenegs and Polovtsians, heathen tribes who would descend on frontier towns and settlements to pillage, murder and kidnap civilians to hold as hostages or trade as slaves. Ukraina, today's Ukraine, means literally 'the land on the edge', and the Rus-ian state was cursed with open borders and no natural defences. The *dikoe polye*, the wild dangerous steppe and the forces lurking within it, became an enduring terror myth in the national psyche.

The Rus-ian princes knew they should end their divisions and join forces to fight a common enemy, but decades of rivalry ran deep. Fifty years before Nevsky's Battle on the Ice, Prince Igor Sviatoslavich, whose territory of Novgorod-Seversk* on the southern frontier was pillaged by raiders from the steppe, had tried and failed to rally support for an expedition against the Polovtsians. Exasperated by the princes' disunity, Igor set off on his own with a small band of men. His brave but doomed mission is lodged in the Russian consciousness just as the heroism of Scott of the Antarctic or the Charge of the Light Brigade are lodged in ours. It is captured indelibly in the lyric epic 'The Song of Igor's Campaign':

> Then Igor gazed upon the sun and said, 'Brothers! Better it would be to be slain than to be a slave; so let us mount our swift horses that we may look upon the blue waters of the Don. I want to break a lance at the limit of the Polovtsian steppe; with you, O Russians, I will lay down my life, or else drink of the Don from my helmet.'

'The Song of Igor's Campaign' is the first great masterpiece of Russian literature. Every schoolchild knows its strange, disturbing images and its

---

* Not to be confused with the northern city state of Novgorod 'the Great'.

rhythmic, muscular verse. It was a mainstay of the Russian oral tradition, intended to be memorised and recited as patriotic propaganda. But far from being a celebration of victory, 'The Song of Igor' is actually a dire warning of the perils of national disunity:

> And, brethren, Kiev began to groan from grief, for the princes had created dissension among themselves. The fortune of the land was destroyed and lives were shortened by the princes' discord. The ravens cawed and grief like a maiden splashed her wings in the River Don. When the princes argued about trifles, calling them important matters, then brother said unto brother, 'This is mine, and that also is mine.' And the infidels from the steppe came to conquer the Russian land.

There's disagreement about when 'The Song of Igor's Campaign' was written, and even about its authenticity – the manuscript was discovered in 1795 and there've been claims that it's an eighteenth-century fake. Given the vividness of the first-hand descriptions, though, and the detail of the historical references, it seems to me that the poem is the testimony of an eye witness, possibly a combatant. The power of the poetry instils a message that has been assimilated into the collective memory: that the motherland is vulnerable and surrounded by merciless enemies; that Russia's borders are open and porous, constantly in need of vigilant defence. The lesson promoted by 'The Song of Igor' is that all must unite in the service of a strong centralised state or the same lamentable fate will befall her again. It helps explain behaviour that can seem strange to us in the West – the readiness to sacrifice the individual (as we saw in the story of Boris and Gleb), the subjugation of personal interests to the good of the whole, and the collectivist ethos that enshrines the state as the supreme national priority. It's seen in the unflinching expenditure of Russian lives in battle, the aggressiveness of a military stance that flows from the certainty of national weakness, and the widespread acceptance that the state has the absolute right to murder its supposed political enemies such as Leon Trotsky or Alexander Litvinenko (see pp. 316 and 523).

Literature, music, art and film have long served as a means of national validation in Russia, a common meeting place, a repository of shared values.

In times of censorship and repression, the arts have provided her sole forum of public discourse. And they'll play an important role in our attempts to explain her history too – for the central theme of Russian culture is Russia herself, reflecting her national identity and also helping to shape it.

Tragically for Kievan Rus, the poetic brilliance of 'The Song of Igor's Campaign' was a gleam of fire in the darkness, after which the lights would go out for many years. The downfall of the divided state, and the foreign domination that Igor's narrator feared, soon became a reality. For the next two centuries, native culture lay low, and the spirit of Russia embalmed in Igor's Song could be preserved only in underground memories. The Mongol hordes were massing on the horizon.

CHAPTER FOUR

Modest Mussorgsky's piano suite *Pictures at an Exhibition* reaches its musical climax in a movement titled 'The Heroes' Gates in Kiev' (usually translated as 'The Great Gate of Kiev' and given various orchestral makeovers by artists ranging from Maurice Ravel to the 1970s progressive rock band Emerson, Lake and Palmer). In reality, Mussorgsky's Gates were never actually built – they were merely an architectural study in a painting by his recently deceased friend Viktor Hartmann – but that doesn't stop Kiev tour guides taking visitors to see them. What the tourists actually see are Kiev's Zoloti Vorota (Golden Gates), a towering brick and wood structure built in the eleventh century as part of the city's defensive wall.

The walls have gone now and the gates are little more than a decorative adornment in a grassy park behind the Opera House. But in 1240 the citizens of Kiev were desperately relying on their protection from a very real enemy. Khan Batu was a grandson of Genghis Khan and commander of the Mongol troops – called 'Tartars' by the Russians – who conquered nearly all of Kievan Rus between 1237 and 1240. According to the chronicler who recorded Batu's seizure of the city of Ryazan, his methods were, to say the least, uncompromising:

> The accursed Batu ... stormed the city with firebrands, battering rams and scaling ladders. In the Cathedral of the Assumption, the Tartars seized Princess Agrippina and hacked her into pieces together with the other princesses. The bishops and the priests they burned alive and set fire to the churches, killing men, women and children with their swords, drowning others in the river. The Tartars burned our holy city with all its beauty and its wealth and spilled our blood on its holy altars. Not one person remained alive. Parents could not mourn their children, nor children their parents, for all alike were dead. All had drunk to the dregs from the same bitter cup.

After Ryazan, Batu marched on the principalities of Suzdal and Vladimir, Kolomna, Chernigov and the still minor city of Moscow. By 1240, the Mongols were approaching the capital of the Russian lands, the great city of Kiev. At the top of the Golden Gates, from the ancient lookout post (recently reconstructed by the city authorities), you can see where the Mongols pitched their camp, surrounding the city on all sides. For the thousand or so defenders of Kiev it must have been a heart-stopping sight because the attackers had many thousands of troops and their tents stretched as far as the eye could see. Unusually, the Mongol commander dispatched envoys offering the chance to surrender, but the Kievans refused. After a week-long bombardment that breached the city walls, the Mongols poured in, wreaking death and destruction.

The terrified civilians sought shelter in the Desyatinna Tserkva (Church of the Tithes), in the Old Town area of the city. The church was a stone structure that housed the remains of Grand Prince Vladimir the Bringer of Christianity, his wife and family, but it was not built to withstand the weight of so many people and its upper floor collapsed. Hundreds died in the crush and the rest were burned to death by the besieging Mongols.* By nightfall, the Mongols had set Kiev ablaze. Some 48,000 of its 50,000 inhabitants were dead and the civilisation that was Kievan Rus, the culture and beauty, the embryonic democracy, the respect for legality and civic values – all had been destroyed for ever. A papal envoy travelling through the Kievan lands in 1245 has left us a vivid snapshot of the Mongols' destructive ruthlessness:

> When we passed through this region, we found lying in the fields countless heads and bones of dead people … The pagans had enacted a great massacre in the Russian lands and destroyed towns and fortresses. Kiev had been large and populous, but now it was reduced to nothing – barely 200 dwellings remain and those inhabitants are held in the cruellest slavery.

---

* The ruins of the Desyatinna Tserkva still remain in Kiev, rather forlorn behind a rusting iron fence.

It was a ruthlessness that had helped the Mongols conquer vast swathes of Asia and would soon bring much of Eastern Europe under their control. Their method was to wage total war, with blitzkrieg tactics of speed and surprise. All the resources of the Mongol state were devoted permanently and exclusively to military campaigning. This was not so much a society as a perpetual war machine.

But what the Mongols didn't have was the manpower to administer the territory they had seized. In Russia they selected puppet rulers from among the princes, demanding penal tribute from them and humiliating shows of servility. Appointed and dismissed at the whim of the Mongol overlords, the princes were summoned to prostrate themselves before the Khan in mocking, degrading rituals. One who refused was summarily executed.

The Mongol yoke would last for 240 years, from 1240 to 1480, subjugating Russia's population, disrupting her economy and setting back her development as a European state. Nikolai Karamzin, the first great Russian historian, writing in the 1820s, identifies Mongol rule as the moment when Russia became separated from the West, when the commercial and cultural links that flourished under Kiev were broken and Russia was plunged into darkness and isolation:

> In former times, we had a civic society that equalled the leading European powers, with the same character, the same laws, customs and state structures ... But see now the consequences of our two centuries of slavery: ... Russia's progress was halted: we stood still as Europe sped forward on the path to enlightenment ... and her rulers willingly conceded civil rights to her citizens. The prison of barbarism cut us off from Europe, just when Europe was acquiring the benefits of knowledge, freedom and civilisation.

Isolated from Europe, Russia missed out on the Renaissance, her national progress interrupted for more than 200 years. In some respects, she would never fully catch up with Western Europe's cultural and social values. The radical political philosopher Pyotr Chaadayev, a contemporary of Karamzin, identifies the Mongol occupation as the genesis of Russia's enduring failure to develop as a European state:

Our history began in barbarity and backwardness, followed by brutal foreign oppression whose values were imbibed by our own rulers. Cut off from the rest of humanity, we failed to acquire the universal values of duty, justice and the rule of law. The new ideas that blossomed in Western Europe did not penetrate our state of oppression and slavery.

Instead, in a strange version of Stockholm Syndrome (where kidnap victims embrace the beliefs of their kidnappers), the Russians began to adopt features of the Mongol system for themselves. Forced to kowtow before the Khan, the princes started to demand the same thing from their own followers. The practice of *chelobitie* (literally beating one's forehead on the ground) was adopted as part of Russian court etiquette and would remain in use for four centuries. Prince vied with prince to prove their commitment to the Mongol cause, becoming zealous collaborators and willing collectors of tribute. Some of them adopted the Tartar language. And, most significantly for Russia's future development, a profound admiration for the Mongol model of an autocratic, militarised state began to enter the Russian psyche. Karamzin described the assimilation of Mongol values:

> The princes crawled on their knees to the Golden Horde and, returning with the approval of the Tartar Khan, began to rule with greater boldness than in the days when we were politically free ... So, uprooting little by little the traditions of the old social order, they introduced instead the beginnings of genuine autocracy.

Karamzin recognises the legacy of the Mongol period as a decisive shift from fragile, embryonic democracy to flourishing and durable autocracy. Mongol viceroys and their client princes abolished Kievan Rus's consultative assemblies – the remarkable *veches* at work in Novgorod, Pskov and Kiev – and assumed unchecked authority to take decisions on war and peace, taxation, conscription and the appointment of state officials. Justice became the plaything of despots; cruel new punishments and judicial torture were introduced. Civic participation and respect for the law, glimpsed in the legal code of Novgorod and elsewhere, were replaced by the absolute, unchallengeable diktat of an all-powerful state.

Russian historians have debated whether the advent of autocracy was a positive or negative development. The commonly held view is the one put forward by the liberal Chaadayev – that the Mongol period was a national catastrophe and the absolutist state model it implanted in Russia was her great misfortune. But some Russian nationalists disagree. Karamzin, for instance, is a convinced defender of autocracy and suggests the strength and political unity it engendered among the formerly feuding Russian lands outweighed all the negative effects:

> Batu's invasion brought destruction, death and slavery to Russia; it was, of course, one of our greatest national woes … but its consequences were undoubtedly a blessing in disguise, for the destruction brought with it the gift of unity. It would have been better if our princes could themselves have established unity and autocracy, but they had failed to do so for two centuries. If another century had passed in princely feuds what would have been the result? Almost certainly the downfall of our country. Our Christian faith and our very survival would have been lost. It may be said, therefore, that Moscow's future greatness was created by the Mongol Khans.

It is true that the need for unity in the face of Mongol oppression would eventually force the rival princes into a national alliance (see pp. 37–8). It is also true that the autocratic, centralised power system they assimilated from their occupiers would endure in Russia long after the Mongols had departed. For a state in constant danger of annihilation, the unifying force of autocracy seemed a necessity. In the centuries beyond the Mongol era, it would become a default position for governance in Russia.

The period of Kievan Rus was the first of Russia's 'moments of unruly destiny', the first key juncture at which she could have gone either way – down the path of civic society and participatory government; or down the route of centralised autocracy, the *silnaya ruka* of Asiatic despotism.

On a rainy autumn day in a muddy field by the River Don, southeast of the city of Tula, I waited with a regiment of fierce-looking Russians in chain mail. We expected the enemy cavalry at any moment. The Russian troops were understandably nervous. They had swords and lances and a few of them were swinging spiky iron maces in a distinctly menacing manner. But word had come in that they were badly outnumbered and that the Mongols had orders to take no prisoners.

The name of the muddy meadow was Kulikovo Polye, literally 'the Field of Snipes', and I had come for the annual re-enactment of the decisive battle of the Mongol occupation, the first time the Russians had found the courage to unite and rise up against their ferocious overlords. In 1380, several princedoms, including Moscow, had refused to pay their tribute and the Mongols responded by assembling a powerful punitive expedition to teach them a lesson. In the past, the feuding princes would have run to protect their own fiefdoms, but now – for the first time – 20 of them agreed to work together. Under the leadership of the 29-year-old Prince Dmitry Ivanovich of Moscow, whose forces had already clashed with the Mongols two years earlier, they crossed the Don and took up position in the fields and woods I could see all around me.

The Mongols attacked from the south. By now we could hear the sound of their horses' hooves growing louder by the minute. The fellows in chain mail exchanged worried glances. Many of them looked a bit old and some-what on the podgy side to be frontline troops. But Prince Dmitry was a tactical wizard. He had chosen to fight on wooded terrain that slowed down the enemy cavalry and robbed them of mobility.

The Mongols finally galloped into view and swept around the field a couple of times in a show of hippodrome bravado. My companions waved their maces in the air and there was a little polite banging of Russian swords on Mongol shields before everyone agreed to call it a day and headed off to share a beer and some *shashlik*.

On 8 September 1380, the real Battle of Kulikovo Polye was distinctly longer and bloodier. For over four hours, 60,000 Russians and 100,000 Mongols slashed and hacked with swords and lances. According to the *Chronicles*, Christian bodies lay like haystacks and the River Don flowed red with blood:

> But Prince Dmitry said, 'Fight on! Yield not to the infidels who destroy our land.' Grey wolves howl at our gates … Prince Dmitry galloped to the

River Don ... and the princes marched united together. Russian swords rain down on Tartar helmets; black is the earth under their hooves, but they sow the field with Tartar bones. Mighty armies trample down hills and fields, uttering mighty cries. Lightning flashes, thunder claps; our golden armour shines, banners flap in the wind. It is awful to hear ... But the infidels run before the princes and Russians cry victory in the field. Trumpets sound; drums are beaten; glory is borne through the land. Dmitry has vanquished the pagans ... for the Russian land and the Christian Faith!

Kulikovo Polye is regarded very much as a Christian triumph over the forces of Islam (the Mongols had adopted the Muslim faith in the early fourteenth century), and a 90-foot column with a gilded Orthodox cross now marks the site of the battle. (I also noticed that a lot of the re-enactors when I was there turned up later in the T-shirts of extreme Russian nationalist – some would say racist – groups.) Back in 1380, Christianity and nationalism were just beginning to be influential forces in the formation of the Russian identity. In Russian folk memory, Kulikovo Polye is the place to which Russians came divided but left as a nation (even though at least one Russian prince offered to fight with the Mongols). The victory on the River Don earned Prince Dmitry his enduring nickname – Donskoy, literally 'man of the River Don' – and created the notion of Russia's sacred calling as the standard-bearer of Christianity against the forces of the infidel. Alexander Blok, the great Symbolist poet writing 500 years later, saw it as the starting gun for a millennial clash of opposing values that would define Russia's historical identity:

O my Rus! My wife! Our path is long
And painfully clear!
Our breast is pierced by the ancient arrow
Of the Tartars' will.
Our path leads through the steppe of endless yearning,
Through your yearning, O Rus! ...
In the smoky reaches a holy banner will shine

Aloft beside the Khan's steel sabre ...
And the battle is eternal! We can only dream of peace
Through blood and dust ...

The events at Kulikovo Polye had three crucial outcomes: national pride at the unexpected victory over the occupiers; confirmation that if Russians acted together they could achieve greater things than when they squabbled among themselves; and a realisation of the importance of Christian faith as a unifying national value.

The victory of 1380 destroyed the aura of Mongol invincibility, but it didn't end Mongol domination. For another century, Rus continued paying tribute to the Golden Horde and seething with resentment. What had changed was that the country was united now by what would soon become a national religious myth and by a pan-Russian consciousness of being a unified nation in opposition to external enemies. The leader of that newborn Russia would no longer be Kiev, but Moscow.

CHAPTER FIVE

The origins of the Moscow Kremlin are found in its central square deep within the walls, where six beautiful cathedrals rise up with gleaming domes and dazzling white façades. Their foundations were laid, and the word 'kremlin' first used (it means 'fortress' or 'citadel') in the early fourteenth century, and they are graphic evidence of how Moscow's fortunes had begun to take off. The man who ordered the construction of those earliest cathedrals, and who launched Moscow on its rise from minor princedom to capital city at the heart of the expanding Grand Duchy of Muscovy, was Prince Ivan I. Nicknamed Kalita, or 'Moneybags', Ivan spent the whole of his reign (1325–40) under Mongol domination, but his skill at wheeling and dealing carved out a rich and powerful place for his city and for himself.

I found Ivan Kalita's tomb in the Cathedral of Archangel Michael at the heart of the Kremlin he founded. With its carved stone covered in decorated brass and standing at the very beginning of the long rows of tsars down the centuries, it looks quite splendid. Ivan would probably have appreciated the flashiness of his memorial. He certainly liked money and he amassed lots of it by cosying up to the Mongol Khans, throwing himself at their feet and offering to oversee the collection of taxes in Russia on their behalf. Ivan Kalita was undoubtedly a toady. He even volunteered to help the Mongols crush a Russian uprising led by a rival prince. But it brought him power, and by his fortieth birthday Ivan had persuaded the Mongols to name him Grand Prince, the pre-eminent ruler of the Russian lands.

On my way out of the cathedral, I paused to take in the breathtaking view across Moscow from the heights of the Kremlin wall. It is hard to imagine that this sprawling city, with its high-rises, traffic-clogged streets and smoking chimneys as far as the eye can see, was until the fourteenth century a mere backwater in the constellation of Russian towns, dwarfed by Kiev, Novgorod, Smolensk, Vladimir and even Polotsk. The speed and scale of

Moscow's rise to pre-eminence makes Ivan Kalita's achievement – and that of his heirs – doubly remarkable.

Typical of Kalita's canny knack for seizing the main chance was his courtship of the Orthodox Church. The *Chronicles* record that in 1325 he persuaded the embattled head of the Church, Metropolitan Pyotr, to move his seat from Kiev, via Vladimir, to Moscow. It bestowed Ivan's city a mantle of authority it could never have gained from political power alone:

> For Kalita won the favour of Metropolitan Pyotr, and Pyotr exhorted him to build a cathedral made of stone, saying: 'My son, if you obey my command to build this shrine to the Holy Mother of God and grant me my final resting place within it, you shall reap great glory – more than all the other princes – and your sons and grandsons shall be glorified. Your city will be praised, for it will be home to the fathers of the Church, and all other cities will bow down to it.'

Andrei Tarkovsky's 1969 film *Andrei Rublev* vividly illustrates the hold that Orthodox Christianity exerted, and still exerts, on the Russian consciousness. Its hero, the fourteenth-century Muscovite icon painter, born in the period soon after Ivan Kalita had begun to establish Moscow as the leading Russian city, struggles to remain true to his art amid the horrors of Mongol occupation. The exquisite sequences of Rublev's work, as the film bursts into radiant colour, bear witness to Tarkovsky's own belief in the transcendent power of religion, and hint at why the endorsement of the Church is so vital to those who would claim worldly authority. The concept of the tsar as God's true representative would become immensely important, and the Moscow princes who ruled after Kalita's death were quick to exploit it. For centuries, Russia's Orthodox Christian faith would remain a vital buttress of her autocratic rulers.

In a disturbing scene in the film, Tarkovsky shows the Mongols torturing Russian priests and sacking their churches. But after the initial invasion, its organised harassment of religion seemed to subside. Orthodoxy became a powerful unifying force for the subject people, a first hint of a pan-Russian identity that would emerge from the Mongol years focused on the Grand

Prince and later the tsar. I remember from my own time as a student in Russia in the 1970s how religious observance took on a similar role in the latter years of the USSR, a shared belief that this was the repository of true Russianness amid the alien Communist occupation. In 1969, Tarkovsky's film hinted at the same spirit of stoic opposition and, not surprisingly, it was banned.

In the fifteenth century, the rise of Moscow gathered pace under Ivan Kalita's immensely pragmatic descendants. They were willing to fight against the Mongols – leading the way in 1380 at Kulikovo Polye (see pp. 32–4) – and then to reverse their position and fight with them, earning rich rewards in the form of vast new territories. Whatever served Moscow's interests, Moscow was happy to do.

In 1453, the destruction of Christian Byzantium by the Turks left Muscovy as the sole remaining bastion of the Orthodox faith, directly exposed now to the expanding empire of Islam. The sense of a God-given mission to defend the civilised world against the infidel was embraced by the emerging nation. It was a time of fear but also of pride and opportunity, and Moscow used the crisis to cement its claim to religious and political supremacy.

A mystical prophetic text known as 'The Legend of the White Cowl' circulated, causing great excitement among the population. The so-called prophecy was probably a forgery created for political purposes. In the growing spirit of symbiosis between the Orthodox Church and the Muscovite state, it claimed to consecrate Moscow as the 'third Rome' (after Constantinople, the 'second Rome'), the true guardian of God's rule:

> For the ancient city of Rome hath departed from the true faith of Christ
> … and the second Rome, which has been the city of Constantinople, hath
> perished through the violence of the Muslim sons of Hagar. But in the
> third Rome, which shall be the land of Rus, the grace of the Holy Spirit
> will shine forth … all Christians will unite into one Russian Orthodox
> realm and the crown of the imperial city shall be bestowed upon the Russ-
> ian Tsar. The Russian land will be elevated by God above all nations and
> under its rule will be many heathen kings. The Russian land shall be called
> Radiant and glorified with blessings. It shall become greater than the two
> Romes which went before it.

Thus armed with the authority of the Church and with the vast material wealth accumulated in the century since Ivan Moneybags, Moscow emerged immensely strengthened when the Mongol yoke was finally thrown off in 1480. Within a few decades, its rulers adopted the title of 'tsar', derived from the Roman 'Caesar', in place of the old appellation of Grand Prince. They called themselves *samoderzhets* (autocrat) and 'sovereign of all the Russias'.

But that claim was premature. The departure of the Mongols left a power vacuum, and there were several contenders vying to fill it. In the west, Lithuania had united with Catholic Poland and their powerful empire was expanding vigorously into the western Russian lands. In the north, Novgorod had avoided direct Mongol occupation, becoming a rich trading state while preserving many of the old quasi-democratic values of Kievan Rus. If Moscow wanted to consolidate its pretensions to sole supremacy among the Slavs, it would need to deal with each of them.

Back in Novgorod, the news from Moscow was becoming increasingly worrying. Threatening rumours of impending military action were emerging daily, and in the summer of 1470 the *veche* bell announced an emergency meeting to consider the looming crisis. The gathering was told a choice would have to be made – either submission to the rule of Moscow or a concerted, potentially perilous, campaign of resistance. Novgorod had become accustomed to existence as a peaceful trading state and its army had been allowed to wither. On their own, the Novgorod forces would stand no chance against the army of the Muscovite Grand Prince, Ivan III. The only way to defend the city would be to sign a military and political accord with Ivan's other potential enemies, the Lithuanians.

The *veche* debate was fierce. Union with Lithuania would mean sacrificing Novgorod's independence and – perhaps more importantly – compromising its Russian Orthodox faith. After their union with Poland in 1385, the Lithuanians had adopted Roman Catholicism, and their price for helping Novgorod against Moscow would most probably have meant conversion. The issue of 'the Latin faith', as it was contemptuously dubbed by its Orthodox opponents, featured heavily in the discussions at the *veche*. Two distinct camps emerged, one advocating the acceptance of Muscovite rule, the other urging joint resistance together with the Poles and Lithuanians. By a small majority, the second group carried the day: the people of Novgorod decided to invite King Kazimierz IV of Poland and Lithuania to take power in their city. It was a radical move, and if the plan had been realised, it would have formed a potent anti-Moscow bloc. A Novgorod–Lithuanian alliance could possibly have kept Ivan at bay. It could have assumed future dominance in the Russian lands. And it could have meant a wholly different course for Russian history, with Novgorod or Vilnius assuming the role of capital and Catholicism replacing Orthodoxy as the state religion.

But before the alliance could be consummated, the news reached Moscow, and Ivan III responded furiously. Muscovite troops arrived on the outskirts of Novgorod in July 1471 and defeated the inexperienced Novgorod army in the Battle at the River Shelon.

At first, Ivan tried to reach a peaceful accord with the city's leaders, but their continuing defiance – and alleged continuing contacts with the Lithuanians – goaded him into punitive action. He sent a powerful army to occupy Novgorod and impose Muscovite rule. The advent of government by Moscow would have profound implications for the city's future and for the embryonic institutions of democracy it had developed.

The *Novgorod Chronicle* had been in existence since 1016, recording events with a critical eye for four and half centuries, pointing out failings in the city's government and shortcomings among its officials, but always taking Novgorod's side when its interests were threatened by outside forces. After 1471, however, the change in the *Chronicle*'s tone is striking. It is immediately clear that it is now being written by the new Muscovite boss. Ivan's men had taken over the running of the city and the dramatic events of the summer were shaped and slanted in the best traditions of political spin to give him the best possible press:

AD 1471. The Grand Prince Ivan Vasilievich marched with a force against Novgorod because of its wrongdoing and lapsing into Latinism [Lithuanian Roman Catholicism] … The Grand Prince Ivan Vasilievich was beloved for his righteous acts, yet the deceitful people would not submit to him. Stirred by a savage pride, the men of Novgorod would not obey their sovereign … Their faces were covered with shame, for they did leave

the light and give themselves over in their pride to the darkness of ignorance, saying they would draw away and attach themselves to the Latin
King … bringing evil to all Orthodoxy. The Grand Prince Ivan Vasilievich
did frequently send messengers to them calling on them to live according
to the old ways. But he suffered much from their vexatious ways … Therefore has he laid his anger upon them, upon Great Novgorod …

Written at the command of Ivan and his successors, the *Chronicle* makes
great play of Moscow's long-suffering efforts to reason with the errant
Novgorodians. But in the end, says the pro-Moscow chronicler, Ivan's
patience ran out and he was forced to teach the traitors a lesson:

Thus did Great Prince Ivan advance with all his host against his domain
of Novgorod because of the rebellious spirit of its people, their pride and
conversion to Latinism. With a great and overwhelming force did he
occupy the entire territory of Novgorod from frontier to frontier, inflicting
on every part of it the dread powers of his fire and sword. As in biblical
times, the prophecy did speak: 'From the rumbling and thunder of his
chariots and from the neighing of his horses the very earth shall tremble,'
so in our time was the same prophecy fulfilled over the wicked men of
Novgorod for their abjuration of the true faith and their ill deeds …

The description goes on for several pages and it is easy to conclude that
Ivan doth protest too much. The *Chronicle* reads like a rather over-insistent
attempt to justify an act of expansionist aggression. But, as we know, it is
the victors who write the history books.*

With Novgorod safely subdued, Ivan set about imposing Muscovite rule
and Muscovite forms of governance. In an act that signalled his intentions

---

* I heard a very different version from a historian at the Novgorod State Museum, where I
went to see the city's remarkable birch-bark documents. She claimed there had never been
a plot to join forces with the Lithuanians, and Novgorod had never seriously contemplated
military aggression against Moscow. Ivan's charges of consorting with Lithuania were a
trumped-up excuse to stage an invasion that was going to happen anyway.

for the future, he tore down the *veche* bell, the ancient symbol of participatory government, civic society and legal rights. The Russian lands had come to another turning point in their history: from now on, Ivan was clearly saying, they would be run on very different principles.

Under Ivan III and his successor Vasily III, the first signs of the modern Russian state began to emerge – the formerly warring princedoms were bought up or conquered by Moscow and a fragile national unity imposed by Ivan's autocratic rule. Muscovy also began to play a role on the international scene, opening diplomatic relations with a series of foreign powers.

Autocracy gave Ivan the strength he needed to embark on a vigorous campaign of territorial expansion. Under his leadership, Muscovy tripled in size. He was glorified as the Gatherer of the Russian Lands, initiating the relentless empire-building that would continue unabated into the twentieth century. Yaroslavl, Rostov, Tver and Ryazan were all gobbled up; Pskov, with its own tradition of *veches* and local democracy survived until 1510, when it too fell to the Muscovite forces. In the west, the Lithuanians were slowly driven out of the provinces they had occupied over the preceding century.

But it was expansion eastwards that was to make Russia the world's greatest land empire; and from the fifteenth century onwards the drive into Asia would bring her face to face with important questions about her identity. In contrast to Novgorod, Muscovy's state structures were broadly Asiatic – centralised, militarised and inherited in large part from the Mongols. But the quasi-European legacy of Kievan democracy still loomed large in how Russians thought of themselves. Even as autocracy took root, Kiev remained in Russians' minds as a sort of romanticised golden age. It was the beginning of an uncomfortable split in the national psyche, an unresolved stand-off between the values of East and West that would endure for many centuries.

PART TWO

EXPANSION AND EMPIRE

CHAPTER SIX

Ivan the Terrible (Ivan IV) is one of those names from Russian history that most of us know, forever redolent of despotic ruthlessness and cruelty. Ivan Grozny (his name means 'formidable' or 'awesome', rather than 'terrible' in the modern sense) was born in 1530, the grandson of Ivan III, and proclaimed Grand Prince of Moscow at the age of three, following his father's death. For fourteen years he watched and brooded as relatives and *boyars* ruled in his name. He later complained that he felt slighted and humiliated by those who dared to act on his behalf. He became introverted and resentful, given to fierce outbursts of rage and malice. It is this propensity for callous brutality that has marked Ivan's historical legacy and it is undoubtedly true that it showed itself in the way he dealt with his enemies and rivals.

Perhaps we shouldn't be surprised that Ivan Grozny was Josef Stalin's favourite historical character (see pp. 318). Towards the end of the Second World War, when the film director Sergei Eisenstein began work on his film about Ivan, Stalin called him to the Kremlin for a pep talk. Since every word Stalin spoke was regarded as a pearl of wisdom and recorded for posterity, we have a verbatim record of their conversation.

Parts of it are amusing. Stalin takes it upon himself to give Eisenstein advice about acting and film-making. He complains that the director has made Ivan's beard too long and pointy: 'S.M. Eisenstein promised to shorten the beard of Ivan the Terrible in future,' the transcript faithfully records. But other criticisms were not so simply answered, and it is easy to imagine Eisenstein's growing panic as he is interrogated in a darkened Kremlin late at night by Vyacheslav Molotov, Andrey Zhdanov and the Great Leader himself:

Stalin: Have you studied history?
Eisenstein: More or less …

Stalin: More or less! Well, I know a bit about history! ... You have made the Tsar too weak and indecisive. He resembles Hamlet. Everybody tells him what to do ... Ivan the Terrible was a great and a wise ruler: he always had our national interest at heart. He did not allow foreigners into his country ... He was a nationalist Tsar and farsighted ... By showing Ivan the Terrible the way you do, you have committed a deviation and a mistake.

Zhdanov: Your Ivan the Terrible comes over as a neurotic.

Stalin: You have to show him in the correct historical style. It is not correct that Ivan the Terrible kissed his wife for so long. At that time it was not permitted ...

Molotov: One may show conversations, repressions but not this ...

Stalin: It is true that Ivan the Terrible was extremely cruel. But you have to show the reasons why he had to be cruel.

Molotov: You have to show why repression was necessary. Show the wider needs of the state ...

Stalin: One of Ivan's big mistakes is that he didn't finish off his enemies, the big feudal families. If he had destroyed these people then he wouldn't have had the Time of Troubles. If Ivan the Terrible executed someone he repented and prayed for a long time. God disturbed him on these matters ... But it is necessary to be decisive ...

It is clear from Eisenstein's film that he is partly portraying Stalin in the figure of Ivan, and from the record of their conversation it seems Stalin was aware of this. The final version of the movie shows Ivan as cunning and decisive, not shrinking from repression and murder – one of its most dramatic scenes shows Ivan having his own cousin stabbed to death in the Kremlin – but always acting in Russia's interests, unifying the country by the strength of his autocratic rule. Stalin thought the film should have made Ivan look even tougher, but he knew its vast propaganda value for a Russian nation locked in a life and death struggle with Nazi Germany.

With a script based loosely on historical documents and on the writings of one of Ivan the Terrible's advisers, Ivan Peresvetov, Eisenstein turns the new tsar's speech at his coronation in 1547 into a vision of how Russia must be governed. Only a ruler with unlimited power, Ivan says, can guarantee Russia's survival:

> For the first time, a prince of Moscow claims the title of tsar of all the Russias, and puts an end to the divisions of the past when the *boyars* fought among themselves. From today the Russian lands shall be united. We shall establish an army with universal military service and all – all! – shall serve the state. Only a strong ruler can save Russia. Only strong rule and a united state can repel the enemies at our borders.

We can't be certain of course that these exact words were really spoken by Ivan, but they encapsulate the autocratic principles that would characterise his rule and that of nearly every ruler after him. In a deeply poignant passage that addresses both the Russia of the sixteenth century and the Soviet Union under Nazi occupation, Eisenstein has Ivan speak directly to the camera:

> For what is our country now? A body with severed limbs! We control the sources of our great rivers – Volga, Dvina, Volkhov – but their outlets to the sea are in enemy hands. Our territories have been stolen from us, but we shall win them back! From this day I shall be sole and absolute ruler, for a kingdom cannot be ruled without an iron hand. A kingdom without an iron hand is like a bridle-less horse. Broad and bounteous are our lands, but there is little order in them. Only absolute power can safeguard Russia from her foes – the Tartars, Poles and Livonians: pray for the unity of our Russian fatherland!

Ivan's Russia was beset by powerful enemies – Catholic Lithuania and Poland in the west; Sweden in the north; Muslim powers in the south and east. Early in his reign he'd experimented with a national consultative council and local assemblies. But in what amounted to a condition of never-ending war, the fist of autocracy seemed Muscovy's only hope for survival.

By the 1550s, Ivan's sole foreign ally was England. He turned to Elizabeth I with epistles that sound almost like love letters; he offered her generous trade privileges in return for artillery and munitions, and he built a luxurious English embassy within the walls of the Kremlin for English merchants and diplomats. One ambassador, Giles Fletcher, wrote in his treatise *Of the Russe Commonwealth* of the astonishing unchecked power of the Russian tsar:

> The form of their government is plain tyrannical! All are behoven to the prince after a most barbarous manner. In all matters of state – making and annulling public laws, making magistrates, the power to execute or pardon life – all pertain wholly and absolutely to the emperor, as he may be both commander and executioner of all.

The German traveller and writer Baron von Herberstein was even more scathing in his *Notes on Muscovite Affairs*, marvelling at how far Russia had diverged from the forms of governance he was familiar with in the West:

> In the power which he holds over his people, the ruler of Muscovy surpasses all the monarchs of the whole world ... He holds unlimited authority over the lives and property of all his subjects: not one of his counsellors has sufficient authority to dare to oppose him or even differ from him on any subject – in short, they believe he is the executor of the divine will.

But Herberstein was not *quite* right. We saw how Muscovy under Ivan III had unified the Russian lands in the fifteenth century, but some of the nobles – the *boyar* families who had previously ruled independent princedoms – continued to resent Ivan's assumption of absolute power. Eisenstein's film dramatises their plotting against him and, in another nod to Stalin, paints an approving picture of the tsar's obsessive rooting out of treachery among his subjects:

> We shall cut off heads without mercy! We shall crush sedition and eradicate treason! ... I stand alone – I can trust no-one ... I will smash the *boyars* – take away their patrimonial estates and award land to only those who serve the state with distinction ...

Ivan moved decisively against his opponents. He abolished the great hereditary estates that had been the powerbase of generations of princes: from now on, land would be granted – and taken away again – at the whim of the tsar, and ownership would be contingent on the recipient providing service to the state. The *boyars* were no longer consulted on affairs of government. All men outside the Church, including the nobility, were bound to lifelong service to the state; conscription was a universal duty, and the tsar's authority in all matters was absolute.

But Ivan was racked with suspicion bordering on paranoia. He murdered his own son in a fit of rage; he blamed the *boyars* for the death of his wife Anastasia, and he was the founder of Russia's first secret police – the Oprichniki – with unlimited powers to crush dissent, recruit informers and mete out summary justice. Under orders from Ivan, the Oprichniki put several thousand people to death in Novgorod because the tsar suspected they'd been talking to his enemies in Lithuania.

At one stage, Ivan's paranoia and hatred of the *boyar* families who challenged his right to rule with dictatorial powers led him to set up his own secretive state within a state, known as the Oprichnina, striking fear into the hearts of his opponents. In its ferocity and capriciousness Ivan's reign of terror anticipated that of Stalin, who enthusiastically approved of his methods (see pp. 318). In his Kremlin interrogation of Eisenstein, Stalin reproaches the director for painting a critical picture of Ivan's secret police, insisting that they were 'a progressive army' and their leader Malyuta Skuratov 'a hero'.

In fact, Ivan's repressions alienated many of his former allies. His closest personal friend and greatest general – Prince Andrei Kurbsky – fled to Lithuania and, just as the exiled Trotsky would later do with Stalin, lambasted his former comrade in epistles from abroad:

> To the Tsar, exalted by God, who *formerly* appeared most illustrious but has now been found to be the opposite! May you, o Tsar, understand this with your leprous conscience … you have persecuted me most bitterly; you have destroyed your loyal servants and spilled the blood of innocent martyrs … You have answered my love with hatred, good with evil, and my blood – spilt for you – cries out against you to the Lord God!

Unlike Stalin, though, Ivan wrote back, and the correspondence between the two former friends is riveting. From the safety of exile, Kurbsky rails at the barbarity of Ivan's autocratic regime, praising the superiority of the European civic society in which he now lives. Ivan replies contemptuously that such a system of government by consent could never work in a land as wide and unruly as Russia:

> To him who is a criminal before the blessed cross of Our Lord, who has trodden underfoot all sacred commands … and completed the treachery of a vicious dog! In view of the power handed down to me by God is it the sign of a 'leprous conscience' to hold my kingdom in my hand and not let my servants rule? … The autocracy of this great Russian kingdom has come down to [me] by the will of God … and it is the Russian autocrat who from the very beginning has ruled all his dominions – not *boyars* and not grandees! … For the rule of many is like unto the folly of women; for if men are not under one single authority, even if they are strong, even if they are brave, it will still be like the folly of women! The Russian land is ruled by us, its sovereign, and we are free to reward our servants and we are free to punish them! … and the rule of a Tsar calls for fear and terror and extreme suppression.

Ivan the Terrible is remembered as a wild-eyed, slightly deranged figure. In his later years, he seems to have swung between volcanic fits of drunkenness and depravity and episodes of terrified repentance when he begged to be allowed to enter a monastery. Shortly before his death he was pestering Queen Elizabeth with marriage proposals and requests for asylum in London. When she ignored him, he flew into a rage, addressing her in most undiplomatic language: 'I spit on you and on your palace!' Ivan's anger at a minor dispute about trade spilled over into a personal attack on the Virgin Queen:

> I thought you were the one who ran your own country. That is why I started this correspondence with you. But it seems other people are running your country besides you … You are still there in your virginal state like any spinster … Moscow can do without English goods …

Yet for all his faults, Ivan IV made a positive contribution to Russian nationhood, unifying a fractious state and dramatically expanding its borders. Under Ivan's leadership, Russia expanded beyond the lands occupied by Orthodox, ethnic Russians. It conquered the Tartar khanate of Kazan, laying the foundations for Russia's future empire: astoundingly, it would grow by 50 square miles a day for the next three centuries, until by 1914 it occupied 8.5 million square miles – a multi-ethnic, multilingual state spanning more than one-seventh of the globe.

By his death in 1584, Ivan had neutered the *boyars* and set Russia on the path of centralised autocracy. In Britain, Magna Carta may have curbed the rights of the monarchy and opened the way for a future of constitutional government, but in Russia the power of the sovereign would remain unfettered.

So deeply had the fear of internal division, and the concurrent menace of foreign invasion, permeated the Russian consciousness that the concept of a supreme ruler wielding absolute power was for the most part willingly accepted. The wealth and resources of society were commandeered for the needs of the state; peasants were tied to the land in the first steps towards full serfdom; villages and town communities were made jointly responsible for guaranteeing the payment of taxes, finding recruits for the army and keeping law and order. As we'll see, this doctrine of joint responsibility – subjugating the individual to the common welfare – would become a permanent feature of the way power was wielded in Russia. The readiness to sacrifice personal interests for the good of the state helped lay the foundations of a collectivist ethic that has remained dominant.

'The Muscovite state,' writes the nineteenth-century historian Vasily Kliuchevsky, 'in the name of common welfare took into its full control all the energies and resources of society, leaving no scope for the private interests of individuals or classes.' Compelling national need – the need for self-defence, for survival in the face of overwhelming odds – laid the foundations for a state that would become increasingly omnipotent. Karamzin, the avowed partisan of autocratic rule, concludes in his *History of the Russian State* (1816–26) that 'Russia owes her salvation and her greatness to the unlimited authority of her rulers'. And Sir George Macartney – who served as British ambassador to Russia in the eighteenth century – would comment, with a mixture of admiration and reproach, in his book *An Account of Russia*: 'To despotism Russia owes her greatness and her dominions, so that if ever the monarchy becomes more limited, she will lose her power and strength in proportion as she advances in virtue and civil improvement.'

Ivan the Terrible's sidelining of the aristocracy left only the autocrat and his subservient people. No independent structures or institutions mediated power between them. The Church saw its property confiscated and its influence wane. No infrastructure of laws and rights and no civic society – no middle class – were allowed to form. This model of society would become a major obstacle to reform in Russia, separating her ever further from developments in Western Europe and defining the character of the Russian state for many centuries to come.

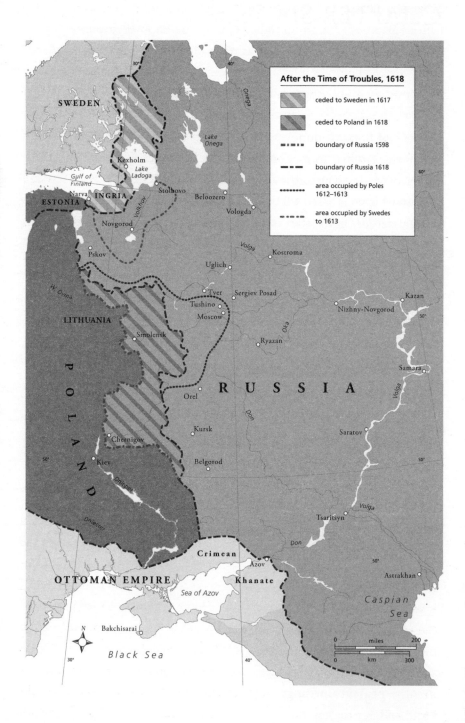

After the Time of Troubles, 1618

- ceded to Sweden in 1617
- ceded to Poland in 1618
- boundary of Russia 1598
- boundary of Russia 1618
- area occupied by Poles 1612–1613
- area occupied by Swedes to 1613

CHAPTER SEVEN

The tale of Boris Godunov, who ruled Russia after the death of Ivan the Terrible, is familiar to modern audiences through the high-octane melodrama of Modest Mussorgsky's magnificent opera. Both it and the Pushkin play on which it is based tell the story of Russia's Time of Troubles, the two fraught decades at the start of the seventeenth century – roughly between the death of Fyodor, the half-witted heir of Ivan the Terrible, and the advent of the Romanovs in 1613 – when famine, revolt, economic devastation and foreign invasions came close to destroying the Russian state for ever. Mussorgsky's libretto paraphrases Pushkin, but both play and opera conjure Shakespearean tragedy from Godunov's tormented conscience:

> Here is conspiracy, sedition of the *boyars*, Lithuanian plots … famine, plague, fear and ruin. The people wander like wild beasts, stricken with disease. Russia groans with hunger and poverty. This dreadful misery is sent by God to punish me for my grievous sin. All blame me for this calamity. Everywhere they curse the name of Boris … Everywhere I see the murdered child!

Both Mussorgsky and Pushkin accept as fact the allegation that Godunov had risen to power by murdering the true tsar, the infant son of Ivan the Terrible, thus terminating the dynastic line of Rurik, the founder of ancient Rus, and creating a catastrophically destabilising power vacuum. In reality, it seems Godunov was innocent and the child – Dmitry – died of natural causes, but the Russian people desperately needed to find some explanation for the apocalyptic fate that had befallen them since Ivan's death. Three successive years of crop failures, sub-zero temperatures even in the summer months, peasant uprisings and lacerating bouts of plague had brought death and destruction on a scale that prompted panic, and prophecies of the end of time. Hungry masses descended on Moscow, blaming Godunov for usurping the crown and provoking the wrath of God:

> What if the murdered Tsarevich Dmitry should suddenly rise from out the grave, should cry, 'Where are ye, children, faithful servants? Help me against Boris, against my murderer! Seize my foe and lead him to me!'

Unbeknown to him, Godunov's nightmare was about to come true. Amid the public unrest, a series of clever conmen stepped forward, claiming they were the tsarevich and true heir to the throne. None of these pretenders could explain how they'd miraculously risen from the grave, but such was the febrile discontent of the times that they won widespread support. The false Dmitrys played on the popular belief that the true tsar was the anointed representative of God and would never let the holy land of Russia fall into danger – so Godunov must by definition be a usurper.

Russia's enemies in the west spotted their chance. The Poles and Lithuanians threw their backing behind one of the pretenders, a young monk named Grigory Otrepev, and furnished him with 3,000 troops. In 1604, he marched on Moscow, picking up thousands of supporters who resented the oppressive rule of Moscow and regarded Godunov as an impostor. They arrived just as Godunov was about to drop dead from a heart attack; false Dmitry made a triumphal entry into the Kremlin and was proclaimed tsar in 1605. He married a Polish princess, installed Polish-Lithuanian forces in the Kremlin and announced plans to convert Russia from Orthodoxy to Catholicism.

Dmitry's reign was to be short and violent, but after his death in 1606 other pretenders emerged, and for seven turbulent years the fate of the nation hung in the balance. The Russian crown was offered to the King of Poland and it seemed another period of hostile foreign occupation was about to begin.

But in 1612, two heroes emerged to save Russia from her foes. Nowadays Muscovites walk past their memorial, by St Basil's Cathedral in the shadow of the Kremlin walls, with barely a second glance. But without their intervention, Russia could today be a Roman Catholic province of Poland and

Lithuania. The heroes' names are Minin and Pozharsky. The latter was a Russian prince, who had fought in earlier battles against the Poles, but Kuzma Minin was the archetypal man of the people, a merchant – a butcher by trade – from the city of Nizhny Novgorod.

When he heard that Moscow had fallen to the Poles, Minin flew into a patriotic rage. He launched a campaign to raise public funds for a national army of liberation and pledged to drive the occupiers out of Russia. Minin enlisted the support of the Russian Orthodox Patriarch, Germogen, who appealed to the leaders of several Russian cities: 'Let us act together of one accord … Orthodox Christians in love and unity. Let us fight unto death to free Muscovy of our enemies, the Poles and Lithuanians.' Germogen gave his official blessing to the army of national resistance, cursing the Roman Catholic Poles for their threats against Orthodoxy. For his temerity he was beaten and starved to death by the occupiers.

In the winter snows of November 1612, Minin and Pozharsky arrived on the outskirts of Moscow at the head of a rather ramshackle army. With an unexpected show of tactical genius, they manoeuvred their improvised militia and pinned down the Polish forces inside the Kremlin. Russia was saved. Surrounded and close to starvation – there were reports of them eating dogs and even of cannibalism – the Poles finally offered to surrender on condition of safe passage back to Poland.

The Russians agreed, and the weak, exhausted Poles filed out of the Kremlin gates at the foot of Red Square. But as they did so, the Russians pounced. The Poles were massacred to the last man. Such was the barbarism of the times and the passionate fervour of national feeling. The success of Minin and Pozharsky in 1612 suggests there was by now an Orthodox Russ- ian nation capable of acting independently of the tsar. Religious faith and a community of shared responsibility in the face of a common enemy were once again the glue that bound Russians together.

But the first act of the victorious people was to restore the legitimacy of the monarchy.

Ivan the Terrible, and his imbecile son Fyodor, who served as a puppet for the *boyar* Boris Godunov, were the last of the Rurik dynasty rulers. Now

Russia was in search of a new dynasty. In 1613, the absence of legitimate power had left the throne to be fought over. The Time of Troubles, first with the tormented Godunov and then the usurping Poles, had undermined the authority of the state. Now, desperate for a strong leader to unite the country against her enemies, the *boyars* called a national council (Zemskii Sobor) of the nobility, clergy and merchants to elect a tsar.

The Romanovs were one among many aristocratic clans at the Russian court. They had a connection with the Crown – Ivan the Terrible's wife Anastasia was from one of the family's branches. But they were about to prove themselves by far the most adept at exploiting the power vacuum left by the contested period of *boyar* rule during the Time of Troubles. No one knew it then, but the Romanov family would rule for 300 years, until the cataclysm of 1917. Several candidates were proposed to the *boyars'* council, including King Karl Philipp of Sweden, but the Romanovs scooped the day by promoting their young prince, Mikhail. He was just 17, but he was – crucially – a grand nephew of Ivan the Terrible and consequently an indirect link with the good old days of military strength and economic order.

The start of a new dynasty was potentially a time for a new style of governance in Russia. The nobility at the Zemskii Sobor might have seized the moment to insist on a role in running the country. And if they had done, Russia might once again have taken a different course.

Instead, the nobles acceded to what they all agreed was the country's overriding priority: the need for an absolute ruler, unshackled by restrictions on his authority, and invested with the monolithic power necessary to safeguard national security. Another opportunity to temper the autocracy that would dog Russia for centuries had slipped by with nothing changed. In the minds of the *boyars*, and almost certainly of the Russian people, the need for national unity and security was the paramount priority that overrode considerations of participatory government and individual rights. The *silnaya ruka* was Russia's default position and, as events were to prove, in 1613 it was clearly the right one.

Mikhail Romanov took office at a perilous time. The Polish occupiers had been driven out of Moscow, but they and other marauding bands of Cossacks, mercenaries and brigands continued to roam the Russian countryside. Tsar Mikhail I had to be escorted to his coronation by heavily armed troops.

But unlike Godunov, the new tsar seemed to enjoy the support of his key constituencies. Popular legends grew up around him, possibly encouraged by the Romanovs. The most famous of them, 'The Tale of Ivan Susanin', stressed Mikhail's closeness to the people, and the people's solidarity in the cause of the state. Immortalised in Mikhail Glinka's opera *A Life [Laid Down] for the Tsar* (1836), Susanin gets wind of an enemy plot: the Poles have dispatched their troops to murder Tsar Mikhail, and our hero is the nation's only hope of saving him. Susanin sends his nephew to raise the alarm, while he himself promises to take the Poles to the tsar. But Susanin leads the Poles off the road and into the depths of the Russian forest where they, and he, perish from the cold. The story's message is clear – and the Russian people understood it then, as they did from Glinka's opera two centuries later – that the individual must sacrifice himself for the greater good; the state is necessary for the survival of the people and the individual is bound to serve it.

The Susanin legend encapsulates the same collectivist ethos we saw in the self-sacrifice of Boris and Gleb, who gave up their throne, and their lives, for the sake of stability in eleventh-century Kiev (see pp. 17–18). And it will recur in the twentieth century, notably in the legend of Matvey Kuzmin, the Soviet partisan who led a Nazi patrol into an ambush at the cost of his own life. The enshrinement of the common good as society's paramount ideal makes possible at the same time some of the worst and the best in the people and the nation. At one end of the scale, it surfaces in the early idealism of twentieth-century Communism and the continuing social solidarity of the Russian people. At the other, it underpins phenomena like the Red Army's reckless sacrifice of men in the Second World War and the post-war pillaging of the civilian economy to serve the needs of the military.

The Bolsheviks didn't know what to make of the Susanin legend. At first they banned Glinka's opera because it glorified the tsar, but when they realised the power of its collectivist message, they relented. Its rousing final chorus, 'Slavsya Ty, Rus' Moya!', later to become briefly the Russian national anthem, is today a standard in the repertoire of the Red Army:

Glory to you, my native Russian land!
May you be forever strong!
Strike down with your mighty hand
All enemies who violate our land!

In 2005, the then president Vladimir Putin declared 4 November – the date Minin and Pozharsky united the nation and drove the Poles out of Moscow – a national holiday. It replaced the former Victory Day of 7 November, too closely identified with the old Communist regime. The new holiday was christened Russian National Unity Day, and it was, I suppose inevitably, hijacked by the black shirt-wearing, Hitler-saluting Russian nationalists, who interpret Russian unity as Slavic unity. The Russian National Unity Party welcomed National Unity Day with its own brand of Slavic chauvinism. 'In 1612,' it announced, 'our enemies were the Poles and Lithuanians; but today they are NATO and the assertive ethnic groups in our own Russian land.'

But that view misinterprets history, for many of those 'ethnic groups' had already been assimilated by Russia in 1612 and were fighting on the same side. Russia was by then a multi-ethnic empire that took in vast swathes of territory well beyond the traditional Slav lands. And it was, ironically, the wealth of that very empire – the northern forests, the agriculture of the Asian south, the mineral riches of Siberia – that had given Muscovy the strength to survive its recurring crises. As we'll see, the relationship between the Russian state and the Russian Empire – between its original Slavic population and its expanding multi-ethnic one – was to become an ever more crucial factor in moulding the country's future identity.

CHAPTER EIGHT

Siberia took me aback. The vastness of it is staggering, almost incomprehensible. Before I ever went there, Siberian friends had tried to explain the character of their native land to me, but words cannot capture it. Russians regard Siberians as a race apart – ethnically, linguistically and culturally Russian, they nonetheless have a bearing that marks them out. It is something to do with calmness, steadiness and openness. I have stood with the pianist Denis Matsuev in the moments before he walks on stage to play to 3,000 people and there is not a flicker of disquiet in his deep Siberian eyes. A great bear of a man, his colossal hands rain down on the keys with boundless power – his colleagues affectionately call him 'the piano smasher' – but there is no hint of effort in his unflappable face. Siberia breeds stoicism, endurance and quietude, qualities born and nurtured in a place of herculean geography, where the extremes of beauty and suffering are the stuff of daily life.

Standing on the eastern edge of the Ural Mountains, I find the distances hard to take in. In shades of green and yellow, the steppe stretches in all directions to the infinity of a barely discernible horizon. In winter, all this will be covered with pure, endless snow. Hardly surprising that this place has spawned legends of space and emptiness and freedom. Hardly surprising that the people of sixteenth-century Muscovy – oppressed under Ivan the Terrible, terrorised and dispossessed in the Time of Troubles – should look to escape eastwards, to find release and air and liberty here in the unfettered Siberian lands. There's a word for it in Russian – *volya*. It means 'freedom', but it also means 'will' or 'independence'; and, as it became ever more associated with the untamed east, it began to acquire overtones of wildness, volatility and the unknown. In later years, Siberia would gain a reputation as a place of deportation, exile and labour camps. Siberia as heaven; Siberia as hell – it has never been a place for the faint-hearted.

The rush into Siberia at the end of the sixteenth century was famously led by the dashing Cossack Yermak Timofeyevich, his memory immortalised in Russian folk poetry and popular ballads:

On the Volga, on the Kama,
Lived the Cossacks as free men!
Their leader – Yermak as they called him –
whispered to his bold comrades:
'True Cossacks, brothers all!
When summer's gone and winter's come,
Where, oh where, shall we live then?
On the Volga, to live as thieves?
Attack Kazan and meet the Tsar?
For he has sent his men,
Forty thousand 'gainst us few —
No, brothers, no!
Let us go … and take Siberia!'

Like many who came to Siberia in those days, Yermak was on the run. The Cossacks acknowledged no master – their very name means 'free men'; their kingdom was the *dikoye polye*, the wild steppe – and Yermak had fallen out with the tsar over his plundering of Russian merchant convoys.

Siberia was the refuge of choice for Russia's outcasts and outlaws. Its virgin lands needed populating and Moscow was not too choosy who did it. Ivan the Terrible handed out 20-year charters to noble families like the Stroganovs to set up colonies, but what he claimed were 'empty lands' were actually the fiefdoms of Islamic khans, successors of the Mongols and the Golden Horde.

The colonisers needed fighting men to drive them out, and Yermak was quickly signed up. In 1582, he led a small band of Cossacks deep into the Siberian hinterland, terrifying the local population with the sound of gunfire and massacring the forces of the Siberian khan Kuchum. But as winter fell, Yermak found himself cut off, far from home and short of food and bullets. With a panache that would write his name in the history books, he sent envoys back across the Ural Mountains with a message announcing that he had 'conquered Siberia'. He apologised for his past crimes against the tsar and told Ivan he was quite willing to be hanged for them, but if pardoned he would 'deliver the Kingdom of Sibir' to the Muscovite crown.

Ivan the Terrible duly pardoned Yermak, conferring on him the title of Prince of Siberia and sending him reinforcements and a superb suit of silver armour. Shortly afterwards, in a skirmish with the forces of the khan, Yermak was pursued across a tributary of the Irtysh River where the weight of the splendid armour dragged him to his death:

It was at the little stream Kamyshinka, friends –
At the little stream Kamyshinka,
Where there lived a people proud and free.
At their head stood Yermak, son of Timofey.
Alas for the son of Timofey … Alas!

Yermak may not have lived to see it, but the conquest of Siberia was to be completed with astonishing rapidity, opening up vast sources of wealth that transformed Muscovy from a state on the brink of collapse to a nation of unparalleled riches. In later years, it would be Siberia's gold, coal, timber and iron – and nowadays her vast stores of oil and gas – that would make Russia a superpower. But, as Elizabeth I's ambassador Giles Fletcher wrote with some envy, Siberia's first gift was fur:

The native commodities of the countrie (wherewith they serve both their owne turnes, and sende much abroad, to the great enriching of the emperour and his people) are many and substantiall. First, furres of all sortes. Wherein the providence of God is to be noted, that provideth a naturall remedie for them, to helpe the naturall inconvenience of their countrie by the colde of the clymat (for it would breede a very frost in a man to look abroad in that place). Their chiefe furres are these: blacke fox, sables, lusernes, dunne fox, martrones, gurnestalles or armins, lasets or miniver, bever, wulverins, the skin of a great water ratte that smelleth naturally like muske, calaber or gray squirrell, red squirell, red and white foxe. Besides

the great quantitie spent within the countrie (the people beyng clad all in
furres the whole winter), there are transported out of the countrie some
yeares by the marchants of Turkie, Persia, Bougharia, Georgia, Armenia,
and some other of Christendome, to the value of foure or five hundred
thousand rubbels, as I have heard.

Furs in the sixteenth and seventeenth centuries were to become a sort of
international gold standard, traded, bartered and creating huge fortunes.
Fur fever in Siberia acted something like the Alaskan gold rush in nineteenth-
century America, drawing in hopeful settlers who by 1648 had established a
Russian presence all the way across the region, as far as the Pacific Ocean.
Like the American Wild West, the ever-retreating frontier of unoccupied
land became a powerful and enduring El Dorado for Russia's self-made men.
In the popular imagination, the virgin lands of southern Siberia even today
inspire tales of daring adventure and romance.

But as well as material gains, Muscovy's expansionism had another goal
– security. The experience of foreign aggression and repeated invasion had
imbued the Russian mindset with an obsessive desire for protection: her
frontiers were long and vulnerable, with no natural barriers such as seas or
mountains, so she drove the danger further and further from her heartlands
by energetic colonisation in all directions. Russia felt she could be safe only
if she controlled her Eurasian hinterland – east and west – and the Soviet
Union's obsessive grip on her East European 'buffer states' suggests that
similar fears lasted well into our own times.

East of the Urals, the vastness of Siberia meant Russia could not at first
settle her new lands. But she did her best to assimilate or subdue the native
populations. Through military force, trading links, the extraction of tribute
and the exploitation of natural resources she laid the foundations of the
multi-ethnic, multilingual empire that would determine her future.

There is, though, another, darker side to Siberia. Shostakovich's opera
Lady Macbeth of the Mtsensk District (1934), with its prisoner's lament on
the journey to the east, poignantly evokes the convict road that so many
Russians would tread over the next four centuries:

Mile after mile creeps by in the endless march.
The heat of the day is done,
The sun on the steppes is setting.
Oh, road, where chains are dragged,
where bones of the dead still lie,
where blood and sweat have flowed,
to the echoing groans of the dying!

Isaak Levitan's painting *The Vladimirka Road* (1892) captures similar emotions. In a desolate landscape, a path has been worn through the steppe. It stretches to the far horizon, where it seems to have no end. There are no human figures in Levitan's canvas, but the power of the work is the unspoken presence of the generations of feet that have created the path, as they marched eastwards along the convict road to exile.

Siberia as land of opportunity has always coexisted with Siberia as land of torment and captivity. From the seventeenth century, they developed side by side. First the tsars, then the Soviet leaders saw it as a safe, distant dumping ground for those who threatened their power. Fyodor Dostoevsky, Lenin, Stalin, Osip Mandelstam and Alexandr Solzhenitsyn were among those who trod its frozen paths, each of them exiled for troubling the Kremlin autocrats. The early Romanovs sent convicted criminals and prisoners of war to forced service in battalions defending the frontier; exile in tsarist times was largely to villages and towns, where offenders would be monitored until the end of their sentence (Lenin was allowed to take his hunting rifles and half his voluminous library with him). But by the1930s, Siberia was covered in a network of labour camps, and the majority of inmates were political prisoners. Even if a prisoner escaped, death awaited him from starvation in the forests and swamps.

I have seen the places where so many suffered in Stalin's Gulag. Most traces of the camps have been erased, but not all of them can be. About 120 miles outside the Siberian town of Tyumen, in the midst of endless birch forests, I found the remains of the Bazhenov labour camp slowly being reclaimed by weeds and saplings. Right beside it, though, a vast hole in the ground – a mile wide and seemingly almost as deep – bore indelible witness to the work of the thousands of prisoners who were forced to quarry asbestos here. Today, the work continues with modern mining methods, but deaths from lung disease in the area are enormously high. Just standing on the edge of the pit makes me uneasy about what I am breathing in. But back in the 1940s and 1950s, camp inmates were forced to chip away at the asbestos with picks and shovels and without any protection. The camp records make poignant reading. At least 7,000 men and 600 women were imprisoned here, and documents list the tasks they were forced to carry out: 'manual work in asbestos quarry; digging of mine shafts; geological explorations; work in asbestos processing facilities; asbestos enrichment tasks; building of road and rail transport facilities; construction of camp buildings and accommodation'.

The archives list the names of the camp commandants over the years of its existence – Colonels Afanasiev and Trofimov; Lieutenant-Colonels Yorkin, Zheleznikov, Filimonov, Perminov; Major Gorbunov – and record that Bazhenov was finally closed on 29 April 1953, less than two months after the death of Stalin. The records testify that Colonel Trofimov was 'relieved of his duties due to ill health', although his illness is not specified. There is no information about the health of inmates either during or after their time in the camp.

Bazhenov was one of nearly 500 ITLs – Correctional Labour Camps – that made up Stalin's Gulag, a vast network of locations mostly here in Siberia, but spreading to nearly all areas of the Soviet Union, where an estimated 14 million people were imprisoned between 1929 and 1953. Conditions were made deliberately harsh. Political prisoners – the *politzeks* – were treated worst of all, and it's thought one and half million died from hunger, disease, cold and exhaustion. The population of the camps was a valuable source of free labour for the Soviet Union as it rushed to build its industrial base. All the great Siberian construction projects – the railways, canals, power stations and gigantic blast furnaces that became the showpieces of the Soviet economy – were built by prisoners. When the central planners ran short of labour, the NKVD (the People's Commissariat for Internal Affairs, or secret police) would always supply them with more freshly arrested 'enemies of the people'. Like Bazhenov, the majority of ITLs were closed after Stalin's death, but some continued to operate well into the 1980s.

A period of openness about the camps came in the 1990s when archives were declassified, but today the Russian state harasses organisations like

Memorial that continue to expose the crimes of the Soviet era. Siberians live daily with the legacy of their past, not just from the twentieth century but from earlier times of exile too. The Siberian poet Yevgeny Yevtushenko, himself a descendant of exiles, captures the ambivalent nature of the place – as freedom or as banishment – in his haunting, autobiographical narrative poem *Stantsiya Zima* (literally 'Winter Station', in fact the name of his home town):

> These involuntary peasant settlers
> took (I suppose) this foreign countryside
> like fate, each to his own unhappiness:
> one's stepmother, however kind-hearted,
> can never be the same as a mother.
> But having crumbled its soil in their fingers,
> and let their children drink of its water,
> they realised it was their own, the flesh
> of their flesh, tied by blood to them.
> So they put on again the yoke of destitution,
> that bitter-tasting life. No one blames
> an old nail sliding into a wall: it's being
> hammered with the butt of an axe!
> There were so many hardships,
> anxieties of survival;
> however much they bent their
> labouring backs,
> it always turned out it was not they
> who consumed the crops –
> The crops consumed them …

It would be many years after the initial sixteenth-century colonies before Moscow could extend her centralised control to the furthest reaches of her empire. In the early years, when Yevtushenko's ancestors first arrived, much of Siberia remained beyond the pale. Many who were exiled there simply disappeared into its endless landscape. The Siberian taiga became a refuge for the discontented, the overtaxed and disaffected peoples of European

Russia – a sort of safety valve for those who harboured resentment against the tsar and his agents. One such group would eventually grow into a major force in Russian history, attracting millions of followers.

On a day of biblical-scale downpours, I waded through the puddles in a rutted cinder track on the edge of Yekaterinburg, a city of around a million people on the eastern slopes of the Ural Mountains. I was looking for a church, the Shrine of the Birth of Christ, and found it tucked away behind a sports field and medical dispensary. My knock at the wooden door at the back of the church was answered by a tall, serious priest, his black beard trailing down his black cassock and his long hair tied tightly back. Father Pavel declined my offer to shake hands, saying the priesthood did not permit it. He looked in his fifties but told me he was 39. I said I had come in search of the Old Believers, and he nodded gravely. 'That is not a name we encourage. We are the true Church, the only Church.'

The Old Believers – *Starovery* or *Staro-obryadtsy* – are the heirs of historical disaffection. Their ancestors were religious dissidents who split from the official Muscovite Church in the 1650s, fled to Siberia and braved centuries of persecution to keep their form of worship alive. Like the Pilgrim Fathers, they opted for exile rather than betray their beliefs. But numerically, and politically, they were much more significant. Many millions of Russians renounced the official Church in a schism that began as a protest against the state-sponsored reform of liturgical rituals – how to make the sign of the cross, how to bow, how many times to say hallelujah – but developed into a power struggle over the role of Church and State.

The Old Believers opposed the hijacking of religious belief by a centralised state-sponsored hierarchy and clung to democratic self-determination in the appointment of priests and the running of parishes. So fierce were their beliefs that thousands of them burned themselves to death rather than submit.

When the Old Believers were declared heretics and excommunicated en masse, the spirit of rage and resentment came close to revolution. And it found a remarkable spokesman in a fiery priest from Nizhny Novgorod called Avvakum Petrov:

What we need to do is spit on all these newfangled rituals and books and then all will be well ... As to my excommunication, it came from heretics so in Christ's name I trample it underfoot. And the curse they have put on me? I won't mince my words – I wipe my arse with it!

As students, we all loved Avvakum's autobiography because it was full of such pithy, vigorous putdowns – there's plenty of straight talk about sex and descriptions of his opponents as 'shit-faced pharisees' wiping their backsides with hellfire – all expressed in a laconic, down-to-earth brand of Old Russian. But as I re-read it now, I see what a marvellous document the *Life of Avvakum* is, and what a remarkable man he was. When Tsar Alexei began to crack down on the schismatics with the cooperation of the official Church under its patriarch Nikon, Avvakum and his family were banished to Siberia. In his *Life,* Avvakum recounts how for 14 years they were imprisoned in a pit dug into the frozen earth. In the face of certain death – he was eventually burned at the stake in 1682 – he meditates on the nature of spiritual belief and earthly authority, in a series of agonised, self-doubting but ultimately triumphant passages:

As they were beating me, I felt no pain because of the prayers I was saying. But now as I lie here the thought comes to me: Oh, Son of God, why did you let them beat me so? When I was living as a sinful man, You did not chastise me, but now I know not in what I have sinned ... Woe for my sinful soul! My daughters dwell in poverty and their mother and brothers lie buried in a dungeon in the earth. But what can be done? Every man must endure pain for the Christian faith, and with God's help I will accept that which has been ordained and will come to pass ... Many have been burned and baked. They burned Isaiah and Abraham and other defenders of the Church. God will count the number of them ... So, are you afraid of that furnace? Take heart, spit on it, and do not be afraid! You may feel afraid, but as soon as you go into the furnace, everything will be over in an instant ... When we all are dead, these words of mine shall be read and we shall be remembered before God ... In very truth I know not how I may endure this thing to the end: but I glorified God and He knows that. I am in His hands now ...

As I walked into the Old Believer Church in Yekaterinburg, I suppose I was vaguely expecting Father Pavel to be a modern-day version of fiery old Avvakum. He spoke cogently about his own experiences – how he had helped reclaim the church building from the state after the Communists had converted it into a museum, how he and two other priests had built up the congregation and engaged local icon painters to restore the iconostasis. But when I asked if relations with the official Orthodox Church were better now, Father Pavel frowned. 'How can we have good relations with them? They have betrayed the truth of Christ.' I must have looked puzzled because Father Pavel launched into a tirade. 'We are the only Church that has remained constant. And those who remain constant will win salvation. How can anyone believe the sign of the cross should be made with three fingers, like they do? Of course it must be made with two fingers, as Our Lord has taught us ...'

As the priest spoke, I thought of the centuries of deaths and suffering, the mass immolations like those portrayed with vivid fury in Mussorgsky's opera Khovanshchina, and I was at a loss to understand. How could the difference between two fingers and three fingers, or saying hallelujah three times instead of two, lead men to murder and die with such alacrity? The answer, undoubtedly, was that people were taught and came to believe that these things made the critical difference between eternal salvation and the burning fires of hell. It put me in mind of the fervent women I had encountered scurrying through the catacombs of Kiev's Monastery of the Caves. From the seventeenth century onwards, the passion that led men to die for such convictions fomented huge resentment against a Muscovite state that was seen as encouraging apostasy.

Two months after Avvakum's death, a new tsar would come to the throne, and the swelling anger of the Old Believers would be part of a daunting set of problems he would have to tackle: a semi-underground Church in sullen opposition to the state, and a yawning gap between an autocratic tsar and a downtrodden people; an empire over-extended in Siberia and in the increasingly troublesome south. The new tsar would have to make changes, and make them fast, if he wanted to avert the looming crisis.

CHAPTER NINE

Readers of a certain generation may recall a pop song called 'The Carnival Is Over.' It was a UK number one for the Seekers in 1965, sandwiched between the Rolling Stones and the Beatles; its words spoke of hearts beating 'like a drum' and pledges to 'love you till I die'. But the haunting melody was copied from a traditional Russian folk song whose lyrics were considerably less anaemic. 'Stenka Razin' is the violent, bloody tale of a Don Cossack who sails across the Caspian Sea to loot, pillage and abduct a Persian princess. When he proposes to make her his bride, Razin is mocked by his comrades for being so soppy. So, 'with one mighty blow of his brawny arm', he proves his manhood by throwing the poor woman overboard to her death.

The murder is probably a legend, but Razin himself was a real historical figure. In 1670, he led a revolt against the tsar and the Muscovite state. Setting out from the Cossack heartland on the River Don, he gathered thousands of followers as he marched north – from persecuted peasants to nomadic tribesmen and religious rebels – in a broad alliance of disaffection. Razin proclaimed himself the true tsar and promised an end to exploitation, with freedom and equality for all men. Taken aback by the strength of the revolt, Moscow watched helplessly as his forces captured a string of major towns, including Saratov, Samara and Astrakhan, ordering the execution of aristocrats and government officials, and turning food supplies over to the common people. Razin's promise of deliverance from the oppression of tsarism and the abolition of class privileges roused the population. By the autumn, his army was nearly 200,000 strong and it took a full-scale military campaign before the Kremlin could subdue him.

Stenka Razin's democratic populism struck a chord with the oppressed lower classes and the non-Russian minorities, exposing a simmering resentment in Russian society and a widening gap between rulers and ruled. When he was hanged, drawn and quartered on Red Square, the crowd stubbornly refused the official order to rejoice – an event commemorated three centuries later in Yevgeny Yevtushenko's poem, 'The Execution of Stenka Razin':

'Why, good folk, are you not celebrating?
Caps into sky – and dance!'
But Red Square is frozen stiff,
the halberds scarcely swaying.
Amid the deadly silence ...
The square had understood something.
The square took off their caps,
and the bells
struck three times
seething with rage.
But heavy from its bloody forelock
the head was still rocking,
still alive.
From the blood-wet place of execution,
there where the poor were,
... hoarsely the head spoke:
'I have not died in vain ...'
and, savagely,
not hiding anything of his triumph,
Stenka's head
burst out laughing at the Tsar!'*

Eleven troubled years after Razin's execution, a new tsar was crowned. Peter I – Peter the Great – was only nine in 1682, and for a decade and a half he would be shamelessly manipulated by relatives and regents in a ruthless,

---

* These verses from Yevtushenko's poem were set powerfully to music in the 1960s by Dmitry Shostakovich, as 'The Execution of Stepan Razin'. Both poem and cantata nominally celebrate the official Soviet version of Razin as a proto-socialist rebelling against tsarist autocracy. But, as with much of their work, Yevtushenko and Shostakovich knew it would have a deeper resonance: the autocrats were still in the Kremlin; they had merely traded in the tsarist crown for a Soviet red star.

violent power struggle. Peter was initially made to share power with his sickly half-brother Ivan, as the contenders for power jostled around him. Some of his closest friends were murdered before his eyes, and Peter was left with a burning conviction that Russia must change. In 1696, when he assumed full authority, he inherited a host of urgent problems that were tearing the nation apart – the legacy of the Razin rebellion, the split within the Church and the Old Believers' continuing opposition, the growing disconnect between the Kremlin and the people, and the curse of serfdom.

Peter the Great was a giant, both physically (he was 6 feet 7 inches tall) and intellectually. His relentless energy and fierce determination would make him the most influential ruler in Russian history; only Lenin would come close to him in the impact he had on society and power. Peter reformed the way Russia was governed, creating its first civil service, building a new capital city and bringing the Russian calendar into line with the rest of the world. He constructed a modern army, and a navy that saved Russia from the very real threat of foreign invasion. And he turned a nation in danger of self-destructing into a European great power, with a vast, stable empire capable of supporting her international ambitions. Just as Britain, Spain and Portugal were founding colonies in the New World, Russia was racing to catch up with the world's great empire builders.

Peter the Great has traditionally been credited with Europeanising Russia; he's remembered as the great moderniser who 'opened a window on the West' and turned the country away from its old Asiatic leanings. In reality, this is only partially true. But what is clear is that his formative years and early education were dominated by progressive, largely civilising European influences. Testimony to Peter's Westernising character is found in the memoirs of Patrick Gordon, an expatriate Scottish soldier who saved him from an attempted coup and was subsequently appointed senior general in the tsar's army. Gordon describes a young man who 'had a great regard for learning and was at much pains to introduce it into the country. He rose early; the morning he gave to business till ten or eleven o'clock.' But he also points out that Peter's prodigious appetite for work was complemented by a prodigious appetite for other things:

He was a lover of company, and a man of much humour and pleasantry, exceedingly facetious and of vast natural parts ... He never kept guards about his person ... He never could abide ceremony, but loved to be spoken to frankly and without reserve ... All the rest of the day, and a great part of the night, [he devoted] to diversion and pleasure. He took his bottle heartily, so must all the company; for when he was merry himself he loved to see everybody so.

Peter's carousing was shared at first hand by Patrick Gordon's son-in-law, Alexander, another of the many Westerners who tutored the young monarch and continued to instil Western ideas in him throughout much of his life. Alexander praises Peter's 'great and singular genius' and testifies that he was 'through the whole of his life a warm friend to the interests of Great Britain'. 'No one who was acquainted with the civil and military state of Russia in Tsar Peter's minority,' he concludes, 'and was a witness of the almost incredible reformation which he introduced in both, could think with indifference of him, or of the great change which he almost instantaneously made upon a barbarous and uncivilised people.'

But for all the high-flown ideals, Peter never lost touch with the earthy side of his character. It comes as no surprise to hear that Alexander Gordon sealed the tsar's friendship via the shared Russian and Scottish fondness for a wee dram:

Soon after his arrival in Russia, [Alexander] was invited to a marriage where a good many young gentlemen of the best families in the land were present ... When the gentlemen were warm with their liquor, some of them spoke very disrespectfully of foreigners in general and of the Scots in particular. Mr Gordon who had a strong passion for his country ... gave the one who sat next to him a blow on the temple, which brought him on the floor. In an instant, he and another five were upon Mr Gordon and seemed determined to make him fall a victim to their national prejudice. But Mr Gordon's fists were so weighty, and bestowed with such goodwill that his antagonists bore the mark of them for several weeks... and he had the glory of the victory in this very unequal combat. Next day a complaint was given in to Tsar Peter, wherein Mr Gordon was represented in the worst light imaginable. His Majesty immediately ordered Mr Gordon to be sent for, [who] owned that this message made him tremble. Putting on a very stern countenance, the tsar asked him how he came to be so turbulent and whether the charge brought against him was just. But Mr Gordon spoke so modestly of his own behaviour and seemed so sorry to have incurred the tsar's displeasure that the affair ended in a manner quite contrary to the expectations of his enemies. The tsar, after hearing him very patiently, said: 'Well, Sir, your accusers have done you justice by allowing that you beat six men: and I also will do you justice' … and on saying this, he returned with a Major's commission which he presented to Mr Gordon with his own hand.

Peter the Great would be a drinker and reveller for the whole of his life. He combined intelligence and wit with an unremitting penchant for debauchery. With a band of close associates he formed the All-joking, All-drunken Synod of Fools and Jesters, a sort of Hellfire Club, with extravagant rituals of feasting, drunkenness and savage mockery of the Church. Like Shakespeare's Prince Hal, he could carouse with the best of them. But, like Hal, he maintained an unwavering seriousness of intent and acceptance of his destiny. Having had to share power for the first 14 years of his reign with his imbecile half-brother, Peter assumed sole authority at the age of 23 and took as his official title 'Peter the First, Emperor and Autocrat of All the Russias'. This was clearly going to be a ruler to be reckoned with.

Peter the Great's private apartments are now reconstituted in the Hermitage in St Petersburg. When I was shown around them, the first thing that struck me was how small the rooms were. A man of his great size would have found them physically very restrictive and theories have been advanced that he suffered from a type of agoraphobia, that made him seek refuge in cosy places. It is true that Peter had an aversion to crowds; a nervous affliction made his head jerk uncontrollably, and sudden seizures sometimes caused him to collapse. But Peter also loved the sea and spent as much time as he could on board ship, so a more likely explanation is that he ordered the rooms to be built small because he wanted them to resemble an enfilade of ship's cabins. Peter studied military matters with an obsessive passion, learning carpentry and seamanship so thoroughly that he could build a vessel with his own hands. Amid the maps and globes and maritime charts in his private rooms, there is a fully equipped workshop with 162 chisels ranged on racks around the walls.

Much of the living room and bedroom furniture in the private apartments is English, and the story of how Peter acquired it sums up the intellectual curiosity, determination and enterprise that would mark his approach to domestic and foreign policy. In 1697, perhaps prompted by Patrick Gordon and his other foreign advisers, the 24-year-old Peter announced he intended to travel incognito through Western Europe dressed as a merchant seaman. The disguise may have been a little thin – he took plenty of royal minders with him – but it allowed Peter to learn at first hand how advanced nations ran their government and their military. In Holland he worked for four months in a shipyard. In England he travelled to London, wrecking the private house where he was lodging, like a modern rock star, and making visits to Oxford and Manchester. He apparently didn't like the Mancunians very much, but he learned a lot from them about city building that he would put to good use when he embarked on the construction of St Petersburg six years later.

Peter took up residence near the Royal Dockyards at Greenwich, where he signed on as a simple carpenter, keen to learn as much as he could about the world-leading skills of British shipbuilders. One of them, Captain John Perry, to whom Peter took a particular shine, commented that the tsar 'conversed with our English builders, who showed him their drawings and the method of laying down by proportion any ship or vessel, of whatever form required, with the rules for moulding and building a ship according to such a drawing, which extremely intrigued and pleased his Majesty, and which he found everywhere practised, in the merchants' yards as well as those of the King'. Another Greenwich shipwright reports that 'the Tsar of Muscovy worked with his own hands as hard as any man in the yard'. And Perry approvingly concludes:

He spent most of his time in what related to war and shipping, and upon the water. He often took the carpenter's tools in his hands and often worked in the Deptford Yard as he had done before in Holland. He would be found at the smiths' and at the gun-founders' and there was scarce any art or mechanic trade whatsoever, from the watchmaker to the coffin-maker, but he inspected it.

On his return home, Peter used the knowledge he had gained to embark on a frenetic building programme for the Russian navy. He had taken back with him to Russia a cohort of British engineers, whom he charged with revolutionising his shipyards. One of them was John Perry, who took a measure of national pride in helping to implement the tsar's plans:

> He now made those Englishmen that he had brought over his chief master-builders and he discharged all the [previous] builders, except those who were to finish the ships that they had begun, and those who were left under the command of the English; and he decreed that for the future there should be no ships built but in the English fashion.

With the help of Perry and his fellow engineers, the Russian navy was transformed from a handful of outdated vessels to a fleet of 300 state-of-the-art warships. It was a remarkable achievement that would bring Peter success in two long-held strategic goals – domination of the Baltic Sea in the north after a gruelling war with Sweden, and a first, tenuous toehold on the Black Sea in the south. From being a landlocked state, Russia would finally make the breakthrough to become an empire with an opening on the world.*

---

* One of Peter's commanders, the Dane Vitus Bering, was dispatched to reconnoitre the eastern coast of Siberia, eventually landing in Alaska, just 50 miles across the strait that now bears his name. For the first time, two groups of European pioneers, one at the western extreme of their frontier, the other at the easternmost, would meet around the other side of the world from their starting point. With fur still a vital trading commodity, the quality of Alaskan sea otter pelts persuaded Moscow to colonise the new territory, and it remained in Russian hands until it was sold to America – for the derisory sum of $7 million – in 1867.

The lesson Peter had learned from his sojourn in the West was that to succeed, Russia needed to change. And if Russia wanted to stay strong abroad, it needed to tackle the problems undermining it at home. The adoption of European knowhow had worked well for the military, and Peter decided the same modernising methods were needed in civil society.

When Peter the Great founded his new capital city in 1703 (named after St Peter the Apostle, not after himself) he was making a grand statement. His Scottish general, Patrick Gordon, and most of the Russian aristocracy were appalled by the location – a swampy, desolate bog in the distant northwest, where the River Neva enters the Gulf of Finland. But the audacity of Peter's choice was charged with an emblematic resonance of renewal and adventure that would inspire future generations, including the greatest of all Russian writers, Alexander Pushkin. His epic poem 'The Bronze Horseman', written a hundred years later, opens with an elegant love letter to the young European city of St Petersburg, 'gem of the Northern world', whose splendour would oust the old, Asiatic-leaning Moscow:

> ... Oh, how I love thee, city of Peter's making;
> I love thy harmonies austere,
> And Neva's sov'reign waters breaking
> Along her banks of granite sheer ...
> A century – and that city young,
> Gem of the Northern world, amazing,
> From gloomy wood and swamp up-sprung,
> Has risen, in pride and splendour blazing ...
> To that young capital now is drooping
> The crest of Moscow – on the ground;
> A dowager in purple, stooping,
> Before an empress newly crowned.

Petersburgers still passionately believe their city is special – different from all others – and I can understand why. When I came to study here in the mid 1970s, I found the imperial scale of the place almost surreal: the never-ending boulevards and even vaster squares; the White Nights when darkness is banished and the city takes on its magical aura of ethereal beauty – you can see why Peter was obsessed with it. And you can see why the opening of a 'window on Europe' has become the defining metaphor of his reign. The oppressive years of Mongol domination had changed Russia. The Muscovy that emerged from the Mongol yoke had become closed and inward-looking. Foreigners were all regarded as potential enemies; the Kremlin kept out European ideas.

But Peter, it seemed, was renouncing all that. Ancient, cramped Moscow, 'a widow in purple', was giving way to the openness and modernity of the new capital. Moscow embodied the old era of Asiatic despotism, Ivan the Terrible and the Time of Troubles. But St Petersburg would be the future. Peter spoke of a 'great leap from darkness into light'. Italian and French architects were engaged to build splendid stone palaces, and the nobles were commanded to move to the new capital en masse.

Nothing could be clearer – Russia was becoming a European state, with all the implications that would have for the way it was governed and the way its people were treated. Now there would be an end to autocracy and repression; now there would be, if not democracy, then justice and the rule of law. Or would there?

The first clues that Peter's reforms might not be all they seemed came in the very way he set about building his new capital. While the city rose, gleaming and splendid, its foundations – laid on gigantic crates of stones sunk by slave labourers into the boggy mire – were literally full of the dead. Peter knew his workforce was perishing by the tens, perhaps even hundreds, of thousands. He knew that punitive labour in the treacherous swamps, freezing weather, starvation and disease were causing human suffering on a massive scale. But he put the interests of the state above the interests of its people. What clearer image could there be of the survival of the old despotism even as it purported to introduce the new, 'modern', civilised Russia? Pushkin, the democrat and liberal, is so aware of this that by the end of 'The Bronze Horseman', his initial praise for Peter is tinged with horror:

> He, who our city by the sea had founded,
> Whose will was Fate – most terrible there
> He sat, begirt with mist and air.
> What hidden power and might he claims!
> What fire on yonder horseback flames!
> Proud charger, whither art thou ridden,
> Where leapest thou? and where, on whom,
> Wilt plant thy hoof? – Ah, lord of doom
> Oh, potentate … in thy hold
> A curb of iron, thou grasped of old
> O'er Russia 'neath thy feet cast down …

In those bitter verses, learned by heart by generations of Russians, Pushkin is addressing – indeed berating – the iconic statue of Peter the Great, the tsar as Bronze Horseman, which stands on Senate Square in the centre of the city. Rising dramatically from a colossal block of granite, the horse's front hooves are suspended perilously above the heads of those who walk beneath it. Peter's hand is outstretched, as if ready to gallop forwards and upwards into the air. The Bronze Horseman has become a symbol of St Petersburg, of the city's founder and all he stood for.

Pushkin clearly has an ambiguous view of Peter, and of autocrats in general. The hero of his poem, Yevgeny, is a representative of the common people – the *malenky chelovek*, (little man) – who bears the brunt of Peter's megalomania, goes mad with anger and despair and, in a daring gesture of revolt, shakes his fist at the tsar on his horse:

> About the statue, at its base,
> Poor mad Yevgeny circled, straining
> His wild gaze upward at the face
> That once o'er half the world was reigning.
> Through his heart a flame was creeping
> And in his veins the blood was leaping.
> He halted sullenly beneath
> The haughty statue; clenched his teeth,

Then clenched his fist …
And shuddered, whispering angrily,
'Ay, architect, with thy creation
Of marvels … Ay, beware of me!'
And then, in wild precipitation
He fled. For now he seemed to see
The mighty Emperor, quietly,
With awesome anger burning,
His visage to Yevgeny turning!

In his fevered, despairing madness, Yevgeny hears the tsar's bronze statue chasing him through St Petersburg, the horse's dreadful hooves thundering on the cobbled squares and streets. Pushkin's image of Peter as vengeful tyrant brutally crushing the hopes of the people is remarkable and chilling. But it is balanced by the poet's unfeigned admiration for all that Peter achieved – the unsurpassed beauty that is St Petersburg and the transformation of Russia into a modern power oriented towards the Western world. It is true that Peter had much of the despot about him. But it was that very ruthlessness that allowed him to push through his drastic and urgently needed programme of modernisation in the face of stern resistance from a society unused to and suspicious of change.

I found the physical embodiment of one of Peter's most significant changes in the costume section of the St Petersburg Hermitage Museum. On a chilly Monday in September, a curator took me to see the museum's stores of eighteenth-century apparel, an array of ornate and painstakingly individuated uniforms, some with epaulettes, some with braid, all sewn from different-coloured silks and satins, and each one corresponding to a specific rank not in the army but in the vast civil bureaucracy Peter created. There were uniforms for ministers of state, civil councillors, borough surveyors, stewards, chamberlains, state registrars and collegiate registrars. Not only that, each rank had its own rights and privileges; each was assigned a specific title and form of address ('Your Excellency', 'Your Nobleness', 'Your High Nobleness' and so on) that had to be rigidly adhered to. It has been calculated that here were 262 distinct gradations of seniority. It was formalisation and codification on a grand scale.

But this was not merely organisation for organisation's sake. Peter had a very real reason for introducing his new civil service system and at its heart was the country's desperate need for order and accountability. For many centuries, Russia had been run as a capricious autocracy – the Tsar at the top, the people at the bottom and little in the way of civic institutions to mediate power between the two. Corrupt, often uneducated placemen appointed through connections and bribery wielded unchecked authority over justice, taxes and daily life. They took their cut from the money they raised from the people, and their abuses fostered resentment and unrest. The pernicious system of *kormlenie* – literally 'feeding' – had seen a long succession of tsars give their friends and favourites unchecked responsibility for administering a geographical region or a sector of the economy. The appointee would receive no salary, but he would have the right to enrich himself from the cash flow his activities generated. It was an unfettered licence to rip off the people.*

Peter the Great was the first tsar to recognise the problem. In a sense he was forced to do so. Russia's system of governance had forfeited the trust of the people. A distinct lack of consent on the part of the ruled had resulted in popular revolts like that of Stenka Razin and the rebellion of the Old Believers. Peter's response was to rebuild the system from head to toe. He set out to create the machinery of what he called 'a regular state', where things would work according to rules, where the will of the sovereign would be mediated by respected institutions, and tax farming replaced by equitable levies. His overriding aim was to engage the population in the interests of the state, to win their support by offering them a stake in society rather than by coercion; to replace resentment with patriotism and civic consciousness.

Peter abolished the old patronage system, the hereditary posts and privileges of the aristocracy, and instituted a new merit-based structure of civil administration.

---

* In some ways, the legacy of *kormlenie* lives on in the Russian lands. Today's masters of the Kremlin reward their cronies with the chairmanship of the great national industries, from gas to oil to transport. They don't own the industry per se, but they control its revenues, and the tales of bulging Swiss bank accounts are legion. Individuals who get in their way are quickly dealt with. The oil magnate Mikhail Khodorkovsky, for instance, dared to challenge the Kremlin and found his company confiscated and himself in a Siberian jail.

The uniforms, grades and titles in the Hermitage Museum were the emblematic manifestations of Peter's famous Table of Ranks, 14 rigidly defined steps of state service through which its members would progress by promotions based solely on personal accomplishments. From now on, there would be an end to string pulling and nepotism. The nobles would have to educate themselves, pass exams and serve in the new civil service, where precedence would depend on their performance and probity.

Peter's vision of a 'regular state' meant eliminating abuses and corruption. Now regulation would replace the capricious rule of petty potentates. He wanted to strengthen the state and make sure it ran properly.*

Remarkably, commoners too were allowed to enter the meritocracy. They had to start at the lowest of the table's 14 ranks, but for the first time ordinary people could aspire to advancement and a higher social station. Under Peter, recognition and rewards would be determined less by birth than by hard work and service to the tsar.

This was not, it should be stressed, democracy. There was no sense in which the people could influence either state policy or the selection of state officials. The tsar would still make those decisions. But Peter had decided it was in everyone's interest that state policy should be implemented in a way that was seen as fair to all. It was certainly in his own interests because the old ways of corruption and abuse had brought the state to the point of crisis.

It might therefore be said that Peter was changing things so things could stay the same. His aim was to strengthen and ensure the survival of the autocratic tsarist system. But in order to do that, he knew he had to reform those elements of the system that were bringing his authority into disrepute and endangering its long-term prospects. It is an intriguing paradox and one encountered again with the reforms of Alexander II, Nicholas II and Mikhail Gorbachev among others.

Peter, unsurprisingly, encountered vehement opposition from those who had prospered under the old system. One of the biggest bones of contention was his programme of Westernisation. When he ordered the nobility to dress

---

* His policies could be termed 'statist' in the same sense that Vladimir Putin – another autocratic Petersburger – put the supremacy of the state at the heart of his policy-making.

in the Western manner, learn French and cut off their beards, many simply refused. So he responded with a 'beard tax' for anyone who failed to become a short-haired, clean-shaven European. Those who clung to the old forms of dress would be forced to change. The French writer Jean Rousset de Missy left a wry description of the battle of wills that ensued:

> The Russians had always worn long beards, which they admired and took much care to preserve, letting them hang down on their chests, without even trimming their moustache ... The tsar ordered that all except priests and peasants must pay a fine of a hundred roubles a year if they wanted to keep their beards, and the common people would have to pay one kopek each. Officials were posted at the gates of the towns to collect the tax. The Russians regarded the [anti-beard campaign] as a terrible sin on the part of the tsar because it was tantamount to an attack on their religion ... As to the reform of clothes, the Russians' garments, like those of the Orientals, were very long, reaching down to the ground. The tsar issued an ordinance banning that style of dress and commanding all the nobles to dress in the French fashion ... A suit of clothes cut in the new style was hung at the gate of every city, with a decree commanding all except the peasants to have their clothes made on this model, upon penalty of being forced to kneel and have all of their garments which fell below the knee cut off by the city guards ... Women's dress was changed, too. English hairdressing was to replace caps and bonnets; bodices and skirts instead of the former undergarments ... His Majesty set the example in all these changes.

If the attack on beards and kaftans symbolised a change in mindset, there were more substantive changes, too. Peter introduced compulsory education, making the children of nobles, clerks and officials study mathematics and geometry. And he sent young noblemen abroad to learn about the West, just as he himself had done. He opened diplomatic missions in major European capitals and invited foreign specialists to come and work in Russia. Jealousy of the incomers often spilt over into violence, but the tsar stood firm. He had opened the window, and the light from Europe was flooding in.

In perhaps his boldest move, Peter took steps to weaken the power of the Church. He abolished the post of patriarch and entrusted the running of Russian Orthodoxy to a council of clergy, which he himself partly controlled.* Secular education was favoured over religious instruction, men under the age of 50 were banned from becoming monks, and the Church's finances were deftly reformed to make it beholden to the state.

As a man, Peter gloried in authority, proclaiming himself emperor – *Imperator Russorum* – a reflection of his determination to have Russia recognised as a great power with a great empire, an aspiration that still resonates today. He succeeded in making Russia a Eurasian empire and a great European power, but only at the cost of the Orthodox Church and Russian nationhood.

When there was resistance to Peter's reforms, he was quick and cruel in crushing it. After a rebellion by his elite guards, the Streltsy, Peter had a thousand of them tortured and executed, personally participating in the slaughter and hanging their corpses on street corners. He ordered his own son to be beaten and eventually beheaded, and he locked up his wife, his sister and his mistress in nunneries.

Discontent with Peter's Westernising, and with his disrespect towards the Church, reached a head in 1708. Another peasant revolt, with ominous echoes of the Stenka Razin adventure, suggested strongly that the people still clung to an older, more conservative image of Russianness based on Christian Orthodoxy and the divine nature of the monarchy, which Peter had betrayed. The leader of the rebellion, a Cossack named Kondraty Bulavin, proclaimed that the tsar was the anti-Christ and urged the peasants to march against him. Peter had the insurgents massacred. Rather than address their legitimate concerns, he moved to make their conditions even harsher, tying the peasants to the land and making them in practice the property of their masters. Serfdom would be a millstone around Russia's neck for another century and a half.

Was Peter a despot or a reformer? In many respects, he was both. He introduced Western standards of behaviour, but he used very un-Western

---

* The council was chaired by a layman, whose appointment was decided by Peter himself.

methods to do so. He praised European values, but clung to Asiatic forms of governance. He rejected notions of parliamentary participation (something that was developing in Britain, for example, following the Glorious Revolution and the Bill of Rights in 1688) and he pursued efficiency, not democracy. He knew change was vital because of the tensions in society – the peasant revolts were a symptom of a system straining at the seams – but he wanted to control that change, and he certainly didn't want any reforms that would weaken the autocratic power he himself wielded.

Indeed, Peter's reign saw the formulation of some of the most powerful justifications of autocracy as a system of government. The 'Spiritual Regulations', written in 1721 by Peter's reforming Archbishop Feofan Prokopovich, state unequivocally that human beings are naturally selfish and disputatious. As a result, the firm hand of autocracy is necessary to restrain their inborn inclination towards conflict and anarchy. The argument, says Feofan, is particularly applicable to Russia because 'the nature of the Russian people is such that the country can be safeguarded only by autocratic rule. If another principle of government is adopted, it will be completely impossible to maintain its unity and wellbeing.' Another Petrine thinker, Vasily Tatishchev, concurs. He advances the contention we first heard voiced in the time of Kievan Rus – that Russia's borders are long and porous; that she is threatened by outside enemies; and that she therefore needs the unifying force of autocracy to prevent internal divisions leading to a weakening of national defences. These are the arguments that would form the ideological justification for autocracy for generations to come.

CHAPTER TEN

Peter the Great died on 8 February 1725. He had been in agony for several weeks, and when doctors operated on his blocked urinary tract they released 4 pints of infected urine. The gangrene that had spread to the tsar's bladder killed him soon afterwards. He was 52 years old; he had reigned for more than 40 of those years and had transformed Russia from a struggling, landlocked state to a major and still-expanding empire. But for a man so dedicated to efficiency, Peter left the country in a muddle. Having decreed that the monarch should appoint his own successor, he had signally failed to do so.

The result was that for more than three decades, the descendants of Peter the Great were locked in power struggles and palace coups. When his niece Anna came to the throne in 1730, a small but influential group of nobles asked her to sign a series of 'conditions' obliging her to consult a council of the aristocracy before raising taxes, fixing state spending, embarking on military action or appointing senior officials. The idea was in tune with developments in parts of Western Europe, including Britain, where the Bill of Rights had set limits on the power of the king. Had Anna agreed to the 'conditions', it might have opened the way for Russia to become a constitutional monarchy, perhaps eventually a Western-style parliamentary democracy.

But Anna refused. She enlisted the backing of the Imperial Guard and insisted on preserving the old system of unfettered autocracy. She spent much of her reign banishing, humiliating and executing those who opposed her.

Ten years later, in 1741, it was the turn of Peter's surviving daughter, Elizabeth, to seize power, again with the help of the military. The story has it that she turned up at the headquarters of the Preobrazhensky Regiment in St Petersburg in a metal breastplate, brandishing a silver crucifix and demanding to know whom the army intended to support. 'Listen, lads!' she is said to have declared. 'You know whose daughter I am. As you served my father, Great Peter, so now you must serve me ... You must choose between your natural sovereign and those scoundrels who have stolen my birthright!' The regimental commanders were so impressed by Elizabeth's bravado that they agreed to march with her to the Winter Palace, where they arrested the stopgap infant tsar Ivan and those claiming to rule on his behalf, and installed Elizabeth on the throne instead.

Elizabeth may have come to power by unconstitutional means, but her style of governing was very different from that of the abrasive, unyielding Anna. She operated through compromise and conciliation. She made a pledge not to execute anyone during her reign, and kept it. At the prompting of her advisers Ivan and Peter Shuvalov, Elizabeth revived the possibility of 'permanent, fundamental laws' that would bind the monarch's conduct and make her at least partially answerable to the nobility. A commission was set up to develop proposals, including guarantees of property rights, a promise that nobles would be tried only by a jury of their peers, and provisions for consultation on key issues of state policy. But in the end Elizabeth, too, fought shy of sharing power. It took the advent of another, quite remarkable woman before the idea of liberal reform would finally gain serious consideration.

The woman history would know as Catherine the Great began life as a German princess, Sophia Auguste of Anhalt-Zerbst, born in the Baltic seaport of Stettin on 2 May 1729. At the prompting of Frederick II of Prussia, the young Sophia was taken to Petersburg by her mother in 1743. She was just 14 and had no experience of life outside her home town. But Frederick knew the childless Elizabeth of Russia was looking for a bride for her nephew and heir, the future Peter III, and he hoped Sophia would find favour. His aim was undoubtedly to arrange a match that might improve Prussia's standing and influence at the Russian court.

In the event, Sophia and Elizabeth took to each other at once. The young Lutheran princess converted to Russian Orthodoxy in 1744 and took the name of Yekaterina, or Catherine. She spent her days learning Russian, which she mastered quickly, although she never lost her German accent. Writing much later in her memoirs, Catherine admitted she would have done 'anything that was necessary … and profess anything that was demanded in order to gain the crown of Russia'.

A marriage was quickly agreed and the wedding took place in August 1745. Catherine was barely 16, and married life was to be a torment for her. Peter was physically repulsive, mentally immature, paranoid and probably impotent. (His portrayal in a memorable 1930s Hollywood epic by Douglas Fairbanks Jr. as a brooding, homicidal Prince Hamlet swinging from manic bursts of energy to periods of darkest gloom seems remarkably close to the truth.) Catherine's diaries list the torments she went through, as Peter spent his time leering at his courtiers, pouring wine over the heads of visiting dignitaries and whipping his dogs with an obsessive sadism. 'I understood very clearly that the Grand Duke did not love me,' she writes. 'Just 15 days after our wedding he told me he was in love with Mademoiselle Karr, the empress's maid of honour … I realised that my life with this man would be very unhappy if I allowed myself to show tender feelings for him that were destined to be so ill rewarded. I concluded that to die of jealousy would be of no use to anyone …'

For a 16-year-old, the logic is remarkable. Spurned and humiliated by her cretinous husband, she simply decided to make a life for herself without him. In response to his cruelty and disdain, it is hardly a surprise that the beautiful, sensuous, intelligent Catherine should have turned elsewhere, and stories of her extramarital activities abound. The noble Counts Saltykov, Poniatowski, Orlov, Vasilchikov, Zavadovsky, Zorich, Lanskoy, Yermolov and Zubov are among many who enjoyed her favours, although the widely quoted figure of 300 lovers has never been substantiated. She hints in her memoirs that her marriage with Peter was not consummated, but Catherine nonetheless produced three children, one of whom was destined to become tsar.

It's unfortunate that Catherine the Great is so universally remembered for her interest in sex. She certainly wasn't shy about taking virile lovers among her court favourites, but most of the more outlandish stories – including the one about the wild stallion and the leather sling – were almost certainly concocted by her enemies. The inveterate misogynist Frederick II of Prussia was being deliberately mischievous in spreading scandalous gossip to belittle Catherine's political acumen ('in government by women, the vagina always has more influence than a sensible policy guided by the light of reason' being one of the more printable of his outrageous claims).

Frederick's bitchiness was a response to Catherine's courageous, and sensible, support for closer relations with England and Austria, to the detriment of her native Prussia. When Frederick helped engineer Catherine's rise to power he had assumed she would repay him by becoming a loyal ally. She had the chance to do so in January 1762, when Elizabeth died and Catherine's husband became Tsar Peter III of Russia. Peter had long been a strong advocate of Prussian interests, and one of his first acts on ascending the throne was to withdraw from the Seven Years War, concluding a peace treaty with Frederick that gave up nearly all Russian gains. The move provoked anger among the Russian nobility and – ever the pragmatist – Catherine seized the moment. Together with her lover Grigory Orlov, she encouraged a palace coup that deposed Peter in July 1762. He had reigned for just six months; a week later he was murdered by guards loyal to Catherine.

From that moment onwards she ruled alone, taking the title Empress Catherine II of All the Russias. Like Elizabeth, Catherine had come to the throne through military force, but it did little to overshadow her reign. She ruled with single-minded dedication, showing tactfulness and skill in domestic policy and choosing international allies to meet the needs of her country. Peter the Great had laid the foundations for Russia's emergence as a European power, but it was Catherine who would bring it to fruition. George Macartney, the British ambassador to Catherine's court in 1765, was among the first to recognise her achievements:

> I never saw in my life a person whose port, manner and behaviour answered so strongly to the idea I had formed of her … Russia is no longer to be gazed at as a distant, glimmering star, but as a great planet that has obtruded itself into our system, whose place is yet undetermined, but whose motions must powerfully affect those of every other orb.

The Ottoman Empire was in decline, and Macartney had no doubt that another semi-Asiatic power, the Russian Empire, was about to take its place.

To Western observers like Macartney, Russia seemed vast and menacing. But the Russian perspective was somewhat different: as always, her show of strength was connected with the ingrained fear of vulnerability that had haunted her since the days of the Mongols.

Catherine launched a rapid expansion to the south that was intended to provide a buffer against the hostile forces on her borders, but would actually sow the seeds of ethnic tensions that have lasted into our own times. To the west, she used Russia's military strength and her flair for alliance building to engineer the partitioning of Poland, ruthlessly annexing Polish territory in collusion with the Prussians and Austrians in a chilling foretaste of the Nazi–Soviet pact of 1939. By the end of Catherine's reign, Poland had ceased to exist as a physical entity, surviving only in the hearts of her people and their burning determination to see their country reborn.* Catherine the Great negotiated and bullied Russia into the role of continental Europe's most feared superpower. But at home, her reign was on shaky ground. An incomer with no hereditary claim to the throne, a Prussian and a convert from Lutheranism, she could easily have been despised by the population. It was a tribute to her unflagging tact and energy that she won the respect of many. When famine sparked rebellions in some Russian provinces, she refused requests from provincial governors to put them down with military force. Instead, she sent emergency food supplies from government stocks with a message that they should reach the people most in need. Where Peter the Great would have tortured and executed, Catherine negotiated and compromised. In the early years of her reign, she was regarded as a progressive reformer very much in tune with the democratic trends of the European Enlightenment.

Walking through the stacks and storage rooms of the Russian National Library on Nevsky Prospekt in St Petersburg is like stepping back into a

---

* Even today, the words of the Polish national anthem commemorate the nightmare of Russo–Germanic oppression – 'Poland has not died, so long as we still live!' I well remember how poignant that sounded at demonstrations of the Polish opposition during the long years of Soviet domination.

previous age. The elegant neo-classical interiors have changed little since Catherine the Great had it built as the Imperial Library in 1795. The catalogue of the library's 35 million items is still kept on cardboard slips in wooden drawers and it can take days for books to be fetched out of vaults that run for many miles under the city streets. I have known the workings of the library for a long time, but I recently discovered a new set of rooms, smelling of fresh varnish and distinctly smarter than the rest of the place. A proud curator told me they had just been renovated with a grant from the government of France. They were, she explained, a reconstruction of Voltaire's library and they now housed the 7,000 books, manuscripts, notebooks and drafts he owned at the time of his death.

The story of how Voltaire's worldly goods ended up in Russia is an intriguing one. Having secured the Russian throne, Catherine seemed determined to put into action the Enlightenment principles she had absorbed in her youth from the writings of liberal French, German and British philosophers. The Hermitage Museum was founded on her orders in 1764 to house her collection of Western paintings and books. She would spend days there, reading and copying out in longhand the works of the French *philosophes*, those revolutionary champions of reason, democracy and freedom. Catherine learned by heart long passages from Montesquieu's *Spirit of the Laws* (1752), the iconic manifesto of constitutionalism, separation of powers, civil liberties and the rule of law. When the French authorities suppressed Diderot's revolutionary *Encyclopédie* (1751–72), she invited him to come to Petersburg to complete its composition. Strange, incendiary bedfellows, you might think, for the ruler of a country where autocracy was the established rule!

But Catherine was her own woman. She welcomed foreign investment, relaxed censorship and encouraged the spread of education. From 1763, the year after her coronation, she embarked on a long, earnest correspondence with Voltaire, the best-known writer of the age and the leading exponent of political liberalism. 'By chance your works fell into my hands,' Catherine wrote in her first letter to him, 'and since then I have never stopped reading them. I have had no desire to have anything to do with books that were not written as well as yours, and from which the same profit could not be derived.'

Voltaire could not resist flattery and replied in similar glowing terms. Their correspondence continued for over a decade, during which he came to regard Russia under Catherine's leadership as the world's best hope for the enactment of the Enlightenment ideals he espoused. She employed Voltaire to write an official history of Peter the Great as a signal that she would honour and expand her predecessor's Europeanising policies. And Voltaire responded by becoming her head of global PR. 'You are greater than the Aurora Borealis,' he gushed, 'you are the brightest star of the North; there never has been a luminary so beneficial ... Diderot and I are the lay missionaries who preach the cult of Sainte Cathérine and we can boast that our Church is almost universal.'

Catherine was viewed, and viewed herself, as a patron of culture, of philosophy and of social change, a 'philosophe on the throne'. It was a brave stance by a brave woman, and it was bound to be controversial.

But the reason Catherine rushed to buy up Voltaire's effects after his death was no longer one of mutual admiration. By then, the two of them had quarrelled in dramatic fashion, after the empress's political views had undergone a remarkable sea change. Catherine's real interest in acquiring his library was because she feared her letters to him would be placed in the public domain and she would be pilloried for the liberal sentiments she had expressed in them. So how did the putative liberal reformer who vowed to enlighten Russia morph into an entrenched conservative for whom her former ideals had become anathema?

Her first steps had been bold ones. In 1767, the young Catherine had been in a hurry to embody the abstract principles of the Enlightenment in legal practice. She convened an All-Russian Legislative Commission with delegates from the nobility, the merchants, the Cossacks and the (non-serf) peasants. She issued them with a *Nakaz* – an Instruction – to create a new code of law that would end the oppression and injustice suffered by the Russian people:

> For it is the wish of all worthy members of society ... to see each individual citizen protected by laws, which – so far from injuring him – will protect him against every attack on his welfare ... to prevent the rich from

oppressing those who are not so wealthy as themselves and converting the employments entrusted to them as state employees to their own private profit ... For liberty can exist only in the ability of doing what everyone ought to desire, and not being forced to do what should not be desired.

Catherine's *Nakaz* proclaimed the equality of all men before the law. It rejected capital punishment and torture. Large parts of it were copied verbatim from Montesquieu. Here at last, it seemed, was an attempt to create a law-governed state, what Catherine called a 'civil society'. It was full of high-flown ideals and aspirations, but other European monarchs found it decidedly disconcerting. The French immediately forbade publication of the *Nakaz* as dangerously revolutionary, and Diderot gleefully commented on it in a phrase that set the tone for much of the rhetoric of the coming revolutions in America and France itself. 'There is no true sovereign except the nation,' he proclaimed. 'There can be no true legislator except the people.'

It seemed to many that Russia was preparing to boldly go where few others would dare to tread. Having been the most backward of the European powers, she now appeared to be leading the way to the enlightened future. But Russia's steps on the road to reform are always fraught with trips and stumbles. Having advanced some way down it, Catherine would soon be scurrying back again.

The Tauride Palace in St Petersburg is one of those half-forgotten behemoths that litter the city's imperial heritage. If you ask Russians what they know about the *Tavrichesky Dvorets* (the name comes from Taurida, the ancient Greek for the area now known as Crimea), they will probably mention its role in the revolutions of 1917. Today the palace is a somnolent backwater, home to the Inter-parliamentary Assembly of Member Nations of the Commonwealth of Independent States, a talking shop with few real powers and little political influence. But the place itself is a marvel, a magnificent, symmetrical two-winged creation of columns and domes, with a central grand entrance of staggering proportions. The main corridor leads to a cavernous, gilded ballroom and the former Winter Garden, now converted into a debating chamber, but originally considered one of the marvels of the age. The poet Gavril Derzhavin described the palace's opening festivities in April 1791, when 3,000 people, the cream of Russia's noble elite, witnessed fireworks, acrobats, orchestras and dazzling illuminations throughout the building:

> At first you doubt your eyes and think this is the work of some magician. Living things are everywhere – trees and plants bloom and works of art proliferate. Everywhere spring reigns, and the greatest achievements of human art vie with the delights of nature … In the rotunda, a statue rises of Catherine the Law Giver …

Zoya, the palace's historian, showed me where the real Catherine had sat during the festivities, on a mighty raised platform at the western end of the ballroom. The royal dais was topped with not one, but two thrones, and the person who sat beside the empress that night was the man for whom Catherine had had the Tauride Palace built. From the moment they had met a decade and a half earlier, Grigory Potemkin had been the love of her life:

> My dear friend, I love you! You are so handsome, so clever, so witty; when I am with you I forget about everything in the world … I love you so much! … Come quickly to my bedroom and prove your love to me!

Catherine the Great had taken many lovers among her court favourites, but when she first invited Prince Potemkin into her bed, in February 1774, she sensed this one would be different. In a welter of passionate letters, he declared his undying love for her and she responded in a frenzy of desire:

> Oh, Monsieur Potemkin, what sorcery have you used to unbalance a mind that was previously reckoned among the best in Europe? … What a scandal for Catherine the Second to be the victim of this crazy passion! … Your power over me is so strong! … Enough! I have scribbled enough – go, crazy, mad letter to that place where my hero dwells … my colossus, my golden cockerel, my tiger! … come to see me so I can tame you with my endless caresses … My heart cannot be content for even an hour without love.

The relationship began when Catherine was in her forties, on the throne for over a decade and one of the most powerful rulers Russia had known. She was looking for more than just an affair; she wanted love in her private life and a counsellor in her role as empress. Her sex life was the talk of the court, but she didn't care to hide it. The British ambassador, Sir Robert Gunning, sent a detailed diplomatic dispatch back to his masters in London:

> A new scene has just opened which is likely to merit more attention than any that has presented itself since the beginning of this reign ... [The former] favourite whose understanding was too limited to admit of his having any influence on affairs or sharing his mistress's confidence is replaced by a man who bids fair for possessing them both in the most supreme degree. Potemkin's figure is gigantic and disproportioned and his countenance is far from engaging, but he appears to have a great knowledge of mankind ... and as much address and suppleness in his station ... Though the profligacy of his manner is notorious ... he may naturally flatter himself with the hopes of rising to that height to which his boundless ambition aspires ... It seems the Empress is going to commit the reins of government to Potemkin.

Grigory Potemkin was tall and very well built (Catherine reputedly kept a plaster cast of one part of his anatomy to console herself when he was away). He was also a war hero, having fought the Turks in the southern campaigns; intellectually sharp, boisterously charismatic and very forceful. Soon they were living as man and wife – they almost certainly held a secret marriage ceremony – and it's clear from their correspondence that Gunning's assessment was only slightly exaggerated: Catherine did indeed trust Potemkin with affairs of state. But their partnership as rulers was about to be put to the test by the most serious crisis Russia had faced in a generation.

In the spring of 1774, the good citizens of Orenburg – the provincial capital and a strategic staging post in the southern Ural Mountains – were in a panic. News had arrived that revolutionary forces led by the Cossack Yemelyan Pugachev were advancing from the south to pillage and loot the city. The rebels had already seized Kazan and Samara; vast swathes of territory from the Volga to the Urals were under Pugachev's control. What had started as a Cossack revolt in the mould of Stenka Razin a century earlier had turned into something close to a national revolution. Hundreds of thousands of peasants, factory workers, Old Believers and serfs had turned against their masters; landowners were being massacred and their estates ransacked. It was a foretaste of the revolutionary terror that was about to sweep away Louis XVI in the French Revolution of 1789. Unlike revolutionary France or America, though, where the people were demanding ever more radical changes to society, in Russia the spark for revolt, paradoxically, was a reaction against reform. Pugachev had convinced the people that Catherine was a false tsar who must be overthrown and executed: she had handed Russia to the Germans, he told them, and they must rise up and seize back their own land. Anyone not wearing traditional Russian dress of kaftans and beards must be a German and therefore slaughtered without mercy. Alexander Pushkin's classic tale 'The Captain's Daughter' (1836) captures the apocalyptic atmosphere of the times. Pugachev was threatening not just Orenburg, but Nizhny Novgorod and even Moscow itself. No one was safe; violent revolution was at hand, and the downfall of the monarchy seemed only a matter of time:

> At that moment great crowds of horsemen appeared, and soon the steppe was covered with a multitude of men. A figure in a red coat, with a bare sword in his hand, was riding among them on a white horse … it was Pugachev! With terrible shouting and yelling, the rebels came rushing towards the fortress … The brigands were inside the fortress now, plundering the officers' quarters. Their drunken shouts resounded everywhere and the gallows, with their freshly hanged victims, loomed menacingly in the dark. Pugachev and a dozen Cossacks … were sitting around a table littered with bottles and glasses, their faces flushed with drink and their eyes aglitter. I couldn't help marvelling: a drunkard who had spent his life wandering from inn to inn was capturing fortresses and shaking the very foundations of the state!

Fortunately for Catherine, her new lover and co-ruler was made of stern stuff. Potemkin faced down the opposition of the Petersburg court and insisted that the empress travel to Moscow as a visible figurehead of resistance. He replaced the squabbling military commanders and dispatched new, bolder generals to fight the rebels. In August, Pugachev was defeated at Tsaritsyn, later to be the scene of another historic battle under its future name of Stalingrad (see pp. 346–51). By mid September, the revolution was in tatters, its leaders betrayed and handed over to the authorities. In January 1775, Pugachev was publicly beheaded on Red Square. The immediate threat to the monarchy was over, but the underlying causes remained.

In the History Museum in Yekaterinburg – a city that came close to sharing the grim fate of Orenburg but was spared when Pugachev fell at Tsaritsyn – the director showed me examples of the roughly produced tracts the rebels had distributed in the region. They announced that Pugachev was really Tsar Peter III, who had miraculously survived the attempt by the usurper Catherine to depose him and was now returning to reclaim the throne:

> Those who rally to me, the true tsar, Peter III, will be rewarded with money and bread and advancement. They and their kin will find a place in my kingdom and will carry out glorious deeds. But those who neglect their duty to support their true ruler and do not rally to my loyal troops with weapon in hand will find the harshest punishment …

The rebels' manifestos reproached Catherine for her secularisation of society and advanced 'Tsar Peter' (Pugachev) as the true standard-bearer of the old national myth of Holy Russia, the defender and champion of Christianity. It was a message that found a ready response from the peasants and common people. Ever since the days of the Mongols, Orthodoxy had been the cement that bound Russia together against its enemies, and now a foreigner – a German! a Lutheran! – was seizing Church lands and making its priests servants of the state. Pugachev himself was an Old Believer (and there were millions of them, estranged from tsarist authority) and his cause was theirs.

The peasants could not, of course, read the rebels' leaflets (and Pugachev and most of his comrades were themselves illiterate), but there was no lack of willing intermediaries. In pulpits throughout the land, disgruntled priests enthusiastically read out Pugachev's manifestos, with their denunciations of Catherine as 'the Devil's daughter'.

The paradox of the Pugachev rebellion is that the peasants and common people had shown themselves to be more conservative than the reformers who set out to improve their lot. They simply didn't want Catherine's newfangled 'Western' ideas. So having spent the first years of her reign winning the support of the Russian people, Catherine was now in danger of losing it. She needed to respond to the Pugachev debacle – and the people's mistrust of change – and she did so by retrenching. Her great Legislative Commission, originally inspired by the Enlightenment ideals of liberty, equality and the rule of law, was wound up. Instead of giving power to the people, as Voltaire and Diderot had hoped, Catherine's final document was a resounding endorsement of the old system of autocracy: uncontrolled authority in the hands of one person, namely herself!

> The possessions of the Russian Empire extend upon the globe to 32 degrees of latitude, and to 165 of longitude. The sovereign is absolute, for no authority but the power centred in his single person can act with the vigour proportionate to the extent of such a vast dominion. The extent of the dominion requires that absolute power be vested in the one person who rules over it. It is expedient so to be, that the quick dispatch of affairs, sent from distant parts, might make ample amends for the delay occasioned by the great distance of the places. All other forms of government whatsoever would not only be prejudicial to Russia, but would provoke its entire ruin.

What clearer statement could there be of the basic, underlying determinant of how Russia must be governed? Russia is too big and too unruly ever to be suited to democracy, it says; only the strong hand of centralised autocracy can keep such a disparate, centripetal empire together and maintain order among her people. It was the same doctrine enunciated by Rurik and Oleg, by Ivan the Terrible and Peter the Great, by Archbishop Feofan Prokopovich and Vasily Tatishchev.

Yet if Catherine was determined to remain a supreme ruler and autocrat, why did she embark on reform at all? Like Peter the Great, Catherine was forced to make changes because her survival depended on it. Her claim to the throne was a slim one, and the Pugachev revolt convinced her she couldn't keep relying on military force to maintain it. So she aimed to create a system of laws and administration that would entrench the authority of the monarch throughout society, making it impossible to uproot.

> In the very nature of things, the sovereign is the source of all civil and imperial power. Intermediate powers, subordinate to the monarch's supreme power and dependent on it, must form an essential part of monarchical government. Through them, as if through smaller streams, the power of the government is poured out and diffused … These laws undoubtedly constitute the firm and immoveable basis of the state.

To ensure what she called the 'efficient diffusion of the monarch's authority', Catherine enlisted the help of the landed nobility. In 1785, she granted them a Charter guaranteeing their property and personal freedom; protecting them from judicial abuse and corporal punishment; exempting them from taxation, and giving them the right to form regional assemblies to run local government. In return, they were bound to eternal loyalty to the throne and to the empress herself:

> Since the honourable title of a noble is acquired by service and efforts beneficial to the empire and the throne … therefore at any time needful for the Russian autocracy, every nobleman is obligated to respond at once to the first summons from the autocratic power and to spare neither his efforts nor his life itself in serving the state …

The freedoms granted in Catherine's Charter were perceived as a sort of emancipation of the nobility. But there was no corresponding emancipation of the serfs – that would have to wait another 76 years. The peasants were aware of, and resented, the new privileges of their masters. They received no such legal entitlements and their lot worsened as that of the nobles improved. The gap between the top and bottom of society was widening, and a century later it would lead to violent confrontation.

When Alexander Radishchev, a Russian liberal with a social conscience, exposed the evils of serfdom and social inequality in his polemical *Journey from Petersburg to Moscow* in 1790, Catherine scribbled angry rebuttals in the margins of her copy, and then had him arrested and exiled. By now, in the final years of her reign, she was simply in denial about the realities of poverty and suffering in her realm, so much so that stories circulated of Potemkin having to build false façades of prosperous buildings along her route when she travelled to the provinces – the so called 'Potemkin villages' that have become a synonym for self-deluding blindness.

Having flirted with the liberal values of the European Enlightenment, Catherine grew horrified by the forces of revolution they were unleashing. The spectacle of another European monarch – Louis XVI – dragged to the guillotine in 1793 by a baying mob of 'enlightened' revolutionaries gave her nightmares. She renounced her previous admiration for Voltaire and Diderot and offered to send Russian troops to quash the Enlightenment ideals she had once espoused. The great reformer had become the great reactionary.

CHAPTER ELEVEN

Tchaikovsky's *1812 Overture* is a sturdy crowd-pleaser, played at summer pops and Albert Hall spectaculars where everyone enjoys the big bangs at the end. But musicians will testify that it is a finely calibrated piece of music. Its alternating themes are developed with the touch of a master craftsman, a musical confrontation that reaches a climactic resolution of cathartic intensity.

We all recognise the first theme: in Tchaikovsky's orchestration the French national anthem becomes a menacing sound picture of Napoleon's armies marching eastwards, bringing the message of revolution to Russia. The years after the French Revolution of 1789 were a period of turmoil on both sides of the Atlantic. The old order was changing in Europe and North America alike. For the monarchs of countries such as Britain, Italy, Prussia, Austria and Russia, it was a time of great fear. Initial attempts to crush the new French Republic had failed, and the rise to power of Napoleon Bonaparte brought French Republican forces advancing into several European and North African countries. By 1812, Bonaparte's fortunes were at their apogee and he was looking for new conquests in the east.

In Tchaikovsky's music, though, a new theme arises, this time steady and measured. The tsarist national hymn is heard quietly at first, then growing in confidence as Tchaikovsky's overture erupts into patriotic fervour. The orgasmic climax, with real cannons firing off, shows where Tchaikovsky's sympathies lie: the French defeat is the cue for national rejoicing ...

Music can be a powerful political weapon, and Napoleon stirred something visceral and atavistic in the Russian psyche. The nation's collective memory had never quite erased the terror of the Mongol yoke five centuries earlier, and the fear of invasion remained an ever-present, ever-menacing nightmare.

The French Enlightenment had had both supporters and opponents in Russia. Even Catherine the Great had been captivated by its liberal ideals. While the French Revolution of 1789 had changed the monarch's mind in dramatic fashion, many Russian radicals welcomed it as a model of liberation for their own country. But when Napoleon turned his sights on Moscow, the threat to the motherland spurred them to bury their differences, forget their grievances and unite. The preservation of the nation became the overriding imperative, just as it had been at Kulikovo Polye in 1380, just as it would be at Stalingrad in 1942.

But how had Russia got itself into such a dire predicament in the first place?

The answer lies in the years before the French invasion of 1812, when a catalogue of opportunities to avert the looming threat had been missed. For two decades, Russia had watched impotently as the seeds of revolution spread abroad from France, caught in the sort of vacillating indecision about how to react that would greet similar crises right down to the twentieth century.

Catherine the Great had died in 1796 (like Elvis, she expired on the toilet, prompting much ribald mirth from her opponents), leaving the throne to her successor and unloved son, Paul I. The narrow-minded Paul had never accepted enlightenment or reform. His resentment of his mother was visceral. He reversed many of the reforms she had agreed to introduce. He ordered the body of her lover Potemkin to be dug up and fed to the dogs, took back the civil liberties granted to the aristocracy, further entrenched serfdom and reintroduced judicial punishments, including flogging, branding and the tearing out of nostrils. The vengeful autocratic state was back.

Paul I seems to have lived a life of paranoia, seeing threats in every quarter. Thirty miles south of St Petersburg, the former royal palace of Gatchina stands today as a sad memorial to his reign. Picking my way through its labyrinthine rooms and corridors, I found most of them in ruins, with ceilings collapsed and walls crumbling, still awaiting repair after the destructive presence of the Nazis here. But their scale and former grandeur are unmistakable. Paul became obsessed with Gatchina, expending vast amounts of time and energy rebuilding and enlarging the palace, embellishing its interiors with sumptuous artworks and furniture, and packing its acres of parkland with follies, bridges and grottoes. Gatchina became his retreat, a safe haven from the dangers of political reality. He spent his days marching his Imperial Guard round and round its courtyards in Prussian-style drills. Rather disconcertingly, I found them still there and still marching when I emerged from the darkness of the palace, brought lovingly back to life by historical re-enactment enthusiasts. Later in the nineteenth century, Gatchina would become the refuge of another conservative monarch, Alexander III, and the legacy of the two reactionary tsars left it with the sinister nickname 'the Citadel of Autocracy'.

Paul I's years in power were devoted to combating the radicals. He appointed his own officials in every region and beefed up the secret police – the *tainaya ekspeditsiya* – to seek out and exterminate political opposition. He tried to close Russia's borders to the French contagion, banning foreign books and journals and forbidding his subjects from travelling abroad. It was a technique that would work for the leaders of the Soviet Union, but for Paul I it ended in blood. On 23 March 1801 he was seized in his private chamber by a group of disgruntled Guards officers, who demanded he sign a decree announcing his abdication. When he refused, he was stabbed, strangled and kicked to death. Paul's 23-year-old son Alexander – waiting in his bedroom down the corridor, and almost certainly aware of the plot against his father – was summoned and told it was time for him to 'grow up and start to rule'.

Alexander was largely raised by his grandmother, Catherine, and he was undoubtedly close to her in his formative years, when she was still enamoured of Voltairean liberalism. But the violent death of a father – especially one brought about with a son's tacit connivance – was bound to have had a psychological impact. Contemporaries report that he disguised his true thoughts and opinions, and may have harboured a lingering sense that he should not betray his father's legacy. The inner conflict between Catherine's youthful liberal beliefs and his father's reactionary conservatism would play itself out in Alexander's psyche. And it would mark the temper of his rule. It was, as we will see, a classic reign of two halves.

*

Despite the brutal circumstances of his accession, Alexander I began his time in power in a spirit of conciliation. He seemed to have imbibed the Enlightenment rhetoric of his grandmother and rejected the Prussian-style militarism of his murdered father. He spoke fluent English and French, and was familiar with the progress of democracy in those countries. The young Alexander resumed the quest Catherine had embarked on – and then abandoned – of building a 'regular state' where fairness and the rule of law would replace corruption and coercion. The gap between Russia's ruler and the Russian people had grown dangerously wide and Alexander feared revolution if it were not addressed.

Like Catherine, he set up a committee to discuss political reform, and in doing so he enlisted the services of one of the most remarkable brains of the century. Mikhail Speransky was a committed liberal, dubbed 'the Russian Voltaire'. His confidential assessment of Russia's system of government, produced for Alexander's eyes only, is an incendiary exposé of the deadening persistence of autocratic rule:

> The fundamental principle of Russian government has always been the autocratic ruler who combines all legislative and executive powers and disposes of all the nation's resources. There are no limits placed on this principle. When the powers of the sovereign authority are unlimited – to such an extent that no rights are left over for the subjects – then such a state exists in slavery and its government is despotical.

Even Catherine's flirtation with liberal values was a sham, says Speransky – mere window dressing for the Asiatic despotism that had continued to exist in Russia since the downfall of Kievan Rus:

> Under Catherine, the government wished to enjoy the glory of philosophical ideals but still maintain all the advantages of despotism. Our laws might sound like they were written in England, but our system of government is that of Turkey.

Speransky concludes that the autocracy had survived every attempt to reform it. The Asiatic model of iron rule learned under the Mongols ('the government ... of Turkey', as Speransky caustically puts it) had become so ingrained in the Russian mind that moves to introduce Western notions of constitutional democracy had all foundered. The absence of justice, law and protection from capricious authority had, he laments, stifled initiative and progress, leaving Russia mired in primitive backwardness:

> Under autocratic rule there can be no code of law, for where no rights exist there can be no impartial balance between them ... there is nothing but the arbitrary decisions of the sovereign, prescribing to the citizens their bounden duties, until such time as the autocrat decides to change them. The law is completely dependent on the autocratic will, which alone creates it, alone establishes the courts, names the judges and gives them their rules ... as the fancy strikes it.*

Speransky told Alexander that only shock therapy could cast off the burden of the past – an overnight plunge into democracy and the sharing of power. He drew up plans for freely elected local councils, a national parliament

---

* It is remarkable how much of Mikhail Speransky's diagnosis of the all-powerful state wielding arbitrary authority is still applicable nowadays, just as it was in the time of Ivan the Terrible. Speransky's contention that Russia has never been a law-governed state ('the law is completely dependent on the autocratic will ...') is still at least partially true today, as the Kremlin continues to dictate the verdicts in key court cases like that of the oligarch Mikhail Khodorkovsky and others. Speransky's complaints about the lack of property rights in a predatory, grabbing state are shared by many who suffered from them in the twenty-first century:

> What is the use of laws assigning property to private individuals when property itself has no firm basis in any respect whatsoever? What is the use of civil laws when their tablets can at any time be smashed on the first rock of arbitrary rule? How can finances be set in order in a country with no public confidence in the law ... and no laws for regulating the financial system? There are no truly free men in Russia except beggars and philosophers!

That quote in particular is striking because it could very easily be from the commercial corporations and businessmen of the twenty-first century – BP, Shell, Yukos, Hermitage, the dispossessed Russian oligarchs – all of whom have suffered from Vladimir Putin's new version of statist autocracy, where the Kremlin can seize private assets at will whenever their owners come into conflict with 'the rock of arbitrary rule'. In today's Russia 'public confidence in the law' still remains a scarce commodity.

and a remarkable draft constitution guaranteeing civil rights and the separation of powers, an end to the police state and freedom of the press.

Alexander listened sympathetically. At one moment he seemed close to endorsing a British-style constitutional monarchy, telling an adviser, 'I would then happily retire to the country and watch my nation prosper.' But alongside the liberal voices, there were hardline conservatives whispering in his ear, like the formidable minister of war, Alexei Arakcheev. He had served under Paul I and continued to champion the cause of military dictatorship. The very word 'Arakcheevshchina' (Arakcheevism) came to signify the worst excesses of a military police state, and Alexander listened to its precepts with all the attention of a son listening to his father.

In the words of Pushkin, Speransky and Arakcheev were the tsar's good and bad geniuses standing at the opposing doors of his reign. Unfortunately for Russia, Alexander was impressionable and vain, easily influenced by the person he'd last spoken to. Perhaps hamstrung by the inherited conflict he felt between the legacy of his grandmother and that of his father, he vacillated so much between the two sets of advice that in the end he did nothing.

His projects for reform became bogged down in indecision; his attitude to the republicanism of the new regime in France swung from admiration to apoplectic denunciation. Alexander sent troops to fight Napoleon in 1805, but then agreed to sit down with him at Tilsit in 1807. Bonaparte had spent the years since seizing power in an unremitting drive to expand French domination across Europe. Allied coalitions had tried and failed to halt him, and Alexander's advisers stressed the danger he represented for the Russian monarchy. But Alexander nonetheless insisted on trying to do business with him. After lengthy negotiations at Tilsit, and again a year later at Erfurt, he decided Napoleon was a charming man and – in a fit of enthusiasm – announced he was ready for a global alliance with his former enemy.

Like Stalin's Non-Aggression Pact with Hitler over a century later, Alexander's alliance with Napoleon secretly divided Europe into spheres of influence they each would dominate. And it, too, was doomed to end badly. After five years of dissembling, Napoleon – as Hitler would – tore up the agreement and marched into Russia. The paranoid Paul I had severely weakened the country's defence forces, purging seven field marshals and 333 generals in a panic of doubt about their loyalty. The half a million French troops were vastly superior to the defending Russians, and advanced rapidly, looting and laying waste until, on 7 September 1812, they reached the village of Borodino, 75 miles west of Moscow. The ensuing battle is at the heart of one of the great set-piece descriptions of Leo Tolstoy's *War and Peace* (1869):

> A shell tore up the earth a couple of paces from Pierre. Brushing off the dirt that had spattered his clothes, he glanced around with a sheepish smile … a fire was blazing and it was, he felt, burning stronger and stronger in his own soul. Everything was strange and muddled. His eyes grew dim. A cannon ball struck the rim of the trench by which Pierre was standing, a black object flashing before his face … He had no time to realise the colonel had been killed, that the soldier yelling for help was a prisoner and that another soldier had just been bayoneted in the back before his eyes … A thin, sallow faced, sweating man in a blue tunic rushed at him brandishing a sword and shouting. Instinctively Pierre put out his hands and grabbed him (it was a French officer) by the throat. The officer, dropping his sword, seized Pierre by collar … By now, several tens of thousands of men in various uniforms and strange angular positions lay dead on the fields where for centuries the peasants of Borodino had harvested their crops …

Pierre Bezukhov's confused apprehension of the horrors of battle took place in what is now a quiet country meadow. On a bright, late summer day, I drove out to Borodino and saw peasants looking much like those Tolstoy describes, still harvesting their crops, although now with combine harvesters rather than horses and oxen. Birds were singing in the trees; cattle chewing grass in the fields. A few memorials mark the high points of the battle and a modest museum displays bloodstained uniforms and regimental standards. It is all far removed from the violence and drama of 1812, but this is where the pivotal battle of the Napoleonic wars took place, the battle Napoleon himself declared to be the most terrible he ever fought. This is where Tolstoy describes the endless piles of bodies, the dead and the maimed, field hospitals amputating limbs without anaesthetic. And this is the ground he says was soaked in so much blood that it became rich and fertile for many years afterwards.

In numerical terms, Borodino was a defeat for the Russians; they lost 45,000 men and had to withdraw back towards Moscow. But after months of fleeing before the invaders, the nation had stood and fought. From being cowed and terrorised, the people had regained hope. A shrewd new commander called Mikhail Kutuzov took charge here at Borodino, and a snappy little jingle was spreading confidence among the troops: '*Priyekhal Kutuzov pobit' Frantsuzov,*' the men were saying – 'Kutuzov's come to beat the French'. According to Tolstoy, Borodino marked the turning point between certain defeat and the beginnings of victory:

> For Napoleon's generals and soldiers were seized with awe and dread of this foe who, after losing one half his men, stood as formidable at the end of the battle as before it. The invaders' confidence was smashed. Russia had won not the sort of victory defined by the capture of territory and enemy flags, but a moral victory, the sort that compels the enemy to recognise the moral superiority of his opponent and his own impotence. Like a maddened beast that in its onslaught receives a mortal wound, the invaders became conscious they were doomed … Its momentum would take the French army onwards to Moscow, but once there, it was bound to perish without further effort on the part of the Russians, bleeding to death from the wound it had received at Borodino!

In political terms, the battle fought at Borodino would provide Russia with an opportunity to restore national pride, to unite a quarrelsome empire and narrow the disabling gap between the rulers and the people, perhaps even to reduce the future potential for discord and revolution. But in Russia such opportunities present themselves only rarely and they are not often taken.

Tolstoy regarded the outcome of the Napoleonic campaigns as such a crucial turning point in the fortunes of mankind that he developed a whole theory of history from it. He sets out his thesis in the Second Epilogue to *War and Peace,* and it informs his explanation of the key events throughout the narrative of the book:

So the French army flows on to Moscow; behind it – hundreds of miles of devastated, hostile country. The more the Russians retreat, the stronger their spirit of fury against the enemy – every step back fuels the flames of anger. The Russian army retires to the other side of Moscow and the invaders enter the city. Like a fatally wounded beast, they lie bleeding and licking their wounds for five weeks. Then suddenly, with no new reason, they turn tail and make a dash back to the west from whence they came …

The decision of the French to withdraw from Moscow, just a month after capturing it, is ostensibly 'for no reason'. But *War and Peace* is all about the mysterious forces that move history. According to Tolstoy, it is not the generals and politicians who push history forward – they just claim the credit post facto – but the ordinary men and women, the insignificant soldiers, workers and peasants who teem through the pages of *War and Peace*, and whose collective will somehow combines to be the driving motor of world events. Tolstoy's is a demotic view of history, not socialist, but definitely collectivist. And it leads him to a theory of historical necessity, in which the wise man, like the Russian general Kutuzov, marches in step with the laws of history, while the foolish man tries to change them. In Napoleon we see the calamitous results of such vaunting ambition: his Grand Army is left cold, hungry and a long way from home, as the Russian people ('spontaneously', according to Tolstoy) abandon Moscow, setting it ablaze behind them. According to the eyewitness testimony of one of Napoleon's generals, Le Comte de Ségur, it was the Russian people themselves who ran through the streets with firebrands, deliberately putting their own city to the torch. Such ferocious resolution, says de Ségur in his memoirs, *Histoire de Napoléon et de la grande armée pendant l'année 1812* (History of Napolean and the Grand Army During the Year 1812), could have sprung only from the greatest of patriotism; even Napoleon could not hide his admiration for this supreme expression of the people's collective will:

> While our soldiers were still contending with the fire, Napoleon, whose sleep no one had dared disturb during the night, was woken by the double light of day and conflagration … He was in a state of extreme agitation, seemingly

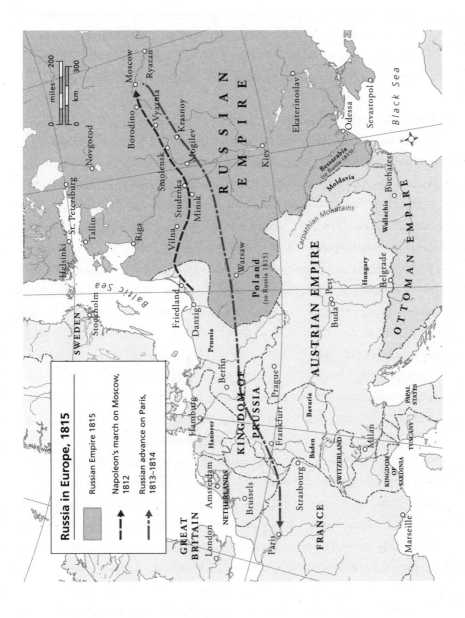

Russia in Europe, 1815

Russian Empire 1815

Napoleon's march on Moscow, 1812

Russian advance on Paris, 1813–1814

parched by the flames that surrounded us. Surprised, after striking at the heart of an empire, to find it exhibit any other sentiment than that of submission, he felt himself conquered and surpassed in determination of will. Every moment he was starting from his seat … and rushing to the windows to trace the progress of the fires, all the while exclaiming: 'What a terrible thing! To have done this to themselves! All those palaces ablaze! What strength of character! What a people! They really are Scythians!'

How fitting that Napoleon should discern the survival of that Asiatic, 'Scythian' ruthlessness and determination that surfaces in the Russian character at times of threat and crisis. This is the flip side of the coin from the civilised 'European' nature Tolstoy has been portraying (and at times mocking) in the aristocratic, French-speaking grandees of St Petersburg. Napoleon and his troops would be on the receiving end of it as they retreated from Moscow.

By the time the remnants of the French army escaped from Russian territory, over 300,000 of its men were dead, fallen in battle or succumbing to hunger, cold and typhus. In the winter snows, soldiers ate their horses and huddled inside the dead animals' bowels in search of warmth. They were harried by regular Russian troops, by the Cossacks and increasingly by partisan detachments of civilians. This was very much a peoples' war – furious, patriotic and ultimately successful – in defence of their common fatherland.

But, worryingly for the authorities, success on the battlefield stirred unfamiliar feelings of confidence and ambition in those who took part in it. There was a spate of uprisings as the people demanded the reward for their service to the state: serfs demanded freedom; peasants demanded the land. Their anger was not directed against Alexander I – the tsar was still venerated as 'our Little Father', godlike and all-powerful – but now the people expected him to use that power to bring them justice and liberty. Similar aspirations were soon to emerge among the regular soldiers who pursued Napoleon across the frontier and all the way back to Paris.

Russian troops fought in the decisive battle of Leipzig in 1813 and led the allied victory parade down the Champs Elysées a year later. Their brief but triumphant occupation of French territory was an eye-opener for men who'd never been outside their own country. The infantry seemingly left their mark with the creation of a new name for a French café – bistro (*bystro*, in Russian, means 'quick; hurry up with the beer'), but the officers imbibed something more than alcohol. Like the Red Army troops who would occupy Germany in 1945, they saw a world their rulers would have preferred them not to see. Their experience of liberty and prosperity in France stayed with them after they returned home, and it set many of them wondering why their own country should not enjoy the same benefits. The bacillus of discontent and the yearning for change had infected an important class of Russian society; soon it would germinate and spread, before flowering in the most dramatic circumstances.

For a while, the seeds of revolt lay dormant. Alexander's leadership in the coalition against Napoleon had strengthened his hand, making Russia the most influential and most feared power in Europe. But after the liberal impulses of his youth, Alexander had been panicked by the French invasion and the spread of domestic opposition into a dour, slightly paranoid conservatism. He consulted oracles and self-styled religious prophets. Perhaps burdened by the murder of his father, he adopted an intense, evangelical Christianity that convinced him he must build a Holy Alliance of European states to maintain the established order, stop the spread of revolution and uphold what he saw as 'high Christian ideals'.

Alexander's determination to impose his ideology on the world earned him the reputation of a tyrant, committed to military intervention when states failed to meet his standards of behaviour. A reign that had begun with hopes of reform was ending in the ugly throes of punitive autocracy. Two amateurish attempts by opposition groups to assassinate or kidnap Alexander convinced him that repression and unbending reaction were Russia's only salvation. He was preparing further crackdowns when he died suddenly in 1825 from typhus in the southern town of Taganrog.

The Russia Alexander I left behind him was backward and conservative. In his later, reactionary years he had built a police state based on spies and denunciations; his wars had undermined the civilian economy; and his unfulfilled promises of reform had fostered a popular disaffection that would grow throughout the century. The unrest that had simmered during

Alexander's lifetime exploded spectacularly soon after his death at the end of 1825. Nikolai Nekrasov's epic poem 'Russian Women' captures the drama that was played out on the wide open spaces of St Petersburg's Senate Square on 14 December:

> See, the crowds are running to the square!
> A regiment is there,
> and others still arriving,
> Till a thousand soldiers stand and cry, 'Hurrah!'
> The crowd scarcely knows
> what's unfolding before its eyes.
> More troops come running:
> 'Yield!' they cry,
> but bullets and bayonets are the only reply.
> Some brave general begins to scold;
> They drag him from his horse.
> Another to the ranks cries out:
> 'Stop now; the tsar will pardon you!'
> But he too is put to death.
> The archpriest himself calls on them to repent:
> 'Bow down before the tsar!' he pleads.
> They cross themselves, but say:
> 'Be gone, old man. This is no place for you.
> Pray for us now ...'
> As the cannons heave into view:
> The tsar himself commands: 'Fire!' ... and they do.

Nowadays, Senate Square is a place of ornamental gardens and statues running from St Isaac's Cathedral to the River Neva, but in the early nineteenth century it was a military parade ground. On that wintry Monday morning in December 1825, 3,000 disaffected troops gathered from early morning to make their demands public. Their leaders were veterans of the French campaigns who'd spent the intervening years building a secret network of liberal-minded cells within the army. These were the men who would go down in Russian history as the Decembrists, leaving a legacy of inspiration for future generations of rebels against autocracy and repression.

The pretext for their military coup was confusion over the succession to the dead tsar. Alexander's brother Konstantin would normally have succeeded to the throne, but had secretly stepped down in favour of a third brother, Nicholas. But the real aims of the rebels were much more fundamental. Their minimum requirements were the introduction of a constitutional monarchy and the abolition of serfdom. Many of them wanted more. Inspired in part by the revolt of the American colonies against the British crown, they were determined to press for an end to tsardom, a republic, and the redistribution of land to the people.

The standoff lasted for most of the day. The rebel soldiers were expecting to be joined by the rest of the Petersburg garrison, but their communications were poor and their leadership badly organised. Amidst sporadic gunfire, the men remained drawn up in battle formation on the square for several hours. Crowds of civilians gathered around them, partly from curiosity, partly in support of their demands,* leaving the new emperor Nicholas in a quandary about how to deal with the situation. He sent a messenger who was promptly shot dead, and he later dispatched a half-hearted cavalry charge, which foundered on the icy cobbles. Finally, in mid afternoon, Nicholas ordered his artillery to smash the rebel ranks. Hundreds died in the shelling, and those who did not were arrested and put on trial. Scores of conspirators were sent to Siberia, and five were sentenced to death in a public hanging.

The site of the Decembrist executions lies on the eastern rampart of St Petersburg's Peter and Paul Fortress. Long used as a prison, the citadel occupies a large island in the Neva and its ramparts are now a tourist destination, a pleasant stroll for a Sunday afternoon. But the place has a sinister past, having housed generations of political prisoners. On 13 July 1826, after months of interrogations, the five leaders of the Decembrist uprising were led out of their cells to be faced with the sight of makeshift wooden gallows

---

* Exactly the same thing happened during the Moscow coup of 1991 and the shelling of the Russian White House in 1993.

surrounded by crowds of excited spectators. A memorial column now marks the spot where the young officers Pavel Pestel, Sergei Muravyov-Apostol, Mikhail Bestuzhev-Ryumin and Pyotr Kakhovsky, all in their late twenties, and the radical poet Kondraty Ryleev, were taken up the steps and nooses placed around their necks. The crowd fell silent in anticipation as the first man, Muravyov-Apostol, was dropped through the trapdoor, but let out a gasp when the rope snapped and he fell unharmed to the floor. Russian tradition has it that a man who survives his execution cannot be re-hanged, and the crowd called for a reprieve. Meanwhile, Kakhovsky was dropped through the trap and, astoundingly, the same thing happened. Cheering burst out from the spectators. It would grow to a mighty roar when Ryleev was also hanged and also saved by a broken rope. As the crowd called out for all the men to be pardoned, the authorities suspended the executions. Ryleev turned to his executioners and hissed, 'Oh unhappy country, Russia, where they don't even know how to hang a man!'

Nicholas was faced with his first big dilemma as tsar, a choice that would set the tone for his reign, and it could be that Ryleev's contemptuous sneer influenced his decision. Nicholas ordered the flower of liberal Russia to be hanged for a second time, and this time none of them survived.

Like the 1916 Easter Rising in Ireland, the Decembrist revolt seemed at the time to have been a shambolic, if heroic failure. But it was a watershed. For Nicholas, it was an ominous warning that all was not well in his empire. And the harsh treatment of those who led the revolt rallied public opinion to their cause. The executed rebels would become the inspiration for future generations of revolutionaries. In a country where poets have long been venerated as the conscience of the nation, Alexander Pushkin's sympathetic verses about the Decembrists did much to establish them as iconic standard bearers of the will for freedom:

> In far Siberia's deepest land,
> Be proud and patient.
> Your bitter labours, and lofty thoughts
> Will not be spent in vain.
> The faithful sister to all woe,

Is hope and joy and courage ...
The hoped-for time will come, e'en so:
Then heavy chains fall by the board,
Then dungeons crack – and freedom's voices
Will greet you at the gate, rejoicing ...

Nicholas I responded to the Decembrist revolt with a retreat into the deepest, most repressive traditions of Russian autocracy. He strengthened the secret police, under the leadership of the dreaded Count Benkendorff, cracked down on dissent and introduced draconian measures to suppress political opposition. Military discipline and fear were his chosen tools of government. The satirist Saltykov-Shchedrin described Nicholas's Russia as 'a desert landscape with a jail in the middle; above it – in place of the sky – a grey soldier's greatcoat'. The populist writer Gleb Uspensky left a similarly vivid picture of the terror that pervaded the lives of its citizens:

> Never to stir ... never to show that one had any thoughts ... always to show that one was afraid, terrified – such were the habits bred by those years. To be afraid was the basic rule of life. It throttled the people's ability to think. No one believed that man had the right to live ... The atmosphere was full of terror: 'You are done for!' shrieked the sky and the earth, the air and the water ...*

Nicholas sent troops to crush popular revolutions in Poland and Hungary. At home, he announced that the official state doctrine would henceforth be *Pravoslavie, Samoderzhavie, Narodnost'* – Orthodoxy, Autocracy and Nationhood – a stark mantra of reactionary values and a deliberate rebuff to the revolutionary triad of *Liberté, Egalité, Fraternité.*

---

* Uspensky's lines are an uncanny foretaste of the poet Osip Mandelstam's 1933 poem about the same atmosphere of terror that gripped Russia under Stalin: 'We are living, but the ground is dead beneath our feet; ten steps away our words cannot be heard. In half whispers we speak of the Kremlin mountain-man ...' Mandelstam's words would condemn him to the camps and ultimately to death, but Uspensky was more fortunate.

The press – heavily censored and state controlled – gave its unstinting support, as did leading writers, including Nikolai Gogol and Fedor Tyutchev. The liberal Pushkin was exiled to his country estate and Nicholas took it on himself to be the poet's personal censor, engaging him in discussions about literature and life, just as Stalin would later do with Boris Pasternak and Mikhail Bulgakov. (Pushkin's 'The Bronze Horseman' and other poems may have denounced the despotic side of the long-dead Peter the Great, but – as with much of Russia's greatest literature – its readers would not fail to recognise its contemporary relevance.)

Nicholas's reign fostered anti-Western sentiment; it favoured the forced Russification of the empire's ethnic minorities, and it stimulated the birth of the Slavophile movement, which would become a powerful force in the century-long tussle between reaction and reform.

But for all its pernicious faults, Nicholas's approach was essentially a reinstatement of the old Muscovite tradition of absolute autocracy and the primacy of the state. It did away with the liberal experiments of previous rulers such as Catherine and Alexander. Nicholas blamed his predecessors for raising the people's hopes of reform and thereby fanning the flames of popular discontent when liberalisation did not follow or the measures enacted were not radical enough to meet their expectations.

The principle is succinctly expounded in the nineteenth century's seminal treatise on autocracy and revolution, Alexis de Tocqueville's *L'Ancien Régime et la Révolution* (The Old Regime and the French Revolution):

> Experience teaches us that the most critical moment for bad governments is the one that witnesses their first steps towards reform. A sovereign who seeks to relieve his subjects after a long period of oppression is lost, unless he be a man of great genius. For evils that are patiently endured when they seem inevitable become intolerable once the possibility of escape from them is hinted at. The very redress of grievances throws a sharp light on those that are left unredressed, and adds fresh poignancy to their smart … It is almost never when a state of things is the most detestable that it is smashed but, rather, when it begins to improve, permitting men to breathe, to reflect, to communicate their thoughts with each other, and

to gauge by what they already have the extent of their rights and their grievances. The weight, although less heavy, seems then all the more unbearable.

De Tocqueville was talking about France in 1789, but his conclusion is remarkably applicable to Russia: *the moment of greatest danger for an autocratic regime is when it begins to reform itself.**

---

* The fear that once a reformist leader of an autocratic state gives the people an inch, he will inevitably see them demand a mile recurs many times in Russian and Soviet history of the nineteenth and twentieth centuries. As we will see, it has usually ended in the exasperated abandonment of attempts at reform by a chastened government, followed by a hasty return to Russia's default position of centralised autocracy.

PART THREE

RISE OF REVOLUTION

CHAPTER TWELVE

The bodies of Russian servicemen killed in the fighting are returned to their families, Russian lives given in the name of Boris Yeltsin's ham-fisted Chechen policies. For the president, these images are a potential political disaster ...

Boris Yeltsin says himself that his style of governing is one of crisis management and in the case of Chechnya he's the one who let the crisis brew, ignoring the republic's growing discontent until conflict was inevitable ...

Boris Yeltsin's war to stop his country disintegrating has left Chechnya in ruins, facing Moscow with a horrendous bill for reconstruction and the prospect of other wars in other republics that may still have to be fought to hold Russia together ...

Now political terrorism has come to Moscow – an explosion on a crowded underground train leaving four people dead and many injured ...

As part of my research for this book I dug out the videotapes of my BBC news reports from Russia between 1987 and 1997. I was startled to be reminded how many of them were devoted to ethnic and nationalist disturbances in the outlying republics of the USSR. I reported on the escalating conflicts in the south of the USSR that drove Armenians, Azeris, Ukrainians, Georgians, Moldovans and others to rebel against Soviet rule. And I reported on the Kremlin's sometimes brutal attempts to hold the Soviet Union together. In the 1990s, another ethnic group rose in anger and revolt. The previous rebellions had been in the non-Russian Soviet republics, but Chechnya was part of Russia itself, and its drive for independence from the hated Russian yoke would become the greatest domestic challenge for Boris Yeltsin and his successors.

The south has always been a problem for Russia, and in many ways a problem of her own making. The ethnic flashpoints of the 1980s and 1990s, and the terrorist bombs that still explode in Moscow today, all sprang from seeds that were sown many centuries earlier. Russia's south is a dangerous frontier – unruly, angry and brutal, but rich in physical resources, geograph-ically beautiful and strategically vital. From the earliest times, Russians eyed its fierce nomadic tribes with suspicion and fear, and the experience of conquest by the Mongols instilled a lasting desire to secure the country's borders (see pp. 28–31). Through several centuries, a succession of tsars tried to drive Russia's potential enemies ever further from her heartlands by expanding the Russian Empire in all directions. In the east, the policy was largely successful, with Siberia becoming a loyal part of Russia itself (see pp. 60–1). In the north and west, buffer states were acquired but failed to prevent invasions by the Swedes, Prussians, Lithuanians, French, Poles and Germans. But it was in the south that Russia's expansionist ambitions met the fiercest resistance and unleashed the longest-lasting problems.

When Ivan the Terrible launched a drive to annex the southern lands in the sixteenth century, he initiated a struggle that would dog Russia for four centuries. He captured the Muslim khanates of Kazan and Astrakhan, but lost territory to the Crimean Tartars, who sacked and briefly held Moscow in 1571, taking many of its inhabitants as slaves. The Muslim warlords were the bogeymen of the Russian psyche; the south was a source of menace, terror and death.

In 1654, Alexei I signed a treaty with the Cossack leader Bogdan Khmel-nitsky enabling Russia to incorporate Ukraine into its empire. In Moscow's eyes it represented a joyful reunification of the old lands of Kievan Rus, the ancient fountainhead of Russian civilisation. But for many Ukrainians the forced union became a source of stored-up anger and resentment that would fester for hundreds of years. Both Ukraine and Russia claimed to be the true inheritor of the golden age of Kiev, and each regarded the other with suspicion and sporadic hostility.

In the 1680s, Peter the Great sent his armies against the Crimean khan, but his enemies' scorched earth tactics sent them scurrying back home. Russia's southern frontier would advance and recede with the following generations.

The eighteenth and early nineteenth centuries were consumed in wars with the Ottoman Turks for control of the fertile lands north of the Black

Sea. Catherine the Great brought the rest of Ukraine, the Crimea and the warm-water ports on the Azov and Black Seas under Russian control. Possession of these southern territories accelerated Russia's rise to Great Power status, and contributed to a sense of national pride that helped glue together a fractious empire.

But the Caucasus region, where Chechen, Georgian, Dagestani and Ingush peoples populated the breathtaking mountains and lush valleys, became a vicious battleground. Resistance to Russian rule brought 50 years of guerrilla warfare in the early nineteenth century that claimed thousands of lives and inspired Russia's writers and poets with tales of cruelty, passion and pride. Pushkin's narrative poem 'A Captive of the Caucasus' (1822) set the tone for generations of writers:

> So shall I sing that glorious hour,
> When the Russian eagle
> Rose above the Caucasus
> And Russian drums did beat in combat bloody ...
> I sing of you o mighty heroes
> Whose feet did trample down the tribes ...
> All to the Russian sword do now bow down.
> – Proud sons of the Caucasus!
> You fought and died most fierce;
> But nothing saved you –
> Not your enchanted armour, nor your mighty steeds,
> Not your mountains, nor your love of freedom wild ...

Pushkin was a liberal and a defender of freedom, yet the oddly jingoistic end to his poem shows how even he became carried away by the exploits of Russian imperialism unfolding as he wrote.

The campaign to subdue the south under Alexander I in the nineteenth century was led by General Alexei Yermolov, a distinguished veteran of the Napoleonic campaigns and commander of Russia's artillery forces. Arriving in the Caucasus in 1816, he quickly established a reputation for ruthlessness and extreme cruelty. His deliberate campaign of terror included the execution without trial of enemy insurgents, the massacre of their families, and the kidnapping and rape of native women. He justified the destruction of millions of acres of forest – just as the Americans would justify the use of Agent Orange in Vietnam in the next century – because it removed potential hiding places for enemy guerrillas. Yermolov said his aim was 'to make the terror of my name a more potent defence of our frontiers than any chains or fortresses':

> I desire that for the natives my word should be a law more inevitable than death ... Mercy in the eyes of the Asiatics is merely a sign of weakness. And the reason for my severity is one of the greatest humanity: I consider that one execution saves hundreds of Russian lives from destruction and deters thousands of Muslims from engaging in treason against the state ...

Yermolov founded the fortress city of Grozny, now the capital of Chechnya. From there he launched punitive expeditions against Chechen villages, ordering his officers to 'destroy their towns, hang hostages and slaughter their women and children'. Many thousands of Chechens were deported and exiled from their homeland. Villages were razed and razed again. One such raid, on the village of Dadi in September 1819, has lodged in the collective memory. The local population, inspired by the legendary Chechen leader Shamil, put up such heroic resistance to the Russians that their deeds are celebrated in Chechen folk ballads. When all the male villagers had been killed by enemy bullets, the defences were manned by women wielding ceremonial daggers; rather than be taken prisoner, they used them to cut their own throats:

> Awake, you braves!
> Wake your families, wake your wives!
> Hurry through the morning prayer!
> Your village now is under siege.
> Three rings of glinting steel,
> Bayonets, daybreak stained with blood.
> The day will shatter in a thousand deaths.

For Yermolov has ordered:

No child, no woman shall be spared!

Open up the great Koran,

Say the prayer of death.

Today, brave men, your souls

Will fly. But the infidels

Will never see your backs in flight.

Allah will take your Holy War

In His embrace …

Each blade of grass, each rock recalls

The pain and rage of our fathers' land.

They shared their death with foes

Who came unbidden, sword in hand.

And happy were our fighters not to see,

Not to weep at the pitiful sight,

Of a Chechen child in tears

By the side of his murdered mother's corpse.

For the Chechen people, General Yermolov remains even today a figure of hatred and revulsion, a symbol of Russian genocide and a spur to some of the most appalling atrocities Chechen fighters have inflicted on captured Russian conscripts in the wars of the past 20 years.*

Even at the time of Moscow's drive into the south, though, the patriotic support of Yermolov's campaigns expressed by Alexander Pushkin was not shared by all. In 1837, Mikhail Lermontov, a young Guards officer with liberal leanings, wrote a coruscating poem full of radical anger against tsarist hypocrisy and the 'hangmen who murder liberty, genius and glory … huddling around the throne in a greedy throng'. Soon after,

---

* In the twenty-first century, Russia continues to take its lead from Yermolov. Villages, towns and – most spectacularly – the Chechen capital, Grozny, have been shelled to rubble. Yermolov's tactics of divide and rule, and the bribing and blackmailing of puppet rulers to wield power on Moscow's behalf have brought a semblance of stability, but only at the expense of repression, murder and state-backed terror. History suggests strongly that it will be many generations before the volcano of Chechen resentment is snuffed out.

he was transferred to a dragoon regiment in the Caucasus, a sort of prison exile in the guise of military service. But in his seminal novel *A Hero of Our Time* (1839), Lermontov implies that for him Russia is the prison, while the wild rebellious Caucasus offers liberty:

> Yesterday I arrived in Pyatigorsk … When there is a storm, it comes right down to the roof of the house … To the west is Mount Beshtu, blue as the last cloud in a dispersing storm. Mashuk, like a shaggy Persian cap, covers the entire northern horizon … Farther away, the mountains are darker, mistier … and at the very limit of sight, a silver chain of snowy peaks runs from Kazbek to mighty Elbrus with its towering peaks. What joy it is to live in such a land!

A Hero of Our Time is bursting with such marvellous, evocative descriptions of the magnificent Caucasus and its fierce, proud inhabitants who fought to protect their homeland. Lermontov's vain, complicated, self-obsessed Russians seem petty by contrast. The book's title is clearly ironic: if anything, it is the noble savages, the Chechens and the Dagestanis, who are the heroes, while the Russians are sterile, cynical wastrels. Lermontov's theme is an oblique indictment of the 'civilisation' that brings slavery and repression.

Writing later in the century, Lev Tolstoy is even more critical. In his youth he served in the Caucasus as a junior officer in the Russian army and wrote in his diary that the campaign was 'ugly and unjust'. His last completed work, the novella *Hadji Murat*, is fired with moral revulsion for the Russians who cheat and butcher their way through Chechnya:

> No one spoke of hatred of the Russians. The emotion experienced by all the Chechens, from the youngest to the oldest, was much stronger than hatred. It could not be hatred, for they did not regard those Russian dogs as human beings; it was such repulsion, disgust and perplexity at the senseless cruelty of these animals that it made the desire to exterminate them – like the desire to exterminate rats, poisonous spiders or wolves – as natural an instinct as that of self-preservation.

The heavy-handed repression of nationalism in the outlying regions of its empire left Russia with problems that would fester for centuries. In recent years Chechnya has been the most visible of these, but other ethnic groups continue to nurse similar grievances that also date back to tsarist times. Periods of crisis and weakness in the governing regime have historically incited nationalist agitation among the empire's minorities, raising the spectre of catastrophic disintegration. In the revolutionary turmoil of the early twentieth century, the liberal prime minister Sergei Witte warned in his *Memoirs* (1921) of the ethnic fault lines that threaten Russia's unity:

> This flood [of revolutionary pressure] is made more dangerous in Russia by the fact that 35 per cent of the population consists of non-Russian, conquered nationalities. Anyone who has intelligently read recent history knows how difficult the development of nationalism in the past century has rendered the task of welding together heterogeneous national elements into a uniform body politic. [In 1905] the border provinces were clearly taking advantage of the weakening of Central Russia to show their teeth. They began to retaliate for the age-long injustices that had been inflicted upon them ... They were ardently waiting for what appeared to them as their deliverance from the Russian yoke. For this situation we alone were to blame. We failed to perceive that since the days of Peter the Great and, especially, since the reign of Catherine II, we had been living not in Russia, but in the Russian Empire ... Our border provinces will never put up with the policy of ruthless Russification. The Georgians, Armenians, Tartars ... wanted autonomy; all longed for the annihilation of the system of deliberate oppression that embittered their existence.

The protracted struggle to subdue her southern territories would be damaging for Russia herself. Ever since Kievan Rus, the self-image of a nation in danger, in a quasi-continuous state of battle or preparedness for battle, had permeated the Russian psyche. The Mongol occupation had inculcated the model of a militarised state that devotes national resources, material and human, predominantly to the waging of war. And the centuries of attritional conflict in the Caucasus and elsewhere confirmed the belief that Russia must remain ever vigilant, ever mobilised for self-defence. The strain of unremitting military readiness would deform Russia's economy and state structures and stand in the way of social reform. The perceived need for a ready supply of military recruits would fatally delay efforts to abolish the curse of serfdom. Ultimately, it would undermine the efforts of reformist tsars in the nineteenth century and lend impetus to the forces of revolution.

Part of the reason why Russia was willing to pay such a heavy price for domination of the Caucasus was to shield her vulnerable southern frontiers, where the Persians, Turks and increasingly the British were jostling for territory. The decline of the Ottoman Empire left Russia and Britain facing off in a struggle to fill the power vacuum left by the departing Ottomans. The so-called Great Game – the *Bolshaya Igra* – would play itself out over a period of 90 years, not coming to an end until the Anglo-Russian Convention of 1907. Before then, the struggle for supremacy in Central Asia would spread to fighting on Russia's own territory. Fear of Russian penetration into the Mediterranean spurred the British and French to land troops in the Crimea in 1854 to destroy the tsar's Black Sea fleet at Sevastopol. Nicholas I, whose belligerence had done much to provoke the Crimean War, died of pneumonia at the height of the fighting, leaving Russia to suffer a devastating defeat. A punitive peace treaty in 1856 forced her to dismantle all her naval bases on the Black Sea, undoing the work of centuries to establish a warm-water port in the south and dashing hopes of access to the Mediterranean.

The scale of the disaster, the tactical blunders and the humiliation of tsarist authority marked the beginning of the end for Russia as the dominant European power. And, crucially, it sparked such public dissatisfaction at home that it gave a new impetus to the emerging forces of the revolutionary opposition. Discontent would grow throughout the century and culminate in the explosive events of 1917.

CHAPTER THIRTEEN

In Nikolai Gogol's novel *Dead Souls*, the central character, Chichikov, is a conman who buys up dead serfs whose names still appear on the census and then makes a fortune by mortgaging them with the state bank.

> 'So tell me, madam,' said Chichikov, 'have many of your peasants died? … You could always let me have them, you know.' 'Let you have what?' said the old woman. 'The dead souls,' said Chichikov. 'I might even buy them from you.' 'But what do you want them for?' asked the old lady. 'I've never sold dead peasants before … You're not cheating me are you? Perhaps other merchants will come and offer me a better price …' 'The woman's a block-head,' Chichikov thought to himself. 'Look here, madam,' he said. 'What do you think they can be worth? They're nothing but bones and dust … now tell me yourself: what use are they?' 'Well,' she said, 'perhaps they could be used for something on the farm … you know, in an emergency …'

Gogol's prose is deceptively simple: the more you read, the more you discover its strange, disconcerting density. *Dead Souls* is not simply a social critique – Gogol veers between his unique brand of absurdist humour and a strange, mystical crusade to regenerate the Russian nation. But its subject matter – the buying and selling of human beings, even after their death, the callousness and incompetence of the tsarist bureaucracy – is a sharp exposé of the practice of serfdom.

Dead Souls was completed in 1852, when the abolition of slavery was under serious discussion both in Russia and the USA. Serfdom had been such a key pillar of the Russian economy, providing the nation's supply of bonded labour and recruits for the army, and underpinning the whole of its social structure, that previous tsars had baulked at the thought of tampering with it.

As early as Kievan times, when Oleg's trading boats would transport captives down the Dnieper to be bartered in Byzantium in the eleventh and twelfth centuries, slaves were a valuable commodity. Historians assume that these were prisoners seized by raiding parties and sold into a lifetime of servitude. But in later years, during the thirteenth and fourteenth centuries, there is evidence of free peasants forced by the burden of their debts to enter into bonded service. By the fifteenth century, the rules governing the acquisition of slaves had been codified in law. The Russkaya Pravda, the first collection of legal documents in Russian history, declares that 'there be three types of slave':

> One may buy a slave before witnesses and pay a judge to register it. If a man do marry a female slave without her master's approval, then shall he also become a slave. If a man do agree to take on the master's tasks, then shall he be his slave. And for a debt of grain that is not worked off in time or paid in full, one will become a slave.

In practice, many peasants agreed to enter slavery voluntarily. A uniquely Russian institution known as *krugovaya poruka* (joint responsibility) had made local communities collectively liable for the payment of taxes, the enforcement of public discipline and the provision of conscripts to the army. In times of crop failure or economic hardship, such responsibilities were difficult to meet, and often the only solution was for whole villages to agree to become the property of powerful landholders.

In the mid sixteenth century, slaves began to be reclassified as serfs, attached to their master's estate but now guaranteed certain rights of tenancy, including the transmission of the land to their sons. Some paid dues to the landholder for the use of the land (known as *obrok*) while others provided service labour (*barshchina*). In many ways, serfdom was beneficial to all concerned; the landholder gained a steady labour force and the peasants were afforded security and protection. Most masters were bright enough to realise it was in their interest not to ill-treat their serfs, and as a result the system spread rapidly. But serfdom cemented a collectivist mentality that would dominate Russia for centuries. The inherited willingness to pull together in the face of shared problems helped the nation expand into an empire and defend itself against its enemies. But it also hindered the development of private property, political freedoms and the law-governed institutions that Western Europe was slowly beginning to develop.

Early on, between the thirteenth and fifteenth centuries, peasant families ran their own communities, engaged in a limited amount of private work for their own benefit and – by common custom – had the right, once a year, to leave their master during the week before St George's Day in November. As long as the harvest had been completed and all their debts paid off, they could simply wave goodbye and take their services elsewhere. But the state had come to depend on the tax revenues that the serfs generated and their movement from one place to another made collection difficult. So in the 1590s Tsar Boris Godunov suspended the right of transfer and within a few decades the peasants were bound irrevocably to the land.

Over the next 200 years, their rights were progressively eroded until serfs began to be bought and sold as personal chattels. In the reign of Peter I (1682–1725) the peasants formally became the property of the landowner, tied to their master rather than to the land, and suffering at his whim. Their remaining civil rights were removed and their condition became more akin to the plight of the Negroes in the United States than to the relatively benign service of earlier years.

In numerical terms, serfdom reached its peak in the late eighteenth century under the supposedly liberal Catherine II. Wealth was commonly expressed as the number of 'souls' a nobleman owned. Both Peter the Great and Catherine adopted the practice of rewarding state service by the gift of human beings – a thousand serfs here, another 10,000 there. The figures involved were stupendous. By 1796, the census showed that 17 million people out of a population of 36 million were in bonded service. A landowner had the right to beat his serfs and to send them to convict labour in Siberia if they failed to obey his commands.

The more the peasants were regarded as property, objects rather than human beings, the more they suffered at the hands of their masters, and the worse the stories of barbarity grew. Just outside the town of Troitsk, 20 miles south of Moscow, I went looking for the former estate of Darya

Saltykova, a wealthy eighteenth-century aristocrat. It took me some time to find it because none of the locals seemed willing to help; most just shook their head and walked away. I was eventually given directions for the hamlet of Krasnaya Pakhra. As I approached, I spotted a blue-domed church on the top of a hill and next to it a neoclassical manor house covered in scaffolding that was clearly being renovated ('for an oligarch', the workmen whispered). The setting was idyllic, but the place had a gruesome history. Darya Saltykova had taken possession of the manor in 1755 (the church was her private chapel) and had spent the next seven years personally torturing and murdering over a hundred of her serfs. Like many landowners of the time, she had a private jail on her estate and in her case it was equipped with torture chambers, where she poured boiling liquids over her prisoners, tied them to burning irons or immersed them in freezing water.

It is clear even today that this was the mansion of a very grand family, and Saltykova had connections in high places. So when the peasants tried to report her crimes, they found themselves put on trial for slander. But two brave serfs managed to smuggle a written complaint directly to the empress, Catherine the Great. It is a sad, pathetic document. One of the men says he was made to watch as Saltykova first accused his wife of failing to wash a floor properly and then systematically beat her to death with clubs and whips. He writes that Saltykova told him: 'If you report this, you will gain nothing except that you yourself will be flogged to death.' The empress read the men's denunciation and Saltykova was put on trial. She was sentenced to an hour in the stocks and then confined to a nunnery. A light sentence, but any punishment of a landowner was quite exceptional.

Serfdom by the nineteenth century had developed into the worst form of slavery. But hundreds of thousands of small landowners risked losing everything if serfdom were abolished, and they stubbornly resisted reform. Despairing of justice, many serfs ran away to Siberia or the wild territories of the south, where they joined rebellious Cossacks in the great peasant revolts (see pp. 60–1).

Like Negroes in the southern United States, serfs had no legal rights, no means of redress and no escape; they and their descendants were slaves in perpetuity. But unlike in the United States, where the rest of society enjoyed freedom and democracy, serfdom in Russia was the ultimate reflection of the despotism and lack of legality that pervaded the whole of Russian society.

Russia's conscience once again resided in its writers, artists and poets. In the Tretyakov Gallery in Moscow, I was shown the magnificent peasant paintings of Ilya Repin. Peasant scenes had been a staple of Russian art down the centuries, but Repin brought to the genre an emotive and obliquely propagandist power. The faces of the toiling labourers in his *Barge Haulers of the Volga* (1870–3) are charged with human dignity in the depths of pain. His *Religious Procession in Kursk* (1880–3) is a masterpiece of conflicting expressions: tsarist soldiers on horseback whip the crowds of peasants as priests in gilded robes avert their gaze. The effect is intentionally shocking, and it brought Repin into conflict with the censor.

Much of Russia's literature in the nineteenth century reads like a despairing attempt to expiate the intelligentsia's guilt over the horrors of serfdom. Nikolai Nekrasov, Ivan Goncharov and Mikhail Saltykov-Shchedrin agonise over it, and, in *A Sportsman's Sketches* (1852), Turgenev pays tribute to the nobility of the serfs while hinting at the moral vacuity of the aristocracy. Tolstoy, in the autobiographical character of Lyovin from *Anna Karenina* (1873–7), and in novellas such as *The Death of Ivan Ilyich* (1886), holds up the Russian peasant as the fount of humanity and wisdom. When, towards the end of his life, Tolstoy was sent a recording device by Thomas Edison, he chose to record his polemic tract 'I Cannot Remain Silent' (1908), which includes a paean of praise to the Russian peasant. His recorded words evoke the sense of shame that had hung over the nation for much of the nineteenth century:

Today I read in the newspaper that we have executed by hanging 20 peasants in the town of Kherson – 20 of the very people by whose labour we all live, the peasants whom we are guilty of degrading with all the forces of society, with the vodka we pour down their throats, the terrible conditions and laws under which we make them live, the military conscription and the false beliefs we impose on them and use to deceive them. These were 20 of the very people whose goodness, simplicity and hard labour are the sole foundation and guarantee of our Russian way of life ... the way we treat them

seems so awful to me that I cannot remain silent ... I for one cannot agree
to go on living in the unspeakable society that does these things.

The intelligentsia idealised the peasants; but few of them had any first-hand
experience of peasant life. Tolstoy, Turgenev, even Nekrasov, all came from
the landed gentry. For them and for the social reformers who followed their
lead, the peasants remained an intellectual cause to be fought for, rather
than real people to be consulted and understood. The Europeanised upper
classes and the illiterate masses were two separate nations living in a single
country. The yawning gap between intellectuals and peasants would result
in a fiasco of mutual misunderstanding when the revolutionaries tried to
incite the masses later in the century. But before then an epochal change
was brewing: the death of the tyrannical Nicholas I in 1855 had brought a
new man to the throne, determined to do something radical about the
crying iniquity of serfdom.

Alexander II had come to power with Russia in turmoil. The Crimean War
had brought the country to its knees and Alexander's first task was to
conclude the humiliating Treaty of Paris, the peace settlement that would
put an end to the fighting in 1856. He seems to have decided very early in
his reign that there would have to be changes in the way Russia was run.
Alexander reformed the army and introduced universal conscription, but
he shied away from the expansionist belligerence of his predecessors.
He began work on a new legal code and granted greater powers of self-
government to rural and municipal authorities. But his greatest reform came
on 3 March 1861. On the sixth anniversary of his accession, Alexander II
issued the 'Manifesto on the Emancipation of the Serfs'. It brought freedom
to 23 million Russians who for centuries had been little more than slaves.

By the Grace of God, We, Alexander II, Emperor and Autocrat of All the
Russias, announce to our faithful subjects: We have become convinced that
the task of improving the condition of the serfs is a sacred mission that
Divine Providence has called upon us to fulfil ... On the basis of these new
arrangements, the serfs will receive in time the full rights of free rural

inhabitants. The nobles, while retaining their property rights on the lands belonging to them, will grant the peasants perpetual use of the land in return for a specified obligation; and, to assure their livelihood as well as to allow the fulfilment of their obligations to the government, will sign over to them a portion of arable land fixed by the said arrangements, as well as other property.

The liberation of the peasants was the biggest shake-up in Russian society since the time of Peter the Great. It affected virtually every member of the population, placed the whole economic and social structure on a new footing, and created shock waves that would rumble through the nation for decades.

The reform was long overdue. Serfdom had been abolished nearly everywhere in Europe, and in the United States, where abolition proposals had split the Union, civil war would break out in the following month. In Russia, peasant unrest had been growing since the end of the Napoleonic invasion, turning to violent uprisings during and after the recent military disaster of the Crimean War. The serfs, who'd fought bravely in both campaigns, expected their 'Little Father', the tsar, to reward them by giving them the land, which they had regarded since time immemorial as the collective property of the Russian people.

But the majority of landowners were opposed to reform, and Alexander had to force it through. It was, he told the aristocracy, 'better to liberate the peasants from above ... rather than wait till they win their freedom by uprisings from below'. The manifesto is full of pleas for restraint that betray the very real fear of conflict and possibly violence.

We count on the nobles to reach a friendly understanding with the peasants and to reach agreements on the extent of the land allotment and the obligations stemming from it ... Russia will not forget that the nobility, motivated by its respect for the dignity of man and its Christian love of its neighbour, has voluntarily renounced serfdom, and has laid the foundation of a new economic future for the peasants ... Until that time, peasants and domestics must be obedient towards their nobles, and scrupulously fulfil their former obligations … Aware of the unavoidable difficulties of this reform, We place Our confidence above all in the graciousness of Divine Providence, which watches over Russia … and We rely upon the common sense of Our people …

At first, the peasants gave the emancipation decree a gleeful welcome, as the future anarchist Prince Pyotr Kropotkin describes in his *Memoirs of a Revolutionist* (1899):

I was still in bed, when my servant, Ivanov, dashed in with the tea tray, shouting, 'Prince, freedom! The manifesto is posted on the walls … People are reading it out aloud so the others can understand it …' In a couple of minutes I was dressed, and out. A comrade was coming in with a copy of the manifesto. 'It was read out at early mass in St Isaac's Cathedral,' he said. 'There were … peasants there and they all understood what it meant. When I came out of church, two of them were standing in the gateway and they said to me with a mocking grin. 'Well, sir? Are you going now?' And he mimicked how they had ushered him out. Years of expectation were in that gesture of sending away the master …

Kropotkin was an opponent of the tsarist regime, but even he was caught up in the mood of rejoicing:

We ran, rather than marched back … The same enthusiasm was in the streets. Crowds of peasants and educated men stood in front of the palace, shouting hurrahs, and the tsar could not appear without being followed by demonstrative crowds running after his carriage … Oh, Alexander, why did you not die on that day? Your name would have been transmitted in history as that of a hero!

But when the peasants learned what was in the fine print of the emancipation – and there were nearly 400 pages of it – the mood soured. In a bid to appease the nobles, Alexander had fatally fudged the whole reform.

*

In the shadow of Moscow's Cathedral of Christ the Saviour, I found evidence of how Alexander's flirtation with reform would eventually be rewarded. A new and rather grandiose statue, 30 feet high and surrounded by bronze lions, fountains and towering white colonnades, had been erected by public subscription, proclaiming in foot-high letters: 'To Alexander, the Tsar Liberator'. Lower down on the plinth were the words: 'Freed millions of serfs from bondage, introduced independent local councils and regional self-government, ended the war in the Caucasus'. Alexander also expanded education, introduced a more impartial court system and eased censorship; Russia, ironically, was the first country to translate and publish Marx's *Das Kapital* (1872). His reforms were a real step towards the creation of civil society and a law-governed state.

But that, sadly, is only half the story. The liberation of the serfs in 1861 failed to satisfy the peasants' hopes because it set a two-year transition period before the measures took effect and, even worse, it didn't give them the land. Instead, it specified that peasants' holdings must be bought from the aristocracy at a price set by the government. Since few serfs had the money, the state offered them an 80 per cent loan, but they were locked into repaying it – with annual interest of 6 per cent – for a period of 49 years.* It meant the peasants were forced to carry on working for their old masters, paying out more than they had done in the past and often with less land to show for it. Soon the government was sending police and troops to enforce their loan repayments, causing clashes and resentment.

Emancipation disappointed and angered nearly everyone. At the bottom of the inscription on Alexander's statue, I read the sorry punchline: 'Perished,' it says, 'on the first of March 1881 … as the result of a terrorist act'.

That 'terrorist act' was carried out in St Petersburg. I found the spot, by the side of the former Catherine Canal leading from the Winter Palace to the city's main thoroughfare, Nevsky Prospekt. It was on the route the tsar habitually took every Sunday morning and at a certain point on the

---

* Alexander and his advisers were aware of the financial burden the loan system would impose on the peasantry, but Russia's finances were in a parlous state after the disaster of the Crimean War and the state could hardly afford to be any more generous.

embankment by the Pevchesky Bridge the roadway becomes particularly narrow, bounded by iron railings and the canal. The royal carriage, guarded by a detachment of Cossacks, was forced to slow down and edge its way through the milling crowds.

Among them was Nikolai Rysakov, a member of the radical revolutionary organisation, Narodnaya Volya ('The People's Will'). He threw a bomb at the royal procession, but in the excitement of the moment, or jostled by the crowd, his aim failed him and the bomb fell short of the tsar's carriage, exploding among the Cossacks and knocking Rysakov into a fence. Alexander was unharmed. Against his bodyguards' advice, he insisted on getting out of his carriage to check on the condition of the injured men. But as he did so, another terrorist, Ignaty Grinevitsky, threw a second bomb. Grinevitsky was standing so close that he was killed instantly by the blast and the tsar was sent flying. The chief of police ran to his aid:

> I was deafened by the blast, burned, wounded and thrown to the ground. Through the smoke and the snowy fog, I heard His Majesty's voice crying weakly, 'Help!' Gathering what strength I had, I jumped up and ran to the Tsar. His Majesty was half-lying, half-sitting, leaning on his right arm. Thinking he was merely wounded, I tried to lift him but I saw his legs were shattered and the blood was pouring out of them. Twenty people lay wounded on the ground. Some were crawling or struggling to throw off bodies that had fallen on them. In the crimson snow I saw bits of clothing, epaulettes, sabres and bloody chunks of human flesh.

Why did the man who brought emancipation, peace and the possibility of democracy to Russia end up with his legs blown off and his face shattered, bleeding to death from a stomach ripped open from his groin to his throat? The question is all the more poignant because in the minutes before he set off on his last, fatal carriage ride, Alexander had just put his signature on a document that could have changed Russia for ever. The draft constitution Alexander signed that Sunday morning in March 1881 was an attempt to reinvigorate and widen the social reform he had begun 20 years earlier with the emancipation of the serfs.

Alexander implicitly recognised that the failure of his previous reforms to satisfy liberal demands had contributed to the growth of social unrest and revolutionary violence. So he was once again, he declared, committed to seeking a widening of consultative democracy.

The so-called Loris-Melikov Constitution, named after the reform-minded minister who wrote it, spoke of 'inviting society to take part in the formulation of policy'. It proposed a further relaxation of censorship and an expansion of the powers of locally elected councils, including the right to send delegates to a national assembly that would play a role in the formulation of legislation. It was not, of course, the constitutional democracy the revolutionaries were demanding, but it was a first step. Alexander's assassination, by the revolutionaries themselves, put an end to any hopes of progress for a generation.

Alexander's initial measures of 1861 had shown the Russian people that change was indeed possible, and they were emboldened by that knowledge to demand an ever wider, ever faster pace of reform. But he failed to respond to their demands, and by the time revolutionary violence persuaded the tsar to experiment again with reform, it was already too late. The leading revolutionary and Narodnaya Volya activist Vera Figner summed up the views of a growing social class that wanted freedom and democracy. Tsarist power, she contended, would never be able to deliver what they were demanding; the only solution was revolution:

> The policies of Count Loris-Melikov deceived no one. The government's real attitude towards society, the people and the party hadn't changed one jot. The count was still determined to repress the people; he was just substituting prettier methods for the usual crude ones.

The rhetoric is similar to that of young radicals down the ages. But in Russia, people believed the rhetoric and acted on it. Where did the young men and women who murdered Alexander and plotted against the tsarist state spring from? What drove them to such violence? And what was the vision of Russia that persuaded them to sacrifice themselves in the name of a political cause?

CHAPTER FOURTEEN

Zhelyabov died smiling, while Rysakov, who had betrayed his comrades under interrogation, was dragged struggling to the scaffold, mad with fear. On the gallows Sofia Petrovskaya kissed Zhelyabov and the two other condemned men, but turned away from Rysakov who died alone, damned by the new revolutionary religion ... They had killed for the sake of ideas ... so death in the midst of their comrades was the justification they needed ... To die cancels out both guilt and the crime itself ... it was the culmination of nihilism, at the very foot of the gallows.

Albert Camus's description of the execution of the revolutionaries who murdered Tsar Alexander II in 1881 is laced with moral ambiguity. His philosophical essay *The Rebel* (1951) hints that he both understands and condemns the act of political murder. It is both necessary and impermissible.

Prison photographs of Nikolai Rysakov, the blond-haired 19-year-old who threw the first bomb but betrayed his friends under interrogation, are full of the same ambiguity. He stares at the camera with fear in his eyes. And the transcripts of his confession are painful to read, so desperate are his pleas for mercy, for 'just another year of life'.

But, like all the others, Rysakov had been a willing assassin, fired by what he saw as the moral imperative of the political cause. In the 1860s and 1870s they carried out scores of bombings, killing and maiming bystanders and sacrificing their own lives with abandon. Their remarkable political anthem, the 'Hymn of the Revolutionary' (1865) sums up the fanatical absolutism of the Narodnaya Volya activists:

Don't cry over the corpses of your comrades,
Who fell with a gun in their hand ...
Just walk without fear through their bodies,
And carry the standard aloft!

Under the banner of ideas,
We must struggle;
We must fight the deadly battle
To the bitterest of ends ...

The blinkered intensity of it all is astonishing – the closest parallel is probably the fanaticism of today's Islamic suicide bombers. This was to be a merciless, bloody war to the death.

To understand the source of the ferocity, we need to look back at the roots of violent opposition in Russia's long history. In earlier times, disgruntled nobles plotted against Ivan the Terrible, pretenders to the throne caused civil war in the Time of Troubles, and military coups and murders raised up and brought down monarchs as late as the nineteenth century (see pp. 00). But these were essentially power struggles within the autocracy, not a challenge to Tsarism itself. The challenge came 'from above', from within the ruling caste, not from the ordinary people 'below'. The first tentative instance of that came with the reformers Alexander Radishchev and Nikolai Novikov, who attacked the social policies of Catherine the Great, agitated for measures to close the gap between the autocrat and the people, including the abolition of serfdom, and were promptly jailed for their trouble.

The Decembrist coup plotters of 1825 fired the starting gun on a century of revolutionary opposition backed by the use of force (see pp. 112–13). Over the following decades a new, archetypally Russian class of disgruntled young men and women began to emerge as its ideological cheerleaders. The intelligentsia were drawn from students, clerks, writers and teachers – all given a relatively liberal education by the state, but repelled by the nature of that state and angry at the yawning gap between rulers and ruled. They were *raznochintsy*, literally 'people of different social grades'. In the 1830s, the writer Pyotr Chaadayev attacked the institution of autocracy in Russia in language so furious that his 'Philosophical Letters' (1831) were denounced and banned, circulating only clandestinely as manuscripts passed from hand to hand – an early form of *samizdat*.

Our history began in barbarity and backwardness, followed by brutal, humiliating foreign oppression whose values were imbibed by our own rulers. Cut off by our extraordinary destiny from the rest of humanity, we failed to acquire the universal values of duty, justice and the rule of law. When we finally threw off the [Mongol] yoke, the new ideas that had blossomed in Western Europe did not penetrate our state of oppression and slavery because we were isolated from the human race. We fell into a condition of ever deeper servitude. While the whole world was being rebuilt and renewed, nothing was built in Russia. Nothing of what was happening in Europe got as far as us. We have remained cowed and cowering in our miserable hovels … Perhaps you find me bitter in speaking thus of our country; but I have spoken only a small part of the whole unpalatable truth.

Chaadayev was declared mad by the regime and sent into exile. His riposte, both ironic and furious, was 'The Vindication of a Madman' (1837).

Chaadayev's diagnosis sparked a fierce ideological debate. He argued for a decisive turn towards Western values – European-style constitutionalism and social justice. It was a view that found plenty of support among the intelligentsia and coalesced into a powerful school of so-called Westernisers.

But an equally vigorous movement emerged, in stark disagreement with Chaadayev's solution and proposing instead a return to the 'basic Russian values' of Orthodoxy, peasant collectivism and national culture. These were the so-called Slavophiles, who saw Russia's strength in its sense of history and shared purpose. In their eyes, communal institutions like the traditional peasant councils, the *mir*, gave Russia an advantage over the individualistic West: Europeans thought of themselves first, but Russians thought in terms of common effort and the common good. The Slavophiles were conservatives who supported tsarism. They too were aware of the growing gap between the monarch and his subjects and they proposed consultative councils to bring the two back into harmony. The Slavophile Konstantin Aksakov defined the essence of Slavophilism as *sobornost'* (togetherness):

All classes and groups of the population are imbued with a single spirit, a single faith, identical convictions, uniform concepts and the same devotion to the common weal; … Russia is a sort of moral choir, in which the individual voice is not drowned out but is heard in all its glory as part of the collective harmony of all voices singing together.

Striking a similar note, Dostoevsky wrote in his 'Writer's Diary' in the 1870s:

Our land may be destitute and chaotic ... but it stands as one man. All 80 million of its inhabitants share a spiritual unity that does not, and cannot, exist anywhere in Europe.

The Slavophiles promoted an inspiring, if heavily romanticised view of Russia's past. They were anti-Western in the sense that they rejected European social values and lamented Peter the Great's attempts to introduce them. Alien Western ideas, they believed, were the cause of the fatal estrangement between the monarch and the people; the old social model of an autocratic, Orthodox society in which everyone knew his or her place was a better recipe for social stability. The Slavophiles disagreed profoundly with Chaadayev's criticisms and proclaimed Russia's moral superiority over the West, reviving the old myths of 'Holy Rus' with its divine mission to save the world. 'Suffering land of the Russian people!' writes the poet Fedor Tyutchev. 'The foreigner's glance will never understand you ... But the King of Heaven, weighed down by the burden of the cross, in the garments of a slave, has walked upon your soil and He has blessed you.' Tyutchev at his best is one of Russia's great lyric poets. He was also a xenophobic nationalist and imperialist whose political writings sound like Rudyard Kipling on amphetamines. His mystical-religious representation of Russia, similar in many respects to that of Dostoevsky, reflects the Slavophiles' vision of a downtrodden nation ennobled by a native faith that will change the world.

With the mind alone,
Russia cannot be understood.
No ordinary measure spans her greatness.
She stands alone, unique;
In Russia you simply must have faith.

The belief that Russia's destiny was to teach humanity how to live would characterise Slavophile teachings in the nineteenth century and surface again in a new guise after 1917. But the Slavophile–Westerniser debate stemmed from a dichotomy that had haunted Russians from the earliest times: the values of Eastern despotism, the legacy of the Mongol yoke, versus the Western model of participatory government and social guarantees. By the 1840s, both Westernisers and Slavophiles agreed change was needed.

On the whole, the generation of the 1840s were political thinkers and theorists, generally unwilling to resort to violence as a political weapon. Writers such as Alexander Herzen and Vissarion Belinsky denounced autocracy, serfdom and the tsarist police state. They advocated European liberal values, but their very Russian form of socialism borrowed from the Slavophile ideal of the peasant commune. Herzen famously predicted that Russia would provide the most fertile ground for socialist revolution:

A storm is approaching; make no mistake about it. Revolutionaries and reactionaries are at one about that. All men's heads are in a spin; a weighty question, a question of life and death, lies heavy on all our chests … The word 'socialism' is unknown to the Russian people, but its meaning is close to their hearts because they have lived for generations in village communes … The peasants have been the guardians of our national character, which is based on the ethos of Communism – the division of the land according to the number of workers, and the absence of private ownership … By good fortune, the life of the commune has survived into the period of the rise of socialism in Europe … making our soil the most suited to the germination of those seeds brought from the West.

Herzen became known as 'the Father of Russian Socialism'; he coined the formula 'land and freedom', which would become the slogan of the populist movement. But faced with demands to take the revolution onto the streets he drew back, vainly hoping to the very last that the tsarist system would reform itself. Disappointed and increasingly marginalised, he ended his life in exile, living in London – in Paddington and Putney – vainly trying to influence Russian politics through his writings in émigré journals.

Herzen's generation was well intentioned, committed to the peaceful introduction of socialism and horrified by political coercion. They opposed dictatorships of any kind, tsarist or revolutionary, and believed in genuine liberty and choice.*

But the Men of the Forties had missed their chance. In a few turbulent years, their brand of idealistic liberalism was swept away by a new generation of angry radicals. The Men of the Sixties were much less squeamish, much readier to use violence to impose their views.

Turgenev captures the moment in his iconic novel of the times, *Fathers and Children* (1862), painting a pained, rueful portrait of the new breed of revolutionary nihilists. The novel's hero, or anti-hero, Bazarov is determined to do away with the old order, vehemently opposed to the gradualism of the previous generation. He fails because his revolutionary zealotry is undermined by the very human emotions of love and affection.

But it was another book, written a year later and now largely unread, that helped to determine the future of the revolutionary movement. Nikolai Chernyshevsky's *What Is to Be Done?* seems today like a clumsy, humourless pot-boiler, but in 1863 it captured the imagination of an entire generation. Composed in prison and disguised as a sentimental romance, the plot glorifies the 'new men', disgusted by tsarist society and selflessly dedicated to socialist ideals. The love affair of the two main characters climaxes not in bed, but in the founding of a women's cooperative!

'I shall speak frankly with you,' Vera said. 'Good and intelligent people have written many books concerning the way we should live in order to create

---

* I remember the great social philosopher Isaiah Berlin – himself born in St Petersburg less than 40 years after Herzen's death and already in his seventies when I met him as a first-year undergraduate – telling me that the men of the 1840s were like very intelligent chihuahuas compared to the ferocious rottweilers who came a generation later. Berlin had no time for the new breed of revolutionary terrorists. I remember him asking me rather disconcertingly, 'You are not, I hope, a revolutionary with a perfumed beard, are you?' But then he added, with a twinkle in his eye, 'Mind you, we shouldn't forget that Herzen was in favour of socialist free love, until his wife decided she would give it a try – and then he changed his mind ...'

universal happiness. And the principal means they recommend ... is the organisation of workshops on a new basis! I have established a workshop in order that all the profits may go to you, the workers ... this is my passion.' How much joy and happiness the idea brought her! What better thing could happen? It was Vera Pavlovna's most passionate dream!

What Is to Be Done? is a dreadful read. It spawned a whole genre of 'come with me to the salt mines' romances. But its message of social liberation, female emancipation and heroic commitment to the political struggle struck a chord. It became an overnight sensation and a revolutionary classic. Its glorification of 'cold-blooded practicality and calculating activity' set the tone for the violence of the coming years, and Lenin himself regarded it as a pivotal precursor of Bolshevism.

Dostoevsky, who had flirted with socialism in his youth and served time in exile for it, took a very different view. The extremism of the 'new men' of the 1860s had turned him against the revolutionary movement. In his novel *Crime and Punishment* (1866), he lambasts their moral bankruptcy in the figure of Raskolnikov, whose creed of amoral pragmatism – anything is permitted as long as it contributes to the triumph of the 'great idea' – is shown to be an untenable sham. In *The Devils* (1872), Dostoevsky uses the dying words of an old socialist, a well-intentioned Man of the Forties, to excoriate the new revolutionary 'swine' who have taken the previous generation's ideas and perverted them with cynicism and indiscriminate violence:

> All the sores and foul contagions, all the impurities, all the devils great and small have multiplied in that great invalid which is our beloved Russia. What we need is a great idea, a great will to cast them out – just like the lunatic possessed of devils ... Then all those demons will come forth, all the impurity, all the rottenness that was putrefying on the surface ... and we shall cast ourselves down, possessed and raving, from the rocks into the sea, and we shall all be drowned – and a good thing too, for that is all we are fit for.

Dostoevsky based the central character of *The Devils* on the notorious terrorist Sergei Nechaev, whose *Catechism of a Revolutionist* (1869) is a chilling expression of absolutist immorality, in which the end justifies any means:

> The revolutionist … has broken all the bonds that tie him to the civilised world with its laws, moralities and customs. He is their implacable enemy… He knows only the science of destruction. His object is always the same: the surest and quickest way of destroying the whole filthy order. He despises and hates the existing social morality. For him, morality is everything that contributes to the triumph of the revolution. Anything that stands in its way is immoral and criminal.

To demonstrate his contempt for conventional morality, Nechaev – like Raskolnikov in *Crime and Punishment* – set out to commit a deliberately gratuitous, immoral act, persuading his fellow revolutionaries to murder an innocent comrade. For Dostoevsky, 'Nechaevism' summed up the sinister cynicism and evil that had come to characterise the Men of the Sixties. His portrayal of Nechaev in the character of Pyotr Verkhovensky in *The Devils* is a powerful denunciation of the whole revolutionary milieu.

It is clear, though, that the radical extremists of Narodnaya Volya, men and women like those who murdered Tsar Alexander II, enjoyed a good deal of popular support. In 1878, one of their members, a 28-year-old woman named Vera Zasulich, carried out a plot to murder the governor of St Petersburg, Fyodor Trepov. She later explained that she was motivated by a desire for revenge because Trepov had ordered the beating of a young prisoner who refused to remove his cap in his presence. In an astonishing show of sangfroid, Zasulich bluffed her way into the governor's mansion and pulled a revolver on him.

Despite being shot at point-blank range, Governor Trepov survived. Zasulich was arrested on the spot. It seemed an open and shut case of attempted murder, and the government ordered a public trial with a jury. But if their aim was to highlight the inhumanity of the revolutionaries, they would be sadly disappointed. With the help of a skilled lawyer, Zasulich based her defence on the 'political necessity' of her act. She used her time in court to fulminate against the iniquities of the regime and argued that the only rational response to a repressive state was righteous political violence. The trial became a widely publicised indictment of the government itself and, despite the overwhelming weight of the evidence against her, Zasulich was acquitted by a jury of ordinary Russians. Public opinion evidently sympathised with the revolutionaries. The tsar ordered a retrial, but Zasulich's supporters spirited her out of Russia and she lived abroad until the 1905 revolution allowed her to return home.

Less lucky was Alexander Ulyanov, a young man from the southern Russian town of Simbirsk. When Ulyanov was hanged for taking part in a Narodnaya Volya plot in 1887, it would leave a legacy of bitterness in his younger brother, Vladimir. He in turn would later take out his anger and resentment … under the name of Vladimir Lenin.

CHAPTER FIFTEEN

The private correspondence of Russia's ruling elite reveals the sheer panic that gripped the monarchy after the assassination of Alexander II in March 1881. Konstantin Pobedonostsev, the right-wing conservative adviser of the new tsar, Alexander III, bombarded his master with agitated letters, arguing passionately that the assassination was the direct result of foolish experiments with liberalism.

> The times are terrible, Your Majesty. It is now or never if you wish to save Russia and yourself. Do not believe the siren voices urging you to yield to so-called public opinion! For God's sake, Your Majesty, do not believe them – do not continue with the liberal reforms!

Pobedonostsev berated both the dead tsar and the Russian interior minister, Loris-Melikov, who wrote the reforming draft constitution that the monarch signed on the morning of his assassination (see pp. 133–7):

> Your Majesty, if you put your trust in this man [Loris-Melikov], like your father did, he will lead you and the whole country into ruin. All he is interested in is liberalisation … He wanted to introduce free, European-style institutions in Russia … For God's sake, Your Majesty, do not let yourself fall under his spell!

The tussle between liberal and reactionary forces didn't last long. Horrified by his father's murder (he had been present as he died in agony), Alexander III replied to Pobedonostsev, accepting his arguments and agreeing to fire the remaining liberals in his government:

ABOVE Rurik the Rus (centre) on the Novgorod Millennium Monument.

RIGHT Thirteenth-century birch bark drawings from Novgorod.

BELOW Alexander Nevsky speaks to his troops ahead of the Battle on the Ice, in Sergei Eisenstein's film of 1938.

ABOVE Nestor the Chronicler.

RIGHT The tomb of Ivan Kalita in the Cathedral of the Archangel Michael in the Moscow Kremlin.

BELOW *Yermak Timofeyevich Conquers Siberia*, by Vasily Surikov (1893).

LEFT *Ivan the Terrible*, by Viktor Vasnetsov.

BELOW Tsar Boris Godunov,
in a scene from Mussorgsky's opera

BELOW Monument to Minin and
Pozharsky in front of St Basil's
Cathedral, Moscow.

Peter the Great, by Paul Delaroche (1838).

Catherine the Great, by Albert Albertrandi (*c.* 1770).

General Mikhail Kutuzov at the Battle of Borodino, by Anatoly Shepelyuk (1952).

The 1825 Decembrist Revolt on Senate Square, St Petersburg, by Karl Kolman (1830s).

Religious Procession in Kursk, by Ilya Repin (1880–3).

ABOVE *Alexander Pushkin,* the founder of modern Russian literature, by Orest Kiprensky (1827).

RIGHT The Monument to Tsar Alexander II at the Cathedral of Christ the Saviour in Moscow.

ИМПЕРАТОР АЛЕКСАНДР II

ОТМЕНИЛ В 1861 ГОДУ КРЕПОСТНОЕ ПРАВО
В РОССИИ И ОСВОБОДИЛ МИЛЛИОНЫ КРЕСТЬЯН
ОТ МНОГОВЕКОВОГО РАБСТВА.

ПРОВЕЛ ВОЕННУЮ И СУДЕБНУЮ РЕФОРМЫ,
ВВЕЛ СИСТЕМУ МЕСТНОГО САМОУПРАВЛЕНИЯ
ГОРОДСКИЕ ДУМЫ И ЗЕМСКИЕ УПРАВЫ.

ЗАВЕРШИЛ МНОГОЛЕТНЮЮ
КАВКАЗСКУЮ ВОЙНУ.

ОСВОБОДИЛ СЛАВЯНСКИЕ НАРОДЫ
ОТ ОСМАНСКОГО ИГА.

ПОГИБ 1 МАРТА 1881 ГОДА
В РЕЗУЛЬТАТЕ ТЕРРОРИСТИЧЕСКОГО АКТА

Prison photograph of Nikolai Rysakov, member of the Narodnaya Volya group that assassinated Alexander II in 1881.

ABOVE The Khodynka tragedy of 1886, in which 1,400 people were crushed to death.

RIGHT The monk Grigory Rasputin, faith healer and confidant to Tsarina Alexandra.

BELOW Tsar Nicholas II with his family: (from left to right) Princess Maria, Tsarina Alexandra, Tsarevich Alexei, Princesses Olga, Tatyana and Anastasia.

Count Sergei Witte, author of the 1905 'October Manifesto' and first prime minister of Russia.

Pyotr Stolypin, prime minister, assassinated at the Kiev opera house in 1911.

Memorial to Tsar Nicholas II on the site where his remains were unearthed in the 1990s.

Yes ... Today's meeting saddened me. Loris [and the others] were still arguing for the same policies. Decidedly, they would like to see representative
government introduced in Russia. But don't worry – I shall not allow it!
... The very idea of electoral government is something I can never accept!

Within days of ascending the throne, Alexander III had denounced his
father's plans for quasi-liberal reform, scribbling on the front page of the
draft: 'Thank God this over-hasty, criminal proposal was never realised and
the whole crazy project has been rejected.' A month later, he shared his feelings with the nation:

A proclamation to all Our faithful subjects: God, in his inscrutable
wisdom, has seen fit to end the glorious reign of Our Beloved Parent with
a martyr's death and thus to lay upon us the sacred duty of autocratic rule
... Our noble Father, having assumed from God the mantle of autocratic
power for the benefit of the people in his stewardship, remained faithful
even unto death ... The base and wicked murder of a Russian Sovereign
by unworthy monsters from the people is a terrible and shameful matter.
It has darkened Our entire land with grief and terror. But in the midst of
Our grief, the voice of God orders Us to take up the task of ruling, with
total faith in the strength and righteousness of Our autocratic power. We
are summoned to reaffirm that power and to preserve it for the benefit of
the people from any encroachment upon it.

Alexander III's pronouncement was titled 'The Tsar's Manifesto on Unshakable Autocracy'. It signalled the end of yet another of Russia's brief flirta-
tions with the ideas of representative government and a return to the
autocratic rule which had become her default position. Its language is strik-
ingly reminiscent of Ivan the Terrible's speech at his coronation in 1547
('From this day I shall be sole and absolute ruler, for a kingdom cannot be
ruled without an iron hand ... Broad and bounteous are our lands, but there
is little order in them. Only absolute power can safeguard Russia ...' (see
p. 46) In Russia, the rhetoric that underpins autocracy has remained
constant for centuries.

Alexander's manifesto was written by Pobedonostsev, who became the driving force in a conservative backlash that would last for two decades. He had been Alexander's tutor from childhood. The huge, bear-like tsar, 6 feet 4 inches tall and almost as wide, and his priestly, cadaverous adviser ruled Russia in tandem. Under Pobedonostsev's influence, censorship was tightened, the secret police reinforced and thousands of suspected revolutionaries packed off to Siberia. Government agents known as Land Captains were appointed in every rural district and given wide-ranging powers to root out sedition.

Pobedonostsev became the bogey man of the liberals: when Tolstoy pilloried his reactionary views and pinched, sinister appearance in the figure of Anna Karenina's husband Karenin, Pobedonostsev retaliated by having Tolstoy excommunicated. But conservatives and nationalists regarded him as a hero. Dostoevsky was a personal friend and described him as the only man who might be able to save Russia from revolution.

In his densely argued collection of essays, *Reflections of a Russian Statesman* (1898), Pobedonostsev makes the case for autocracy in Russia with passionate conviction. As a committed Christian, he maintains that men are innately sinful and that the firm hand of an all-powerful monarch is the only means to restrain their natural rapacity:

> It is a gross delusion to regard parliamentary government as a guarantee of freedom. The absolute power of the sovereign is replaced by the absolute power of parliament, with this difference only – that the sovereign may embody a rational will, while in parliament all depends on accident … When liberal democracy triumphs, it brings into society disorder and violence with the principles of infidelity and materialism … Such conditions lead inevitably to anarchy, from which society can be saved only by dictatorship – that is, by the return of autocracy.

In an argument as relevant today as it was in 1881, Pobedonostsev contends that the vast size of Russia and its many ethnic minorities mean Western-style democracy can never work there:

These deplorable results [disorder and violence] are all the more manifest where the population of a country is of heterogeneous composition, comprising nationalities of different races. The principle of nationality is the touchstone that reveals the falseness and impracticability of parliamentary government ... The various races are animated by passionate feelings of intolerance towards the political institution that unites them in a single body, and an equally passionate aspiration to independent government with their own, generally fictitious, culture ... Each race would send to parliament representatives not of common political interests, but of racial instincts, of racial hatred, not only to the dominant race but to the sister races and to the political institution that unites them all ... Only autocracy succeeds in evading or conciliating such demands and outbreaks. Democracy cannot settle these questions, and the instinct of nationality thus serves as a disintegrating force.*

Not surprisingly, his and Alexander's response to ethnic aspirations within the empire was a brutal campaign of forced Russification, repressing native languages and cultures and crushing nationalist ambitions. It fostered resentment and sowed the seeds of future conflict in regions like the Caucasus, central Asia and the Baltics. Alexander's policy towards the Jews also bore the stamp of Pobedonostsev's fierce anti-Semitism. The so-called May Laws banned Jews from living in certain areas and entering certain professions. Quotas were imposed on Jewish access to higher education, and anti-Semitic sentiment, never far below the surface in Russia, was deliberately stirred up. Successive waves of pogroms in the years between

---

* This, of course, is what the leaders of the Soviet Union, and of present-day Russia, long feared. In the 1980s and 1990s, Gorbachev's reforms triggered an upsurge of nationalism in Soviet republics like Georgia, the Baltic states and Ukraine, followed by independence demands from ethnic minorities on the territory of Russia itself. As long as the belief in the permanent, unchallengeable nature of Soviet power was maintained, the nationalities had broadly accepted their fate. But when Gorbachev raised the possibility of concessions, the illusion was broken. The nationalities saw that change was, after all, possible, and pushed for change of the most radical sort. Pobedonostsev's diagnosis echoes Alexis de Tocqueville's warning that the relaxation of autocracy ultimately leads to disintegration (see pp. 116–17).

Alexander's accession and the 1917 revolution killed thousands of Jews and forced an estimated 2 million to emigrate, mainly to the United States. Pobedonostsev was reported to have sneered that 'a third of Jews will be converted, a third will leave and the rest will die of hunger'.

Alexander III wanted to unify the country by turning a Russian empire into a Russian nation, with a single nationality, a single language, religion and sovereign authority. His values were a return to the old triptych of *Pravoslavie, Samoderzhavie, Narodnost'* – Orthodoxy, Autocracy and Nationhood – which the last reactionary tsar, Nicholas I, had relied on. Alexander had a pathological fear of political opposition and was quick to declare emergency rule, suspend the law and restrict the civil liberties introduced by his father. For a while, revolutionary activity was driven underground, but it never went away.

In the decade leading up to Alexander's reign, the intelligentsia had taken its gospel of social revolt to the peasants and workers in a campaign that became known as *Khozhdenie v Narod* or 'Going to the People'. In the countryside around Moscow and other big cities, the peasants were amazed to see cohorts of young townsfolk – students, clerks, sons and daughters of merchants and aristocrats – suddenly pitching up in their villages. The new arrivals knocked on the doors of the peasant huts, stripped off their fancy clothes and offered themselves as agricultural labourers. The locals were bemused, then *am*used to see the posh townsfolk struggling under loads of hay, blistering their tender hands with scythes and shovels. But the incomers were also bearing a message. The intelligentsia had concluded that however much they talked and theorised, however many bombs they planted and government officials they assassinated, a popular revolution was never going to happen unless and until the masses supported it.

So their aim was to awaken the peasants' revolutionary consciousness and to foment spontaneous uprisings across the country. The idea seemed sensible. The botched Emancipation of 1861 had left most of the peasants still working for their former masters and saddled with state-imposed debts that had generated widespread anger. It should have been fertile ground. But if the revolutionaries were hoping for a warm welcome, they were in for a shock. In the diaries and memoirs of those young idealists a tone of baffled disappointment crops up again and again. Alexander Mikhailov was a 21-year-old student when he went to work outside Saratov:

> I left college with my instruction manual in my bag and happy hopes in my heart … I met the others who were going to the people and changed into peasant clothes. For the whole summer I worked as a labourer, sleeping under open skies, burned to a cinder by the sun and mercilessly bitten by mosquitoes. The peasant footwear cut my feet till they bled …

Solomon Lion, a Jewish intellectual, was only 19. He quickly became discouraged by the lack of response from the peasants:

> Of course the peasants hated the burden of taxes and the persecution they suffered from the landowners … of course they would have agreed with me that this all needed to be overthrown, but they were so cautious and mistrustful that I never even got the chance to talk to them about an uprising or the tsar or revolution …

A young Praskovia Ivanovskaya, who would later become a professional terrorist in the ranks of Narodnaya Volya, recalled a less than impressive start to her early revolutionary career:

> The peasants reacted to all radical talk with distrust and incomprehension. Our talks usually ended with them saying: 'That's our fate. We were born that way and we'll die that way.' So we didn't actually conduct any socialist propaganda at all! … we were an alien element in a world we scarcely knew. In fact, we were rarely able to talk at all: after the day's work, our limbs shrieked with weariness, our exhausted bodies demanded rest and peace.

Solomon Lion's disillusionment with the peasants was complete. Like all the others, he eventually returned to the city with his hopes for a popular revolution in tatters:

> The peasant masses were so apathetic and so mistrustful that they took us revolutionaries, who were ready to lay down our lives for them, for aristocrats trying to bring back serfdom and reverse the tsar's liberation of the serfs. Basing our hopes for socialist revolution on attempts to galvanise the masses is like trying to build a house on sand …

In many instances, mistrustful, conservative peasant elders turned the incomers over to the police. Hundreds were arrested, and dozens more were murdered by peasant mobs. The experience was enough to convince the revolutionaries that the people were never going to be a reliable basis on which to stage a revolution.

It was a realisation that would have a dramatic impact. From that point onwards, the conviction began to grow that the revolution must be brought about and imposed on society by a clique of dedicated professionals. The man who did most to entrench this view – and who would exert a powerful influence on the thinking of Vladimir Lenin – was the political theorist Pyotr Tkachev:

> The people are incapable of building a new world that would move towards the communist ideal. That can be done only by the revolutionary minority … The people can never save themselves. Neither in the present nor in the future could the people, left to themselves, carry out the socialist revolution. Only we, the revolutionary movement, can do this – and we must do so, as quickly as possible.

The 'people's revolution' was going to be based not on the will of the people, but on the determination of a small group of activists. The concept of the 'invisible dictatorship' of the revolutionary brotherhood, originally propounded by the anarchist Mikhail Bakunin, gained widespread acceptance. After 1917, the Bolsheviks would claim to be the 'vanguard of the people', exercising dictatorship on behalf of the proletariat. But in none of these models was there any room for the people to express their opinion of what was being done in their name. Democracy, elections, representative government – all were condemned as liberal Westernism, a tool for the interests of the bourgeoisie. In the revolutionaries' vision, the rule of law was not to be an impartial instrument of justice under which the interests of every citizen would be equally guaranteed; it was to be more like the judicial model favoured by Catherine the Great, a machine to impose the will of the autocracy on the subjugated masses.

Even among the revolutionaries themselves there was unease at such cynical absolutism. Pyotr Lavrov, champion of the Going to the People movement, was appalled:

> The belief that a party, once it has seized power, will voluntarily renounce it can be entertained only before the seizure … State power, whoever wields it, is hostile to a socialist system of society. Any minority power means exploitation, and a dictatorship can mean nothing else. We cannot accept a programme of revolution through a minority dictatorship. This is not the programme of the true socialist revolution.

Lavrov recognised that the revolutionaries were taking on the same character as the regime they were fighting against. The Russian tradition of autocratic rule was simply reasserting itself under another name.

CHAPTER SIXTEEN

On a chilly winter's day, I walked across a scrubby expanse of grass in northwest Moscow, about 4 miles from the Kremlin and just over the road from the Moscow Dynamo football stadium. The typical high-rise housing blocks of the Soviet era and a newly built sports complex defined the edges of the field. The place was quiet, apart from a few tramps drinking vodka. But in mid May 1896, Khodynka Field was noisy and crammed to bursting. Nearly 400,000 Muscovites had come here, attracted by the promise of free food and drink, and gifts to celebrate the coronation of the new tsar, Nicholas II.

The crowds had been building up for two days. Stalls doled out beer and sausages, pies and ice cream, souvenir coins and mugs. Singers and choirs provided entertainment, and fairground carousels were mobbed with excited children. Then, early on the morning of 18 May, it was announced that the newly crowned Nicholas and his young wife, the beautiful Princess Alexandra of Hesse, were on their way to greet their faithful subjects. The crowd became agitated; people began to rush forward. In his eyewitness account of what happened next, the journalist Vladimir Gilyarovsky refers to a deep ditch that cut Khodynka Field in two. It has been filled in now, but from Gilyarovsky's description I spotted where it must have run, along the side of the new housing estate:

> The crowd was pushing madly forwards. You couldn't resist its momentum. The crush was building up and people were screaming ... Then, as they poured down the sides of the ditch, there was a howl of horror: the opposite wall was tall and vertical, higher than a man's head, and those at the front were being crushed ... There was a mass of screaming people, desperately trying to lift their children out of danger, but more and more people were pouring in, falling onto the heads of those below – a second

layer, and a third, until death, terrible death, was all around us. Blue, sweating faces, people vomiting, gasping for air, the cracking of bones, and corpses held upright by the crowd with nowhere to fall ...

An estimated fourteen hundred men, women and children perished and many more were maimed for life. The authorities were informed of the disaster, but decided after agonised debate to press ahead with the coronation celebrations. Flickering newsreels of that day in May show Nicholas and Alexandra processing serenely through Red Square, surrounded by elegant men with bearded faces like their English relatives George V and today's Prince Michael of Kent. In smart uniforms and flowing white dresses, the royal party are seen dancing gracefully under sunlit marquees.

Elsewhere in the city, rumours were beginning to spread. Newspapers were banned from writing about the Khodynka tragedy, but by the end of the day Muscovites were talking of 'the calamity', whispering that it was an omen, and declaring that 'no good will come from the reign of this tsar'.

By all accounts, Nicholas was not a hard-hearted man; he visited the injured in hospital and donated ninety thousand roubles to the families of the dead. But he was young – only 26 when his father's unexpected death from kidney failure catapulted him to power – and largely inexperienced in the ways of state. 'What shall become of me, and of Russia?' he is said to have asked.

The hardline conservatives who had guided Alexander III missed no opportunity to warn his impressionable son of the danger of making concessions that would weaken the monarchy. When a delegation of provincial assembly members came to Moscow to pledge their allegiance to the new tsar, they asked if he might graciously consider the introduction of a small measure of devolved authority, ceding certain powers to democratically elected local councils. Nicholas rejected the idea in a scathing speech:

I understand that some people, carried away by senseless dreams, have been heard to suggest that local councils might be allowed to participate in the government of this country. I wish to make it clear that I am determined to maintain, for the good of the nation, the principle of absolute autocracy, as firmly and as resolutely as did my late lamented father ...

Nicholas's hostility towards representative democracy was not the result of ignorance. He had observed the Western parliamentary system at first hand during a visit to the British Houses of Parliament in 1895 and he had spoken to Queen Victoria, his wife's grandmother, about the merits of constitutional monarchy. But the bombings and assassinations carried out by Russia's revolutionary opposition had convinced him that reform must be resisted at all cost. The conservative Konstantin Pobedonostsev – who had served Nicholas's father and was now the new tsar's most trusted adviser – encouraged this view, but even he admitted privately that public opinion was unhappy with the tsar's intransigence:

> I fear the tsar's speech has caused all sorts of muttering. I'm told our young
> people and the intelligentsia are agitated and annoyed with His Majesty ...
> I think ordinary folk out in the country liked what he had to say ... But
> some people had completely unrealistic expectations – God alone knows
> what they wanted him to do ... and it all bodes ill for the future.

The moderate liberal opposition, who sought to introduce democracy by constitutional means, feared the tsar's stubbornness would play into the hands of the extremists. Viktor Obninsky was a leader of the Constitutional Democrats, known by their party's initials as the KaDety or 'Cadets':

> When he called our hopes for reform 'senseless dreams' there began to be
> a widespread disenchantment with Nicholas ... It unified the opposition
> forces and made them even bolder ... His speech was the first step on a
> slippery slope, and Nicholas is still sliding down it in the opinion of his
> subjects and of the whole civilised world.

Within a year, disturbances had broken out in Russian universities, and the authorities had to use force to quell the unrest. The Socialist Revolutionaries, or SRs – inheritors of the terrorist Narodnaya Volya movement – formed a 'fighting detachment' to disrupt government by targeted assassinations. They murdered senior government figures close to the tsar, including two consecutive ministers of the interior in 1902 and 1904, as well as scores of lesser officials. After blowing up Vyacheslav von Plehve, the second of the two interior ministers, the SRs issued a long-winded communiqué explaining the reasons behind their terror campaign. The assassination was the only means to end Russia's repressive autocratic rule:

> Von Plehve was the pillar that was supposed to prop up the crumbling wall of autocracy. He did everything to suppress the people, lavishing the people's money on police, prisons and kangaroo courts. On his orders, troops were used to protect the autocracy against the robbed and oppressed people. Workers and peasants were beaten, cut down, shot and exiled to Siberia. All this was to reinforce the crumbling bastion of autocracy. It seemed as if justice had been driven off the face of the Earth, and that the dark reign of injustice would last in Russia for ever. But the power of the people is great. Surrounded by a wall of police, the minister thought he was beyond the reach of the people's judgement. But that judgement came. The thunder of the people's anger has struck this contemptible enemy. Von Plehve has paid with his life for the hunger, the misery, the robbery, the torture, the groans and the deaths of millions of working people. Von Plehve was one of the pillars that held up the wall of autocracy, a wall that blocked the people's path to freedom and happiness. If you chop down the pillars, the wall will fall.

The security police infiltrated the terrorist organisations, but with perverse results. The men whom they thought were acting as their double agents were in fact using their privileged position to mount further assassinations. The most infamous of them, Evno Azef, even helped murder his own employers in the Interior Ministry. With consummate cynicism, Azef played each side off against the other for an astounding nine years before finally being unmasked.

By the end of 1904, Russia was close to turmoil. Political violence was spreading, the economy was foundering, and harvest failures and a sharp rise in food prices were stirring discontent among the people. A strike at the Putilov engineering works in St Petersburg spread quickly to other factories, and within a month 100,000 workers had downed tools.

St Petersburg was suffering from a winter of discontent, with electricity cuts and growing shortages of essential goods.

On Sunday 9 January 1905, a procession of around 20,000 workers, led by the priest and trade union organiser Father Georgy Gapon, defied a ban on demonstrations to march with a petition to the Winter Palace in the centre of St Petersburg. The petition asked Nicholas II to grant concessions to the hard-pressed labouring classes in language that was vivid but still respectful to the tsar:

> Sire! We the workers, our children, families and defenceless aged parents, have come to you to seek justice and protection. We are in deepest poverty and oppressed with labours beyond our strength. We are treated like slaves who must suffer in silence ... Despotism and arbitrary rule are suffocating us. Sire, our strength is exhausted and our patience has run out. Things have become so terrible for us that we would prefer death to the unbearable torment we are being forced to suffer.

The ambiguous tone of the petition – both humble and threatening – reflected a strange duality in Father Gapon's own character. He seems genuinely to have wanted the tsar to be the people's saviour, to avoid revolution by granting them higher pay and better working conditions, civil liberties and a constituent assembly. Gapon had assured the authorities that the march would be peaceful – the workers carried icons and Nicholas's portrait, and they sang patriotic hymns, including 'God Save the Tsar'. But tension was high. When the march passed a designated point, nervous soldiers opened fire, leaving more than a hundred people dead in the snow.

The Russian prime minister, Count Sergei Witte, watched the massacre:

> From my balcony, I could see a large crowd moving along Kamenno-Ostrovsky Prospekt. It contained many women and children. Before ten minutes had passed, shots resounded in the direction of the Troitsky Bridge ... A bullet whizzed past my head, another one killed the porter of the Alexander Lyceum. I saw a number of wounded being carried away from the scene in cabs, and then a crowd running in disorder, with crying

women here and there. I learned afterwards that it had been decided not to allow the marchers to reach the Palace Square, but apparently instructions were not issued in time to the military authorities. There was no one present to speak to the workers and make an attempt to bring them to reason … The troops fired rashly and without rhyme or reason. There were hundreds of casualties … and the revolutionists triumphed: the workers were completely alienated from the tsar and his government.

Bloody Sunday, as it became known, had a profound effect on public opinion. Like the marchers, the vast majority of Russians had regarded the tsar as their friend and protector; the peasants called him their 'Little Father', second in veneration only to God himself. So the massacre of those who had come to seek his help was seen as a fatal betrayal.

Ironically, Nicholas was not at the Winter Palace, having been persuaded by advisers not to accept the demonstrators' petition. (His diaries after the event speak of his pain at the killings but fail to condemn the military for opening fire.) Adding to the confusion was the possibility that Father Gapon was himself playing a double game. He had certainly had dealings with the secret police and reported to them on the activities of the trade union movement he helped to found and run. The Socialist Revolutionaries believed he was a provocateur, and popular ballads began to circulate accusing Gapon of leading the people to their death to discredit the political opposition. ('He pretended to be the people's friend,' run the lyrics, 'but then he scarpered with a shout of *onwards friends to freedom!* … as he took to his heels and ran.') Suspicion about Gapon was widespread, but it seems in hindsight that his motives were not as malicious as the Socialist Revolutionaries believed. Count Witte himself confirms in his memoirs that Gapon had 'gone native':

[The government] began to organise workmen's societies … to try to keep the labouring masses under the influence of the department of police. The task of organisation was entrusted to Father Gapon, who succeeded in gaining the confidence of the governor of St Petersburg. Then, of course, the inevitable happened. The preaching of the socialists and anarchists radicalised the workmen, and they began to strive to implement the extreme programme of socialism. Not only was Gapon unable to stem this movement, but he, too, became infected with the revolutionary spirit …

After the disaster of Bloody Sunday, Gapon fled abroad to Geneva and London. Early in 1906, he returned to Russia and approached the leadership of the Socialist Revolutionaries, denying he was a traitor. He tried to persuade the others to join him in his contacts with the police, but the SRs disbelieved him and after a 'revolutionary trial' they condemned Father Gapon to death and hanged him.

Bloody Sunday sparked two years of strikes and unrest throughout the Russian Empire. Workers, peasants, students, ethnic minorities and soldiers and sailors staged angry protests, to which the government responded with arrests and executions. For Russia's revolutionaries, discouraged after the failure of the Going to the People movement, Bloody Sunday was a welcome, if unexpected boost. Many of their leaders had been languishing in exile and one of them, Vladimir Ulyanov – now known by his revolutionary name of Lenin – gleefully welcomed its effect on revolutionary consciousness among the Russian people:

> Before the uprising the proletariat had been happy enough with the government … [Then] the troops crushed unarmed workers, women and children. They shot people as they lay on the ground. With unutterable cynicism, they pronounced that they 'had taught them a good lesson'. The slaughter of 9 January changed everything. Even those Petersburg workers who had believed in the tsar started to call for the immediate overthrow of the regime.

For Nicholas II and his government, trouble at home was joined by disaster abroad.

By the 1890s, the Russian Empire stretched from Poland in the west and Afghanistan in the south to Vladivostok and Kamchatka in the east. The construction of the Trans-Siberian Railway had emboldened Nicholas to seek further territory in Manchuria, and when this raised the prospect of conflict with Japan he rejected his ministers' advice to seek a negotiated settlement. Nicholas's refusal to back down suggests he was happy to provoke a war that most observers assumed Russia would win with ease. His prime minister, Count Witte, wrote that the tsar was expecting a quick victory to divert attention from his problems at home:

> At heart, His Majesty was for an aggressive policy, but, as usual, his mind was a house divided against itself. He kept on changing his policy from day to day ... He became involved in the Far Eastern adventure because of his youth, his natural animosity against Japan ... and, finally, because of a hidden craving for a victorious war ... Suffice it to say that he alone is to be blamed for that most unhappy decision ...

In early 1904, a surprise Japanese attack had inflicted severe damage on the Russian naval force at Port Arthur in Manchuria. In a panic, Nicholas responded by sending the Baltic fleet on an 18,000-mile journey around the world to come to their rescue. But the Russian warships had got only as far as the coast of north Yorkshire when disaster struck. Their commander mistook a gaggle of British trawlers fishing close to Dogger Bank for Japanese torpedo boats and ordered the fleet to open fire. In the panic that followed, two Russian ships signalled that they had been hit by torpedoes and the battleship *Borodino* reported it had been boarded by Japanese marines. Four trawlers were hit, and one sank with the loss of three English lives. Britain was gripped by national outrage that led to demands for war against Russia. An inquiry determined that much worse damage had been avoided solely because the Russians were so drunk that they ended up firing at each other.

On 14 May 1905, the Russian fleet entered the Straits of Tsushima, between Korea and Japan. The memoirs of Vladimir Kostenko, a ship's engineer on the cruiser *Oryol*, describe the grim sequence of events that followed. An outmoded, underequipped fleet, untrained peasants manning the guns and a series of blunders by the men in charge, led by Admiral Zinovy Rozhestvensky, were about to trigger the worst naval defeat in Russian history:

Our ships were crowded together in a single, inflexible column. As the Japanese approached, the commander of the *Oryol* disobeyed orders and fired a single shot. The enemy vessels immediately retaliated. The Japanese were quick to encircle us. The battleship *Suvorov* was the first to be hit … and we soon followed. The *Oslyabya* was hit in the prow and we in the stern. The enemy's cruisers were firing at us from 6-inch guns, steadily intensifying their fire. The *Suvorov* and the *Oslyabya* were subjected to a hail of shells and suffered horrific damage. The *Oslyabya* sank within ten minutes … the *Suvorov* was literally a wall of flames. And then it was our turn. The *Borodino* went down; then the *Alexander III* … We continued firing as well as we could until Admiral Nyebogatov gave the signal that the Russian fleet was surrendering.

By the time the smoke cleared, the Russians had lost eight battleships and four cruisers, with 4,000 men dead and 7,000 taken prisoner. The Japanese, led by Admiral Tōgō Heihachirō, lost just three torpedo boats. It was an unmitigated disaster for the tsar and his state. Vladimir Kostenko summed up the indignation felt in virtually every part of Russian society:

> While there is no doubting the bravery and dedication of our sailors, all their heroism and self-sacrifice counted for nothing. Our best ships went down one after another in agony and flames. Only now do we see what an unparalleled crime was committed by those who so heedlessly sent us to our deaths. Our decrepit, degenerate tsarist monarchy was blindly hoping for a miracle, but instead it begot the catastrophe of Tsushima. It is tsarism that has been smashed by the guns of Admiral Tōgō! It is tsarism that bears the shame of this defeat. Tsushima stands as the boundary between two eras of our history, the final, indisputable demonstration of the bankruptcy of the whole absolutist system!

Within weeks of the Tsushima disaster, discontent began to spread through the armed forces. In the southern port of Odessa, sailors of the Black Sea fleet staged a protest against the harsh conditions and cruel discipline to which they were subjected. According to the version of the story made famous by Sergei Eisenstein's 1925 film, sailors on the battleship *Potemkin* brought things to a head in early June. Served with maggot-infested meat, the ratings protested and were threatened with a firing squad, sparking a mutiny that spread to the whole fleet and even to the inhabitants of Odessa itself. The film's most celebrated scene shows tsarist troops slaughtering innocent civilians on the steps that lead to the docks. The drama is compelling and *Battleship Potemkin* is a powerful film; it was banned in Britain until 1954 on the grounds that it might foment social unrest. But as with so many revolutionary legends, the *Potemkin* events were almost certainly less dramatic than their subsequent portrayal. In Russia, the victors' history has never lacked for self-aggrandisement.

What is undisputed is that defeat at Tsushima sent shockwaves through the nation. It brought financial and territorial losses and personal humiliation for Nicholas II. Revolutionary groups were emboldened and even the poet Konstantin Balmont, leader of the normally other-worldly Symbolists, weighed in with a bitter elegy:

Our tsar is Tsushima, a bloody stain;
The stink of gunpowder and smoke,
Where reason goes dim.
Our tsar is blind poverty,
Prison and firing squads.
Tsar of the gallows, doubly low,
Who makes promises he dare not keep;
A coward who thinks with a stammer.
But just you wait: the hour of reckoning is near.
He whose reign began with Khodynka
Will end it on the scaffold.

After the events of Bloody Sunday and the disaster of Tsushima, Nicholas was forced to rethink his unbending insistence on absolute autocracy. He offered concessions in the hope of defusing the building revolutionary tension. Had he taken such steps at the outset of his reign, he might have been successful. But now his concessions were perceived as a grudging response to irresistible pressure from the people, rather than the voluntary act of a reforming monarch. If the people could force the government to concede this much, many concluded, another push might bring the whole edifice crashing to the ground.

CHAPTER SEVENTEEN

On 18 October 1905, a young Jewish intellectual with a goatee beard, thick black hair and intense dark eyes rose to address an assembly of striking workers in the Technological Institute in St Petersburg:

> Citizens! We've got the ruling clique with its back to the wall! Nicholas II says he will promise us freedom and the right to vote. But he isn't doing so from the goodness of his heart or because he wants to. Oh, no! He began his reign by murdering the workers ... and stepping over their corpses until he arrived at Bloody Sunday in January this year. The man who sits on the throne is a murderer and if it now seems he's making promises, it's only because we have forced him to do so!

Today whiteboards and computer screens have replaced the revolutionary banners. When I visited, students were listening earnestly to a lecture on nuclear physics in the lecture hall where Lev Bronstein, known to posterity as Leon Trotsky, addressed the crowd in 1905:

> Citizens! If anyone among you believes in the tsar's promises, let him say so! Look around you! Has anything changed? Have the gates of our prisons been opened? Have our brothers returned to their homes from the Siberian deserts? No! The dictator still rules over us with the aid of the army. The guardsmen covered in the blood of January the ninth are his support and his strength. It is he who orders them not to spare their bullets against your breasts and heads ... Bloody Sunday has swept away the spring and replaced it by a military dictatorship.

The group Trotsky was addressing in such inflammatory terms was the *Soviet Rabochikh Deputatov* of St Petersburg. 'Soviet' in Russian means 'council', so this was the Council of Workers' Deputies, directly elected in the factories by the workers themselves and immensely popular with the people. So closely identified with the revolutionary cause did the word 'soviet' become that it would stand for over 70 years as the name of the greatest empire of the twentieth century, the Soviet Union.

That first St Petersburg Soviet has been romanticised by generations of revolutionary historians, beginning with Trotsky himself. To read his memoirs, you'd think the Soviet was solely responsible for the protest strikes that gripped Russia after Bloody Sunday:

> As the October strike developed, the importance of the Soviet grew literally hour by hour. The industrial proletariat rallied around it and the Soviet united the revolution around itself. It resolved to transform the working class into a revolutionary army ... A tremendous wave of strikes swept the country from end to end, convulsing the entire body of the nation. Every striking factory elected a representative and, having equipped him with the necessary credentials, sent him off to the Soviet. The Soviet was the axis of all events; every thread ran towards it, every call to action emanated from it.

In fact Trotsky, who'd just returned from exile in London, had missed the start of the strikes and was arrested after only two months back in Russia. On 3 December 1905, the St Petersburg governor, Dmitry Trepov (whose father Fyodor was the target of Vera Zasulich's assassination attempt in 1878), sent troops to crush the Soviet. They stormed the building. All those present were arrested and put on trial. Trotsky was sentenced to exile in Siberia, but conditions were lax and after a few weeks he escaped and made his way back to England. Lenin, who had been in exile since 1900 following a jail sentence in Russia for plotting against the tsar, had come back to St Petersburg even later than Trotsky, in November 1905. He managed to avoid arrest, but he too was forced to flee when the tide turned against the revolutionaries in 1906.

In terms of immediate results, the Soviet had achieved little. Lenin and Trotsky went back into exile and returned to the frustrated bickering that characterised much of the revolutionaries' existence before 1917. Both men had been members of the Russian Social Democratic Labour Party, dedicated to proletarian revolution, but the RSDLP had split at its Second Party Congress, held in London in 1903. The delegates had quarrelled over the structure of the revolutionary movement. One group, known as Mensheviks (the word in Russian means 'minority', despite their followers actually being the majority) advocated a widely based, popular organisation. Trotsky sided with the Mensheviks, but Lenin led the Bolsheviks (Majority), calling for the revolution to be led by a small, ruthless group of professionals. It was Lenin's vision of a rigidly run revolutionary elite – euphemistically referred to as 'democratic centralism' – that would triumph.*

The 1905 Soviet failed; but the impact of that failure was immense. The Soviet proved the need for centralised coordination of strikes and protests; it brought practical experience of the distribution of arms to the workers; and it showed Russians that challenging the government through violent insurrection was possible.

For the regime, the events of 1905 – from Bloody Sunday in January to the strikes and the Soviet in October – were a warning that the monarchy could no longer ignore. If Trotsky inflated his account of the opposition's activities, his depiction of a murderous tsar was also exaggerated. There were many arrests, but the number of executions was low – official figures put it at ten for the whole of 1905, while even the radical opposition lawyer Oskar Gruzenberg claimed only 26. Those numbers would rise dramatically to over 200 in 1906, over 600 in 1907 and over 1,300 in 1908, before declining in subsequent years. The figures suggest that the monarchy was willing at first to try conciliation before eventually resorting to repression.

Nicholas II had reacted to the tragedy of Bloody Sunday with his usual vacillation. He had agreed to meet a delegation of workers ten days after the massacre, and his speech to them – like his diaries – reveals not a ruthless calculating dictator, but a weak man, overwhelmed by events:

---

* Even the choice of party names reflected Lenin's unscrupulous pragmatism. The split at the 1903 Congress originated in a disagreement about narrow personnel issues, and Lenin won that vote by a slim margin. He immediately appropriated the name of Bolshevik, despite his faction holding a minority of the delegates.

I have asked you here so you can hear my words directly from me and tell your friends what I have to say … I know your life as working people is not an easy one. Lots of things need to be improved and put right … I would ask you please to have patience … But you know it is wrong of you – criminal, in fact – to come in a mutinous crowd, as you did, to tell me about your needs and desires … I believe in the good intentions of the working people – and in your lasting devotion to me – so I am nonetheless willing to pardon you for what has happened.

Nicholas and Alexandra donated 50,000 roubles to the families of those who died on Bloody Sunday. Three weeks later the tsar's uncle, Grand Duke Sergei, the military governor of Moscow, was blown to pieces as he left his office in the Kremlin. The sight of his uncle's severed head on the cobblestones, the blood and fingers spattered on the Kremlin walls sent Nicholas into shock. For the next eight years the tsar failed to appear in public. His hysterical German wife lived in terror. Alexandra had produced four healthy daughters, but the tsar's only male heir – the tsarevich Alexei, born in 1904 – was afflicted with life-threatening haemophilia. In desperation, Alexandra enlisted the aid of a charismatic but dissolute Siberian holy man, Grigory Rasputin, who convinced her he could heal her son. Nicholas too fell under the charlatan's spell, calling him 'a good, religious, simple Russian … the voice of the people'. He closed his eyes to Rasputin's drunken lechery and told his advisers, 'When in trouble or assailed by doubts, I like to have a talk with him and invariably I feel at peace with myself afterwards.' At the same time, the tsar seemed oblivious to the real voices of rising popular protest. The prime minister, Count Witte, wrote despairingly:

> When in the course of my official conferences with His Majesty, I referred to public opinion, he frequently would snap, 'What do I care about public opinion?' He considered that 'public opinion' was solely that of the intelligentsia … 'How I detest the word intelligentsia,' he declared. 'I would like the Russian Academy to strike it out of the dictionary.'

Like Louis XVI before the French Revolution, Nicholas was swept along by escalating calamities, incapable of consistent thought or action. Witte tried to persuade the tsar that only an immediate programme of reforms – modernisation, constitutional democracy and respect for civil freedoms – could defuse the pressures threatening to tear Russia apart. In August 1905, he convinced him to accept an embryonic parliament, known as the Duma, but was appalled when at the last minute Nicholas insisted on restricting it to an advisory role:

> Such a contrivance was typical! The Duma had all the prerogatives of a parliament except the chief one. It was a parliament and yet, as a purely consultative institution, it was not a parliament! The law of 6 August satisfied no one. Nor did it in the least stem the tide of the revolution, which continued steadily to rise.

The August reforms failed; the Soviet was formed and a general strike threatened, forcing the tsar into further concessions. Nicholas's 'October Manifesto', composed for him by the liberal Witte, conceded the constitutional democracy he had previously resisted. It granted legislative powers to the Duma and opened it to all classes of society:

> We, Nicholas II, Emperor and Autocrat of all Russia declare that … the unrest and disturbances in our empire fill Our heart with heavy grief … They threaten to cause disorder in the masses and undermine the integrity and unity of the state. We therefore instruct the Government to … grant the population the unshakable foundations of civic freedom on the basis of inviolable personal rights, freedom of conscience, of speech, assemblage and association … to admit to participation in the Duma those classes of the population that have hitherto been deprived of the franchise … to establish as an unshakable rule that no law can be made without the sanction of the Imperial Duma, and that the people's elected representatives should be guaranteed real participation in supervising the lawful behaviour of our appointed authorities.

The manifesto of October 1905 was an astounding leap forward. After centuries of autocracy, Russia was – overnight – to become a parliamentary democracy. It was, in broad outline, what the moderate opposition had been demanding and, had it been offered earlier and more willingly, it might have worked. But now it was seen as too little, too late, even by Witte:

> In the years 1903–1904, one definite idea had fermented in the minds of the people – namely, that to avoid the miseries of a revolution it was necessary to carry out a number of liberal reforms in keeping with the spirit of the times ... When the people becomes conscious of its dignity and needs, it is impossible to persist with the patently unjust preferment of the privileged minority at the expense of the majority. Rulers and politicians who do not grasp this simple truth prepare a revolution with their own hands. At the first weakening of the government's power and prestige, it bursts out with the violence of an uncontrollable explosion.

Even in October 1905, the moderate opposition – the Constitutional Democrats or KaDety – were prepared to welcome the tsar's proposals and accept the offer of a constitutional monarchy. But the moderate democrats had been undermined by the years of prevarication and delay. The momentum now was with the revolutionary extremists, men like Lenin and Trotsky, who demanded the whole tsarist system be swept away. Trotsky's memoirs mock the regime's attempt at reforms:

> The onslaught of the revolutionary proletariat turned us Marxists from a so-called 'political fiction' into a powerful reality ... and the tsarist autocracy, in its utter confusion, began to make concessions ... When the tsar issued his manifesto, those liberals all shouted, 'Victory!' But we said, 'No! it's only half a victory. The tsar is still there with his army; he can still take back what he's conceded or promised to concede.' The tsar's manifesto is nothing more than a scrap of paper. Here it is – crumpled in my fist! Today they've issued it – tomorrow they'll tear it into pieces, just as I am now tearing up this 'paper freedom' before your eyes!

Trotsky's dismissal of 'those liberals' reflects the final separation of the opposition into its constitutional and extremist branches – the 'liberals' who were prepared to cooperate with the tsarist vision of a constitutional monarchy were reviled as bourgeois, capitalist lackeys by the Marxist Social Democrats – Mensheviks and Bolsheviks. They demanded the complete destruction of the old order and the transfer of absolute power to the forces of the socialist revolution.

When the uprising's momentum petered out in 1906, Nicholas's ever-fluctuating intentions once again betrayed the moderate opposition. His long awaited constitution, issued on 23 April, reversed many of his concessions. It gave the tsar a veto over the decisions of the Duma and announced that the emperor would retain 'supreme autocratic authority'. Freedom of speech was severely regulated and the Tsar held the right to appoint ministers and dissolve the Duma. Witte suggested Nicholas had agreed to a parliament and a constitution only because the events of 1905 had scared him into it:

> His Majesty is afflicted with a strange nearsightedness. He experiences fear only when the storm is actually upon him, but as soon as the immediate danger is over, his fear vanishes. Thus, even after the granting of the constitution, Nicholas considered himself an autocratic sovereign in a sense that might be formulated as follows: 'I do what I wish, and what I wish is good. If people do not see it, it is because they are plain mortals while I am God's anointed.' He usually ends in a puddle of mud … or a pool of blood.

When elections in April 1906 produced a left-wing majority demanding further reforms (including the transfer of all agricultural land to the peasants), Nicholas ordered the dissolution of the Duma after just 73 days. He dismissed Witte and appointed a tougher prime minister, Pyotr Stolypin. Stolypin agreed to fix the election rules to guarantee a right-wing majority, but he resisted the tsar's demands to abolish the Duma completely. Nicholas expressed his annoyance in a letter to his mother:

> A stupid delegation is coming over from England to see liberal members of the Duma. Uncle Bertie told us he was very sorry but he couldn't stop them coming. It's the fault of their famous English 'liberty', of course. I bet they'd be pretty angry if we sent a delegation to the Irish to wish them

success in their struggle against their government … It wouldn't be so bad if everything that was said in the Duma stayed within its walls. But every word comes out in the papers, which everyone reads, and now the people are starting to get restive again. I get telegrams from all over the place asking me to dissolve the thing, but apparently it's too early for that. Just let them do something really stupid, though, and Whack! they'll be gone!

Over the next five years, Stolypin would govern Russia with a combination of ruthless repression and dogged attempts at reform. He introduced legislation to improve the rights of the peasants and help them acquire the land; but he also stepped up the executions of the regime's opponents; the hangman's noose became known as 'Stolypin's necktie'. As unrest abated, the Russian economy recovered: industrialisation and capitalism began to take root; the railways carried prosperity to the people; state finances revived and living standards rose. The period between 1905 and the First World War was a brief golden age for Russian industry, with factory output growing by 5 per cent per annum. The population of St Petersburg swelled as it became an important centre of metalworking, textiles and shipbuilding. In the south, the iron and steel industries boomed. Output of coal more than doubled, and the expansion of oil extraction in the Caucasus brought prosperity to Baku and other cities.

But Stolypin's efforts did not save the monarchy, or himself. Tsarist Russia's last attempt at political liberalism came to a bloody halt on 5 September 1911. By then, the prime minister had received threats against his life and suffered at least one assassination attempt; but he ignored his bodyguards' advice to stay away from public events and declined to wear a bulletproof vest. On that Tuesday evening, he attended a production of Rimsky-Korsakov's opera *The Tale of Tsar Saltan* at the Kiev Opera House. During the *entr'acte*, Stolypin sat in his private box, chatting to the tsar and his two eldest daughters, Olga and Tatyana, who were in the box next to his. Below them, in the front row of the stalls, an anarchist revolutionary named Dmitry Bogrov had been watching. He walked up to the prime minister and fired two quick shots, hitting him in the arm and the chest. Witnesses say Stolypin rose from his chair, unbuttoned his gloves and calmly removed his jacket to reveal his white shirt stained red with blood. With the fatal bullet lodged in his chest, he sank down again, muttered the words, 'Happy to die for the emperor' and made the sign of the cross over Nicholas and the royal party. Stolypin was taken to the Kiev central hospital where he survived for another four days. The tsar visited several times and reportedly begged Stolypin to 'forgive' him. Those words, and the fact that Nicholas ordered the curtailment of the judicial investigation into the shooting, gave rise to rumours that the prime minister's assassination had been ordered not by the revolutionaries but by conservatives in the royal entourage who wanted to put an end to Stolypin's programme of liberal reforms. It emerged that the assassin Bogrov had had contacts with senior figures in the tsarist secret police, but he was executed before he could be properly questioned.

Stolypin was buried in Kiev's Monastery of the Caves. His death signalled the end of reform and the return to reaction. The cataclysms of the next decade meant all thoughts of reform would be put away for many years to come.

CHAPTER EIGHTEEN

Tchaikovsky's *1812 Overture* was written decades after Napoleon's invasion of Russia, but in 1876 another of Tchaikovsky's compositions rallied national pride and passion over a conflict that was unfolding even as he wrote. His *Marche Slave* is full of swelling Tchaikovskian emotion, but it had a very practical purpose. That year, the Balkan peoples rose up against the Ottoman Empire that had ruled them for four centuries, unleashing a wave of pan-Slav nationalism. Thousands of Russians volunteered to fight with their Serbian brothers against the Muslim Turks.* Tchaikovsky wrote the *Marche Slave* as his contribution to the war effort and it was premiered at a concert to raise funds for the wounded.

The Balkan crisis of the 1870s led to a full-scale war between Russia and Turkey, the Russo–Turkish War of 1877–8, which ended with the liberation of Serbia, Bulgaria and most of the South Slav lands. The emergence of Russian-led pan-Slavism as a powerful force provoked Britain and Austria to action. At the Congress of Berlin in 1878, they undid many of the Russian gains and decreed that Bosnia and Herzegovina should be administered by Vienna. The resentment caused by that decision culminated famously in June 1914 with the assassination by Bosnian Serb nationalists of the Austrian archduke Franz Ferdinand in Sarajevo. Vienna blamed Serbia for the assassination; Russia supported her Slav allies. Within weeks, treaties and alliances were invoked and Europe was at war.

Alexander Solzhenitsyn's novel *August 1914* (1971) is to the First World War what *War and Peace* (1869) was to the Napoleonic invasion – a vast swathe of history seen through the eyes of dozens of characters, fictional and real. The shattering defeats that decimated the Russian army in the first

---

* Including Anna Karenina's lover, Vronsky, in Tolstoy's 1877 novel.

weeks of hostilities are described through the eyes of those caught up in the tumult of battle:

> Information arrived that the whole Kashir Regiment had been destroyed at the village of Morken ... The retreating forces were more like a confused and defenceless gypsy camp than an army ... It was an extraordinary thing this mélée of units drawn up higgledy-piggledy with no one to tell them what to do or where to go ... What was there left to do? ... It was too late now, and no use ... His dazed mind was clearing but Vorotyntsev could still not grasp the full dimensions of the catastrophe – it was immeasurable.

There is an echo here of Tolstoy's Pierre Bezukhov, wandering dazed through the Battle of Borodino. But Solzhenitsyn engages in a running polemic with Tolstoy about the nature of history: where Tolstoy believes individuals cannot shape history, Solzhenitsyn argues fiercely that they have a moral imperative to try. Writing in the late 1960s, he saw the failures of the First World War as a weakening in the moral resolve of Russian society that would pave the way for the triumph of the morally pernicious Bolsheviks. There was nothing inevitable about the Bolshevik revolution of 1917, Solzhenitsyn says – greater determination and better leadership could have achieved a different outcome – and he castigates the Tolstoyan fatalism of the Russian generals:

> Only now did Vorotyntsev notice the doomed look imprinted on General Samsonov's face, the look of a 16-stone sacrificial lamb being led to the slaughter ... He sat with his heavy body slumped wearily in the saddle, his cap dangling in his hand, the look on his face not one of authority, but of sadness and resignation ... The army commander's approach was extraordinary. He did not reproach the soldiers for deserting from the front line, he did not try to make them go anywhere, he made no demands on them ... The disaster that had befallen the Second Army, indeed the Russian army as a whole, could still have been prevented ... In a well-defended spot like this, why had the troops become little more than a gypsy rabble? Why were they trickling away in ineffectual little groups?

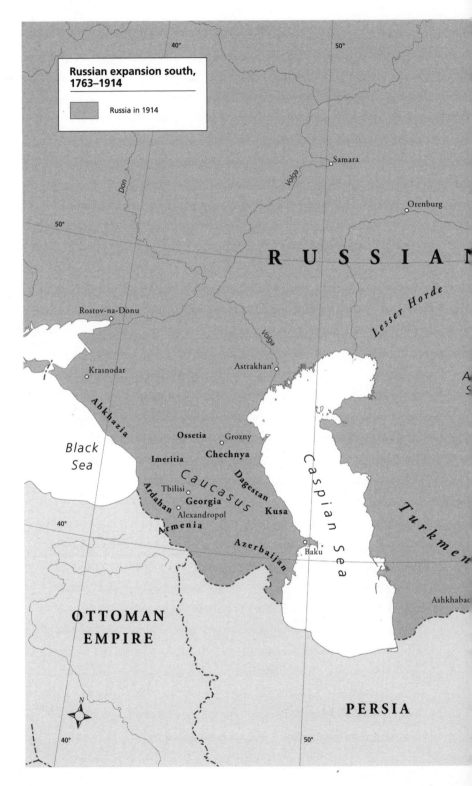

Russian expansion south, 1763–1914

Russia in 1914

40°
50°

Samara

Orenburg

50°

Don

Volga

RUSSIA

Lesser Horde

Rostov-na-Donu

Volga

Krasnodar

Astrakhan'

Abkhazia

Ossetia
Grozny

*Black
Sea*

Imeritia
Chechnya

Caucasus

Dagestan

Tbilisi

Ardahan

Georgia

Kusa

Alexandropol

40°

Armenia

Azerbaijan
Baku

Caspian Sea

Turkmen

Ashkhabad

**OTTOMAN
EMPIRE**

N

PERSIA

40°
50°

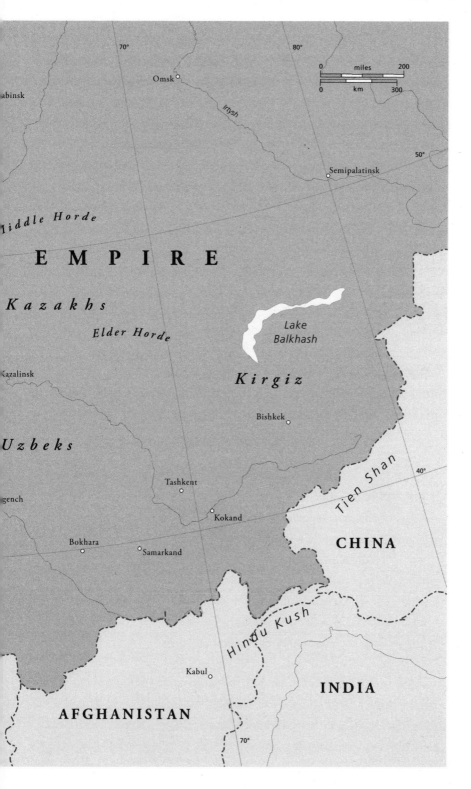

abinsk

70°

Omsk

Irtysh

80°

Semipalatinsk

50°

Middle Horde

E M P I R E

K a z a k h s

Elder Horde

Kazalinsk

Lake
Balkhash

K i r g i z

Bishkek

U z b e k s

Tashkent

gench

Kokand

40°

Bokhara

Samarkand

Tien Shan

CHINA

Hindu Kush

Kabul

INDIA

AFGHANISTAN

70°

0   miles   200

0   km   300

1914 offered a last opportunity for the tsarist regime to save itself. The war was popular. For a brief moment, peasant resentment and workers' demands took second place to the imperative of defending the motherland. In the capital, now renamed Petrograd because Petersburg sounded too German, huge crowds cheered the tsar. Six million men enlisted in the first four months.

But the mood of national unity was soon to be shattered by political infighting and setbacks on the battlefield. The Battle of Tannenberg and the Battles of the Mazurian Lakes left 70,000 Russian casualties. Nearly 100,000 Russians were taken prisoner. The news had a devastating effect on public confidence, comparable to the catastrophe of Tsushima in 1905. Rather than report the rout of the Russian army to the tsar, Samsonov committed suicide by shooting himself in the head. Poland, which had been part of the Russian Empire since the late eighteenth century, fell to the Germans in the summer of 1915, and Russian forces were obliged to retreat along the whole front, from Latvia in the north to Ukraine in the south.

The Russian army was made up of poorly trained soldiers led by incompetent officers. Guns were so scarce that many recruits went into battle without a rifle. General Anton Denikin, commanding the Galicia front in the southwest, wrote bitterly in his memoirs:

> I shall never forget the tragedy of 1915. We had neither cartridges nor shells. We fought pitched battles and made gruelling marches. We were exhausted both physically and mentally. From initial hopes we were plunged into the depths of despair ... The German artillery roared without cease, literally blowing away rows of our trenches with all who were in them. We barely replied at all, for we had nothing to reply with. Our totally exhausted regiments were beating off assault after assault with little more than bayonets. Blood flowed endlessly; our ranks were growing thinner and thinner; graveyards grew by the day ...

At home, there were food shortages, profiteering and inflation. Discontent with the government and the tsar bubbled to the surface. In August 1915, the centrist parties in the Duma demanded the replacement of the tsar's cabinet by a government appointed by parliament, a guarantee of workers' rights, legal trade unions, full citizenship for the peasants and an amnesty for political prisoners.

But Nicholas II continued to believe in the values of Orthodoxy, Autocracy and Nationhood, which had underpinned tsarist rule for generations. He rejected the parliamentarians' demands, suspended the Duma and announced that he would personally take command of the army, directing the war from military headquarters. His decisions showed him to be hopelessly out of touch.

In a famous speech to the Russian parliament in November 1916, Pavel Miliukov, the leader of the Constitutional Democrats, denounced the tsarist regime, its ministers and the tsarina. The fact that the denunciation came from the moderate KaDety, who had previously supported the tsar's ideas for a constitutional monarchy, revealed the depth of the country's anger and disillusionment:

> This regime does not have the wisdom or the capacity to deal with the current situation! ... Gentlemen! This regime has sunk lower than ever before! The gap between it and us has become a yawning chasm that can never be bridged! ... Throughout the Russian lands rumours are circulating of treachery at the highest levels of the state ... of dark forces working in the interests of Germany, preparing the way for a shameful peace accord with the enemy ... A handful of shady personalities are manipulating the affairs of state with treacherous intentions: the so-called 'court party' grouped around the empress ... Are they motivated by treachery or by stupidity? You can take your pick – the results are the same!

Miliukov's attack on the tsarina Alexandra reflected the repugnance she aroused in the Russian people. Her German origins, her rumoured desire to capitulate to the kaiser and her closeness to the religious charlatan Rasputin were damaging the monarchy. Alexandra had always been the dominant force in the royal marriage and, with Nicholas frequently absent at army headquarters at the front, she and Rasputin were widely believed to be running the country. For over a year Russia suffered the vagaries of 'tsarina rule'. Alexandra made decisions based on whims or messages from God, mediated by Rasputin. Ministers were appointed and fired in an unpredictable game of cabinet leapfrog. The empress and her holy man got through four prime ministers, five interior ministers, five agriculture ministers and three each of foreign, war and transport. General Denikin complained of the 'German-Rasputin clique' that had 'surrounded the emperor, brought about paralysis of the government and threatened to bring about the collapse of the army'. And Count Sergei Witte lamented the 'craze of occultism … the mysticism complex with which Alexandra infected her husband'.

In December 1916, a group of right-wing noblemen led by Prince Felix Yusupov invited Rasputin to the Yusupovs' palace on the Moika Canal in St Petersburg and plied him with wine laced with cyanide. The doctor who provided the poison assured them it was enough to kill several men. But Yusupov writes in his wonderfully over-the-top memoirs that Rasputin was a 'diabolical figure' and the only effect of the cyanide was to make him feel a little sleepy:

> Rasputin stood before me motionless, his head bent and his eyes fixed on the crucifix. I slowly raised the revolver. Where should I aim, at the temple or at the heart? A shudder swept over me; my arm grew rigid, I aimed at his heart and pulled the trigger. Rasputin gave a wild scream and crumpled up on the bearskin … The doctor declared there was no possibility of doubt: Rasputin was dead … Our hearts filled with hope; we were convinced that Russia and the monarchy would be saved from ruin and dishonour … Then a terrible thing happened: with a sudden violent effort Rasputin leapt to his feet, foaming at the mouth, rushing at me and sinking his fingers into my shoulder like steel claws …

The gothic horror of Rasputin's death (the plotters eventually finished him off with more bullets, blows to the head with an iron bar and drowning in the icy canal) came too late to save the monarchy. The news from the front was grim, support for the war evaporated, and revolutionary mutterings grew louder. Workers at a key munitions factory, the Lessner plant in Petrograd, issued a proclamation of discontent, declaring they would not fight for Russia until the regime accepted their demands for civil rights and the redistribution of land. The talk in the streets was of impending insurrection.

CHAPTER NINETEEN

By the beginning of 1917, tsarism was rotting from within. The spark that ignited the February Revolution came from an unlikely source. Nevsky Prospekt, the main boulevard of St Petersburg, now dotted with chic boutiques and expensive restaurants, was then the home of butchers, bakers and fishmongers. It was at bread shops on the Nevsky and in the streets nearby that discontent turned into revolt. By the third year of the war, the civilian economy had collapsed and chronic food shortages forced women to spend hours every day queuing for bread that often never came. Some set up improvised beds on the pavement outside the bakeries. On 23 February 1917, International Women's Day, thousands of women left their places of work in a spontaneous protest. On the streets, they joined forces with the bread queues and with strikers from the giant Putilov engineering works. The women organised themselves into groups to go around factories all over the capital and urge the workers to down tools. Their demands were not specifically formulated, but bread, freedom and an end to the war is a fair summary. Dr E.M. Herbert, a foreign visitor to Petrograd, witnessed the explosive consequences:

> There were riots and disorder in the streets, and I think this is the best description of a revolution: people were smashing up shops, looting bread-shops; women, particularly. Tramcars were being overturned, barricades were being built out of wood blocks and paving stones. Obviously something was imminent …

Like the great peasant revolts of Stenka Razin and Pugachev in the seventeenth and eighteenth centuries, the February Revolution of 1917 was a spontaneous uprising against a hated regime, driven by an avalanche of grievances: peasants demanding the land, workers sick of exploitation, soldiers disgusted by the war, ethnic minorities jostling for independence and almost all enraged by food shortages and spiralling prices. It was unplanned, uncoordinated, and it left the professional revolutionaries trailing in its wake. In his novel *Lenin in Zurich* (1975), Alexander Solzhenitsyn mockingly describes how Lenin, observing events from the safety of his Swiss exile, refuses to believe a revolution has broken out. 'A revolution in Russia?' he exclaims, 'What rubbish!' and goes on eating his boiled beef, making sure he gets a good slice of the fatty bit.

Daily demonstrations in the streets of Petrograd grew more violent; Russians died in the streets. The police had used clubs and rifle butts to beat back demonstrations on the Nevsky Prospekt. On Sunday 26 February, a quarter of a million people converged on the centre of the capital: workers from the big engineering plants chanting 'Long live the revolution!'; women protesting at the bread shortages; and thousands of students waving banners, singing 'La Marseillaise' with ferocious Russian lyrics:

> We renounce the old world!
> We shake its dust from our feet!
> We hate the golden idols,
> We hate the palace of the tsar!
> Arise, arise, you labouring masses!
> Rise against the foe!
> Forward! Forward!
> Let the people's cry of vengeance go!
> The greedy rich exploit your work,
> They take your last piece of bread.
> The tsar, the vampire, drinks from your veins;
> The tsar, the vampire, drinks the people's blood.
> Arise, arise, you labouring masses!
> Against thieves, the dogs – the rich,
> Against the evil vampire tsar!
> Kill the cursed the criminals!
> Bring on the dawn of a better life!

In late afternoon, faced with escalating chaos and an absence of orders from their political masters, the troops opened fire. The Cossacks, always the most ruthless of the tsarist forces, sent volleys of rifle shots into the crowd, killing about 200 men, women and children. Nearly 200,000 would die before the uprising was over. Osip Yermansky, a Menshevik journalist, witnessed one of the clashes, when soldiers intercepted a column of demonstrators near the Moika Canal:

> As the masses approached, the soldiers were ordered to kneel and aim their rifles. The crowd saw what was happening and stopped. But those at the back of the march, unaware, continued to push them onwards. There was a moment of hesitation. Then the troops fired two volleys. The front row of marchers fell to the ground, with many dead. The demonstration broke up in panic. People fled, slipping in pools of blood, stepping across the bodies of the dead and dying sprawled in the roadway. Their faces were full of bitterness and anger.

The massacre disgusted many of the soldiers who'd been rushed back from front-line combat to put down the uprising. The sailors' regiments in particular were close to mutiny. By Sunday evening hundreds of troops had defected to the demonstrators. Within a couple of days the whole Petrograd garrison was in open mutiny against the tsar, murdering those officers who tried to restrain them. Tsarist insignia were torn down, prisoners released and police arsenals looted, with the guns handed out to the crowds. Even the Cossacks began to desert to the revolutionaries.*

---

* As the Bolshevik worker Ivan Gordienko noted, it was again the women of Petrograd who took the situation in hand: 'The working women took the initiative. They surrounded the Cossacks in a sort of solid wall. "Our husbands and fathers and brothers are all at the front!" they shouted, "and here at home we are hungry, insulted and humiliated. Think about your own mothers and wives and children! Come and join us – we're demanding bread and an end to the war!" The officers were alarmed how the men might react, so they ordered them to charge. The Cossacks rode forward and people were preparing to defend themselves, but the Cossacks rode past and didn't touch us ... Some of them smiled and one actually winked at us. Cries of "Long live the Cossacks!" rose from a thousand throats.'

With angry crowds on the streets and the army divided, Petrograd was descending into anarchy. The State Council, the conservative upper house of the Duma, wrote to Nicholas II to warn him of the danger. Nicholas seemed strangely detached. His letters to his wife Alexandra barely mention the revolution:

> Military Headquarters, 24 February. My sweet, darling sunshine! My brain is resting here – no ministers, no troublesome questions demanding thought ... I got your telegram telling me of Olga and Baby having measles. I could not believe my eyes – this was so unexpected ... At dinner I saw all the foreign generals – they were very sorry to hear this sad news ... For all the children, and especially for Alexei, a change of climate is absolutely necessary after their recovery ... We shall think this out in peace on my return home ... I greatly miss my half-hourly game of patience every evening. I shall take up dominoes again in my spare time.
> Your loving little hubby, Nicky.

The tsar's advisers were at their wits' end. The Duma and the British ambassador, George Buchanan, had been urging him for weeks to make concessions to placate the mob. Even Nicholas's own brother Mikhail warned him that cataclysm was at hand ('The monarchist system is tottering. Loyal defenders of the idea that Russia cannot exist without a tsar are seeing the ground cut out from under their feet.') But all the warnings and entreaties were dismissed with disdain. When the chairman of the Duma, Mikhail Rodzianko, had gone to warn the tsar that revolution was imminent, Nicholas answered: 'My information is completely different. And if the Duma allows contentious debates to be held on the subject, I shall dismiss the Duma.' When Rodzianko tried to explain that he had the tsar's interests at heart, Nicholas waved his hand and said, 'Hurry up! The grand duke is waiting to have tea with me.'

On 27 February, with the tsar away at army headquarters, Rodzianko sent him a last despairing telegram:

The situation is growing worse. Measures must be taken at once; tomorrow will be too late. The hour has struck in which the fate of the country and the monarchy is being decided. The government is powerless to stop the disorders. Troops of the garrison cannot be relied upon. The reserve battalions of the Guard regiments are in the throes of rebellion; their officers being killed. They have joined the mobs and the revolt of the people; they are marching on the Interior Ministry and the Duma. Your Majesty, do not delay! If the agitation reaches the army … the destruction of Russia and the dynasty is inevitable.

Nicholas's response was to order the dissolution of the Duma and a military crackdown.

The idiocy of such a course was so evident that the parliamentarians ignored his command and dispatched a delegation of deputies, led by the former Duma chairman Alexander Guchkov, to try to reason with him. With the tsar's train stranded in a siding near the city of Pskov, it was late on the evening of 2 March when they reached him. In the meantime, Alexandra had been sending telegrams playing down the seriousness of the situation in the capital and urging her husband 'not to sign any paper or constitution or other such horror'. But the deputies told Nicholas he had no choice: only his abdication could now defuse the revolutionaries' anger.

Struggling to remain impassive as he listened to their accounts of the bloodshed and chaos, the tsar finally accepted the end: 'There is no sacrifice I would not bear for the salvation of our Mother Russia,' he told them. 'I am ready to abdicate the throne.'

The Romanov dynasty that had begun in 1613 and celebrated its third centenary with great pomp just four years earlier came to an end in a provincial railway siding.

The announcement of the abdication was delayed while discussions were held on who should take Nicholas's place. The natural successor would be the tsar's son, the haemophiliac tsarevich Alexei. But Nicholas feared for his son's health and insisted instead that the crown go to his brother,

Mikhail. The tsar's abdication decree was hastily typed out and transmitted back to the Duma in Petrograd:

> In the days of the great struggle against the foreign enemies, who for nearly three years have tried to enslave our fatherland, the Lord God has been pleased to send down on Russia a new heavy trial … In these decisive days in the life of Russia, We believe it Our duty to facilitate for Our people the closest union possible and a consolidation of all national forces … In agreement with the Imperial Duma, We have thought it well to renounce the Throne of the Russian Empire and to lay down the supreme power. As We do not wish to part from Our beloved son, We transmit the succession to Our brother, the Grand Duke Mikhail Alexandrovich … We direct Our brother to conduct the affairs of state in full and inviolable union with the representatives of the people in the legislative bodies on those principles that will be established by them … We call on the faithful sons of the fatherland to fulfil their sacred duty, to obey the [new] tsar in the heavy moment of national trials, and to help Him, together with the representatives of the people, to guide the Russian Empire on the road to victory, prosperity and glory. May the Lord God help Russia!

But the last Romanov tsar would never rule. Mikhail didn't want the throne. A Duma delegation, led by Vladimir Dmitrievich Nabokov, a moderate liberal and a founder member of the Constitutional Democrats, failed to convince him to do other than sign a document saying he might accede to the throne when things calmed down. Nabokov would later lament the lost chance of a constitutional monarchy:

> Mikhail stressed his resentment of his brother's 'thrusting' the throne upon him without even asking his consent … When he signed the document I had prepared, he seemed somewhat embarrassed and disconcerted. Perhaps he did not fully realise the importance of the step he was taking … Now, standing before the ruins of a broken, dismembered, defiled Russia; having experienced all the abominations of the Bolshevik

nightmare, I ask myself if there would not have been a better chance of a happy outcome if Mikhail Alexandrovich had accepted the crown...*

On 3 March, the Petrograd Soviet's newspaper, *Izvestiya*, reported: 'Nicholas II has abdicated the throne in favour of Mikhail Alexandrovich, who has in turn abdicated to the people. Great rallies and ovations are taking place in the Duma. The rapture defies description.' In the Tauride Palace in St Petersburg, Nicholas's portrait was ripped from the wall of the Duma chamber. Tsarism was dead. The Duma deputies announced that a new 'Provisional Committee' would run the country.

The men who formed the Provisional Government were liberals and moderate socialists, Constitutional Democrats and others, who had agreed to collaborate with the tsar's ideas for a constitutional monarchy. This made them deeply untrustworthy in the eyes of the people. The new prime minister was a prince – Georgy Lvov – which didn't go down well at workers' rallies, as the Provisional Government minister Alexander Ivanovich Guchkov discovered to his peril:

> Guchkov had been addressing a rally of railway workers, when a shop steward took the floor. 'What do we think of this new provisional government, comrades? Does it have representatives of the people in it? Fat chance! Look, it's led by Prince Lvov. I ask you – why did we bother making a revolution at all? We've all suffered at the hands of these princes and counts ... All these new ministers are rich landowners. Maybe we shouldn't let Alexander Ivanovich out of here, comrades!' The crowd responded to the

---

* When he got home from the negotiations, Nabokov explained the momentous events he had been involved in to his 17-year-old son, also called Vladimir. Nabokov Junior would become one of the twentieth century's greatest authors and his autobiographical writings pay homage to the deep affection he felt for his father. He speaks of his father's devotion to 'humane, heroic, liberal' values, his subsequent 'resolute plunge into anti-despotic politics' and his championing of freedom and democracy. When called upon to speak against Bolshevism in a Cambridge Union debate during his time as a student in England, the younger Nabokov says he simply memorised verbatim a speech his father had given on the same theme. As we will see, his father's untimely death would reverberate throughout Nabokov's work.

speaker's demands by shutting all the doors. It was becoming most unpleasant …

But another centre of power, untainted by compromise with the old regime, was also emerging. By 1917, the Tauride Palace, the former mansion of Potemkin and Catherine the Great, had been converted to accommodate two great assembly chambers, and in the months after the February Revolution they would become home to Russia's competing seats of power. In the right wing of the palace, in the magnificent Duma chamber, the constitutional democrats tried to create a liberal, parliamentary democracy. A short walk down a corridor lit by gold chandeliers and lined with white marble columns, hundreds of workers, soldiers and peasants gathered in the left wing with a very different plan for Russia's future. Here the people proclaimed the Petrograd Soviet of Workers' Deputies, the direct heir of those organs of workers' power that sprang up after Bloody Sunday in 1905 (see pp. 160–2). Peasants across Russia had elected local councils, or soviets, to seize the land from the landowners and run the villages themselves, sometimes murdering their former masters and burning down their manor houses. Workers in factories and workshops had named their soviets. And in most army units soldiers had done the same: many allowed their officers to take command in actual combat, but some insisted on nominating their own officers and, on occasion, murdering their predecessors.

All of these soviets sent representatives to the Tauride Palace: this was direct democracy par excellence, reminiscent of the ancient *veches* in Kievan Rus. The meetings were noisy and disorderly; votes were fiercely, sometimes violently contested. The revolutionary groups that had refused to cooperate with the tsar were all represented here – Mensheviks, Socialist Revolutionaries and a handful of Bolsheviks. All agreed that the ultimate goal must be workers' power and a revolutionary dictatorship, but they were disorganised, divided and surprisingly cautious. After some debate they decided that for the moment they would cooperate with the Provisional Government 'as long as it didn't hinder a democratic revolution'. The leaders of the Petrograd Soviet had the might of the people behind them, but seemed reluctant to use it.

This became known as the period of *dvoevlastie* (dual power), when the Provisional Government feared the raw strength of the Soviet of Workers' Deputies, but the Soviet apparently feared the responsibility of governing. The liberal government was in office, but constantly looking over its shoulder for the approval of the revolutionary Soviet, which could exercise at least a modicum of control over the rampaging masses and feral soldiers who terrified the country's supposed leaders.

The situation cried out for someone to seize the initiative. Unbeknown to the majority of those who sat and argued in the Tauride Palace, he was already on his way.

CHAPTER TWENTY

In the spring of 1957, a box of documents was released under the forty-year secrecy rule by the German state archives in Bonn. They were a verbatim record of telegrams between German diplomats in Switzerland and the Foreign Ministry in Berlin:

> *Bern, 23 März 1917. Hervorragende russische Revolutionäre hier, hätten den Wunsch über Deutschland nach Rußland heimzukehren...* [Bern, 23 March 1917: Leading revolutionaries here wish to return to Russia via Germany... Please send instructions...]
>
> Da wir Interesse daran haben, daß Einfluß des radikalen Flügels in Rußland Oberhand gewinnt, scheint mir eventuelle Durchreiseerlaubnis durch Deutschland angezeigt... [In Germany's interests for radical wing of revolutionaries to prevail in Russia ... arrange train transportation for them ... provide money ...]
>
> *Wir müssen unbedingt jetzt suchen, in Rußland ein größtmögliches Chaos zu schaffen...* [We must try to create utmost chaos ... facilitate the triumph of the extremists and another shattering upheaval ... then military intervention by us will guarantee the collapse of Russian power ...]

Since 1914, German agents had been keeping a close eye on the groups of exiled Russian revolutionaries in Bern and Zurich. When tsarist power was overthrown by the forces of the February Revolution in 1917, Lenin and co were desperate to get back to their homeland. It appeared that the exiles could be of service to the German cause. If Berlin could help get them back home, they would almost certainly stir up so much trouble for the Russian government that Russia would be forced to withdraw from the war and concede a peace accord favourable to German interests. According to Winston Churchill, the Germans aim was to send Lenin into Russia 'in the same way that you might send a vial containing a culture of typhoid or of cholera into the water supply of a great city. And it worked with amazing accuracy ....'

In late February, the German Foreign Ministry provided money and a single-carriage train to take the revolutionaries eastwards across Europe. From Bern, Lenin, his wife Nadezhda Krupskaya and 30 others sped through Frankfurt, Berlin and Stockholm, unable to leave their compartment because of the locks on the doors, sealed by the German authorities to prevent the contagion of revolution seeping out en route. The sealed train arrived at the Finland Station in Petrograd shortly before midnight on 3 April 1917 and is still standing there today.

I saw Locomotive 293, in a glass box under a rather twee canopy next to platform one. It has been preserved – venerated, almost – for the best part of a century, but it draws fewer crowds today than in the Soviet past: a helpful lady railway official spent 20 minutes looking for the key to let me through to see it.

In April 1917, Lenin was half expecting to be arrested as he stepped out of his carriage. He had not been in Russia for 12 years and he himself admitted he knew 'very little' about what had been happening there. But he had the unshakable confidence of a true believer, a revolutionary fanaticism born from a lifetime's commitment to the cause.

Lenin was born in 1870 to a wealthy, liberal-minded family in Simbirsk. His elder brother's execution for involvement in a plot against the tsar imbued him with an enduring hatred of the regime. His early political activism earned him time in prison and banishment to Siberia, where he married his fellow revolutionary, Krupskaya. From 1900 to 1917, Lenin lived abroad, returning to Russia only briefly in 1905. He was a professional revolutionary, leading a shadowy existence, supported by funds from his mother's estate. His lack of experience of everyday work and human suffering, said Maxim Gorky, had left Lenin 'ignorant of the lives of ordinary people … He does not know them. He has not lived among them.'

When he stepped off the train at the Finland Station, Lenin was not arrested but greeted by a raucous, slightly tipsy bunch of soldiers and workers who waved red flags and cheered his every word. 'The Russian revolution created by you,' he proclaimed to the crowd, 'has opened a whole new epoch! … The worldwide socialist revolution is dawning; European capitalism is on the brink of collapse. Soldiers, comrades! We must fight for a socialist revolution in Russia! We must fight until the total victory of the proletariat! Long live the worldwide socialist revolution!'

I followed in Lenin's footsteps and was caught up in a noisy pro-Communist demonstration on the spot where he was greeted nine decades earlier. Men were shouting slogans much as they have done since the day he arrived, only now with the aid of megaphones. Lenin's Soviet-era statue still stands in front of the Finland Station, a little the worse for wear since a protestor's bomb blew a hole in his backside in 2009, but with the iconic arm still outstretched and the unwavering expression of single-minded confidence still on his face.

His confidence was largely sham. Lenin was stepping into a country in chaos. Tsarism had gone but the revolutionaries were far from united, and the Bolsheviks were minor players, knowing what they wanted to destroy but not what they wanted to create. Lenin was not in control. No one was.

The Provisional Government was planning for free and fair national elections, and introducing a remarkable series of liberal reforms. It released political prisoners and promised civil liberties, ended religious and ethnic discrimination, and abolished both the death penalty and the discredited tsarist police. The Provisional Government's liberal idealism was impeccable, but the middle of a world war with revolutionary chaos on the streets was not the easiest moment to introduce democracy.

For its part, the Petrograd Soviet, the explosive assembly of workers, peasants and soldiers, was biding its time. Among its leaders, the Socialist Revolutionaries were quarrelling over land reform, split between those who wanted to grant the land to the peasants immediately and those who wanted to wait until the end of the war. The Mensheviks were sticking to the Marxian doctrine that society must go through a phase of capitalist democracy before a true revolution can usher in socialism. So the Soviet took the position that the Provisional Government should be allowed to get on with it: the revolution would have to wait until Russia's bourgeois liberal phase had run its course.

Lenin had other ideas. His first act in the chamber of the Petrograd Soviet was to proclaim a manifesto known as the 'April Theses', which set out a much more urgent blueprint for revolution. The soviets, he said, should stop waiting for history, stop cooperating with the Provisional Government and step forward at once to install a dictatorship of the proletariat.

'All Power to the Soviets!' was Lenin's dramatic conclusion that day in April 1917, and it has resonated down the years. It was actually an odd thing for him to demand, because the Bolsheviks were no more than a minor faction in the soviets' leaderships. But Lenin knew that the soviets were the closest thing to a true representation of the will of the people, and he was already plotting a Bolshevik coup to take control of them. His April Theses addressed the demands coming from the different sectors of society and gave them the answers they wanted to hear:

> The first stage of the revolution [in February] ... placed power in the hands of the bourgeoisie. The second stage must now place it in the hands of the proletariat and the poorest peasants! ... There must be no support for the bourgeois Provisional Government. We must expose its capitalist, imperialist nature ... as the worst enemy of peace and socialism. No! to a parliamentary republic. Yes! to a republic of the People's Soviets ... An end to the imperialist war ... abolition of the police, army and bureaucracy ... confiscation of the landowners' estates, nationalisation of the land and its redistribution by the soviets ... the salaries of state officials not to exceed those of an average worker ... the banks to be nationalised under the control of the soviets ... the creation of a new revolutionary *Internationale*!

Lenin's speech that day showed he had understood the radicalism of the popular mood. The February Revolution had emboldened workers and peasants all over the country to oust tsarist officials and set up their own centres of power. The peasants' yearning to own the land was finding violent expression in the burning of landowners' estates; the workers were seizing factories and creating workers' committees to run them; the ethnic minorities were demanding independence and an end to Russian imperial domination. Above all, there was growing opposition to the war, which the

Provisional Government had pledged to continue fighting; and there was universal anger at the food shortages.

Other revolutionaries hesitated. Lenin boldly promised the people what they wanted to hear: Land, Peace, Bread and Freedom. In practice it meant an abdication of any responsibility for law and order, or for the crumbling Russian Empire. But it was a masterstroke of PR: the Bolsheviks became the standard-bearer for the aspirations of the people, and it would give them the popular support they needed to have a real chance of taking power.

By June 1917, Lenin was ready to make his move. At the Congress of Russian Soviets, held in the Large Hall of the Tauride Palace, the Mensheviks and most of the SRs were still arguing that the time was not ripe for a social-ist revolution. 'There is no political party that can say to the Provisional Government, "Give power to us and leave the scene – we will take your place", said the Menshevik leader Irakli Tsereteli. 'Such a party does not exist in Russia.'

Lenin seized the moment. He stood and uttered the phrase that would signal the advent of Bolshevism as a force to be reckoned with: '*Yest takaya partiya!*' he declared: 'There is such a party!'

> To those who say there is no political party ready to take full responsibility for power in Russia, I say 'Yes, there is! … We Bolsheviks will not shirk the task. We are ready here and now to assume the fullness of power!'

It was brilliant political theatre. Those three words – *Yest takaya partiya!* – became part of Bolshevik legend, repeated endlessly for the next seven decades. They would appear in manifestos and on banners, in children's textbooks and in Soviet literature and music.

By the summer of 1917, Russia was falling apart and circumstances were playing into Lenin's hands. Prince Lvov had resigned as prime minister and the Provisional Government had a new leader. The mercurial socialist lawyer Alexander Kerensky was committed to social justice, democracy and the rule of law, but events outran him. The KaDet minister Vladimir Nabokov supported the government's liberal ideals, but concluded that Kerensky was not big enough for the job:

The man was gifted, but not of the highest calibre. He had the appearance of a dandy, the face of an actor and an unpleasant smile that bared his upper teeth ... He combined abnormal vanity with a love of posing, ostentation and pomp ... It is difficult to imagine how the dizzying heights to which he was carried during the first months of the [February] Revolution reacted on Kerensky's psyche. In his soul he must have realised that all the admiration and idolisation were mere mass hysteria, for he had neither the merits nor the intellectual and moral qualities to deserve them. He was a fortuitous little man, to whom history assigned a role in which he was destined to fail so ingloriously, without a trace ...

As minister of war, Kerensky had kept Russia's promise to Britain and France to carry on fighting the Germans. In June he had launched a new offensive to take the pressure off the allies in the West, but it was beaten back with heavy losses. Lenin, by contrast, advocated immediate withdrawal from the war. Nabokov was harshly critical of Kerensky for failing to recognise the growing anti-war sentiment playing into the hands of the Bolsheviks:

I expressed my opinion that one of the basic causes of the [impending] revolution was weariness of the war and the people's reluctance to continue it ... No sage could have ended it without colossal damage, both material and moral. But if there had been an acceptance that the war was hopelessly lost, catastrophe could perhaps have been avoided ... I maintained that there was no other conclusion than the necessity of a separate peace with Germany.

History proved Nabokov right. In early July, angry soldiers and workers took to the streets. A famous series of photographs taken on 4 July 1917 on Nevsky Prospekt shows protesting crowds being gunned down by government troops in Petrograd. Heaps of bodies were left lying in the middle of the road, at a crossroads under a maze of trolley bus cables, while the rest of the crowd ran desperately for cover. Nabokov witnessed the tragedy unfold:

Armoured cars and vehicles darted through the streets ... Shooting broke out from various directions. When the crackle of shots started up, the multitude of people overflowing the pavements of the Nevsky Prospekt dashed to one side, fleeing in a headlong rush, knocking down those they ran into ... The days were lovely and warm; the sun was shining – a striking contrast with the alarming effect of what was happening ...

Radical mobs of soldiers and workers were roaming through the capital. Inflamed by Lenin's rhetoric, the Petrograd garrison had refused to be sent to the front. The sailors of the Kronstadt fortress were in open revolt, and a quarter of a million people had besieged the Tauride Palace calling for the soviets to seize power and end the war. Terrified and fearing anarchy, the Provisional Government had ordered those troops who remained loyal to open fire.

With Russians now gunned down on the streets, the Bolsheviks could claim that Kerensky and the 'bourgeois liberal' government were just as great enemies of the people as the tsar had been. It seemed that Lenin's moment had come: another revolution was under way. Then, inexplicably, he fled.

I have always been puzzled by Lenin's decision to disown the July uprising; after his fiery exhortations to seize power, it seemed a startling change of tack. But the journalist Nikolai Valentinov, who knew Lenin as a friend, suggests an explanation in a manic depressive side to Lenin's character:

> He would be gripped by a state of rage, of ferocious passion, a frenzy of enthusiasm and extreme nervous energy ... but then would come a sudden drop in his spirits, a sort of exhaustion, a very obvious wilting and depression ... Looking back, it's clear that these two alternating states were the psychological essence of his behaviour.

Overtaken by self-doubt, gripped by fear of what he had unleashed, Lenin suddenly announced that the uprising of the July Days was premature, that the whole thing would end in disaster like the short-lived working-class government of the Paris Commune of 1871. Following a government raid on Bolshevik headquarters on 5 July, he went underground.

For the next three months Lenin hid, first in Petrograd, then in a primitive straw hut on Lake Razliv north of the city. 'Lenin's hut', in the middle of a birch forest a hundred yards from the lakeshore, was preserved and made into a national shrine after 1917, and for most of the twentieth century it was visited by Communist pilgrims. Today the elaborate visitor centre, with its museum, billboards, pergolas and restaurants looks shabby and neglected. The pile of straw in which Lenin sheltered, allegedly original, seems to have survived suspiciously well in this harsh northern climate for nearly a century. The museum has his forged identity documents, with his red beard shaved off and his bald head disguised under a thick wig. It preserves the tree stump at which Lenin is supposed to have sat and plotted the future course of the people's uprising in his treatise *The State and Revolution* (1917), before finally fleeing abroad to Finland, where he stayed until October.

With Lenin in hiding, the Provisional Government celebrated victory prematurely. Kerensky told his ministers the Bolsheviks had missed their chance and were now a spent force. Their party newspaper, *Pravda* (Truth), was banned and a government commission announced that Lenin and his comrades were German provocateurs. Their return to Russia in a German train and their acceptance of funds from Berlin were splashed on the front page of pro-government newspapers under the headline: 'Lenin and Co are spies!'*

Those Bolsheviks who hadn't gone to ground, including the recently returned Leon Trotsky, were arrested on suspicion of treason. But the Provisional Government was committed to the rule of law, and when it turned out there was insufficient evidence to charge them, it let them go. Vladimir Nabokov offered this despairing comparison:

> The Provisional Government could have used [the July Days] to eliminate Lenin and co. But it failed to do so. The government simply made concessions to the socialists ... The Provisional Government had no sense of real power. This was a struggle between two forces: on the one side, those public elements that were sensible and moderate, but – alas! – timid and

---

* On 5 July 1917, the pro-government newspaper *Zhivoe Slovo* (The Living Word) printed an article by a former Bolshevik, Grigory Aleksinsky, 'revealing' that Lenin was in the pay of the Germans. Four days later, the allegations were repeated by the State Prosecutor's Office.

unorganised; and, on the other, organised immorality with its fanatical, absolutist leaders ... The Lenins and the Trotskys are completely indifferent to the fate of individuals. 'When you chop down a forest, chips must fly' is their convenient answer to every question.

By disbanding the instruments of state power – the police, the secret police and the death penalty, even in the armed forces – the Provisional Government had voluntarily renounced its coercive control over society. In the months after July 1917, it was effectively at the mercy of the 'maximalist' revolutionaries who denounced bourgeois liberal democracy and demanded nothing less than a revolutionary dictatorship. By October, the pressure for change would be unstoppable.

CHAPTER TWENTY-ONE

Vladimir Lenin was a less than intimidating orator. Recordings of his speeches reveal that he had a high-pitched voice and couldn't pronounce his 'R's. In one of the earliest recorded examples, he can be heard explaining how the First World War and the 'bourgeois' revolution of February 1917 had opened the way for a genuine proletarian revolution:

> The whole world is turning to revolutionary struggle! The war has shown that capitalism is finished and a new order is ready to take its place ... The liberals have betrayed the workers and become the enemies of socialism ... Those who are faithful to the cause of liberation from the yoke of capitalism are known by the glorious name of Communists! Soon we shall see the triumph of Communism throughout the whole world!

Lenin's predictions were only partially right. The ferocious power struggle between liberals and socialists in Russia after the February Revolution would decide the fate of the nation, if not the world. The most vivid account of the period is by the American journalist, John Reed, who witnessed the October Revolution. Reed's book, *Ten Days That Shook the World* (1919) was so outrageously pro-Bolshevik that Lenin was quick to endorse it as the official truth. 'I unreservedly recommend this book to the workers of the world,' he wrote. 'I would like to see it published in millions of copies and translated into every language.' History, as always, is written by the victors.*

---

* Reed died of typhus in 1920 and was given a hero's funeral under the Kremlin wall, but his book suffered a very Russian fate: when Stalin came to power he noted angrily that Reed fails to mention him as a leading player in the revolution and fulminated against the positive portrayal accorded to Trotsky, by then Stalin's enemy and rival: 'It scarcely needs proof that all these and similar "Arabian Nights" fairy tales are not in accordance with the truth ... But after Trotsky's latest pronouncements, it is no longer possible to ignore such fairy tales ... and I must counter these absurd rumours with the actual facts.' Soon after Stalin's speech, Reed's book was banned in Russia and all copies were pulped.

We have inherited widely differing accounts of 1917 from the revolutionaries' side, and even more from the defeated members of the tsarist regime and the Provisional Government. So the question of what really happened in October and who made the revolution has sparked fierce, sometimes lethal disputes.

Lenin had been hiding in Finland since the failure of the July insurrection, and his influence was confined to vociferous 'letters from afar' urging armed revolt. Stalin, who'd been in Petrograd the longest, was a junior figure in the Bolshevik leadership: he had shared prison and exile with Trotsky and Lenin, but was never regarded as anything more than a useful enforcer and party fundraiser (mainly through bank robberies). Grigory Zinoviev and Lev Kamenev, the two other leading Bolsheviks, actively opposed a renewed attempt to seize power at a famous Bolshevik Central Committee meeting on 10 October (voting was ten for and two against, with Lenin smuggled in incognito to attend).

It was left largely to Trotsky to organise the revolution. He had been arrested in July and switched his allegiance from the cautious Mensheviks to the more radical Bolsheviks while in jail. On his release in September he was elected chairman of the Petrograd Soviet and took personal charge of the Military Revolutionary Committees, assembling Red Guard militias of former soldiers and policemen. Trotsky was the military brains of the revolution and he had a strategy ready when Lenin emerged from hiding to take charge at the end of October.

But the official Soviet accounts of 1917 give the opposite impression. The iconic Soviet film of the revolution, Sergei Eisenstein's *October* (1927), is a case in point. Eisenstein had based the film on John Reed's book, with Lenin and Trotsky occupying the starring roles. But Stalin ordered him to re-cut it and portray Trotsky as a coward. So the final version depicts a rather sinister-looking Trotsky, with exaggeratedly Jewish features, hesitating over the start of the revolution and cowering feebly in a doorway as the Bolsheviks march boldly onwards to seize power.

In truth, many groups were competing for influence in the period leading up to October: the liberals of Alexander Kerensky's Provisional Government were nominally in charge; but the directly elected revolutionary

Soviets of Workers and Soldiers had overwhelming public support. The Bolsheviks' promise to end the war had increased their support among the public and, with a little manipulation of the membership regulations, they gained a majority in the Petrograd Soviet. When Trotsky was elected chairman in September, he set about turning the Soviet into an instrument of the Bolshevik Party.

Conservative forces were active, too. At the end of August, the army commander General Lavr Kornilov advanced on the capital with six regiments of troops from the ferocious Caucasian Native Division, pledging to restore order by crushing the soviets, instituting full military discipline and hanging Lenin and co from the lampposts.

Kerensky vacillated, first supporting Kornilov but then panicking when he received reports that the coup might topple him too. He offered to do a deal with the Petrograd Soviet. In return for their help in fighting off the advancing Kornilov, Kerensky agreed to release all remaining Bolsheviks arrested after the July Days and to arm the Soviet with weapons from the government's armouries.

The Bolsheviks agreed. They used their influence over the railway and communication workers to disrupt the coup, severing Kornilov's supply lines and diverting the trains carrying his troops towards Petrograd. But when the coup was defeated and its leaders arrested, the Bolsheviks refused to hand back the guns. The episode left Lenin's party armed and increasingly popular with the masses. By the end of October, they were ready to strike.

On the banks of the River Neva as it flows through the centre of St Petersburg, an armour-plated battleship sits permanently at anchor. Nowadays tourists swarm over its decks and wedding parties pose for photographs beside it. When I toured its oak-panelled cabins and engine room, a Russian pop group was playing noisily on the stern deck. The battleship *Avrora* was launched in 1900 and played its part in the ill-fated Battle of Tsushima five years later (see pp. 163–4). But the reason it has avoided the scrapheap is that this is the ship that fired the guns that launched the Bolshevik Revolution.

On the evening of 25 October, sailors on board the *Avrora* sent up a series of blank shots from its 6-inch cannons. The Baltic fleet was notorious for its revolutionary fervour, and the sound of the gunfire from the port area terrified the ministers of the Provisional Government holed up in the Winter Palace. The story propagated later by the Bolsheviks is that the *Avrora*'s salvoes were a prearranged signal that triggered fierce fighting throughout Petrograd as the masses rose up to seize power. Eisenstein's *October* depicts the storming of the Winter Palace with such realism and so many thousands of extras that his black and white sequences are still frequently mistaken for real footage. The former residence of the tsar was the holiest symbol of the old regime, detested as much as the Bastille in revolutionary Paris, so you can understand why Bolshevik propaganda wanted its fall to be dramatic, passionate and bloody.

But, in reality, it was none of those. The Winter Palace was hardly defended: apart from a motley corps of teenage cadets and women soldiers, the troops had all drifted away or defected to the revolutionaries. The people just wandered in, got lost in the endless abandoned rooms and helped themselves to the tsar's wine cellars. John Reed was there:

On both sides of the main gateway the doors stood wide open, light streamed out and from the huge pile came not the slightest sound. Carried along by the eager wave of men we were swept into the right-hand entrance, opening into a great bare vaulted room … A number of huge packing cases stood about, and upon these the Red Guards and soldiers fell furiously, battering them open with the butts of their rifles, and pulling out carpets, curtains, linen, porcelain plates, glassware. One man went strutting around with a bronze clock perched on his shoulder; another found a plume of ostrich feathers, which he stuck in his hat. The looting was just beginning when somebody cried, 'Comrades! Don't touch anything! Don't take anything! This is the property of the People!' In the meanwhile unrebuked we walked into the Palace. There was still a lot of coming and going, of searching for garrisons of Junkers [soldiers], which did not exist … We penetrated at length to the gold and malachite chamber with crimson brocade hangings where the Ministers had been in session all that day and night and where they had been betrayed to the Red Guards. The long table covered with green baize was just as they had left it, under arrest. Before each empty seat was pen and ink and paper; the papers were scribbled over with beginnings of plans of action, rough drafts of proclamations and manifestos. Most of these were scratched out as their futility became evident, and the rest of the sheet covered with absent-minded geometrical designs, as the writers sat despondently listening while Minister after Minister proposed chimerical schemes. I took one of these scribbled pages, in the hand writing of [Deputy Prime Minister] Konovalov, which read, 'The Provisional Government appeals to all classes to support the Provisional Government'.

Kerensky himself had fled, promising to return with fresh troops to put down the revolution.* Instead, he escaped to a lifetime of exile in Paris and New York, leaving his ministers behind to await arrest in the Winter Palace. They were rounded up in the imperial breakfast chamber and forced by the illiterate revolutionaries to write their own arrest warrants, before being carted off to prison without any serious resistance. In fact, there wasn't much heroism or bloodshed anywhere in St Petersburg. Bolshevik tales of the masses storming the Winter Palace in the face of stiff resistance were myths; more damage was done to the palace during the shooting of Eisenstein's film than in the storming itself. In contrast to the first two Russian revolutions in 1905 and February 1917, which were genuinely populist uprisings with widespread support from the people, October was very much a palace coup, a political putsch. The majority of people in Petrograd, let alone in the rest of Russia, barely knew it had happened. The coup was over in 24 hours with only two recorded deaths, far fewer than in the February Revolution, the July Days or, indeed, in 1905.

That evening, Lenin appeared before the Congress of All-Russian Soviets of Workers' and Soldiers' Deputies in the Smolny Institute, a former ladies' finishing college on the edge of the city. He had been in exile for so

---

* Nabokov commented tartly that 'even to the very end, Kerensky completely failed to understand the situation ... Four or five days before the Bolshevik coup, I asked him if he considered a Bolshevik uprising a possibility and he replied, "I am praying for an uprising ... I will crush it utterly".'

long that few delegates knew him by sight, but all knew him by reputation. Alexandra Kollontai, the most powerful woman in the Bolshevik leadership, described his appearance in the language of reverential hagiography that would soon become de rigueur when speaking of the great leader:

> And there was Lenin at the door of the conference hall. A whisper of voices rippled through the room: 'Lenin!' For a long time the enthusiastic applause of the deputies prevented him from speaking. Lenin made an extraordinarily powerful speech that literally electrified the will of the Soviet's deputies…

Lenin's speech that 'literally electrified' the deputies was a declaration of victory and a promise of swift action to satisfy the demands of the people:

> Comrades! The revolution of workers and peasants, which the Bolsheviks have always supported, has been achieved! … The cause for which the people have fought so long and hard – immediate negotiations for a democratic end to the war, the abolition of the aristocracy's ownership of the land, workers' control over the means of production and the installation of a Soviet government – this cause has been won!

In Soviet accounts like those of Kollontai, Lenin is portrayed as confident and unwavering, single-mindedly directing the revolution from Bolshevik headquarters in the Smolny. His metamorphosis into the infallible genius of later historiography was already under way. But Western eyewitnesses tell a different story – that no one was in charge of the chaotic October events and Lenin himself was never sure how it would all end. Morgan Phillips Price, a British journalist reporting for the *Manchester Guardian*, recorded his memories of the days after the Bolshevik coup for the BBC:

> There was tremendous tension of course. Lenin appeared there for the first time since he'd gone into hiding. I think he had shaved off his moustache. I just forget: either he'd shaved it off or he'd grown one; he looked different. And he made a speech in which – I was rather surprised – he didn't

show any very great enthusiasm. He'd been having to meet opposition in his own party to taking this action of seizing power, and he seemed to me to be a little uncertain of himself. About an hour later news arrived that the regiments had surrounded the Winter Palace and arrested the Provisional Government and that Kerensky had got into a disguise and escaped in a motorcar. And of course there was tremendous enthusiasm then, and it was felt that things were making progress …

When Lenin addressed the Congress of All-Russian Soviets the following day, he was heckled by the Mensheviks and one faction of the Socialist Revolutionaries. They complained that the Bolsheviks had been usurping control of the soviets by forcibly barring opposition delegates, especially in provincial areas outside the big cities. Lenin had used his party's new dominance to set up a cabinet of ministers completely dominated by Bolsheviks, in effect an unelected government, known as the *Sovnarkom* (Council of People's Commissars). Accusing the Bolsheviks of illegally seizing power, the Mensheviks stormed out in protest. As they left, Trotsky famously snarled, 'You're finished, you pitiful bunch of bankrupts. Get out of here to where you now belong – in the dustbin of history.'

The Mensheviks' concerns were well founded. Most supporters of the revolution had assumed that Lenin's formula of 'All Power to the Soviets' meant government by some kind of socialist coalition, involving all the revolutionary factions, ready to offer them peace, land and workers' control. But the Bolsheviks had begun to exert a stranglehold over the leadership of the soviets and they didn't intend to relinquish it. One of the Sovnarkom's first acts had been to create a new secret police, chillingly entitled the Extraordinary Commission for Struggle against Counterrevolution, which quickly became known as the Cheka from its first two initials. The secret police were instructed to round up and imprison the Bolsheviks' opponents, including their former allies among the SRs and Mensheviks themselves. The crackdown on political pluralism had begun. Lenin's government also passed genuinely popular measures, such as the Decree on Peace, and the Decree on the Distribution of Land to the Peasants. It nationalised the banks, seized church property, and turned the factories over to the workers.

With a stick and a carrot, the Bolsheviks were consolidating their monopoly on power, and it would last for over 70 years.

The events of 1917 have long been regarded as a turning point in Russian history and in one sense they were. February put an end to tsarist rule and October inaugurated the era of proletarian socialism. But I believe the real chance for change came in the brief period *between* the revolutions. Lenin himself, with a hint of a sneer, called Russia between February and October 'the freest country in the world'. The Provisional Government was committed to the introduction of liberal parliamentary democracy, respect for the rule of law and guarantees of individual civil rights – things that Russia has rarely known.

Lenin, by contrast, scorned such 'bourgeois' freedoms. 'The Bolsheviks,' he liked to say, 'make no fetish of democracy.' The dictatorship of the proletariat would be imposed by a small group of revolutionaries who understood things better than the proletariat itself; democracy had no inherent value apart from its usefulness in promoting the socialist transformation of society. According to Maxim Gorky, Lenin had a 'ruthless contempt, worthy of an aristocrat, for the lives of ordinary individuals'. And Morgan Philips Price reported that even revolutionary leaders like Rosa Luxemburg were alarmed by his plans for a new dictatorship in Russia:

> She did not like the Russian Communist Party [Bolshevik] monopolising all power in the soviets and expelling anyone who disagreed with it. She feared that Lenin's policy had brought about, not the dictatorship of the working classes over the middle classes, which she approved of, but the dictatorship of the Communist Party over the working classes.

In a broader sense, 1917 was much less of a turning point. Russia's thousand-year history of autocracy was going to continue. Only the name had changed.

The great Soviet author Vasily Grossman, writing shortly after the death of Stalin, identifies Russia's two brief chances of freedom – the liberation of the serfs in 1861 and the 'bourgeois' revolution of February 1917 – both of which were tragically spurned. His late novel *Everything Flows* (1964), recognises in the October Revolution another 'moment of unruly destiny' when Russia again turned back:

> Dozens, perhaps hundreds of ... teachings, creeds and programmes came as suitors to the young Russia who had cast off the chains of tsarism. As they paraded before her, the advocates of progress gazed passionately and pleadingly into her face ... Invisible threads bound these men to the ideals of Western parliaments and constitutional monarchies ... But the slave girl's gaze, the great slave girl's searching, doubting, evaluating gaze came to rest on Lenin! It was him she chose... In February 1917 the path of freedom lay open for Russia, but Russia chose Lenin ... The debate opened by the supporters of Russian freedom was ended. Russian slavery had once more proved invincible ...

The terrible paradox of 1917 was that the Russian people's striving for freedom and self-government was to deliver them up to a new and even more oppressive despotism.

PART FOUR

DICTATORSHIP (OF THE PEOPLE?)

CHAPTER TWENTY-TWO

Boris Pasternak's novel *Doctor Zhivago* (1957) captures the cruelty, chaos and violence of the revolutionary whirlwind of 1917. Through Yuri Zhivago's poetic sensibility we feel the visceral changes tearing the entrails of his native land. At first the imagery is positive and hopeful, anticipating a new beginning:

> Everything was fermenting, growing, rising with the magic yeast of life. The joy of living, like a gentle wind, swept in a broad surge indiscriminately through fields and towns, through walls and fences, through wood and flesh. Not to be overwhelmed by this tidal wave, Zhivago went out in the square to listen to the speeches ... 'Just think what extraordinary things are happening all around us!' Yuri said. 'Such things happen only once in an eternity ... Freedom has dropped on us out of the sky...'

But Pasternak chronicles the speed and violence with which those expectations of a new world were crushed. From initial hopes of freedom and democracy, Yuri Zhivago grows alarmed at the random brutality of the Bolshevik Revolution, its unthinking destructiveness and utopian megalomania:

> 'It just seems to me that with all that's going on – the chaos, the disintegration, the pressure from the enemy – this isn't the moment to start dangerous experiments,' said Yuri. 'The country has to get over one upheaval before plunging into another one ...' 'That's a very naive statement,' said his travelling companion. 'All the destruction is right and proper ... Society must be smashed to pieces; then a genuinely revolutionary government can put the pieces together on a completely new basis.' Yuri felt sick; he went out into the corridor ...

Zhivago's hesitation over how to greet the October Revolution – as joyous rebirth or national catastrophe – reflected the attitude of many Russians. After February 1917, the short-lived Provisional Government had begun to introduce Western-style parliamentary democracy; and even after he seized control in October, Lenin continued to promise 'All Power to the Soviets', the directly elected local councils of workers, peasants and soldiers. To the surprise of his opponents and many of his own supporters, Lenin stood by the Provisional Government's promise of free elections to a national constituent assembly, a body that was intended to pave the way for a constitution and a parliament based on universal suffrage. But Vladimir Nabokov Senior sensed this was a cynical ploy:

> Everyone expected the Bolsheviks to start a campaign against the Constituent Assembly. But they proved to be more cunning. As is well known, they tried to blame the Provisional Government for delaying the convocation of the assembly, and made a great show of their own commitment to convening it. They were waiting to be certain of their own strength, and of their opponents' weakness ... before acting in a very coarse and brutal way.

The millions who turned out to vote on 25 November 1917 knew nothing of the Bolsheviks' plans and probably believed that democracy in Russia was finally dawning. After a largely peaceful election, in which two-thirds of the population voted, 707 men and women from across Russia were chosen to represent the interests of the people. The Constituent Assembly convened in the Tauride Palace in St Petersburg at four o'clock in the afternoon of 5 January 1918. It was the first freely elected parliament in Russia's history, an historic moment by any standard. The reformist dreams of liberals down the ages – Witte, Speransky, Chaadayev, Loris-Melikov, the Decembrists and all the others – seemed finally to be coming true.

But like so many democratic experiments in the past, this one too was doomed to failure.

The Bolsheviks had not done well in the elections, and their rivals, the Socialist Revolutionaries, had a majority in the assembly. With more than twice as many seats as the Bolsheviks, the SRs should have been dominant. But Lenin had already installed a government dominated by his Bolsheviks, and he wasn't about to let an election remove them from power.

> To relinquish the Soviet Republic won by the people, for the sake of the bourgeois parliamentary system of the Constituent Assembly, would now be a step backwards and would cause the collapse of the October workers' and peasants' revolution ... We must not be deceived by the election figures. Elections prove nothing. The Bolsheviks can and must take state power into their own hands ...

The Constituent Assembly was allowed to exist for just over 12 hours. The Bolsheviks walked out after the first votes went against them. The other parties carried on until four in the morning of 6 January and were then evicted by pro-Bolshevik guards fuelled with vodka and brandishing rifles. When the deputies came back the next day, they found the Tauride Palace locked and surrounded by soldiers.

Lenin's Bolsheviks had hijacked the embryonic institutions of freedom and democracy. Now they were about to impose a centralised dictatorship even harsher than the one they'd overthrown.

Like the zealots of the French Revolution, the Bolsheviks adopted a 'year zero' policy, declaring the country a republic, renaming her cities and streets, recasting the Russian alphabet and revising the calendar. The capital was moved from Petrograd to Moscow. The foreign and domestic debts of the old regime were disowned. Religion was persecuted and independent newspapers banned; free love, divorce and abortion were allowed. Titles and ranks were abolished. Old forms of social etiquette were abandoned – instead of using 'Sir' or 'Madam', people were told to call each other *Grazhdanin* (Citizen), while party members addressed each other as *Tovarishch* (Comrade).

In the name of 'protecting the revolution', legality and justice were jettisoned. In pronouncements signed personally by Lenin, the Bolsheviks declared their political opponents – the liberal KaDety, the Mensheviks and most of the SRs – enemies of the state:

The Right Socialist Revolutionary and Menshevik parties are carrying on a desperate struggle against Soviet power, calling openly in their publications for its overthrow and describing it as arbitrary and unlawful. They are defending the saboteurs, the servants of capital, and are going as far as undisguised calls to terrorism ... All leaders of the Constitutional Democratic Party, a party filled with enemies of the people, are hereby to be considered outlaws. They are to be arrested immediately and brought before the revolutionary court ...

These were men who had played a distinguished role in the struggle against tsarism, but now they were demonised, arrested and murdered. All who failed to obey the Bolshevik line, including former comrades in arms, were branded bourgeois provocateurs. It would not be long before all opposition parties were banned and a one-party state introduced. It would last until 1991.

Most damagingly, when demonstrators marched in support of democracy and the Constituent Assembly they were fired on by Bolshevik Red Guards. Twelve marchers were killed. In a coincidence resembling a portent, the dead were buried on 9 January, the anniversary of the tsarist murders of Bloody Sunday in 1905. Even the official bard of Bolshevism, Lenin's favourite writer Maxim Gorky, was outraged:

For almost a hundred years the finest Russians have lived by the idea of a constituent assembly that would allow the free expression of democracy in Russia ... Rivers of blood have been spilled for this idea. But now the so-called People's Commissars have given orders to shoot the democrats who march in its honour ... The Petrograd workers were mowed down, unarmed ... by cowards and murderers ... Do the 'People's Commissars', among whom there must be decent and sensible people, not understand ... that they will end up strangling the entire Russian democracy?

Lenin was trying to do precisely that. 'Everything has turned out for the best,' he wrote. 'The dissolution of the Constituent Assembly means the complete and open repudiation of democracy in favour of dictatorship. This will be a valuable lesson.'

Although Gorky remained publicly loyal to the Bolshevik cause, his private letters of the time reveal both his personal disillusion with the revolutionary leadership and an unflinching awareness that Lenin had no interest in freeing Russia from its millennial history of autocratic rule:

> Lenin and Trotsky do not have the slightest idea of the meaning of freedom or the rights of man. They have been poisoned with the filthy venom of power, and this is shown by the shameful attitude towards freedom of speech, the individual and all those other civil liberties for which the democrats have struggled … It is clear that Russia is heading for a new and even more savage autocracy.

Russian historiography continued to revere Lenin even as it denounced Stalin for the crimes of the Soviet system, but those crimes originated with the first Bolshevik leader. Lenin seemed to care more for ideas than for people. He pursued the cause of the revolution exclusively, single-mindedly, whatever the cost in human suffering. It was he, not Stalin, who founded the one-party state; he who created the feared secret police and the system of forced labour camps later known as the Gulag; and he who first gave the order for summary executions of suspected political opponents. Writing in the 1960s, Vasily Grossman reflected on Lenin's Mephistophelian attraction:

> Lenin's intolerance, his contempt for freedom, the fanaticism of his faith, his cruelty towards his enemies, were the qualities that brought victory to his cause … and Russia followed him – willingly at first, trustfully – along a merry intoxicating path lit by the burning estates of the landowners. Then she began to stumble, to look back, ever more terrified of the path stretching before her. But the grip of his iron hand leading her onwards grew tighter and tighter. Imbued with apostolic faith, he walked on, leading Russia behind him … While the West was fertilised with freedom, Russia's evolution was fertilised by the growth of slavery.

But the Bolshevik regime was fragile, beset by powerful enemies. The state had ground to a halt as civil servants, the banks and the treasury, railway and communications workers all went on strike in protest against the new government. Wages were unpaid; the economy was crumbling. The Bolsheviks had support in the cities, but the countryside overwhelmingly backed their rivals, the SRs. At home, anti-Bolshevik forces were preparing armed opposition and abroad the Western powers were growing ever more hostile, alarmed by the Bolsheviks' pledge to withdraw from the war against Germany.

Bold measures were needed, and Lenin took them. He issued a decree that abolished all private ownership of land with no compensation; peasant communities were to distribute it among themselves. The Bolsheviks failed to mention that this was actually the Socialist Revolutionaries' land programme. But it was the greatest shift in land tenure in Russian history, and it persuaded many peasants to fight in the Red Army because they feared the anti-revolutionary White Army would take back the land. (The Bolsheviks, of course, would do exactly that when they imposed collective farms in the 1930s.)

Then, in early 1918, Lenin dispatched his commissar for foreign affairs, Leon Trotsky, to negotiate a peace treaty with the Germans, recognising that an end to the war would be hugely popular. Trotsky was categorical:

> We cannot, will not and must not continue a war begun by tsars and capitalists in alliance with monarchs and capitalists. We will not and we must not continue to be at war with workers and peasants like ourselves. We are not signing a peace of landlords and capitalists. Let the German and Austrian soldiers know who exactly is sending them into the field of battle and let them know for whom they are being asked to fight … Let them know also that we refuse to fight against them.

Sensing the Bolsheviks' weakness, the Germans insisted on punitive conditions, and the Treaty of Brest-Litovsk, signed in March 1918, brought huge territorial losses for Russia. The new Soviet Republic had to forfeit Poland, Finland, the Baltic states, Belorussia and much of Ukraine, losing a quarter of her population and vast swathes of her coalfields, agricultural land and heavy industry. Lenin was criticised, but maintained that immediate peace was the only way to save the revolution:

Either we sign the peace terms or we sign the death warrant of the Soviet government ... Their knees are on our chest, and our position is hopeless ... We are compelled to submit to a distressing peace. But it will not stop the forthcoming revolution in Europe. We can now begin to prepare a revolutionary army ... a serious, mighty, people's army. This peace must be accepted as a respite enabling us to prepare a decisive resistance to the bourgeoisie and imperialists. The proletariat of the whole world will come to our aid. Then we shall renew the fight.

But before thinking about exporting revolution abroad, the Bolsheviks had to deal with a growing menace at home. Supporters of the old order were spoiling for revenge. A violent civil war was about to erupt, and its consequences would be terrible.

CHAPTER TWENTY-THREE

Tsar Nicholas II and his family had been held prisoner by the revolutionaries since his abdication in March 1917. The Provisional Government had offered to send them to London, but Nicholas's cousin, George V refused, fearing their presence might foment revolution in an already strife-ridden Britain. After the Bolsheviks came to power, the royal family were held in a confiscated merchant's house in the Siberian city of Yekaterinburg.

For the new regime, the Romanovs, alive, were a burden and an embarrassment. Something had to be done.

At midnight on 16 July 1918, the royals were woken by loud knocking on their bedroom doors. Two Yekaterinburg secret policemen told them they were being taken to the cellar, 'where they would be safer'. The tsar and empress were allowed to wash and dress, eventually emerging from their rooms at 1 a.m. A local party member, the teenaged Pavel Medvedev, was among their guards and seems to have established cordial relations with some of the family. Certainly, his account of the events of the early hours of 17 July 1918 betrays elements of sympathy:

> The tsar was carrying his young son Alexei in his arms … They were dressed in soldiers' shirts and wore caps. The empress, her daughters and the others followed the tsar and the secret policemen led them down to the cellar. During my presence none of the tsar's family asked any questions. They did not weep or cry … It seemed as if all of them guessed their fate, but not one of them uttered a single sound …

Yakov Yurovsky, a Yekaterinburg Bolshevik, was the secret policeman in charge of the operation. His official report on the events that followed is matter-of-fact:

Nicholas had put Alexei on a chair and stood as if to shield him. I said to Nicholas that the Soviet of Workers' Deputies had resolved to shoot them. He said, 'What? What?' and turned towards Alexei. But I shot him and killed him outright. Then the firing started ... Bullets began to ricochet off the walls. The firing intensified as the victims' shouts rose. When it stopped, the daughters, the empress and Alexei were still alive. Alexei remained sitting, petrified. I killed him. The others shot the daughters but did not kill them. They resorted to a bayonet, but that didn't work either. Finally they killed them by shooting them in the head.

The spot in Yekaterinburg where the last Tsar of Russia met his fate is now occupied by a recently built cathedral, the Shrine of Redemption through Blood. The old merchant's house where the murders took place was torn down (ironically, by Boris Yeltsin when he was the local Communist Party boss in the 1970s) to stop it becoming a place of pro-monarchist pilgrimage. But times change, and in 1981 Nicholas was canonised by the Orthodox Church. The new cathedral is surrounded by billboards showing life-sized images of the dead Romanovs and asking for prayers to 'the holy martyrs'.

After the shootings, the corpses were thrown onto the back of a lorry and dumped in a disused mineshaft outside the city. According to Yurovsky, rumours began to circulate about the location of the bodies. He was ordered to retrieve the remains and take them elsewhere for reburial. On the way to the new site his lorry broke down, so he and his men decided to bury them where they were in the forest. As a result, the resting place of the last tsar and his murdered family remained unknown for over 70 years. When the grave was finally discovered in 1991 by local amateurs, the royal bodies were identified by DNA from their relatives in the British royal family, including Prince Michael of Kent. Also buried with them was the royal physician, Botkin, who had voluntarily stayed with the tsar's family, as well as a maid and two servants.

A well-signposted Orthodox monastery has now sprung up on the spot, 12 miles from the city, with photo displays, shrines and cafeterias to cater to the many pilgrims who come here to pay homage. In hushed reverence, some with tears in their eyes, men and women offer up their love and respect to the tsar who was once so widely reviled.

There has been debate about exactly who ordered the executions, but recent research suggests the decision was taken personally by Lenin. At first the Bolsheviks gloried in the murders. The anniversary was declared a public holiday and Soviet officials came to Yekaterinburg to have their photograph taken in the bloodstained cellar with its bullet-scarred walls. But in later years the official version became almost apologetic. Now it was claimed that the murders were the panicked reaction of low-level functionaries as the escalating civil war closed in on Yekaterinburg, with the dangerous possibility that the tsar might be rescued by the monarchist Whites.

Civil war had been raging for several months before the killings took place. The October Revolution had divided the country. Former officers of the Imperial Army, furious at the capitulation to the Germans in the First World War, were leading the armed opposition. They were joined by a host of other groups, including dispossessed landowners, anarchists, national minorities – Cossacks, Finns, Ukrainians and others – as well as the Bolsheviks' former comrades, now enemies, from the other revolutionary factions. The conflict between Bolshevik Reds and anti-Bolshevik Whites was immensely bloody, the atrocities committed by both sides appalling. The poet Marina Tsvetaeva, whose husband fought with the Whites but later became a Red agent, evoked a war that pitted Russian against Russian:

The field sways, a chant of 'Rus!'
rises over it.
Help me, I'm unsteady on my feet.
This blood-red is making my eyes foggy …
They all lie in a row,
no line between them,
I recognise that each one was a soldier,
But which is mine? Which one is another's?
This man was White now he's become Red.
Blood has reddened him.
This one was Red now he's become White.
Death has whitened him …
And so from right and left
behind ahead

together. White and Red, one cry of
– 'Mother!'

The anti-Bolshevik campaign – or, rather, series of campaigns – began well. Lenin's newly named Russian Communist Party (Bolshevik) controlled Petrograd, Moscow and most of the big cities, but its opponents controlled vast areas of the country. The south was in the hands of Cossack governments; the Ukrainian nationalists were growing in strength; and White volunteer armies, led by the tsarist generals Kornilov and Denikin were beginning a menacing march northwards. Admiral Kolchak's forces held Omsk in the east; and from their base in Estonia, General Yudenich's troops were threatening Petrograd itself. The Bolsheviks were surrounded.

The Western powers – the British, French, Americans and Czechs – were helping the Whites with supplies and men. Tens of thousands of foreign soldiers were pouring in to fight the menace of socialism, sparking Lenin's fury in a series of passionate speeches:

> Comrade soldiers of the Red Army! The capitalists of England, America and France are waging war against Russia. They are taking revenge on the Soviet Peasants and Workers' Republic because she overthrew the power of the landlords and capitalists and set an example for the peoples of the rest of the world to follow. With money and munitions, the capitalists of England, France and America are helping the Russian landlords lead their armies from Siberia, the Don and the Caucasus against the Soviets, seeking to restore the power of the tsar, of the landlords, of the capitalists!

In the crackly recording that has come down to us, you can hear the anger in Lenin's voice as he demands global class struggle. You can understand how he became the prototype for the twentieth-century demagogue. But, despite the rhetoric, Lenin privately feared the Bolshevik state might not survive the civil war. The Bolshevik propaganda effort was focused on demonising the Whites and the foreign interventionists, particularly the English. Songs with anti-British words suddenly became widely performed and improbably popular.

Our former masters begged the foreigners
To save their land and their banks ...
So the crafty old English sent in troops and tanks!
But to the bourgeois devils our people say:
We'll take death over slavery any day.

The 40,000 British troops were war weary and keen to get home. One division sent to the Russian far north had all been declared unfit for service in France, but they successfully blockaded the ports of Archangelsk and Murmansk to prevent supplies getting through to the Communist government. The men hated the harsh climate and were revolted by the brutality of the civil war, as a British seaman, Tom Spurgeon, recorded in his diary in March 1918:

> While I was there I met a Russian officer who could speak better English than I could. One day, we were walking together, talking away as we always did about the Western way of life. Without noticing too much, we strolled into a park where there were a number of soldiers and dissidents, including women and children. When the soldiers saw us approach the civilians were all lined up. Then, as calm as anything, the officer I had been talking to walked down the line and shot every one of them through the back. He then went back down the line and if any of them were breathing he shot them through the head. To him it was like having breakfast. There were women and small children but it didn't seem to worry him at all. I remember clearly some of the bodies quivering on the ground. I can never forget. I am haunted by it even now.

Other British troops spent weeks or months waiting for action. Those sent to Baku in Azerbaijan learned to barter in the local markets, referring to it as 'skolko-ing' (*skolko* – 'how much?' – was the only Russian word many of them learned), but to a man they hated the 'fish jam' (actually, caviar) that they were given as rations. When they eventually fought, the British acquitted themselves well, earning the respect of those who fought with them and against them.

Trotsky wrote later in his memoirs that Lenin had felt intimidated by the British forces, which were armed with guns and equipment far more modern and efficient than those of the Red Army. In October 1919, as army commander, Trotsky issued an order of the day designed to fan the flames of hatred against the foreign interlopers:

> Red warriors! On all the fronts you meet the hostile plots of the English. The counter-revolutionary troops shoot you with English guns. On the southern and western fronts, you find supplies of English manufacture. The prisoners you have captured are dressed in uniforms made in England. The women and children of Archangel and Astrakhan are maimed and killed by English airmen with the aid of English explosives. English ships bomb our shores …

French troops showed less enthusiasm than the British. Many mutinied in the Black Sea ports, demanding to go home. But the 70,000 Czechs fought fiercely. As the Bolsheviks had feared, they did indeed seize Yekaterinburg, just nine days after the tsar was murdered there. Within a few months they had helped capture a string of Siberian cities and advanced all the way to Vladivostok. The Allies supplied General Denikin and Admiral Kolchak with a million rifles, 15,000 machine guns and 8 million rounds of ammunition. The Whites were in the ascendancy. Their forces came to within 100 miles of Moscow and even closer to Petrograd.

In October 1919, the White general Nikolai Yudenich arrived in the town of Gatchina with 20,000 troops. Gatchina had been a traditional monarchist stronghold, with its magnificent royal palace and loyal tsarist history dating back to Catherine the Great. Now it was the perfect launching pad for a White assault on Red Petrograd just 30 miles away. Bolshevik power was tottering; if the regime could not retake Gatchina, the new state would be staring annihilation in the face.

But the Red Army was led by a military genius. Leon Trotsky had worked tirelessly to transform the raggle-taggle Red Guards into a proper fighting force. He reversed the disastrous 'democratisation' of the army, which had allowed soldiers to debate military orders and countermand their officers. He imposed political commissars in every battalion to maintain discipline. He introduced conscription, and shot those who refused. By early 1919, the Red Army had doubled in size to 1.6 million men; by the end of the year it had doubled again.

Now, in the face of the threat from Yudenich, Trotsky raised new fighting units from the revolutionary suburbs of Petrograd and rushed in many more by rail from Moscow. The defence of Petrograd made Trotsky an iconic, terrifying figure, dashing from battle to battle in his own armoured train, haranguing and inspiring the troops, meting out summary execution to cowards and deserters. He ordered the construction of barricades and trenches to halt the British tanks fighting with the Whites and marshalled thousands of foot soldiers to advance towards Gatchina. After three days of fierce fighting, the Whites retreated; Petrograd was saved. Trotsky's reward was the Order of the Red Banner and the renaming of Gatchina in his honour: it would be called Trotsk until he fell from grace in 1929.*

Gatchina and the defence of Petrograd was a turning point in the civil war. Now Lenin's speeches sounded an optimistic note:

> The Red Army has united, it has risen up, it is chasing the landlords' armies and the White Guards officers out of the Volga region; it has taken back Riga and nearly all of Ukraine; it is getting close to Odessa and Rostov. Just a little more effort; just a few more months of struggle and victory will be

---

* Trotsky's own memoirs of the defence of Petrograd suggest it was a close run thing: 'For the one and only time during the entire war I had to play the role of a regimental commander. When I saw our men were retreating ... I mounted the first horse I could lay my hands on and turned them back. For the first few minutes, there was nothing but confusion. Not all of them understood what was happening, and some of them continued to retreat. But I chased one soldier after another, on horseback, and made them all turn back. My orderly, a Muscovite peasant, and an old soldier himself, was racing at my heels. Brandishing a revolver, he ran wildly along the line, repeating my appeals and yelling for all he was worth: "Courage, boys, Comrade Trotsky is leading you!" The men were now advancing at the pace at which they had been retreating before. Young workers and peasants, military students from Moscow and Petrograd, were utterly reckless with their lives. They advanced against machine-gun fire and attacked tanks with revolvers in their hands. The general staff of the Whites wrote of the "heroic frenzy" of the Reds ...'

ours. The strength of the Red Army is that it consciously and unitedly goes into battle – for the land of the peasants, for the power of the peasants and the workers, for Soviet power!

Germany's defeat in the First World War allowed the Bolsheviks to recoup much of the territory they had ceded under the Treaty of Brest-Litovsk in 1918 (see pp. 217–18). Finland and the Baltic states were gone, but much of Ukraine, Belorussia and the southern territories were back in the Soviet fold.

Poland was another matter. Seizing on the chaos caused by the Russian civil war, the Poles, under the command of the charismatic Jozef Pilsudski, launched an invasion of Soviet Ukraine. Their aim was to reclaim those lands that had historically belonged to Poland, and in collusion with anti-Soviet Ukrainian nationalists they advanced remarkably quickly, capturing Kiev itself. The writer Isaak Babel, who himself served in the Soviet cavalry, wrote of the callous cruelty of the Russo–Polish War (1919–21):

> On that day, 22 July 1920, the Poles tore into our rear in a series of light-ning manoeuvres. They swooped down on the Eleventh Division and took many prisoners … Numb with despair, I stumbled into the fighting around Khotyn … My horse was killed … the universe was rent with wails and screams … In the darkness I stopped to relieve myself … and when I finished I saw I'd spattered the corpse of a dead Pole with my urine. It was trickling from his mouth and empty eye sockets …

Babel's *Red Cavalry* stories of the 1920s are harsh portraits by a battlefield reporter. This was a ferocious, nationalistic struggle for territory that the two nations had fought over since the sixteenth century. Startled by the Polish successes, the Bolsheviks ditched the rhetoric of class conflict and international revolution, and returned instead to Russian nationalism. They no longer urged the workers of all nations to wage war against capitalism; they urged Russians to wage war against Poles.

The 100,000 volunteers who responded were enough to halt the Polish advance and send Soviet forces marching to within a few miles of Warsaw. The communiqués of the Red Army's commander, General Mikhail

Tukhachevsky, were euphoric. He declared his intention to march onwards and bring Communism to the streets of London and Paris 'over the corpse of White Poland on the road to worldwide conflagration'. But in a battle that became known as the Cud nad Wisłą (Miracle of the Vistula) Poland won an unlikely victory over the encircling Russian forces. Warsaw was saved and so, for the time being, were the streets of London and Paris. With the Soviets forced out of Polish territory, the two sides agreed an armistice that split the disputed areas in Ukraine and Belorussia between them. For Moscow, the war imposed a tacit acceptance that the export of Communism would, at least temporarily, have to be abandoned. For the moment, the Soviets needed to concentrate on ensuring the triumph of revolution at home.

Peace with Poland and the departure from Russia of the Western intervention forces meant Trotsky could turn his attention to the remaining White Army of General Pyotr Wrangel, now bottled up in the Crimea. In November 1920, with the Red Army advancing and horrific tales of torture and executions proliferating, the White soldiers and their families scrambled for a place on the British and American ships that would take them to exile in Turkey. In scenes foreshadowing the US evacuation of Saigon, the Soviet writer Konstantin Paustovsky described the desperation and panic of those determined not to be left behind as the last vessels departed the port of Odessa:

Gaping mouths, torn open by cries for help, eyes bulging from their sockets, faces livid and deeply etched by fear of death, of people who could see nothing but the one, blinding, terrible sight: rickety ships' gang-planks with handrails snapping under the weight of human bodies, soldiers' rifle-butts crashing down overhead, mothers stretching up their arms to lift their children above the demented human herd ... People were senselessly destroying each other, preventing even those who reached the gangway from saving themselves. The moment anyone gained a hold on the plank or the rail, hands grabbed and clutched at him, clusters of bodies hung on him ... Ships listed under the weight of people clinging to the deck rails ... ships sailed away without stowing the gangplanks, which slid into the sea, with people still clinging to them. It was impossible to listen to the cries, curses and wails of those left on the quayside, parted from their families.

Fifty thousand men, women and children left behind were summarily executed by the incoming Bolsheviks. In Mikhail Bulgakov's play *Flight* (1928), two White officers fall into conversation on board a ship fleeing the port of Sevastopol. They discuss the destruction of the old Russia, and the failure to save her from the Bolshevik yoke:

What do you see out there? Ship after ship steaming away, the decks filled with defeated men ... It's over; it's the end of the road ... Everything, everybody smashed to pieces for once and for all ... And you know what the problem's been? We've all been play-acting. Everybody except the Bolsheviks: because they knew exactly what they wanted all along ...

CHAPTER TWENTY-FOUR

One of the most widely viewed Soviet films of the 1930s was the historical biopic *Lenin in 1918* (1939). Directed by Mikhail Romm, it was a sequel to his earlier *Lenin in October* (1937), which told the story of the Bolshevik leader's role in the 1917 revolution. This time, the plot is darker and more nuanced. Midway through the movie, Lenin is shown on a visit to a Moscow factory, where he delivers a rousing speech to the workers. But as he steps outside, gunshots ring out. The camera cuts to a menacing-looking woman skulking amid a crowd of people. With a cry of horror, the crowd realises that her victim is Lenin himself. With a stoical look on his face, Vladimir Ilyich clutches his chest and subsides into the arms of his companions.

The film is based on a real event, and I found the place where it happened, in the Zamoskvoreche district of Moscow, a stone's throw from the apartment where I lived in the 1990s. What is now known as the Vladimir Ilyich Electromechanical Plant had originally been built in the mid nineteenth century by an Englishman called Hopper. I spotted a commemorative plaque on the wall recording the several occasions on which Lenin visited the building. It makes no reference to the dramatic events of 30 August 1918, but the guards at the gate happily told me stories of 'the day Lenin nearly died'.

Romm's movie shows the would-be assassin, a disenchanted Socialist Revolutionary named Fanny Kaplan, firing three bullets into Lenin's arm, neck and jaw. His bodyguards bundle him into a car and rush him back to the Kremlin, unconscious and seemingly close to death. The Bolsheviks were gripped by panic and fear. The country was in the throes of civil war, surrounded by enemies, and the fragile new regime saw threats everywhere. There was an immediate assumption that this was an enemy conspiracy. News came in of another attack, this time fatal, on the head of the Petrograd secret police, Moisei Uritsky. Scores of suspects were rounded up, tortured and shot.*

With Soviet Russia enraged by British support for the Whites in the ongoing civil war, it was little surprise that the finger of blame should be pointed at London. The British diplomat Robert Bruce Lockhart and his fellow spy Sidney Reilly were accused of masterminding the plot on behalf of the Western imperialists. Red Guards ransacked the British embassy and shot dead a British official. Bruce Lockhart was dragged from his bed and arrested. With the dragnet closing in, Sidney Reilly fled north via Petrograd to Finland, finally reaching London on 8 November. Meanwhile, Bruce Lockhart was being interrogated by the Cheka in the Lubyanka prison. His memoirs are the epitome of English calm under duress, but there is little doubt that his life was hanging by a thread:

> My term of imprisonment lasted for exactly one month. It may be divided into two periods: the first, which lasted five days and was marked by discomfort and fear; the second, which lasted for 24 days and may be described as a period of comparative comfort accompanied by acute mental strain. My one comfort was the official Bolshevik newspapers, which my gaolers took a propagandist joy in supplying to me. Certainly, as far as my own case was concerned, they were far from reassuring. They were still full of the Bruce Lockhart Plot. They contained numerous resolutions, passed by workmen's committees, demanding my trial and execution … and still more fearsome accounts of the Terror, which was now in full force. From the first day of my captivity I had made up my mind that if Lenin died, my own life would not be worth a moment's purchase.

---

* There was a reason why *Lenin in 1918* should be given such prominence in the USSR of the late 1930s. This was the period of Stalinist witch-hunts, of alleged plots and conspiracies in all parts of society, and of purges and show trials. So a movie depicting dark forces at work to overthrow Soviet power was just what Stalin had ordered. And if you look closely, you can spot that one of the men the film shows plotting to murder Lenin is the Bolshevik leader Nikolai Bukharin. Again this was no coincidence: Bukharin had just gone on trial for his life, on trumped up charges, as the film hit the cinemas.

Luckily for Bruce Lockhart, Lenin clung to life. His injuries were grave, and blood from the wound to his neck had spilled into his lungs, making breathing difficult. Surgeons decided it was too dangerous to remove the bullets from his body, and all they could do was dress the wounds to stave off infection. But the Bolshevik media played down the seriousness of Lenin's injuries, fearing any threat to his life might engender public panic or encourage opposition forces plotting a coup against the regime. *Pravda's* headline read: 'Lenin, shot twice, refuses help. Next morning, he reads papers, listens; continues to guide the locomotive of global revolution.' The Lenin myth was gathering momentum; the intimations of saintly stoicism and the extravagant personality cult that would attend him in life and in death, are already evident in *Pravda's* words.

Bruce Lockhart, who almost certainly did have a hand in the plot, was held in the Lubyanka, threatened with execution and confronted with the terrified Fanny Kaplan:

> At six in the morning a woman was brought into the room. She was dressed in black. Her hair was black, and her eyes, set in a fixed stare, had great black rings under them … Her features were strongly Jewish … We guessed it was Kaplan. Doubtless, the Bolsheviks hoped she would give us some sign of recognition … But she went to the window and … looked out into the daylight. There she remained, apparently resigned to her fate, until the sentries came and took her away. She was shot before she knew if her attempt to alter history had failed or succeeded.

Bruce Lockhart was luckier. After a month in the Lubyanka, London exchanged him for a high-ranking Soviet diplomat. On his return, the British media were quick to portray him and Sidney Reilly as heroic Western agents nobly trying to smash the Communist menace. A radio play starring Errol Flynn and a Warner Brothers movie with Leslie Howard, entitled *British Agent* (1934), took a decidedly anti-Bolshevik stance, portraying our plucky 'diplomats' as the prime movers in a daring operation sanctioned by London.

Lenin recovered from his injuries, though they would ultimately contribute to his death five years later. But the immediate effect of the

August shootings was a terrible hardening in the Bolshevik regime. On 2 September 1918, Yakov Sverdlov, chairman of the Bolshevik Central Committee, called for 'Merciless mass terror against all opponents of the revolution!' It was, he proclaimed, imperative to strike ruthlessly at those who had tried to murder Lenin and at those who supported them.

Sverdlov's words signalled the beginning of the Red Terror, which was to last for months and claim the lives of thousands. In response to the attack on Lenin, so-called class enemies were rounded up and executed for no other crime than their social origin. In operations that foreshadowed the Gestapo, hostages were selected from former tsarist officials, landowners, priests, lawyers, bankers and merchants to be used as reprisals. The British journalist Morgan Philips Price recorded his horror at the Bolsheviks' methods:

> I shall never forget one of the *Izvestia* articles for Saturday, September 7th. There was no mistaking its meaning. It was proposed to take hostages from the former officers of the tsar's army, from the KaDety and from the families of the Moscow and Petrograd middle classes and to shoot ten for every Communist who fell to the White Terror. Shortly after, a decree was issued by the Central Soviet Executive ordering all officers of the old army within territories of the Republic to report on a certain day at certain places … The reason given by the Bolshevik leaders for the Red Terror was that conspirators could only be convinced that the Soviet Republic was powerful enough to be respected if it was able to punish its enemies, but nothing would convince these enemies except the fear of death. All civilized restraints had gone …

Lenin himself signed the execution lists. The aim seemed to be the physical annihilation of a whole social class. Being modestly well off made you guilty; soft hands unused to manual labour could get you shot. Martin Latsis, the head of the Cheka in Ukraine, revealed the real aim of the Terror:

> Don't go looking in the evidence to see whether or not the accused fought against the Soviets with arms or words. Just ask him which class he belongs to, what is his background, his education, his profession. These are the

questions that will determine the fate of the accused. That is the meaning and the very essence of the Red Terror.

As paranoia became the norm, the Bolsheviks relied more and more on the murderous henchmen of the Cheka. The organisation's methods, cynically acknowledged by its fanatical leader, 'Iron' Felix Dzerzhinsky, were extrajudicial: confessions extracted by torture followed by immediate execution. 'We stand for organised terror,' Dzerzhinsky claimed, 'this should be frankly admitted. Terror is an absolute necessity during times of revolution. Our aim is to fight against the enemies of the Soviet government and of the new order of life. We judge quickly … Do not think that I seek forms of revolutionary justice; we are not in need of justice now – this is war …'

In the name of Lenin's Utopia, an estimated half a million people were killed in the three years following the initial period of the Red Terror. But even that pales by comparison with the 9 million or more who died in the same period in the civil war. The death toll from combat, typhus, starvation and drought was appalling; and with another 1–2 million Russians fleeing abroad, the country was close to collapse. The economy was devastated, the currency worthless, and people reduced to primitive barter. The writer Yevgeny Zamyatin described Petrograd as 'a city of icebergs, mammoths and wasteland … where cavemen, swathed in hides and blankets, retreat from cave to cave'. People sold their possessions and family heirlooms for scraps, or bartered them for firewood. Horses, dogs and cats disappeared from city streets to be made into 'civil war sausage'. Shortly before he himself starved to death, the philosopher Vasily Rozanov wrote presciently:

With a clank, a squeal and a groan, an iron curtain has descended over Russian history: the show is over, the audience has risen. It's time for people to put on their coats and go home. But when they look around they see there are no coats any more, and no more homes …

With factories closing down and wages losing 90 per cent of their value, even the proletariat was deserting the Bolshevik cause. 'Down with Lenin and horsemeat,' scrawled the Petrograd graffiti. 'Give us the tsar and pork!'

Strikes broke out in several Petrograd factories. The government crushed them with tsarist methods – mass firings, arrests and executions.

As his hold on power became more fragile, Lenin abandoned his promises of freedom, justice and self-determination. From May 1918, the rhetoric of liberation gave way to what came to be known as War Communism – harsh, enslaving and repressive. Lenin had ridden a popular wave of unrest with his slogans of Peace, Bread, Land and Workers Control. But the Bolsheviks would rescind every one of these promises within months of coming to power. As early as November 1917, *Golos Truda* (The Voice of Labour), the official organ of the anarchist labour unions, had warned of the impending crackdown:

> Once their power is consolidated and 'legalised', the Bolsheviks who are
> … proponents of centralist, authoritarian rule, will begin to rearrange the
> life of the country and of the people by dictatorial methods, imposed by
> the centre. The centre, in Petrograd, will impose the will of the party on
> the whole of all Russia and command the whole nation. Your soviets and
> your other local organisations will become, little by little, simply executive
> organs of the will of the central government. We will see the installation
> of an authoritarian and statist apparatus that will act from above and set
> about wiping out everything that stood in its way with an iron hand.

This is indeed what happened. In the name of War Communism, society was turned into a centralised command economy; the state was run as a militarised machine, where all must obey and deserters are shot. The nominally independent Factory Committees, to which Lenin had promised full workers' control, were progressively subjugated to the Bolshevik-run trade unions. From mid 1918, workers' control was reduced to monitoring rather than management. Between 1918 and 1921, forced labour was systematically imposed on the population, with breaches of discipline punishable by death. The labour camps began to fill up with 'anti-revolutionary elements'. Industry was nationalised, private enterprise banned. Food was rationed and only workers and soldiers were guaranteed adequate sustenance. A siege mentality now informed the government's every act. The families of former tsarist officers were held hostage to force them to build the new Red Army. Workers were no longer seen as agents of the revolution but as raw material, an expendable resource to be exploited in the great experiment of building socialism. The programme of War Communism had more than a touch of the Pol Pot about it.

Instead of peace, Lenin had brought devastation. Instead of bread – starvation. Instead of land – requisitions. Instead of workers' representation – terror. Winston Churchill commented tartly that Lenin's 'purpose [was] to save the world, his method to blow it up'. The British consul in Petrograd, Colonel R.E. Kimens reported on the effects of War Communism:

> The only work done by the Soviet authorities is the inciting of class hatred, requisitioning and confiscation of property, and destruction of absolutely everything. All freedom of word and action has been suppressed; the country is being ruled by an autocracy that is infinitely worse than that of the old regime. Justice does not exist and every act on the part of persons not belonging to the 'proletariat' is interpreted as counter-revolutionary and punished by imprisonment and in many cases execution … The Soviet authorities' one object is to overthrow the existing order of things and capitalism, first in Russia and afterwards in all other countries, and to this end all methods are admissible as long as the masses remain satisfied … The danger is very great that Bolshevism will spread to neighbouring countries. In that case it will be impossible to stop the movement that presents a danger to the civilisation of the whole world.

Members of the former middle class were denounced as *bourzhoui*, 'bourgeois parasites', and 'non-persons'. Their homes were confiscated, their furniture seized and their clothes requisitioned for the state. They were placed in the lowest category for food rations, on the border of starvation, and forced to do cruel, often deadly labour. Petrograd lost two-thirds of its population as people fled to the countryside to try to find food. City streets were filled with war orphans and child thieves. Begging, black marketeering and prostitution were rife.

In the countryside, peasants were divided into three categories – 'poor' and 'medium', and therefore allies of the proletariat; or *kulaks*, literally 'grasping fists', who had made some personal wealth from their farming and were therefore enemies of the people. These were the better farmers, the efficient businessmen or the village elders who took prominent roles in the rural community. As the class of peasants who had the most to lose under Bolshevik rule, and were considered the most likely to oppose it, the *kulaks* were made scapegoats for the disruption in food supplies. In speech after speech, they were demonised by Lenin:

> A wave of *kulak* revolts is sweeping across Russia. The *kulak* hates the Soviet government like poison and is prepared to strangle and massacre hundreds of thousands of workers. We know very well that if the *kulaks* were to gain the upper hand they would ruthlessly slaughter hundreds of thousands of workers, in alliance with the landowners and capitalists, restore back-breaking conditions for the workers, abolish the eight-hour day and hand back the mills and factories to the capitalists. These blood-suckers have grown rich on the want suffered by the people in the war; they have raked in thousands and hundreds of thousands of roubles by pushing up the price of grain and other products. These leeches have sucked the blood of the working people and grown richer as the workers in the cities and factories starved. So we declare ruthless war on the *kulaks*! Death to them! ... The workers must crush the revolts of the *kulaks* with an iron hand!

The Bolsheviks handed power to armed 'committees of the poorest peasants' with a licence to plunder and murder the now hated *kulaks*. Within weeks, neighbour was killing neighbour. It may have rallied the poor to the Bolshevik cause, but it destroyed the class of peasants who had brought initiative and efficiency to the rural economy. Agriculture regressed to disastrous levels. Grain supplies dwindled. The cities starved.

With famine looming, the Bolsheviks' most pressing problem was how to feed the workers and soldiers who were their key support. If hunger turned these classes against the regime, Bolshevism would perish. So the

party decreed that armed food brigades should be sent out into the countryside to force the peasants to hand over their crops.

Red Guards appeared out of the blue demanding grain; peasants were
tortured until supplies were handed over; those who resisted were shot,
their homes burned and their families deported. For the Bolsheviks' accusations against the *kulaks* – that they were guilty of hoarding supplies and
deliberately starving the workers – were directed indiscriminately at all who
managed to eke out anything more than a subsistence living. In reality, most
peasants had barely enough to feed themselves. Knowing that their produce
would be confiscated, the response of many was to down tools in protest.
A third of the land went to seed, and cattle and horses were slaughtered in
vast numbers.

From 1918 onwards, the regime's brutality was met with armed resistance. The peasants murdered 15,000 members of the Bolshevik food
brigades. One community impaled their decapitated heads on spikes, until
a bombardment by government artillery razed the entire village to the
ground. Escalating unrest in the Tambov region, 300 miles southeast of
Moscow, culminated in the formation of a 70,000-strong Peasant Army,
prepared to fight for freedom and the right to the land. Over a period of
nearly two years, the rebellion spread to vast areas of southeastern Russia,
recalling the great revolts of Razin and Pugachev (see pp. 69–70 and 94–6).
It took 100,000 troops and poison gas to massacre the rebels as they hid in
the forests, with survivors and their families consigned to the growing
network of prison camps.

By early 1921, crop failures were endemic, and famine spread across
Russia. In the Volga region, 10 million people were on the verge of starva-
tion and 22 million livestock were lost. The British writer and novelist Sir
Philip Gibbs saw it at first hand:

The harvest had been annihilated by two terrible droughts. And the
reserves of grain which had always been kept by the peasants had been
used up to feed the Red Army. There were twenty-five million people
threatened by starvation and many of them were dead and dying. I went
into cottages where a whole family would be lying down to die. I really

saw some terrible sights which filled my heart with pity for a great people. The children looked like fairy-tale children and it was most pitiful to see them dying of hunger with their stomachs swollen out.

Lenin seemed unmoved. It is hard to find a word of human sympathy or concern anywhere in his collected works. But he was quick to exploit the misery of the nation, to create scapegoats to deflect popular anger from the regime. Directives that he signed personally called for ever greater repression and the incitement of class hatred in the name of Bolshevism:

> The insurrection of the *kulaks* must be suppressed without mercy. We need to set an example. You need to hang (I repeat, hang, without fail, in full public view) at least a hundred *kulaks*, the rich, the bloodsuckers. Then publish their names and take away all of their grain. Also, execute the hostages – in accordance with my previous telegram. Do it in such a way that people for hundreds of miles around will tremble and cry out, 'Let us choke and strangle those bloodsucking *kulaks*!' P.S. Use your toughest people for this.

When the clergy resisted the Bolshevik campaign to close down the churches and confiscate Church property, Lenin's response was once again terror. 'We must … put down all resistance with such brutality that they will not forget it for decades,' he wrote. 'The greater the numbers of reactionary clergy and bourgeoisie we succeed in executing … the better.'

Russia was slipping into anarchy. Strikes were crippling the towns; the countryside riven by revolt. Lenin's response was more terror. When two other members of the government, Grigory Zinoviev and Nikolai Bukharin, tried to moderate the powers of the secret police Lenin overruled them. As late as 1921, he was still expanding the Cheka's powers of summary execution.

But terror was not enough. Russia was teetering on the brink of another revolution. And in March 1921 an event of colossal importance would force the Bolsheviks to rethink the whole way they exercised power.

CHAPTER TWENTY-FIVE

Much surprised me when I first arrived in the Soviet Union as an idealistic but ill-informed grammar-school boy. The temperature of the Cold War was moving from deep freeze to tepid indecision, yet the country remained another world, where citizens were denied civil rights and Soviet television was still in thrall to Vladimir Lenin. Night after night he burst onto the screen. A choir of cute children sang the praises of the first Soviet leader – 'We are all young Leninists! We dream that we will live and work as Lenin did! Our love is for him and for our homeland …' It was disconcerting, reminiscent of the Christian hymns I had sung in my own childhood – just substitute Christ for Lenin. But how strange that a man who spent his days signing death warrants and inciting mass terror should be idolised as a kindly father figure for little children.

Then there was the grown-up version that blared from the radio with lyrics that reminded me of standing in the Kop at Anfield singing 'You'll Never Walk Alone'. 'Lenin is always with you,' said the words of a show tune with swelling strings and a *heldentenor* hitting the top notes. 'In grief, in hope and joy. Lenin is your springtime, Your every happy day. He's in you and he's in me … In every moment Lenin's with us … bringing joy to the world.'

The overblown sentimentality of Lenin worship was the butt of jokes. My new Russian friends warned me we could never be alone, even in the most intimate moments, then burst into laughter as they explained that *Lenin vsegda s nami* – Lenin is always with us.* But the saint-like personality cult was still taken seriously by the masses. For decades his image and words were glorified in films, songs and posters. A party that had destroyed religion

---

* Another take on the same joke was that 'in the USSR you can't buy double beds, only triple beds'!

in a deeply Christian country needed something to replace it in the people's minds, and holy Lenin, dedicated, ascetical and self-denying, was in tune with the times.

The civil war had made the Bolsheviks a party of autocratic power, uninterested in debate or divergent opinions. They considered themselves a paramilitary fraternity surrounded by an untrustworthy population that must be re-educated to understand the new reality. To achieve their ends, the party's leaders would need to steel themselves to be austere, disciplined zealots, untroubled by ordinary human emotions.

Lenin acknowledged that the fanatical Rakhmetov in Chernyshevsky's *What Is to Be Done?* – the man who refused food and slept on a bed of nails to make himself tough – had been a role model for his own development. 'I can't listen to music,' Lenin said, 'because it makes me want to say sweet, silly things, and pat people on the head … but you have to beat people's heads, beat them mercilessly! … What a devilishly difficult job I have.'

Four years on from 1917, the revolution was still far from secure. When its leaders gathered in Moscow for what should have been the triumphal Tenth Party Congress in March 1921, they did so against a backdrop of menacing unrest. Peasant revolts, famine and strikes were crippling the Russian economy. The Petrograd workers, who'd been the touchstone of the February and October revolutions, were once again on the streets; but now they were marching against the Bolsheviks. The grievances listed in the workers' strike declaration were an open protest against Communist repression:

> We, the representatives of the factories and socialist parties in Petrograd, despite much that we disagree on, have united to pursue the following goals: overthrow of the Bolshevik dictatorship, free elections to the soviets, freedom of speech, press and assembly for all, and the release of political prisoners.

In a panic, the government declared martial law. Troops dispersed the strikers with rifle fire. But another, even more dangerous storm was brewing just outside Petrograd, and soon it would shake the regime to its foundations.

*

On a blustery autumn day, with a salty wind blowing in from the sea, I picked my way through a deserted warren of stone fortifications on an island in the Gulf of Finland. The crumbling walls and gun emplacements, now overgrown with weeds and creepers, are part of the fortress of Kronstadt, the former home of Russia's Baltic fleet and first line of defence of St Petersburg, just 30 miles away over the chilly waters to the east.

After the February Revolution of 1917, the Kronstadt sailors rose up and murdered their tsarist officers; as the revolution's shock troops, they fought with ferocious zeal and helped secure the Winter Palace in October. But by 1921, things had changed. Here in Kronstadt's underground tunnels and on the cruisers and battleships lying at anchor, meetings were being held. The mood among the fortress's 30,000 sailors was ugly, and their anger was directed against the Bolsheviks. The democracy of the Soviets had been crushed by a one-party, Communist dictatorship. The sailors sent a delegation to meet the Petrograd workers and heard tales of anger, despair and growing demands for direct action. A spokesman for the workers told them the people's patience was close to breaking point:

> Since you are from Kronstadt, and you are the revolutionary sailors they threaten us with all the time, and you want to know the truth, well here it is: we are starving. We have no shoes and no clothes. We are physically and morally terrorised. Each and every one of our requests and demands is met by the authorities with terror, terror and yet more terror. Look at the prisons of Petrograd and you will see how many of our people are locked up in there. No, comrades! The time has come to tell the Communists openly: 'You've done enough speaking on our behalf. We say, Down with your dictatorship which has driven us into this dead end! Now move over and make way for non-party men. Long live freely elected soviets! They alone can get us out of this mess!'

When the delegation returned to Kronstadt, mass meetings discussed how the sailors should respond to the crisis. There was resentment that Lenin's call for 'All Power to the Soviets' had been replaced by an insistence on 'All Power to the Bolsheviks'. In a mark of protest, 5,000 Kronstadt sailors burned their party cards. Their leaders drew up a manifesto claiming the Communists had 'lost the trust of the people' and demanding immediate concessions, including free elections open to all parties:

> The working class expected the revolution to bring freedom, but it has brought enslavement whose horrors far exceed those of tsarism ... The power of the monarchy, with its police and its gendarmerie, has passed into the hands of the Communist usurpers, who have given the people not freedom but the constant fear of torture by the Cheka ... The Communists have inflicted moral servitude, too, even forcing the people to think the way they want them to ... Through the state control of the trade unions they have chained the workers to their machines so that labour is no longer a source of joy but a new form of slavery. To the protests of the peasants, expressed in spontaneous uprisings, and those of the workers, whose living conditions have compelled them to strike, they have answered with mass executions and a bloodletting that exceeds even that inflicted by the tsarist generals. The Russia of the proletariat, the first to raise the red banner of liberation, is now drenched in blood.

When news of the manifesto reached Lenin at the Party Congress in Moscow, he understood the danger for the Bolsheviks. He sent Trotsky to Kronstadt with orders to crush the revolt.

On 8 March 1921, the day the Congress opened, with the sea still frozen solid, Bolshevik forces set out to march 5 miles across the ice. Trotsky's artillery opened up from the shore, but the Kronstadt sailors were ensconced in fortified pillboxes. I found them still standing on the water's edge. From inside I could see how the rebel gunners had the advancing Bolshevik troops firmly in their sights, exposed and visible for more than a mile, with nowhere to hide on the inhospitable ice. With a withering barrage of fire, the sailors mowed down thousands of Red Army men and forced the rest to retreat. The Bolsheviks were staring disaster in the face.

But Trotsky was merciless. A week later, he gathered 45,000 fresh troops and lined up machine-gunners to fire on any who refused to go into action. Around 300 delegates from the Party Congress volunteered to come to help with the assault. This time Trotsky's forces gained a foothold around Kronstadt and, after 24 hours of bloody fighting, with Red Army losses reaching nearly 10,000 men, the fortress fell to the Bolsheviks. Many of the rebels escaped across the ice to Finland, but 15,000 were taken prisoner, to face immediate execution or a lifetime in the camps. Lenin denounced the Kronstadt sailors as 'White traitors', and rushed in extra bread supplies to calm the angry public.

The immediate crisis was over, but Kronstadt was a warning that Lenin could not ignore. It gave a focus to the anger of workers and peasants, who felt the Bolsheviks had robbed them of the fruits of the revolution. A peasant uprising in Tambov reached its height just as the sailors of the Kronstadt naval base were mutinying. Lenin admitted the Bolsheviks were 'barely hanging on'. He told the opening session of the Tenth Party Congress that the peasant wars and the Kronstadt revolt were 'far more dangerous than all the Denikins, Yudeniches and Kolchaks put together'. The people were sick of his repressive War Communism, weary of hunger and economic meltdown, no longer willing to suffer in the name of some future Utopia. Military force and mass terror were no longer enough to keep the lid on; Lenin needed a different, longer-term solution.

The solution Lenin proposed to the Party Congress just days after the Kronstadt rebellion was the New Economic Policy – the NEP. It would soften the dictatorial control of the state, and reintroduce some elements of capitalism to try to improve the nation's disastrous economic conditions: 'The New Economic Policy we are introducing today is a substantial one. It will last for a long time,' Lenin famously promised. 'Comrade peasants! Today we announce openly, honestly and with no deception: in order to maintain the march towards socialism, we are making a whole series of concessions to you … There will be limits, but you will be told what these are so you can judge for yourselves …'

Lenin's 'concessions' included an end to the hated practice of grain seizures by the state, which had sparked bloody resistance and a collapse in Russian agriculture. Now, in return for handing over a fixed portion of their produce, peasants would be allowed to sell the rest for their own profit. Unsurprisingly, harvest yields rocketed.

In industry, too, some private enterprise was to be permitted, with cooperatives or trusts allowed to make money for themselves instead of for the state. Aid and investment would be sought from abroad, and better international relations would reduce the isolation Russia had suffered since 1917. Banks, military production and strategic industries would remain in state hands, but a mixed economy would be tolerated in most other sectors. Small-scale and light industries would be entrusted largely to the hands of private cooperatives.

It was the only way to placate the people. But it was an ideological bombshell and it split the party. Many Bolsheviks saw the NEP as a betrayal. The weakening of the state, the reversion to capitalist methods were perceived as a travesty of Communist ideals, a capitulation to the *bourzhoui*. Even Vladimir Mayakovsky, the Bolsheviks' fiery, semi-official poet, lampooned the NEP in verse:

> They asked me if I love the NEP.
> I said I do,
> when it's not so darned absurd.
> Come on, comrades!
> Get out there
> And slug it out with the merchants ...
> Lenin says it's 'here for good':
> But who knows?
> Another revolution could be along soon ...

But the New Economic Policy was a great success. Within a few years, agriculture and industry were back to their pre-war levels, with improved living standards that deflated much of the popular anger against the regime. Limited private enterprise spurred the Russian people to work harder in pursuit of personal gain. The peasants produced more food because they knew it was in their interest to do so.

The NEP averted the threat of a counter-revolution and consolidated the Bolsheviks' hold on power. But Lenin never really liked it. For him it was a strategic retreat, a necessary trick to preserve Communist rule on the way to true socialism. He undoubtedly sympathised with the hardliners who resented its elements of renewed dalliance with capitalist methods. But he also knew that he had to push it through. With the NEP arousing fierce debate in the party, he moved decisively to crush all opposition to it, and to the authority of the party leadership. On the same day the NEP was announced and the revolt in Kronstadt was finally defeated, Lenin presented a motion to the Congress demanding party unity. 'There must be an immediate dissolution of all dissenting groups that have been formed on the basis of some platform or other,' it said. 'Failure to comply with this Congress resolution will result in unconditional and immediate expulsion from the party.'

The 'On Party Unity' motion was carried, and it would have fateful consequences. The remaining elements of pluralism within the party were swept away. From now on debate would be stifled and any challenge to the leadership would be denounced as treacherous 'factionalism', a tactic Josef Stalin would later exploit to establish his dictatorial hold on power. The motion paved the way for the intolerant, monolithic Communist Party that would rule the country for the next 70 years.

Lenin was acutely aware that even limited reform runs the risk of unleashing demands for more. So he accompanied the concessions of the NEP with a crackdown on dissent that included show trials of political opponents and deportations of the Russian intelligentsia, beginning in 1922.

Like Augusto Pinochet's Chile, or China today, Lenin pulled off the feat of liberalising the economy without loosening the grip of the political dictatorship (something Mikhail Gorbachev would signally fail to do 60 years later, with serious consequences for himself and his party).* The NEP offered breathing space, giving Lenin the time he badly needed to consolidate the Bolsheviks' hold on power. But if 1921 marked an upswing in the party's political health, Lenin's own was becoming increasingly fragile.

---

* It is clear that the model for Gorbachev's *perestroika* reforms was at least in part the New Economic Policy of the 1920s. For both Lenin and Gorbachev, it was the threat of economic collapse that made them experiment with capitalism. And in both cases the experiment transformed society. The NEP and *perestroika* both created a new class of speculators – the so-called NEP men in the 1920s and the oligarchs in our own time – who grew rich from exploiting the new economic freedoms. Both were reviled by the rest of the population, both had a reputation for the tasteless flaunting of personal wealth, and both represented a threat to the survival of the Communist system. I believe that Gorbachev, like Lenin, saw economic liberalisation as a means to preserve and strengthen socialism, but – unlike Lenin – he failed to impose the political tightening that would stop change spiralling out of control and ultimately destroying the system it was designed to save.

The USSR, 1922

CHAPTER TWENTY-SIX

There is a lot of silent film footage of Vladimir Lenin. The Soviet Union regarded cinema as its most powerful propaganda tool, and in 1969 the Soviet Institute of Marxism-Leninism brought it all together in a sort of retrospective director's cut. Watching it now, the film's painstaking chronological sequencing provides an insight into the evolving public and private existence of the Soviet leader.

In the period after 1917, we see Lenin haranguing crowds, addressing congresses, chatting self-consciously in the Kremlin (lip-readers can make out his rather impatient 'How much longer will this take?'), stroking his pet cat and signing letters at his desk. But the films run out suddenly at the end of 1921. After that, nothing. A blackout.

Lenin's disappearance from public view was the result of two serious strokes, possibly the legacy of injuries sustained in the assassination attempt of 1918. The cover-up of ill health would be a familiar story with later Soviet leaders. But Lenin's illness would have serious consequences for Russia and the world.

During the last two years of his life, paralysed and barely able to speak, with only one hemisphere of his brain still functioning, he struggled to express his instructions for the country's future. In a document that became known as 'Lenin's Testament', produced in the seclusion of his dacha in the village of Gorki outside Moscow, he ran the rule over those who were lining up to succeed him. He has warm words for the young Nikolai Bukharin, 'the darling of the whole party'. He's less certain about Trotsky, who, although 'distinguished by outstanding ability', has 'displayed excessive self-assurance'. But he reserves the greatest doubts for Josef Stalin:

> Comrade Stalin, having become General Secretary, has too much power
> in his hands; and I am not sure that he always knows how to use that power

with sufficient caution … Stalin is too coarse and this fault is unsupportable in the office of General Secretary. Therefore I propose to the comrades to remove Stalin from the position and appoint to it another man who will in all respects differ from Stalin – more patient, more loyal, more polite, more attentive to comrades … The character of the two main leaders [Trotsky and Stalin] … could inadvertently lead to a split. And if the party does not act to prevent it, the split may come without warning …

If Lenin had lived to present his warning to the party, history could have been very different. But, with his testament still in the drawer of his desk, he suffered a third, devastating stroke and died on 21 January 1924. Lenin was 53, and the revolution was less than seven years old. The British novelist Arthur Ransome, who knew Lenin personally and was well disposed to the Bolshevik cause, was present at the Party Congress in Moscow when news of the leader's death was announced:

When Congress met at eleven this morning, [Central Committee President] Kalinin, who was hardly able to speak, announced Lenin's death in a few broken sentences. Almost everybody in the great theatre burst into tears, and from all parts came the hysterical wailing of women. Tears were running down the faces of the members of the Presidium. The funeral march of the Revolutionaries was played by a weeping orchestra. The elders of Congress will go to Gorki to-night and bring the body to Moscow to-morrow, where it will lie in state in the hall of the trade unions, which from six to-morrow will be open to the public … His death is a blow not only to the Communist party, but to all Russia. Even the irreconcilable enemies of the Revolution are unable to disguise their respect for one of the greatest figures in Russian history.

Lenin's body was carried in an open coffin from his dacha to the railway station at Gorki, and then by special train, decked with garlands of flowers, to the Kievskaya Station in Moscow. Ransome was in the Kremlin for his lying in state:

The body of Lenin … lay on a crimson catafalque guarded by a group of his old comrades … Stalin stood with arms folded, iron like his name. Bukharin, beside him, was still for once, like a figure carved in wax. Gradually the hall filled with Communists … Lighting for the benefit of the kinematograph operators lit up the white faces of bearded peasants and leather-jacketed workmen … There was absolute silence: then funeral music … while soldiers stood at attention. I had a curious feeling that I was present at the founding of a new religion.

On Red Square under the Kremlin wall, Lenin's mausoleum is a squat, foursquare building in black and burgundy marble, a now familiar sight to all who know the Russian capital. But in January 1924 there was nothing here except a flimsy wooden platform draped in red and black cloth. Lenin's coffin was carried out and placed on it in the intense winter cold, while thousands of Muscovites filed past in reverential silence.

Standing on Red Square, I can well understand what Arthur Ransome meant about the founding of a new religion. I have descended the steps inside the mausoleum to view Lenin's body probably 20 times or more since I first came here as a schoolboy, but you still shiver every time you see that unmistakable waxy face glowing like a holy relic. The dimmed lights, the chilly silence, the reverential guards all tell you that this is the very epicentre of a messianic force that spread its tentacles across the whole world.

Just as Christian Russia believed for centuries that it had a God-given mission to bring truth and enlightenment to mankind, so Russian Communism believed in its own holy destiny to change, educate and perfect the human species. The party would lead us from the grim, corrupted present to the cleansed, harmonious future. But in return it demanded unquestioning obedience from its followers: any deviation or dissent would be mercilessly punished.

The 'kinematograph' footage that Arthur Ransome saw being shot at Lenin's funeral has survived. The corpse and the mourners are dramatically, indeed rather spookily, lit. The staging is masterful, with a touch of Wagnerian apocalypse about it. But there's something even more striking: barely a shot goes by without the dark, brooding, moustachioed figure of Josef Stalin sliding into the frame. He unloads the coffin from the train; he stands guard over the bier; he takes his position as chief pallbearer.

Stalin was not the party's senior leader, but his role as General Secretary put him in charge of organisational matters and he gave himself the starring role. So anyone looking at the films and photographs of the funeral could be forgiven for concluding that he was Lenin's anointed successor. Trotsky, by contrast, is noticeable by his absence. He didn't make it to the funeral because Stalin had lied to him about the time and date it was taking place! It was a move worthy of Machiavelli.

'Lenin's Testament' was damning about Stalin – the two men had quarrelled as Lenin lay dying – but Stalin attempted to overrule Lenin's widow Nadezhda Krupskaya and conceal the document from public view. With Krupskaya demanding her husband's wishes be respected and the testament published, the party leadership met for a tense, private discussion. Eyewitness accounts of the meeting speak of Stalin 'sitting on the steps of the rostrum looking small and miserable … In spite of his self-control and show of calm, it was abundantly clear that his fate was at stake …' Many of those present, including Trotsky, would undoubtedly have liked to see the remarks about Stalin made public. This was their chance to be rid of the man whose ruthless ambition would eventually destroy them all, but they failed to take it. The problem was that they too were criticised by Lenin, and they too had much to lose. In the end they decided not to publish the testament but merely to read extracts from it to trusted party officials. Krupskaya leapt to her feet in protest, but to no avail. Stalin, said Trotsky later, sat there quietly wiping the sweat from his brow.

After he consolidated his grip on power, Stalin decreed that Lenin's testament did not exist; attempts to refer to it were denounced as treachery. So Lenin's warning about the danger of handing power to Stalin went unheeded. When Winston Churchill commented that 'the Russian people's worst misfortune was Lenin's birth; their next worst, his death', he already knew that the way had been opened for the horrors of Stalinism.

It is tempting to think of Josef Stalin as the accidental dictator, the low-level functionary who somehow usurped the boss's chair. His early role for the Bolsheviks was certainly one of brawn rather than brains: he ran bank raids, kidnappings and murders for the party in his native Georgia. But if the intellectuals of the revolution looked down on him, they badly underestimated the resentment and need for vindication that drove him on. It would manifest itself in the ruthlessness with which he swept them all aside.

Stalin played only a minor part in the revolutions of 1917, but he later expended vast amounts of energy rewriting history to glorify his role and belittle that of his rivals. In the five years of infighting that followed Lenin's death, Stalin controlled the party's files and administration, a position he used systematically to appoint his own supporters to positions of influence. The old practices of corrupt personal patronage that had undermined the rule of law in tsarist times were reincarnated now in the Bolsheviks' all-powerful *nomenklatura* system, under which they arrogated the right to make all appointments to key posts in both party and government. As the man in charge of it, Stalin made it his business to know the blemishes on everyone's record, and he used them to blacken his opponents.

Trotsky, for instance, was attacked as a former Menshevik; Zinoviev and Kamenev denounced for their hesitation over the launch of the 1917 uprising. Logical debate was replaced by the hysteria of a witch-hunt. When Trotsky published a memoir in 1924 suggesting that he and Lenin were the main architects of the revolution, he was hounded out of his post as minister of war. The slightest deviation from Bolshevik orthodoxy became a mortal sin, and the man who increasingly defined that orthodoxy was Josef Stalin.

From the mid 1920s, Stalin and Trotsky clashed over the key issue that came to obsess the leadership – how to secure Communism. Marxist doctrine held that this could be done only by spreading revolution throughout the world, and right up to his death Lenin had remained convinced that global revolution was about to happen. A recording of a speech he made in late 1919 reveals the unshakable intensity of his faith:

The word Soviet has become known and popular all over the world. It is the favourite word of all working people. So despite the persecution to which communists are subjected in so many countries, Soviet power must necessarily, inevitably, and in the not distant future, triumph all over the world.

It is hard to imagine it now, but after 1917 the message of world revolution began to grip many European countries. Reminiscing more than half a century later, the veteran British Communist Harry Young spoke of the shared belief in left-wing circles that it was only a matter of time before capitalism was ousted by the red flags of the Soviets:

> We had a great big banner, 'The world revolution will be led under the banner of the Communist International', and in 1924, we really believed it ... The work was done in a spirit of heroic idealism. Glory and romance and drama, and what we all hoped for: that in a few short months the last bastion of capitalism would fall in Europe and the Soviets would be in power throughout the entire continent. It was a time of hysterical meetings, of shouting, 'Up the Councils of Action!' I rushed up to Glasgow and all over with the *Daily Worker* and addressed endless meetings. We thought great revolutionary events were under way ...

The general strike in Britain in 1926 and the depression in the Western economies in the 1930s reinforced those hopes. But as years went by and global Communism failed to materialise, enthusiasm began to falter. The only states to experiment with communist government were Hungary and Bavaria, and they soon returned to the capitalist fold.

The Bolshevik leaders wavered and split. Trotsky continued to advocate world revolution, with a dogmatic certainty that made the concept synonymous with his name. But Stalin was more pragmatic. He advanced a new doctrine of 'Socialism in one country', claiming that the Soviet Union could build Communism on its own, and appealing to Russian national pride to do so. It meant the denial of Marxist ideology, which rejected nationalist values in favour of international class struggle. But Stalin had gauged the mood well, and it paid dividends.

Trotsky's dedication to classic Marxism lost out. The Party Congress agreed that deviation from official policy (as decided by Stalin and his allies) would not be tolerated. In 1927, Trotsky was expelled from the party and posted to Kazakhstan. By 1929, Stalin felt his position as party leader was secure enough to deport Trotsky from the territory of the USSR. He went into foreign exile, first in Turkey, then in France, Norway and finally Mexico. Zinoviev, Kamenev and Bukharin hung on for another few years but would eventually fall victim to the purges of the 1930s. Stalin was beginning to airbrush his rivals from the record of history. Few had actively wanted him as leader; everyone knew he was manipulative and ruthless, but no one had been strong enough to stop him.

If world revolution had been put on hold, Communism still had to be secured at home. The newly formed Union of Soviet Socialist Republics was made up of a hundred or so national groups, and many of them were far from convinced. Stalin had been People's Commissar for the National-ities – or NarKomNats – since the revolution, and Lenin evidently hoped that as an ethnic Georgian he would deal sensitively with the problem. The tsars had repressed the nationalities in their empire, fostering resentment and revolt, but Lenin favoured a more conciliatory approach.

As early as 1917, the Bolsheviks passed a resolution guaranteeing indi-vidual peoples the right to national self-determination, with linguistic, cultural and administrative freedoms, and at least a theoretical right to secede from the Union. Autonomous regions were created, and a growing number – beginning with Russia, Ukraine and Belorussia – were granted the status of Union Republics, all supposedly co-equal. There would even-tually be 15 of these, of which the Russian Republic was by far the biggest, occupying three-quarters of the Soviet territory and containing two-thirds of its population. In addition, scores of so-called Autonomous Republics were established for smaller ethnic groups, the vast majority of them located on Russian soil.

It was a potentially explosive mix. Many nationalities had been pressing for independence under the tsars and had expected the revolution to grant it to them. They were encouraged when the Congress of Soviets proclaimed its Declaration of the Rights of the Peoples of Russia, under which the 'self-determination of peoples' was guaranteed 'up to and including secession and the formation of an independent state'. Finland, Latvia, Lithuania and Belorussia gratefully declared independence as early as 1917. Ukraine, Poland, Estonia, Azerbaijan, Armenia and Georgia were not far behind.

But as the disintegration of Russian society and the national breakdown of order in the civil war fanned the flames of nationalism within the tottering empire, the Bolsheviks quickly revised their policy. Independence movements were now denounced as 'bourgeois' and 'counter-revolutionary'. Stalin in particular was suspicious of the nationalities. His instinct, as a Georgian himself, was that they were bound to rebel against Moscow and would use any treacherous method to oppose Soviet rule. If the unsettled territories and ethnic groups were now to be persuaded that loyalty to the Soviet Union was in their natural interests, it would require patience, understanding and sensitivity. Stalin had none of those. He set the tone in 1922 when he initiated moves to crush Georgian demands for greater independence within the Union. Lenin favoured conciliation, but Stalin went for brute force. His own Georgian roots seemingly counted for nothing.

Great-Russian dominance and an unrelenting drive to subsume minority groups and cultures into a collective Soviet identity would be the principle that underpinned his nationalities policy for the next 30 years. When the USSR was first formed in December 1922, Stalin had opposed Lenin's federative model of a Union of Republics, arguing instead that all the remaining territories of the former tsarist empire should be forcibly incorporated into the Russian Federation. (His suspicion of the nationalities would reach a peak of frenzied paranoia during the Second World War.) It was largely decisions taken by Stalin during his time as party leader that entrenched the national and ethnic conflicts that would dog Russia right down to the twenty-first century.

The Georgia crackdown was an indication that the rhetoric of greater freedom for the national minorities ran counter to the increasingly centralised structure of state and party rule. Moscow seemed simultaneously to be both encouraging and suppressing non-Russian national movements – a fatal contradiction that would cause decades of smouldering conflict.

CHAPTER TWENTY-SEVEN

The collectivisation of Soviet agriculture in the years from 1928 to 1940 caused human misery on an unprecedented scale. It brought with it the worst excesses of Communist social engineering. Millions would lose their lives because of it; virtually no one in the country escaped its effects. The experiences of 84-year-old Masha Alekseevna are typical of a whole generation:

> Oh yes, dear. It happened in 1930, when I was four years old. In Tambov. Well! They just started to take everything away from us – the grain, the horses, the cows … They took everything away to their collective farm. And even those who went to work in the collective farm, they still took everything away from them! It was the authorities, you know … My mother had a big trunk, where she hid some bits and pieces of food. She sat me on the trunk to try and hide it from them. But they even found those things in the trunk and took them away, too. Everything – even down to a tiny bit of soap …

Collectivisation was perhaps the most divisive and destructive of all the utopian experiments imposed on Russian society in its long history of authoritarian government. But Stalin's announcement of the new policy, at the Fifteenth Party Congress in December 1927, makes it all sound so sensible:

> The solution to our problems lies in making agriculture large-scale … The socialist way is to unite the small peasant farms into large collective farms, sharing machinery and employing scientific farming methods … We can either go back to capitalism, or forward to socialism; there can be no third way … The collective farms are the principal basis for remoulding the peasant, for changing his whole mentality in the spirit of socialism.

One of the key pledges that helped sweep the Bolsheviks to power in 1917 was that the land would be given to the peasants. It was, almost certainly, the measure that did the most to garner support for the new regime. But the party's long-term plans never envisaged the survival of private farming. Lenin's New Economic Policy, which ran from 1921 to 1928, allowed those who cultivated the land to sell part of their produce for personal profit, but it was widely regarded in Communist circles as a temporary measure designed to combat the acute food shortages in the years following the civil war. To the hardliners in the Bolshevik leadership, the NEP smacked of a concession to capitalism, and when Stalin felt his grip on power was strong enough, he ditched it. Now, he told the country, the drive for real Communism would be launched in earnest:

> We are turning the main mass of the peasantry away from the old, capitalist path … to the new, socialist path, kicking out the rich, the capitalists. We are re-equipping the middle and poor peasants with tractors and machinery for the collective cultivation of the land … Is it not obvious that the peasants would jump for joy at this assistance and join the collective-farm movement en masse!

By late 1929, two years of disappointing harvests had seen crop yields plummet. A 2 million-ton shortfall in grain supplies to the state had been met with requisitioning and punitive measures against those who resisted. The Central Committee concluded in November that a radical acceleration of the pace of collectivisation was the only solution, with the forced reorganisation of peasant communities into gigantic collective farms, or *kolkhozy*, and state farms, *sovkhozy*. Stalin made the announcement sound like a story of fabulous success, rather than a desperate response to a desperate situation:

> The peasants are joining the collective farms by whole villages, districts and regions! Even the blind can see that if there is any serious dissatisfaction among the main mass of the peasantry, it is not because of the collective-farm policy of the Soviet government … The peasants are

abandoning en masse the lauded banner of 'private property' and are going over to the lines of collectivism, of socialism. The last hope for the restoration of capitalism is collapsing. We know that by the spring of the coming year, 1930, we shall have over 60,000 tractors in the fields, a year later we shall have over 100,000 tractors, and two years after that, over 250,000 tractors ... Despite the desperate resistance of retrograde forces of every kind ... we are now able to accomplish and even to exceed what was considered 'fantasy' several years ago. And that is why the middle peasant has turned towards Communism.

Collectivisation was the regime's flagship policy, crucial to the creation of the New Soviet Man moulded in the ways of socialism, and Stalin couldn't afford to see it fail. The new system was welcomed by the poorest peasants – they literally had nothing to lose, and the shiny new tractors appearing on the state farms were a big draw. But Stalin's confident announcement of victory was premature. The 'retrograde forces' he identifies as opposing collectivisation were growing in strength, and far from being capitalist lackeys, they were actually composed of millions of ordinary peasants, men and women who'd made a success of their farming. People like Grandma Masha and her family simply did not want to hand over their worldly goods to the collective.

Many peasants viewed collectivisation as a return to serfdom. As well as having to give up their land and property, they lost their right to sell their produce for personal gain. Now they were forced to sell the vast bulk of the food they produced to the state, at artificially low prices set by the state itself. In an echo of the policies of tsars dating back to Boris Godunov, the peasants were tied to the land by a system of 'internal passports', which prohibited the movement of agricultural workers from the countryside to the towns. In many ways, collectivisation meant swapping the yoke of the tsarist private landlords for the new yoke of the Communist state.

Stalin was acutely aware of the growing resistance to his policies, and to combat it he resorted to his usual mixture of inducements and repression. The problems of collectivisation were blamed on the *kulaks*, 'grasping fists' allegedly determined to sabotage the will of the Soviet state. The *kulaks* were Stalin's scapegoat, just as they had been Lenin's (see pp. 236–8). They could be hounded and repressed. Ordinary, 'good' peasants could observe the fate of the *kulaks* with the *schadenfreude* of seeing their rich neighbours done down. But they also knew that anyone who opposed collectivisation, or anyone who so much as complained about it, could be swiftly reclassified as a *kulak* himself. In January 1930, Stalin famously pledged to 'liquidate the *kulaks* as a class', in rhetoric similar to that of Lenin a decade earlier:

> The collective-farm movement is a mighty and growing avalanche sweeping the *kulak* resistance from its path, shattering the *kulak* class, paving the way for socialism in the countryside ... We must smash the *kulaks* and eliminate them as a class ... We must strike so hard they will never rise to their feet again. That is what we Bolsheviks call a real offensive ... We must break the *kulaks'* resistance ... and replace their output by the output of the collective farms ... They must be smashed in open battle and deprived of the means to exist – use of the land, instruments of production and the right to hire labour. That is the policy of eliminating the *kulaks* as a class.

Soviet culture presented the '*kulak* smashing' in rosy hues. Paintings, poetry, songs and movies overflowed with burgeoning wheat-fields and happy peasants on their new collectivised tractors. A 1930s musical called *The Rich Bride*, for instance, is a sort of Ukrainian *Oklahoma!*, in which muscular young men sing about their tractors as great steel horses and rhapsodise about the glory of cultivating the virgin lands. Brigades of women from the communal farm march through fields, flying flags and shouldering farm implements like weapons. *The Rich Bride* is a joyous celebration of a socialist rural idyll every bit as fictional as its schmaltzy romantic plot.

The reality was different. Three-quarters of Soviet territory was eventually collectivised, but the fearsome rhetoric of Stalin's call to 'liquidate the *kulaks'* gave rise to abuse and suffering on a massive scale. Because there was no clear definition of who exactly was a *kulak*, the term came to denote any successful farmer, any peasant who opposed collectivisation or – in many cases – any person the local authorities didn't like. Tens of thousands were executed, and millions shipped off to labour settlements in barren areas of Siberia and Central Asia, where they perished in huge numbers.

The exact number of peasants who died as the direct result of collectivisation is impossible to define, but recent Western scholarship puts the number at somewhere between 4 and 10 million.

The Bolsheviks had never had much support in the countryside. The peasants didn't trust them and they didn't trust the peasants, an uncomfortable position for a revolution supposedly based on the will of the people. The regime saw the deeply religious, conservative peasants as the last bastion of the old order, hankering for their 'Little Father', the tsar, and unmoved by the appeals of the revolution. So imposing centralised control on the countryside was almost as important as securing the grain supply. Collectivisation was tantamount to war on the recalcitrant peasantry. By the winter of 1930, the problems of Soviet agriculture had deepened. The collectivisation effort had made only limited progress, with a mere 15 per cent of peasant households incorporated into the new system. With socialism's fate hanging on the result of efforts to secure food for the urban workforce, Stalin launched a concerted campaign to bring the countryside to heel.

Israel Chernitsky was one of 25,000 shock troops – class-conscious urban workers, former soldiers and young Communists – sent by Moscow to wage war on the *kulaks* and enforce collectivisation:

> We went into the house, and the secretary of the party organisation announced, 'According to the decision of our meeting, your family is to be de-kulakised. Put all your valuables on the table. I warn you no hysterics – I've got strong nerves. We'll stand firm.' A woman burst into tears and cursed the authorities.

The Bolshevik Central Committee decreed that the 'Twenty-Five Thousanders', as they became known, should be selected on the basis of their organisational and political experience. They were given rudimentary training and dispatched to rural areas to strengthen work discipline, production and distribution on the *kolkhozy*.

The Twenty-Five Thousanders were celebrated as heroes. Vladimir Mayakovsky wrote poems in their honour, and the bestselling novel of the early 1930s was Mikhail Sholokhov's *Virgin Soil Upturned*, with its Twenty-

Five Thousander hero Semyon Davydov, who overcomes stubborn resistance and *kulak* sabotage to create a model collective farm, before perishing heroically in the final chapter. One real-life Twenty-Five Thousander, Lev Kopelev, writing with the benefit of hindsight, recalled the ideals that motivated him:

> Stalin had said, 'The struggle for grain is the struggle for socialism.' I was convinced that we were warriors on an invisible front, waging war on *kulak* sabotage for the sake of grain that the nation needed for the Five Year Plan (see p. 268–9, 273–6). For grain above all, but also for the souls of the peasants whose attitudes were bogged down in ignorance and low political consciousness, and who succumbed to enemy propaganda, not grasping the great truth of Communism.

The peasants were set in their ways, mistrustful of outsiders. So the arrival of strangers ordering them to break up their farms and hand over their possessions was met with fury. Thousands of towns and villages rose up in protest, and one of the fiercest rebellions was in the Pitelinksy district 250 miles southeast of Moscow. I drove to the village of Veryaevo, where the revolt was centred. Nowadays it is a quiet, ramshackle community of painted wooden houses and barns with zinc roofs, clustered around a ruined brick church with weeds growing from its bell tower. But in February 1930 its streets were full of angry, raucous peasants. The collectivisation brigades had begun to seize cattle and confiscate grain. Families designated as *kulaks* had been expelled from their homes. Government patrols raided the locals' houses during the night, insulting the men and abusing the women. Rumours were circulating that all wives and children were to be declared state property and shipped off to Moscow.

Soon the peasants were speaking of Soviet power as the agent of the devil, and alarming, caustic folk rhymes began to do the rounds:

> Akh, brethren! Akh, sisters!
> Don't go to the kolkhoz,
> For the anti-Christ is there.

Thrice upon you will he put his mark,
On your hand,
Your forehead for all to see,
And deep within your breast ...

Prophecies appeared, with warnings about what awaited people in the dreaded *kolkhoz*:

In the kolkhoz they will brand you with a branding iron. The churches will be closed down and praying will be forbidden. The christening of children will be forbidden. The dead will be cremated. The old and sick will be killed. Marriage will be abolished and all men and women made to sleep together under one long blanket.

On 22 February, Veryaevo took up arms. The rebels had machine guns and hand grenades, left over from the fighting in the civil war, and they were preparing to use them. Peasant elders rang the church bells to summon reinforcements from neighbouring villages, which were also in revolt. Hundreds came on horses and sleighs, or skied over the frozen ground. A detachment of Red Army men attempting to restore calm was surrounded by an angry mob. When a policeman was seized and badly beaten, the violence began.

Official accounts speak of 3,000 rebels led by a redoubtable woman warrior called Alyona. Two government officials were beaten to death. When Alyona taunted the troops by baring her breasts to them, she was shot down in a volley of gunfire that sparked a full-scale battle.

The mob chased the government forces out of town and set up barricades on all roads in and out. Sensing victory, they stormed the collective farm, killing the chairman and taking back their grain and cattle. Those peasants who had been evicted as *kulaks* were returned to their homes and the village priests, who had been thrown into jail, were released. Slogans appeared on walls and fences proclaiming 'Down with the Soviet commune! Down with Soviet power! Down with the robbers and pillagers! Up with the tsar! Bring back the old ways!' It took several weeks before the authorities regained control, and repression followed. Hundreds of those involved in the uprising were arrested, but resentment and resistance bubbled on for months.

Veryaevo was far from an isolated incident. Peasants all over the Soviet Union rebelled against collectivisation. Many elected to slaughter their livestock rather than hand it over to the commune, and, in the first half of 1930, millions of cattle, horses, pigs and sheep were lost – something like a quarter of the nation's total. Peasants refused to plant crops and often sabotaged the machinery of the hated collective farms, smashing tractors and pouring grit into the diesel fuel. The impact on Soviet agriculture was so great that it didn't fully recover for 20 years. The immediate result was appalling – widespread famine. Malcolm Muggeridge was one of the few Western journalists courageous enough to travel to the affected areas and report the truth:

> It was the big story. This was in thirty-two, thirty-three, and I went down to the Ukraine and the Caucasus and my pieces appeared in the *Manchester Guardian*. It was a scene of horror I had never seen before – villages with no one in them, peasants at a railway station being hoofed off. People starving; people swollen. And it was awful, not least because it was manmade.

Between 2 and 4 million people died in the *Holodomor*, the great famine that swept through Ukraine in 1932 and 1933. At the very time Soviet cinema was turning out films about singing peasants dancing through golden wheat-fields, cases of cannibalism were being reported throughout the republic. Moscow suppressed all information about the famine for 50 years, but the British diplomat Gareth Jones bore witness to the misery and death it inflicted:

> This ruin I saw in its grim reality. I tramped through villages in the snow of March. I saw children with swollen bellies. I slept in peasants' huts, and I talked to every peasant I met ... I walked alone through villages and twelve collective farms. Everywhere was the cry, 'There is no bread; we are dying.' This cry came to me from every part of Russia. In a train a Communist denied to me that there was a famine. I flung into the spittoon a crust of bread I had been eating. A peasant fished it out and ravenously ate it.

I threw orange peel into the spittoon. The peasant again grabbed and devoured it. The Communist subsided.

Shamefully, there was no shortage of Western luminaries willing to swallow Moscow's propaganda that the garden was rosy and that any suggestions to the contrary were anti-Soviet slander. Jones, whose reports were ridiculed as lies and falsification, was furious that Western visitors to Russia allowed themselves to be taken in by the Soviet PR campaign:

> After Stalin, the most hated man in Russia is Bernard Shaw. To many of those who can read and have read his descriptions of plentiful food in their starving land, the future is blacker than the present. There is insufficient seed. Many of the peasants are too weak to work the land. In short, the Government's policy of collectivisation and the peasants' resistance to it have brought Russia to the worst catastrophe since the famine of 1921 swept away the population of whole districts ... Today the famine is everywhere ...

As well as George Bernard Shaw, H.G. Wells, Beatrice Webb and Walter Duranty of the *New York Times* accepted and propagated the Kremlin's lies. Gareth Jones was murdered in Mongolia two years later, in circumstances that have never been properly explained.

Even more chillingly, it appears that Stalin deliberately worsened the famine by withholding vital supplies from allegedly anti-Soviet areas in Ukraine. In the centre of Kiev in a prominent position beside St Michael's Monastery, a display of 6-foot billboards catches the eye of visitors and passers-by. Erected in 2006 during the presidency of the nationalist president Viktor Yushchenko, they bear a text in Ukrainian and English headed 'Holodomor – Genocide against the Ukrainian people'. Disturbing photographs of skeletal children and corpses lying in rows outside Ukrainian peasant huts are accompanied by a commentary that leaves little doubt about whom the Ukrainian nationalists hold responsible for the famine. Recent scholarship has suggested the accusations against Stalin and his colleagues do have some truth to them. It is, for instance, undeniable that Ukrainian Communists had warned Stalin that famine was looming.

Roman Terekhov, the party secretary in Kharkiv, wrote to the Soviet leader to ask for urgent measures to be taken, but Stalin replied:

> I see you are a good storyteller. You seem to have invented this tale about a famine to try to frighten us. But I tell you, it won't work!

In 1932, Mikhail Khataevich, first secretary of the province of Dniepropetrovsk, warned Vyacheslav Molotov, the politburo member in charge of collectivisation, that 'the minimum needs of the peasantry must be met, or there will be no one left to sow and produce'. Molotov passed his remarks on to the other Bolshevik leaders, but the decision was taken to carry on requisitioning grain even in the worst-affected areas. Demands for concessions to alleviate the hunger of the population, said Molotov, were 'unBolshevik': 'Such a view is incorrect because we cannot put the needs of the state – needs which have been precisely defined in party resolutions – in tenth, or even in second place.' As a result, the party continued to requisition the peasants' grain. At one point, 8 million tons of it – enough to feed 5 million people for a year – was sold abroad, while Ukrainians and Russians starved at home.

As well as the decision to continue exporting vitally needed grain, measures were taken to prevent peasants leaving the famine-afflicted areas of Ukraine. Explanations that this was necessary to prevent the spread of disease are not credible. By banning travel, the regime was in effect condemning large numbers of people to death.

At the same time, Moscow took the attitude that those suffering in the famine had somehow brought it on themselves. They were referred to as 'idlers', 'thieves' or 'counter-revolutionaries', and Nikita Khrushchev later remarked that 'for Stalin, the peasants were scum'. Some parts of Stalin's correspondence hint that he deliberately encouraged terror-starvation as a means to punish an unreliable population:

> Unless we begin to straighten out the situation, we may lose Ukraine. Keep in mind that [enemy] agents in Ukraine are many times stronger than [ours]. The Ukrainian Communist Party, with its 500,000 members – ha,

ha, ha! – includes quite a lot – yes, quite a lot! – of rotten elements, conscious and unconscious …

From being a campaign of class hatred against the *kulaks*, grain requisition-ing and the starvation it induced now appeared in Stalin's mind as a tool to be used against the Ukrainians, a way to break nationalist resistance to rule from Moscow. By the early 1930s, Stalin had begun to doubt the loyalty of the non-Russian nationalities and suspected foreign influences were at work, stirring up anti-Soviet sentiment. His suspicions would grow until they ripened into the bloody purges that would leave their mark on the rest of the decade.

CHAPTER TWENTY-EIGHT

The People's Economic Achievements Exhibition in northern Moscow is Russia's answer to Disney World, but without the rides. Founded by Stalin in 1935, it was laid out on the grandest of scales – the site is bigger than Victorian London's Great Exhibition; bigger than Monaco, in fact. I first came here as a child with my parents in the 1960s when the VDNKh, as it was known, was at the height of its glory. Proud guides showed us foreigners around the extravagantly decorated pavilions showcasing the achievements of Soviet industry and technology: Engineering, Astronautics, Atomic Energy, Radio-electronics, and another 78 of them for good measure. The broad vistas were crammed with visitors. The towering entrance arch, visible for miles, was crowned with the most famous statue of the Stalin era: the monumental *Worker and Peasant* (1937), holding aloft their gleaming hammer and sickle in a soaring gesture of confidence in the future.

By the 1990s, however, the pavilions were empty, the plaster falling from the walls; and the 80-foot statue lay in pieces on the ground. Huge sections of its outer skin – steel fingers, muscular arms and naked breasts – had fallen away, its inner skeleton on view to the world, like the bones of a decaying dinosaur. The 6-foot-high letters that spelt out 'CCCP' – 'USSR' – for all to see and admire were dumped forlornly behind the parapet of the roof. Only in the last two years has the site been tidied up and restored to something like its original condition. The VDNKh makes a neat, if depressing, metaphor for the rise and fall of the vast industrialisation programme the Soviet Union embarked on from the late 1920s, and intended this place to commemorate and glorify. By 1928, Russia had overcome the immediate threats of civil war and foreign invasion. The revolution had been consolidated, and the USSR was gaining grudging recognition from the international community. But its economy was in a mess. While Lenin's New Economic Policy had encouraged small traders and revived some branches of production, heavy industry had regressed. The large-scale strategic sectors – manufacturing, iron and steel, machine and shipbuilding, electrification, mining and armaments – had not recovered from the chaos of the collapse of tsarism and the depredations of the First World War. The Soviet Union's weakness made it vulnerable, and the need for radical measures was becoming ever more apparent.

In 1928, Stalin announced the first Five Year Plan for industrialisation, describing it as a new revolution from above (initiated by the party leadership), just as vital as 1917. Industrialisation was a central theme in his speeches for the next four years. It was, he warned, a matter of national survival:

> The history of Russia is one of continual beatings she suffered because of her backwardness. She was beaten by the Mongol khans, by Turkish beys, the Swedish lords, the Polish and Lithuanian nobles and by the British and French capitalists. The reason they beat her was her backwardness, her military, cultural, political, agricultural and industrial backwardness … We are fifty or a hundred years behind the advanced countries. We must make up this distance in ten years … Either we do it, or they will crush us!

The rhetoric surrounding the drive for industrialisation was couched in the terminology of a military campaign. The fears of Russian vulnerability, the spectre of powerful enemies at the gates, were centuries old, and Stalin's appeal tapped into them to mobilise the nation in the face of overwhelming odds.

> Do you want our socialist fatherland to be beaten and to lose its independence? If you do not want this, you must put an end to its backwardness in the shortest possible time. You must adopt a truly Bolshevik pace in building up its socialist system of economy. There is no other way. That is why Lenin said on the eve of the October Revolution: 'Either we overtake and outstrip the advanced capitalist countries, or we perish!'

The ultimate test of that prediction would come soon enough, with the Nazi invasion of 1941; and the outcome of that terrible reckoning would provide at least a partial justification of Stalin's methods in the intervening years.

The destruction of the civil war had reduced industrial output to a mere 13 per cent of its pre-war level – Trotsky admitted 'we have destroyed the country to defeat the Whites' – and the anti-Communist blockade by the Western powers was strangling Moscow's access to trade and investment. So industrialisation would have to be financed by heroic sacrifices on the part of the workers, and by the ruthless confiscation of wealth from the former privileged classes. During the first Five Year Plan, real wages fell dramatically. A continuous working week was introduced. Millions of prisoners from the labour camps, and members of the Komsomol (the Young Communist organisation) were used as unpaid labour. The Five Year Plans, with their rigid system of central control and economic planning, set impossibly high targets and punitive timetables in every sector of industry. Yet the Soviet people rose to the challenge.

The first two Plans, between 1928 and 1937, achieved genuinely impressive results, with the emphasis on heavy industry. The Soviet Union became the world's second largest industrial producer, behind only the United States. Output doubled and gigantic new industrial centres were built almost from nothing. The River Dnieper was harnessed by a hydroelectric dam, fuelling plants that employed half a million people. The 140-mile Belomor Canal, linking the White Sea to the Baltic, was built by slave labour, at the cost of 9,000 lives. The lightning-fast construction of the gargantuan blast furnaces of Magnitogorsk in the Urals inspired a novel about the world record for pouring concrete, a feature film, and the iconic music – *Vremya Vperyod* (Time Go Faster) – that would introduce Soviet television news bulletins right up to 1991.

The surging energy of those years, the frantic drive to modernise Soviet industry, made machines and technology favoured subjects for the nation's culture. Music like Alexander Mosolov's driving, pounding overture *The Iron Foundry* (1926), with its splendid socialist bombast, all jagged rhythms and musical onomatopoeia, reflected the urgency of the industrialisation campaign. Novels such as Fyodor Gladkov's *Cement* (1925) and Nikolai

Ostrovsky's *How the Steel Was Forged* (1936) became best sellers. With no experience of modern industry, Russia was forced to recruit Western specialists to help build the thousands of tractors and tools needed to mechanise agriculture through collectivisation. But when targets were not met, they quickly became convenient scapegoats – branded 'wreckers' and saboteurs – whose well-publicised trials reminded the people that foreigners were still the enemy. In March 1933, five British engineers from the electrical contractor Metropolitan-Vickers were arrested on charges that they had used their cover as businessmen to spy on the USSR. After intensive interrogation by the Cheka secret police (now known by the acronym OGPU), one of the men, Leslie Charles Thornton, signed a remarkably detailed confession:

> All our spying operations on U.S.S.R. territory are directed by the British Intelligence Service, through their agent, C.S. Richards, who occupies the position of Managing Director of the Metropolitan-Vickers Electrical Export Company, Ltd. Spying operations on U.S.S.R. territory were directed by representatives of the above-mentioned British firm, who are contractors, by official agreements, to the Soviet Government, for the supply of turbines and electrical equipment and the furnishing of technical aid agreement. British personnel were gradually drawn into the spying organisation after their arrival on U.S.S.R. territory and instructed as to the information required.

The trial of the five men met with a furious reaction from Britain. Prime Minister Stanley Baldwin declared that the accused were innocent, and MPs demanded the breaking off of commercial and diplomatic relations with Moscow. The British press was unanimous in condemning the Russians for torturing confessions out of their prisoners. 'This is an ordeal conducted in the name of justice,' the *Observer* declared, 'but bearing no resemblance to any judicial proceedings that civilisation knows.' The Soviet prosecutor, Andrei Vyshinsky, making the first of what would be many high-profile appearances in Stalin's political trials, was described by the *Daily Express* as a 'carroty-haired, red-faced Russian [who] spat insults ... and pounded the table'. And *The Times* fretted, 'Great anxiety is felt as to what is happening to [the prisoners] in prison between the sittings of the court. Those long acquainted with Chekist methods think their lives are in danger.'

The response from Moscow was to publish declarations from all the Britons declaring that they had never been treated with greater politeness and courtesy. Allan Monkhouse's statement was positively gushing:

> They were extraordinarily nice to me and exceedingly reasonable in their questioning. My examiners seemed first-rate men who knew their job. The OGPU prison is the last word in efficiency, entirely clean, orderly and well organised. This is the first time that I have ever been arrested, but I have visited English prisons and can attest that the OGPU quarters are much superior. The OGPU officials showed every concern for my comfort …

But the accused engineers withdrew their 'confessions' in court. London threatened a trade embargo and the case ended with three of the men being deported and two others given short jail sentences.

For native Soviet workers, the bullying was much worse. Breaches of work discipline could be punished by death, or the withdrawal of ration cards, which sometimes meant the same thing. Workers who criticised the pace or the purpose of industrialisation schemes – driven by distant bureaucrats in Moscow with no understanding of the reality on the ground – were labelled ideologically unsound. Relentless purges instilled constant anxiety – a great motivating factor, as the playwright Alexander Afinogenov pointed out in 1932 in his remarkably outspoken play *Fear*:

> We live in an era of great fear … The overriding motivation for 80 per cent of Soviet citizens is fear … the workers are called the masters of the country now, but their mind is afraid: the manual labourer develops a persecution complex, constantly striving to catch up and do better, gasping for breath in the endless race for production.

Unlike the Metropolitan-Vickers case, show trials of Soviet citizens rarely ended with token sentences. In the so-called Shakhty trial of March 1928,

53 coalmine managers whose pits had failed to meet the party's production targets were accused of deliberately sabotaging the Soviet economy. They were alleged to have conspired with 'class enemies' inside the USSR and hostile governments abroad to undermine the country's progress towards socialism, a charge that was classed as treason and subject to the death penalty. On 13 April, Stalin told the politburo that 'this counter-revolutionary group of bourgeois "experts" [the defendants] carried out their work for five years, receiving instructions from the anti-Soviet organisations of international capital … For five years this counter-revolutionary group of "experts" was engaged in sabotaging our industry, causing boiler explosions, wrecking turbines and so on. And all this time we were oblivious to everything …

The reason the authorities were oblivious to the defendants' sabotage was almost certainly because it did not exist; the failure to meet production quotas was most likely the result of incompetence and outdated equipment. But the state needed scapegoats for its economic failings and it needed high-profile punishments *pour encourager les autres*. Five of the Shakhty defendants were executed and 44 others sent to the Gulag. The new crime of 'economic wrecking' was added to the Soviet penal code as part of Article 58 (Counter-revolutionary activity), punishable by death for the offender and ten years in jail for his relatives.

Two years later, another show trial was deemed to be necessary, and this time leading Soviet economists and engineers were put in the dock. They were charged with belonging to a shadowy 'Industrial Party' backed by the governments of France and Britain for the purpose of overthrowing the Soviet regime. The defendants were said to have plotted to sabotage industry and communications in strategic areas in order to pave the way for an invasion by foreign forces. Again, five were sentenced to death and the rest sent to the camps. The following month, Stalin told the Congress of Socialist Industry that they must draw the correct lessons from the 'prolific growth of wrecking activities' in the country: 'The underlying cause of wrecking activities is the class struggle,' he told the conference. 'The class enemy furiously resists the socialist offensive … We must remain vigilant in the battle against capitalism.'

To help keep the people striving to fulfil the Five Year Plans, Soviet propaganda created a new national mythology. Its heroes were the workers themselves, and they were celebrated in literature, art and music. Trotsky boasted that the New Soviet Man would 'point out places for mountains and for passes, change the course of rivers and lay down rules for the ocean'. Almost immediately, a popular song hit the streets, picking up on Trotsky's words, deifying the working man:

> Ships sail and bridges rise aloft.
> You alone made the buildings,
> You change the rivers' course
> This is not the work of god,
> But the work of you alone ...
> There is no higher power than the working man.

The unmistakable message was that workers must live up to the godlike image that had been created for them. By the mid 1930s, the focus was on a new breed of superheroes, the shock brigades, who would lead the charge of industrial expansion. The semi-official bard of the revolution, Vladimir Mayakovsky, was again on hand to give them a resounding launch:

> Onwards, shock brigades!
> From workshops to factories!
> Today the revolutionary fights
> On the barricades of industry!
> Puff out our collective chest ...
> And deep into the Russian darkness
> Hammer in the lights
> Like nails ...
> Pour out electric power
> Like a river.
> Keep up, keep up!
> Outpace the Five Year Plan!
> Onwards, with no rest days;

Onwards, with a giant's steps.
The Five Year Plan
Complete in four!
Now socialism will rise,
Genuine, real, alive.

'March of the Shock Brigades' is Soviet agitprop at its best – in Russian it is marvellously inventive poetry with a powerful, intoxicating message. With the state urging the people to fulfil the Five Year Plans in four years – and then even in three – the concept of 'socialist competition' drove factory to race against factory; worker against worker. In August 1935, Alexei Stakhanov, a coalminer in the Donbass region, mined 102 tons of coal in a single shift, vastly more than his 7-ton quota. The following month, he mined a staggering 227 tons. A public holiday was named in his honour; films and songs lauded him as the new breed of worker hero. Stakhanov was promoted to manage a coalmine and then to help run the industry as a state official and member of the Soviet parliament. In December, his exploits earned him a place on the cover of *Time* magazine.

The Soviet authorities used his example to encourage others to exceed work quotas and break production records. 'Stakhanovite' workers were rewarded with better pay, apartments and holidays; some were given the untold luxury of a car. In reality, many of their achievements were embellished or even made up. It seems that while Stakhanov did indeed mine the remarkable amounts of coal claimed by the authorities, he was assisted during his shift by a team of other miners and newly introduced extraction machinery. But his feats and those of other record breakers allowed Stalin to raise production targets for everyone else and to denounce those who criticised the breakneck pace of industrialisation. The Stakhanovites were paraded at mass gatherings and lauded personally by Stalin. At a Kremlin banquet in May 1938 in honour of the 'miracle' of Stakhanovism, he could hardly restrain his enthusiasm:

Here, sitting at this table, are Comrades Stakhanov and Papanin. They have no scientific degrees, but who does not know that in their work in industry

Stakhanov and the Stakhanovites have upset the existing standards, which were established by well-known scientists and technologists, have shown that they were antiquated, and have introduced new standards that conform to the requirements of real science and technology? There you see what so-called miracles can still be performed! ... I give you a toast to Lenin and Leninism! To Stakhanov and the Stakhanovites!

Tatiana Fyodorova was a member of the Komsomol and grew up idolising the workers of the shock brigades. She became a Stakhanovite worker herself when her team set a record for tunnel construction in building the Moscow metro. Her speech of thanks in 1932 reflected the energy and enthusiasm the movement inspired:

We live so well, our hearts are so joyful, in no other country are there such happy young people as us, we're the happiest young people, and on behalf of all young people I want to thank our party and our dear comrade Stalin for this joy that we have.

Tatiana Fyodorova was personally congratulated by Stalin. Even 60 years later, after all the revelations of the iniquities of the Stalinist system, she continued to express her admiration for the ideals of Stakhanovism and the man who created it:

Stalin set a task, build this or build that ... and thanks to the fact that people trusted him and this enthusiasm of young people, it was possible. Remember this was a country where people were illiterate, were in virtual darkness, wore birch-bark shoes. Even now I think it's something out of a fairy tale. How was it possible in one of the most difficult times to raise these great construction sites? It was only possible through the unity of the people, and the love of the people for their idol. Because for us Stalin was an idol.

The Five Year Plans continued, remarkably, until 1986. The first thing I saw plastered on the street walls when I visited Moscow as a child was Lenin's exhortation that 'Communism is socialism plus the electrification of the whole country!' By then, the dead hand of centralised planning had plunged the Soviet economy into crisis. But even as early as 1934, when the party's so-called 'Congress of the Victors' met to celebrate the achievements of collectivisation and industrialisation, the reality behind the myth was tarnished.

The lot of the ordinary Soviet worker was far from the glamorous life of the Stakhanovites. Jobs and labour were abundant, but wages low. Crash industrialisation had doubled the urban population and cities were straining at the seams. Little new housing was being built, so the state squeezed workers into smaller and smaller spaces. Members of the former bourgeoisie, the so-called 'non-people', were evicted to make way for the workers. To maximise space, a system of communal living was introduced, with several families billeted in one apartment, sharing kitchens, bathrooms and even bedrooms. The *kommunalka* concept echoed the Bolshevik rejection of 'bourgeois' values such as private property and the nuclear family. In practice it was a nightmare. Feuds broke out between residents, property was stolen and murders committed. With police informers everywhere, people felt spied on in their own homes. Mistrust was rife; tensions rose. Workers on big industrial projects were forced to live in tents.

As a further measure of control, the party introduced internal passports in 1932, listing the bearer's ethnic origin, employment and social status. A new system of compulsory residence permits – the so-called *propiska* – made it hard to change address or move to desirable cities like Moscow and Leningrad (as Petrograd was now known). And all the while, as the average city dweller struggled, Communist Party officials in the *nomenklatura* accumulated privileges, from dachas to cars, fancy goods and food. Popular resentment was bubbling beneath the surface. Stalin's drive for industrialisation had modernised the national economy at the cost of widespread misery for the Soviet people. It provoked both admiration and furious condemnation, often split on generational lines. The British diplomat Gareth Jones summed up the clash in an article he wrote for the London *Evening Standard* in March 1933:

A few days ago I stood in a worker's cottage outside Moscow. A father and a son, the father a skilled worker in a Moscow factory and the son a member of the Young Communist League [Komsomol], stood glaring at one another. The father, trembling with excitement, lost control of himself and shouted at his Communist son: 'It is terrible now. We workers are starving. Disease is carrying away numbers of us workers and the little food there is is uneatable. That is what you have done to our Mother Russia.' The son cried back: 'But look at the giants of industry which we have built. Look at the new tractor works. Look at the Dneprostroy [a giant dam]. That construction has been worth suffering for.' 'Construction indeed!' was the father's reply: 'What's the use of construction when you've destroyed all that's best in Russia?'

CHAPTER TWENTY-NINE

The arts have long been Russia's other world, a flourishing garden of creativity when political discourse was choked by intolerant autocracy. They defied and triumphed over censorship and repression, offering Russians a better vision of themselves.

The revolutions of 1917 had sparked hopes of a golden age for the arts. Painters, writers and composers seized the opportunity of untrammelled freedom with febrile innovation. The poets Alexander Blok, Andrei Bely and Vladimir Mayakovsky produced some of their most important work; the writers Mikhail Zoshchenko and Mikhail Bulgakov pushed at the bounds of satire and distorted realism; Kasimir Malevich and the Suprematists took painting into new regions in search of abstract geometric purity; the Constructivists, Alexander Rodchenko, Vladimir Tatlin and others strove to square the circle between the concrete forms of architecture and photography and the values of 'art for art's sake'; musical experimentalism broke through the barriers of harmony, overflowed into jazz and orchestras without conductors. The trend was avant-garde, dispensing with the constraints of the old realism, looking ever more intensely to unleash the power of pure imagination. At first the regime was tolerant, preoccupied with other more pressing matters. But by the mid 1920s, the Communist leadership was looking disapprovingly at the radicalism and the abstraction, beginning to shape the doctrine that would eventually insist on all art being made to serve the aims of socialism.

From 1932, literature was brought under the control of the Soviet Writers' Union, and the bureaucrats who ran it took it upon themselves to police the work of authors, poets and playwrights, defining what was acceptable and what was not, according to the dictates of the party. In 1934, the First Congress of Soviet Writers' Union adopted the doctrine of Socialist Realism. From now on, it decreed, all art must depict man's struggle for socialist progress towards a better life. The creative artist would now serve the proletariat by being realistic, optimistic and heroic. All forms of experimentalism were degenerate and un-Soviet. Only official art – and only official artists – would be tolerated.

Stalin's claim to ownership of the arts and his insistence on art serving the state were nothing new in Russia. But the autocracy now exercised a stranglehold on society unprecedented in history, and it left writers, composers and artists with stark choices: to stay and do the tyrant's bidding; to flee; or to stay and oppose. In Stalin's Russia, a stray word could bring a death sentence; a poem could explode with the power of a bomb. The poet Osip Mandelstam wrote that 'Russia is the place where poetry really matters – here they shoot you for it.' He revelled in the power of his art, but he feared the man who did the shooting:

> We are living, but the ground is dead beneath our feet;
> Ten steps away our words cannot be heard.
> In half whispers we speak of the Kremlin mountain-man,
> The murderer, the peasant slayer …

Most of Mandelstam's poetry consists of exquisite, finely wrought verses lamenting the loss of culture and humanity in the new era of the revolution; their tone is restrained and understated, dedicated to redemption through art. Just once, however, he let rip with a savage expression of his hatred for Stalin, the *destroyer* of art and the hangman of the Russian soul:

> His fingers are oily as maggots,
> Words fall from his lips like lead weights.
> With his gleaming leather boots
> And his laughing cockroach whiskers,
> He flings decrees and diktats,
> Heavy as horseshoes, into peoples'
> Groins and eyes and foreheads.
> Every killing is a treat
> For the broad-chested Ossetian.

By 1934, the revolution was 17 years old and determined to exert its authority; the slightest word of criticism could mean the Gulag. Mandelstam was well aware of the danger. But still he read his 'epigram' about Stalin to friends and acquaintances, in a state of exultation, with an almost triumphant warning to all of them: 'Not a word about this or they'll shoot me.' Within weeks he was arrested.

For the ruler of one of the world's greatest empires, a man who murdered millions with little compunction, Stalin took a strangely obsessive interest in the fate of individual writers and artists, personally weighing and meting out rewards and punishments, seemingly consumed by the thought that his actions would be judged by a higher authority.

Even though Mandelstam had insulted and humiliated him, Stalin sought guidance on whether this was a truly great poet or whether he could exterminate him with impunity. He rang Boris Pasternak, late at night and with no warning, to ask for his opinion. Terrified by the Georgian voice on the end of the line – the voice of the man Bukharin described as 'Genghis Khan with a telephone' – Pasternak equivocated. He answered ambiguously and spoke about the values of poetry. He asked Stalin if they could talk about life and death. But he didn't have the courage to say, 'Yes, Mandelstam is a great poet.' Stalin lost patience and put the phone down. Within a few days, Mandelstam had been sent to a labour camp, where he would perish. Pasternak's son, Yevgeny, told me his father was haunted by the memory of that phone call for the rest of his life:

> Stalin wanted to know if my father knew about Mandelstam's poem, but he avoided a straight reply … By telling Stalin he wanted to talk about life and death, he was really saying he wanted to talk about all the crimes that were being carried out in Stalin's name; it was a terrible, dangerous conversation … Luckily Stalin hung up the phone when he did; otherwise it would have meant death for my father.

Stalin's own tastes in music and literature were notoriously staid; although well-read and interested in the arts, he disliked experimentation and the avant-garde. Ultimately, he was interested only in what could further the cause of the Communist revolution. And to be effective as propaganda, art had to be comprehensible by the masses of ordinary people; anything more complicated, innovative or original was by definition useless and, worse still, potentially dangerous.

The Futurist poets – most importantly, Vladimir Mayakovsky – embraced the revolution and proclaimed the power of art and imagination. The Fellow Travellers produced modernist prose, not always to the taste of the arch conservatives in the Kremlin. The self-described Proletarians demanded that literature be subjugated to party control, claiming for themselves the right to speak for the party, but in the end they too fell foul of the Bolsheviks' shifting standards. Independent writers, including those who at first welcomed the revolution, found themselves marginalised and threatened.

A common reaction was simply to stop writing, to 'step on the throat of one's own song', as Mayakovsky put it. Isaak Babel defiantly told the First Congress of the Soviet Writers' Union in 1934, 'I am practising a new genre … perfecting the genre of silence.' It was a deliberately provocative statement, highlighting the regime's stifling of creative freedom. Babel had been a Bolshevik since the early days and his *Red Cavalry* short stories had received great public acclaim (see pp. 226). But he had become increasingly critical of Stalin and found it virtually impossible to have his work published. In addition, the witty, urbane Babel had had a sexual liaison with the wife of the head of the secret police, Nikolai Yezhov.

In May 1939, Babel was arrested. His common-law wife, Antonina Pirozhkova, was taken with him in the car to the Lubyanka, but released at the prison gate. In her moving memoirs of her husband, *At His Side* (1996), she recounts his last minutes of freedom:

> In the car, one of the [police]men sat in the back with Babel and me, while the other one sat in front with the driver. 'The worst part of this is that my mother won't be getting my letters,' Babel said. Then there was silence for a long time. I couldn't bring myself to say a single word. Babel asked the secret policeman sitting next to him, 'So I don't suppose you get too much sleep, do you?' And he even laughed. As we approached Moscow I said to Babel, 'I'll be waiting for you; it will be as if you've gone to Odessa, only

there won't be any letters.' He answered, 'I ask you to see that the child not be made miserable.' ... We drove to the Lubyanka prison and through the gates. The car stopped before the massive, closed door where two sentries stood guard. Babel kissed me hard and said, 'Some day we'll see each other.' And without looking back, he got out of the car and went through that door. I turned to stone. I could not even cry. I kept thinking, 'Will they not even give him a cup of tea? He can't start the day without it.'

Babel's unfinished works were confiscated and destroyed. His name was expunged from all reference works and he became a 'non-person' in the Soviet Union. His family was told he had been sent to a labour camp in Siberia, 'without the right of correspondence'. Left alone in Moscow, Pirozhkova heard nothing about her husband's fate for another 15 years, when she was curtly informed that he had 'died of cardiac arrest on 17 March 1941'.

But even that was a lie. Babel's bloodstained 'confession', ludicrously admitting to being a Western spy in the pay of the French secret services, was released after the collapse of the Soviet Union in 1991, together with a record of his trial and verdict. The proceedings, held in the private chambers of the NKVD director, Lavrenty Beria, lasted less than 20 minutes, at the end of which the prisoner was sentenced to death. A typed submission from Beria, requesting Stalin's permission to execute 356 'enemies of the USSR' is dated January 1940. Babel's is the twelfth name on the list and Stalin has scribbled in blue crayon, 'Agreed'.

In the stifling atmosphere of repression that descended on Russia in the 1930s, poetry took on a new, almost religious significance. Yevgeny Pasternak says his father was well aware of the secret, subversive power of what he wrote:

The knowledge of free poetry was the only thing that could take the place of free speech. Poetry came to encompass everything that was most important to us; everything we believed in, everything we yearned for ... It allowed us to keep alive the freedom of memory and independence of thought in the dark years when 'they' were trying to reduce us to nothing ... Because Stalin knew about my father, it meant his fate did not depend on the murderous petty bureaucrats who were able to crush so many other poets. But, you know, the terror was so thick and all-enveloping that who survived and who did not depended largely on the work of chance … or on the hand of God …

It seems that Stalin's personal interest in Pasternak's works saved him from extermination. When the NKVD asked for guidance on how to deal with Pasternak, Stalin wrote on the margin of the secret police report, 'Leave that cloud-dweller in peace.' Stalin's decisions were arbitrary and unpredictable. He thought of himself as the supreme authority on art, theatre, music and even linguistics. And it was that blinkered confidence in his own judgement that led him to spare one great poet and condemn another.

It was only a matter of time before the Great Leader would bring his philistine tastes to bear on a Russian musical scene that had been bursting with vitality and brilliance since the early years of the century. Russia had been blessed with a flowering of musical genius that included Alexander Scriabin, Sergei Rachmaninov, Igor Stravinsky and, in the years after 1917, the young Dmitri Shostakovich.

Stalin's first attempt to bring the composers to his socialist heel, in 1936, was sparked by a controversial opera. Shostakovich's musically daring, politically dubious *Lady Macbeth of the Mtsensk District* had been running to encouraging reviews for nearly two years when Stalin decided to go and see it for himself. So appalled was he by the modernity of the music and the sexually charged nature of the action that he stormed out of the auditorium. Two days later, *Pravda* published a withering condemnation of the work under the headline 'Muddle instead of Music', an article that signalled the end of artistic freedom in musical life. From now on, the joyful celebration of the proletariat was to be the only theme acceptable in Soviet culture.

When Shostakovich read the *Pravda* article, he was in no doubt it was written by Stalin himself. He knew he had become an enemy of the people and the conviction that his days were numbered never left him. When I visited Shostakovich's widow Irina in the Moscow apartment they shared, off Tverskaya Street just north of Red Square, his grand piano was there and she was still classifying the documents of his final years. Irina told me that after the *Pravda* attack fear became his constant companion. Even after Stalin's death he continued to look over his shoulder:

> It's terrible when an artist is persecuted. My husband was always under pressure. He was like the little bird in the old Russian poem: they capture him and squeeze him by the throat ... and then they tell him to sing! ... He was a nervous man ... physically frail ... he hated public appearances ... But it's wrong to say he was weak. He had great inner strength. All the attacks on him left him traumatised. But he had constancy and great decency. Morally he was strong.

For the rest of his life, Shostakovich felt he must constantly appease the authorities' lust for blood. He wrote the music they requested, but filled it with secret defiance: to those who listen carefully, there is a bitter, mocking strain in much of his work. He writes the triumphant music the regime demanded of him, but undermines it with an ironic flourish, or a cheeky quotation of his own initials 'DSCH' encoded in the notes (in German notation, 'S' is E flat and 'H' is B natural). His music says one thing, but means another.*

---

* If art can kill its creators, in the strange world of the old Soviet Union it seems it could also kill its tormentors. In 1969 the 'pre-premiere' of Shostakovich's Fourteenth Symphony – a private performance for Soviet officials, where the regime's musical enforcers would root out any deviations from official socialist doctrine – was attended by Pavel Apostolov, a critic who for years had persecuted Shostakovich and other composers. Shostakovich was by then a sick man, and in the recording of his introductory speech you can hear how weak his voice has become. Talking about his new work, the ailing composer says he has chosen to write a piece about death and takes Soviet society to task for refusing to talk about the subject as if it didn't exist. It was clearly not a welcome discourse to the official arbiters of public taste in the audience. When the symphony was played, with its settings of poems all concerned with the subject of death, Apostolov rose to his feet and forced his way down the row of seats to walk out of the hall. As the door crashed behind him, Shostakovich and most of the audience thought the critic was demonstrating his disapproval of the content of the symphony and that political retribution would follow. But when they came out, they found an ambulance outside. Apostolov had been having a heart attack and had died as the last notes of the symphony were being played. For the Moscow intelligentsia, who had suffered so much at the hands of bureaucrats like Apostolov, this was the blackest of black comedy. The apparatchik killed by a symphony. Such was the power of art.

After the scandal over *Lady Macbeth*, Shostakovich made a show of atonement by writing a new symphony – his fifth – that would be tuneful and uplifting, in line with the party's demands. He even gave it the subtitle 'A Soviet artist's response to just criticism'. And it seems to have calmed Stalin's rage. The work's finale, with its bombastic D major fanfares is, on the face of it, upbeat and optimistic, a very 'Soviet' moment of triumph. But listen and hear the hollowness and stifled anger within. The composer is not cheering, but screaming against the system.

In the scherzo of his Tenth Symphony, written at the time of Stalin's death in 1953, Shostakovich unleashes the lifetime of pent-up fury he has nursed against the man who tried to stifle his music. It is the symphonic equivalent of Mandelstam's fatal poem denouncing Stalin and his crimes. The wild, hammering rhythms of the music are relieved only by the appearance in the following movement of Shostakovich's own four-note musical signature. Now the composer seems to be offering his personal testimony: 'This I have experienced; this I have witnessed. I have seen the barbarity and survived to tell the story.' Even though Stalin had been dead for six months by the time the symphony was first performed, Shostakovich remained haunted by the fear of him. He confirmed the true meaning of the portraits in his work only in interviews that he insisted be kept secret until after his death.

Like Shostakovich, Anna Akhmatova knew the full ferocity of the dictator's rage. She was the first of the great poets to be banned by Stalin, in 1925. Her husband, the poet Nikolai Gumilev, had been executed in 1921 as part of the random killings carried out by the state in response to an imagined anti-revolutionary plot.* Her son Lev was arrested in 1935, when Akhmatova was at the height of her poetic powers. She spent years trying to free Lev from the Gulag, a personal Calvary that her great poem *Requiem* (1935–40) made into an enduring memorial for all those who trod the same lonely path. In

---

* Gumilev was arrested in August 1921 on fabricated charges of plotting to overthrow the state. Numerous appeals were made on his behalf, but Lenin and Dzerzhinsky remained unmoved. When Dzerzhinsky was asked if they were entitled to shoot one of the leading poets in Russia he replied: 'Are we entitled to make an exception for a poet and still shoot the others?'

one of the work's most remarkable passages, Akhmatova describes standing in the endless prison queue of mothers and wives. When someone in the queue, a woman with blue lips, recognises her and asks 'Can you describe this?' she replies, 'Yes, I can.' As with Shostakovich, the poet announces, 'I am a witness and I am a writer; perhaps something will survive of what I write':

> Not under foreign skies
> Nor under foreign wings protected,
> I was with my people in those hours,
> There where unhappily my people were ...
> I pray not only for myself,
> But also for all those who stood there
> In bitter cold, or in the July heat,
> Under that red blind prison-wall ...
> I should like to call you all by name,
> But they have lost the lists ...
> I have woven for them a great shroud
> Out of the poor words I overheard them speak.
> I remember them always and everywhere,
> And if they shut my tormented mouth,
> Through which a hundred million of my people cry,
> Let them also remember me ...

The verses of *Requiem* were so incendiary that they could not be written down; Akhmatova and her friend Lydia Chukovskaya committed them to memory and burned the manuscript. Akhmatova speaks of the power of poetry and the need to keep it alive under the harsh conditions of Stalinist Russia. 'We will preserve you, Russian speech,' she writes, 'from servitude in foreign chains, keep you alive, great Russian word, fit for the songs of our children's children...' Akhmatova's colleague, Nadezhda Mandelstam, the widow of Osip, said later that all over Russia there were little old ladies who hardly dared go to sleep at night for fear of forgetting their husband's verses. Despite years of abuse from the regime, which derided her sensual-sacred poetry as the ravings of a 'half nun, half harlot', Akhmatova's poetry

retained an astounding level of popularity among the Soviet public, circulating widely in *samizdat* or simply learned by heart.

Then, in 1941, with the Nazis at the gates, Stalin relented. Knowing the
resonance of her voice for a nation under threat, he allowed her to publish
and to broadcast on state radio. Akhmatova was suddenly useful for the
regime. She responded with the glorious patriotic verses of her lyric poem
'Courage' (1942). Recognising her popularity, Stalin had her flown out of
besieged Leningrad to the safety of Tashkent. On the aeroplane, she became
aware that below, across the endless terrain of Russia, her exiled son had
taken the same journey under very different circumstances. In her epic
Poem Without a Hero (1940–65), she writes:

> Opening before me was the road
> Down which so many have trod,
> Down which my son was led.
> And that funeral procession was long,
> Amid the festive and crystal
> Silence of the Siberian land …

As she foresaw, Akhmatova's triumph was through her art. She wrote that
Pushkin's glory was to be remembered and known and loved by successive
generations in all the details of his life, while the monarchs and officials
who tormented him – for all their great titles and ranks – have been forgotten, or reduced to footnotes in Pushkin's work. She hardly doubted that she
would enjoy the same posthumous vindication.

Akhmatova survived into her seventies, along with Nadezhda Mandelstam, who said she had 'drawn a winning lottery ticket that allowed her to
live out her days'. Between them they memorised and preserved the poetry
of a generation: they were, literally, keeping the culture of Russia alive in
their heads until the great barbarism had passed.

For Boris Pasternak, however, a more public trial awaited. His seminal
novel *Doctor Zhivago*, smuggled to the West and rewarded with a Nobel
Prize in 1958, thrust him into the international spotlight. Zhivago's questioning of the collectivist ideals of Soviet Communism enraged the Kremlin

and brought a public campaign of vilification against its author. In Pasternak's dacha in the village of Peredelkino outside Moscow, the museum's curator showed me the desk at which he had received, accepted and then refused the prize under fierce pressure from the Soviet leadership. The furore, she said, left him a broken man. He was expelled from the Writers' Union, threatened and called a traitor because he had had his novel published abroad in the 'hostile' West. Yevgeny Pasternak told me the pressure weakened his father's already fragile health:

> He was delighted and happy when he got the letter offering him the Nobel Prize. He naively thought he would be able to accept it. But the authorities threatened him. If he went to collect the prize, they would never let him back in the country ... They would arrest those close to him ... I saw him that day, and it was quite clear what a terrible blow it had all been to him.

Pasternak fell ill. When the doctors were called, they diagnosed a heart attack, but also a previously undetected and very aggressive cancer of the lungs. On the day of Pasternak's death, 30 May 1960, there was no official announcement in the Soviet media, but handwritten notices were posted in Moscow saying that his funeral would take place two days later in Peredelkino. The authorities had the notices torn down, but they appeared again and thousands of people arrived on 2 June to pay homage. The poet's coffin was carried by his son Yevgeny, and by Yevgeny's half-brother Leonya, across the fields to the place where he's buried in the local cemetery.

Mandelstam, Babel, Pasternak, Akhmatova and Shostakovich had chosen to remain in Russia after 1917. But in the immediate aftermath of the revolution, another road had been open to those who had doubts about the new regime, and many artists, writers and musicians took it. The wave of émigrés who left Russia in those early years before the Bolsheviks closed the country's borders settled chiefly in Western Europe. Russian colonies sprang up in Berlin, Prague and the south of Italy. But the largest number settled in France, colonising certain *arrondissements* of Paris that are still noticeably Russian even today.

The exiles brought with them all the acrimony and hatred that had riven Russian society at home. Rival political groupings continued their feuds on the streets of Paris. Neighbours mistrusted neighbours. And, after 1924, everyone feared the vengeance of Stalin. Rumours of Red agents carrying out murders and kidnaps circulated constantly. Few slept easy in their beds.

The young Sergei Efron was a former soldier with the White Army. He had impeccable anti-Communist credentials and he was trusted in émigré circles. But unbeknown to his friends and family, he had been recruited by Soviet intelligence. Efron was asked by his Communist controllers to take part in the murder of a Soviet defector, Ignace Reiss, and he agreed to do so. But when the French police discovered he had been involved in the plot, his Soviet spymasters smuggled him out of France and took him back to Russia.

Efron's story was far from unique; treachery and defections were rife among the émigrés. But Sergei was also married to one of the great poets of modern times, Marina Tsvetaeva, author of some of the most remarkable and passionate lyric verse in the Russian canon.

After a series of youthful affairs with both men and women, she had fled Russia with Efron, the man she called Seryozha, and whom she spoke of as her only true love. When his involvement with the Reds was revealed, Tsvetaeva's friends in the Paris émigré community regarded her as an enemy. She was shunned and alone. Her daughter Alya had already gone back to Russia, and now her husband had gone too. Tsvetaeva felt she had no choice but to follow them.

She undoubtedly knew the dangers. She had had a brief affair with the literary critic Dmitry Svyatopolk-Mirsky, who later returned to the USSR and was executed by the Bolsheviks. But Tsvetaeva now found herself being forced down the same path. It was 1939, and Stalin's purges were swallowing their victims; she was going back into the heart of the Terror.

Efron had initially been rewarded for his services to the regime and given a dacha not far from Moscow. Tsvetaeva lived there with him for a while. But in early 1940, Alya and another friend were arrested. Under torture, they incriminated Efron as a French spy and he too was arrested. With her family in jail – her husband soon executed and her daughter sent to the Gulag –

Tsvetaeva's life was unbearable. She had found peace neither in exile nor back in Russia, and the theme of suicide began to appear in her poetry:

> What tears in eyes now,
> Weeping with anger and with love …
> What a black mountain
> Has blocked the world from the light.
> It's time – it's time – it's time
> To give God … his ticket back.

Later she wrote: 'The world considers me possessed of courage. But no one is more timid. I fear eyes, blackness, footsteps … for a year I have been taking the measure of death …'

Deprived of her family, with no means of support and too depressed even to write poetry, she hanged herself on 31 August 1941 in the provincial town of Elabuga, where she had been evacuated from the invading Nazis.

As well as poets like Tsvetaeva, the 3 million Russians who fled abroad after the revolution included great painters – Marc Chagall and Wassily Kandinsky; writers – Nabokov and Ivan Bunin; and composers such as Igor Stravinsky, Sergei Prokofiev and Rachmaninov. All were haunted by the knowledge that they could live neither in their native land nor without it. 'When I left Russia,' wrote Rachmaninov, 'I lost my desire to create. Devoid of my Homeland I have lost myself.'

The exiles felt keenly that the true Russia had ceased to exist in October 1917 and that they must keep the flame alive until the barbarians were driven out. They regarded themselves as the custodians of the real Russia, a society and a culture in exile. At their enforced distance from the physical Russia, they created an imaginary Russia, a Russia that never changed, in which they could live. The writer Ivan Bunin turned his villa in Grasse in the south of France into a sort of closed world where Russian was spoken and contemporary life was excluded. Unlike Rachmaninov, Stravinsky never lost the will to compose, but his works of the 1920s – in particular the ballet *Le Baiser de la fée* (The Fairy's Kiss) – appear as a despairing attempt to recreate a world that is lost. The music is filled with nostalgia, with children's songs from his youth and Tchaikovskian melodies saturated with longing for the comforting past.

In his memoir, *Speak Memory* (1951), the writer Vladimir Nabokov describes the pain of being cut off from that past, the constant unexpressed yearning to return. He speaks of exiles who never unpacked their suitcases, who 'imitated in foreign cities a dead civilisation, now remote, almost legendary'. His writing celebrates the Russia he knew as a child and idealised in exile in Europe and the United States. But the sweet nostalgia is tinged with the bitter knowledge that the object of his love has been desecrated by the new rulers of Russia. He always said he would never go back, even if he were able to:

> The revolution was blood, deceit and oppression. All it can promise now is material articles: second-hand, philistine values; copies of Western gadgets and caviar for the generals … I detest it. Any palace in Italy is better than that [going back]. I do not wish to spoil the picture of the haunts of my childhood which I have kept in my mind.

But in the early days of his exile, many of Nabokov's stories do deal with the desire and the fear of going back. In his Gogolian fantasy 'A Visit to the Museum' (1938), the narrator searches for an old Russian painting in a French art gallery. The visit turns into a dreamlike fantasy in which he wanders through endless, nightmarishly expanding corridors until he opens a final door and emerges not in France but in the snowy streets of St Petersburg, now transformed into a terrifying alien place by the Bolshevik regime:

> At first, the quiet and the snowy coolness of the night, somehow strikingly familiar, gave me a pleasant feeling after my wanderings … but there was a twinge in my heart … Alas! It was not the Russia I remembered, but the factual Russia of today, forbidden to me, hopelessly slavish and hopelessly my native land …

Nabokov's terror at the Sovietisation of his homeland and the destruction of his childhood paradise by the Bolsheviks was reinforced by the fate of his own father, who had been an official in the Provisional Government between February and October 1917. Nabokov's affection for his father permeates the pages of his work, and the circumstances of his violent death would make a traumatic impression on him. After taking his family into exile in 1918, Nabokov Senior had continued to campaign for the liberal democratic values of his party, the Constitutional Democrats or KaDety. In March 1922, he travelled to Berlin to chair a KaDet conference at which the party's former leader Pavel Miliukov was due to speak. The two men had quarrelled and were now political opponents, but Nabokov believed in tolerance and gave his colleague a warm introduction. As he was speaking, two former tsarist officers ran towards the stage singing the tsarist anthem and shooting from revolvers at the startled Miliukov. Nabokov was in his fifties, unfit and overweight, but he jumped off the stage and wrestled one of the men to the floor. His action undoubtedly saved Miliukov's life. Nabokov himself was not so lucky. The other assassin fired two shots into his chest, killing him instantly.

For some émigrés, the pull of home was overwhelming. Sergei Prokofiev had left Russia after the revolution, carving out a successful career for himself as a pianist and composer in Western Europe and North America. But in 1936, at the height of Stalin's terror, steadfastly refusing to acknowledge the danger he was putting himself in, he elected to return to Moscow. Prokofiev's son Sviatoslav, who was a young child at the time and remembers the train journey eastwards as a great adventure, told me that Russia's lure was too great for his father to resist:

> He blamed the vandalism of the Bolsheviks ... My father writes in his diary, 'I thought it [the revolution] was inevitable, but it will soon stop boiling and the sickness will finish.' Like all Russians living abroad, the real émigrés, they all were very homesick, nostalgic for their motherland. He said in his diary, 'What the hell am I doing in the West, while my music is so much needed in my country?'

Going back showed a naivety on Prokofiev's part about what was happening in Russia, or – perhaps more likely – deliberate self-delusion. For him and other exiled artists the feeling of isolation in a Western world where their work was misunderstood, where the intellectual classes admired Stalin and disdained those who fled from him, was simply too much to bear. The Bolsheviks promised Prokofiev wealth, fame and privilege if he came back. He believed them ... and went.

At first his life in the Soviet Union went well. He felt valued as a composer performing an important public function. He was initially allowed to write what he wanted with no official interference. He composed *Peter and the Wolf* (1936) to great success and, according to Sviatoslav, believed he could remain apolitical, detached from the realities of the Soviet world. 'In the beginning he was just very happy. He saw his friends and literally plunged into the Soviet musical life. But soon came the terrible 1937 years with their purges. He was perplexed when he learned about the arrests of some of his friends.'

Chief among them was Prokofiev's old ally, the distinguished theatre director Vsevolod Meyerhold, who was working on the composer's opera *Semyon Kotko* (1940) at the time of his arrest in June 1939. Meyerhold's 'crimes' were never formally identified, but his work in the theatre was experimental and avant-garde. He was deeply opposed to the restrictive dogma of socialist realism and made a speech in which he lamented the artistic straitjacket culture was being placed in. After he was arrested and taken to the Lubyanka, unknown men broke into his flat and smashed everything in sight. His wife, the distinguished and beautiful actress Zinaida Raikh, was left dead on the floor of the kitchen with her eyes gouged out. It was a stark image of the cultural desecration practised by Stalin's regime.

Meyerhold's prolonged torture at the hands of the NKVD left him a broken man. He was reduced to writing terrified pleas for clemency that were made public only in 1991 when the KGB archives were opened by the government of Boris Yeltsin:

They are torturing me. They make me lie face down and beat my spine and feet. Then they beat my feet from above ... when my legs are covered with internal haemorrhaging, they beat the red-blue-and-yellow bruises ... it feels like boiling hot water. I howl and weep from the pain ... I twist

and squeal like a dog. Death, oh most certainly, death is easier than this.
I begin to incriminate myself in the hope I will go quickly to the scaffold.

Meyerhold went to his execution in February 1940, reportedly shouting 'Long live Stalin', believing, like many others, that the great Father of the Nation could not possibly be aware of the crimes that were being carried out in his name.

Sergei Prokofiev himself was spared arrest, possibly by his international reputation, possibly by the efforts he made to write the sort of socialist realist music the regime demanded from him. Prokofiev's *Cantata for the 20th Anniversary of the October Revolution* (1936–7) was written spontaneously, without official pressure. The composer was thrilled by the scale and ambition of the task, and he created a masterpiece, using several orchestras, a folk ensemble and settings of the words of Karl Marx's *Das Kapital*. The work has only recently been revived in the West, to great critical acclaim. It languished unheard for many years, possibly – according to Sviatoslav Prokofiev – because of its overt Communist message:

> People like to say, 'Oh, he wrote music for the Bolsheviks,' but they forget that Mozart and Bach, they also wrote cantatas by command. But it seems to me that some parts sound quite satirical and even ironical. For example, there is a personage Lenin and he is shouting out revolutionary slogans and the orchestra also plays very loud and Lenin with his typical accent shouts, 'The revolution began!' or something like that. Well, of course, the party bosses did not like it …

Prokofiev's miscalculation over the *October Cantata* was to set words by Lenin and Stalin. The party apparatchiks, who already nursed a personal resentment against him because of his successful time in the West, denounced this as a presumptuous sacrilege and had the work refused. It was never played during the composer's lifetime. Prokofiev, in the words of his son, finally began to realise 'something very bad is happening in this country'. But it was too late. His requests to travel abroad were refused and, in 1948, Stalin's cultural commissar, Andrei Zhdanov, condemned his music at the Congress of the Soviet Composers' Union. A few days later, during the conference, his wife was arrested. Lina Prokofiev, Sviatoslav's mother, spent the next eight years in the Gulag. His father's reputation – and his health – were shattered. Prokofiev died the same day as Stalin, on 5 March 1953. There were no flowers for his funeral because they'd all been requisitioned for the Great Leader and Teacher.

On one of the best streets in central Moscow sits an unusual and beautiful private house. It has glazed brick walls, a *style moderne* frieze of irises, spectacular stained glass and a fantastic staircase of polished limestone. It had belonged to a millionaire banker who fled from Russia after the 1917 revolution, but in 1931 Stalin presented it to the writer, Maxim Gorky, the head of the Soviet Writers' Union and favourite of the Bolshevik regime. As always, Stalin expected something in return for his largesse. He was determined to see the arts serving socialism, and Gorky was a major author who lent considerable weight to the regime's case.

Initially a fervent supporter of the revolution, Gorky had been appalled by the abuses of power under the Bolsheviks and had gone into exile in 1921. He spent eight years in southern Italy, wavering between genuine revulsion at the revolution's cynical violence and regret that he had left behind the trappings of power and influence. From the mid 1920s, Stalin tried to seduce Gorky back to Russia with promises of material wealth and high positions in the Soviet cultural world. The big new house, as well as dachas outside Moscow and in the Crimea, were some of the enticements the regime was offering. And Stalin knew how to appeal to Gorky's vanity. He was already a famous, wealthy writer, and would undoubtedly be a historic figure in Russian literature. But he agreed to serve as Stalin's henchman, despite knowing well the crimes his regime was committing.

As head of the Soviet Writers' Union from 1934 until his death in 1936, Gorky became an apologist for Soviet Communism. He championed collectivisation, the secret police and the repressions. He was a personal friend of Genrikh Yagoda, the bloodthirsty director of the NKVD. He wrote approvingly about the construction of the Belomor Canal, linking the White Sea to the Baltic, which was built by slave labour at the cost of 9,000 lives. Like the Western stooges who allowed themselves to be fooled by Stalin's rosy PR, Gorky too was a willing dupe. When taken on a visit to the Solovki labour camp, one of the Gulag's most feared prisons, he wrote glowingly of the good conditions the convicts were kept in. The camp had been specially prepared for Gorky's visit and the prisoners were given extra food, clothes and luxuries, including newspapers. The prisoners had been warned not to let on to their visitor that this was a show put on for his benefit, and none of them dared to risk doing so. But if you examine photographs of Gorky in the camp, you can see that the inmates are deliberately holding the newspapers upside down in a tacit signal to the outside world that all is not what it seems.

In return for his willing help, Gorky was fêted by Stalin and the other Soviet leaders, who were frequent visitors at his Moscow mansion. The main thoroughfare leading north from the Kremlin was renamed Gorky Street in his honour, and he became the regime's author number one: his books were published in vast numbers, and his work was taught in every school.

Within the constraints of his official position, it seems Gorky did what he could to protect fellow writers who were in danger of arrest and repression. His efforts were not always successful, and he never risked his own wellbeing, but compared to others, Gorky retained some elements of humanity and integrity. His murderous successor as head of the Writers' Union, Alexander Fadeyev, who personally signed death warrants for the extermination of his colleagues, had no such compunction. Yevgeny Pasternak, whose father was persecuted by Fadeyev, recalled an incident when his mother Zinaida went to plead for mercy:

> Fadeyev was superficially friendly: he had the dacha next door to us. When he was drunk, which was often, he would recite my father's poems by heart and praise them. But that day when Zinaida went to him to plead for clemency towards my father, he told her, 'Listen. I love your husband. But if they tell me to crush him, I shall do it without a moment's hesitation.'

In the Soviet Union, artists and writers who saved their own skins were understood. Those who did so at the cost of persecuting others were universally reviled.

The question of who collaborated with Stalin's regime is a vexed one. Hundreds of unprincipled, untalented painters, writers and composers produced reams of worthless propaganda. Tyrants like Fadeyev were complicit in crimes and repressions. But even the greatest artists went some way towards collaboration. Anna Akhmatova wrote a poem to Stalin to try to save her son from the camps. Osip Mandelstam did the same: it failed to save him, but it may have saved his wife Nadezhda. Much later, she said of those terrible years:

> People who had voices had their tongues cut out, and with the stump that remained they were forced to glorify the tyrant. The desire to live is insuperable and people accepted even this if it meant a little more life ...

Riddled with guilt and fearing retribution after the death of his protector Stalin, Alexander Fadeyev shot himself in 1956, prompting Boris Pasternak to comment, 'So, it seems Alexander Alexandrovich has rehabilitated himself.'

Fadeyev can no longer answer to the court of public opinion, but his opposite number at the Soviet Composers' Union lived on into his nineties and died only in 2007. Tikhon Khrennikov was personally appointed by Stalin in 1948 and – astoundingly – remained active in the post until 1991. For nearly half a century, he ruled Soviet music just as the ruthless Fadeyev ruled literature. In 1948, Khrennikov leapt to do Stalin's bidding by denouncing Shostakovich, Prokofiev and other leading composers after Stalin decreed that Soviet music must be cleansed of anti-socialist, bourgeois-Western elements. His diatribe resulted in humiliating public recantations from Shostakovich, Prokofiev, Nikolai Miaskovsky and Aram Khatchaturian. They were made to apologise for their musical 'crimes' and promise to write socialist music in the future. Khrennikov's defence, offered to me in an interview in his Moscow apartment shortly before his death, was that he was just following orders:

> Well yes, we had the decree of the Central Committee in 1948, when all the big names – Shostakovich, Prokofiev, Khatchaturian – were attacked for writing un-Soviet music. They were accused of writing music that had Western tendencies and was inimical to the Soviet people. As far as I am

concerned, they just told me – they forced me – to read out that speech attacking Shostakovich and Prokofiev. What else could I have done? If I'd refused, it could have been curtains for me … death. Stalin's word was law.

As with Gorky, opinions about Khrennikov are divided. 'Anti-Soviet' tendencies are less easy to identify in music than in written art forms, and composers suffered correspondingly less persecution than writers and poets. I have encountered more than one Russian musician willing to testify that Khrennikov did what he could to protect composers like Prokofiev and Shostakovich.* But, despite his initial hints at contrition, he remained proud of the power he wielded:

> My word was law! People knew I was appointed personally by Stalin and they were afraid of me. I was Stalin's commissar. When I said No! it meant No. They all treated me with respect. But, you know, under me no composer or musician was ever executed! Other unions, the writers and so on, they all had people arrested and executed. But not in my union. No one was ever executed.

Execution was not the only tragedy to befall Russia's artists and writers. The fate of the poets Vladimir Mayakovsky and Sergei Yesenin epitomises the destiny of many who loved, or tried to love the revolution. For the greatest among them it was a passionate, almost carnal *affaire*, shot through with euphoria, betrayal, despair and – all too often – suicide, an astoundingly common fate among poets and writers in the years after 1917. It was as if the revolution had heightened the intensity of existence until everything – art, poetry, love and politics – became a matter of life and death.

---

* Khrennikov's defence evokes some limited sympathy even from Shostakovich's widow Irina: 'Well, Dmitry used to say: "If it wasn't Khrennikov, someone else would have done it … maybe someone even worse." But Khrennikov was malicious and vindictive. He caused a great deal of harm. A great deal. He was always scheming. And now he tries to say it wasn't his fault … All the attacks on Dmitri left him traumatised. In 1948, it was really tough. They banned his music, he lost his job at the conservatoire. Life was hard. But he wrote his secret revenge: his music …'

Mayakovsky's verse heaves with the themes of love – love for a woman and love for the revolution. His early poetry is a vigorous, inventive call to arms, a fervent appeal to his own generation to rise up against the old world and hurry on the advent of the new. His epic poems 'Vladimir Ilyich Lenin' and 'Good!'; his poetic exhortations 'Left March!' and 'Ode to the Revolution'; and his ringing political slogans became the common currency of a generation. They are brimfull of confidence in the power of poetry and its central role in building the new society:

> The song and the verse
> Are a bomb and a flag;
> And the voice of the poet
> Raises the class to arms.
> Whoever sings today apart,
> He is against us.

But in the years after 1917 a skulking fear begins to appear, at first tangentially, then with greater insistence; an ever more powerful theme of unrequited sexual love, and a suggestion that the poet's love for the revolution may suffer the same fate.

Mayakovsky's poetry was innovative, fiercely individualistic and technically brilliant. The Futurists were the poets of the modern age. They declared their intention to 'throw Pushkin, Dostoevsky and Tolstoy from the steamship of modernity'. 'It is time for bullets to pepper the museums,' Mayakovsky announced. The Futurists wanted to renew language, revitalise society and create a new humankind, so their aims seemed perfectly in tune with those of the Bolsheviks.

But the leaders of the revolution were cultural conservatives. Lenin considered Mayakovsky's work to be 'nonsense, stupidity, double stupidity and pretentiousness'. By the late 1920s, Mayakovsky was out of love with the revolution. He wrote plays attacking the philistinism of Soviet society and the deadening bureaucracy of officialdom. By 1930, he had had enough. In a third-floor room in an apartment building just behind the Lubyanka, he took off his shoes and overcoat, sat down on the bed and shot himself.

For three-quarters of a century the room has been preserved exactly as he left it – his shoes on the floor, his overcoat on the bed and the complete works of Lenin on the bookshelf. His suicide note, in the form of a poem, suggests the poet's unrequited love had overwhelmed him:

> It's past one o'clock. You must have gone to bed.
> The Milky Way streams silver through the night.
> I'm in no hurry; with lightning telegrams
> I have no cause to wake or trouble you.
> And, as they say, the incident is closed.
> Love's boat has smashed against the daily grind.
> Now you and I are quits. Why bother then
> To balance mutual sorrows, pains and hurts.
> Behold what quiet settles on the world.
> Night wraps the sky in tribute from the stars.
> In hours like these, one rises to address
> The ages, history and all creation.

Mayakovsky's death sent shock waves through the Soviet Union. He had been the official poet of the regime, his verses were the soundtrack of the revolution. If *he* were disillusioned ...

Five years earlier, Yesenin, the mercurial peasant genius, had trod the same path of despair. A boisterous, spontaneous poet who toured the bars of Moscow reciting his verses, Yesenin too was a man of inexorable passions. He drank too much, got into fights and was briefly married to the American dancer Isadora Duncan, even though they didn't speak each other's languages. He tried his hardest to love the revolution and write the poetry it wanted from him, but kept coming back to the songs of love and nostalgia and respect for human beings that were supposed to have been left behind in the old world of the 'former' Russia. In his poems, you can hear Yesenin desperately trying and failing to come to terms with the new social order ('I want to be a poet/And a citizen/In the mighty Soviet state'). But ultimately, it was Yesenin's refusal to sing the dull, socialist song of Stalinist mediocrity that turned him into the *poète maudit* of literary legend, and ensured the undying affection in which Russians still hold him:

I am not your tame canary!
I am a poet!
Not one of your petty hacks.
I may be drunk at times,
But in my eyes
Shines the glorious light of perception!

Yesenin's lyrical evocations of the Russian countryside brought him fame. Schoolchildren learned his poetry by heart. But, like Mayakovsky, Yesenin fell out of love with the revolution. His poems started to express doubts about the new order, and his work met official disfavour. Alcoholism and a series of failed love affairs ended with him hanging himself in a Leningrad hotel in 1925, having written a poem in his own blood.

Yesenin's grave in the Vagankovskoe Cemetery in Moscow has been a place of pilgrimage ever since. His last lover killed herself on his tombstone on the first anniversary of his death. And even today I know that whenever I go there, a troupe of Moscow down-and-outs will eagerly recite Yesenin's verse in return for a little vodka money. The writer and critic Viktor Shklovsky lamented in the 1930s, 'Art must move organically, like the heart in the human breast, but they [the regime] want to regulate it like a train.' There was always something monomaniacal about the Bolsheviks. The love and lyricism of poets like Mayakovsky and Yesenin left them indifferent. Poetry was useful only if it was socialist poetry. Lenin famously said, 'I'm no good at art: art for me is a just an appendage, and when its use as propaganda – which we need at the moment – is over, we'll cut it out as useless: snip, snip!'

CHAPTER THIRTY

In St Petersburg, I was shown around a rather splendid five-room apartment in the central Petrogradsky district of the city. My guide was a local history enthusiast, and the flat was striking. The large entrance hall with its fine parquet floor leads into an enfilade of high-ceilinged rooms, including a voluminous library with leather-bound books in mahogany cabinets and hunting trophies on the wall. But the teak wireless set gives it away: the place has been suspended in time, preserved exactly as it was when the last inhabitants walked out of the door many decades ago. So luxurious are the furnishings and fittings that the first thought is of a noble family or a rich merchant living here in pre-revolutionary days. But why are there portraits of Stalin and Lenin hanging on the walls?

The answer lies in one of the great stories of Communist history. This was indeed the home of a pre-revolutionary millionaire, but in 1917 it was appropriated by the new Bolshevik government for a very important purpose. In an era when most families counted themselves lucky if they had a single room to themselves, this spacious apartment was allocated to just one man. Sergei Kirov was the Leningrad party boss, a politburo member and a key figure in the Soviet leadership. The elite group to which Kirov belonged enjoyed luxuries and privileges that the rest of the population could only dream of. Their cosseted lives were far removed from the everyday struggles of Soviet existence – as well as the comfortable apartments, they had access to private restaurants, health resorts and special shops filled with produce and goods.

But party membership was to be no protection for Kirov. In the middle of the 1930s, when he had been living in his grand apartment for a little over eight years, the revolution began to consume its own. The party elite would discover that losing the trust of Stalin could mean losing their jobs, their flats and very often their lives.

Kirov had been a loyal ally of Stalin in the 1920s. During the civil war, he had organised the Bolshevik campaign in the northern Caucasus, gaining a reputation for ferocity in his suppression of White resistance. He was rewarded in 1926 with the appointment to run Leningrad, as St Petersburg was now known. He gained a reputation for his efficiency as an administrator, winning genuine popularity among ordinary Leningraders for his work in tackling food shortages. As his popularity grew, Kirov became a rallying point for independent opinion in the party leadership, admired for his apparent willingness to stand up to the increasingly authoritarian Stalin.

Independence, though, was a mixed blessing and Kirov's position was put to the test at the Seventeenth Party Congress in January and February 1934. Although dubbed the 'Congress of the Victors' in honour of the putative successes of industrialisation and collectivisation, the proceedings were overshadowed by urban and rural unrest. Stalin had become increasingly morose and quarrelsome since the death of his wife Nadezhda Alliluyeva 15 months earlier. She had shot herself in her Kremlin bedroom after storming out of a dinner party where she and Stalin had had a very public row. Although the official version was that Nadezhda had died of appendicitis, persistent rumours pinned the blame for her death directly or indirectly on her husband.

His personal problems and the misfortunes plaguing the country seemed to affect Stalin deeply. His colleagues spoke of his increased suspicion of those around him, his more frequent use of alcohol and readiness to fly into a rage at the least provocation. His obsessive determination not to loosen his grip on power was tinged with growing paranoia.

Stalin warned in his Congress speech that this was no time for the party to rest on its laurels. He pointed the finger at those in the leadership who were advocating moderation in the fight against bourgeois elements and reconciliation with those who had questioned the supremacy of the party line.

There is a danger that certain of our comrades, having become intoxicated with success, will get swollen heads and begin to lull themselves with boastful songs, thinking that victory is easy and all threats have been overcome. There is nothing more dangerous than sentiments of this kind, for they weaken the party and disarm its ranks. If such sentiments gain the upper hand in our party, we may be faced with the danger of all our successes being wrecked. There will be difficulties and we must continue to struggle. We must not lull the party, but sharpen its vigilance; we must not sing it to sleep, but sharpen it for action; not disarm it, but arm it; not demobilise it, but keep it in a state of constant readiness ...

When he rose to speak, Kirov took a different tack. A small, powerfully built man with a flair for public oratory, he addressed the Congress with a confidence that bordered on swagger. While praising Stalin in his opening remarks, he claimed that the time had come for more sensitivity in the way the country was governed. 'The main difficulties are already behind us,' he told his audience, in an apparent rebuff to the leader's speech. He appealed for a more tolerant approach to dissenting voices in the politburo, even extending an olive branch to opposition movements within the party.

In all areas of socialist construction, the proper socialist principles are now in force. So did we need to worry about the pronouncements of the former opposition leaders within the party? The Congress has heard their speeches ... and I think we need to look at the fate of these people in a more human way. I don't want to go into the theories they put forward – and they no longer hold their old views ... Now they want to join us in the universal triumph of socialism ... They sat in the rear while the party was fighting for socialism. But I think that soon they will merge back into our victorious Communist army. The opposition leaders have been defeated, but now they wish to join us in our victory ...

Kirov's remarks were ambiguous. He seemed to be offering reconciliation instead of repression, and his speech drew enthusiastic applause. When the Congress delegates voted to elect the Central Committee, Kirov received only three negative votes, by far the fewest of any candidate. Stalin, by contrast, was opposed by over a hundred delegates (although the true number was never announced: according to the official media, he too was said to have received three votes against).

At the end of the Congress, a group of party members approached Kirov in the hope that he would challenge Stalin for the party leadership. Kirov declined and informed Stalin of the conversation, but the General Secretary had been alerted to a potential rival and his mood was far from forgiving.

On the afternoon of 1 December 1934, Sergei Kirov left his flat to drive to his office in the Smolny Institute, a former convent school in a leafy part of town on the banks of the River Neva. Nowadays, it is a half-hour crawl through traffic jams, but in the 1930s with no private cars on the roads, he arrived in minutes. As Kirov approached his office, a small, thin man walked up to him, drew a Nagant revolver and shot him in the back of the neck. The Leningrad party boss was dead within a minute. The assassin, a young worker named Leonid Nikolaev, had been expelled from the party with the result that he lost his job, and he apparently blamed Kirov.

There is no conclusive evidence that Stalin arranged the murder of his colleague, but rumours have long circulated that he had a hand in the affair. Nikita Khrushchev, speaking in 1956, seemed to lend them credence. Nikolaev, who was known to the NKVD, had gained access to the Smolny a month earlier and a guard had discovered the pistol in his briefcase. Nikolaev was arrested, but after being interrogated, he was released and, inexplicably, allowed to keep his gun. Seemingly on Stalin's instructions, Kirov's personal security was subsequently reduced and he was alone with no bodyguard at the moment of his death.

Stalin took the unusual step of travelling to Leningrad to be present during Nikolaev's questioning. He ensured that the murderer signed a confession admitting he had acted as part of an opposition plot inspired by Stalin's enemies – Trotsky, Zinoviev and Kamenev – and he arranged for the immediate implementation of the death sentence. An acquaintance of Kirov's who had been present at the shooting was also killed when the NKVD had him picked him up and allowed him to fall from the lorry in which they were transporting him. The only two witnesses to the murder had been silenced.

Whatever the truth behind Kirov's assassination, its effect was to unleash years of paranoia, terror and suffering for millions of people across the Soviet Union. Kirov was promptly sanctified as a Soviet martyr; the Leningrad ballet, towns and even battleships were named after him. In his name the Soviet Union was to be made 'safe' again. 'Deviationism' was now conflated with 'terrorism' and Stalin's comments on his colleague's murder have a sort of 'I told you so' ring to them, a riposte to Kirov's call for tolerance of diverging political views:

> The foul murder of Comrade Kirov was proof that the enemies of the people would resort to double-dealing and that they would mask themselves as Bolsheviks, as party members, in order to worm their way into our confidence and gain access to our organisations ... The Central Committee emphatically warned party organisations against political complacency and lack of vigilance! Such complacency is fundamentally wrong. It is an echo of those who assured us that our enemies 'would become real Socialists in the end'. We do not need complacency, but vigilance! Real Bolshevik, revolutionary vigilance! ... Every Bolshevik under present conditions must have the ability to discern an enemy of the party and unmask him no matter how well disguised he may be.

Within days, hundreds of people had been arrested and executed without trial. Stalin decreed that due process of law could be ignored in order to guarantee rapid justice. The corpses piled up in the basement of the Leningrad NKVD. The great purge years were beginning.

Chistki (purges) of the Communist Party had been common occurrences in the Soviet Union from the early 1920s onwards. Party members would be instructed to hand in their membership cards and asked to answer a number of questions to show that they deserved their place amongst the privileged elite. Undesirables were expelled and lost the perks afforded to members. One purge, in 1933, had resulted in the withdrawal of party cards from 854,000 people on the grounds that they were 'careerists', 'drunkards', 'idlers' or 'opportunists'. Leonid Nikolaev, the embittered assassin, had probably been one of them.

Only after the murder of Kirov did the purges take on the more sinister form we associate them with today. Throughout 1935 and the first half of 1936 Stalin moved to tighten his grip on the party. He had become frustrated with those who opposed his plans to accelerate the pace of economic growth, and a report from the NKVD that Trotsky had been secretly liaising with opposition groups in the party served as the excuse Stalin needed to crush his 'opponents' decisively. He announced to local party committees that large numbers of party cards had fallen into the hands of political enemies and spies. Those removed from the party in all subsequent *chistki* could therefore be convicted of espionage, a capital offence in the Soviet Union. Former or suspected members of the so-called Left Opposition were arrested and interrogated, often brutally, until they admitted they had been part of a Trotskyite plot to overthrow the Soviet leadership. Under torture, they were induced to incriminate others, many of them undoubtedly innocent. The circle of denunciations grew ever larger, until the NKVD felt it had enough 'evidence' to carry out a piece of political theatre that would become emblematic of this period of Soviet history.

In the summer of 1936, Kamenev and Zinoviev, who had already been sentenced to prison terms for their 'moral complicity' in Kirov's death, were re-tried. This time they were accused of leading a terrorist organisation that had eliminated Kirov and was intent on killing Stalin. It would be the first in a series of show trials designed to whip public opinion into a frenzy of paranoia and denunciations.

Holding a public trial was a risk. There was no objective evidence to back up the conspiracy claims; success would depend entirely on the confessions of the accused. Without confessions, the trials would be seen as a sham. It would have been simpler to hold the proceedings behind closed doors, but Stalin's aim was to crush his 'enemies', both physically and in the court of public opinion. And to do that he needed to transform the defendants from lauded heroes of the Bolshevik revolution into evil saboteurs bent on the destruction of the people's socialist society.

Before their trial, the NKVD assured Kamenev and Zinoviev that their lives, and those of their families, would be spared as long as they admitted their guilt and implicated other Old Bolsheviks, including Nikolai Bukharin, Mikhail Tomsky and Karl Radek. The goal appeared to be the elimination of all those who had played key roles in the events of 1917, leaving Stalin as the sole link and successor to Lenin. All remaining party members would owe their positions and their careers to him alone.

After months of preparations, the trial began on 19 August 1936. It was held in the October Room of the House of Unions, formerly the Assembly of the Nobility, a blue neoclassical building in the centre of Moscow, built during Catherine's reign. The theatrical master of ceremonies was Andrei Vyshinsky, the Soviet state prosecutor who had conducted the Metropolitan-Vickers case (see pp. 270–1) and was now beginning his remarkable career as the driving force in the political trials of the pre-war years. His eventual reward would be to serve as chief Soviet prosecutor in the Nuremberg War Crimes Trials and to become Soviet foreign minister in the final years of Stalin's reign.

Vyshinsky understood perfectly that the aim of the show trials was to incite the people's hatred of the defendants. In speeches full of anger and disgust, he described Zinoviev and Kamenev as dogs, perfidious enemies of the people, the lowest form of life:

> The enemy is cunning, and a cunning enemy must not be spared. The people leapt to their feet in indignation at these ghastly crimes. The people are quivering with rage. And I, as the representative of the state prosecution, join my indignant voice to the rumbling of the voices of millions! I remind you, comrade judges, that it is your duty, once you find these people, all sixteen of them, guilty of crimes against the state, to apply to them in full measure those articles of the law that the prosecution has demanded. I demand that these rabid dogs be shot – every one of them – until the last of them is wiped out!

Vyshinsky's fulminations were read out in factories and on collective farms. Workers cheered and celebrated the unmasking of such evil traitors. Telegrams poured in demanding the death penalty.*

---

* A telegram, from the workers of the Meshchovsky Region near Kaluga, 100 miles southwest of Moscow, is typical of the tone of indignation and lust for vengeance: 'The workers of the Meshchovsky Region demand merciless retribution against the terrorists and anti-party vermin of the Trotskyite apposition [sic] groups. An end to the counter-revolutionary activities of Zinoviev, Kamenev et al! Death to the enemies of the working class! Annihilate all who try to overthrow the dictatorship of the proletariat! Long live the invincible working class! Long live the Communist Party and its mighty leader, Comrade Stalin!'

LEFT 'There *is* such a party!' Lenin urges the seizure of power in June 1917.

BELOW Demonstrators in Petrograd mowed down by pro-Government troops in July 1917.

RIGHT Leon Trotsky in his uniform as Commander of the Red Army.

BELOW Lenin addresses the workers in 1917.

BOTTOM *Taking of the Winter Palace on 25th October 1917,* by Nikolai Denisov (1940s).

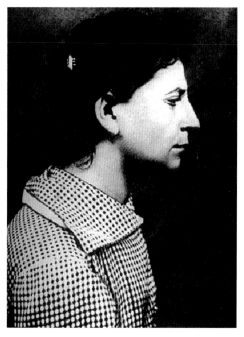

'Iron' Felix Dzerzhinsky, founder of the Cheka secret police.

Fanny Kaplan, the woman who shot Lenin.

Huge crowds gather on Red Square to mourn the death of Lenin.

LEFT Stalin, the second
Soviet leader.

ABOVE Alexei Stakhanov with his
record-breaking miners.

LEFT 'Our forces are inexhaustible!'

НАШИ СИЛЫ
НЕИСЧИСЛИМЫ

Soviet cultural figures of the early twentieth century: Boris Pasternak,
Vladimir Mayakovsky, Dmitry Shostakovich, Osip Mandelstam, Sergei
Prokofiev, Maxim Gorky, Anna Akhmatova, Isaak Babel, Marina Tsvetaeva.

ABOVE Soviet troops advance in the ruined streets of Stalingrad, 1942.

BELOW The Red Army hoists the Hammer and Sickle on the Reichstag, Berlin, in May 1945.

RIGHT Vyacheslav Molotov signs the Nazi–Soviet Pact on 23 August 1939 as Stalin looks on.

BELOW Churchill, Roosevelt and Stalin at the Yalta conference in February 1945.

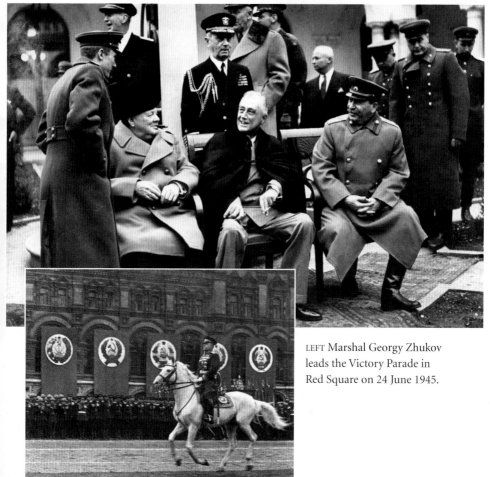

LEFT Marshal Georgy Zhukov leads the Victory Parade in Red Square on 24 June 1945.

Stalin leads the way, with (left to right) Mikoyan, Khrushchev, Malenkov, Beria and Molotov following closely behind.

Stalin lying in state, March 1953.

The outcome of the trial was never in doubt. Remarkably, Kamenev, Zinoviev and the 14 other defendants played their parts perfectly. In confessions that seemed to have been learned by rote, so exactly did they corroborate each other, they freely admitted their guilt. On 24 August, after five days of hearings, the court announced that all 16 defendants had been found guilty. All were sentenced to death. The executions were carried out the following morning. Zinoviev and Kamenev became the first members of the Central Committee to be executed; they would not be the last.

The standard had now been set. In January 1937 Karl Radek, one of Lenin's closest allies, appeared in the dock along with 16 others accused of terrorism and sabotage. All but four were sentenced to death and immediately executed. Radek himself avoided the death penalty because he agreed to implicate others, an act that would open the way for the biggest of the show trials two years later. But by that time Radek too would be dead, murdered by an NKVD assassin in the labour camp where he was sent to serve his sentence.

By 1937, the Soviet Union was gripped by fear. Many genuinely believed that spies, wreckers and saboteurs were in their midst and that they must remain constantly on the lookout for enemy agents. The atmosphere of suspicion was seized on by some to settle old scores or move up in the world. If they denounced a rival or an immediate superior, their chances of taking over their job increased. People denounced others out of fear of being denounced themselves. Anyone even suspected of being a *kulak*, a White sympathiser, a member of a non-Communist political party, or of a suspect nationality (German, Polish, Jewish or similar) was now at risk. It took very little for people to be sucked into the carnage.

Suddenly there were no longer 'accidents' in the Soviet Union. If a fire broke out, a machine in a factory or a tractor on a farm broke down, then someone was to blame and would be held responsible. Once arrested, their fate was swiftly decided by the dreaded *troika*, an extrajudicial system of express justice where a party member, an official from the Prosecutor's office and an NKVD man had the power to dispense life and death. Laws introduced in 1934 had made families collectively responsible for crimes committed by a relative, so the wife and young sons of Lev Kamenev survived him by barely a few years; Zinoviev's family suffered a similar fate.

Most monstrous was the brainwashing of the young. Under the influence of the omnipresent propaganda, a 13-year-old schoolboy in the West Siberian village of Gerasimovka denounced his father for 'falling under the influence of *kulak* relations'. The year was 1932 and the boy's name, Pavlik Morozov, would become celebrated across the Soviet Union. The denunciation of family members was not in itself a rarity – by the middle of the decade, newspapers were full of small ads announcing 'I denounce my brother' or 'I break off relations with my mother' and so on – but Pavlik's subsequent fate made him an enduring hero. With his father safely packed off to ten years in a labour camp (where he would eventually be shot), Pavlik Morozov was himself murdered. The circumstances of his killing have never been satisfactorily explained, but the Kremlin propaganda machine was quick to turn it into an instructive morality tale for all other Soviet children.

According to the official version of events, Pavlik was murdered by angry relatives of his justly imprisoned father. His uncle and grandfather were accused of the crime and portrayed in the media as corrupt *kulaks*. With the case gaining widespread publicity, thousands of telegrams poured in demanding the death penalty, which was duly handed down and carried out. Pavlik became a martyr for the party, celebrated as a hero citizen and an example for all. In a remarkable reversal of natural morality, the state proclaimed that loyalty to family must take second place to loyalty to the ideals of the state. Maxim Gorky praised Pavlik's 'selflessness', concluding that by 'overcoming blood kinship, he discovered spiritual kinship'.

The tale of Pavlik Morozov became compulsory reading in schools; songs, plays, a symphony and an opera were composed in his honour. Sergei Eisenstein's film *Bezhin Meadow* (1937) was named after the location of Pavlik's murder. The school in Gerasimovka became a shrine to his memory, and statues of the boy who was honoured with the title 'Informer Number One' sprang up in parks all over the country.

Thanks to Comrade Pavlik, family members were placed under a legal obligation to inform. If they knew of the criminal intentions of a 'traitor to the homeland' and failed to report it, they could be sentenced to five years in the Gulag. Even if they didn't know, they could still be exiled. By now people were disappearing without a trace, taken away by the secret police in the middle of the night, never to be heard from again. People lived in such constant fear of the knock at the door that they slept fully clothed with a packed suitcase under their beds. No one was safe from the 'black crows', the name given to the NKVD cars in which the secret police drove around at night, silently abducting their victims.

The true extent of the purges is illustrated by the fate of the men who administered them. Genrikh Yagoda had officially been the head of the NKVD since 1934, although he had effectively run the organisation since the death of its founder Felix Dzerzhinsky eight years earlier. In late 1936, he was replaced for falling behind in uncovering 'Trotskyite saboteurs' – in effect, for not arresting enough people. His successor, Nikolai Yezhov, a dwarf of a man with a piercing voice and bandy legs, quickly earned the nickname of 'Iron Hedgehog' (*yezh* in Russian means 'hedgehog') for his bloodthirsty enthusiasm in the job. In early 1937, he announced targets for the purges, similar to the quotas imposed on industry and agriculture. Numbers were fixed for arrests in each sector of society and it was decreed that 28 per cent of these should be shot. Yezhov set himself the goal of arresting 260,000 'anti-Soviet elements'; the actual offences were less important than fulfilling the quota.

In early 1938, partly to protect his own life, Yezhov agreed to arrest his predecessor. After a year's anxiety-ridden retirement, Genrikh Yagoda appeared in the final and most famous show trial alongside Nikolai Bukharin, Alexei Rykov and Nikolai Krestinsky, all former members of the politburo. The Trial of the Twenty-One, as it was known, was designed to tie up the loose ends of the two previous trials and kill off the remaining Old Bolsheviks. The defendants were accused of being part of the 'Right Trotskyite Bloc' and of committing a dizzying array of crimes, including murdering Kirov and Maxim Gorky, attempting to assassinate Stalin, Lenin, Sverdlov and Molotov, conspiring to wreck the economy, spying for the West and making secret agreements to partition the Soviet Union between its enemies in the East and West. They confessed, and on 14 March 1938 18 of them were sentenced to death, leaving Vyshinsky to proclaim triumphantly:

The weed and the thistle will grow on the graves of these execrable traitors. But on us and on our happy country, our Glorious Sun will continue to shed His serene light. Guided by our beloved Leader and Master, the Great Stalin, we will go forward to Communism along a path that has been cleansed of the remnants of the last scum and filth of the past.

Strangely, for a man who had himself arranged show trials, and knew the inevitable outcome, Yagoda had continued to believe to the very last moment that Stalin would not allow him to be executed. Alexander Solzhenitsyn in his magnum opus *The Gulag Archipelago* (1973), describes the torturer's last moments in court:

This murderer of millions simply could not imagine that his superior murderer, up top, would not, at the last moment, stand up for him and protect him. Just as though Stalin had been sitting right there in the hall, Yagoda confidently and insistently begged him directly for mercy: 'I appeal to you! For you I built two great canals!' And a witness reports that at just that moment a match flared in the shadows behind a window on the second floor of the hall, apparently behind a muslin curtain, and, while it lasted, the outline of a pipe could be seen ... In light of the Oriental despot in Stalin's character, I can readily believe that he watched the comedies in that October Hall. I cannot imagine that he would have denied himself this spectacle, this satisfaction.

Fitzroy MacLean, the Scottish diplomat and adventurer, claims in his splendid memoirs of his time in Moscow (*Eastern Approaches*, 1949) that the dictator was indeed there, the invisible *metteur-en-scène* of the whole performance:

At one stage of the trial a clumsily directed arc-light dramatically revealed to attentive members of the audience the familiar features and heavily drooping moustache peering out from behind the black glass of a small window, high up under the ceiling of the courtroom.

Visible or not, however, the defendants in the show trials would have been acutely aware of Stalin's hand guiding their fate. And that may shed some light on the question I find the most puzzling of all. As I read through the transcripts of proceedings, I found myself asking why these intelligent and strong-willed men agreed to falsely incriminate themselves. It is quite clear from the self-excoriating speeches of the Old Bolsheviks in the dock that they are confessing to imaginary crimes, to things they could not possibly have done. Why did they confess to attempting to destroy all they had worked for?

One answer is that they were tortured mercilessly, deprived of sleep, beaten and interrogated for days on end until they confessed. That is undoubtedly what happened to the majority of them. In addition, they were warned that their families would be killed if they did not do what they were told to do. But in many cases, there seems to be more to their confessions than simply a surrender to physical and mental coercion. Bukharin, the man Lenin had described in his testament as 'the darling of the party' (reason enough, no doubt, for Stalin to want rid of him), gave a hint in his final plea to the court:

> If one were to die without repenting, it would mean one was dying for absolutely nothing at all. But repentance makes everything positive that glistens in the Soviet Union acquire new dimensions in a man's mind. This in the end disarmed me completely and led me to bend my knees before the party and the country. When you think such thoughts, all the personal considerations, all the bitterness, rancour and pride fall away, disappear.

The desire for one's death to have meaning, to make a positive contribution, is a natural one. But why would Bukharin and the others wish to serve the cause of a Communist Party that was now bent on destroying them?

The answer, perhaps, lies in the mindset of the Socialist Revolutionary. These were men who had spent their life in the service of a cause, and even if they disagreed with some aspects of the party line (in fact, their only real crime was that of disagreeing with Stalin), the triumph of the party remained the ultimate good. Opposing the party now would mean negating all that had gone before.

Arthur Koestler's novel *Darkness at Noon* (1940) is based on the Trial of the Twenty-One, and it addresses the question of repentance in light of the author's own experience as a political prisoner facing execution. Koestler notes wryly that the Bolshevik revolutionary had 'become a slaughterer in order to abolish slaughtering; to sacrifice lambs so that no more lambs would be sacrificed; to whip people with knouts so that they may learn not to let themselves be whipped; to strip himself of every scruple in the name of a higher scrupulousness'. The Bolsheviks had sacrificed millions of lives 'for the greater good', making it an article of faith that the party was more important than any individual's doubts. While Bukharin and the others had not committed the ludicrous anti-party crimes of which they were accused, they were no longer fully supportive of the direction the revolution had taken. So by the logic of the party, the logic by which they themselves had lived, their annihilation by the party was something that had to be accepted.

Bukharin seems to have consciously agreed to play the role of traitor in the hope that it would help the party, in time, to find its way back to the true path. (Rubashov, the defendant in *Darkness at Noon*, accepts the same fate.) Bukharin's wife, who herself spent 20 years in Stalin's camps, later confirmed that 'one reason for his preposterous confession in the dock was precisely this: he hoped that the idea to which he had dedicated his life would triumph'. Bukharin told the court: 'Know comrades, that the banner you bear in a triumphant march towards Communism contains a drop of my blood, too!' and his final letter, which his wife memorised before his death, began: 'I address this appeal to you, the future generation of party leaders, whose historical mission will include the obligation to take apart the monstrous cloud of crimes in these frightful times.' It would take 50 years, but that future generation of Communist leaders answered his appeal. In 1988, under Mikhail Gorbachev, Bukharin was rehabilitated, exonerated of all the charges against him.

After the Trial of the Twenty-One, the rate of executions started to slow. But two defining moments of the Terror were still to come. In late 1938, Nikolai Yezhov seemed to suffer a nervous breakdown. His fellow NKVD officers reported that he was no longer controlling the work of the department, that he was behaving oddly at meetings, staring out of the window and playing with paper aeroplanes. It seemed as if the years of torturing and murdering had driven him insane. Others speculated that he was feigning madness in order to escape from the horrors of his job, or that he wanted out before he too was purged. Yezhov was called in by Stalin and it was announced that he had 'asked to step down' as head of the NKVD, to be replaced by his deputy, the rapidly rising star, Lavrenty Beria. A year later, with Beria firmly installed as master of the Lubyanka, Yezhov too was arrested and treated to the same punishment he had inflicted on his predecessor. Like the dead Genrikh Yagoda, he too was stripped naked, beaten repeatedly and finally shot in the back of the head. It was beginning to look as if each successive head of the secret police was living under a potential death sentence: as each of them did Stalin's dirty work, the secrets they accumulated and the power they wielded made them an ever greater liability, too much of a potential threat for Stalin to let them live.

With Yezhov dead, Stalin did his best to blame him for the Terror: any excessive zeal in the purges, he claimed, was due to the infiltration of the NKVD by 'fascist elements' and to Yezhov's personal bloodlust, for which he had now been punished. Beria was instructed to purge the NKVD itself and scores of senior officials were executed.

To this day in Russia the years 1937–8, when the Terror was at its peak, are known in popular memory as the 'Yezhovshchina' (regime of Yezhov). As had happened with the Old Bolsheviks, his image was removed from official photographs, and the pages of his entry in *The Great Soviet Encyclopaedia*, which had celebrated him as a protector of the revolution, were ripped out. To fill the gap, a very long article was inserted on the subject of hedgehogs.*

With the death of Yezhov, the Terror seemed to be winding down. But Stalin had one last opponent to deal with. Leon Trotsky, public enemy number one in the Soviet Union, had kept up his vendetta against Stalin

---

* The same thing would happen in 1953 when Yezhov's successor as head of the secret police, Lavrenty Beria, fell from grace. In his case, readers of *The Great Soviet Encyclopaedia* would find themselves very well informed about the Bering Strait.

from his exile in Mexico. In vehement letters and damning public pronouncements reminiscent of Prince Andrei Kurbsky's polemic against Ivan the Terrible (see pp. 48–9), Trotsky had continued to denounce the murderous policies of his former comrade and condemn the show trials. 'Stalin's trial against me,' he told the international public via radio and newsreel addresses, 'is built upon false confessions, extorted by modern inquisitorial methods, in the interests of the ruling clique. There are no crimes in history more terrible in intention or execution than the Moscow show trials. They are the product not of Communism, not of socialism, but of Stalinism, that is, of the irresponsible despotism of the bureaucracy over the people … The true criminals hide behind the cloak of the accusers … The Stalinist secret police has sunk to the level of the Nazi Gestapo.'

In the summer of 1940, Trotsky was working on an excoriating biography of Stalin. It would never be completed. On 20 August, after numerous failed assassination attempts, Stalin achieved his aim. Trotsky had invited a young Spaniard into his villa in Mexico City, believing him to be one of the many political groupies who had congregated around him in the years since he left Russia. But Ramón Mercader was a Soviet agent, recruited by the NKVD during the Spanish Civil War (1936–9) and trained in Moscow in the art of assassination. As Trotsky worked in his study, Mercader hit him with savage force on the back of his head with an ice axe he had smuggled in under his raincoat. The former hero of the Russian civil war survived long enough to know that he had perished at the merciless hands of his great rival. His last words before dying the following day in hospital were reportedly, 'I know I shall not survive this. Stalin has finally accomplished the task he attempted unsuccessfully before …'

Mercader would serve 20 years in jail. On his release he was made a Hero of the Soviet Union, living out his final years in Moscow, where his story still occupies a prominent place in the displays of the KGB Museum in the Lubyanka.

The purges of the 1930s changed the face of the USSR. In political terms, they allowed Stalin to achieve his aim of removing all actual or potential rivals for power. The effect on the Communist Party's higher echelons is illustrated by the fate of those who attended the Seventeenth Party Congress in 1934, the so-called Congress of the Victors. Eleven hundred of them, more than half those present, were arrested; and by 1939 two-thirds of those arrested had been executed. The Central Committee fared even worse: 119 of its 139 members were executed. The Congress of the Victors had become the Congress of the Condemned.

According to the NKVD's own records, they detained 1.6 million people during 1937 and 1938, of whom 681,692 were shot for 'counter-revolutionary and state crimes'. The true figures are undoubtedly much higher. By comparison, in the 85 years from 1825 to 1910, the tsarist regime executed 3,932 people for political crimes.

The mass arrests of the purge years destabilised the Soviet economy. Industrial and agricultural production went into sharp decline. By 1939, the number of inmates in the Gulag ran into the millions. The *zeki*, as they were known, were put to work as part of the planned economy, labouring in mines, timber forests and on construction sites. Hundreds of thousands died from overwork and starvation. In a morbid variation on the Russian tradition of joint responsibility, they would receive their full ration of food only if their group accomplished its daily target. One inmate later wrote, 'The hungrier we were, the worse we worked. The worse we worked, the hungrier we became. From that vicious circle there was no escape.'

Perhaps the most disastrous consequence of the purges was the damage they did to national security. Stalin had not limited the bloodletting to his political rivals. The military high command also suffered heavy losses. In 1936, Stalin had claimed that elements of the Red Army were plotting against him. The truth or otherwise of the charge has never been established, and subsequent claims that the Kremlin was duped by Nazi disinformation are also unproven. But in June 1937, eight of the Red Army's top commanders were charged with conspiracy with Germany. All were convicted and executed, including the army's leading military strategist, Marshal Mikhail Tukhachevsky. The search for traitors spread rapidly through the lower ranks, and between 1937 and 1939 some 15,000 army officers and political personnel were shot. Of the 85 members of the Military Army Council, 68 were executed.

Stalin's timing could not have been more catastrophic. He had destroyed the elite of the Soviet Union's armed forces at the very moment that the clouds of world war were gathering on the horizon. But he appeared unconcerned. The record of his remarkable conversation with Sergei Eisenstein suggests that he saw himself as a modern-day Ivan the Terrible, doing whatever was necessary for the good of the nation, untroubled by mundane considerations of justice and morality. He approved of Ivan's willingness to murder his rivals, and reproached him only for 'praying and repenting'. 'God disturbed him too much in this matter,' he concluded. 'He ought to have been even more decisive!' In his copy of a biography of Genghis Khan, Stalin underlined the sentence 'The deaths of the vanquished are necessary for the tranquillity of the victors.'

CHAPTER THIRTY-ONE

Photographs taken on the night of 23 August 1939 show a grinning Stalin standing beside the German foreign minister, Joachim von Ribbentrop in the large reception hall of the Great Kremlin Palace. Behind them, a portrait of Lenin looks down from the wall; in the foreground, Vyacheslav Molotov, the Soviet commissar for foreign affairs, is sitting at a desk signing one of the most notorious international accords in history. According to Molotov's grandson, Vyacheslav Nikonov, the commissar recalled von Ribbentrop greeting the signing with a curt 'Heil Hitler!' The room, he says, fell suddenly silent; then Stalin gave a little laugh and made a curtsey. The 'Treaty of Non-Aggression between the German Reich and the Union of Soviet Socialist Republics' guaranteed that both nations would remain neutral if either were attacked by, or themselves attacked, a third party. The Molotov–Ribbentrop Pact, as it came to be known, would lead to the deaths of millions and the division of Europe.

The treaty was hastily typed up on flimsy paper with none of the usual seals and flourishes. The whole thing looks a little makeshift, perhaps because it was so unexpected. Hitler had spent the preceding years denouncing Stalin's regime as 'a band of international criminals'. And Soviet propaganda had been preparing the way for confrontation with the 'Nazi menace'. So deep had been the enmity between them that they had fought what was in effect a proxy war, supporting opposing sides in the Spanish Civil War.

But after 23 August, Germany was no longer an enemy. Suddenly Hitler was a friend, and Soviet public opinion would have to be told that the Nazis were now a good thing. Books and tracts denouncing Hitler and the Nazis were withdrawn from Soviet libraries. Fascism was no longer mentioned in the press. German cultural centres were opened in major cities, and German music, films and plays began to appear everywhere. Sergei Eisenstein's film *Alexander Nevsky*, which had been ordered by Stalin to portray

Russian resistance to German aggressors in a previous historical era, was withdrawn from cinemas overnight and Eisenstein was instructed instead to direct a new version of Richard Wagner's *Die Walküre* (1870). The Soviet Union had spent the last few years executing thousands of people on charges of being fascist agents or spies. So why did Stalin opt for a pact with the former 'devils'?

Attached to the back of the treaty was a second, secret agreement, kept hidden from the Soviet people and the rest of the world. The 'secret protocol' of the Molotov–Ribbentrop Pact was a deal between Stalin and Hitler to carve up Eastern and Central Europe between them. Its paragraphs delineate 'spheres of influence' in which each dictator would be free to do as he liked. Stalin would get Latvia, Estonia, part of Lithuania, Finland and Bessarabia; as so often with Russo–German treaties, the biggest loser would be Poland:

> Of the areas belonging to the Polish state, the spheres of influence of Germany and the USSR shall be bounded approximately by the line of the rivers Narew, Vistula and San. The question of whether the interests of both parties make desirable the maintenance of an independent Polish state can only be defini- tively determined in the course of further political developments.

Hitler now had the green light to invade the western part of Poland; Stalin was being given a free hand to annex the rest of the country, all the territory east of the River Vistula. To Stalin's delight, Moscow would be regaining the land it had lost in the Russo–Polish war of 1919–21, and more besides. As with the partitions of the nineteenth century, the state of Poland was again destined to be wiped off the map (see pp. 322–3).

Even with its covert addendum concealed from public knowledge,[*] the treaty shocked the world. *Time* magazine insisted on referring to it as the

---

[*] The existence of the secret protocol was officially denied in the Soviet Union until 1989, when a demonstration by 2 million people in the Baltic states to mark the fiftieth anniver- sary of the signing of the treaty prompted Mikhail Gorbachev to set up a commission of inquiry and eventually to apologise for the consequences of the pact on those countries affected by it.

'Communazi Pact' and its participants as 'Communazis'. Churchill declared, 'The sinister news broke upon the world like an explosion,' and he had good reason to be surprised. At the same time as they were preparing to sign the Molotov–Ribbentrop Pact, the Soviets had been carrying on parallel negotiations with London and Paris. On 23 July, just a month before Stalin's curtsey to von Ribbentrop, the Kremlin leadership had told the British and French ambassadors in Moscow that they were ready for a deal. For a moment it looked as if the three nations would fight together in the war that Germany seemed bent on triggering.

But Stalin had always been flirting with two potential suitors. For Hitler, the advantages of avoiding, at least for the time being, war on two fronts were great – Berlin believed the First World War had been lost because its forces were split between two theatres of combat – and Hitler was prepared to offer Stalin terms that seemed expansively generous. The Allies, by contrast, had not pursued Stalin's hand with anything like the same alacrity. While Germany had been flying its top officials, including von Ribbentrop himself, to Moscow, British Prime Minister Neville Chamberlain seemed to think the matter was considerably less urgent. He didn't send his foreign secretary, and those officials he did send were dispatched by one of the slowest ships in the British navy: HMS *City of Exeter* took five days to get to Leningrad, and the British delegation then took another two to reach Moscow. Its leader, Admiral Sir Reginald Drax, was merely competent (the British embassy wrote to ask why someone more senior had not been sent). He made little impression at the Kremlin. The day after the signing of the pact with Germany, the British and French delegations asked for an urgent meeting with the Soviet military negotiator, Marshal Kliment Voroshilov, who told them bluntly, 'In view of the changed political situation, no useful purpose can be served by continuing this conversation.'

The main stumbling block to an agreement with the Western powers was a lack of trust dating back to the Russian Civil War. Stalin had not forgotten Britain and France's intervention on the side of the Whites, and the Allies remained wary of the Bolsheviks' proclaimed desire to foment worldwide revolution and overthrow capitalism. In addition, Moscow had understandable doubts about the strength of the Allies' resolve to stand up to the Nazis. The Munich conference of 1938, to which Stalin had not been invited, and the subsequent policy of appeasement had bred suspicion in the Kremlin that the West might be willing to collude with the Nazis, or leave Germany and the Soviet Union to fight themselves into the ground.

By 1939, Stalin felt time was running out. He wanted to ensure the Soviet Union would be protected from German expansionism. If he could not do so by making a deal with France and Britain, then he would do one with Germany.

Did Stalin believe Hitler's promises? Soviet historians have argued that the Nazi–Soviet Pact was a deliberate ploy by Stalin to win him time to rearm and prepare for war. His purges had left the Soviet military terribly weakened – and he might have hoped Germany would exhaust itself in the struggle against the Allies – but his conduct over the next two years hardly suggests he was prepared for war when it broke out. Stalin distrusted Hitler, but felt he had the measure of him. 'Hitler wanted to trick us,' he told the politburo, 'but we got the better of him.' That was wishful thinking.

On 1 September 1939, Germany invaded Poland. France and Great Britain declared war two days later. Not wanting to be seen to be acting in league with Germany, the Red Army waited two weeks before moving into eastern Poland, allegedly 'in order to aid and protect the Ukrainians and Belorussians living on Polish territory'. The rest of Europe observed Moscow's behaviour with undisguised puzzlement. It was unclear if the Russians were preparing to confront the advancing Germans or merely profiting from Poland's disarray. In a speech to the House of Commons on 1 October 1939, First Lord of the Admiralty Winston Churchill declared: 'I cannot forecast to you the action of Russia. It is a riddle wrapped in a mystery inside an enigma. But perhaps there is a key. The key is Russian national interest … Russia has pursued a cold policy of self-interest.'

Churchill said it succinctly. The Soviets soon bullied the Baltic states into signing treaties of 'mutual assistance' allowing the Red Army to build bases on their territory. In Latvia, Lithuania and Estonia, as well as in western Ukraine and Belorussia, rigged elections produced Communist-dominated assemblies, which 'spontaneously' voted to become part of the Soviet

Union. For nearly two years, from 1939 to 1941, Stalin imposed rigid Soviet control on the territories in his 'sphere of influence'. In the Baltic states, opposition was crushed and potential nationalist leaders repressed. Thousands of politicians, trade unionists, intellectuals and teachers were arrested and deported or executed. Their homes and jobs were given to ethnic Russians as Stalin revived the worst excesses of the old tsarist 'Russification' policies. The punitive repressions of those years would condition the attitudes of many when the Germans arrived to oust the Soviets a couple of years later.

In Poland, resistance to Soviet rule, or even the suggestion of resistance, was met with ruthless ferocity. Four hundred thousand Poles were arrested. Over 20,000 of them – army officers, officials, doctors and intellectuals – were taken to prison camps close to the city of Smolensk in western Russian. After six months of interrogation by the Soviet secret police, the men were earmarked for execution. The head of the NKVD, Lavrenty Beria, informed Stalin that the prisoners were dangerous elements who 'are engaged in counter-revolutionary activity and anti-Soviet agitation. Every single one of them is waiting only to be released in order to begin an immediate fight against Soviet power.' Stalin showed no mercy. The executions of the cream of Polish society began on 3 April 1940, each man shot through the back of the head at close range with a single bullet from a revolver: 21,857 bullets; 21,857 dead. The murders were carried out in various locations, but have come to be known collectively as the Katyn Forest massacre. In 1941, when the treachery of the Germans would turn Poland back into an ally of Moscow, the Soviets were faced with demands to explain what had happened to the missing Polish officers. Stalin first suggested they had been shipped to Manchuria; later he blamed the Nazis for the crime. It would not be until 1990 that Mikhail Gorbachev finally acknowledged the truth of Soviet guilt.

But it was not only in the west that Moscow was looking for new conquests. In October 1939, Stalin offered a 'mutual assistance' pact to Finland. In it he demanded that the two countries' shared border, just 20 miles north of Leningrad, be shifted further northwest. The Finnish government rejected the demand; Moscow called that a hostile act.

In late November 1939, nearly half a million Soviet troops advanced onto Finnish territory, outnumbering their opponents by three to one. So confident was the Red Army of victory that it warned its forces not to advance too far and stray into Sweden. Dmitry Shostakovich was ordered to write a *Suite on Finnish Themes*, to be played by Soviet military bands as they marched through Helsinki. But in temperatures that dropped to minus 45 degrees Celsius, the Red Army proved itself considerably less effective than Alexander Nevsky's men had been on the ice of Chudskoe Lake seven centuries earlier.

The Finnish forces had dug in along a less than impregnable defensive position known as the Mannerheim Line. There was little in the way of fortifications and the Finns lacked much basic military equipment, but they fought tenaciously, proving themselves adept at guerrilla warfare.* Many of the Russian invaders had no winter uniforms and were easily spotted against the snow, giving the Finnish snipers an easy target. One of them, Simo Häyhä, killed over 500 Red Army men; the Russians came to know the sniper's bullet as the 'white death'. After a month of fighting, a Soviet general noted bitterly: 'We have conquered just enough territory to accommodate the graves of our dead.'

In January 1940, Stalin ordered a renewed offensive under the leadership of Marshal Semyon Timoshenko, and by March the Red Army had advanced far enough into Finland to force a peace on Soviet terms.** Stalin

---

* The Soviets found themselves assailed by a surprising improvised weapon, a bottle filled with petrol and topped with an extra-long wick, which was thrown at close range and proved remarkably effective at setting lorries and tanks on fire. The Finns gave it a nickname, the 'Molotov cocktail', which became known throughout the world. When challenged about the Soviet bombing of Finnish towns, Molotov had declared that Moscow was dropping not bombs but food parcels for the starving population. The Finns decided to repay the Soviet generosity by giving the Red Army 'a drink to go with their food'. Half a million Molotov cocktails were produced before the war was over, and hundreds of Soviet tanks were destroyed by them.

** In the final weeks of the fighting, Britain and France had been actively planning to send troops to help the Finns. The likely consequence would have been a catastrophic war between the USSR and the Western Allies. Fortunately, the Norwegians refused permission for the Allied forces to cross their territory.

got most of the territory he had demanded, but the Soviet Union had lost 100,000 men and been embarrassed by the army of a 'small' nation. The 'Winter War' of 1939–40 further stained Moscow's international reputation. The Soviet Union was thrown out of the League of Nations and placed on its list of aggressors alongside Germany, Japan and Italy.

The Winter War showed the Red Army to be far from an invincible force. When France collapsed in June 1940 and Britain stood alone and vulnerable against the Nazis, Stalin faced the prospect of a Germany free to attack the Soviet Union in a single-front war. He had already ordered measures to reinforce the armed forces – conscription was broadened to increase the army from 2 million to 5 million men, and the production of aircraft, artillery and rifles was boosted – but more time was needed. Stalin confided to Molotov that they would 'not be ready to confront Germany on an equal basis until 1943'.

Moscow was locked into a Faustian pact. To placate the Nazis, the Soviet Union was supplying Germany with thousands of tons of oil and grain. In early 1941, Stalin agreed to increase the level of material assistance, just months before Hitler would use it to invade the USSR. After the debacle of the Molotov–Ribbentrop pact, Britain had tried to improve relations with the Kremlin, but found its efforts rebuffed by a Soviet leadership terrified of anything that might alienate Hitler.

Stalin seems to have convinced himself that Hitler would not risk a war against Moscow (or at least not while he was still fighting the Allies in the west). He simply ignored evidence to the contrary. In early 1941, Winston Churchill informed him that British intelligence had indications of German preparations for an imminent attack, but Stalin dismissed the message as a ploy to trick the Soviet Union into helping Britain. Richard Sorge, a Soviet spy in the German embassy in Tokyo, reported that he had seen plans for an invasion of the USSR. By early May, he had sent Moscow the outline plan of the attack and even the exact date on which it was to be launched. Still Stalin refused to mobilise his troops along the country's western border. As late as 21 June he told Defence Minister Timoshenko: 'This is all a panic over nothing.' But Nikita Khrushchev would later report that everyone knew an attack was coming. 'The sparrows were chirping about it at every crossroad,' he recalled in 1956, suggesting that Stalin had lost his nerve following the Finland setback and was deliberately deluding himself. On the very eve of the invasion, a German sergeant-major who swam across the River Bug in Poland to warn the Red Army was shot as an enemy provocateur.

Operation Barbarossa, the largest military operation in history, began in the early hours of 22 June 1941. The Soviet army was unprepared for the magnitude and ferocity of the attack. With 4 million men and over 750,000 horses, 47,000 artillery pieces, 5,000 aircraft and nearly 3,000 tanks, the invaders advanced rapidly against the disorganised Soviets. Hitler described the Soviet Union as a rotten building – once they kicked the door down, he said, the whole edifice would crumble. On the first morning alone, Luft-waffe bombers destroyed 1,200 Soviet aircraft on the ground, German special forces sabotaged the Red Army's communications, and heavy shelling decimated its front-line defences.

When Stalin was informed, he refused to believe Hitler had ordered the attack. He told the chief of the general staff, Marshal Georgy Zhukov, that no countermeasures were to be taken until they had spoken to the German embassy. 'Do not give in to any provocations and do not open fire,' was the order relayed to the troops on the ground. Within minutes, General Boldin, the deputy commander of the Western Military District, was on the line to the Kremlin. 'How can that be?' he shouted down the phone. 'Our troops are being forced to retreat. Cities are burning; people are dying!'

The centralisation of Soviet power, the discouragement of initiative from below and the memory of the years of purges meant nothing could be done without authorisation from the top. All depended on Stalin and at the critical moment he failed. When it was finally confirmed that Germany had indeed declared war, Stalin collapsed in despair, incapable of action. Molotov was left to announce the outbreak of war:

> Citizens of the Soviet Union! Today at four o'clock in the morning, with-out addressing any grievances to the Soviet Union, without a declaration of war, German forces fell on our country, attacked our frontiers in many places and bombed our cities ... an act of treachery unprecedented in the

history of civilised nations … Our people's answer to Napoleon's invasion was a Patriotic War … And now once again the Red Army and the whole nation will wage a victorious Patriotic War for our beloved country …

Only on the afternoon of 22 June, more than eight hours after the invasion had begun, were front-line commanders ordered to launch 'heavy counter-attacks to destroy the enemy's main forces, to drive operations back into enemy territory'. It was an impossible demand. Many Soviet units were already isolated and encircled. But the Red Army fought bravely. The fortress of Brest-Litovsk, the nineteenth-century castle where Trotsky had signed the armistice with Germany in March 1918, offered particularly fierce resistance. Three thousand Soviet troops held out against overwhelming German forces for ten days of bloody fighting, until every one of them had perished. The heroic defenders of Brest had shown the Wehrmacht was not infallible – the German chief of staff remarked, 'Everywhere the Russians fight to the last man. They rarely capitulate.' But in other areas the Red Army was in headlong retreat.

Stalin remained in a state of shock, and on 28 June he fled to his dacha outside Moscow. For three days, isolated from the world, he issued no orders and received little news. His refusal to prepare for war had exacerbated the scale of the disaster; his purges of the Red Army's top commanders had emasculated the Soviet military command. Eventually Molotov, Mikoyan and Beria drove out to see him. When they arrived, Stalin reportedly muttered, 'Why have you come?' He appeared to believe they were there to arrest him. When Molotov suggested the creation of a State Committee for Defence, Stalin timidly enquired, 'And who should head it?' Molotov's immediate response – that he, Stalin, should of course be in charge – seemed to snap him out of his torpor. On 3 July, he made his first address to the nation since the outbreak of war 11 days earlier.

'Comrades! Citizens! Brothers and sisters! I appeal to you, my friends,' he began, in terms he had never used before when addressing the people. 'History shows that invincible armies do not exist and have never existed. Napoleon's army was considered invincible but it was beaten … The same must be said of Hitler's German fascist army today …'

In the radio recording of his speech he sounds muffled and tired. His tone is initially defiant, but then a note of doubt creeps in, a convoluted self-justification that hints at a sense of guilt:

> It may be asked how could the Soviet Government have consented to conclude a Non-Aggression Pact with such treacherous fiends as Hitler and Ribbentrop? Was this not an error on the part of the Soviet Government? Of course not ... No peace-loving state could decline a peace treaty with a neighbouring state, even one headed by fiends and cannibals like Hitler and Ribbentrop ... By concluding the Non-Aggression Pact with Germany, we secured our country peace for a year and a half, and the opportunity of preparing our forces to repulse fascist Germany should she risk an attack on us ... All the finest men and women of Europe, America and Asia approve the conduct of the Soviet government ... This war is not an ordinary war. It is a great war of the entire Soviet people against the German fascist forces. This is a national war in defence of our country.

The old Communist rhetoric of class warfare was abandoned. Stalin's speech was a return to the language of patriotism, to the nationalist spirit of 1812, an appeal to a divided nation to unite in defence of the motherland.

It seemed to work. As in 1812, popular militias were formed across the land. Recruitment stations were flooded with volunteers, as many as 120,000 signing up in Moscow alone. Stalin demanded that 'conditions in the occupied territories must be made unbearable for the enemy. He must be pursued and destroyed at every step.' Partisan movements, aided by Red Army troops caught behind enemy lines, sprang up everywhere. Young workers and students were trained to sabotage German operations. One of the most famous of them, Zoya Kosmodemyanskaya, was only 18 when she was caught cutting German field telephone cables. Zoya was so brutally tortured that even some of the Nazi soldiers were disgusted by it, but she steadfastly refused to reveal her identity or that of her comrades. On the makeshift gallows with the noose already around her neck, she appealed to the civilians who had been assembled to see her die:

Hey, comrades, don't look so glum! Now's the time for courage! I am not afraid. It is my joy to die for the motherland – and for all of you. They will hang me, but I am not alone. There are 200 million of us. They can't hang us all! Goodbye comrades! Don't be afraid!

Zoya Kosmodemyanskaya became the first woman of the Great Patriotic War to be made a Hero of the Soviet Union. The Nazis had taken photographs of her execution and of her semi-naked body dumped in the snow. In Soviet hands they became a powerful tool, undeniable proof of the barbarity of the invaders. Now all the anti-Nazi propaganda that had been hastily withdrawn in August 1939 was brought out of storage. Eisenstein's film *Alexander Nevsky* was re-released and received a rapturous reception.

Logistical problems vitiated the war effort. There was not enough time to train the masses of volunteers, and not enough guns to arm them. Nikita Khrushchev recalled trying to get rifles for new recruits in Kiev and being told there were none. He was advised to equip them with 'pikes, swords, homemade weapons, or anything you can make in your factories'. To send untrained, poorly armed volunteers against the Wehrmacht was an act of desperation, but when gaps in the lines needed to be filled, the leadership didn't hesitate. Entire Red Army divisions were wiped out in wave after wave of suicidal counterattacks, ordered by officers so afraid of Stalin that they dispatched tens of thousands of men to near-certain death.

Hitler had told his generals in March 1941 that 'the war with Russia will be such that it cannot be conducted with chivalry; the struggle is one of ideologies and racial differences and will have to be conducted with unprecedented, unmerciful, unrelenting harshness.' All captured commissars (the political officers attached to every army unit) were to be executed on the spot. Stalin responded in August by declaring it an offence for any Red Army soldier to be taken captive. POWs would face punishment if and when they returned; and while they were in captivity their families' military ration cards were to be confiscated. In Stalin's eyes there were 'no Soviet prisoners of war, only traitors'.

The Germans made little effort to feed captured Soviet soldiers. Of the 3 million taken by the end of 1941, 2 million had died from starvation, disease or maltreatment by February 1943. The few who survived had Stalin's camps to look forward to. Barbarossa was a fight to the death, more brutal and more terrible than anything seen on the Western Front, perhaps even in the history of war.

The Wehrmacht's three-pronged attack advanced rapidly towards Leningrad in the north, Moscow in the centre and Kiev and Rostov-on-Don in the south. By mid July, they were in Smolensk, halfway to Moscow. By the end of August, Army Group North directly threatened Leningrad, and Kiev had fallen by September. Hitler knew he could not afford a long war of attrition. The Wehrmacht's fuel had so far been provided by the Soviet Union itself, but supplies would not last. The Germans needed to cripple the enemy quickly, and that meant taking Moscow, Leningrad and the vital oil fields of the Caucasus.

But despite the early setbacks, the Red Army did not collapse as Hitler had predicted. Neither did the majority of the Soviet population welcome the German troops as saviours. Some, notably in occupied Estonia and Lithuania – where the Germans were perceived as allies in their struggle to throw off the Russian yoke – did join the Nazi cause, but in the main the Soviet people remained loyal to Stalin. The Nazis treated the local populations so brutally that few were likely to be won over. In Ukraine, where millions resented Soviet domination and hoped Hitler would set them free, villages had initially welcomed German soldiers with the traditional greeting of bread and salt. They were repaid with brutality. The Germans confiscated food and livestock and forced the peasants to continue working on the hated communal farms. The retreating Red Army had employed the same scorched earth policy that had helped starve Napoleon's men in 1812, so the burned fields yielded little, to the fury of the Nazi occupiers. In response to anti-German sabotage, hostages were rounded up by the Gestapo and shot. For every German slain by the partisans, between 50 and 100 'communists' (usually ordinary citizens seized at random) were executed.

The mass killings of Soviet Jews were also explained to rank-and-file soldiers as part of the 'anti-partisan' campaign, with the slogan 'A Jew is a Bolshevik is a partisan'. The results were horrifying. An alleged attack on some German officers in September 1941 was the pretext for the worst massacres. On 26 September, notices appeared in newspapers and on the streets of Kiev announcing that the city's Jews were about to be resettled elsewhere in Ukraine.

> Yids* of the city of Kiev and vicinity must assemble on Monday 29 September by 8 a.m. at the corner of Melnikova and Doktorivskaya streets, next to the cemetery. They must bring with them all money, documents and valuables, as well as warm clothing and underwear. Any Yids who fail to carry out this order and are discovered in any other location will be shot.

What followed was the largest single mass killing of the Holocaust. The thousands who responded to the announcements were assembled into groups and marched to the Kiev suburb of Babi Yar. The Nazi report on the operation is full of self-congratulation: 'We had expected only five to six thousand, but thirty thousand appeared. Thanks to our clever organisation, they continued to believe right up to the moment of their execution that they were being resettled …' As the columns approached Babi Yar, the Jews were channelled towards the edge of a deep ravine, where they were forced to strip and put their belongings in a pile. A German soldier watched what happened next:

> It was all done so quickly. The Ukrainian guards hurried those who hesitated with kicks and shoves … The Jews were led down narrow paths into the ravine, and when they got there the Schutzpolizei [security police] grabbed them and forced them to lie down on the corpses of those who had already been shot. It took no time. As soon as a Jew lay down, a Schutzpolizei man came with a machine gun and shot him in the back of the head. The Jews who were going down into the ravine were so terrified by what they saw that they lost all hope. Some of them even chose to lie down of their own accord and waited for the shot to come … There were three rows of bodies, each about 60 metres long. I couldn't tell how many layers there were beneath each of them. The bodies were twitching and covered in blood.

---

* The Russian word *Zhidy* is used.

By the end of the war, more than a million Soviet Jews had died in the Holocaust. In autumn 2010, on the sixty-ninth anniversary of the massacres in Ukraine, I visited Babi Yar where so many were murdered. A small memorial marks the spot, but nowadays little attention is paid to the massacre – the involvement of ethnic Ukrainians in the persecution of the Jews, and directly in the events of September 1941, has left a vague sense of unease about what happened here.

Seventy miles west of Kiev, in the city of Berdichev, however, I stumbled across a living link to the Holocaust. Close to the town's Carmelite Convent a small gathering of elderly Jews – the last remnants of the 30,000 who used to live here – were marking the anniversary of the day the Gestapo began 'cleansing' the city. In the course of September and October 1941, the Berdichev ghetto was liquidated and more than 20,000 of its inhabitants murdered.* One of the speakers at the anniversary meeting was herself part of the convoy of Jews taken to be murdered in October 1941. Her voice trembling, she told how she had somehow avoided the executioners' bullets and fallen alive into the communal grave. Covered by other bodies, she lay still and silent until night fell, before crawling out of the pit and dragging herself to safety. The years had not lessened her anger. 'We must never forget what the fascists did to us and to our country!' she shouted. 'People talk of forgiveness, but how can we ever forgive what those monsters did? Young people! Never forget, never forgive!'

On the edge of Berdichev, a reminder of the murdered generation remains. It is the abandoned Jewish cemetery, the last resting place of the city's Jews for hundreds of years, rich in ornately crafted gravestones and sculpture. But suddenly there was no one left alive to tend it, and now it is overgrown and abandoned, the silence interrupted only by a train rumbling past and the cries of birds perching on the tombs.

---

* The dead included the mother of the celebrated Soviet author Vasily Grossman, who was away serving as a war correspondent for the Red Army newspaper. He would never forgive himself for not doing more to save his mother, and in his most famous novel, *Life and Fate* (1959), he imagines the letter she might have written to him as death approached.

The summer and autumn of 1941 brought the Germans impressive military gains. Eastern Poland, Estonia, Latvia, Lithuania, Belorussia and western Ukraine were all in Nazi hands. But the 180,000 German casualties in the three months to September exceeded the Wehrmacht's entire losses in the whole West European campaign of 1940. Soviet casualties were vastly higher, but the Germans were beginning to believe their enemies had an endless supply of men. General Halder, the head of the German High Command, commented bitterly on the Red Army's ferocious ability to keep fighting:

> The whole situation makes it increasingly plain that we have underestimated the Russian colossus ... Their divisions are not armed and equipped according to our understanding of these words and their tactical leadership is not very satisfactory. But if we destroy a dozen, the Russians present us with a dozen more. They are near their own resources, while we are moving farther and farther from ours. Our troops, sprawled over an immense front line, are subjected to incessant attacks from the enemy.

Hitler pressed his generals to expedite the capture of Moscow and Leningrad. His directive of 22 September made it clear that he wanted the latter to become an example of Nazi invincibility:

> The Führer has decided to erase the city of Petersburg from the face of the Earth. I have no interest in the further existence of this large population point after the defeat of Soviet Russia ... We propose to blockade the city and erase it from the Earth by means of artillery fire of all calibre and continuous bombardment from the air.

So began the 900-day siege of Leningrad. For the next two and a half years the city would exist in a state of terror, shelled around the clock and starved of fuel and supplies. Only the food brought on convoys across the frozen Lake Ladoga provided the minimal rations that kept the population alive. When spring came and the lorries began to fall through the ice, the situation became even more precarious. Nearly one in three of the city's 2.5 million inhabitants would starve to death and Leningrad's fate would hang in the balance, caught between Hitler's obsessive fury and the heroic endurance of her people.

While the German Army Group North battered at the defences of Leningrad, Army Group Centre was advancing along the route taken 129 years earlier by Napoleon's Grande Armée. Their goal was Moscow, and the lessons of history had not been lost on them. The key aim of Operation Typhoon, launched in early October, was to capture the capital and gain shelter for the invading forces before winter set in. Many of the German commanders had read the grim accounts of Napoleon's retreat and were determined not to suffer the same fate. In the first week of Typhoon, Army Group Centre won stunning victories in Vyazma and Bryansk, encircling the defending forces and capturing half a million Soviet troops. The route to Moscow was open; its fall seemed only a matter of time.

With the capital gripped by panic, Stalin ordered the immediate evacuation of ministries, government officials, industrial managers and key economic personnel. Fleets of aircraft ferried them to the safety of Kuibyshev, 500 miles southeast of Moscow on the Volga. In scenes reminiscent of the days before Napoleon's arrival in 1812, government papers and sensitive documents were hastily burned; power plants, bridges and public buildings were rigged with explosives. Ordinary Muscovites packed what they could carry and struggled for a place on the trains still leaving the city. In an astounding feat of logistics, industrial equipment, machinery and even whole factories were dismantled and shipped eastwards to the Urals, where they were set up and resumed production in record time. By the end of the operation, an estimated 500 factories and 2 million people had been evacuated from the capital. Lenin had been among the first to leave, his body secretly removed from the Red Square mausoleum in early July and shipped to safety in the west Siberian city of Tyumen.

In mid October, the Germans reached Borodino. The historical significance was lost on no one. The Soviet 82nd Rifle Division under Colonel Polosukhin managed to hold out for five days before being forced to retreat by superior German forces. A memorial now stands at the scene of the battle, almost as big as the one from 1812, and the heroism of Borodino's defenders was promptly celebrated in a rousing popular song:

Borodino! Your ground stands firm!
Your name alone brings triumph,
Conjures the fallen back from the dead,
Inspires the living to mighty deeds.
If our forefathers could only see
Through the eternal gloom of the grave
How keenly their honour is defended
By their descendants in worthy immortality!

But by early November, the Germans had advanced to within 50 miles of Moscow. Stalin ordered Marshal Georgy Zhukov, who had been organising the defence of Leningrad, to come and save the capital. Zhukov weighed up the advantages of abandoning Moscow, as Kutuzov had done in 1812, but finally told Stalin the city could and would be saved. Stalin, nominally the supreme commander of the Red Army, broadcast to the nation that he would stay in Moscow to supervise its defence. Over half a million Muscovites answered the call to help construct fortifications on the periphery of the city, and tens of thousands more volunteered to defend it. Without heating and with food in short supply, the people of Moscow now seized their chance to fight back. Four hundred thousand women, many of them with husbands at the front, went to work in arms factories making Molotov cocktails, flame-throwers and machine guns.

The author Konstantin Simonov realised in the early days of the war that people were fighting not for Stalin, the revolution and the Soviet Union, but for the Russian land – the city, town or village they regarded as home, and the people who lived there.

The villages were small, with dilapidated little churches and large graveyards, and the old wooden crosses each looking like the next. It was then that I understood how strong within me was the feeling for my motherland, how much I felt that the land itself was my own, how deeply rooted within the land were all those people who had lived there. The bitterness of the first two weeks of the war convinced me it was impossible that this land could ever become German. In these graveyards were so many grandfathers and great-grandfathers, ancestors we had never seen, that the land was Russian. Not only on the surface but down and down for yard after yard into the very depths.

Stalin too knew the importance of the past and the appeal of nationalistic patriotism. His Revolution Day speech on 7 November took place with the sound of German guns as a backdrop. Afterwards, the troops marched straight from Red Square to the front, less than 40 miles away.* Stalin linked the fighters of 1941 with Russia's national heroes from the past:

> All the peoples of our country support the efforts to smash the invading hordes. Our reserves of manpower are inexhaustible! ... Let the manly images of our great ancestors – Alexander Nevsky, Dmitry Donskoy, Kuzma Minin, Dmitry Pozharsky, Alexander Suvorov and Mikhail Kutuzov – inspire you! Death to the German invaders! Long live our glorious motherland!

The German assault on Moscow had been slowed down by the annual period of *rasputitsa*, the season of rain and mud that makes Russian roads impassable before the winter freeze. When temperatures fell in mid November, the German tanks could once more advance along the frozen roads. But the Soviets still held one important advantage. The Red Army had learned from its mistakes in Finland the previous year. Its soldiers had trained to fight on skis, and they had white camouflage, fur jackets and warm felt boots. Most German soldiers had none of these, as Berlin had gambled on them being in Moscow before the worst of the winter weather. As in 1812, winter came to the Russians' aid. Frostbite claimed thousands of German casualties as Zhukov's forces fell back as slowly as possible towards the capital. Soviet losses were great, but the Wehrmacht's advance was finally halted on 19 November, with its forward units reporting they could see the domes of the Kremlin.

---

* For security reasons, the traditional eve-of-parade meeting had to be held in Mayakovskaya metro station, with trains used as cloakrooms and dining rooms.

Just how close the Germans got to Moscow is evident to any visitor who flies in to the city's Sheremetyevo international airport. By the side of the main road into town, giant tank traps from 1941 still mark the farthest point of the German advance, just 10 miles from Red Square. The Wehrmacht had enjoyed two years of uninterrupted triumph across Europe, but the failure to take Moscow was a critical moment. The Germans had advanced 600 miles into Soviet territory, capturing an area the size of Britain, France, Spain and Italy combined. Two-fifths of the Soviet population was under enemy control; the USSR had lost nearly 4 million dead or wounded. But it had stopped the Wehrmacht before Moscow. The German troops were close to exhaustion now, facing a bitterly cold winter with stretched lines of communication and lacking vital supplies of winter clothing, boots, fur hats and antifreeze. The Soviet Union had come close to annihilation, but it had survived. As the French general Antoine-Henri Jomini remarked on the eve of Napoleon's invasion, 'Russia is a country that is easy to get into … but very difficult to get out of.'

CHAPTER THIRTY-TWO

Moscow had held out. Christmas and New Year celebrations in the exhausted capital were muted. Yet Stalin seems to have exchanged acute depression for manic optimism. He told the British foreign secretary, Anthony Eden, that the war had reached a turning point:

> The German army is exhausted. Its commanders hoped to end the war before winter and made no proper preparations for a winter campaign. They are poorly clothed, poorly fed and losing morale. But the USSR has massive reinforcements, which are now going into action ... We will continue to advance on all fronts.

Stalin's exuberance was not shared by the military. Marshal Zhukov's troops had pushed the Germans back some 80 miles, but the momentum had not yet swung to the Soviets. Zhukov pleaded that the Red Army needed time to regroup; Stalin ordered an all-out counter-offensive. He told his generals they must emulate Kutuzov in 1812 and chase the invading armies out of the Russian lands. But the attack launched in January 1942 made little impact. The Soviet forces were too weak to dislodge the Germans, and by April the offensive was bogged down in the mud of the spring *rasputitsa*. Four hundred thousand more men were captured or wounded. Stalin was forced to abandon the campaign. The conflict settled into a brief stalemate.

The men at the front were not the only ones to suffer. Those left behind endured their own hardships. It was a rare family that did not have a father, son or brother away in battle, and by the end of the war few would escape without losing a relative. The longing and anxiety of the separated was captured in a poem by Konstantin Simonov, *Zhdi Menya* (Wait for Me), which became as popular in Russia as the songs of Vera Lynn in Britain or Marlene Dietrich in Germany. Its hypnotic rhythms are a half-comforting, half-despairing prayer for the safe return of millions who would never come back:

> Wait for me, and I'll come back!
> Wait in patience yet,
> When they tell you off by heart
> That you really should forget.
> Even when my dearest ones
> All say that I am lost,
> Even when my friends give up,
> And sit and count the cost,
> Drink a glass of bitter wine
> To their absent fallen friend –
> Wait! And do not drink with them!
> Wait until the end!

But the women of the Soviet Union did more than just wait. It fell to them to fill the gaps left in industry and agriculture. In December 1941, a new law mobilised all undrafted workers for war work. Overtime was made obligatory, holidays were suspended and the working day increased to 12 hours. Women between the ages of 16 and 55 took up the jobs left by the fighting men, stoking furnaces, driving tractors and operating heavy machinery.

More and more factories were being dismantled and relocated to the east, hastily reassembled in the Urals, Siberia, Kazakhstan and Central Asia. Millions of people were evacuated with them, plunged into a new life in an unknown region. Living conditions were harsh: factories were rebuilt first and accommodation second. Through the bitter winter of 1941–2, hundreds of thousands lived in mud huts and tents, as society responded to the slogan that appeared everywhere in posters, newspapers and speeches: 'Everything for the front!' In some cases, the machines were assembled immediately so production could begin, and only then would factory walls be built around them. But by mid 1943 industrial production had outstripped that of Germany. The output of munitions quadrupled between 1940 and 1944. In areas where Soviet industry was weak, such as the production of lorries, tyres and telephones, lend-lease supplies from the USA and Britain helped make up the deficit.

Food, though, remained a huge concern. The Germans now controlled much of the Soviet Union's most fertile land and the Soviets needed to adapt quickly if they were to feed the army, let alone the rest of the population. Agricultural production had fallen catastrophically; the grain harvest of 1942 was only a third of 1940 levels. The Kremlin imposed demanding quotas on the collective farms but, unlike in the civil war, the peasants were allowed to keep their limited private plots and to sell their produce. As in industry, it fell to the women to take up the slack on the *kolkhozy*. The author Fedor Abramov wrote of the superhuman effort from all parts of society that kept Soviet agriculture afloat:

> They dragged out the old men, they dragged teenagers from their school desks, they sent little girls with runny noses to work in the forests. And the women, the women with children, what they went through in those years! No one made any allowances for them, not for age or anything else. You could collapse and give up the ghost, but you didn't dare come back without fulfilling your quota! Not on your life! 'The front needs it!'

City dwellers cultivated every spare patch of earth to supplement their meagre diets with home-grown vegetables, and the Allies provided meat in the form of huge quantities of tinned Spam. Rations were now allocated only to those who turned up for work. The whole of Soviet society was regarded as a military machine, and unauthorised absence from work was classed as desertion, punishable, as it was at the front, by death. Local defence units and citizen fire wardens were recruited from women, adolescents and the elderly. Street fortifications were hastily built and militias assembled from factory workers. Private radios were confiscated for the duration of the war, and those who failed to hand theirs in were liable to be punished. 'Praising American technology' was declared an arrestable offence. (The USA may have become an ally, but old attitudes of wariness and mistrust died hard.) A whole new class of 'crimes', punishable by forced labour, was created, including 'spreading rumours' and 'sowing panic'. Those who were convicted and dispatched to the Gulag joined the hundreds of thousands who had been deported from Poland and the Baltic states, all of them put to work helping the war effort, assigned to units building airports, landing strips and roads in the far north and east.

By the spring of 1942, the Nazi invaders had lost over a million men, and Hitler accepted he could not relaunch the three-pronged attack of Barbarossa. He decided instead to focus on taking the Caucasus oilfields, a vital goal if the Wehrmacht were to have enough fuel to continue the war. The Germans' first task was to reach the Rivers Don and Volga, where they could cut off the supply route to the Soviet forces and cover their own flank as they pushed south towards the oil cities of Grozny and Baku. In early summer, Hitler's forces repulsed a renewed Soviet offensive in Ukraine and began the advance eastward into the Don steppe. At the end of June, they planted the swastika on the peak of Mount Elbrus, the highest point in Europe. The Wehrmacht had ventured farther into Russia than any Western army before it, capturing nearly 2 million square kilometres of Soviet territory. In July, Hitler confidently told his generals 'The Russian is finished.'

Stalin's optimism of late 1941 was beginning to waver. By the end of July 1942, he was resorting to methods of the utmost ruthlessness to ensure the Red Army fought to the last drop of blood. His Order Number 227 was distributed to all units, with instructions that it be read to every fighting man.

The people of our country, for all the love and respect that they have for the Red Army, are beginning to feel disappointment in it; they are losing faith in it. Many curse the Red Army for giving our people over to the yoke of the German oppressors while the army runs away to the east. Some foolish people say we have much territory and can continue to retreat ... But it is time to stop retreating ... 'Not a single step backwards!' must be our motto. Each position, each metre of Soviet territory must be stubbornly defended, to the last drop of blood. We must cling to every inch of Soviet soil and defend it to the end. We must throw back the enemy whatever the cost. Those who retreat are traitors to the motherland. Panic-mongers and cowards must be exterminated on the spot.

Stalin ordered the summary court martial of any officer who allowed his men to retreat without express instructions from military headquarters. Offenders were to be stripped of their commission and medals and shot. To deter 'cowards and panic-mongers', penal battalions were created. 'Those who have been guilty of a breach of discipline due to cowardice or bewilderment,' said Stalin's order, would be 'sent to the most difficult sectors of the front to give them an opportunity to redeem by blood their crimes against the motherland.' To prevent retreat in the face of the enemy, 'blocking squads' armed with machine guns were to be placed behind unreliable divisions. 'In case of panic or scattered withdrawals of elements of the division, the squads must shoot them on the spot and thus aid the honest soldiers of the division to fulfil their duty to the motherland.'

Order Number 227 drew on the historical Russian precept that the individual must be prepared to sacrifice himself for the greater good of the state. Its rhetoric of 'redemption through blood' – *iskupit' krov'yu* in Russian – is that of the medieval chronicles, redolent of Russian history right back to the martyrdom of Boris and Gleb (see pp. 17–18). Penal battalions were assigned to the most perilous tasks, such as clearing minefields in front of Soviet advances or laying mines in the path of German tanks. Inmates from the labour camps were offered the chance to expunge their convictions by serving in them. Casualty rates were as high as 50 per cent, and the chance to win redemption was often a moot point.

More than 150,000 men were sentenced to death for 'panic-mongering, cowardice and unauthorised desertion of the battlefield'. Stalin took to phoning commanders to ask why they were not implementing his orders. Order Number 227 had the desired effect. It imposed discipline and unity, boosting morale among the troops. Its twin mottos – 'Not a step back!' and 'Victory or death!' – would define the ethos of the Red Army for the rest of the war.

The state was more than willing to use fear to get the necessary results. When Nikolai Baibakov, who later became the head of the State Planning Committee Gosplan, was put in charge of the oil installations in the Caucasus, he was warned by Stalin 'If you leave the Germans even 1 ton of oil, we will shoot you. But if you destroy the installations and we are left without fuel, we will also shoot you.'

Soviet Counteroffensive, 1942–1945

—— Soviet front, December 1941

—— Soviet front, November 1942

—— Soviet front, December 1944

········ Soviet front at German surrender, 7 May 1945

------- Allied front at German surrender, 7 May 1945

But self-sacrifice could be motivated by love as well as by fear, and the Kremlin was adept at tapping into the deep well of Russian patriotism. The conflict was given the official title 'The Great Patriotic War' to summon up thoughts of 'The Patriotic War' against Napoleon. New decorations were created with the names of historic heroes – the Orders of Suvorov, Kutuzov and Nevsky – and gold braid reintroduced on military uniforms. Political commissars were made subordinate to military commanders; and troops were instructed to go into battle with the cry 'For the motherland and for Stalin!' The appeal to Russianness threw up a problem. It excluded the non-Russian nationalities, who were also fighting in the armed forces. Appealing to 'Soviet-ness' had a much less powerful ring to it; for many ethnic minorities, it even had distinctly negative connotations. The propaganda machine went into contortions to try to resolve the dilemma. The non-Russian nationalities were encouraged to 'join in with your Russian brothers'. 'The home of the Russian is also your home,' they were told. 'The home of the Ukrainian and Belorussian is also your home!' Stalin, himself a Georgian, spoke of the Russian people as the outstanding force and the leading nation among all the Soviet peoples. The unspoken promise to the lesser nations seemed to be that they would enjoy freedom and equality if they pulled their weight during the war. And, to an extent, it worked. Cooperation among the nationalities increased in the face of a common enemy. For 20 years the 'brotherhood of nations' envisaged by the revolution had been little more than words, but during the Great Patriotic War, for a brief moment, it looked close to being realised.

It was, though, always Russia at the heart of the equation. In 1943, the politburo decided to replace the 'Internationale' – with its appeal to supra-national values of class struggle – with a new national anthem that proclaimed Russia's leading role in the Union:

> An indestructible union of free republics,
> Was bound together by Great Rus!
> Long live the land created by the will of the peoples:
> The united, powerful Soviet Union!
> Sing to the motherland, home of the free!
> Fortress of peoples in brotherhood strong!

Stalin's priority was the need to unite the nation. That is why he hinted at concessions to the nationalities and why he made compromises in other areas of society. He permitted more freedom in culture. Artists could create what they wanted, as long as their work avoided direct criticism of Marxism–Leninism. Previously banned poets were allowed to publish again. Anna Akhmatova broadcast her emotional, patriotic verse on Soviet radio. Composers who not so long ago had been denounced by the Kremlin contributed music to the nation's cause. Shostakovich began writing his Seventh Symphony, a tribute to his native Leningrad, while he was serving as a part-time fire warden in the besieged city. Like Akhmatova, he was evacuated to safety and finished the work in the town of Kuibyshev, announcing over the radio: 'All of us are soldiers today, and those who work in the field of culture and the arts are doing their duty on a par with all the other citizens of Leningrad.' When the symphony was performed in the Large Hall of the Leningrad Philharmonia on 9 August 1942, the city had been blockaded for nearly a year and audience and musicians alike were close to starvation. The brass section had to be given extra rations to play. The Soviet leadership announced that the symphony represented an artistic denunciation of the evils of Nazism. They ordered a bombardment of German positions to halt the shelling of the city during the performance, which was broadcast on loudspeakers in the streets and subsequently around the world. The *Leningrad* is far from Shostakovich's most accomplished work, and he later claimed it was a denunciation of all dictatorships – communist as well as fascist – but it gave a powerful boost to Soviet morale.

Even the Orthodox Church, the reviled target of Communist disapproval, long driven underground, was allowed to resume open worship. The Russian patriarchate, abolished by the tsars, was restored. Priests were encouraged to say prayers for the triumph of the Soviet army and to raise money for the war effort. Tanks on the way to the front were often blessed. Stalin insisted that priests and bishops be subjected to official vetting and they had to swear loyalty to the Soviet state. But the Church did not resist his demands and a tacit pact was reached between Church and State – some would call it collaboration – which has endured until today. The then Metropolitan of Moscow, Nikolai, customarily referred to Stalin as 'our common father'.

The concessions by the Kremlin, and the carefully fostered atmosphere of national reconciliation, convinced many that they could at last have a say in the destiny of their own country. The novelist Vyacheslav Kondratiev, himself a veteran, wrote: 'For us, the war was the most important thing in a generation... You felt as if you held the fate of Russia in your hands. It was a real, genuine feeling of citizenship, of responsibility for your fatherland.'

The German Sixth Army, under the command of the experienced General Friedrich von Paulus, reached Stalingrad on the banks of the River Volga in August 1942. Hitler made no secret of his determination to capture the city that bore the name of his hated enemy. It was as if the two dictators were about to engage in a personal duel to the death.

Stalin told his generals, 'The defence of Stalingrad is of decisive importance to all Soviet fronts. The Supreme Command orders you to spare no effort, to shirk no sacrifice in the struggle to defend it and destroy the enemy.' The battle had been given added urgency following a visit to Russia a few days earlier by Winston Churchill and the US representative Averell Harriman. The noise from the engines of the US Liberator bomber in which the two men flew from Cairo to Moscow had evidently made conversation impossible, and they communicated by notes written in pencil. Reading those scribbled pages now, it is clear they were bringing bad news: Churchill and Harriman informed Stalin that the Western Allies were still not ready to open a second front in Europe. The Red Army would have to face the Germans alone in the East for at least another year.

The defence of Stalingrad was entrusted to the newly formed 62nd Soviet Army under the command of General Vasily Chuikov, a grizzled 42-year-old who had fought in the October Revolution of 1917 and later in Poland and Finland. Chuikov's memoirs, *The Battle of the Century* (1963), are a rather deadpan account of his role in the fighting – you would hardly guess the heroism of the man – but he did allow himself the odd flash of emotion. The first came on the eve of the battle, when he made a personal promise to Stalin. 'We will save this city,' he pledged, 'or all of us will die at our posts.'

One of the 62nd Army's political commissars – the party officials attached to every regiment to root out subversion and instil discipline –

was Nikita Khrushchev. Khrushchev had previously served as head of the Ukrainian Communist Party, distinguishing himself by the alacrity with which he purged and executed his fellow officials. He had been with the Red Army as it invaded eastern Poland and had later helped organise the defence of Kiev in 1941.

Even before the German ground forces arrived at Stalingrad, the Luftwaffe had bombed the city to the point of devastation. The port facilities on the River Volga, which the Soviets relied on for supplies, had been destroyed. One Soviet soldier, Nikolai Razuvayev, wrote in his diary:

> A voice boomed from the loudspeakers: 'Air-raid warning!' and two or three minutes later the anti-aircraft guns opened up. Five minutes after that thousands of bombs began to drop. After ten minutes the sun was blocked out. The ground beneath my feet was shaking. Everything was covered in smoke and dust. There was a continuous roar from all sides, and fragments of bombs and broken stone were falling from the sky. It went on like this until darkness fell. The city was in flames. And with dawn, the air raids resumed.

Stalin had decided not to evacuate Stalingrad, believing the troops would be less inclined to defend a deserted city. In the first two days of the bombardment 25,000 civilians were killed. Over the next six months, 2 million soldiers would battle for a city that was already in ruins. The Germans initially had more men, more tanks and more planes, but Chuikov kept his pledge. His men fought for every house and every yard of shell-holed street. The more the city was reduced to rubble, the harder it became for the invaders. Street fighting did not suit the Wehrmacht; its tanks and motorised units could not operate in the constricted space. But the Soviet forces learned quickly how to use the conditions to their advantage, splitting into small mobile units, moving rapidly from location to location, harrying the enemy. Chuikov instructed his men to 'hug the enemy close', always keeping the two front lines on top of each other so the Germans could not call up artillery support fire without destroying their own forces.

Stalin pressed Marshal Zhukov to mount a counteroffensive to cut off the German army around Stalingrad and in the Caucasus to the south, but Zhukov told him nothing could be done for at least two months. In the meantime, Chuikov would have to hold the city without reinforcements, as all reserves of troops, tanks and aircraft were needed for the coming offensive. By now the fighting had descended into the most brutal hand-to-hand combat. At times the Germans controlled the upper floors of a building while the Russians held the basement, battling for the floors above or below them. One German soldier wrote, 'Stalingrad is no longer a city. By day it is a cloud of burning, blinding smoke. When night arrives, the dogs plunge into the Volga and swim desperately to the other bank.* Animals flee this hell. Even the hardest stones cannot bear it. Only men endure.'

Women served as messengers, signallers and as combatants on the front line. The most renowned were the regiments of 'Night Witches', women pilots who flew ancient Soviet biplanes under cover of darkness. The planes made little noise and their bombs fell without warning. Bridges and forward airfields were their preferred targets, terrorising the Germans with the suddenness of their attacks.

Snipers, using the rubble as cover, killed hundreds and were glorified. The young Siberian, Vasily Zaitsev, was credited with over 300 kills, his exploits widely celebrated by the Soviet propaganda machine. Mila Pavlichenko matched Zaitsev's tally, and German troops dubbed her 'the Russian Valkyrie'. They felt she decided who lived or died on the battlefield. Pavlichenko was paraded through the Soviet Union, and taken on tours of Britain and the United States. The message she relayed on behalf of the Kremlin was that the Allies should show as much courage as she had, by opening a second front in Western Europe. The author Vasily Grossman was in Stalingrad for the six months of the battle and describes it in harrowing detail in *Life and Fate* (1959). In one of his less known works, 'An Everyday Stalingrad Story' (1942), he follows a 19-year-old sniper, Anatoly Chekhov, as he plies his deadly trade:

---

* The dogs had good reason to flee, as the Germans had orders to shoot them on sight. The Soviets had trained Alsatians to seek out food from under vehicles, and dispatched them with explosives on their backs to detonate under German tanks.

A German carrying an enamel plate turned the corner. Chekhov had learned that the soldiers always came out with their pails at this time to fetch water for the officers. He turned the distance wheel, raising the crossed hairline of his sights; he shifted them 4 centimetres forward from the soldier's nose and fired. A black spot suddenly appeared beneath the soldier's cap, his head jerked backward, and the pail fell with a clatter from his hand. Chekhov felt a shudder of excitement. A minute later, another German appeared around the corner with a pair of field glasses in his hands. Chekhov pressed the trigger.

The world watched the battle, and the conviction grew that if Stalingrad could be held, the war could be won.

Slowly the Wehrmacht extended its hold over the city. The Soviet forces clung to the eastern suburbs and the thin strip of land between Stalingrad and the River Volga. Von Paulus had already informed Hitler that the Nazi standard was flying over Stalingrad; it only remained to force the last defenders over the river. But the Germans had not reckoned with the tenacity and self-sacrifice that had driven Russians to defend their homeland for nearly a thousand years. 'There is no place for us behind the Volga!' was the motto drummed into the troops. 'Not one step back!' was a warning as well as an exhortation – retreat over the river would be met with reprisals. The Soviets suffered huge numbers of casualties. The 13th Guards Division under General Alexander Rodimtsev had lost 95 per cent of its 10,000 men by the end of September. In his memoirs, Chuikov says mass military sacrifice led to victory:

At the end of the attack the enemy had advanced only a mile. They made their gains not because we retreated but because our men were killed faster than we could replace them. The Germans advanced only over our dead. But we prevented them from breaking through over the Volga. The Germans lost tens of thousands of dead in half a mile of soil and they couldn't keep it up. Before they could renew their ranks with fresh reserves we launched a general offensive.

The Soviets did not retreat beyond the Volga. Perhaps the most heroic action of the campaign came with the defence of 'Pavlov's House', a central apartment block fortified and defended by a force of just two dozen soldiers under the command of Sergeant Yakov Pavlov. The men had captured the four-storey building at the end of September and held out for two months against wave after wave of enemy attacks. German military dispatches referred to it as a fortress and assumed it had an endless supply of defenders. Pavlov was surprised when he was later acclaimed as a hero and showered with medals. His casual valour was very much in the tradition of War and Peace's gunner Tushin and all the 'little men' whose deeds Tolstoy believed to be the driving force of history. Chuikov said that more Germans died trying to take 'Pavlov's House' than had done in taking Paris. The fate of Stalingrad was decided by such deeds.

The tenacity of the defenders of Stalingrad had won Zhukov the time he needed to gather his forces, and the Soviet counteroffensive, codenamed Operation Uranus, was launched on 19 November 1942. Vasily Grossman described it as 'two great hammers, one to the north and one to the south, each composed of millions of tons of metal and human flesh'. Amazingly, the Red Army had managed to keep the build-up of thousands of tanks, guns and men concealed from the Germans. For once, Stalin had not hurried his commanders, and the offensive was efficiently prepared. Blinded by his desire to capture Stalingrad, Hitler had taken forces from the flanks of his army, leaving them badly weakened. Zhukov's pincer movement took advantage. By 23 November, some 300,000 Germans and their Romanian allies had been surrounded in a sealed enclave they christened the Kessel or 'cauldron'. Hitler instructed the commanders of the 6th Army not to try to break out, but to dig in and wait for the Luftwaffe to fly in weapons and supplies. The decision proved disastrous. The Luftwaffe was unable to transport anything like the necessary quantities of material, and the trapped men quickly found themselves isolated and close to starvation. For the majority of them, the Christmas of 1942 would be their last. The diaries and letters of the men in the Kessel, with their talk of snow and Christmas trees and Schubert on the piano, make poignant reading as they realise they have been abandoned to their fate. Hunger and frostbite took their toll. In early January, von Paulus reported, 'Army starving and frozen. No ammunition. No longer able to move tanks.' When a Luftwaffe general flew in to the *Kessel* to announce that supply operations were no longer possible, von Paulus told him, 'Don't you realise the men are so hungry that they pounce on the corpse of dead horses, split the head open and devour the brains raw!'* By 2 February 1943, when they finally ignored Hitler's threats and surrendered, only 90,000 of the initial 300,000 men remained alive. Of these just 5,000 would make it back home, having endured captivity in Soviet camps for many years after the war. The 6th Army, which had marched triumphantly through Belgium and France, was annihilated. Over a million people died in the battle for Stalingrad. But its outcome turned the war in favour of the Allies. The Soviets had ensured that the Germans would retreat from now on.

In the north the blockade of Leningrad continued. The city had been shelled remorselessly since August 1941, enduring 254 days of bombardments in 1942 alone. Its population was suffering terribly. On Nevsky Prospekt, the city's main thoroughfare, there are still reminders of the dark times, including a sign painted on a wall. 'Citizens!' it reads. 'During air raids this side of the street is more dangerous!' The Germans were so close that their music could be heard playing over loudspeakers; announcements in Russian called on Leningraders to surrender. On the outskirts of the city, Nazi troops laid waste to the great royal palaces – Peter the Great's summer residence at Petrodvorets, the Catherine Palace at Tsarskoe Selo and the royal estate at Gatchina. Repeated attempts to break the siege had failed, and thousands were dying of hunger every month. People ate dogs and cats; the animals disappeared from the Leningrad zoo. The bodies of those who collapsed from exhaustion were left lying in the street where they fell. Of the approximately 2.5 million residents at the start of the blockade, nearly 800,000 are thought to have starved to death, with 200,000 more killed by bombing raids. The physical destruction was immense. The city of Peter had been

---

* After the defeat at Stalingrad, Hitler urged von Paulus to commit suicide, but he refused. During his time as a prisoner of the Soviets, he became a strident critic of the Nazis and was finally released in 1953.

reduced to a shell of its former self. On returning to Leningrad in May 1944, Akhmatova wrote of her anguish at finding 'a terrible, terrible ghost that pretended to be my city'.

But Leningrad had not fallen. The heroism and 'Asiatic' stubbornness of the Russian people had repelled the Nazi hordes. I remember as a schoolboy staying at the city's famous Astoria Hotel (not then restored to its traditional – and expensive – splendour) and seeing some faded documents framed under glass in the hotel lobby. They were invitations from Adolf Hitler to the victory party he had confidently planned to hold in the Astoria. They had been printed in advance and even gave the date in 1942 on which the party was scheduled to take place.*

As the Germans were pushed back, Hitler ordered what would be his final offensive on the Eastern Front. The Soviet forces had been moving westwards at differing speeds in different sectors, and those around the city of Kursk, 300 miles south of Moscow, had advanced considerably further than the sectors immediately to their north and south. The effect was to create a bulge, or salient, of Soviet troops that Hitler decided was a vulnerable target. On 4 July 1943, some 900,000 German soldiers and nearly 3,000 tanks launched Operation Citadel. The aim was to attack the Kursk salient in a pincer movement from north and south and cut off the advanced Soviet forces. It was the first move in what was to be the largest tank battle in history. Zhukov had received intelligence reports of Hitler's intentions and was able to prepare defensive positions involving a million men, 4,000 tanks and 3,000 aircraft. The battle lasted for 50 days. Never before had a German blitzkrieg offensive failed to pierce the enemy's defensive line, but this time the Soviets stood firm. Just as at Borodino in 1812, the Russians lost more men than their foes, but the psychological victory was undoubtedly theirs. With the German advance halted, the Soviets sent penal battalions to clear the enemy minefields and thousands of T-34 tanks poured forward into the gap in the German lines. Hitler was again forced to retreat.

---

* When I visited the hotel again more recently, I was told Hitler's party invitations had been removed after complaints by German guests. They can now be seen in the State Memorial Museum of the Siege of Leningrad.

The Soviet victory at Kursk coincided with the American and British landing in Sicily in July 1943. The Axis Powers were now under siege from east and south, and the Allies were increasingly confident of success. In November 1943, the leaders of the big three Western Allies met for the first of their wartime conferences in Tehran. Stalin repeated his demand that Winston Churchill and Franklin D. Roosevelt open a second front in Western Europe and they agreed to do so, by May 1944 at the latest. More controversial was the question of what to do with Poland after the war. Stalin was adamant that the Soviet Union should hold onto Western Ukraine, Belorussia and the territory in eastern Poland that had once belonged to ancient Rus. He argued that Poland could be compensated with land on its western border that was currently part of Germany. Churchill and Roosevelt provisionally agreed that the post-war Soviet–Polish border would be along the Curzon Line of 1919. This would give the Soviet Union most of the Polish territory it had annexed under the secret protocol of the Molotov–Ribbentrop Pact, including the cities of Lvov, Brest-Litovsk and Vilnius. The Polish Government in Exile in London, officially recognised by the Allies as the country's legitimate government, were not even consulted. Their outrage at the proposed loss of Polish land met with little sympathy.

By the summer of 1944, the Germans had been driven out of the last square mile of Soviet territory. Operation Bagration, launched two weeks after the D-Day landings in Normandy, succeeded in dislodging the Axis forces from Belorussia and eastern Poland. Fifty-seven thousand captured Germans were paraded through Moscow in front of jeering crowds.* The Red Army swept through Romania, Hungary and Slovakia, and in early August it neared the eastern suburbs of Warsaw.

In anticipation of the approaching battle, the non-Communist Polish resistance movement, the Armia Krajowa (Home Army), loyal to the exiled

---

* For many years after the war, these men would remain in the USSR, working on construction projects and other public works to 'expiate their crimes'. The few who survived did not return to Germany until 1955. The building that used to house the BBC office in Moscow had been built by German POWs, and I remember Russians being envious of its high quality. Apartments built by 'the Germans' were considerably more desirable than Soviet-built blocks.

government in London, staged a concerted uprising against the Nazi occupiers. The timing of the uprising, which began on 1 August, was intended to stake Poland's claim to independence: the fighters wanted to have a hand in liberating Warsaw, to prevent Moscow claiming that it alone had rescued Poland. The Poles knew the Red Army stood on the eastern bank of the Vistula River and they expected the Soviets to join them in expelling the Germans. Indeed, Radio Moscow had been broadcasting appeals for Poland to rise up. But the Russians did nothing. For the next two months, the Red Army sat and watched as the Poles fought alone. At first the Armia Krajowa (AK), supported by the city's civilian population, enjoyed a measure of success, gaining control of large areas. But their forces were limited and inadequately armed. In mid August, the tide turned: the Germans had regrouped and were inflicting serious damage on the Poles. On instructions from Heinrich Himmler, the SS declared all inhabitants of the city to be legitimate military targets and went from house to house shooting men, women and children. Up to 50,000 civilians were executed by the Nazis and many more died in bombardments and exchanges of fire. The AK appealed for help, but Moscow did not respond. Churchill pleaded with Stalin to help the Poles, but he refused. By early September, the uprising was doomed. The partisans tried to escape through Warsaw's sewers, but many of them were rounded up and shot.* After the surrender of the remaining resistance forces, the Nazis decided to punish the Poles by systematically destroying their city. When the Soviets finally arrived in January 1945, around 85 per cent of the capital lay in ruins, making Warsaw the most damaged city in the war. A poem by a young Polish partisan, Jozef Szczepanski, was discovered in the ruins, with a defiant message for the Russians who had left him and his colleagues to die:

> Know this! You cannot harm us!
> You can choose to help us, deliver us,

---

* Andrzej Wajda's 1956 film *Kanal* (Sewer) is a chilling reconstruction of the uprising's last days. In Communist-ruled Poland, Wajda could not tell the full story of the Soviet treachery, but his film did enough for Poles to feel their sacrifice had not been forgotten.

Or still delay and leave us to perish …
Death is not terrible; we know how to die.
But know this! From our tombstones
A new Poland will be born in victory,
And never will you walk our land,
You Red ruler of bestial forces!

Sadly, Szczepanski was wrong. By deliberately postponing the seizure of Warsaw, Stalin had allowed the leading representatives of Polish nationalism to be wiped out en masse. The AK's rival, the much smaller Communist resistance group, the Armia Ludowa (People's Army), had been instructed by Moscow not to take part in the uprising, and its forces had survived intact. At Stalin's insistence, they would now provide the country's postwar pro-Soviet government, laying the foundations of the Communist yoke that would weigh on Poland for the next four decades.

After Warsaw, the Red Army resumed its rapid advance. By February 1945, it was within 50 miles of Berlin and facing desperate resistance from German forces. In the final months of the war, an astounding 300,000 Soviet soldiers were killed and over a million wounded on German soil. The Soviets were bent on revenge for the Nazi atrocities carried out in the Soviet Union. There was widespread rape, looting and the killing of civilians. Soviet commanders intervened only sparingly and only when such activities jeopardised discipline. Stalin himself was aware that Red Army soldiers raped tens of thousands of German women and tried to justify it in a conversation with the Yugoslav leader, Josip Tito, in April 1945:

I take it you have read Dostoevsky? So you know how complicated a thing the human psyche is? Well, imagine a man who has fought from Stalingrad to Belgrade, over thousands of kilometres of his own devastated land, across the dead bodies of his comrades and dear ones. How can you expect such a man to react normally? And, anyway, what is so awful in him having a bit of fun with a woman after such horrors? The Red Army is not composed of saints, nor can it be … The important thing is that it fights Germans.

The author Ilya Ehrenburg, who together with Vasily Grossman was among the greatest Soviet war correspondents, had spent the preceding years documenting German atrocities. Writing in the Red Army newspaper, *Red Star*, he had a stark message of revenge:

> The Germans are not human ... If you have killed one German, kill another. There is nothing better than German corpses. Don't count the miles you have travelled; count the number of Germans you have killed. Kill a German – that is what your mother asks of you. Kill a German – that is what your child begs of you. Kill a German – the earth that bore you is crying out for you to do it. Don't miss. Don't hesitate. Kill.

Ehrenburg, like Grossman, was Jewish and the two of them undertook a project to detail the Nazis' crimes against Soviet Jews. Their 'Black Book of the Holocaust' in the USSR bears exhaustive witness to the massacres and persecution, but for many years it remained unpublished. The Soviet authorities' ambivalent attitude towards anti-Semitism, and their unwillingness to 'divert attention from the suffering of the Soviet people', led them to ban it. From January 1945, the Red Army began to liberate the Nazi concentration camps in Central Europe: Auschwitz, Belzec, Chelmno, Sobibor and Treblinka. Vasily Grossman's article 'The Hell of Treblinka' (1944), for which he interviewed survivors and local inhabitants, would be used as evidence that helped convict the men responsible at the Nuremburg Trials.

With Soviet troops approaching Berlin, the Allies met again. This time, at Stalin's insistence, the conference was held at the Black Sea resort of Yalta, on 4 February 1945. It was here that the fate of Europe would be finally decided, and the foundations laid for the division between East and West that would last almost half a century. Roosevelt was by now a sick man, with only two months left to live. The newsreel footage of the Yalta conference shows him looking drawn and weak, barely able to lift his arm to shake hands with the other participants. Stalin took advantage, bullying FDR into accepting his vision of Europe's future, freezing out Churchill whenever he objected. It was agreed that the Polish Government in Exile would return from London to join the Communist-dominated Provisional Government already installed in Warsaw. Stalin accepted that elections would be held as soon as possible, secure in the knowledge that pro-Communist forces were already in charge. Together with the confirmation that the Curzon Line would be recognised as the border between Poland and the Soviet Union, the measures were a sell-out of Polish interests. Even today, Poles regard 'Yalta' as a synonym for treachery and double dealing.

In mid April, the final assault on Berlin began. The forces of Marshals Zhukov and Konev raced each other to take the prize, pounding the Nazi capital with ceaseless artillery barrages, firing a greater tonnage of ordnance than the Allied bombers had dropped on the city in the whole course of the war. After a week of street-to-street fighting, the Soviets arrived in central Berlin on 2 May. Hitler had committed suicide two days earlier in his bunker under the Reich Chancellery. The troops who discovered his charred corpse – together with those of Eva Braun, Josef Goebbels and his family – reportedly destroyed the evidence to prevent the relics becoming a focus for Nazi sympathisers. The famous photo of Soviet soldiers raising the Communist flag with the hammer and sickle over the Reichstag was taken that same afternoon, a re-enactment of the scene that had taken place the night before, when no camera had been on hand. Even the staged photo did not entirely please the Soviet censors. One of the two soldiers could clearly be seen wearing two watches, a sure sign that he had been looting. The watches were edited out before the picture was released to the world.

In the early hours of 8 May, Germany signed an unconditional surrender to the Western Allies. Stalin toasted the victory at a reception of Red Army commanders at the Kremlin:

> Comrades, I would like to raise a toast to the health of our Soviet people and, most of all, to the Russian people. [*Loud, continuous applause; shouts of 'Hooray!'*] I drink, most of all, to the health of the Russian people because they are the most outstanding nation of all the nations of the Soviet Union ... the leading force among all the peoples of our country.

On 24 June, four years and two days after the Nazis had poured across the Soviet border, Zhukov led the victory parade on a white stallion across Red

Square. The drama of the galloping horse and the deafening shouts of *Oorah!* – 'hooray' – were a magnificent spectacle, full of joy for the survivors, redolent with the pain of the bereaved. (Stalin had been determined to lead the parade himself, but had twice been thrown by the stallion and cursed, 'Fuck this. Let Zhukov do it!') As the Red Army troops marched past the Lenin mausoleum, throwing down the piles of Nazi standards and banners captured from the foe, the Soviet Union celebrated its greatest moment of triumph.

The nation had shown its heroism and now it hoped for its reward. As in 1812, the Russian people waited for the state to recognise their sacrifice by granting them freedom and the right to participate in the running of their country. But their aspirations for civic participation after the war were again to be thwarted. Stalin intended to return to his old methods.

CHAPTER THIRTY-THREE

The Soviet Union lost between 20 and 25 million people in the Second World War – over 10 per cent of its population. By comparison, Germany had lost some 7 million, Great Britain 500,000 and the United States 300,000; the Soviet Union suffered as many casualties in the fighting at Stalingrad as did the US and the UK in the whole of the war. The huge death toll resulted in a damaging imbalance of women to men, and the birth rate of the post-war generation plummeted. The formerly occupied lands of the Soviet Union had been devastated. The scorched earth tactics of the retreating Red Army had rendered the soil infertile and wrecked agricultural production; when the Germans departed, they flooded mines, destroyed train tracks and blew up factories. Much of western Russia was a wasteland, where homeless millions wandered through the ruins of towns and villages.

Stalin demanded massive reparations. At the Potsdam conference in late July and early August 1945, the Allies divided Germany and Austria, along with their capital cities, into four zones of occupation to be administered by the US, UK, Soviet Union and France. Each of the victors would be awarded a share of German assets, and the Soviets promptly shipped 11,000 tons of industrial equipment to the east. Stalin was the only one of the Big Three leaders still in power at Potsdam. Harry Truman had replaced the recently deceased FDR, while Clement Attlee ousted Winston Churchill as prime minister in elections held during the conference.* Stalin felt he had the measure of his neophyte partners, and his bargaining position was strong. The Red Army's advances in the final months of the war

---

* Voting in the election took place on 5 July, but the results were not announced until 26 July, partly because the votes of British servicemen still serving overseas needed to be counted. So while Churchill attended the first ten days of the conference, he was replaced by Attlee for the final week.

had established it as the occupying power in the Baltic states, Poland, Czechoslovakia, Hungary, Bulgaria and Romania. The division of Europe existed de facto, and at Potsdam Stalin pressed the British and Americans to recognise it de jure. He advanced the age-old argument that Russia must protect its vulnerable borders. To do so, it needed to acquire influence over the territories surrounding it; so the countries of Central and Eastern Europe would become Moscow's 'buffer states', a sphere of influence in which the Western Allies would have little or no say. For nations such as Poland, whose soldiers had fought alongside the Allies for nearly six years – and whose Government in Exile would now play no role in running their newly 'liberated' homeland – it was an unspeakable betrayal. For their part, the Baltic countries, Latvia, Lithuania and Estonia, would lose their statehood altogether and become mere republics in the 'brotherhood of nations' that was the Soviet Union.

Men and women of all the Soviet nationalities – not just Russians – had fought bravely to ensure the survival of the USSR; there was a widespread expectation that life would be better now and society freer. Stalin's public rhetoric was encouraging. In a speech broadcast on 9 February 1946, he went out of his way to praise the manner in which the nationalities had pulled together during the war. 'The Soviet Union has proved to be a model multinational state,' he claimed, 'a state organisation in which the national question and the problem of the collaboration of nations have found a better solution than in any other multinational state ...' But the warm words and self-congratulation masked a darker reality. Now that the external enemy had been defeated, Stalin's attention turned to the (real or imagined) 'enemy within'.

From the very start of the war, Moscow had embarked on a concerted campaign of ethnic engineering within the borders of the USSR, arresting, expelling and deporting members of national groups that Stalin viewed as potential Nazi collaborators. In August 1941, he had begun with the Volga Germans. These were the descendants of scholars, artists, engineers and military advisers invited to settle in Russia nearly 200 years earlier by the German-born empress Catherine the Great. Their families had been in

Russia so long that they were Russian in all but name. In the years since 1930 they had won high praise for being at the forefront of the collectivisation effort. Yet Stalin convinced himself that these people would welcome Hitler's troops and help destroy the Soviet Union. He ordered the Volga German Autonomous Republic liquidated and its inhabitants deported. Approximately 400,000 people were rounded up, evicted from their homes and taken in forced transports to the deserts of Kazakhstan in Central Asia or the Altai Region in Siberia. On arrival, the majority of them were drafted into the Trudarmiya, the Labour Army, effectively a network of work camps designed to boost the war effort.*

Stalin seemed to view the war as an excuse to move against any nationality he viewed with suspicion. The Nazi occupation of the Caucasus and the Crimea in 1942 had fuelled his paranoia about the native peoples of the area. In confidential memos, he declared that the local nationalities were not to be trusted and made clear that he expected stern measures to be taken against them.** Just as he had done in the Baltic states in 1939, Stalin

---

* As late as the 1980s, I had friends in Moscow whose families were still in exile: the father of one of them was the editor of the Volga German newspaper *Vozrozhdenie* (Rebirth) which had campaigned for 40 years for the right to return. Oddly, the problem was partly solved in the Gorbachev era when the Volga Germans were allowed to emigrate and the West Germany embassy was suddenly besieged by queues of people with German-sounding names, all of whom were promptly issued with visas. Few questions were asked and no immigration quotas imposed. The West German authorities were acutely sensitive to the plight of their fellow citizens 'trapped' in Russia from all periods of history, from the eighteenth century to the Second World War. Their liberal Law of Return opened the way for thousands to make new lives in the West.

** Typical is Stalin's confidential Order Number. 5859ss regarding the Crimean Tartars, which was issued on 11 May 1944: 'Many Crimean Tartars betrayed the motherland, deserting Red Army units that defended the Crimea and siding with the enemy, joining volunteer army units formed by the Germans to fight against the Red Army; as members of German punitive detachments during the occupation of the Crimea by German fascist troops, the Crimean Tartars particularly were noted for their savage reprisals against Soviet partisans, and also helped the German invaders to organise the violent round-up of Soviet citizens for German enslavement and the mass extermination of the Soviet people. Taking into account the facts cited above: All Tartars are to be banished from the territory of the Crimea and resettled permanently as special settlers in the regions of the Uzbek SSR. The resettlement will be assigned to the Soviet NKVD. The Soviet NKVD (comrade Beria) is to complete the resettlement by 1 June 1944.'

decided that the USSR's southern borders needed to be populated by 'more reliable' (Russian or Ukrainian) elements. Beginning in early 1944, hundreds of thousands of Chechens, Ingush, Balkars, Karachai, Kalmyks and Crimean Tartars were deported from their ancestral homelands in the north Caucasus and Crimea, allegedly as punishment for collaborating with the Nazis. In fact, only a small minority had collaborated, not significantly more than in Ukraine or other parts of the Soviet Union.* The vast majority of Caucasian males had been drafted into the Red Army just like everyone else and had fought bravely for its liberation. While they were fighting for the USSR, their families – women, children and the elderly – were piled into cattle trucks and taken off to be 'resettled indefinitely' in Siberia, the Urals, Uzbekistan and Kazakhstan. The deportations were carried out at great speed, often with no warning. Those who were ill or who refused to go were shot, as one Chechen deportee recorded in his unpublished diary for February 1944:

> The chairman of one of the village soviets, 80-year-old Tusha, assisted in the removal of his fellow villagers, his family being shipped off as well. Only his daughter-in-law remained with him, with her child at her breast. Addressing a Georgian officer, Tusha said in his broken Russian, 'Me born here, me here die. Me no go anywhere!' Tusha spread his arms out and

---

* While it is true that Chechen independence groups had seized on the German invasion as a chance to rise up against Soviet rule, active collaboration had actually been more widespread in other parts of the Soviet Union. The Baltic states, western Belorussia, western Ukraine and Moldavia all had incipient resistance movements opposed to Soviet rule. When the Germans arrived, some of them volunteered to collaborate in the misguided hope of reasserting their national identities. Nationalist forces in some areas attempted to fight against both sides at once, vainly hoping to free their homeland from both communists and fascists, and even after the Germans had been defeated, resistance to Soviet rule continued. In a little-known episode of history (the Soviet authorities banned all reference to it), the Organisation of Ukrainian Nationalists and the Ukrainian Insurrectionary Army continued full-scale military operations long after the end of the war to try to prevent the reintegration of Ukraine into the USSR. The scale of the fighting was remarkable: in 1946, the Red Army had over half a million troops in action against the partisans and it took another wave of mass deportations to end Ukrainian resistance.

stood before the gate of his home. The daughter-in-law understood. She cried out and, pressing her child to her breast, took hold of her father-in-law. She pulled him and pulled him towards our group, crying all the while, 'Daddy, Daddy, come on! They'll kill you.' It all happened in an instant. The officer gave an order to a Russian soldier standing with his automatic at the ready. 'Shoot! All three.' The soldier blanched and trembled. He said: 'The man I will shoot but not the woman and the child.' A pistol flashed in the officer's hand. Before the soldier had finished his last word he lay on the ground, shot through the head. Within the same instant, the officer had killed Tusha, his daughter-in-law and her child. They drove us in haste down the path to the roadway. There trucks were waiting for us. Those who lagged behind were shot. That is the way it was.

The journey eastwards took over a month and many died from starvation and disease. The dead were buried by the side of the road or railway line. Those who survived found little or no preparation had been made for them at their destination. They were confined in 'special settlements' in the most primitive conditions, and NKVD figures suggest 20 per cent of them were dead within a year. The Kremlin was punishing those ethnic groups, often Muslims, who had resisted integration into the Soviet way of life. The deportees were banned from using their native languages, and access to education was severely restricted.

Throughout the Soviet Union the question of nationality became one of vital importance. The atmosphere of xenophobia during the war and the rumours of sinister foreign forces at work within Soviet society meant everyone was suspect. Official propaganda denounced individual ethnic groups – Crimean Tartars, Chechens, Germans and, increasingly, Jews – urging Soviet citizens to be on their guard against them. The old rhetoric of class enemies had been replaced by that of ethnic enemies. In *Life and Fate*, Vasily Grossman highlights how nationality replaced social origin as the most sensitive entry on people's internal passports:

Point five: 'Nationality'… This had been so simple and insignificant before the war; but now it was acquiring a particular resonance. Pressing heavily on his pen, Viktor wrote boldly and distinctly, 'Jew'. He wasn't to know what price hundreds of thousands of people would soon pay for answering Kalmyk, Balkar, Chechen, Crimean Tartar or Jew. He wasn't to know what dark passions would gather year by year around this point. He couldn't foresee what fear, anger, despair and blood would spill over from the neighbouring sixth point, 'Social Origin'. He couldn't foresee how in a few years' time many people would answer this fifth point with a sense of doom – the same sense of doom with which the children of Cossack officers, priests, landlords and factory owners had once answered the sixth point.

The official media whipped up public anger against 'foreign' influences that were said to undermine the people's sense of their homeland, denouncing the offending ethnic groups as 'cosmopolitans'. It was a term that came increasingly to be identified with the Jews. There had been a resurgence in anti-Semitism during the rapprochement with Nazi Germany, but it was temporarily submerged in the chaos of war and the sense of common cause against the foe. After 1941, Stalin had given the Kremlin's blessing to Jewish organisations that rallied opposition to the Nazis. The most influential of them was the Jewish Anti-Fascist Committee (JAC), led by the popular actor Solomon Mikhoels. He was the artistic director of the Moscow State Jewish Theatre and famous throughout the USSR for his role in the 1936 musical *Circus*, which celebrated the brotherhood of the Soviet nationalities. Mikhoels and other JAC members travelled to the West to drum up support for the Soviet Union amongst the Jewish Diaspora, raising millions for the war effort. But at home there were ominous developments. In 1943, Jews were systematically removed from the army's political apparatus and baseless rumours were spread about Jewish cowardice and desertion. In 1948, the creation of the state of Israel, seen as an ally of the now reviled West, sharpened old prejudices. Those Jews who had survived the war in occupied territories were accused of collaborating with the Nazis. How else could they have survived? Approximately half of the Soviet Union's pre-war Jewish population had been murdered in the Holocaust, more than 1 million people, yet the JAC's attempts to highlight the tragedy did not please the Kremlin. Like Grossman and Ehrenburg's 'Black Book', the JAC's focus on

Nazi mistreatment of Jews was considered incompatible with the official line that the whole of the Soviet Union suffered equally. Information on the Holocaust was suppressed, and in the heightened nationalism of the post-war years Jews suffered once again.

Once the war ended, the JAC's propaganda value vanished. The ties its members had forged with other Jewish organisations across the world made it an object of official suspicion, and Stalin ordered the JAC to be shut down in 1948 on the pretext that it was a 'centre of anti-Soviet propaganda'. It was announced that Mikhoels had been run over and killed by a truck in Minsk, and a state funeral was held for him in the Donskoy Monastery in Moscow. In reality, he had been beaten to death by the Belorussian security services on the direct orders of the Kremlin. The murder of Mikhoels signalled the start of an intensive period of state-sponsored anti-Semitism that would last until Stalin's death. In June 1949, 15 other members of the JAC executive committee, prominent actors, poets, writers and doctors, were arrested on Stalin's orders and taken to the cells of the Lubyanka. For three years they were held in isolation, beaten and tortured. Their interrogation records reveal the extent of the Kremlin's fury against men and women who just a few years earlier had been praised as loyal allies. 'The Jews are foul, dirty people,' an investigator named as Colonel Vladimir Komarov yelled at the prisoners. 'All Jews are worthless scum. The entire opposition to the party is made up of Jews. All Jews throughout the Soviet Union spit on Soviet power. The Jews want to annihilate every Russian.' One of the arrested men is said to have received over 2,000 blows. In August 1952, the 15 were charged with treason, espionage and bourgeois nationalism. With the state media whipping up a campaign against 'rootless cosmopolitans', the verdicts were barely in doubt. On 12 August 1952, in what would become known as 'the night of the murdered poets', 13 of the defendants were condemned to death and immediately executed.

Anti-Semitism was now a semi-official state policy. Jews were frozen out of many jobs; access to higher education was severely restricted. Textbooks no longer mentioned that Karl Marx was Jewish. Films, including the musical *Circus*, were re-edited to cut out the appearances of Mikhoels. And further repressions would follow.

If there was one group that might have expected things to improve after the war, it was the ethnic Russians. Since the middle of the 1930s, the Russians had been singled out as the favoured nation amongst the Soviet people. A *Pravda* editorial in 1936 is typical of the official rhetoric:

> All the peoples – participants in the great socialist construction – may be proud of the results of their labour; every one of them, from the smallest to the largest, are Soviet patriots. But first among these equals are the Russian people ... whose role throughout the whole Great Proletarian Revolution has been exceptionally important, from the first victories to today's magnificent period of development.

Just as the workers had been praised as the vanguard of the class war, the Russians were now the leading nation of the Soviet Union. Russian teaching was made compulsory in the non-Russian republics, and during the war Russia was held up as the example to inspire and unite the peoples of the Union. In *Life and Fate*, the decent, courageous Major Yershov, captured by the Nazis, sums up what he and countless others were fighting for:

> He was certain that he was not only fighting the Germans, but fighting for a free Russia: certain that a victory over Hitler would be a victory over the death camps where his father, his mother and his sisters had perished ...

But Stalin had no intention of rewarding the Russian people. He was a student of Russian history and determined to avoid what he saw as the mistakes of his predecessors. Just a few days after the fall of Berlin, Stalin had told the novelist Konstantin Simonov that he did not want a repeat of what had happened after Russia's victory over Napoleon. 'Stalin feared a new Decembrist movement,' Simonov wrote. 'He felt he had introduced Ivan to Europe and Europe to Ivan. Just as Alexander I had done in 1813–14 ...'

Stalin knew that Alexander I's troops had been impressed by the freedom and prosperity they encountered during their occupation of Paris, and that this had inspired them to fight for change in their own country. The Decembrists' desire for reform had its roots in their experience abroad, and that same experience had just been granted to the Red Army. In 1945, Soviet soldiers in Germany had collected as many consumer goods as they could lay their hands on, from wristwatches and radios to carpets. They had come into contact with British and American troops, with Western ways of doing things, and with Western freedoms. In Stalin's eyes, they had undoubtedly been infected with all the dangerous values he had striven to keep out of the Soviet Union and he resolved not to let this contagion affect his own reign.

Most at risk from the wrath of the dictator were those Red Army soldiers who had been captured by the Germans. The Soviet state maintained its line that surrender was a criminal offence, and all troops taken prisoner were viewed as traitors. The Kremlin had refused to sign the Geneva Convention, effectively disowning its own men and preventing the International Red Cross from protecting them. Of the nearly six million Soviet POWs, less than half survived to the end of the war.

The Nazis had played on their captives' fear, hunger and desperation, offering them food and clothing if they would switch sides and join the German forces. Some accepted the offer, including most notably General Andrei Vlasov, one of the heroes of the Battle of Moscow. In a major propaganda coup, the Nazis appointed Vlasov to create a 'Russian Liberation Army' of former POWs, which he would lead into battle against the Soviet Union. Vlasov said his aim was to build 'a Russia without Bolsheviks and capitalists', denouncing Communism for its brutal collectivisation measures, repression of the peasants (he was himself the son of a repressed *kulak*) and what he called the 'trampling underfoot of everything Russian'. History has regarded Vlasov as a traitor and an opportunist, but his detailed 'Prague Manifesto' of November 1944 made clear that his views were anti-Bolshevik, not anti-Russian. He toured the POW camps spreading the message that Germany was waging a war against Communism, not against the motherland, but he failed to gain widespread support. Despite the threat of death from starvation, fewer than one in ten of the POWs signed up. Vlasov's army never engaged in anything more than a limited skirmish with Soviet forces and ultimately switched sides again to fight against the Nazis.

To Stalin, though, the fact that *some* Red Army men had betrayed the Soviet Union tarred them all. In his Manichean mind, every returning POW was a potential enemy. NKVD filtration camps were set up to quiz returning POWs about how they had been captured and why they had not fought to the death like real patriots. No one was trusted: by the end of 1946, millions of Soviet citizens had been through the filtration camps and 300,000 had been sentenced to summary execution or long terms in the Gulag. More than half a million were consigned to hard-labour battalions rebuilding the devastated Soviet Union, and over a million were sent back for further service in the Red Army. All of them, even those released without punishment, would live the rest of their lives under the stigma of having been captured by the Germans.*

Many POWs were aware of the possible fate that awaited them in the Soviet Union, and large numbers tried to remain in countries held by the British and Americans. The agreements reached at the Yalta conference, however, included an undertaking that all those designated as Soviet citizens – civilians and soldiers alike – would be forcibly repatriated. In the course of Operation Keelhaul (1946–7), the Allies handed over more than 2 million people to the Soviet authorities. The ominous title of the operation suggests the Allies knew what might happen to them, but they wanted their own citizens back from the USSR. France, for instance, had nearly 100,000 Soviet citizens on territory it controlled at the end of the war, made up of men who had joined the Wehrmacht, forced labourers and some escaped POWs who had fought with the French resistance. Paris was under pressure to mollify the Soviets as it was pressing for the return of 13,000 French citizens, mainly from the Franco–German border areas of Alsace-Lorraine, who had been captured on the eastern front fighting in the Wehrmacht. As a result, the French made no attempt to distinguish between the categories of Soviet citizens they were holding and simply sent them all back to face whatever destiny awaited them.

---

* Until the 1980s, the question 'Have you or your family lived in occupied territory or been taken captive?' was a routine enquiry on job applications, with the clear implication that a positive response would indicate guilt or the suspicion of guilt.

Stalin also demanded the return of all Russian émigrés, including those who had lived abroad for many decades.* To his surprise, the Allies agreed to cooperate. The NKVD was allowed to set up a detention camp at the Château de Beauregard on the outskirts of Paris, where thousands of POWs and others who refused to return voluntarily were handed over to Soviet control. NKVD agents roamed the streets of Paris forcibly abducting Russians, while the French authorities turned a blind eye. Those who had fled from the revolution and spent the intervening years opposing Bolshevik rule would be returning to certain death in the Soviet Union. Andrei Vlasov, who had surrendered to the Americans, was handed over when Soviet troops surrounded the car in which he was being transported. After a year's interrogation in the Lubyanka, he and seven other generals were hanged in August 1946. In return for French, British and American cooperation, the Soviets freed Allied prisoners they had liberated from Nazi camps in eastern Germany.

The somewhat unexpected return of so many Soviet POWs caused Moscow problems. The Gulag rapidly filled with Red Army officers and soldiers, as well as prisoners from the re-occupied Baltic states. They all had good reason to detest the Soviet regime. Service in the war, often under desperate conditions, had taught them discipline, independence of thinking and a fierce loyalty to one another. They refused to be broken by Stalin's camps. They did not inform on one another and they dealt mercilessly with individuals who collaborated with the camp authorities. By the late 1940s and early 1950s, disturbances and uprisings in the Gulag were becoming increasingly common.

Outside the camps, those returning soldiers unaffected by Stalin's 'special measures' were also finding life tough. They found themselves demobilised in a land devastated by war. There were chronic shortages of food and basic goods, and not enough housing or jobs. Many former soldiers were forced to dig temporary shelters in the ground, much as they had done at the front. After four years fighting for the Soviet cause, they

---

* Many of them had been born in pre-revolutionary Russia and had never been Soviet citizens, so technically were not covered by the Yalta agreement.

returned to find their home towns destroyed, and their wives and children unable to comprehend what they had gone through. The harrowing experiences of those who fought at the front and those who stayed behind often made it impossible to start again where they had left off.*

In some ways, former soldiers were perceived as a threat to the regime. These were men whose shared experience had created an emotional bond between them, a bond that the Kremlin feared might outweigh their loyalty to the state. There was a prohibition on the formation of veterans' groups. Soldiers were actively discouraged from taking part in public life, expressing their opinions or writing their memoirs. The perception that they were being prevented from talking about their experiences – with the veiled suggestion that these experiences were somehow reprehensible – left many of them feeling frustrated and abandoned. The state was now seeking to suppress the very qualities it had encouraged during the years of fighting. Qualities such as courage, initiative and enterprise had been vital during the war; now they were again deemed to be worthless – or, even worse, dangerous – in a society that insisted on conformity, obedience and subservience. Alcohol rates rose alarmingly among ex-soldiers and civilians alike as the sense of disillusionment increased.

For the civilian population, too, post-war life was full of disappointments. The war seemed to have changed little; there were few improvements in either material standards or citizens' rights. In 1946, famine struck, as the diminished availability of arable land, the shortage of able-bodied men and the disruption of production left nearly 100 million people hungry. Two million starved to death, including half a million Russians in the traditional

---

* A grave shortage of hospital beds and doctors made the care of injured soldiers difficult; many were denied both medical treatment and social care. In the 1970s, I was shocked by the number of amputee veterans on the streets of Russian cities. Little had been done to help them after the war and many had been reduced to begging. Most distressing were the so-called *samovars*, men who had lost both arms and both legs and were wheeled around in crude wooden carts, often with a handwritten sign asking for charity. Instead of making proper provision for people who had sacrificed themselves in the Soviet cause, the Kremlin had callously sent many of them to be resettled in the far north, where their abandonment by the state would be less publicly obvious.

agricultural lands of the Volga. The increased religious freedom of the war years ended, and practising Christians once again faced discrimination. The liberalisation in the arts that had done much to inspire patriotism and loyalty was reversed. In August 1946, it was decreed once again that all literature, art and music must serve the purposes of Marxism–Leninism–Stalinism, rejecting Western, bourgeois influence. (The crackdown became known by the name of 'Zhdanovshchina', after the commissar for culture, Andrei Zhdanov.) Anna Akhmatova, following her brief period of acceptance by the state, was effectively banned from publishing, and the satirist Mikhail Zoshchenko was heavily criticised. The crime of 'formalism' – anything that did not match the state's recipe for simple, uplifting conformity – was used to reprimand Shostakovich, Prokofiev and Khachaturian. Stalin himself upbraided writers and film directors, including the already terrified Sergei Eisenstein. Hopes were being crushed; the Soviet Union was returning to its old stereotypes.

CHAPTER THIRTY-FOUR

On 22 May 1945, just two weeks after the German surrender, Winston Churchill received a top secret document he had commissioned from the Joint Planning Staff of the British Military Command. Labelled 'Operation Unthinkable', the document laid out the plan of attack for a major renewal of hostilities. On the front page, the words 'Russia: Threat to Western Civilisation' were written by hand in ink, followed by a bald statement of the plan's objective: 'To impose upon Russia the will of the United States and the British Empire'. The paper explored the possibility of a pre-emptive strike against the Soviet Union. 'A quick success might induce the Russians to submit to our will at least for the time being. But if they want total war, they are in a position to have it ... The only way in which we can achieve our object with certainty and lasting results is by victory in a total war.' Under the headings 'Decisive Defeat of the Russian Forces' and 'Occupation of Vital Areas of Russia', it discusses the pros and cons of Britain and the US committing to such a 'total war'. Not surprisingly, the need for secrecy was paramount: 'Owing to the special need for secrecy,' it noted, 'the normal staffs in Service Ministries have not been consulted.'

The offensive never took place. The British generals concluded with typical understatement that an invasion of the Soviet Union would be 'hazardous'. But the implication was clear: Europe, and to a lesser extent the world, was once again divided, this time between communist and capitalist camps. Pro-Soviet governments were in power in Poland, Czechoslovakia, Hungary, Yugoslavia, Bulgaria, Romania and Albania. The West had hung on to Greece, but even there its grip was tenuous. Communist movements were gaining ground in Italy and France.

The Soviet Union and the Western Allies had fought together in a coalition of convenience, and once the fascist threat had been defeated, the pre-war suspicion returned. Churchill's personal distrust of Stalin was clear, but the reasoning behind Operation Unthinkable was based on more than just intuition. In 1945, the size of Soviet forces in Europe was enormous; Stalin had made clear that he would not relinquish the grip Moscow now exerted in the eastern part of the continent, and there was a very real fear that he had designs on the West, that he too might be thinking the unthinkable.

By the end of July, Churchill was out of office. The man who had led Britain to victory had been replaced by the reformist, left-leaning Labour government of Clement Attlee. Churchill did not go quietly. Just as he had railed against the growing Nazi menace in the 1930s, warning against the complacency of the civilised nations, now he turned his Cassandra gaze on the menace of Communism. His speech, 'The Sinews of Peace', delivered in Fulton, Missouri, on 5 March 1946, etched an image in the imagination of the world that would define the realities of post-war Europe for the next 40 years:

> From Stettin in the Baltic to Trieste in the Adriatic, an iron curtain has descended across the Continent. Behind that line lie all the capitals of the ancient states of Central and Eastern Europe. Warsaw, Berlin, Prague, Vienna, Budapest, Belgrade, Bucharest and Sofia, all these famous cities lie in what I must call 'the Soviet sphere', and all are subject in one form or another, not only to Soviet influence, but to a very high, and, in some cases, increasing measure of control from Moscow ... The Communist parties have been raised to pre-eminence and power far beyond their numbers and are seeking everywhere to obtain totalitarian control ... This is certainly not the liberated Europe we fought to build up, nor is it one which contains the essentials of permanent peace.

The warning was unambiguous, and Stalin reacted angrily. On 12 March, in an interview in *Pravda*, he spoke in bellicose terms of Western imperialism's desire for war, claiming, 'Mr Churchill and his allies resemble Hitler and his allies. They have concluded that the English-speaking nations should rule the world.' With no access to news or information other than the official state media, all of which were full of Stalin's pronouncements, the vast majority of Soviet people believed that Britain and America were now warmongers, most probably future enemies. Stalin's reply to Churchill's charge of 'Soviet expansionism' was one that every Russian understood: in light of Russia's long history of foreign invasions, the creation of 'buffer states' in the countries of Eastern Europe was a natural objective.

> Mr Churchill speaks of 'unlimited expansionist tendencies' on the part of the Soviet Union. But the following circumstance should not be forgotten. The Germans were able to make their invasion of the USSR through these countries because they had governments hostile to the Soviet Union ... So what can there be surprising about the fact that the Soviet Union, anxious for its future safety, is trying to see to it that governments loyal in their attitude to the Soviet Union should exist in these countries? How can anyone, who has not taken leave of his wits, describe these peaceful aspirations of the Soviet Union as expansionist tendencies? ... If Mr Churchill and his allies succeed in organising a new armed campaign against Eastern Europe – as they did 26 years ago [during the Western intervention against the Bolshevik regime after the revolution] – it may confidently be said that they will be thrashed, just as they were thrashed the last time.

It was a blunt warning, but Stalin's swagger masked an inner panic. Despite the Red Army's size and successes in the war, the Soviet Union did not possess what the US did: the nuclear bomb. The spectacle of what the new American weapon had done to the Japanese cities of Hiroshima and Nagasaki in August 1945 had convinced Stalin that the Red Army's numerical strength was now meaningless. Soviet society was gripped by the sudden, dreadful knowledge that the warmongers in London and Washington had the means to wipe out Moscow, Leningrad and innumerable other cities. Alexander Werth, the *Sunday Times*'s correspondent in Moscow, reported that the nuclear terror was all-pervading:

> The news [of Hiroshima and Nagasaki] had an acutely depressing effect on everybody. It was clearly realised that this was a New Fact in the world's power politics, that the bomb constitutes a threat to Russia, and some Russ-

ian pessimists I talked to that day dismally remarked that Russia's desperately hard-earned victory over Germany was now 'as good as wasted'.

Werth was permitted to ask Stalin about the bomb, and the dictator had a studiously upbeat reply. 'Atomic bombs are meant to frighten those with weak nerves,' he told his questioner, 'but they cannot on their own decide the outcome of wars. Of course, monopoly ownership of the secret of the atomic bomb creates a threat. But there are at least two remedies. Monopoly ownership of the bomb cannot last for long. And use of the atomic bomb will be prohibited.'

Stalin clearly did not trust prohibition. Moscow had declined to join Washington's newly created Atomic Energy Commission, which was given the task of regulating nuclear weapons, so only one option remained. The Soviet Union would have to develop its own bomb and quickly. The need became even more pressing when, in March 1947, President Truman announced his doctrine of US support for nations struggling for liberty and democracy, a doctrine aimed initially at preventing Greece and Turkey falling into communist hands, but with the wider target of the East European nations already under the Soviet yoke. It was confirmation that the US and the Soviet Union were on a collision course.

Three months later, Washington announced a programme of economic and technical assistance to European states struggling to rebuild their economies after the war. The European Recovery Program, popularly known as the Marshall Plan, offered to make aid available to countries on both sides of the Iron Curtain. The total eventually provided exceeded $13 billion, or 5 per cent of the United States' annual GDP, but Washington's largesse brought obligations with it. Recipient nations would have to furnish details of their national economy and cooperate with US advisers in a programme of modernisation and restructuring. While West European nations eagerly signed up to the Marshall Plan, Stalin was wary. Vladimir Yerofeyev, a member of the Soviet team that negotiated with the Americans, felt Stalin would have liked to take the money but mistrusted Truman's motives. 'Stalin was always suspicious,' he wrote, 'and he wasn't keen on it from the very start. He said: "Just you watch. The situation is quite different from the wartime Lend-Lease American assistance to us. With the Truman Doctrine in place as well, they don't really want to help us. This is a ploy by Truman. They want to tear the People's Democracies away from our sphere of influence, to win them over, infiltrate them, and pull them away from the Soviet Union.'" When Czechoslovakia and Poland said they might take the American money, Stalin ordered them to refuse. He was determined to shape the previously capitalist economies of his 'buffer states' to the Soviet model of socialist central planning; American influence was seen as hostile interference.

To counter the Marshall Plan, Moscow created Comecon, the Council for Mutual Economic Assistance, in January 1949. The new body issued a defiant statement to the Western powers:

> The governments of the United States of America, of Great Britain, and of certain Western European states have imposed a trade boycott on the countries of People's Democracy and the USSR because these countries did not consider it appropriate that they should submit themselves to the dictatorship of the Marshall Plan, which would have violated their sovereignty and the interests of their national economies. In the light of these circumstances ... the countries of People's Democracy [Bulgaria, Hungary, Poland, Romania and Czechoslovakia] and the USSR, consider it necessary to create the Council for Mutual Economic Assistance, on the basis of equal representation between the member countries ... to accelerate the restoration and development of their national economies.

The Eastern Bloc was pulling up the drawbridge. But, for Stalin, socialism would be safe only when Moscow had the bomb.

Work had begun on nuclear fission in the Soviet Union in the late 1930s, but purges of scientists and the outbreak of war had hampered progress. Soviet spies had alerted Stalin to Western progress on the bomb in the early days of the war, and in 1943 the Soviet Union set up its own research programme. It would be led by the brilliant physicist Igor Kurchatov, known to his colleagues as *boroda* – 'the beard' – because of his long, shaggy whiskers and amiable, shambolic personality. Less than a week after the United States dropped the bomb to end the war in the East, Stalin called Kurchatov and his team to the Kremlin. 'I have only one demand to put to you, comrades,' he told them. 'Build us an atomic weapon in the shortest possible time! Hiroshima has shaken the world. The balance of power has been destroyed. You must build the bomb to save us from a grave danger.' As they were leaving, Stalin called them back. 'Ask for whatever you want, comrades. You won't be refused. As the saying goes: if a child doesn't cry, the mother won't know what he needs.'

The state of Soviet science was far from rosy. Before the revolution, Russia had produced some of the world's great scientific minds, from Dmitry Mendeleev, inventor of the periodic table, to Konstantin Tsiolkovsky, the pioneer of astronautics. But, as in so many areas of Soviet life, science had been undermined by ideological dogmatism. The USSR's wheat farming had been nearly destroyed when Stalin insisted on implementing the crackpot theories of the agronomist Trofim Lysenko, largely because Lysenko was himself a peasant and had caught the dictator's attention by denouncing the 'kulaks of science'. Einstein's theory of relativity, on the other hand, was rejected as 'bourgeois, reactionary and incompatible with Marxism–Leninism', probably because its inventor was a German–American Jew. Only when Kurchatov informed the Kremlin that they would be unable to develop an atomic weapon without Einstein's research did Stalin relent, telling Beria to 'leave them in peace – we can always shoot them later'.

To speed the research, a new atomic weapons laboratory was created in 1946. Known by the code name Arzamas-16, it was located in the closed town of Sarov, 250 miles east of Moscow. Kurchatov nicknamed his new home 'Los Arzamas', a pun on the Manhattan Project's Los Alamos facility in New Mexico, where the bombs dropped on Japan had been created. Support facilities were built across the Soviet Union, and the physicists were well looked after, their salaries doubling or tripling as their work was ever more highly prized. They were shielded from the deprivation and food shortages endured by the rest of the population after the war, prompting politburo member Lazar Kaganovich to grumble that the atomic cities were 'like health resorts'.

But life for the scientists was far from a holiday. An exclusion zone was set up around Arzamas-16; the town of Sarov was removed from publicly available maps; and guards patrolled barbed-wire defences around the facility. Even leaving Arzamas was far from easy. Security agents accompanied the leading scientists everywhere they went, and informers were infiltrated into the work teams to keep tabs on employees. The base and its outlying units across the country became known as the 'White Archipelago', a more comfortable, privileged version of the Gulag Archipelago, but no less claustrophobic.

The scientists knew they faced harsh reprisals if they failed to deliver what Stalin wanted. A number of Kurchatov's staff were Jewish, and they were doubly threatened as state-approved anti-Semitism grew after the war. One of Arzamas's key figures, the scientific director Yuli Khariton, was especially vulnerable. Khariton was not only Jewish, but had spent two years studying at Cambridge University before the war. Both his parents had fled the Soviet Union and he was forbidden to have any contact with them; his father would later be recaptured and sent to his death in the Gulag.

With as many as 10,000 engineers and scientists working at Arzamas, secrecy was of the utmost importance. Andrei Sakharov, who would go on to play a key role in the Soviet Union's drive for the hydrogen bomb, was warned by a fellow scientist on his first visit to Arzamas. 'There are secrets everywhere, and the less you know that doesn't concern you, the better off you'll be. Luckily for us, Khariton has taken on himself the burden of knowing everything.'

The motivations of the Soviet physicists working on the nuclear project were complex. There was the underlying fear of Stalin and the NKVD, of course. But memories of the country's terrible suffering in the war were still fresh and there was patriotism in their minds too. Sakharov, who would later have doubts about the moral and political implications of his work on the bomb, had none at the time. 'We believed that our work was absolutely necessary,' he wrote. 'It was the means of achieving a balance in the world … I had invested so much of myself in that cause and accomplished so much. At that time … the state, the nation and the ideals of Communism remained intact for me.' Khariton agreed that developing an atomic bomb was 'necessary to secure the defence of the country' – it was a continuation of the war, a means of protecting the motherland from the ever-present external threat. Kurchatov had not fought in the war but now, he said, 'I regard myself as a soldier in this new scientific war,' and often signed his letters 'Soldier Kurchatov'.

In 1948, when the first Soviet nuclear reactor capable of manufacturing weapons-grade uranium was completed at the newly built Urals town of Chelyabinsk-40, Kurchatov quoted Pushkin's poem 'The Bronze Horseman' in his celebratory speech:

> You remember that Peter the Great said [of the founding of St Petersburg], 'Here a town will be established, To spite our arrogant neighbour.' Well, unfortunately, we still have quite a few arrogant neighbours. So, to spite them we too have founded a town. In your time and mine we will have everything: kindergartens, fine shops, a theatre, and, if you like, a symphony orchestra. And then in 30 years' time your children, born here, will take into their own hands everything that we have made. And our successes will pale before the scope of theirs. And if in that time not one uranium bomb explodes over the heads of people, you and I can be happy! And our town can become a monument to peace. Isn't that worth living for?

To build a stockpile of nuclear weapons the Soviet Union needed industrial quantities of uranium and plutonium. It was precisely the sort of project for which the Stalinist command economy was suited; the reserves of slave labour from the prison camps meant tens of thousands of men could be set to work. From 1946 onwards, prisoners dug for uranium in central Asian mines with little or no protection against radiation. Workers were drafted to do the same in East Germany and Czechoslovakia. In 1950, a report by the US Central Intelligence Agency (CIA) estimated that between 150,000 and 200,000 men were 'working' on the nuclear project in Soviet-controlled East Germany alone, with a far higher number in the Soviet Union itself. Many of them died slow, agonising deaths caused by exposure to radioactive radon gas. Radiation sickness began to appear in the population living near the Chelyabinsk reactor, as rivers in the region were steadily contaminated. By 1951, over 75 million cubic metres of radioactive waste had been discharged from Chelyabinsk-40. All this remained unreported and the sufferers were given no information on the cause of their illness. When labourers died, more were simply brought in.

The Soviet intelligence services also recruited communist sympathisers within the American and British atomic programmes who passed on valuable information throughout the 1940s. Klaus Fuchs, a German-born physicist working on the Manhattan Project, supplied the Soviets with the design for the Nagasaki bomb. His data had to be verified under rigorous testing, as Moscow feared the West might be passing on deliberate disinformation, but Fuchs's information undoubtedly helped expedite the construction of the first Soviet weapon.

On 29 August 1949, in a trial given the codename 'First Lightning', the Soviet Union tested its first atomic bomb RDS-1* at Semipalatinsk in the deserts of Kazakhstan. Professor Vladimir Komelkov, who had worked on the triggering device, watched the overground explosion from the northern observation post, 6 miles away:

> On top of the tower an unbearably bright light blazed up. For a moment it dimmed and then with new force began to grow quickly. The white fireball engulfed the tower and, expanding rapidly, changing colour, it rushed upwards. The blast wave at the base swept away structures, stone houses, machines, rolling like a billow from the centre, mixing up stones, logs of wood, pieces of metal and dust into one chaotic mass. The fireball rose, revolved; turned orange, red. Streams of dust, fragments of brick and board were drawn in after it, as into a funnel. Overtaking the firestorm, the shock wave, hitting the upper layers of the atmosphere, passed through several layers of inversion, and there, as in a cloud chamber, the condensation of water began ... The sound reached us like the roar of an avalanche.

---

* The significance of the initials was never officially confirmed, but many took them to mean *Rossiya delayet sama* (Russia has done this alone).

As the mushroom cloud rose, Lavrenty Beria, head of the Soviet secret police and the political controller of the project, kissed Kurchatov and Khariton on the forehead. For Khariton it was a moment of triumph and salvation. 'We felt relief,' he wrote, 'even exultation. Now that the USSR had this weapon, we knew that others could no longer use it against us with impunity.'

The Soviet test shocked the Americans. The CIA had told President Truman that Moscow couldn't build a bomb before mid 1950, and more likely not until 1953. Stalin deliberately made no public announcement of the Semipalatinsk blast and in reply to foreign speculation declared that the Soviet Union had had the bomb since 1947. His aim was to convince the Americans that the USSR already had stockpiles of atomic weapons.*

The Soviet nuclear bomb cemented the new bipolar world geometry and brought a tense stalemate to the international scene. The two superpowers had no territorial disputes, but the clash of capitalist and communist dogmas would lead to rivalry and proxy conflicts in the coming years. The threat of nuclear devastation now hung over the world, with only the bleak reassurance of what came to be dubbed Mutually Assured Destruction (MAD) – the certainty that neither side could prevail unscathed and that both would therefore be deterred from initiating a war.

The first skirmish came in occupied Germany. The British, French and Americans were finding it increasingly difficult to work with the Soviets and there had been confrontations at the intersection of the occupied zones. The West's aim was to restore stability and boost the German economy as a bulwark of European post-war recovery. But Stalin preferred to keep Germany weak, partly to punish her and partly to ensure she would never again be in a position to start a war. In early 1948, the Western Allies proposed the creation of an independent Federal German Republic

---

* By doing so, he also sowed suspicion that the USSR might have made progress towards the next goal in the escalating arms race, the development of the hydrogen bomb. The quest for the new weapon would run until 1961, when the Soviet Union tested a 100 megaton bomb, five times more powerful than anything the US had ever tested and a thousand times more powerful than the Hiroshima bomb. The 'Tsar bomb', as it was known, had the capability to wipe out an area the size of Greater London.

(Bundesrepublik Deutschland) from the French, British and American sectors. The Soviets accused the West of pandering to former Nazis. Their sector would not join the new country, they said, but would instead form a separate state, the German Democratic Republic (DDR), where socialism would provide a guarantee against revanchist fascist tendencies.

On 18 June, the Allies announced that a new currency, the Deutschmark, was being introduced in the Western zones. The Soviets responded that it could not be used in Berlin, where the occupying powers held joint authority. Within a few days, the DDR announced that it was introducing its own currency, the Ostmark, and that this would be the official currency of the whole of Berlin. To underline the point, the Soviet authorities halted all Western shipments into the city, citing unspecified 'technical difficulties' with transport links. Allied supplies had to travel by train across the hundred miles of Soviet controlled territory that separated the capital from the West. Now, with train links blocked by Moscow, the Western sectors of Berlin began to run out of food and coal. This 'island of capitalism in a sea of Communism' had rankled with Stalin, and his aim was to squeeze the West out of the city. Khrushchev later admitted, 'We wanted to exert pressure on the West to create a unified Berlin inside a DDR that would then close its borders.' Stalin, he said, was 'prodding the capitalist world with the tip of the bayonet.' But he had underestimated the West's determination.

Truman ordered B29 bombers to fly to US bases in Germany and Britain, hinting (falsely) that they were armed with nuclear weapons. At the same time, the British and US air forces began to ferry in supplies to the blockaded city. In the second half of 1948 and the early months of 1949, they completed nearly 300,000 flights, bringing in more than 2.3 million tons of cargo. It was enough to prevent West Berliners from having to seek aid from the Soviets, which would effectively have ceded control over their sectors to Moscow. The Soviet military tried to impede the airlift, buzzing the incoming planes and shining bright lights to dazzle the pilots, but they stopped short of shooting them down. By the spring of 1949, the Berlin airlift had succeeded. Moscow announced the lifting of the blockade on 12

May. The first flashpoint of the post-war years left a legacy of bitterness and mistrust. The Cold War had begun.

By the late 1940s, Stalin was also dealing with a wave of simmering discontent within the 'countries of People's Democracy' that made up his East European buffer states. The Federal People's Republic of Yugoslavia was the most unruly of these. Its president, Josip Broz Tito, had been the leader of the Communist partisan movement that fought bravely during the war to liberate the country from the Nazis. Unlike the other East European states, the Yugoslavs had not had to rely on the Red Army for substantial assistance, and although the new government considered itself Communist, Yugoslavia felt it deserved more autonomy than the other members of the Cominform (the Moscow-sponsored organisation of Communist nations).

Tito increasingly refused to bow to orders from Moscow. Contrary to Stalin's instructions, he tried to seize several Italian towns on the Yugoslav border, and actively supported the Greek Communists in that country's civil war. Stalin was furious, telling the politburo, 'I will shake my little finger and tomorrow there will be no Tito any more.' In 1948, Yugoslavia was expelled from the Cominform, with Moscow accusing it of bourgeois nationalism and of having links to the Trotskyite movement. Tito was reviled in the Soviet media, which habitually referred to the Yugoslav government as 'Tito and his bloodthirsty clique'.* According to the Soviet army general and military historian Dmitry Volkogonov, plans were laid to assassinate him with bubonic plague. But the plot was never implemented.

Tito went on to pursue what he labelled the 'Yugoslav road to socialism', a show of independence that was considered an affront to Communist orthodoxy. He informed Moscow of his intentions in a letter of May 1948:

---

* This led to an amusing example of how eagerly, but sometimes clumsily, the Soviet public tried to support the official line on political matters. In 1956, during a brief rapprochement between the two countries, crowds turned out to welcome the Yugoslav leader on a visit to Moscow with banners enthusiastically proclaiming 'Long live Tito and his bloodthirsty clique!'

While we study and take as an example the Soviet system, we are developing Socialism in our country in somewhat different forms. We do this …
because it is forced on us by the conditions of our daily life …'*

After its expulsion from the Cominform, Yugoslavia embarked on a savage
purge of its own communist party, in which as many as 50,000 Moscow
loyalists were tortured and killed. Tito pursued the 'Yugoslav road to socialism' by implementing a fierce policy of political non-alignment,** which
allowed him to court both communist and capitalist support. (Moscow
tried to lure him back into the socialist camp after Stalin's death, but he
continued to benefit from US economic aid and was famously entertained
at Buckingham Palace by Queen Elizabeth II in 1972, where he was awarded
the Order of the Bath.)

Determined not to allow other states to follow Tito's example, Stalin
ordered purges across the Eastern Bloc to remove potential rebels. In
Hungary and Czechoslovakia, there were show trials of the party leadership,
reminiscent of the Soviet purges of the 1930s. In Prague, 14 members of
the politburo, including the party's general secretary, were convicted of
'Tito-ist' subversion and treason. The evidence was fabricated but 11 of
them were executed and the others sentenced to life in jail.

Elsewhere, communism's march appeared to be gathering pace. Mao
Zedong's communists had beaten the nationalist Kuomintang in the
Chinese Civil War (1947–9) and founded the People's Republic of China in
October 1949. But this victory for Marxism was greeted with mixed
emotions in the Kremlin. Stalin had not been convinced that Mao's uprising
would be successful and had supported other figures in the Chinese

---

* By splitting from Moscow and living to tell the tale, Tito pulled off the trick that Hungary
and Czechoslovakia would signally fail to do in the following two decades. Indeed, the
memory of Yugoslavia's defiance almost certainly contributed to the Kremlin's determination
to crush later revolts when they arose elsewhere.

** As early as 1945, Tito had warned the two superpowers: 'We demand that everyone be
allowed to be master in his own house … we do not want great powers to involve us in some
policy of spheres of interest …'

Communist Party. Even when Mao had seized the initiative, Stalin was less than generous in supplying him with aid. When Mao came to Moscow in December 1949, he was not given the welcome of a man bringing the world's most populous nation into the Communist camp. Khrushchev recalled being informed that someone called 'Matsadoon' had come to see him. When he asked 'Who?' he was told, 'You know, that Chinaman.' Mao was made to wait six days for an appointment in the Kremlin. He was well aware he was being insulted, yelling at a Soviet official, 'I have come here to do more than just eat and shit!'

But within a year Stalin was seeking Mao's help. In 1945, Korea had been divided along the 38th parallel, with Soviet troops occupying the north, and US troops the south. Three years later, the north became the Democratic People's Republic of Korea and the south the Republic of Korea. In 1950, when North Korea's leader Kim Il-Sung asked Moscow's permission to invade the south, Stalin agreed. The Soviet Union offered to provide arms and equipment for the North Koreans, but made clear that Soviet troops would not play a direct role in the fighting. On 25 June 1950, the Korean War began. Kim's army won a series of quick victories and Seoul fell within three days, forcing the South Korean troops to retreat into a small zone in the southeastern tip of the peninsula.

But to the Soviets' surprise, the US came to the south's aid. Profiting from the absence of the Soviet ambassador to the United Nations,* Washington pushed through a resolution to send UN troops to help the South Koreans. The American army helped the south retake Seoul and crossed the 38th parallel into the north. Stalin realised he had misjudged the situation: he must now decide if he was willing to risk all-out war with America. Kim appealed to Moscow for help, but Stalin refused. According to Khrushchev, when Stalin was asked about the prospect of the US troops reaching the Soviet border he shrugged and replied: 'What of it? Let the USA come and be our neighbours in the Far East. They will come there, but we will not fight with them. We are not ready to fight.'

---

* Moscow had been boycotting the UN since the start of the year in protest at Taiwan's presence on the Security Council.

Instead Stalin turned to China. He put pressure on Mao to send Chinese troops, disguised as volunteer units, into the combat zone, and Mao agreed. Fighting continued for over a year until a stalemate was reached at the end of 1951. It took another two years before an armistice was signed. No formal peace treaty was ever agreed. With the border dividing the two Koreas again reverting to the 38th parallel, a tense stand-off began, which lasted into the twenty-first century.

When Chinese Prime Minister Zhou Enlai visited Moscow in 1952, Stalin claimed that the war had been a success because it had shown up the Americans' weaknesses. 'The Americans are not capable of waging a large-scale war at all,' Stalin told him, 'especially after the Korean War … They were just fighting little Korea, and already the American people were weeping about it. What would happen if they started a large-scale war? All their people would be weeping and wailing!'

In fact, the Korean War had been a tactical failure for Stalin. Very few of the estimated 2 million casualties were Soviet, but Moscow had signally failed to get what it wanted in Korea. This had been the first proxy conflict of the Cold War and the Communist aggressors had been repelled. In addition, Stalin's failure to commit troops to the North Korean cause had strained his relations with Kim Il-Sung and, more importantly, with Mao Zedong.

Despite the setbacks in Berlin and Korea, the USSR's standing in the world had never been higher. It had proved its military strength in the war, and it had developed a nuclear arsenal. But the Soviet Union's 'glorious leader' seemed to be losing his edge. In 1952, Stalin was 73. His memory and native cunning were beginning to fail him; at times he seemed lost. Khrushchev recalled one incident when Stalin, seemingly unaware of those around him, muttered over and over, 'I'm finished. I trust no one, not even myself…'

Doctor Vladimir Vinogradov had been Stalin's personal physician for several years. He had treated him after the heart attack he suffered in the summer of 1945, and had helped keep his illness secret from the public. But now he faced an even trickier challenge. It was 19 January 1952, and for several months the leader had been showing signs of memory loss, mood swings, irrational behaviour and debilitating fatigue. Vinogradov advised

Stalin that he was suffering from hypertension and arteriosclerosis. It was a matter of some urgency that both conditions should be treated, and for the treatment to be effective there would need to be complete rest. In other words, he said, if the leader of the Soviet Union wished to avoid the possibility of imminent death, he would have to retire from public activity.

Stalin reacted with rage. He ordered Vinogradov out of the room. He informed his aides that the doctor should be dismissed from his post and arrested. But Vinogradov was right. The dictator's lifestyle was finally catching up with him. He rarely exercised and though he drank only occasionally, his nocturnal lifestyle meant he seldom got to bed before the small hours. All this and the stress of leadership had taken their toll. Where once he strode up the mausoleum steps on parade days, now he shuffled, struggling for breath. The more Stalin's health deteriorated, the more he seemed prey to paranoia. He had taken advantage of Lenin's long illness in the 1920s to usurp the old leader's power and now seemed fearful that those around him would do the same to him.

Stalin moved from blaming his own doctor to distrusting all doctors. He had long feared assassination, and now he believed that the doctors trying to preserve his health were bent on killing him and all his comrades. 'They perish one after another,' he told a politburo colleague after several leading Bolsheviks had died from natural causes. 'Shcherbakov, Zhdanov, Dimitrov – all of them died so quickly! … We must replace the old doctors with new ones!'

In Stalin's fevered imagination, Vinogradov's suggestion that he should retire became a treacherous plot to remove him from power. In the following months, he ordered the arrests of other physicians who had treated the party leadership. It was no coincidence that a high proportion of them were Jewish – 1952 was the high-water mark of anti-Semitism in post-war Russia: in August, the members of the Jewish Anti-Fascist Committee would be wiped out; in December, the defendants chosen by Moscow to be executed in the Prague trials would also be Jewish.*

---

* Klement Gottwald, the President of Czechoslovakia, declared: 'During the investigation and trial of the anti-state conspiratorial centre, we discovered a new channel by which treachery and espionage penetrate into the Communist Party. It is Zionism.'

Stalin's sick and suspicious mind had fixed on the medical profession and on the Jews. With a sinister neatness, he announced that a wide-ranging conspiracy had been uncovered: the security of the Soviet Union was being undermined by a 'Jewish Doctors' Plot'. On 13 January 1953, *Pravda* ran a front-page article under the headline 'Vicious Spies and Killers behind the Mask of Academic Physicians':

> This terrorist group of saboteur-doctors were conspiring to shorten the lives of the Soviet leadership by means of medical sabotage. Exploiting their position as doctors, they deliberately and viciously undermined their patients' health by making incorrect diagnoses, and then killed them with bad and incorrect treatments ... All the participants of the terrorist group of doctors were in the service of foreign intelligence, having sold their bodies and souls. Most of them were recruited by the international Jewish bourgeois-nationalist organisation, an arm of American intelligence. The filthy face of this Zionist spy organisation and its vicious actions are now completely unmasked ... Comrade Stalin has repeatedly warned us ... We must liquidate sabotage and purge complacency from our ranks.

Hundreds of people were arrested, most of them Jews. Leading Jewish writers and intellectuals were told they must sign an open letter, already drafted for them by the Kremlin, calling for stern measures against the 'plotters'. Many agreed to do so but some, including the writer Ilya Ehrenburg, had the courage to refuse. As usual, the secret police used torture to extract confessions from their prisoners. Stalin called the judge in the case and told him to 'beat them, beat them and beat them again', and he warned the security minister that if the doctors did not all confess, he would himself be 'shortened by a head'. When the arrested men were coerced into signing false admissions of guilt, Stalin told the politburo, 'See! You are like blind kittens! What would have happened without me? The country would perish because you don't know how to root out our enemies!'

The next purge was being planned. A show trial was being prepared for the doctors, but its aim was to draw in many more victims, up to and including top party leaders. At the Nineteenth Party Congress in October

1952, Stalin had attacked Mikoyan and Molotov for their 'shoddy work', seemingly paving the way for their replacement by younger, less threatening figures. Beria too had reason to fear the dictator was planning to remove him from his post. Stalin seemed to be preparing a repeat of the so-called Leningrad Affair of two years earlier, in which party leaders whom Stalin perceived as rivals were accused of corruption and embezzlement. Six of them had been executed and over 2,000 removed from their posts.

But Vinogradov, his fellow doctors and the hundreds of others under arrest would never come to trial. On 5 March 1953, Stalin died.

On 17 February, Stalin had left the Kremlin to spend time at his dacha in the Kuntsevo district on the western outskirts of Moscow. For the next ten days, all state business was conducted by telephone to the Kremlin and by documents transported back and forth by official car. Nowadays the large green-walled dacha stands uninhabited amid Moscow's birch forests, its two perimeter fences and security guards dissuading any curious visitors. In Stalin's time it was even more securely protected, with camouflaged anti-aircraft guns and machine-gun nests manned around the clock by NKVD special troops. On Saturday 28 February, Stalin told his guards he would not be going out, but then changed his mind. He ordered his chauffeur to drive him into town, where he spent the evening with his politburo colleagues Malenkov, Beria, Khrushchev and Bulganin, watching an American western in his private cinema in the Kremlin.

The five of them arrived back at the dacha at around 11 p.m. According to the security men, 'the boss' was in good spirits and the kitchen staff were told to prepare dinner. Often, Stalin would ply his guests with booze, waiting for any drunken remark he could use against them as proof of their disloyalty. If he was in a spiteful mood, he would mock his colleagues for their gluttony and alcoholism. Sometimes he would force the corpulent Khrushchev to dance the traditional Ukrainian *gopak*. On this occasion, the boss ordered two bottles of wine and rang a little later for some more. He saw off his visitors at 3 a.m. and retired to his room an hour later, having told the security men to 'go and get some sleep. I'm also going to bed, I won't be needing you today.'

Stalin usually rang the bell for attention when he woke. But on the morning of Sunday 1 March, there was silence. The staff were in a quandary: the boss's instructions were not to come into his room until he rang, but as the hours went by they began to worry. At 6 p.m. a light came on in his room, much to everyone's relief. But Stalin still did not emerge or call them in. Eventually at ten in the evening Pavel Lozgachev, the deputy commissioner of the dacha, was selected to take a package into Stalin's room. He found him slumped on the floor, barely conscious, in a pool of his own urine. The leader of the Soviet Union had been lying helpless for hours; a stroke had left him hovering between life and death, but no one had dared disobey his orders to come and check on him.

According to Lozgachev, Stalin was conscious but unable to speak. They lifted him onto the chaise longue from which he had fallen and called the Kremlin. The news caused panic. The first minister who received the call refused to take it. Eventually, Beria came on the line and asked for details, but it was over two hours before he and Malenkov finally arrived at the dacha.* By then, Stalin was lying unconscious with his eyes closed, and the two men approached him cautiously on tiptoe. Lozgachev recalled Beria telling Malenkov to 'wake him up!' When Malenkov refused to do so, Beria turned around to those present and said, 'What are you looking at? Can't you see that Comrade Stalin is sleeping? You're all panicking for nothing. If anything happens, then you can ring me and we'll come with the doctors.'

It was already 2 a.m. and the dictator was slipping away. The dacha staff were so cowed by his authoritarian rages that they froze, incapable of making a decision. No doctor was called until mid morning on Monday 2 March, by which time it was too late.** After lying unconscious for another three days, Stalin suffered a brain haemorrhage and on the morning of 5 March he vomited blood. Those present took turns to pay their final

---

* The journey in those days would have taken around 15 minutes, and their delay has been the subject of subsequent speculation. Were Beria and his colleagues too scared to go, or were they secretly hoping to give Stalin enough time to die before they got there?

** There is irony in the fact that many of the country's leading doctors were locked up in the cells of the Lubyanka as a result of Stalin's own actions.

respects. According to Stalin's daughter, Svetlana, Beria kissed the dying man's hand and sobbed pitifully, but immediately afterwards seemed full of glee. Svetlana's account of her father's final moments is horrifying:

> For the last 12 hours the lack of oxygen became acute. His face and lips blackened as he suffered slow strangulation. The death agony was terrible. He literally choked to death as we watched. At what seemed like the very last moment, he opened his eyes and cast a glance over everyone in the room. It was a terrible glance, insane or perhaps angry, and full of fear of death. He suddenly lifted his left hand as though he were pointing to something up above and bringing down a curse on all. The gesture was incomprehensible and full of menace.

At 9.50 p.m., Josif Vissarionovich Djugashvili, the son of a Georgian cobbler who had ruled over the largest empire in the world for nearly 30 years, died at the age of 74. The following day, 6 March, newspapers were printed with black borders and Soviet radio replaced its transmissions with funereal music. A morose Yuri Levitan, the USSR's most famous newscaster, announced Stalin's death:

> Dear Comrades and Friends. The Central Committee of the Communist Party of the Soviet Union ... announces with profound sorrow that Josif Vissarionovich Stalin, chairman of the USSR Council of Ministers and secretary of the Central Committee of the Communist Party of the Soviet Union, has died after a grave illness. The heart of Lenin's comrade-in-arms and the inspired continuer of Lenin's cause, the wise leader and teacher of the Communist Party and the Soviet people, has stopped beating ... The immortal name of Stalin will live for ever in the hearts of the Soviet people and all progressive mankind. Long live the great, all-conquering teachings of Marx, Engels, Lenin and Stalin!

Four days of mourning were announced, during which public figures outdid each other in the extravagance of their praise for the dead dictator. The names by which his immense vanity had been flattered over the years were repeated again and again: 'Leader and Teacher of the Workers of the

World', 'Father of the Peoples', 'Friend and Teacher of All Toilers', 'Wise and Intelligent Chief of the Soviet Nation', 'Greatest Genius of All Times and Peoples', 'Shining Sun of Humanity', 'The Lenin of Today' and 'Mountain Eagle and Best Friend of All Children'.

On 9 March, a bitterly cold, grey day, nine pallbearers carried Stalin's coffin from the House of Soviets, the scene of his show trials, to the newly renamed Lenin–Stalin Mausoleum on Red Square. Malenkov led the procession with Zhou Enlai, the Chinese foreign minister at his side. Beria and Khrushchev followed behind, and eulogies were read by Molotov, Beria and Malenkov. Then Joseph Stalin was laid to rest beside his 'comrade-in-arms', the man who in his testament had warned in vain of the danger Stalin represented (see pp. 248–9).

For the Soviet population, brought up on decades of propaganda glorifying their Great Leader, Stalin's death was a cause of genuine grief. A huge crowd braved the elements to attend the ceremonies, covering Red Square with a carpet of flowers.* Many spoke of feeling 'orphaned' by Stalin's death and fearing the Soviet Union without his guiding hand would now be overwhelmed in a world of menacing capitalist forces. The novelist Alexander Zinoviev would later comment on the mass hysteria that underpinned the people's sorrow:

> The Soviet people, conditioned by decades of lies and pretence, effortlessly, freely and gladly made themselves feel sincere grief ... just as they would later, and with all the ease of well-trained creatures of Communism, put themselves into a state of sincere rage at the thought of the evil actions of their former idol and his vile henchmen, actions about which they had seemingly known nothing, although it was they who had helped Stalin's henchmen carry them out.

In an incident redolent of the Khodynka disaster, which cast a shadow over Nicholas II's reign (see pp. 156–7), Stalin's funeral was attended by its own

---

* Sergei Prokofiev, who had died on the same day as Stalin, would have no flowers for his funeral; all had been requisitioned for the official ceremonies. Only a kindly neighbour, who brought her potted plants to Prokofiev's graveside, ensured he was not entirely forgotten.

tragedy. With hundreds of thousands of people converging on Red Square, the police tried to control them by erecting barriers of trucks across the capital's main arteries. But as crowds built up at these bottlenecks, people became trapped. More than 500 of them were crushed to death. News of the catastrophe was suppressed and, like Khodynka, it became a taboo subject. The poet Yevgeny Yevtushenko said it was the moment he realised something was very wrong in his country:

> The breath of tens of thousands of people jammed against one another rose up in a white cloud … New streams poured into the human torrent from behind, increasing the pressure … We were caught between the walls of houses on one side and a row of army trucks on the other. 'Get the trucks out of the way!' people howled. 'Get them away!' 'I can't. I've not been given any orders,' a very young, bewildered police officer called back, almost crying with desperation. People were being crushed against the trucks by the crowd; their heads were being smashed; the sides of the trucks were running with blood. And all at once I felt a savage hatred for everything that had given birth to that 'I have no orders', when people were dying of someone's stupidity. For the first time in my life I thought with hatred of the man we were burying. He could not be innocent of the disaster. It was that 'I have no orders' that had caused the chaos and the bloodshed.

The target of Yevtushenko's anger was Soviet autocracy, the way in which society was indoctrinated not to think for itself, and the sinister ease with which chaos and bloodshed were consequently inflicted upon it. Estimates of the balance sheet of death for Stalin's reign vary tremendously. Alexander Solzhenitsyn claimed that as many as 60 million had perished as a result of Stalin's brutality – from warfare, famine, torture and execution; Robert Conquest, the ground-breaking chronicler of the Terror, puts the figure at 20 million; and the British historian Norman Davies, writing with the benefit of recent research, offers an estimate of 50 million.

At the time of Stalin's death, the USSR was suffering from a desperate shortage of young men, principally because of the war, but also because so many had disappeared into the Gulag. Heavy industry was returning to pre-war levels, but the economy as a whole was in dire straits. Soviet agriculture was struggling to feed an ever-increasing urban population; there had been little improvement in consumer goods and services, and transport remained chaotic. Housing was still desperately inadequate, and the labour force lived under grim conditions with no incentive to improve the quality of their work. Stalin's successors would be faced with deep-rooted material problems, as well as a population that had been physically decimated and psychologically traumatised. And looming over everything was the question of how to address the legacy of the man who had run the country so brutally for so long.

CHAPTER THIRTY-FIVE

Stalin had permitted no talk of succession. In the confusion after his death, Lavrenty Beria, Vyacheslav Molotov, Georgy Malenkov and Nikita Khrushchev hastily assumed the collective leadership of the country. One of their first acts was to halt the proceedings in the 'Doctors' Plot' and try to moderate the rhetoric of anti-Semitism. They set about putting Stalin's papers 'into necessary order', a sensitive and potentially dangerous task for men who had themselves been involved in the excesses of Stalinism. All of them had something to hide, and all were concerned to protect their own interests. Stories abound that Beria stole the document safe from Stalin's dacha in order to destroy the compromising material the dictator had accumulated about him (and to squirrel away the compromising data about his colleagues). While the 'collective leadership' was ostensibly happy to share the responsibilities of power, in reality each was desperate to be the sole man in charge.

Malenkov, a loyal follower of Stalin, described by Yevtushenko as 'a man with a womanish face and a studied diction', emerged as the most powerful candidate. He was promptly named chairman of the Council of Ministers, effectively prime minister. In September, Khrushchev took over Malenkov's former role as secretary of the party, and a period of duumvirate power began. Beria, though, remained ominously in the background as head of the security services, with an intimate knowledge of where the skeletons – literal and figurative – were buried. The unspoken fear was that another dictator might gather as much power as Stalin, and Beria was seen as the most likely potential tyrant. Svetlana's description of his delight at Stalin's death was later confirmed by Khrushchev, prompting speculation that Beria had poisoned him.* An autopsy was carried out, but the results were 'lost' and no official cause of death was ever established.

---

* In his memoirs, Molotov claims Beria himself boasted that he poisoned Stalin, telling the politburo that Stalin had been planning to remove them, and that he – Beria – had 'saved us all'.

Immediately after Stalin's death, Beria had declared an amnesty for all convicts serving sentences of less than five years, excluding political prisoners. By the summer of 1953, the streets were full of petty criminals freed from the camps, and rumours were circulating that Beria intended to use them to help him take power. Khrushchev didn't wait. He warned Malenkov that 'Beria is getting his knives ready for us,' and proposed that they form an alliance to avert the threat. Malenkov, who had worked closely with Beria in the last years of the purges and had much to hide, agreed. Khrushchev enlisted the help of Marshal Zhukov and several members of the Central Committee Presidium (as the politburo was now known). At its next meeting, on 26 June, Khrushchev took the floor to accuse Beria of being a British spy. He moved to have him dismissed from the Central Committee and the motion was swiftly passed. Taken aback, Beria could only mumble, 'What's going on Nikita Sergeyevich? Why are you picking fleas from my trousers?' before Zhukov and a group of armed officers burst into the room to arrest him. At his trial in December 1953, Beria was convicted of treason, terrorism and counter-revolutionary activity. On hearing the sentence, he collapsed to his knees and begged vainly for his life. He was taken at once to be executed by firing squad. His body was incinerated and the ashes scattered outside Moscow. There was a hint of relief in Khrushchev's quip that 'Beria was killed at the Presidium meeting that he had expected to sweep him to power.' The security services were brought under the control of the party and renamed the KGB (Committee of State Security). Beria's former allies were removed from their posts.*

---

* Beria was certainly not a British spy, but his fate should not inspire pity. In 1998 there was a grim reminder of what kind of man he had been. At his trial, Beria had been accused of a number of rapes and sexual assaults, but such accusations had been common practice during Stalin's reign as a means of disgracing the accused, and not everyone believed them. When Beria's house on Moscow's Garden Ring later became the Tunisian embassy, however, work was carried out on water pipes in the garden and the bones of five young girls were uncovered. Declassified archives have confirmed what many suspected: there are statements from Beria's bodyguards that he would drive them around Moscow pointing out girls they were to abduct for him to rape. Those who resisted too vigorously or threatened to expose Beria's deeds ended up buried in his wife's rose garden.

As head of the secret police, Beria had been responsible for sending countless numbers of people to the labour camps and for the running of the Gulag. In camps across the country, inmates greeted the news of his death by throwing their *shapki* (fur hats) into the air in celebration. Since the end of the war, groups of imprisoned soldiers and partisans had been causing trouble in the Gulag, and Beria's downfall unleashed a spate of uprisings. The biggest of them was at the Kengir camp in Kazakhstan where, in the summer of 1954, some 13,000 prisoners went on strike. According to Alexander Solzhenitsyn's *Gulag Archipelago*, the political uncertainty following the death of Stalin left the prison authorities unsure how to respond. 'They had no idea what was required of them,' Solzhenitsyn wrote, 'and mistakes could be dangerous. If they showed excessive zeal and shot down a crowd they might end up being punished as henchmen of Beria. But if they weren't zealous enough, and didn't energetically push the strikers out to work – exactly the same thing could happen!'

As the authorities vacillated, the rebels seized control of the camp. They set up their own provisional government led by former army officers, demanding shorter working days, better conditions and a review of all sentences. They were not simply rioting criminals; they wanted justice from the regime and an element of humanity in the way the state treated its people. After forty-two days of hesitation, Red Army troops with T-34 tanks were sent to crush the revolt, killing 700 rebels. But the sacrifice of the Kengir prisoners and others across the country was not entirely in vain. The uprisings made it clear to the Soviet leadership that there was a serious problem in the judicial system. An investigative commission was set up under the Central Committee secretary, Pyotr Pospelov. Its report, delivered in early 1956, laid bare the abuses of summary justice in the USSR since the 1930s, a period in which none of the current leaders of the party had been entirely innocent.

The Pospelov Report put the leadership in a quandary. If they suppressed it, they would be covering up the crimes of Stalinism and possibly leaving the way open for a new dictator in the future. But if they published it, they would open themselves to accusations of complicity in the abuses. The Twentieth Party Congress, the first since Stalin's death, was scheduled for

February 1956, less than a month away. A decision had to be made quickly. Khrushchev made it.

Nikita Sergeyevich Khrushchev was an unlikely Machiavelli. He had begun life as a shepherd, before becoming a miner in the Don Basin. During the First World War, he was active in the labour movement and fought for the Reds in the revolution, joining the Bolsheviks in 1918. Khrushchev rose through the local party network and in 1938 was appointed first secretary of the Ukrainian Communist Party. By 1949, he had become Central Committee secretary in Moscow.

Sir William Hayter, the British ambassador to the Soviet Union in the 1950s, found Khrushchev full of native wit, energy and ambition. He was no intellectual, Hayter told me three decades later, and his character was rough and unrefined, but Khrushchev had a dogged persistence that served him well. His conversation was peppered with folksy sayings and his Ukrainian background sometimes made his remarks hard to follow, but even this he used to his advantage, wrong-footing his opponents with colourful – often scabrous – comments. In his memoirs, Hayter wrote that Khrushchev was 'like a little bull who, if aimed in the right direction, would charge along and be certain to arrive with a crash at his objective, knocking down anything that was in his way'. He had initially underestimated Khrushchev, misled by his rough, peasant-like manners. At a dinner in 1954, Khrushchev seemed to struggle to follow the conversation and needed Malenkov to explain things to him in 'words of one syllable'. Along with the other British embassy staff, Hayter felt that Malenkov, a man of aristocratic background, well-spoken and with impressive academic qualifications, was the most likely of the collective leaders to win the power struggle. They were soon to realise how wrong they were.

Even before the Party Congress in February 1956, Khrushchev had outmanoeuvred his rivals. Like Stalin before him, he had used his position as first secretary to put his supporters into positions of power. Malenkov had been forced to stand down as chairman of the Council of Ministers, and Khrushchev's ally Bulganin took over the post. Sensing danger, Malenkov had aligned himself with his fellow old-guard Stalinists, Molotov and Kaganovich, opposing Khrushchev's drive for power.

Khrushchev needed to respond, and the Pospelov Report was a useful weapon. His opponents were all implicated in the purges of the 1930s; they were the ones with the most to lose if the report came out, and Khrushchev began to argue in favour of publishing it. 'If we don't tell the truth at the Congress,' he told them, 'we'll be forced to do so at some time in the future. And then we won't be the people making the speeches – we'll be the people under investigation.' But Malenkov and the others objected, and by the time proceedings opened on 14 February, the leadership had not reached a consensus.

On the very final day of the Congress, 25 February, Khrushchev announced that an unscheduled, closed session would be held without foreign delegates or observers. Khrushchev approached the microphone in the Great Kremlin Palace and hesitated for a moment before beginning. The text in his hand, which history would come to know as 'The Speech on the Personality Cult and its Consequences' – or simply 'The Secret Speech' – was based on a draft that Pospelov had supplied. But Khrushchev had expanded and widened the scope of its revelations. For the first time, Lenin's Testament condemning Stalin, and Lenin's letter threatening to sever all relations with him, were read aloud. There was a stir in the hall, but Khrushchev pressed on. Stalinism, he said, had been a damaging perversion of the ideals of Communism; the cult of personality, in which one man was so powerful that his decisions alone were enough to distort true Communist values, had violated the norms of collective leadership and brought the party into disrepute.

> Comrades, it is foreign to the spirit of Marxism–Leninism to elevate one person, to transform him into a superman possessing supernatural char-acteristics, akin to those of a god. Such a man supposedly knows every-thing, sees everything, thinks for everyone, can do anything, is infallible in his behaviour. Such a belief about a man, and specifically about Stalin, was cultivated among us for many years. The cult of Stalin became the source of a whole series of exceedingly serious perversions of party prin-ciples, of party democracy, of revolutionary legality ...

The result, Khrushchev said, was unchecked lawlessness and injustice, including repressions and murder on a mass scale. Now there was a murmur in the hall: the speech was becoming inflammatory.

> Comrades! Stalin was a very distrustful man, full of sickly suspicions. He would look at a man and say: 'Why are your eyes so shifty today?' or 'Why are you not looking me directly in the eyes?' Everywhere he saw 'enemies', 'two-faced deceivers' and 'spies' ... There was the cruellest repression against anyone who in any way disagreed with Stalin. 'Confessions' were acquired through physical pressures. Innocent individuals – who in the past had defended the party line – became victims. Mass arrests and deportations of many thousands of people, execution without trial and without normal investigation created conditions of insecurity, fear and even desperation.

Stalin had had a hand in the murder of Sergei Kirov, Khrushchev claimed; the Doctors' Plot and the Leningrad Affair were both fabrications. The murderous purges of the 1930s and the terrible reprisals against delegates to the Congress of Victors in 1934 were all carried out at Stalin's behest; even his handling of the war had been a bungling disaster. 'He was a coward,' said Khrushchev. 'He panicked. Not once did he go to the front during the whole war.'

For four hours the delegates listened in something approaching a state of shock. The end of the speech was followed by 'a deathly hush'; then people stood up and began to disperse, unsure of what to say to one another. Some of those present were excited that the shadow of the dictator was being lifted, at least in part; others feared exposure for their collusion in the abuses. There were reports of heart attacks among the delegates and suicides in the days and weeks that followed. The speech was not published in the Soviet press, but it was read out to party members at special meetings. The foreign communists, who had not been allowed to hear the presentation, soon learned about it and leaked much of its contents abroad. Polish delegates sent the text to the *New York Times* and the *Observer*.

Khrushchev had undoubtedly been courageous in confronting the legacy of Stalinism, but the speech was a compromise. Its focus was on the repression of Communist Party personnel, rather than the sufferings of the ordinary people; it dealt only with events that occurred after 1934, and it pinned all the blame on Stalin. Khrushchev suggested that he and some of the other party leaders did not know enough about Stalin's doings at the time to be able to intervene and stop him. He did, though, make a point of criticising Beria, and he hinted that Malenkov was closely connected to Stalin's misdeeds.

The speech was a huge gamble for Khrushchev. It risked turning the party against him and it opened him to criticism for his own actions in the past. There were stormy discussions across the country and some fierce demonstrations against the speech's 'slurs' on Stalin's good name. A young Mikhail Gorbachev was shocked by the reaction to the speech in his native Stavropol, where many people still regarded Stalin as the protector of the people, not their oppressor. In Georgia, protesters took to the streets in defence of the dead leader's honour. Thousands chanted 'Glory to Great Stalin!' and 'Down with Khrushchev!' The protests escalated into riots, in which dozens were killed or injured. Years of propaganda and misinformation had left the population confused and incapable of differentiating truth from lies.

Despite the protests, Khrushchev's actions won him substantial support. Junior and mid-level party-state officials, many of whom were too young to bear any direct responsibility for the crimes of the Stalin era, rejoiced that terror and the 'cult of personality' were to be banished in favour of 'collective leadership' and 'socialist legality'.* They wanted guarantees that the abuses of the past would never return and that democratisation would be the way of the future. The bedrock support he gained in 1956 would aid Khrushchev in his future struggles for power, while weakening the position of his future opponents, the old-guard Stalinists Molotov, Malenkov and Kaganovich.

---

* Forty years later, Mikhail Gorbachev organised a conference to commemorate the Twentieth Party Congress. He praised Khrushchev's 'political courage' and marvelled at the 'huge political risk' he had taken. Gorbachev said Khrushchev had shown himself to be 'a moral man' by beginning the process of unmasking Stalin's crimes. A modern Soviet reformer was acknowledging his debt to a kindred predecessor.

The 'secret speech' had immediate and unwelcome consequences in Central and Eastern Europe. There had already been disturbances in Czechoslovakia and Hungary after Stalin's death, as people sensed an opportunity to win greater freedom from Soviet domination. In East Germany, 500 striking workers were killed when they demanded the resignation of the pro-Stalinist government. Now Khrushchev's speech breathed new life into reformist and opposition groups across Eastern Europe. In Poland, intellectuals demanded change, and workers went on strike; 38 people were killed in clashes between protestors and police in Poznan. Khrushchev threatened to send tanks into Warsaw if the authorities failed to restore order. Tensions were eased when Wladyslaw Gomulka became party leader in October 1956, replacing the former Stalinist government and introducing a more liberal brand of 'national' Communism. Peasants were allowed to leave collective farms, and the Catholic Church was no longer barred from teaching religion in schools. Perhaps mindful of Stalin's acerbic conclusion that 'imposing Communism on Poland is like trying to put a saddle on a cow', Moscow backed off.

The crisis in Hungary would be far deeper. Since the end of the war, the country had suffered under the dictatorship of 'Stalin's Best Hungarian Disciple', Matyas Rakosi. But the concessions won by the Poles raised hopes that Hungary too might be allowed a degree of autonomy. In parallel with the changes in Poland, Rakosi was removed from power in the summer of 1956. It was not enough. Limited reform sparked demands for more. On 23 October, 20,000 students took to the streets of Budapest, demanding free speech, open elections with genuine opposition parties and the withdrawal of Soviet occupation forces. By evening the crowds had swollen to nearly 200,000. They toppled a 30-foot bronze statue of Stalin, paraded Hungarian flags with the Communist emblem cut out from the centre and attacked the headquarters of the Hungarian secret police. The police fired on the crowd, and street fighting broke out between the demonstrators and Soviet and Hungarian troops. The prime minister, Imre Nagy, had a revolution on his hands. A reformist himself, Nagy had some sympathy with the protestors' demands and, after a fraught discussion with his cabinet, he announced that the government supported the people's cause. Nagy remained in contact with Moscow, and by 28 October he seemed to have brokered a deal. A ceasefire was announced and Soviet troops were withdrawn from Budapest.

In the Kremlin, the Presidium were divided. In an effort to preserve Communist unity against the West, Khrushchev had made overtures to Tito to repair Soviet relations with Yugoslavia. He had agreed a compromise in Poland. But now Hungary threatened to undermine all the progress that had been made. After some hesitation, the Presidium decided to act. Members of the Warsaw Pact were told that military action would be taken against the 'counter-revolutionary forces' threatening Hungary. (In an exchange with Tito, Khrushchev asked plaintively: 'What option do we have? If we let things take their course, the West would say we are either stupid or weak, and that's one and the same thing. We cannot possibly permit it, either as Communists or internationalists, or as the Soviet state. We would have capitalists on the frontier of the Soviet Union.')

The Warsaw Pact had been created by the Soviet Union in 1955 as a military response to NATO and a means of binding Eastern Europe to the Soviet Union. Its founding charter had promised 'respect for the independence and sovereignty of member states' and 'non-interference in their internal affairs'. Hungary was soon to discover just how empty the rhetoric was.

On 4 November, Red Army troops with 3,000 tanks led by Marshal Konev, one of the heroes of the Battle for Berlin, embarked on Operation Whirlwind, with orders to retake Budapest. (The resolution adopted by the Soviet Central Committee justified this by saying it would be 'unforgivable' for the Soviet Union 'not to help the working class of Hungary in its struggle against the counter-revolution'.) The invasion took the Hungarians by surprise. Imre Nagy had been negotiating with Yuri Andropov, Moscow's ambassador to Hungary, oblivious to the fact that the tanks were already on their way. He immediately declared Hungary's withdrawal from the Warsaw Pact and called on the UN for assistance. The West, however, was embroiled in the crisis over Suez and, with British and French forces invading Egypt, the United States could hardly condemn the Soviets. Left to face the Red Army alone, the Hungarians fought bravely. Pockets of resistance held out for a week. But on 10 November, with thousands dead and much of central Budapest in ruins, the revolution was stifled. Nagy was arrested, held by the Soviet authorities for 18 months and hanged in June 1958.* The general secretary of the Hungarian party, Janos Kadar, who had cooperated with the Soviet invaders, was installed as the head of the government. Moscow had made an example of Hungary and preserved its 'buffer states' intact. But its actions had disgusted many Western communists and damaged Khrushchev's standing at home and abroad.

Khrushchev's secret speech had created uncertainty in the Soviet Union and unrest in Eastern Europe. Its denunciation of Stalinism alienated traditionalist Communist states such as Albania and, more importantly, China. Beijing's version of Communism was hardline and doctrinaire, in tune with Stalinist ideology. The more Khrushchev spoke of peaceful coexistence with the West, the more Mao Zedong feared a weakening of Communist orthodoxy and a lack of resolve to support him in his opposition to the United States. Within a couple of years, Beijing would be formally denouncing the 'treacherous revisionist clique of the Soviet leadership'.

Khrushchev's position as the dominant force in Moscow's collective leadership was beginning to look precarious. Apparently unaware of the gathering storm clouds, he acted with the ebullient self-confidence, verging on arrogance, that had served him well in earlier years. Despite his attack on the 'cult of the individual', he made sure his picture appeared every day in the press. He demanded adulation from radio, television and cinema. He insisted on making a show of his authority and was delighted when his grandson asked him: 'Grandad, are you the tsar?' But his bullying, condescending style alienated potential supporters, and his fondness for alcohol and crude anecdotes led to fears that he would embarrass the Soviet Union on the international stage.

Molotov, in particular, had long wanted rid of Khrushchev. As a close ally of Stalin, he resented and feared the revelations made in the ongoing

---

* In 1989, on the thirty-first anniversary of Nagy's execution, I attended a ceremonial reburial of his remains in Budapest's Municipal Cemetery. Unexpectedly, hundreds of thousands of Hungarians turned out to witness the righting of one of the wrongs of Communism's past. The impact of the ceremony helped accelerate the overthrow of Communism in Hungary.

process of liberalisation. In June 1957, together with Malenkov and Kaganovich, Molotov persuaded a majority of the Presidium to demand Khrushchev's resignation. At a meeting of the Council of Ministers they confronted him and demanded that he step down. But Khrushchev refused. Stalling for time, he argued that he had been elected by the whole of the Central Committee and he would not go without their agreement. He had won a breathing space, but he needed to garner enough support to survive the impending vote. He turned once more to Marshal Zhukov, now minister of defence, and asked him to mobilise the air force to fly in as many sympathetic Central Committee members as possible from across the country. Their support was enough to save Khrushchev and secure his position as General Secretary of the Party. Turning on his opponents, he accused them of complicity in Stalin's crimes, dubbing them the 'Anti-Party Group'. Zhukov was drafted in to denounce Molotov and Malenkov as the main accomplices of Stalin's purges. Together with Lazar Kaganovich, they were removed from the Central Committee, a fate that in previous times would have been accompanied by arrest and possible execution. (When Kaganovich called Khrushchev to plead for mercy, Khrushchev gleefully replied: 'Your words yet again confirm what methods you intended to use for your vile ends ... You measure other people by your own standards. But you underestimate me.') Khrushchev announced that Molotov would be sent as Soviet ambassador to Mongolia, while Malenkov was to run a power station in Siberia, and Kaganovich was made head of the cement industry in Sverdlovsk. All three had been banished to obscure posts, their political careers effectively ended, but in refusing to jail them, Khrushchev was signalling that Stalinist methods were no longer admissible. Bulganin, who had played a part in the conspiracy, was forced to resign as chairman of the Council of Ministers and Khrushchev now became both first secretary and prime minister. His position as supreme ruler was safe, but his erratic, unpredictable nature would be writ large in the erratic, unpredictable course of his country in the years ahead.

PART FIVE

DEMOCRATS WITH COLD FEET

CHAPTER THIRTY-SIX

On 12 April 1961, at 9.06 a.m. Moscow time, Yuri Gagarin turned the launch key of his *Vostok* spacecraft to the 'go' position and lifted off from the Baikonur Cosmodrome in Kazakhstan, shouting '*Poekhali!*' (Let's go!). 'I heard a whistle and an ever-growing din,' he wrote. 'I felt how the gigantic rocket trembled all over, and slowly, very slowly, began to tear itself off the launch pad. The noise was no louder than one would expect to hear in a jet plane, but it had such a range of musical tones and timbres that no composer could hope to score it, no musical instrument or human voice could ever reproduce its magnificence.'

For 108 minutes, Gagarin orbited the Earth, travelling at 18,000 mph, shooting eastwards across his homeland, then onward over the Pacific and North America. Above West Africa, *Vostok*'s retro-rockets kicked in for a jolting 40-second burst and the spacecraft decelerated, turned and began its descent back to the Earth's atmosphere, back to its everlasting place in the history of scientific endeavour and human achievement.

When the Soviet media announced the mission's success, it was the first time the Soviet people had even heard of the project. So dubious were the Kremlin leadership of the quality of their space technology that the very existence of a manned rocket had been kept secret. Gagarin's own parents learned that their son had become the first man in space only when they heard the news on the radio. Before the launch, three envelopes had been sent to the Soviet news agency TASS, each containing a different statement depending on the outcome of the mission: one for success, one for the possibility that Gagarin had been forced to land outside the Soviet Union, and one for complete failure.

When he ejected from *Vostok* and landed safely in the countryside outside Saratov in central Russia, Gagarin found himself surrounded by villagers who approached him with fear and suspicion. They took Gagarin for a spy, and their apprehension was allayed only when he pointed to the letters 'CCCP' emblazoned on his helmet. 'I am Russian,' he told them proudly. 'And you have just met the world's first spaceman!'

Yuri Gagarin was an instant celebrity. He was made a Hero of the Soviet Union, and paraded through the streets of Moscow in an open-top limousine with Khrushchev at his side. As with the launch of *Sputnik* in 1957, the USSR had again beaten the USA, and for Khrushchev it was a chance to claim vindication. 'Arrogant commentators told us that Russians with their bast [birch bark] shoes and footcloths would never be a great power,' he said as he toasted the new cosmonaut. 'But once-illiterate Russia has pioneered the path into space. That's what you've done, Yuri! Let everyone who has sharpened their claws against us know this! Let them know that Yurka was in space; that he saw everything; that he knows everything!'

Gagarin was dispatched on a global victory tour. When he met Queen Elizabeth II at Buckingham Palace, thousands turned out to greet him and *The Times* reported that he received 'a welcome bordering hysteria'. Gagarin was a natural: he handled the media with charm and good nature. And he was an effective ambassador for Soviet collectivist values, saying repeatedly that he may have been the man in the capsule, but that his success would have been impossible without the dedicated work of thousands of Soviet scientists, workers and technicians over many years.

The history of space exploration in Russia had begun even before the revolution. The visionary Konstantin Tsiolkovsky, who lived from 1857 to 1935, was the pioneer of multi-stage rockets and is widely acknowledged to be the father of astronautics. His work was taken up by Soviet scientists in the 1930s and one of them, Sergei Korolyov, would go on to develop both the rocket that took Gagarin into space and the Soviet Union's first intercontinental ballistic missiles. But science under Stalin was a dangerous occupation and any hint of disloyalty was ruthlessly punished. In 1938, Korolyov was denounced by a rival physicist: sentenced to ten years in a labour camp, he was so severely beaten under interrogation that his jaw was broken and he lost most of his teeth. For the rest of his life he would find it hard to open his mouth and to turn his head.

With the outbreak of the Second World War, Korolyov was transferred to a special camp for engineers, where he worked on the development of military aircraft, and at the end of the war he returned to rocket building. His identity, and that of his fellow scientists was kept secret, so Korolyov received no public recognition for his role in Gagarin's triumph. The *Vostok* spacecraft was also hidden from view in order to preserve the secrets of its design. Only years later was it revealed that Soviet spaceships were almost fully automated; cosmonauts had few tasks to carry out and were discouraged from using their own initiative to solve problems. There is no record of Gagarin touching the controls at all after take-off, and Korolyov boasted that *Vostok* was so sophisticated that even 'rabbits could fly it'. Cosmonaut training at the secret Star City complex outside Moscow focused on repetition, emotional stability and the capacity to remain calm under stressful conditions. Gagarin's main rival to be the first in space had been Gherman Titov, an educated man who liked to recite Pushkin in the isolation chamber; but Gagarin was preferred partly because he came from a peasant background, which better reflected the Soviet Union's image as a proletarian state.

By 1963, Valentina Tereshkova had become the first woman in space, allowing Khrushchev to vaunt 'the equality of men and women in our country'. But the race with the Americans to put the first man on the moon drove the Kremlin to demand ever greater advances from its scientists and to take ever bigger risks with the safety of its cosmonauts. Korolyov was ordered to launch the first multi-manned space missions and did so by stripping *Vostok* of all its safety features, cramming three men into a capsule designed for one and sending them into orbit with no means of rescue in an emergency.

In March 1965, Alexei Leonov became the first person to 'walk' in space during the *Voskhod II* mission, but once again Korolyov had been hurried into launching a spacecraft before its technical problems had been properly tackled. A flimsy detachable airlock attached to the side of the capsule meant Leonov was almost stranded in space as his suit expanded and prevented him re-entering. He was forced to manually lower the pressure of his suit, nearly causing him to pass out as he squeezed back into the craft.

The automatic guidance system then failed and the cosmonauts were forced to pilot their way home manually, eventually landing in Siberia 1,500 miles away from their target, where they spent a night stuck in trees, in freezing conditions with wolves circling below them.

By now, the whole Soviet space programme was flying on a wing and a prayer. In October of that same year Leonov, Gagarin and Titov signed a letter to the Soviet leadership warning that 'the situation has changed: the US has caught up and even surpassed us in certain areas ... Unfortunately in our country there are many defects in the planning, organisation and management of vital work.' They received no response. In January 1966, Sergei Korolyov died at the age of 59, his life shortened by the merciless beatings he suffered in the Gulag. It was the beginning of the end. The space scientists had been working towards a flight that would see two *Soyuz* crafts meet and dock in space, but the programme had been dogged with technical problems. The Kremlin insisted that the mission should go ahead to coincide with the 1967 May Day celebrations, and the experienced cosmonaut Vladimir Komarov was chosen to lead it. Komarov knew the ship was not space-worthy. His KGB minder, Venyamin Russayev spoke to him shortly before the launch and later recalled the conversation:

As [Komarov] was seeing us off, he said straight out, 'I'm not going to make it back from this flight.' I asked him, 'If you're convinced you're going to die, why don't you refuse the mission?' He answered, 'Because if I don't make the flight, they'll send Yura [Gagarin], and he'll die instead of me. We've got to take care of him.'

Film of the launch pad on 23 April 1967 shows an unsmiling Komarov, a downcast Gagarin and some subdued technicians. Soon after take-off, the craft's guidance computers failed and mechanical failures began to occur. Komarov complained to ground control: 'This devil ship! Nothing I touch works properly.' After 26 hours, the mission was aborted and Komarov was told to re-enter the atmosphere, but when he tried to alter course he found it impossible to line the ship up correctly. In Washington, an agent of the

National Security Agency who was monitoring communications between Komarov and ground control heard the drama play out.

> They knew they had problems for about two hours before Komarov died, and were fighting to correct them. [Deputy Premier Alexei] Kosygin called Komarov personally. They had a video-phone conversation and Kosygin was crying. He told him he was a hero ... Komarov's wife got on too, and they talked for a while. He told her how to handle their affairs, and what to do with the kids. It was awful. Towards the last few minutes, he was falling apart.

As *Soyuz* plummeted into the steppe at 400 mph, Komarov called out to those who had sent him into space in an unready craft, 'You have killed me ...'

After the *Soyuz* tragedy, Gagarin returned to his former job as a fighter pilot, and on a routine training flight the following year was involved in a near collision that sent his plane crashing to the ground. His remains were cremated and his ashes placed in the Kremlin wall close to those of Komarov, his friend and comrade. The Soviet space programme was in meltdown. The dead hand of central planning, excessive meddling from the leadership and a focus on propaganda victories at the expense of long-term development had undone all the scientific achievement and all the individual heroism. In 1969, the Americans put the first men on the moon; no Soviet cosmonaut would ever follow in their footsteps.

The space race typified the best and worst of the Khrushchev era, promising much but ending in failure. As first secretary, Khrushchev strove to revive the Soviet Union after the dark days of Stalin, to modernise a country whose development had been stifled by decades of repression; but he was weighed down by the legacy of the past and by the fatal flaws of the system he inherited.

The consequences of Khrushchev's 'secret speech' of 1956 reverberated through Soviet society. Millions of Stalin's victims would eventually be rehabilitated, many of them posthumously; barely a family in the country was unaffected. Prisoners released from the camps began returning to their homes, recounting their experiences and revealing the full extent of the injustices and abuses. Anna Akhmatova wrote of a nation divided between victims and torturers: 'Now the arrested will return and two Russias will look each other in the eye: the one that sent people to the camps and the one that was sent away.' The secret speech convinced a generation of Communists that the party was abandoning oppression as a means of control and returning to what Khrushchev dubbed 'Lenin's true path'. (Years later Mikhail Gorbachev would describe himself and his reformist allies as 'the children of the Twentieth Congress'.)

Expectations were high, and Khrushchev was quick to raise them higher. In 1961, he announced that the conflict between the social classes had now been won; society was united, and the state was ruling for 'all the people'. Since 1936, when Stalin declared that socialism had been achieved in the USSR, Kremlin leaders had urged the Soviet people to strive to build Communism; Communist perfection was viewed as a distant nirvana. But the irrepressible Khrushchev announced that nirvana was at hand. The building of Communism, he declared, would be completed in the Soviet Union by 1980. A new Communist Party Programme (the third of its kind) even set out a specific 20-year timetable:

> In the course of the 1970s, housing, public transport, water, gas and heating will become rent-free for all citizens. There will be free medical services, free use of sanatoria and free medicines. The transition to free meals at factories and collective farms will begin. Prices will fall ... Income tax will be abolished ... There will be a 34-hour week (30 hours for those doing arduous work) ... and a 500 per cent rise in output, giving the USSR the highest output per head in the world. Real incomes will rise by three and half times so that the Soviet people will have the highest standard of living in the world.

The concluding sentence of the Third Party Programme became a national slogan, appearing on posters and banners:

The party solemnly declares that today's generation of Soviet people will live under Communism!*

Khrushchev continued his campaign of de-Stalinisation, pinning the blame for the newly revealed atrocities on Stalin alone, playing down his own role and that of his allies. The dictator's body was removed from Lenin's mausoleum and buried under a marble bust beside the Kremlin wall. Streets and towns were renamed: Stalingrad, symbol of Soviet resistance during the Great Patriotic War, became Volgograd. The legal system was reformed and the ad hoc 'emergency tribunals', which had convicted so many innocent people, were abolished. The favourite charges of Stalin's show trials, 'counter-revolutionary activity' and 'terrorist intentions', were removed from the criminal code.

But one institution not reformed was the KGB. The Soviet Union was still a police state. Freedom of speech and association remained severely restricted and critics of the regime were likely to be expelled or, increasingly, declared insane. A condition known as 'creeping schizophrenia' was invented; it was impossible to disprove that you suffered from it and it allowed the state to confine sufferers in hospitals for 'psychiatric treatment'.** The Serbsky Institute in Moscow was one of several *psykhushkas* (mental hospitals) that acquired grim reputations for the abuse of dissidents. As a result, Khrushchev was able to declare in 1961 that there were 'no more political prisoners' in the Soviet Union.

---

* It was not until the Twenty-Seventh Party Congress in February 1986 that the party finally acknowledged the hopeless over-optimism of Khrushchev's claims. 'Much has changed in our life since the adoption of the Third Party Programme,' Mikhail Gorbachev would admit. 'Not all the estimates and conclusions turned out to be correct. The idea of translating the tasks of the full-scale building of Communism into direct practical action has proved to be premature … And as for the chronological limits in which the party's targets are to be attained, they do not seem to be needed.' The advent of Communism was being postponed indefinitely.

** It was never overtly stated, but the underlying assumption was that 'if someone opposes the people's state, which is destined to bring happiness to all mankind, he or she must by definition be mad.'

Under Stalin, the Soviet Union had largely ignored Western opinion about its internal politics. Military power was reputation enough. The party's monopoly on the dissemination of information kept the Soviet people in ignorance of Western achievements, including the superior living standards in Europe and North America. Khrushchev continued to deride the failings of capitalism in order to glorify the advantages of Communism (with characteristic pithiness he described capitalism as 'a dead herring in the moonlight, gleaming brilliantly as it rots'), but he showed a new enthusiasm for competition with the West.

In May 1957, he told a conference of agricultural specialists that the USSR would 'catch up with and overtake America'. When the phrase was reported in the West, it was taken as an indication of military aggressiveness in the escalating nuclear arms race, but the context makes clear that Khrushchev was talking in economic terms. His goal was to raise Soviet standards of living above those of America; posters implored the Soviet people to work together to 'Catch up and overtake the United States in per capita production of meat, milk and butter.' Soviet pride was at stake – the target of 'beating the Americans' was intended to boost performance in all sectors of the economy. It was a gamble by Khrushchev: as Soviet leader, he had at least a broad grasp of the economic realities on both sides of the Iron Curtain and he knew how far Moscow was trailing behind; but his enthusiasm and pugnacity got the better of him.

. Khrushchev needed to deliver on his boast. In the early 1960s, he launched a large-scale programme of house building. Thousands of concrete tower blocks were erected across the country and by the middle of the decade the availability of housing in cities had been greatly improved. In his memoirs, Khrushchev would proclaim, 'To use the words of John Reed, we "shook the world" with our massive drive to build housing for our people.' But the success was only relative and the results remained poor by US standards. The average Soviet city dweller still had only 9 square metres of living space and in 1965 more than half the urban population was still living in the cramped *kommunalki* (communal flats). The new apartments had been put up fast and suffered for it. Many of the prefabricated multi-storey blocks would need replacing only a few years later, and

they quickly gained the nickname of *khrushcheby* – 'Khrushchev's slums'.*
The building boom inspired jokes and urban myths; even Shostakovich
was moved to use it as the subject of an operetta, *Cheryomushki* (1958),
where a young couple fight Soviet bureaucracy to secure a new apartment,
with satirical results.

The economy was slow to respond to Khrushchev's urgings. He had
repealed many of Stalin's draconian labour laws: workers could no longer
be punished as criminals if they changed jobs without official permission
or if they arrived at work more than 20 minutes late. But there were few
financial incentives to make people work hard and there was more than a
grain of truth in the familiar joke that 'they pretend to pay us and we
pretend to work'. By 1961, Khrushchev was again flirting with Stalinist
methods of coercion. His 'Moral Code of the Communist Worker' rein-
stated the old warning 'He who does not work shall not eat' and created a
new offence of 'parasitism', punishing those who shirked work or did not
work hard enough with imprisonment or menial jobs in distant regions.
People were once again encouraged to 'be intolerant towards the violation
of public interests', in effect to inform on work colleagues who did not pull
their weight.

Khrushchev's biggest challenge was agriculture. He was the son of peasants himself and he took personal responsibility for improving the country's
disastrous food production. He set specific targets in the race to 'catch up
with America', but the collective farms responded tepidly. His demand in
1957 for a threefold increase in meat production was so unrealistic that
most agricultural specialists declared it impossible. Khrushchev needed an
example to prove himself right, and he found it in the leadership of the
Ryazan region south of Moscow. The local party boss, Alexei Larionov,
pledged that he would meet the target within a year, and in January 1959
Khrushchev unveiled the promise in *Pravda*, challenging other regions to

---

* In the course of his construction programme, Khrushchev tore down the historic Arbat
district of Moscow, with the loss of many valuable buildings. The series of apartment blocks
that now protrude incongruously on the main avenue of the district are still referred to as
'Khrushchev's false teeth'.

do the same. Larionov was awarded the Order of Lenin and held up as an example for others, but he had little idea how he was going to fulfil his pledge. His solution was to slaughter the whole of the region's beef stock and much of its dairy herd; cattle reared privately by collective farm workers were expropriated and additional meat supplies were bought from neighbouring districts. The measures bankrupted the Ryazan budget and left its agricultural infrastructure in ruins. But at the Communist Party plenum of December 1959 Khrushchev triumphantly announced that the target had been met and that the quota for the following year was being raised even higher. Larionov's irresponsible methods were soon exposed and the region's meat production plummeted to a fraction of its previous levels. He was fired and committed suicide soon afterwards.

The Alice in Wonderland character of Khrushchev's miracle cures extended to much vaster agricultural projects. His Virgin Lands scheme, launched in 1954, was designed to open up the uncultivated steppes of western Siberia and northern Kazakhstan. In a large-scale mobilisation not seen since the 1930s, a quarter of a million young people migrated to create what they hoped would be a major new grain-growing area for the Soviet Union. The campaign was glorified in novels and songs; films and posters reminiscent of the collectivisation era showed happy young men and women working the land, joyfully ensuring that the USSR would never again go hungry. There was enthusiasm and idealism in the spontaneous expression of the Russian frontier spirit. But what the propaganda failed to show was that alongside the mainly Slav volunteers, the ethnic groups deported by Stalin during the war were also being exploited. Chechens, Volga Germans, Ingush and Crimean Tartars all contributed to the early successes of Khrushchev's scheme. Although some of them were allowed to return to their native lands after the 'secret speech' of 1956, the Tartars and Germans were deemed invaluable to the success of the project and had to stay.

By 1960, tens of millions of hectares of new land had been ploughed and national wheat output was up by over 50 per cent. The Virgin Lands scheme was trumpeted as a success, but a few years later success had turned sour. The new lands were fertile, but lay on the edges of the central Asian desert. In the rush for quick results, the soil had not been properly prepared or fertilised and a 'dustbowl' effect developed, similar to that seen in America in the 1930s. As the soil crumbled, ever greater areas of land became barren. Bad weather in the spring and summer of 1962 produced a poor harvest across the whole of the Soviet Union, and of the 37 million hectares of land sown with corn, only 7 million were successfully harvested. Despite Khrushchev's promises of self-sufficiency, Moscow had to buy 20 million tons of grain from Canada to avoid the threat of famine.

In parallel with the Virgin Lands campaign, Khrushchev embarked on another speculative scheme. Soviet delegations to the United States had returned with awestruck accounts of huge and highly productive cornfields in the American Midwest. The superior yield of the US growers was attributed to a hybrid strain of corn developed by a farmer and seed company executive from Iowa named Roswell Garst. Garst was invited to visit the Soviet Union and struck up an unlikely friendship with the Communist Party first secretary, persuading Khrushchev to purchase 5,000 tons of hybrid corn seeds to be planted across the country. When Khrushchev made the first state visit by a Soviet leader to the US in 1959 he insisted on visiting Garst's farm and was photographed smiling broadly amid the towering cornfields, waving a corncob and declaring that the Soviet Union would make an even greater success of its agriculture. 'Up to now, you Americans have worked better than we do,' he announced. 'So we will learn from you. And once we've learned, we'll work even better than you do. So you will have to jump onto the running board of the train of socialism, which is about to leave for the future. Otherwise you'll be left far behind, and we will wave goodbye to you from the rear platform of the last carriage.'

Khrushchev's enthusiasm for corn earned him the popular nickname *kukuruznik*, 'little corn-man' or 'corn nut'; his optimism was infectious, but his self-belief led him to disregard any advice that contradicted his own convictions. When Soviet agronomists warned him to plant corn only in the warm southern regions of the Soviet Union, he refused to listen, ordering it to be sown in the climatically unsuitable area of European Russia. The decision led to disastrous harvests and catastrophic shortages in other, more traditional crops, such as wheat and potatoes, that the new cornfields had displaced.

Khrushchev had gambled on disastrous schemes, and the vast scale of his mistakes brought Soviet agriculture to the edge of catastrophe. The cheap food the Soviet people were accustomed to was no longer available. When meat and dairy prices were raised, a wave of discontent spread through the country. At the Novocherkassk locomotive works in southern Russia, several thousand workers went on strike, and in June 1962 many of them took to the streets, demanding the return of cheap food and better wages. When the workers refused to disperse, troops shot indiscriminately into the crowd, killing at least 16 people and wounding dozens more. Over a hundred people were arrested and brought to trial; seven alleged ring-leaders were sentenced to death for fomenting 'banditry'.*

Bread queues appeared across the country, and the state was forced to spend precious foreign currency reserves to buy food from abroad. Before the revolution, Russia had been a net exporter of grain, but now the Soviet Union could not even feed itself. Khrushchev's son Sergei recalled that the food crisis convinced his father something was deeply amiss with the Soviet system:

> Father didn't understand what was wrong. He grew nervous, became angry, quarrelled, looked for culprits but didn't find them. Deep inside, he began subconsciously to understand that the problem was not in the details. It was the system itself that didn't work. But he couldn't change his beliefs.

The economic crisis forced Khrushchev to take tough decisions. The military budget was cut to fund spending on food imports and on the massive housing programme of the early 1960s. Khrushchev concluded that the Soviet Union could not afford to compete with the United States on all fronts. He consequently announced that the East–West antagonism of Stalin's final years would be replaced by a new doctrine of 'peaceful coexistence'. It was a difficult policy to explain to the Soviet military leadership,

---

* The Novocherkassk events were never referred to in the Soviet media, and details of the massacre remained classified until 1992.

and Khrushchev seems to have done it in a singularly insensitive way, telling the commanders of the armed forces that they were largely redundant now that the Soviet Union had developed the atomic bomb, and that there was no longer any need to 'waste' money on conventional weapons.

To replace the traditional Soviet reliance on the strength of its usual military forces, Khrushchev developed a two-pronged approach to international relations. He sought to create allies out of newly independent African and Asian states, touring India, Afghanistan and Burma in 1955, and befriending Egypt's President Nasser by helping him build the Aswan Dam. The victory of Fidel Castro's Communist forces in the Cuban revolution of 1959 brought Moscow another strategically placed ally that could be exploited to exert pressure on Washington. At the same time, Khrushchev attempted to disguise the pressures on the Soviet defence budget by a campaign of bluff and intimidation. He told a gathering of Western ambassadors in Moscow that the triumph of Communism was inevitable. 'Like it or not,' he said, 'history is on our side. We will bury you.' The remark was a restatement of the classic Marxian belief contained in the Communist Manifesto that 'the proletariat will be the gravedigger of capitalism', but Khrushchev did little to discourage Western speculation that he was threatening nuclear conflict.

Sergei Khrushchev recalls that during his father's visit to England in April 1956, 'he casually enquired ... if his hosts knew how many nuclear warheads it would take to wipe their island off the face of the Earth. An awkward silence followed. But Father did not drop the subject, and with a broad smile on his face, he informed those present that if they didn't know, he could help them, and he mentioned a specific number. Then he added, quite cheerfully, "And we have lots of those nuclear warheads, as well as the missiles to deliver them."' In his usual colourful language, Khrushchev announced that the Soviet Union was 'producing missiles like sausages', but his son later wrote that this too was a bluff:

> When I asked him how he could say that, since the Soviet Union had no more than half a dozen intercontinental missiles, Father only laughed: 'We're not planning to start a war, so it doesn't matter how many missiles we have.

The main thing is that Americans think we have enough for a massive strike in response. That'll make them think twice about attacking us.'

In 1959, an American trade exhibition was held at the Sokolniki Park exhibition halls on the outskirts of Moscow, where the latest US domestic technology, including fridges, washing machines, televisions and dishwashers was laid out in dazzling displays. Khrushchev got into a very undiplomatic and very public exchange of views with the US vice-president Richard Nixon, who had come to open the exhibition. Khrushchev refused to believe Nixon's claim that the average American could afford a home equipped with all the devices on show and argued fiercely but implausibly that Soviet television sets were better than American ones. He mocked the American obsession with 'gadgets' and asked if they had invented a machine to 'stuff food into people's mouths'. As the argument grew more heated, Khrushchev famously told his guest, 'We'll show you Kuzma's mother!' – a piece of Russian slang meaning roughly, 'We'll show you what for!' The exchange, which was shown in part on Soviet television, annoyed many viewers, who felt ashamed at their leader's peasant manners and lack of culture. The sophistication of the US exhibits had impressed those who saw them, and the free glasses of Pepsi Cola handed out to visitors were a big hit. A popular joke recounted how people, when asked for their opinion of this capitalist drink, would reply 'Revolting!' before running to the back of the queue to get another glass.*

When Khrushchev visited the US later that year, he was determined and proud to sing the praises of Soviet accomplishments. 'Who would have guessed it,' he wrote in his memoirs, 'that the most powerful capitalist country in the world would invite a Communist to visit? Who would have thought that the capitalists would invite me, a worker? This is incredible. Today they have to take notice of us. They have to recognise our existence and our power. Look what we've achieved … From a ravaged, backward,

---

* Thirteen years later, Pepsi would sign a reciprocal deal with Stolichnaya Vodka to sell their products in each other's country. Throughout the Brezhnev era, Pepsi was one of the few Western commodities that could be freely bought in the USSR.

illiterate Russia we have transformed ourselves into a Russia whose successes stun the world.'

In a speech in Pittsburgh he repeated his pledge to 'catch up with and overtake America', laughingly adding, 'I think this slogan has frightened some of you. But why? ... We will stand up for ourselves and we will overtake you. We are warning you to buck your ideas up if you don't want to be lagging way behind us ...' Khrushchev got annoyed when journalists attacked him for the invasion of Hungary three years earlier, but in general the visit was a good-natured one. He was determined to control his temper and not to express too much admiration for what he saw. In Los Angeles he went to the 20th Century Fox studios, where he met Frank Sinatra, Gary Cooper, Elizabeth Taylor and Marilyn Monroe, who had been told to wear her tightest, sexiest dress and to leave Arthur Miller at home. Much to his chagrin, he was not allowed to visit Disneyland, because the Los Angeles police said they could not guarantee his safety. In the Soviet Union, Khrushchev's visit was given blanket coverage. His feisty treatment of his hosts played well with the hardline nationalists, but others found it embarrassing. His competiveness was widely mocked. A popular joke imagined Eisenhower responding to Khrushchev's jibes by suggesting they run a foot race to see who would 'catch up with and overtake' whom. When the athletic Eisenhower wins easily, the Soviet media are forced into some ingenuity to put the correct gloss on it. 'Our leader Nikita Khrushchev has captured second place in a world-class field,' *Pravda* reports, 'while the US president finished a humiliating second to last.'

Khrushchev's visit to the US had been credited with taking some of the heat out of the Cold War, but soon the temperature rose again. On 1 May 1960 an American U-2 spy plane operating from a secret US base in Pakistan was shot down as it flew over Siberia photographing intercontinental ballistic missile sites. When the pilot, Gary Powers, ejected and was captured by the Soviets, it gave Khrushchev a perfect opportunity to take the moral high ground. He announced the shooting down of a spy plane, but did not mention the pilot. Eisenhower assumed Powers had died in the explosion and authorised a cover story, that an American 'weather plane' had 'crashed somewhere north of Turkey'. Washington declared that 'there was absolutely no deliberate attempt to violate Soviet airspace and never has been'. On 7 May, in a speech to the Supreme Soviet, Khrushchev revealed the truth with a triumphant flourish. 'I must tell you a secret … When I made my first report, I deliberately did not say that the pilot was alive and well … and now just look how many foolish things the Americans have said.'*

The US and Soviet leaders met two weeks later for a 'Peace Summit' in Paris, where Khrushchev used the U-2 incident to attack Eisenhower, demanding an apology, a formal promise that it would never happen again and punishment for those responsible. When the Americans refused, Khrushchev made an intemperate speech, haranguing Eisenhower for his 'betrayal', and stormed out of the meeting. Many in the Soviet delegation found his conduct hugely discomforting, and Khrushchev would later claim that the U-2 crisis marked the beginning of the problems that would ultimately end his political career. In 1969, he told a visiting American doctor that 'Things were going well until that happened. But from the moment Gary Powers was shot down I was no longer in full control. Those [Kremlin hardliners] who felt America had imperialist intentions and that military strength was the most important thing now had the evidence they needed. After the U-2 incident, I no longer had the ability to overcome that feeling.'

Further evidence of Khrushchev's volatile behaviour was displayed at the UN General Assembly in October 1960, when he repeatedly interrupted a speech by the British prime minister Harold Macmillan. When Macmillan criticised the Soviet Union for its oppressive policies in Eastern Europe, Khrushchev banged a shoe on his desk in protest. (Film of the event seems to show Khrushchev still wearing both shoes, suggesting perhaps that he had borrowed a shoe from one of his aides.) He seemed pleased with the effect his ranting had produced, telling his adviser Oleg Troyanovsky, 'You really missed something! It was great fun!' Later he would claim he was inspired by stories he had heard about the Duma of 1905 in which people

---

* Powers was tried in Moscow for espionage and sentenced to three years' imprisonment followed by seven years' hard labour. He was released early, in 1962, in exchange for a captured Soviet spy.

were not afraid to use extreme measures to get their point across. But several members of the Soviet delegation, as well as Khrushchev's opponents in the Central Committee back in Moscow, were appalled. There was a growing consensus that his actions were beginning to undermine his reputation and that of the Soviet Union.

When Khrushchev next met an American president, the newly elected John F. Kennedy in Vienna in June 1961, he set out deliberately to show the younger man who was boss. He was condescending and domineering, relentlessly complaining about the recent Bay of Pigs fiasco, in which a CIA-trained force of Cuban exiles had been vainly dispatched to overthrow Castro's Communist regime. The two leaders also clashed about the status of Berlin, as Khrushchev continued to demand its incorporation into the DDR. Ever since the division of Germany after the Second World War, citizens of the DDR had been using Berlin's open borders to escape to the West, and Walter Ulbricht, the East German Communist leader, had urged Khrushchev to take action to stop the exodus. Khrushchev agreed: in August 1961, barbed wire was erected between the Western and Soviet sectors. When the West did nothing to remove it, he authorised the construction of a permanent wall surrounding the Western sector on all sides, blocking access from any part of East German territory. Again the West didn't respond. Khrushchev concluded that he had tested Kennedy and come out on top. The successful building of the Berlin wall would foster a misplaced confidence that Moscow could bully the young American leader with impunity.

In fact, Kennedy and his administration were increasingly worried by Khrushchev's unpredictable behaviour and bellicose rhetoric. In October 1961, the USSR's test of the so-called 'Tsar bomb' (see p. 381), the largest nuclear weapon so far produced, heightened tensions throughout the world; the nuclear clock seemed to be approaching midnight. Khrushchev's memoirs suggest he regarded the nuclear arms race in terms of a personal game of chicken with the US leader.

I remember President Kennedy once stated that the United States had the nuclear missile capacity to wipe out the Soviet Union two times over, while the Soviet Union had enough atomic weapons to wipe out the United

States only once … When journalists asked me to comment, I said jokingly, 'Yes, Kennedy is quite right. But I'm not complaining … We're happy to finish off the United States first time round. What good does it do to annihilate a country twice? We are not a bloodthirsty people.'

Khrushchev may have been ready to employ nuclear weapons only as a bargaining tool, with no intention of actually using them. But his outbursts had convinced the US administration that he was erratic and possibly unbalanced. Washington's belief that Moscow might, under certain circumstances, trigger a nuclear conflict would lead to the most dangerous moment of the Cold War.

Castro's takeover in Cuba had given the Soviets the opportunity to challenge the Americans close to home. The US had deployed missiles in Turkey, within striking distance of Moscow, and Khrushchev wanted to rebalance the nuclear equation. In early October 1962, US spy planes spotted unusual building work at Soviet bases and identified what looked like batteries of surface-to-air missiles (SAM), capable of carrying nuclear warheads. The US military chiefs of staff argued strongly for a pre-emptive airstrike to destroy the missile bases, but Kennedy hesitated. By mid October, the world was on the brink of nuclear war; JFK made clear that he did not want to fight, but if the Soviets forced him into it, he would not hesitate. His brother Robert Kennedy confirmed later that the American threat was real:

We had to have a commitment by tomorrow that the bases would be removed. I was not giving them an ultimatum but a statement of fact. They should understand that if they did not remove those bases, we would remove them. Perhaps [they] might feel it necessary to take retaliatory action; but before that was over, there would be not only dead Americans but dead Russians as well.

Khrushchev's aim, as he later wrote, was 'to protect Cuba's existence as a socialist country' and 'provide an example to the other countries of the region'. Khrushchev's personal credibility was at stake, and he seemed committed to seeing things through to the end. 'We hadn't had enough time to deliver all our shipments to Cuba', he recalled, 'but we had already installed enough missiles to destroy New York, Chicago and the other industrial cities, not to mention a little village like Washington. If any of our big missiles survived [an attack], there wouldn't be much of New York left ... I don't think America had ever faced such a real threat of destruction.'

After his success in Berlin, Khrushchev apparently expected another bloodless victory. He asked rhetorically, 'How can I deal seriously with a man who is younger than my own son?' but he had underestimated Kennedy. The White House announced that US warships would impose an exclusion zone around Cuba and that any Soviet vessels trying to breach it would be destroyed. A Soviet flotilla en route to the island with a presumed cargo of more missiles was within days of triggering military confrontation. But with the endgame seemingly at hand, Washington and Moscow simultaneously came up with proposals to defuse the crisis. If the Soviets would dismantle the missiles, the US would guarantee never to stage another invasion like the Bay of Pigs; in return, the Soviet Union promised not to attack Turkey if the US weapons stationed there were removed. On 28 October, Radio Moscow carried a statement by Khrushchev that all Soviet missiles in Cuba were being withdrawn. The US kept its promise to remove its missiles from Turkey, but refrained from announcing this publicly, with the result that Moscow seemed to have accepted a humiliating climb-down. Kennedy told his staff that he had 'cut Mr K's balls off' and the US news media declared victory for America.

The Soviet Presidium were far from impressed with Khrushchev's handling of the affair. It had been his miscalculation to deploy the missiles in the first place, and it was he who wrongly believed he could bully Kennedy into submission. Moscow had been made to appear weak in the eyes of the world; their ally Castro was furious that his country's future had been decided without consulting him, and China – still smarting from the perceived humiliation of Moscow's de-Stalinisation process – denounced the whole episode as 'misguided adventurism followed by capitulation'.

The Cuban debacle and the failure of his agricultural schemes had undermined Khrushchev's authority. By the time the space programme started to implode, he was already yesterday's man. His last official act as Soviet leader was to congratulate the crew of the first multi-manned *Voskhod* mission on 12 October 1964. He made the call from his holiday home on the Black Sea, and later the same day he received a message from the Presidium in Moscow. They had arranged an emergency Central Committee meeting to discuss the agricultural situation and asked him to return for it. When he got there, his reception was brutal. The instigator of the coup was Khrushchev's own protégé, Leonid Brezhnev, and the rest of the Presidium supported it. The ideology chief, Mikhail Suslov, read out an indictment of Khrushchev's mistakes as party secretary, lambasting his erratic, self-aggrandising behaviour, denouncing his failures over agriculture, the Cuban missile crisis and the break with China, and calling for his resignation. Khrushchev was alone; he asked for the same mercy as he had shown the plotters of 1957. 'Comrades, forgive me if I am guilty of anything,' he said. 'We worked together. It's true that we didn't accomplish everything we had hoped for ... Now obviously it will be for you to do as you wish. What can I say? I've got what I deserved.' He then offered his resignation 'for reasons of health'. It was accepted, and the next day the Central Committee, which Suslov had already won over, gave its vote of approval.*

The *Pravda* editorial on 16 October spoke of 'subjectivism and drift in Communist construction, hare-brained scheming, half-baked conclusions, hasty decisions and actions divorced from reality, bragging and bluster, a penchant for rule by fiat, and unwillingness to take into account what science and practical experience have already worked out'. This was

---

* In 1964, the Soviet system of 'democratic centralism' was still functioning smoothly: the web of party domination radiating out from the Kremlin ensured that the commands of the Communist Party of the Soviet Union (CPSU) would be obeyed throughout the land. Whoever controlled the top Communist bodies also controlled the vast administrative structure that filtered down into all levels of society, bringing with it the obedience of the civil service, the army, the militia and the state security services. So it took only a limited 'palace coup' like the one carried out in October 1964 to effect an automatic and total transfer of authority. It is worth noting, as the next time such a coup would be attempted – in August 1991 – conditions would have changed so fundamentally that the plotters' expectations of a similar smooth transition would be dramatically dashed.

ignominy. Khrushchev was viewed by many as a brutish peasant who had embarrassed the Soviet Union on the international stage and nearly blundered into a war that could have ended the world. His boundless self-belief, allied to the limitless power conferred on him in the post of first secretary, had led him to pursue disastrous schemes.

But he had managed the transition from the dark abuses of Stalinism to a society that was more open, less haunted by the spectre of arbitrary repression. 'I am old and tired,' he told a friend on the night of his dismissal. 'Let them cope by themselves. I've done the main thing. Could anyone imagine telling Stalin that he wasn't wanted any more and telling him to retire? He would have annihilated them. Everything is different now. The fear has gone; we can talk as equals. That is my contribution.'

CHAPTER THIRTY-SEVEN

The new regime was determined to distance itself from what had gone before. Leonid Brezhnev, the new party leader, was a characterless man lacking clear ideological goals, who arrived at decisions in counsel with his advisers, Yuri Andropov, Konstantin Chernenko, Mikhail Suslov, Alexei Kosygin and Andrei Gromyko. Where Khrushchev was colourful and eccentric, Brezhnev was grey and dull; where Khrushchev strove to change things, to move the country forward, Brezhnev was content to let it stagnate and flounder. For a while he was viewed as a stopgap leader; few would have predicted his reign would last 18 years, second only to Stalin's.

Leonid Ilyich Brezhnev was the son of a Ukrainian steelworker. Born in 1906, slender and handsome in his youth, the antithesis of the bloated, beetle-browed wreck who would stumble through speeches at the end of his life, Brezhnev trained as an engineer, joining the party in 1929. In the years after 1941 he served as a political commissar with the Red Army in Ukraine, and the post brought him into close contact with the republic's party boss, Khrushchev, whose wartime role as Stalin's representative to the Red Army commanders placed him in daily communication with the Kremlin. Brezhnev himself saw little direct military action, but his contact with Khrushchev, and through him with Stalin, served him well. After the war he had Khrushchev to thank for his rise through the party ranks, and in 1952 he was made a member of the Central Committee. When Khrushchev became General Secretary after Stalin's death, he appointed Brezhnev first secretary of the Kazakh Republic, where he oversaw the early, successful years of the Virgin Lands campaign. In 1960, Khrushchev was instrumental in appointing him chairman of the Presidium.

Having evicted his mentor, Brezhnev set about undoing Khrushchev's reforms, returning the country to the wary conservatism of the past and setting in train a process of decay that would eventually bring the Soviet

Union to its knees. The Brezhnev years would become known as the 'era of stagnation' – in politics, in the economy and in culture.

In the 'thaw' years under Khrushchev, the Soviet population had enjoyed a degree of relative freedom, as de-Stalinisation eased the restrictions on thought and expression. Khrushchev personally allowed the publication of Alexander Solzhenitsyn's *One Day in the Life of Ivan Denisovich* (1962), an account of life in a Stalin-era camp. But liberalisation remained patchy. Khrushchev was not prepared to allow wide-scale criticism of the current Soviet regime, and in later years his liberalism began to waver. Solzhenitsyn's subsequent work was banned, and other writers continued to suffer. Poets like Andrei Voznesensky and Yevgeny Yevtushenko were wildly popular, selling out whole football stadiums for their recitals, but their ambiguous attitude to the regime earned them enemies in the Kremlin. At a modern art exhibition in 1963, Khrushchev announced that the paintings were 'worse than a donkey could smear with its tail'; and when one of the artists, the sculptor Ernst Neizvestny, told him that being first secretary didn't make him an art critic, Khrushchev began a blazing, public row, eventually storming out in a rage.*

Khrushchev was capricious in his attitude towards creative freedom, but his reign came to be viewed with nostalgia in the years of suppression under Brezhnev. With literature and art now rigidly censored, writers who refused to produce the monochrome pap of socialist realism were forced underground. *Samizdat* blossomed, with poems, novels and memoirs passed from hand to hand in laboriously typed carbon copies, each copy growing fainter as the sheets approached the bottom of the pile. Independent voices made themselves heard in an oppressive society, although the *samizdat* writers also ran risks. The veteran dissident Vladimir Bukovsky wrote of the isolation and anxiety the profession brought with it: 'I write myself, I edit myself, I censor myself, I publish myself, I distribute myself and I go to jail for it myself.'

---

* Alexander Shelepin, the head of the KGB, hissed at the sculptor, 'You'll rot in a camp,' but he was never arrested. After Khrushchev's death, his widow asked Neizvestny to sculpt the former leader's tombstone and he created a striking memorial, split from top to bottom between black and white marble to reflect the human and political contradictions of Khrushchev's complex personality.

When the Leningrad poet Joseph Brodsky was put on trial in 1964, the judges belittled him as a 'pornographer' and a 'pseudo-poet in velvet trousers' who had 'failed in his duty to work for the motherland'. His alleged crime, that he 'did not fulfil a useful social purpose', led to a surreal court discussion on the nature of poetry. 'Who has certified that you are a poet?' asked the judge. 'Who has appointed you to be a poet?' 'Nobody,' Brodsky replied. 'Who has appointed me to be a human being?' 'Did you study to be a poet? Did you not try to finish a high school course where they teach this?' 'I didn't think I could learn this from high school.' 'Well, how then?' 'I think … that it comes from God.'

Brodsky was sentenced to five years' hard labour. His persecution caused unease, but it was the trial of the authors Andrei Sinyavsky and Yuli Daniel two years later that brought international condemnation and spurred the growth of the dissident movement. The pair were accused of 'anti-Soviet agitation and propaganda', but the only evidence against them consisted of views expressed by characters in their works of fiction. At their trial they pleaded not guilty, forensically exposing the prosecuting lawyers who tried to prove that an author must agree with the views of his characters. In his final plea to the court, Sinyavsky questioned why such a trial was necessary. 'I am different,' he acknowledged. 'But I do not regard myself as an enemy … In the fantastic, electrified atmosphere of this place, anybody who is "different" may be regarded as an enemy, but that is not logical. I do not see why enemies have to be invented, why monsters have to be piled on monsters by means of a literal-minded interpretation of literary images.' Daniel was sentenced to five years' hard labour and Sinyavsky to seven.*

---

* After serving his sentence, Sinyavsky emigrated to France and was allowed to return to Russia only in 1989 to attend Daniel's funeral. When I spoke to him in Daniel's Moscow apartment after the service, he told me that the real nature of their crime had been to expose the fragility and illegitimacy of the Soviet system. He said the regime needed enemies and 'monsters' to serve as scapegoats for its own failings, to the extent that even works of creative imagination were considered legitimate targets for the oppression of the state. But he had no regrets about what he had done or about the punishment he had received. He was heartened by the Gorbachev reforms, but maintained that Russia would always need poets and writers who were willing to stand in the way of autocracy.

The Sinyavsky and Daniel trial was a crucial moment in the history of dissent in the Soviet Union. From now on, the struggle would focus on the issue of human rights and the absence of a law-governed state. A letter of protest about the Daniel–Sinyavsky trial, signed by the physicist Andrei Sakharov and a host of other leading intellectuals, circulated widely in *samizdat*, and public demonstrations were held. Protestors would gather for 'silent vigils' in Pushkin Square in the centre of Moscow, taking care not to act illegally, and holding banners that read, 'Respect the constitution, the fundamental law of the USSR'. The tacit accusation was that the Soviet regime respected *no* laws, not even its own, and ruled as an unchecked totalitarian autocracy. As if to prove the protestors right, the Kremlin responded by creating a new offence of 'violating public order', which granted the police powers to disperse any public gathering the regime did not like. Writers and academics who took part in the demonstrations were told their careers would suffer; those who ignored the warnings found themselves dismissed from their positions and forced to take menial jobs as cleaners, cloakroom attendants or boiler-stokers. Increasingly, the KGB used networks of informers to infiltrate dissident groups and turn their leaders over to the authorities.

The repression became worse after the Soviet invasion of Czechoslovakia in 1968. Alexander Dubcek's policy of a 'separate road to socialism' for his country had proposed increased freedom of expression, decentralisation of power and possibly the creation of a multiparty system. The 'Prague spring' threatened the tranquillity of Communist rule in Eastern Europe and Brezhnev's alarm grew as his admonishments went unheeded. In the early hours of 21 August 1968, 200,000 troops and 2,000 tanks of the Warsaw Pact, drawn from the USSR, Bulgaria, Poland and Hungary advanced into Czechoslovakia. Seventy civilians were killed as they tried to resist the invaders; road signs were painted over and towns renamed Dubcek or Svoboda (meaning 'freedom', but also the name of the Czechoslovak president) to confuse the advancing troops. But the scale of the fighting was considerably less than in Hungary 12 years earlier, and the Kremlin was quickly able to announce that 'order' had been restored.

When the defeated Dubcek was taken under guard to Moscow, Brezhnev berated him for rocking the socialist boat. 'I believed you; I defended you against others,' he complained. 'I said that our Sasha [Alexander] was a good comrade. But look: you have let us all down!'* A *Pravda* editorial soon after the crisis made clear that independent political thinking in Eastern Europe remained subject to stringent limits. 'Separate roads to socialism', said the newspaper, were legitimate only so long as they disturbed 'neither socialism in their own country nor the fundamental interests of the other socialist countries, nor the worldwide workers' movement.' The so-called Brezhnev Doctrine, confirmed in a speech in November by the General Secretary himself, specified that Warsaw Pact member states were 'free to apply the basic principles of Marxism–Leninism and of socialism in its country, but cannot depart from these principles'.

In Moscow, the invasion was denounced in dissident *samizdat* publications and, on 25 August, eight protestors attempted to stage a sit-in on Red Square, an unprecedented act in an intensely policed and very public area. As soon as they raised their banners proclaiming 'Hands off Czechoslovakia!' and 'For your freedom and ours!' they were surrounded by baton-wielding militia, beaten and dragged away. Four of the demonstrators were sentenced to jail, three to exile and one to a psychiatric hospital. But their courage did much to inspire and consolidate the increasingly assertive dissident groups. Throughout 1968 the Soviet media had given considerable prominence to the May student riots in Paris and to the anti-Vietnam War demonstrations in the United States and Britain. The coverage served, ironically, to encourage opposition forces in the USSR to believe that they too should find ways of making their voices heard.

The invasion of Czechoslovakia also provoked condemnation from the more independent-minded members of the Communist Bloc itself, including Yugoslavia, Romania and Albania. Relations with China, already rocky, were damaged further. In March 1969, tensions between Moscow and

---

* Unlike the leaders of the Hungarian rebellion in 1956, Dubcek escaped with his life, spending many years as a forestry official in rural Slovakia before returning briefly to politics after the 'Velvet Revolution' of 1989.

Beijing erupted in a series of armed skirmishes along the Russo–Chinese border, which left hundreds of troops from both sides injured and dozens dead. The threat was eventually resolved through diplomatic negotiations, but the legacy of mistrust remained strong. The Sino–Soviet split led both sides to look elsewhere for potential allies, and both Moscow and Beijing subsequently embarked on a course of rapprochement with their hitherto common enemy, the United States.

A number of US–Soviet agreements limiting the production and deployment of nuclear weapons were signed on Brezhnev's watch, including the Nuclear Non-Proliferation Treaty of 1969, two Strategic Arms Limitation Treaties (SALT I and II) and the Anti-Ballistic Missile Treaty of 1972. Brezhnev visited New York in 1973 and Presidents Richard Nixon and Gerald Ford both travelled to the Soviet Union in the cause of détente, or *razryadka* as it was known in Russian. The tensions of the Cold War began to ease, but neither side believed there would be a lasting peace.

The Kremlin's chief motivation for pursuing détente was a financial one. Since taking office, Brezhnev had made military parity with the US a priority, allowing the defence budget to rise by 40 per cent in his first six years in power. The stagnating Soviet economy could scarcely bear the strain, and the civilian sector suffered badly. Brezhnev's aversion to change led to perverse decisions that compounded the damage to industry. Technical improvements, such as the introduction of new machines in factories, were put off or avoided completely because the rigid planned economy could not afford the brief dips in production that would occur while the machines were being installed and the workers trained to use them. Indeed, increasing productivity rates was viewed as disadvantageous by many enterprises: if productivity rose, targets would be increased for the following year or workers would be transferred out. People knew that if they worked harder or more efficiently, they would be given more work to do for no more reward; so most saved their energies for their time off, when they would need to queue for food and goods and attempt to make some money on the side. The official economy was shadowed by a second 'black' economy as people supplemented their incomes by working *po-levomu* (on the left), bartering services and goods with one another. Often they did this in collusion with their bosses, using tools or exchanging products taken from their places of work and paying off their superiors for protection. The abuses were widely known and generally tolerated; even Brezhnev acknowledged that 'Nobody lives on just his wages'.

Official propaganda labelled the 1970s the 'Period of Developed Socialism', one step closer to Communism, though it warned that this was likely to be a 'historically protracted period'. Unlike Khrushchev, Brezhnev did not make grand promises he knew he could not fulfil, so only gradual progress in consumer goods and living standards was predicted; improvements in wages and productivity were negligible. The outside world had only minimal access to the secrets of the Soviet economy, however, and Moscow's Panglossian propaganda, insisting that all was 'for the best in the best of all possible socialist worlds', succeeded in convincing many that the USSR was prospering. The oil crisis of 1973, when the OPEC countries cut back on supplies, helped Moscow achieve higher prices for its own oil, and it remained the world leader in steel, iron and cement. But beneath the surface the reality was less rosy.

When Brezhnev hailed the ninth Five Year Plan as a remarkable success, the Georgian first secretary, Eduard Shevardnadze, responded with a more realistic assessment: 'One out of every four consumer articles we produce is of unsatisfactory quality,' he wrote in *Pravda* in February 1976. 'For the first four years of the Five Year Plan, an average of just 91 apartments were built for every 10,000 people across the Soviet Union.' Brezhnev had announced that in the next Five Year Plan 172 billion roubles would be spent on agriculture, but Shevardnadze noted, 'For every rouble we invest in agriculture, we get back a total of 39 kopeks.' Labour productivity was 50 per cent lower than in the US; agricultural productivity was 75 per cent lower. Andrei Sakharov estimated that the purchasing power of the average Soviet worker was about one-tenth that of an American worker. At times the acute shortages of goods made even those few roubles worthless: what was the point of having money if there was nothing to buy? The only people who could rely on a steady supply of food and consumer goods were members of the Soviet *nomenklatura,* party officials and politicians who had access to a range of special shops, carefully hidden behind unmarked doors so as not to enrage the rest of the population who went without. The complete collapse of the Soviet economy was being staved off only by the unbridled export of raw materials, making it as dependent on oil and gas as Russia had been before 1917.

But unlike pre-revolutionary days, there was no longer any grain surplus to feed the population and sell for foreign currency; now the USSR was a net importer of grain. Collectivised agriculture remained as unproductive as ever; the limited private plots that *kolkhoz* workers were allowed to cultivate in their spare time were considerably more efficient, accounting for 28 per cent of the country's gross agricultural output despite covering only 1 per cent of cultivated land. In order to keep prices down for the urban population, the state was forced to pay huge subsidies to the collective farms, reaching the astronomical figure of $33 billion a year by 1981.

As living standards plummeted, alcoholism, mental illness, divorce and suicide rates rose. In 1964, Lithuanians consumed an average of 8 litres of vodka a year; by 1973, the figure had risen to 28.5 litres. Women in particular suffered under the double burden of trying to care for a family while also having to go out to work. The need for a second income placed marriages under stress; the numbers of abortions and divorces rose, and many families in urban areas limited themselves to a single child because of the lack of available living space. Thus the birth rate continued to fall. The populations of Russia, Ukraine, Belarus and the Baltic republics were declining in real terms, and the Slavic race's dominance of the Union was coming under threat. In 1959, ethnic Russians accounted for 55 per cent of the population, while in 1979 the number had fallen to 52 per cent. At the same time, the Tajik, Uzbek and Kazakh populations were growing rapidly, sparking fears among some Russians that they would be outnumbered by 'Orientals'.

Nationalist ill feeling was increasing: the ethnic minorities resented what they saw as the Kremlin's Russian chauvinism, while Russian nationalists accused the Kremlin of ignoring their cultural and social interests. The combination was potentially explosive, but under Brezhnev the problem, like so many others, remained unaddressed. Regional leaders were satraps, corruption ran uncontrolled and the 'tribal tsars' who ran the republics promoted family and clan members into key positions. Local elites began to follow increasingly national lines, while ethnic Russians who had lived in the republics since the 1930s were sidelined and discriminated against. Virtually every republic and every nationality, including the Russians, had grievances against the centre. In the late 1960s, there were disturbances in Yerevan in Armenia, Tartu in Estonia and Kiev in Ukraine. The fault lines that would make themselves felt in the final, tempestuous years of the Soviet Union were beginning to open.

Brezhnev may have been reluctant to tackle the national problem directly, but he was not averse to looking for scapegoats. TV shows, books and films depicted 'Zionism' as a serious threat to the Soviet state, and a Permanent Commission was established at the USSR Academy of Sciences 'to coordinate research dedicated to the exposure and criticism of the history, ideology and practical activity of Zionism'. Jews became an increasingly high-profile target after the Six Day War in 1967, suffering discrimination in the workplace, difficulties in access to higher education and physical aggression in the streets. More and more Soviet Jews sought to emigrate to Israel, but found daunting obstacles placed in their way. The Soviet government had always been reluctant to allow large-scale emigration, partly because it undermined the desired image of the USSR as a socialist paradise where people lived happily and well. But the official reason given to many Jews for the refusal of their exit visa was that they were 'a risk to state security'.*

Under Western pressure, Moscow might reluctantly grant exit visas to Jews who could prove they had family abroad, but other applicants joined the ranks of the *Otkazniki*, or 'Refuseniks' as they were known in the West. The very act of asking to emigrate made a person suspicious in the eyes of

---

* The absurdity of the excuse was mocked in a joke told by the prominent Jewish dissident Nathan Sharansky. 'A Jew approaches a KGB officer,' runs the joke, 'and asks why he has been refused a visa. "We can't allow you to leave because you know state secrets," says the KGB man. "But what secrets?" asks the Jew. "Where I worked we were ten years behind the West." "Exactly!" said the officer. "*That's* the secret."'

the authorities, and Refuseniks became pariahs, removed from their jobs, harassed by the authorities and defamed in the press.

Both Refuseniks and dissidents, insinuated the official media, were agents of the imperialist West, determined to undermine the Soviet Union. Freethinkers, such as Andrei Sakharov, Andrei Amalrik, Vladimir Bukovsky, Roy Medvedev and Alexander Solzhenitsyn, were denounced as extremists, probably in the pay of sinister foreign powers.

In reality, they were neither. The name they adopted for themselves and people like them was *inakomyslyashchie* – literally 'people who think differently', people who wanted to bring about positive change in the Soviet Union. In 1970, Sakharov helped found the Human Rights Committee, a group that declared itself 'A creative association *acting in accordance with the laws of the land*'. They condemned the unlawful use of psychiatric incarceration and medication against opponents of the regime and championed the need for adequate defence provisions for those put on trial. Their modus operandi was to expose the illegal behaviour of the authorities by holding them to account under Soviet legislation that the authorities themselves had introduced. The Kremlin responded with yet more arrests and repression, justified by the KGB chief Yuri Andropov with Orwellian sophistry. 'All Soviet citizens whose interests coincide with those of society as a whole enjoy the highest democratic liberties,' he thundered. 'But it is an entirely different matter for those whose interests do not so coincide.' In other words, 'You are free to think whatever you like, as long it is what we want you to think.'

Alexander Solzhenitsyn made no secret of his belief that Soviet Communism was doomed. In 1973, he wrote *A Letter to the Soviet Authorities*, in which he urged Brezhnev and his colleagues to 'throw away the dead ideology that threatens to destroy us militarily and economically'. 'When you open your newspapers or switch on your television,' he challenged the Kremlin ideologues, 'do you yourselves really believe for one instant all those speeches that you find there? No, you yourselves stopped believing in it long ago, I am certain of it. And if you did not, then you must have become totally cut off from the real life of this country.' It was the height of hubristic folly, Solzhenitsyn wrote, for Russians to try to solve the world's problems when their own native land was in such a mess. And in a conscious nod to the nineteenth-century Slavophiles, he claimed that Russia's hope of salvation lay in its traditional peasant villages, the repository of the true collectivist spirit of the ancient peasant *mir* (self-governing councils), shielded from the noxious ideas of progress and modernity that had brought so much misfortune on the motherland. Solzhenitsyn was a traditionalist, an Orthodox nationalist, and his ideas have much in common with the conservatives of the late nineteenth century. Like the tsarist apologist of autocracy Konstantin Pobedonostsev, Solzhenitsyn maintained that democracy is not the solution to Russia's woes and that authoritarian rule is necessary for her wellbeing. 'For an unprepared people, to jump directly from the cliff [of totalitarianism] into democracy,' he wrote, 'would mean a fatal slam that would result in an anarchistic pulp.' The following year, Solzhenitsyn was arrested and banished to the West. The official media spread false rumours that he was a Jewish Refusenik and that he had himself asked to leave Russia.

With Solzhenitsyn gone, the spiritual leadership of the Soviet dissident movement passed to Andrei Sakharov. He supported the principles of détente and argued that the Soviet state was harming itself by restricting the freedom of the intelligentsia, leaving science and technology to lag behind the West. 'The anti-democratic traditions and norms of public life established in the Stalin era,' he wrote, 'have not been definitively eliminated to this day ... The intelligentsia's attempts to increase its freedoms are legitimate and natural.' Despite intimidation from the authorities, Sakharov refused to back down. 'A man may be deprived of all hope,' he concluded, 'but he must nevertheless speak out because he cannot, simply cannot, remain silent'. It was the dissident's duty 'to be honest, principled, unselfish and ready for self-sacrifice'.

In 1975 Sakharov was awarded the Nobel Peace Prize, a decoration that would sit incongruously beside his Lenin Prize, his Stalin Prize and three Hero of Socialist Labour medals, all awarded for his previous service to the Soviet state's development of the atomic bomb. Sakharov's actions helped to draw worldwide attention to the plight of dissidents in the Soviet Union, and when the West initialled the Helsinki Accords that same year it insisted on the inclusion of a chapter binding all signatories to 'respect human rights and fundamental freedoms'. Moscow agreed to the human rights obligations solely because it was determined to safeguard the other provisions of the treaty, which committed the West to recognising the post-Second World War boundaries of Eastern Europe; Brezhnev would later dismiss outside attempts to enforce Soviet compliance with the Helsinki protocols as 'interference in the internal affairs of the socialist countries'. But the treaty gave the beleaguered human rights groups of the Soviet Union an anchor in international law. It inspired Sakharov and his colleagues to found the Moscow Helsinki Group, which strove to hold the Soviet state to the promises it had made, and it gave Western leaders visiting Moscow a legitimate basis on which to raise cases of abuse. Ronald Reagan and Margaret Thatcher both did so, and they managed to secure concessions from the Kremlin on the issue of Jewish exit visas and on the release of individual political prisoners.

Sakharov would eventually be punished for his refusal to remain silent. In 1980, he was exiled with his activist wife Yelena Bonner to the provincial town of Gorky, but his high profile in the West and his previous fame as a hero of Soviet military research saved him from the labour camps or the psychiatric hospitals.

The Kremlin's leniency towards Sakharov reflected in part the Soviet Union's increased dependence on the West. It was not just grain that Moscow needed now: Western technology and foreign expertise had become vital to the functioning of the Soviet economy, and huge loans from Western banks were keeping the country solvent: in 1974, the USSR had taken out $13 billion in credits, a figure that by 1978 had risen to $50 billion, a third of which was provided by British banks. The capitalist world and the Soviet Union were bound together in a mutual financial embrace that had altered attitudes on both sides. In a volte-face from the early years of the revolution when the West sent military forces to overthrow the Bolshevik state and refused to grant it international recognition, Europe and America were now obliged to preserve the stability of the socialist world so that Moscow could carry on repaying its debts. For their part, the Soviets had not solved their military spending crisis by signing the arms limitation treaties of the early 1970s, and the SALT II agreement, which would have allowed Moscow to reduce expenditure on long-range missiles, was scrapped by Washington when Soviet troops entered Afghanistan in December 1979. The invasion brought détente shuddering to a halt and signalled the resumption of the superpower arms race; when the US decided to ramp up its military spending once more, the Kremlin felt it had to do the same. The troubled occupation of Afghanistan would prove a millstone around the Soviet Union's neck for the next decade, restricting even further the money available for improving living conditions at home.

The next challenge to Soviet absolutism came from Poland. In 1980, sharply increased food prices sent dockworkers in the Baltic port of Gdansk onto the streets, and during the summer the strikes spread to other industries and other areas of the country. The spirit of revolt found an inspirational leader in the moustachioed shipyard electrician Lech Walesa: his Solidarity movement led the confrontation with the Communists and transformed the rebellion from one of material demands to a struggle for liberty, freedom of choice and national dignity. Brezhnev considered but rejected another military invasion, prevailing on the Polish president, Wojciech Jaruzelski, to declare a state of emergency to be enforced by Poland's own armed forces. Martial law lasted from December 1981 to July 1983, during which time thousands of opposition activists were sent to jail and a hundred or more protestors killed in clashes on the streets. A semblance of order was subsequently restored, but the people's grievances continued to fester and would surface again at the end of the decade.

By the time of the Polish crisis, Brezhnev was in decline: his health was poor, he had grown fat and often appeared confused during his public appearances, slurring his speech and forgetting his lines. The Soviet people mocked him with cruel humour. Brezhnev had always been a vain man. In the late 1970s, he developed a passion for honours and medals, declaring that the country's leader should not be content with the rank of a mere lieutenant general. 'People are writing to me,' he announced to the politburo. 'They are demanding that as supreme commander, I ought to have a rank consistent with my position ... The pressure of public opinion, especially among the military, is very strong.' No one believed for a moment that there had been any such 'demands', but Brezhnev was nonetheless made a marshal of the Soviet Union in 1976. By 1979 he had accumulated over 60 decorations, outdoing the heroic Marshal Zhukov by some distance. When Brezhnev's memoirs were published they 'revealed' that the minor skirmishes he had taken part in around the southwest Russian city of Novorossiysk during the war had in fact been the decisive moments of the struggle against fascism. The memoirs themselves were duly rewarded with the Lenin Prize for Literature. Brezhnev's cult of personality made him a figure of ridicule. Aware of the humour he aroused in the Soviet public, he calmly told his colleagues that 'if they make up jokes about me, it must be that they like me'.

A lifetime of heavy smoking and drinking left the ageing Brezhnev with physical and cognitive problems. Debates in the Central Committee went over his head. With each faltering appearance he was becoming a physical incarnation of the system he ruled over: no matter how broken or decrepit things were, the risk of changing them was considered too great; by the early 1980s, the average age in the politburo was approaching 70. The one exception, the spritely Mikhail Gorbachev, was shocked by the doddery state of the country's leader, but when he confronted Andropov about it he was told that the General Secretary had to be kept on as 'a matter of stability within the party and the state, as well as an issue of international stability'. For much of 1982, Brezhnev failed to appear in public, and he eventually died on 10 November. When the *Sun* newspaper discovered he had been in a coma for the last few weeks of his reign, it ran the headline: 'Revealed: Red Cabbage Ruled Russia'.

The era of stagnation would continue; in Brezhnev's place the politburo appointed the former head of the KGB, Yuri Andropov. He was 68 years old, and his record as the man who directed the crushing of the Hungarian uprising bound him irrevocably to the principles of the old regime. He was nonetheless presented to the Western media as a liberal, a reformer and a lover of jazz; in his 15 months in power he made some efforts to end the corruption and mismanagement of the Brezhnev era. But when he died in February 1984 it emerged that his liberalism was that of a KGB apparatchik, that his reforms were little more than tentative tinkering with an economy in need of total overhaul and that he hated jazz.

Even the minimal changes of Andropov's reign were reversed by his successor. The 72-year old Konstantin Chernenko had been Brezhnev's closest ally and remained a devoted disciple of his policies of stagnation. He was already so ill that he could barely deliver the eulogy at Andropov's funeral, and he too died just over 12 months later, the third Soviet leader to go in less than three years. When Ronald Reagan heard about Chernenko's death he quipped to his wife Nancy, 'How am I supposed to get anyplace with these Russians if they keep dying on me!'

US–Soviet relations had been frozen since the invasion of Afghanistan in 1979; each side boycotted the other's Olympics (in Moscow in 1980 and Los Angeles in 1984), and the US continued to supply weapons and training to the Afghan Mujahidin guerrillas. Reagan also decided to press ahead with a new laser-based anti-missile shield known as the Strategic Defense Initiative (SDI), or more commonly 'Star Wars'. SDI sowed anxiety in the minds of the politburo: if the system were to give Washington the capacity to shoot down incoming Soviet ballistic missiles, it would shred the doctrine of Mutually Assured Destruction, leaving the USSR vulnerable to an American nuclear first strike. The Soviet Union's cash-strapped state budget meant it could ill afford to be drawn into a race to match the new American technology, but such was the fear of SDI that both Andropov and Chernenko agreed to increased spending. The reckoning was approaching.

CHAPTER THIRTY-EIGHT

The art of Kremlinology was never a precise one; to deduce who was moving up the Kremlin pecking order and who was falling from favour meant reading barely scrutable signs, such as who stood where in official politburo photographs, who was closest to the General Secretary at Red Square parades, and who got the most mentions in *Pravda*. The façade of unanimity that the leadership maintained made it harder to discern who might harbour reservations about the party line. Private lives, hobbies, families – sometimes even who was married and who was not – were opaque subjects.

So when a member of the politburo arrived in Britain for an official visit in December 1984 and took his attractive young wife on a very public sightseeing tour, it raised eyebrows and expectations. Mikhail and Raisa Gorbachev went together to pay homage at the London haunts of Lenin and Marx; then, while he was meeting the British prime minister Margaret Thatcher, she went shopping in Oxford Street. It seemed a tacit acknowledgement that the bourgeois materialist society Moscow had long ridiculed and condemned might have something to offer after all. Mrs Thatcher, an astute judge of character, was quick to spot the significance of her visitors' behaviour, as she recalled in her memoirs:

> Raisa Gorbachev was making her first visit to Western Europe and she knew only a little English – as far as I could tell her husband knew none; but she was dressed in a smart Western style outfit, a well tailored grey suit with a white stripe – just the sort I could have worn myself, I thought. Our advice at this time was that Mrs Gorbachev was a committed, hardline Marxist … But I later learned from her – after I had left office – that her grandfather had been one of those millions of kulaks killed during the forced collectivisation of agriculture under Stalin. Her family had no good reason for illusions about Communism.

As for Raisa's husband, Mrs Thatcher discerned a similarly nuanced hinterland behind his orthodox, even hardline, Communism:

> Mr Gorbachev insisted on the superiority of the Soviet system. Not only
> did it produce higher growth rates, but if I came to the USSR I would see
> how the Soviet people lived – 'joyfully' ... If I had paid attention only to
> the content of Mr Gorbachev's remarks, I would have to conclude that he
> was cast in the usual Communist mould. But his personality could not
> have been more different ... He smiled, laughed, used his hands for
> emphasis, modulated his voice, followed an argument through and was a
> sharp debater. He was self-confident and though he larded his remarks
> with respectful references to Mr Chernenko, he did not seem in the least
> uneasy about entering into controversial areas of high politics. His line
> was no different from what I would have expected; his style was. I found
> myself liking him. As he took his leave, I hoped that I had been talking to
> the next Soviet leader. For, as I subsequently told the press, this was a man
> with whom I could do business.

Margaret Thatcher had uncovered a little of the complexity that underpinned Mikhail Gorbachev's character and would determine many of his
actions in the years ahead. She had spotted, correctly, that he was a true
believer in the communist system ('We both believe in our own political
systems,' she confirmed. 'He firmly believes in his; I firmly believe in mine
...'), but she hinted that his 'respect' for the Brezhnevite dinosaurs in the
Kremlin was somewhat forced. And she identified two of the key factors
that were already persuading him that big changes would be needed to save
and strengthen the communist system: his 'distrust of the Reagan administration's intentions in general and of their plans for a Strategic Defence
Initiative (SDI) in particular'.

Mrs Thatcher told the BBC that the reason Gorbachev was so set
against SDI was that it was ratcheting up a military spending race that was
ruining the Soviet economy. Successive Kremlin leaders had felt compelled
to match every new generation of US weaponry; but Gorbachev saw it was

strangling the civilian economy, driving down living standards and threatening to bankrupt the state. He told Raisa and his close comrades, 'We cannot go on living like this.' Breaking the spiral of decline would require tough decisions, and Mikhail Gorbachev would be faced with the challenge of implementing them.

When Konstantin Chernenko died on 10 March 1985, an extraordinary plenum of the Central Committee was convened within 24 hours to appoint his successor. The choice was between more of the same – Viktor Grishin, an elderly conservative and very much in the mould of the three previous leaders – or a more youthful candidate. Mikhail Gorbachev had just celebrated his fifty-fourth birthday and he had energy in spades. He was not, however, regarded as a radical reformer. He was proposed by one of the Kremlin's arch conservatives, the veteran foreign minister Andrei Gromyko, who spoke of the strength of Gorbachev's 'party-mindedness'. And when the vote went unanimously in his favour, Gorbachev responded with a speech that made him sound like a Communist hardliner: 'Our party has vast potential ... We must not change our policy. It is a true, correct, genuinely Leninist policy!' Gromyko commented approvingly, 'This man has a nice smile, but he has teeth of iron.' It was the obverse of Margaret Thatcher's conclusion that the smiling personality was more important than the professions of orthodox Communism.

The notion of an underlying duality in Gorbachev's character is an important one. While there is no argument about the trajectory the country travelled on his watch – from a tightly controlled one-party state to a chaotic, quasi democratic free-for-all; from a centralised command economy to the raging capitalism of an unregulated market; from a multinational, multi-ethnic union held together with unrelenting discipline to a centripetal collection of competing states and would-be states – there is genuine disagreement about how it got from A to B. Some Western historians have argued that Gorbachev was a liberal reformer *ab initio*, that he came to power with a reformist goal in his mind and that he proceeded to oversee the transformation of his country, if not according to a predetermined master plan, then at least in accord with his own liberal democratic convictions. That explanation echoes Mrs Thatcher's hunch that Gorbachev's expression of loyalty to the tenets of orthodox Communism was a dissemblance, a smokescreen that concealed the instincts of a social democrat. Russian writers, on the other hand, tend to favour the Gromyko line, that Gorbachev was a Communist and stayed a Communist, and while some of his actions may have facilitated the forces of change, he never intended to do anything more than modernise and strengthen the Soviet Communist system.*

Having lived through the Gorbachev years in Russia, it seems to me that Gorbachev was obliged to embark on a policy of change because of the Soviet Union's parlous economy, but that he intended this to be only 'within system' change, revitalising the one-party state by unleashing a measure of initiative, energy and enterprise. In a political culture that refused to acknowledge its shortcomings, he was unwilling even to use the word 'reform', referring instead to *uskorenie* (acceleration) or *perestroika* (restructuring).

When his policies met resistance from vested interests in the party hierarchy, he appealed over their heads to public opinion: his policy of *glasnost* (openness) was intended to give the Soviet people access to the information they needed to see that what he was proposing was a good thing, and to denounce those who opposed *perestroika*. His aim was to mobilise society's support for his measures of economic and organisational modernisation; but, contrary to Gorbachev's intentions, the people used their new empowerment to demand more radical and more rapid reform than he had contemplated.

From this point onwards, Gorbachev was no longer leading the process of change; he was being dragged along behind the speeding locomotive of public opinion, which he himself had fuelled. The intoxication of discovering

---

* The historian Archie Brown argues that Gorbachev consciously fostered transformational change of the Soviet system and concludes that he was a 'systemic transformer'. By contrast, Dmitry Volkogonov argues that Gorbachev was, and always remained, an orthodox Communist, who inadvertently set off processes that resulted in changes he never intended to bring about.

that the hated autocracy could be changed spread through society until the whole edifice was brought crashing down, very much against the intentions of the man who first set things in motion and who would – given his wish – have remained at the helm of a strengthened and reinvigorated, united and Communist USSR.

There has been much *post facto* rationalisation of what happened in the years between 1985 and 1991, not least by the men – including Gorbachev himself – who led the country. By going back to the daily chronicle of those times, however, it is possible to trace how plans, strategies and commands were pre-empted by those Tolstoyan movers of history: people and events.

Gorbachev's reign began with little hint of the tectonic shocks to come. Three weeks after the new leader's election, the US ambassador in Moscow, Arthur Hartman, briefed President Reagan that 'Gorbachev is a narrow fellow, of set views' whose main concern would be to consolidate his own power. With hindsight that judgement sounds ludicrous, but few of us in 1985 knew we were embarking on one of the great 'moments of unruly destiny' that have peppered Russia's thousand-year history with the chance for lasting change.

Mikhail Gorbachev had been born into a peasant family in 1931 in the Stavropol region of southern Russia. He retained the distinctive accent of the region, with its soft Gs (he pronounces his own name 'Horbachov') and the southern warmth of character with its ready smile and open humour. As a child, he was remarkably bright and unwaveringly conformist. At school he was praised for his 'political awareness', and he was a model member of the Young Communist organisation, the Komsomol. He was admitted to full membership of the party at the unusually early age of 18. His father and grandfather had both been collective farm activists, and young Mikhail earned the Order of the Red Banner for his work in the fields during school vacations. In 1950, he enrolled on a law degree at Moscow State University, where Raisa was already writing her thesis on the life of the peasantry under collectivisation. After they married in 1953, she became a lecturer in Marxist theory and he began his party career. Posts in the leadership of the Stavropol

Komsomol allowed him to demonstrate his talent for administration and won him influential friends. By the age of 35, he was the region's first secretary, with special responsibility for agriculture; a year later he was a member of the Soviet Central Committee, travelling regularly for meetings in Moscow. He met Yuri Andropov, then the KGB chief, who took the rising young star under his wing. Andropov's aim of modernising the Soviet economy found a ready disciple in Gorbachev; in 1984, with death approaching, Andropov, now Soviet leader, tried unsuccessfully to have his protégé named as his successor.

When he did become leader, a year later, Gorbachev's rhetoric betrayed little evidence of reformist tendencies: his speech at his first Central Committee plenum in April 1985 was the epitome of orthodox – and patently sincere – Marxism–Leninism. 'The whole of life and the entire course of history,' he told the assembled delegates, 'confirm the truth of Leninist teaching. It remains the guiding principle behind all our actions, our inspiration and the true compass for our strategy and tactics as we move forward now.' He was explicitly endorsing the principles of the state that Lenin had created: a one-party system, a command economy and a dedication to class struggle, with the goal of instituting global Communism.*

Gorbachev, though, began his time as General Secretary with a signal that the party would be run differently. He wanted to show that he was not a Brezhnev or a Chernenko, and he did so by attacking the style of their

---

* Throughout his political career, Gorbachev stressed repeatedly that he remained a Communist and a Leninist. The first time he met Ronald Reagan, he told his colleagues that the American president was 'the class enemy with whom we are fighting'. In October 1987, he told the politburo that 'Lenin's dialectics is the key to how we must solve the problems of our own age.' Two years later he marked the anniversary of Lenin's birth by denouncing the growing revelations of the first Soviet leader's crimes and failures. 'To turn away from Lenin,' he said in a speech in April 1990, 'would be to hack away the roots of our society and our state, to devastate the hearts and minds of whole generations.' Even in August 1991, after he had been imprisoned and humiliated by the forces of orthodox Communism, he still refused to condemn the Communist Party, warning Boris Yeltsin against 'anti-Communist hysteria and a witch hunt'. His professions of Communist faith were not deliberate play-acting. His aim as a reformer was to revitalise and strengthen Communism, not to destroy it.

rule. In April 1985, he told the politburo that there must be an end to the 'ostentation, arrogance, eulogies and bootlicking' that had characterised the behaviour of the party leadership in recent times. Fawning flattery and glorification of the leader were to become things of the past. Gorbachev declared war on corruption within the party *nomenklatura*, and announced the curtailment of undeserved perks and privileges for party officials. The turnover in party personnel in his first years in power was substantial.

Perestroika at this early stage was very much trial and error. Gorbachev made no secret of his aim – he wanted to reinvigorate the Soviet economy and Soviet society; it was just that he did not know exactly how to do it. In a speech to party officials in April 1985, he endorsed Andropov's unimplemented plans for greater financial independence for factories, but explicitly maintained the centralised economic and planning controls inherited from Stalinist times. He made clear that he did not favour the mechanisms of an unchecked market economy, telling the representatives of Moscow's 'fraternal' countries in Eastern Europe:

> Many of you see the solution to your problems in resorting to market mechanisms in place of direct planning. Some of you look at the market as a lifesaver for your economies. But, comrades, you should stop thinking about lifesavers and think about the ship: the ship is socialism.

Gorbachev quite quickly introduced a limited amount of free enterprise *within* the framework of the centralised command economy. In 1987, his Law on State Enterprise gave more freedom to factory managers, devolving decision-making and allowing them some leeway in fixing prices and production quotas with the aim of increasing efficiency. But the overarching structure of the centrally planned economy remained in place, and the profit motive that drives the capitalist system remained absent. Results were patchy.

In 1988, Gorbachev went further. His Law on Cooperatives specified that in certain areas of economic activity, largely the service industries, the private ownership of small businesses would be tolerated. There were considerable restrictions on size and turnover; the number of employees was strictly limited, and they were all to be co-owners. In addition, the 'cooperatives' were to be heavily taxed, but it was immediately evident that a new entrepreneurial spirit had been unleashed. The streets of Moscow and other cities saw new restaurants opening; private bakeries, hairdressers and taxi firms sprang into existence. Like the rest of the foreign press corps, I was fascinated by the cooperatives. At every new business I visited, I found something I had never seen in the Soviet Union: people who were determined to work hard and do well.* It was the first time since Lenin's New Economic Policy of 1921–8 that capitalism had raised its head, and it all seemed remarkably hopeful.

There was an expectation that economic restrictions would be progressively eased and free enterprise given its head. But Gorbachev had other ideas. He announced that central planning would remain, as would state ownership of the means of production. His aim was not a market economy but the rejuvenation of the sluggish command economy through discreetly capitalist methods. It seemed an unlikely hybrid.

Even this limited flirtation with 'capitalist' methods, however, had aroused fierce opposition from the conservative wing of the party, just as Lenin's NEP had done in the 1920 (see pp. 243–5). Gorbachev's reforms in military and foreign policy met the same resistance. As the first Soviet leader seriously to tackle the crippling arms spending (more than a third of the country's resources was going on the military), he faced a daunting task. The more he negotiated with the Americans about limiting and then reducing arms production, the more he was opposed by the powerful representatives of the Soviet military-industrial complex.

Their criticism of Gorbachev increased after he decided to withdraw Soviet forces from Afghanistan. The USSR was spending billions of roubles

---

* I also discovered evidence of the growing menace of organised crime. The Soviet Union had always had powerful crime groups, but now the *mafiozniki* flourished by demanding protection money from the new small businesses. Those who refused to pay found themselves targeted for reprisals. One cooperative bakery I had visited in its early days was subsequently fire-bombed, and the owner of another business had to sell up in order to raise the ransom the criminals were demanding for the release of his kidnapped daughter.

and suffering thousands of casualties in a foreign adventure that had gone on longer than the Second World War. As early as 1986, Gorbachev issued instructions for a plan of disengagement to be drawn up, but opposition from the hardliners in the defence and security ministries meant it was not until February 1989 that the last Soviet troops were withdrawn, and even then there was barely concealed anger in sections of the military.*

In the face of conservative resistance to his reforms, Gorbachev took an unprecedented step: he appealed directly to public opinion to back his policies. Even more than *uskorenie* or *perestroika*, both of which had precedents under Khrushchev and Andropov, *glasnost* was a radical departure from Soviet tradition. The Bolsheviks had long regarded the control of information as a mainstay of power; the people could not be trusted with the facts about their history or the present because it might inspire them to oppose the regime. From the early days of the revolution, the media were rigidly censored; newspapers printed only the news the Kremlin deemed 'useful'; literature and the arts were forced to serve the cause of Soviet power, and history was brazenly rewritten to remove inconvenient truths. Mikhail Gorbachev wasted little time in loosening the informational straitjacket. He allowed the publication of previously banned works, including Solzhenitsyn's *Gulag Archipelago*, Pasternak's *Doctor Zhivago* and Grossman's *Life and Fate*. But that was the easy part: those books dealt with the crimes of the Stalinist past, from which the party had already distanced itself. More problematical were issues of current politics. In previous times, the Communist monopoly on information meant that difficult facts, problems with industrial or agricultural production, news of disasters, failures,

---

* I have vivid memories of travelling on the last Soviet convoy to leave Afghanistan. The Mujahidin had celebrated victory by shelling the convoys that had gone before us, and the young conscripts were overcome with relief when we reached the Soviet frontier town of Termez. As the army commander Boris Gromov walked over the border to be the last man to leave Afghan territory, I asked one of his senior aides how it felt to be coming home. 'It is a humiliation,' I was told with a bitter grimace. 'The traitor Gorbachev has sold us out.' Like everyone, I had been aware of opposition to Gorbachev's reforms, but it was not until that moment that I realised the deep-seated, visceral contempt in which he was held by some sectors of the Soviet establishment.

ABOVE The USSR's space pioneers, Gagarin, Leonov, Belyaev and Komarov.

RIGHT Nikita Khrushchev meets John F. Kennedy in Vienna, June 1961.

ABOVE Khrushchev's ill-fated corn drive begins.

LEFT An ageing Leonid Brezhnev weighed down by his numerous medals.

Raisa and Mikhail Gorbachev are greeted by the Thatchers at 10 Downing Street.

General Secretary Gorbachev objects as Andrei Sakharov addresses the Congress of People's Deputies, 1989.

Self-proclaimed Soviet president Gennady Yanayev (third from right) and his allies announce their takeover in August 1991.

Boris Yeltsin defies the coup plotters in front of the Moscow White House.

Tanks on the streets of Moscow during the August coup of 1991.

Pravda front pages from during and after the failed coup.

ABOVE The Chechen capital, Grozny, after Russian bombardments in 1995.

RIGHT A businessman shows off the spoils of his voucher-buying spree in 1992.

BELOW Yeltsin waves goodbye to the Russian people and ushers in the reign of Vladimir Putin (front left) in December 1999.

RIGHT Mikhail Khodorkovsky (right) hears the judge sentence him to 14 years in jail at his second trial in December 2010.

BELOW Former FSB agent Alexander Litvinenko on his deathbed, after being poisoned by his former colleagues.

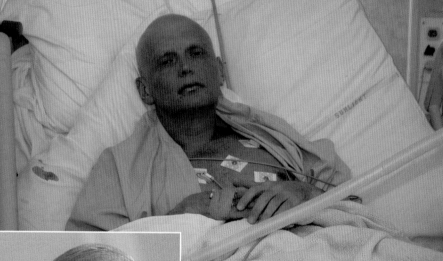

LEFT Vladimir Putin, Russia's second president.

Presidents Dmitry Medvedev and Barack Obama toast the 'reset' in Russian–American relations.

Russia in the twenty-first century remains precariously perched between its Asiatic and European heritage. The path it takes will have consequences for the whole world.

political discontent or state crimes and corruption, would never find their way into the public domain. Information about the successes of the West was concealed by a ban on foreign publications and the jamming of the BBC Russian Service, the US Radio Liberty and the Voice of America.

After a period of initial hesitation, Gorbachev began to relax many of those restrictions. He had spoken bitterly about the forces of opposition to his policies within the party – 'a new clan of people who resort to endless phrase-mongering in order to avoid having to act' – and he saw *glasnost* as a way to bypass that resistance. 'The widening of *glasnost* is a key measure,' he told the Twenty-seventh Party Congress. 'It is a *political* question. *Glasnost* will create democratic awareness and political creativity among the masses and encourage their participation in the process of government.' He knew what he was doing: stirring up the public was intended to break down resistance to reform in the party. What he did not foresee was that, once unmuzzled, public opinion would be a difficult force to control.

Two unexpected events boosted Gorbachev in his struggle. On 26 April 1986, the nuclear reactor at the Chernobyl power station exploded, killing several workers and sending a plume of radioactive fallout into the atmosphere. The authorities reacted as they always had done in the past: they imposed a news blackout. It was two days before any mention of the explosion was made on Soviet television, by which time thousands of people had been fatally contaminated and foreign monitoring stations had detected radiation drifting over the Soviet border. Chernobyl highlighted many of the structural weaknesses in the Soviet system that Gorbachev had been railing against. He used the tragedy – and the embarrassment it had caused the Kremlin – to press home the need for greater transparency. Chernobyl, he said, had 'shed light on many of the sicknesses of our system as a whole. Everything that has built up over the years had converged in this drama: the concealing or hushing up of accidents and other bad news, irresponsibility and carelessness, slipshod work and wholesale drunkenness.'

Then, on 28 May 1987, a young German named Mathias Rust flew a Cessna 172 light aircraft from Helsinki to the centre of Moscow, landing on the Vasilievsky Spusk at the bottom of Red Square. Rust had flown hundreds of miles through Soviet air space and buzzed the Kremlin itself without being detected or challenged. For the West it seemed a *Boy's Own* adventure story, but for the Soviet leadership the breaching of the country's air defences was a source of shame. Gorbachev called in the country's military commanders. 'How could you fail to detect the offending aircraft when it was in the zone of the Sixth Army for two and a half hours?' he asked General Pyotr Lushev. 'Was this reported to you?' 'No,' answered the general. 'I knew about it only when the plane landed in Moscow.' 'And I suppose it was the traffic cops who told you!' Gorbachev shot back. Before the meeting ended, the head of the Moscow Air Defence District had been fired, along with the defence minister and the commander-in-chief of the Soviet Border Troops. The purge would continue. By 1990, more than a hundred generals and colonels had been replaced, allowing Gorbachev to bring in officers sympathetic to the aims of *perestroika*.

In the months after his appointment as General Secretary, Gorbachev had begun advancing liberal allies to positions of influence. Dinosaurs like Gromyko and Grishin were eased out of office. Trusted lieutenants, men who had helped Gorbachev formulate the principles of *perestroika* and *glasnost*, were brought into the central leadership. Eduard Shevardnadze, the Georgian party chief and a confidant of Gorbachev's, succeeded Gromyko as foreign minister in July 1985, despite having little or no experience of foreign policy. In August Alexander Yakovlev, the former Soviet ambassador in Canada and a convinced Westerniser, became a senior adviser on ideology and foreign policy. Grishin's replacement as Moscow party boss was Boris Yeltsin, a charismatic politician from the Urals city of Sverdlovsk (later to revert to its former name of Yekaterinburg). Gorbachev had had dealings with Yeltsin since the mid 1970s and thought him energetic, sometimes unpredictable, but on the side of change. In 1985, he seemed a natural ally for the forces of *perestroika*.

Yakovlev, Shevardnadze and Yeltsin, along with advisers Georgy Shakhnazarov, Abel Aganbegyan, Tatyana Zaslavskaya and Anatoly Chernyaev made up the vanguard of reform in the Kremlin leadership. But other, less liberal figures also wielded influence. Yegor Ligachev, a silver-haired, blue-eyed Siberian ten years older than Gorbachev, was appointed second secretary of the CPSU, effectively becoming deputy leader of the party and the country. With a friendly smile and an unusual willingness to talk to foreign reporters, Ligachev was avuncular, but his politics were distinctly hardline. While supporting Gorbachev's efforts to combat corruption and paying lip service to the ideals of *perestroika*, he came increasingly to be seen as the leader of the forces of conservative Communism. Ligachev opposed even the limited private enterprise allowed under Gorbachev's Law on Cooperatives, as he would make clear in a speech two years later:

> Public ownership unites. Private ownership divides people's interests. It causes social stratification of society … For what purpose was *perestroika* started? For the purpose of unleashing the full potential of socialism! Does private enterprise promote the development of socialist potential? It does not. The only way to move forward on the path of socialist renewal is with the party in the lead. Without the Communist Party, *perestroika* is a lost cause … There are forces in our country fighting against the socialist system, against the Communist Party. They act energetically and they use the mass media. They applaud efforts to undermine socialism and undermine the party. They present this as '*perestroika*'.

Such open anti-*perestroika* rhetoric emerged only in the late 1980s. In the early years, the battle between reformers and hardliners was carried on behind the scenes, but it was no less intense. With Boris Yeltsin leading the liberal voices calling for acceleration in the pace of radical reform, and Ligachev and other conservatives opposing them at every step, Gorbachev was forced to reckon with competing demands from both ends of the political spectrum. His own 'middle course' seemed to satisfy no one.

In 1986, Andrei Sakharov was in his sixth year of internal exile in the closed town of Gorky, 250 miles east of Moscow. Sakharov and his wife Yelena Bonner had become symbols of resistance to Soviet despotism, attracting international support and rallying domestic opposition. Gorbachev had initially justified Sakharov's punishment in language redolent of old-style Communist intransigence. In February 1986, he told the French Communist newspaper *L'Humanité*, 'Dr Sakharov has committed illegal acts. Normal measures of justice were taken in his case. He has been properly punished.' But by the end of the year, after months of vacillation between the radicals and the conservatives in his entourage, Gorbachev was ready to make a dramatic gesture. On 15 December 1986, an electrician appeared at Sakharov's apartment and announced he had orders to install a telephone. When it rang the next morning the voice on the end of the line was Gorbachev's, informing him that his exile was over. Sakharov raised the cases of other political prisoners and asked for their release. When Gorbachev was non-committal, Sakharov put down the receiver. He would return to Moscow in the New Year and immediately resume his political activities, eventually allying himself with Boris Yeltsin and the other radicals to press for full democracy and liberty in the Soviet Union.

The release of Andrei Sakharov brought a backlash from the conservatives. Reports grew of the deliberate obstruction of Gorbachev's policies by hardline members of the *apparat* – the party bureaucracy that controlled all areas of Soviet life and could foil policy initiatives simply by failing to act on them. He complained to the Central Committee that *perestroika* was being slowed down, and named individual ministries that were hampering the reforms. By the beginning of 1987, he was publicly calling on workers to support his initiatives against party bureaucrats who tried to oppose them. In a speech to trade unions in Moscow, he talked openly of disputes within the top party leadership over the pace of reform.

Yegor Ligachev responded with a speech in the city of Saratov that contained a barely coded call for a brake on the *perestroika* process. Instead of condemning the old style of Communist leadership as a 'period of stagnation', he said, modern politicians should recognise its positive achievements. At the January plenum, Gorbachev proposed multi-candidate elections with secret ballots for the directors of factories, but the measure was opposed by the conservatives and Gorbachev backed down.

Now the liberals, led by Boris Yeltsin, turned on him. At a closed-door Central Committee plenum in October 1987, the two men quarrelled furiously. Yeltsin claimed Gorbachev had not responded to his ideas for intensifying the *perestroika* campaign, and launched a scathing personal attack on the Soviet leader's character. 'Recently,' he said, 'there has been a noticeable increase in what I can only call the adulation of the General Secretary by certain members of the politburo ... this tendency to adulation is absolutely unacceptable ... to develop a taste for adulation can lead to a new "cult of personality". This must not be allowed.' Gorbachev's response was equally vicious. 'Boris Nikolaevich,' he said, 'you have reached such a level of vanity and self-regard that you put your ambitions higher than the interests of the party. At a time when *perestroika* has reached such a critical stage, I consider this highly irresponsible.' Yeltsin took umbrage, claimed he no longer felt at home in the politburo, and resigned.

Gorbachev did not banish Yeltsin from the political arena, but offered him the post of deputy chairman of the State Construction Committee with the rank of a junior minister. Yeltsin accepted, but the humiliation he felt after the clash at the plenum ripened into a personal hatred. Over the next three years, his attacks on Gorbachev and his demands for immediate radical change would become increasingly extreme. The battle lines were set. The showdown would not be long in coming.

Liberals and hardliners were both dissatisfied with *perestroika*, and each camp was manoeuvring to pull Gorbachev in their direction. In March 1988, with the Soviet leader away on a visit to Yugoslavia, the newspaper *Sovietskaya Rossiya* published what amounted to a manifesto for hardline resistance to *perestroika*. Presented as a letter from a teacher in Leningrad by the name of Nina Andreeva, but almost certainly published at the behest of Ligachev and his allies, it was titled 'I cannot forsake my principles'. The letter summed up the discontent felt by millions of Communists who regarded *perestroika* as an abomination:

> *Perestroika* ... and *glasnost* are inciting emotions in the masses (especially in our young people) about issues that are concocted by the voices of Western radio stations or by our own compatriots who do not understand the true nature of socialism: a multiparty system, freedom of religious propaganda, emigration to live abroad, the right to broad discussion of sexual problems in the press, the need to decentralise the leadership of culture, abolition of compulsory military service. Controversies are raised among students about the facts of our country's past ... I am puzzled to be told

that 'class struggle' is now an obsolete term, as is 'the leading role of the proletariat' … Does the international working class no longer oppose world capital as embodied in its [capitalist] state and political organs?

It took three weeks before *Pravda* published a response to the Nina Andreeva letter, and there was much speculation that the hardliners had gained the upper hand in the Kremlin power struggle. Gorbachev decided he must seize the initiative. He was ruling the USSR as General Secretary of the Communist Party, a position to which the party had appointed him and from which it could equally remove him. To stave off a potential challenge from the hardliners he needed to widen his power base, to win a mandate to rule from a source that would be less likely or less able to cast him off. At the Nineteenth Party Conference in June 1988 he proposed that the old 'rubber stamp' parliament, the Supreme Soviet, should be replaced with a new body, to be known as the Congress of People's Deputies. The Congress would elect a chairman, who would serve as head of the Soviet state and be referred to as president. To give the new system a measure of democratic legitimacy, the Congress of People's Deputies would be chosen in a partially free national election; it would meet for two sessions each year, between which a smaller body, appointed from members of the Congress, would sit as a semi-permanent national parliament.

The new state president would take over many of the powers previously held by the leader of the CPSU, including control of foreign policy, security and defence, overall responsibility for the adoption of new legislation, economic strategy and the right to nominate the prime minister. The chosen candidate – whom everyone assumed would be Gorbachev – could hold the office of Communist Party General Secretary concurrently, but could now be removed from office only by the whole parliament. He would no longer be threatened by the same fate as Khrushchev, who was sacked as Communist leader (and hence as leader of the country) by a small clique within the party elite.

Despite some misgivings, Gorbachev's proposal 'On the Democratisation of Soviet Society and the Reform of the Political System' was approved in principle by the conference. Conservative delegates continued to hope they could later nullify the proposals by the usual methods of red tape and delay. But Gorbachev pulled off a master stroke: at the very end of the conference, as everyone was preparing to go home, he pulled from his pocket a crumpled piece of paper. In a matter-of-fact tone he said, 'By the way, comrades, I have a timetable for my proposals here. Shall we vote to accept it?' Seemingly without fully understanding what they were letting themselves in for, the delegates raised their hands in favour. Gorbachev thanked them and declared the conference closed. The first multi-candidate elections in the history of the Soviet Union would take place in March 1989, and the resulting parliament would meet to elect a new president immediately afterwards.

The rules laid down for the elections to the Congress of People's Deputies made clear that this was not Western-style democracy. No political parties other than the Communist Party of the Soviet Union would be allowed to field candidates, and one-third of the seats would be reserved for organisations officially sanctioned by the CPSU. Gorbachev stressed that his aim was '*socialist* pluralism', the development of different political platforms within the Communist community,* and not pluralism *tout court* (the right to establish a multiparty system, in which the CPSU would be just one party among many).

His deft footwork at the party conference gave the impression that Gorbachev was still leading and controlling the process of reform. But the 1989 elections would mark the point at which he lost control, and the forces of popular opinion took over.** The election campaign in the months running up to polling day was marked by the most startling outpouring of

---

* Thus putting an end to the ban on 'factionalism' imposed by Lenin at the Tenth Party Congress in 1921.

** Gorbachev himself understood the veracity of Alexis de Tocqueville's maxim that any concessions by an autocratic regime will be seized upon by the people as a reason to demand ever greater change. 'I am doomed to go forward and only forward,' he told his adviser Anatoly Chernyaev at the height of *perestroika* in 1989. 'For me, the path backwards is closed. If I retreat, I will perish …' But when the pace of reform accelerated, Gorbachev forgot his own words. Instead of going forward, he tried to hold back the tide of change with vacillations and equivocations.

energy, passion and anger from a previously cowed population. As I attended the massive public rallies in Moscow's squares, fields and car parks, addressed by Sakharov, Yeltsin, Sergei Stankevich, Gavriil Popov and all the future stars of the liberal movement, I felt that a form of popular democracy was dawning in the Soviet Union. Every activist who had a pile of political tracts to distribute was surrounded by hundreds of hands fighting to read his views; every speaker, no matter how esoteric, was carefully listened to, discussed, applauded or booed with the enthusiasm of a nation that was discovering the right to an unfettered civic existence. The tide of popular revolution would soon be lapping at the Kremlin.

If Gorbachev had viewed the elections to the Congress of People's Deputies as a means to strengthen his and the party's legitimacy, he got more than he bargained for. In Moscow, Leningrad, Kiev and Minsk, scores of party nominees were humiliated. Even in seats where the Communists had barred independent candidates from standing against their man, the electorate frequently crossed out the single name on the ballot paper, denying the candidate the 50 per cent he or she needed to get elected. In independence-minded republics, separatist candidates had a field day. Followers of the Lithuanian Sajudis movement won 31 of the republic's 42 seats; in Latvia, Popular Front sympathisers won 25 out of 29; and in Estonia, they picked up 15 out of 21. In Moscow, Gorbachev's most prominent critic, Boris Yeltsin, swept the board with 90 per cent of the votes cast.

From now on, Gorbachev's most powerful opponents would no longer be the hardliners in the Communist Party, but the radicals who wanted to take reform further and faster than he was prepared to allow. The radicals' demands for freedom and democracy had been heard by the Soviet people and they were rallying to the cause.

Gorbachev reacted slowly to the results. Three days after the elections, he was still trying to defend the party and justify its poor showing. He still believed in the reformability of the Communist system, and he ruled out the possibility of political pluralism. A multiparty system in the Soviet Union, he said, would be 'absurd under our conditions'.

In May 1989, the newly elected Congress of People's Deputies met in the Kremlin for its inaugural session. It was a more diverse and more power-ful parliament than any in the Soviet Union's history, but a large number of the deputies were nonetheless from the old guard. Eighty-six per cent of them were members of the Communist Party; only 300 or so of the 2,250 delegates were genuine supporters of liberal reform.

The vote by the Congress to name Gorbachev as chairman (that is, to make him state president) went according to plan. But in the minds of many liberals doubts remained. The reason Gorbachev had given for the introduction of the new parliamentary and presidential system was to create a law-governed state ruled by authorities that were responsible to the people. The Congress was elected by the people in a way the old Communist apparatchiks never had been. But Gorbachev himself had faced no democratic scrutiny: he had been one of the party's guaranteed nominees to the Congress of People's Deputies, which had in turn nomi-nated him as President. The liberals were beginning to ask why the man who spoke of democracy wouldn't face a popular election.

The Congress selected 542 deputies to form the smaller, standing parlia-ment (which was to inherit the name of its discredited predecessor, the Supreme Soviet). Like its parent body, it too was dominated by Commu-nists. Boris Yeltsin failed to win enough votes, and got through only when another deputy relinquished his place in Yeltsin's favour.

The sessions of the Congress were electric. Its first meeting lasted for two weeks and was shown live on national television. There was mass absen-teeism from the workplace as people stayed home to watch the unheard of spectacle of free speech. Deputies from around the country were suddenly putting into words what ordinary folk had long felt but been too scared to say. Speaker after speaker railed against the iniquities and failings of the Soviet system, attacking the KGB, the military, the censors, the falsifiers of history, and even Gorbachev himself. For a Western observer, those days spent in the Palace of Congresses listening to the debates, wandering the corridors, meeting openly with former dissidents – Sakharov, Yeltsin, Roy Medvedev – as well as with previously inaccessible Kremlin insiders, were a source of marvel. It seemed inconceivable that the repressive, totalitarian system we had reported on for so many years could suddenly have opened the floodgates. The genie of liberty was out of the bottle and, we thought, no amount of repression could force it back in again.

Despite the ban on opposition parties, radical delegates led by Yeltsin, Sakharov and the liberal historian Yuri Afanasyev formed a bloc of reformers known as the Interregional Group of Deputies (IRGD). Its founding conference in July attracted 316 of the Congress's 2,250 members, men and women united in their support for fundamental democratisation. They agreed that political pluralism, the abolition of the one-party state and the granting of self-determination to the separatist-minded Soviet republics would be the main planks of their programme, together with the creation of a market economy and the right to own private property.

Gorbachev feared the IRGD. Their statements, he said, were 'irresponsible and inflammatory', their leaders 'little more than a band of gangsters'. He made clear that he would not tolerate the formation of any political party other than the CPSU. When I spoke to Boris Yeltsin in 1989, as he was emerging as the opposition's most visible spokesman, he was cagey about admitting his real aims. 'Some people say I am not trying to improve the system, but to abolish it,' he told me. 'Well, I cannot confirm that. But I can say that I am in favour of a whole series of things that are – in all senses of the word – revolutionary.' As with most of the conversations I had had with him in the past, this one again had Yeltsin speaking in the coded language that dissidents had been forced to use by fear of the state. Now, though, the state had lost its omnipotence. Tens of thousands of people were demonstrating their support for Yeltsin on the streets of Moscow; coalminers were striking in Vorkuta and the Don Basin, demanding political as well as economic concessions. When asked if he was ready to answer their call for an end to Communism, he replied cautiously:

Multiparty democracy is such a serious thing that we need to listen to the views not only of Gorbachev and Yeltsin – that's not so important – but to the views of the people. And if the whole of society wants it [multiparty democracy], then that is a serious matter. Multiparty democracy shouldn't be a taboo: the people must be allowed to talk about it; then we can draw the necessary conclusions …

Multiparty democracy, championed by Yeltsin and the radicals, but steadfastly refused by Gorbachev, Ligachev and the Kremlin *apparat*, was about
to become the decisive battleground for the country's future. The Communist monopoly on power had been enshrined in the Soviet Constitution
since the 1930s. Article Six of the current constitution stated:

> The leading and guiding force of Soviet society and the nucleus of its polit-
> ical system, of all state organisations and public organisations, is the
> Communist Party of the Soviet Union. Armed with Marxism–Leninism,
> the CPSU determines the direction of society and the course of its domes-
> tic and foreign policy. It directs and controls … the struggle for the victory
> of Communism.

The campaign to repeal Article Six was led by Andrei Sakharov. His petition
for abolition gathered support from all over the country and, on 12 December 1989, he rose to address the Congress of People's Deputies. In a piece of
political theatre, Sakharov produced the petition with 60,000 signatures and
telegrams in cardboard boxes, challenging Gorbachev to deny the legitimacy
of the request. 'The Soviet Union must decide,' he said, 'if it wants to be an
empire or a democracy.' The Congress was being televised live, and
Gorbachev looked aghast at such a public ambush. 'Come over here,' he
called to Sakharov, 'and I'll show you thousands of other telegrams [support-
ing the retention of Article Six]. Let's not try to intimidate each other, Andrei
Dmitrievich; let's not stoop to manipulating public opinion.' There were
slow handclaps from the floor as Gorbachev struggled to silence the challenge from Sakharov. But with Gorbachev arguing fiercely to preserve the
one-party system, the Congress's inbuilt conservative majority carried the
day – the motion to repeal Article Six was defeated by 1,138 votes to 839. In
the corridor after the vote, Sakharov told reporters, 'If necessary, we shall
have to defend *perestroika* from the founders of *perestroika* if their position
becomes reactionary or if they drag their heels unjustifiably.'

Two days later, Andrei Sakharov was dead. On the evening of 14 December, while he was preparing a speech responding to Gorbachev's intransigence, he suffered a fatal heart attack at his desk. Along with 80,000

mourners, I stood by Sakharov's coffin as tributes were read to the 'voice of the nation's conscience'. Yevgeny Yevtushenko compared him to the great humanitarians of Russian history, Tolstoy, Dostoevsky and Chekhov. 'He was,' he said, 'the embodiment of all that is best in the great tradition of the Russian intelligentsia.' Muscovites carried handwritten placards with the words, 'Sakharov, forgive us' for not having had the courage to support his stand on behalf of civil rights. A copy of his speech demanding multiparty democracy was laid on the top of his coffin.

It was an intensely emotional moment, and Gorbachev seems to have been personally affected by it. He came to pay his respects to Sakharov's widow, Yelena Bonner, and praised the former dissident's contribution to reform. With demonstrations growing in support of the repeal of Article Six – including a rally of a quarter of a million people outside the Kremlin in February 1990 – he accepted the inevitable. On 14 March, the constitution was altered to read, 'The Communist Party of the Soviet Union *and other political parties*, labour, youth and other public organisations and mass movements may participate in the policy-making of the Soviet state ...' After more than 70 years, the Soviet Union had become a multiparty state.

By the spring of 1990, Gorbachev's loss of control of the political process was plain to see. We had gathered as always for the annual May Day parade in Red Square. The country's leaders had climbed the steps to the review-stand on top of Lenin's mausoleum, and we correspondents were penned in by its side, in front of the Kremlin wall. The march past began unremarkably, with the usual happy children and floats celebrating the joys of Soviet life. But as the parade continued, we became aware of a commotion in the ranks. Shouts of 'Down with Gorbachev' began to ring out, and we heard the sound of organised chanting calling for democracy and freedom. Reports reached us that a contingent of Yeltsin supporters had joined the end of the official workers' procession; they had, astoundingly, been allowed to march right into Red Square, literally under the noses of the politburo. Up above us we could see Gorbachev's fingers tapping agitatedly on the parapet of the mausoleum, and then – in a flash – he stormed down the steps with his colleagues in tow to disappear in humiliating retreat back into the Kremlin.

From now on, Gorbachev was barely able to keep up with events. He proposed a further strengthening of the presidency: the new rules would grant the officeholder powers comparable to those enjoyed by the US and French presidents. But he refused again to hold an election for the enhanced post. Instead, Gorbachev had himself reappointed as president by a session of the Congress of People's Deputies. In retrospect, it was his last chance to stand for election and to gain a genuine mandate from the country. Such a demonstration of popular approval would have made it impossible for Boris Yeltsin or any other rivals to challenge his right to rule; but, as it was, he remained an unelected politician tarred with the brush of the old-style Communism he had struggled to reform.

Gorbachev had progressively surrounded himself with a government made up of conservatives and hardliners. The Supreme Soviet had voted to refuse several of his ministerial nominees, including Marshal Dmitry Yazov as defence minister and Gennady Yanayev as deputy president, but Gorbachev insisted on further votes until he got his way. Interior Minister Boris Pugo, Prime Minister Valentin Pavlov and the Speaker of the Supreme Soviet, Anatoly Lukyanov, also owed their advancement to Gorbachev's personal recommendation. In virtually every instance there had been prominent liberal voices warning against giving such men access to the levers of power; some deputies had spoken of the dangers of a military coup with them in the Kremlin.

Torn between criticism from the radicals that he was standing in the way of reform and threats from the hardliners that he was betraying the USSR and the CPSU, Gorbachev vacillated and stalled. He was trying to placate both camps and failed to satisfy either. He began to switch his teams of advisers with alarming frequency.

Yeltsin, by contrast, was demonstrating political insight. At the end of May, he got himself nominated as chairman of the Russian Supreme Soviet. Under Gorbachev's reforms of 1989, each of the 15 Soviet republics had been granted its own parliamentary body with limited but real powers. While Gorbachev himself would run the national parliament (the union-wide Supreme Soviet), certain responsibilities were devolved to the individual republics. Yeltsin was now the de facto leader of Russia, while Gorbachev was the leader of the Soviet Union. Nominally, the Soviet president was the senior figure – he ruled all 15 republics, while Yeltsin ruled only one of them. But the system was a new one, no one really understood the demarcation lines, and politics was developing through trial and error. Russia was the dominant force within the Union – bigger and more populous than any of the other republics – and Yeltsin sensed he could push the boundaries of his authority. A new period of dual power was in the offing, similar to the *dvoevlastie* of 1917 (see p. 191), and both Yeltsin and Gorbachev would do their utmost to come out on top.

Yeltsin's greatest weapon was his political dexterity, allied to the fact that the Soviet people knew he had defied the Communist authorities as early as his quarrel at the October 1987 plenum. Since then he had re-invented himself as a populist politician, ostentatiously travelling by public transport, appearing in bread queues to ask ordinary folk about their hopes and concerns, and railing against the abuses and corruption of the Communist *apparat*. While Gorbachev was still defending the CPSU, clinging to the belief that the party could be reformed and revived, Yeltsin was condemning it. At the Twenty-Eighth Communist Party Congress in July 1990, he announced that he could no longer remain a member of the party. 'Having been elected as chairman of the Russian Supreme Soviet,' he told a hushed hall, 'and in light of my responsibility to the peoples of Russia, taking into account the country's transition to a multiparty system, I can no longer submit myself to carrying out the commands of the Communist Party of the Soviet Union. I therefore submit my resignation …' As murmurs rose from the floor, Yeltsin left the podium and walked slowly up the long aisle of the Palace of Congresses, through the rows of delegates to the exit at the back of the hall. Jeers, whistles and cries of 'Shame!' accompanied him on his way. His future, and the country's, no longer lay with the CPSU.

Yeltsin stepped up the battle with Gorbachev by adopting a (largely symbolic) declaration of Russian sovereignty. The two men argued over which laws, Soviet or Russian, should take priority on the territory of the Russian Republic. But they agreed to work together on a strategy to rescue the disintegrating economy. In August 1990, a combined team of economists nominated by Gorbachev and Yeltsin produced a radical reform plan designed to lay the foundations of a modern market economy in 500 days. The '500 Days Programme' proposed mass privatisation, the end of state subsidies, prices determined by the market instead of by the state, a rapid integration into the world economic system and the devolution of many economic powers from the Union to the individual republics. Yeltsin accepted the programme enthusiastically and announced that Russia would implement it. But Gorbachev equivocated. His conservative advisers condemned the plan as capitalism by the back door and Gorbachev abandoned it. Yeltsin wanted radical reform and he wanted it immediately; Gorbachev also wanted change, but his approach was much more gradualist. Their failure to cooperate left the door open for the revanchist forces of hardline Communism, and their enemies were now planning to take dramatic action.

In late November, Defence Minister Dmitry Yazov appeared on national television to announce an extension of the powers of the military. Because of recent incidents of harassment of Soviet troops, particularly in the Baltic states where separatist demonstrations were growing more boisterous, Yazov said soldiers were being granted the right to defend themselves and the property of the Soviet state by using their weapons. Political tensions were high, and the prospect of Soviet troops firing on Soviet civilians raised the stakes another notch. In early December, KGB chief Vladimir Kryuchkov made a long, televised speech using Cold War rhetoric rarely heard since the Brezhnev years. There was, Kryuchkov claimed, an imminent danger to the Soviet motherland: anti-Communist elements, at the instigation of sinister forces from abroad, were stirring up unrest and violence. The nation should be aware that the KGB was prepared to use all the powers at its disposal to defeat these 'enemy forces' and to send their 'foreign masters' packing. As a first step, joint patrols of militiamen and soldiers would be deployed on the streets of major cities to prevent crime and disorder. The implication was clear: demonstrators and protesters would be considered legitimate targets.

Hints of a coming crackdown were hard to ignore, yet Gorbachev did. In mid December, the president's liberal adviser Alexander Yakovlev wrote an article for the newspaper *Moskovsky Komsomolets* in which he warned, 'The conservative and reactionary forces are mercilessly seeking revenge.

They are preparing to mount an offensive. I am deeply disturbed by the inertia that is being shown by the forces of democracy.'

Eduard Shevardnadze's appearance before the Congress of People's Deputies on 20 December was even more dramatic. 'The reformers have gone into hiding,' he said. 'A dictatorship is approaching. I tell you this with full responsibility. No one can say what this dictatorship will be like, or what kind of dictator will come to power ... I have come here to tell you that I am resigning from the government ... I want this warning to be my contribution, my protest against the dictatorship that is about to come into being ...' Shevardnadze made no direct criticism of the Soviet president – the two men were long-time friends and colleagues – but he hinted that Gorbachev should have acted more decisively to oppose the rise of the hardliners: 'I express my sincere gratitude to Mikhail Sergeyevich Gorbachev. I am his friend and fellow thinker. But I have no choice but to resign ... I cannot reconcile myself to what is happening in my country and to the trials that await our nation.'

At the time, when I asked Alexander Yakovlev if he felt the rumours of a military coup against Gorbachev were credible, he showed me a pamphlet that he said was being circulated among soldiers of the Soviet army. 'We need a new Hitler, not Gorbachev,' the pamphlet declared. 'A military takeover is urgently required to save our country. There is plenty of room in Siberia for the people who brought us this cursed *perestroika* ...' The liberal commentator Alès Adamovich added that the hardliners were 'surrounding the president with colonels and generals ... surrounding him and making him a hostage'.

The first sign that Yakovlev and Shevardnadze were right came in January 1991, and the Baltic states were the chosen battleground. The hardliners were alarmed and angry at the threat to Soviet unity posed by the growth of separatist movements in the republics. Latvia, Lithuania and Estonia – which had all been incorporated into the USSR only after the Second World War – had declared their independence. Nationalist sentiments, once stifled by the threat of force, had been unleashed under *glasnost*.

The spectre of disorder and violence was used to demand action. In an article in the army newspaper, *Krasnaya Zvezda*, the former chief of the general staff, Marshal Sergei Akhromeyev called on the armed forces 'to act to protect the unity of our homeland ... The time has come,' he wrote, 'to defend our state with courage and resolution.' The Soviet interior minister, Boris Pugo, was himself a Latvian; in his former post as head of the KGB in his native republic he had won a reputation for the suppression of nationalist sentiment. Now he had nearly half a million special forces soldiers at his disposal. With the world's attention distracted by the impending war in the Gulf, Moscow sent in the troops. In the Latvian capital, Riga, a printing works that had been used to publish separatist newspapers was stormed and occupied. Clashes broke out around the Lithuanian parliament in Vilnius, forcing the nationalist government to barricade itself inside. The special forces seized more buildings, including the headquarters of Lithuanian television, and 13 civilians were killed. Only a week after he had received the Nobel Peace Prize, Gorbachev was presiding over a massacre of his own citizens. Boris Yeltsin denounced him as a murderer. 'I warned in 1987 that Gorbachev was addicted to power,' he said on national television. 'Now he has a dictatorship with a pretty name ... we demand his immediate resignation.'

The violence finally provoked Gorbachev into action. A week after the killings, Moscow ordered its troops to pull out. Gorbachev apologised for the violence in Vilnius and Riga, telling the Supreme Soviet, 'We never wanted this to happen,' but he failed to remove the men who had ordered the attacks. Pugo, Yazov, Yanayev, Pavlov and Akhromeyev remained in their jobs and continued to blame the separatists for the bloodshed. The consequences of their next attempt to seize power would be far more serious.

CHAPTER THIRTY-NINE

The killings in the Baltic republics cast a pall over the New Year of 1991. No one believed the threat of a hardline coup had disappeared when the troops were withdrawn; the plotters in the Kremlin were merely biding their time. A series of unusual events in the first months of the year raised tensions even higher.

In January, Prime Minister Valentin Pavlov announced that all 50 and 100 rouble denomination banknotes were being withdrawn from circulation: citizens could redeem a limited amount of them at the state bank, but anything over the limit would be forfeited. The declared aim was to punish black-marketeers who kept their illegal profits in high-denomination notes, but the criminals found ways to circumvent the measure, while ordinary people saw their life savings wiped out. The public were infuriated by the government's ineptitude, and the hardliners in the Communist Party blamed Mikhail Gorbachev.

Worse was to follow. Shops in Moscow were hit by repeated shortages of basic foodstuffs; on two occasions bread disappeared completely from the city, leading to long queues while bakeries waited for deliveries that never came. When some limited supplies did appear there was panic buying, then arguments and fist fights. The threat of public unrest seemed a genuine possibility, and the parallels with St Petersburg in 1917, when bread shortages sparked the February Revolution (see p. 183), were not lost on the politicians. Moscow had elected a reformist city council, led by Mayor Gavriil Popov, and there were suggestions that the shortages were being engineered to undermine his authority: the old-style Communists who ran the rural districts that produced the city's food were accused of deliberately withholding supplies. First milk, then eggs, then meat would suddenly disappear. At times, the big food stores in the city centre were left with nothing more than tinned sardines on their shelves.

Periodic rumours of military build-ups on the outskirts of Moscow threw the city authorities into a panic. Yeltsin reported to the Russian Parliament that he was concerned about the army's intentions, and Popov at one stage called a news conference to share his fears. 'Our information,' he told us, 'is that a group of extremists is preparing to take military action on the understanding that the hardline political forces will use this as a reason to impose a state of emergency.'

With the state budget sliding into debt, salaries were going unpaid; increases in pensions and benefits were cancelled; public discontent was growing, and the public blamed the Soviet president. When Gorbachev travelled to London to lobby the G7 group of industrialised nations to invest in the Soviet economy, he was rebuffed. At the urging of the Americans, British and Japanese, the G7 refused to put any cash on the table. In Moscow, Gorbachev's enemies played the humiliation card adroitly. They portrayed Gorbachev as the man who had brought the Soviet Union to its knees, transforming it from superpower to basket case, trampling on national pride and emasculating the once-mighty Soviet military. The hardliners hinted darkly that none of this was an accident, but that Gorbachev had deliberately ruined the country because he was a paid agent, a sinister traitor in the service of the malevolent West. Television footage of 'Gorbymania' in the US, Britain and other European countries, where excited crowds poured adulation on the visiting Soviet leader, was cited as proof that he was a Western stooge. The more he was adored in the West, the more he was loathed by a Soviet population that had seen their standard of living plummet and their pride in their country destroyed since he came to power.

The 'loss' of Eastern Europe in the years after 1989 was a huge blow to many who regarded Moscow's domination of the 'fraternal states' as an expression of Soviet potency; and the man who presided over the dismantling of the Warsaw Pact was derided for his weak-willed – or treacherous – willingness to surrender them to the clutches of the West. When Gorbachev's spokesman joked that the Brezhnev Doctrine had been superseded by the Sinatra Doctrine (Eastern Europe would be allowed to do things 'their way'), the Western press corps saw it as a graceful acceptance of geopolitical reality;* but the phrase was cited angrily by Communist loyalists as evidence of Gorbachev's collusion with the capitalist enemy. His failure to prevent the removal of the Berlin wall, the reunification of Germany and the 'defection' of the former Soviet satellites was crucial in stimulating conservative opposition to him and to *perestroika*.

When the Soviet republics began to emulate the example of the Eastern Bloc countries, putting pressure on Moscow to let them also 'do it their way', Gorbachev seems to have realised that things had got dangerously out of hand. If his opponents had pilloried him for leniency towards foreign states such as Poland or Hungary, how much greater would their anger be if he sanctioned the loss of integral territories of the USSR such as Latvia, Lithuania or Estonia.

The 'nationalities problem' had existed under the tsarist empire and throughout the years of Bolshevik rule. While the state remained a monolithic autocracy, the problem could be kept under control, even if Moscow had at times to resort to extreme measures, such as Stalin's mass repressions and deportations. But when Gorbachev's 'new thinking' cast doubt on the state's willingness to murder and repress, when *glasnost* gave the subject peoples access to the truth about their histories, the separatists found a new boldness. From the Baltics to Georgia, Moldova, Armenia and Ukraine, demands to secede from the 'voluntary' union of the USSR grew daily more vociferous.

The prospect of the imminent collapse of the Soviet state was by far the most powerful factor stoking the conservatives' anger. Even before the crackdowns in Latvia and Lithuania, the hardliners in the Kremlin leadership had sent troops to smash nationalist demonstrations in Georgia and Azerbaijan. Twenty pro-independence demonstrators were killed by troops in Tbilisi in April 1989; and in January 1990 the Soviet army killed up to a hundred Azeris after anti-Armenian pogroms in the Azerbaijani capital,

---

* In fact, the politburo had discussed the possibility of armed intervention to stop the 'fraternal countries' leaving the Soviet bloc, but Gorbachev made it clear that he would not countenance the use of force. As early as June 1988, he told the Nineteenth Party Conference that 'our concept of "new thinking" means a commitment to freedom of choice ... the policy of force has outlived its time.'

Baku.* Ethnic unrest in the disputed enclave of Nagorno-Karabakh, in the Trans-Dniestr region of Moldova and in Uzbekistan added to the conservatives' alarm that the USSR was being allowed to disintegrate. The violence put pressure on the army, and its commanders resented being placed in the front line by civilian politicians, whom they regarded as weak and ineffectual.

To mark the fiftieth anniversary of the Molotov–Ribbentrop Pact, which had consigned Lithuania, Estonia and Latvia to Soviet domination, 2 million people had joined hands in a human chain of protest across the three republics. By January 1991, all three had declared their independence and others were beginning to following suit.

Russia itself was becoming restive. The Russian Republic had traditionally been a mainstay of the Union: Russians had been deployed as senior officials in the 14 other republics to ensure loyalty to Moscow; they were the 'big brothers' among the peoples of the USSR, enjoying power and privileges that other groups did not; the Russian language was taught throughout Soviet territory and Russian culture was used as a tool to weaken local, potentially nationalist identity. But there was a lingering resentment that Russian sovereignty had been subordinated to the overarching authority of the Soviet Union, that native 'Russianness' had somehow been submerged in a homogenous Soviet identity.

While Gorbachev struggled to hold the Union together, Boris Yeltsin had no such concerns. The period of dual power had pitched him into a battle for supremacy with the Soviet leader, and he regarded Russian nationalism as one of his trump cards. The clash between the two men became inextricably enmeshed with the struggle of the republics against the centre, with Yeltsin making the issue of Russian independence – and the right to independence of all the republics – a central theme of his political platform. It was a deliberate challenge to Gorbachev's aim of preserving the Union, and it would play into a violent endgame.

*

---

* The Tbilisi massacre happened while Gorbachev was out of the country on a visit to London and Yegor Ligachev was chairing the politburo. The measures in Baku were initiated by the Kremlin envoy Yevgeny Primakov.

When he spoke of his early years, Yeltsin portrayed himself as a young man in conflict with authority. He quarrelled with his teachers, with his peers and with his political mentors. But he makes clear in his memoirs that in all these clashes he regarded himself as being right and the others always wrong. If Yeltsin lost an argument, it was always because he was being unfairly victimised; he stored up his rancour and strove for revenge. He was possessed of an overriding self-belief that spilled over easily into bullying; a smouldering determination to right the wrongs, real or imagined, that others had inflicted on him; a desire for personal recognition, even adulation; and an implacable ruthlessness towards his enemies once they had been laid low.

In the flesh he was an overpowering presence, a great Siberian bear who oozed gruffness and charm. Women fell for him and men admired his natural authority. He had the battered face of a heavyweight boxer, but when he smiled it was the smile of a mischievous boy. Mikhail Gorbachev had an intellectual presence and a nimble mind, but he lacked Yeltsin's underlying sense of menace: 'If you disagree with me,' Yeltsin's eyes seemed to say, 'I will crush you.' When Gorbachev got angry, he went red in the face; but Yeltsin stayed calm, directing his rage coldly, unblinkingly at its target. He could work a crowd with supreme skill; he had the capacity to inspire rare loyalty and implacable hatred in equal measure.

Born just four weeks before Gorbachev, in February 1931, Yeltsin as a young man joined the only political party allowed to exist in his country. With his characteristic drive and need for recognition, he rose swiftly through the ranks of the CPSU; by 1976 he was already the regional party boss in his native Sverdlovsk. His speeches from the 1970s and early 1980s contain no indication of the radical liberalism that would come later. 'The people are full of gratitude,' he told the Sverdlovsk May Day parade, 'for the titanic efforts of Comrade Brezhnev. We thank him for his outstanding role in perfecting and implementing all aspects of our national policy at home and abroad ...' But it was a new style of Soviet leader who gave Boris Nikolaevich Yeltsin the promotion he had long been seeking. It was Mikhail Gorbachev, who in 1985 brought him to Moscow as a secretary of the Central Committee, who made him Moscow party boss and then, in February 1986, a junior member of the politburo. For two years, he worked as part of the Gorbachev team, until his ambition got the better of him. The stand-up row between the two men at the October 1987 plenum was caused at least in part by Yeltsin's inordinate sensitivity to perceived slights. The letter he wrote to the Soviet leader setting out his grievances makes clear that he felt Gorbachev was not paying enough attention to him or to his ideas: 'I have felt a discernible change from an attitude of friendly support to one of indifference towards matters concerning Moscow and coldness towards me personally.'

After the humiliation he suffered at the plenum, close colleagues reported that Yeltsin tried to kill himself. He was summoned from his hospital bed a few weeks later to be stripped of his party post, an indignity for which he never forgave his former patron. For the next three years, Yeltsin was fired by a desire for vengeance, taking delight in Gorbachev's travails and adding to them by sniping at the slow pace of reform. When Gorbachev pointed out the obstacles in the way of political and economic changes, Yeltsin ridiculed him in the most cutting language. His rabble-rousing populism was based on promises that could never be fulfilled; his driving motivation was to embarrass and diminish his rival. In confidential documents, the US administration described him as 'flaky'.

But Yeltsin had the people's support. When the Kremlin-run media attacked him for being drunk on a lecture tour to the United States, he went up in most Russians' estimation. When he was fished out of a river with a bouquet of flowers in his hand, people smiled and nodded, archly hinting that he must have been rumbled in the course of some nocturnal gallantry by a jealous husband. On one occasion, we filmed him reviewing paratroopers going through their training routine, which included a spectacular leap from a high building into a pool of burning petrol. 'I was thinking to myself whether I would have jumped into that fire,' he mused to the camera. 'Perhaps not, but you never know – I'm such a hooligan at heart that maybe I would have jumped after all.'

It was precisely that hint of the hooligan that endeared Yeltsin to many Russians. They admired his courage in standing up to the Communist Party bullies and they respected his independence of thought. When the troops were sent into Latvia and Lithuania, Yeltsin flew to Riga to pledge Russia's support for the cause of self-determination. He appealed to the soldiers not to fire on civilians and won the hearts of independence movements everywhere when he told them they should 'take as much sovereignty as you can swallow'. In his determination to do down Gorbachev and his policies, Yeltsin proclaimed that the Kremlin now stood for repression, an end to reform and the forcible imposition of Soviet rule. 'But we have the strength to stop the forces of reaction,' he told his Russian parliament. 'It is within our power to halt the Soviet authorities' plunge into lawlessness and the use of force. We must show that democracy is irreversible.'

Yeltsin announced that he would respond to the threat of autocracy with the sword of democracy. He would stand in a free and open election for the post of Russian president. The new office would give the incumbent wide-ranging executive powers, and – unlike Mikhail Gorbachev – the winner would have the backing of a democratic mandate from the people.

Gorbachev was quick to recognise the danger. He mobilised the Communist forces in the Russian parliament to try to thwart the initiative, and on 28 March 1991 the battle took to the streets. With the new presidency proposal blocked by his political opponents, Yeltsin called an extraordinary session of the Russian Congress of People's Deputies to get it onto the statute books. Tens of thousands of Yeltsin supporters gathered during the course of the meeting. By late afternoon, with the constitutional crisis still unresolved, a quarter of a million people had crammed into Moscow's main thoroughfare, Gorky Street, and were threatening to march on the Kremlin.

As the crowds descended the hill, detachments of riot police moved into place, blocking their path: the showdown that had long been threatened between Gorbachev and Yeltsin seemed certain to erupt into violence. But as the first ranks of demonstrators squared up to the militia, the crisis was mysteriously defused. Both sides seemed to have received last-minute orders to back off, and while there was some wielding of police batons that night, a potential bloodbath was transformed into a political watershed. Yeltsin won the majority he needed to call a presidential election and the date was fixed for 12 June 1991. On a wave of popular acclaim, he trounced the men who stood against him, including the Kremlin's candidate, former prime minister Nikolai Ryzhkov. Yeltsin's platform of democracy, a free-market economy and self-determination for the Soviet republics won him an overwhelming mandate from the Russian people. Gorbachev could no longer argue with the facts: the Russian parliament had granted Yeltsin the right to rule by decree, and if it came to a straight choice between obeying Yeltsin's decrees or those of Gorbachev, the election had shown which way most people would go. The Soviet president had little choice but to seek an alliance.

The most tangible result of the truce was Gorbachev's acceptance that the Union would have to cede greater powers to the individual republics. Following negotiations with Yeltsin and the leaders of eight other republics (the Baltic states, Moldova, Georgia and Armenia refused to take part), he brought his plans for a new Union structure before the USSR Supreme Soviet in July. Gorbachev's Union Treaty proposed a much looser confederation of states, to be known as the Union of Soviet *Sovereign* Republics; individual members would have wide national autonomy, control over their natural resources, including oil, gas and mineral deposits, and a guarantee that republican laws would take precedence over Union legislation. As Soviet president, Gorbachev would retain control of defence and foreign policy, but he would lose much of his legislative authority, performing instead a coordinating role more akin to the president of the European Union.

Despite the misgivings of its conservative members, the Supreme Soviet approved the plan, and Gorbachev announced that the treaty would be formally signed on 20 August. In the meantime, he would take Raisa, their daughter and two granddaughters for a rare holiday at the presidential dacha in the Crimean resort of Foros on the Black Sea.

Gorbachev's enemies took advantage of his absence. Horrified by what they regarded as the wilful destruction of the USSR and the renunciation of Communist goals (the replacement of the word 'socialist' by 'sovereign' in the title of the new confederation was a particular bone of contention), the hardliners in the Soviet leadership plotted their last offensive. Anatoly Lukyanov, chairman of the Supreme Soviet, was active in rallying opposition to the treaty, contacting a range of colleagues to ascertain how far they were prepared to go. A core of committed old-style Communists held a series of secret meetings, where the rhetoric was one of patriotism and self-sacrifice: the country their fathers and forefathers had fought to preserve was being dismembered; it was their duty to defend it, even at the cost of their own lives. With the date for the signing of the Union Treaty approaching, a dozen of them put their names forward to serve on a State Emergency Committee that would declare itself the legitimate power in the country and restore old-style Bolshevik rule. The members of the committee were all men whom Gorbachev had promoted to positions of power: his vice-president Gennady Yanayev, KGB chief Vladimir Kryuchkov, Prime Minister Valentin Pavlov, Interior Minister Boris Pugo, and Defence Minister Marshal Dmitry Yazov had all been praised and trusted by the man they were about to betray.

On the afternoon of Sunday 18 August, Gorbachev was working in the study of his holiday home when the head of his bodyguards came to tell him a delegation from Moscow had arrived. Gorbachev was suspicious; he decided to make enquiries by telephone before receiving them. 'I had a whole series of phones,' he would later recall. 'A government phone, an ordinary phone, a strategic phone, a satellite phone and so on. When I picked them up I found they were all disconnected. Even the internal phone had been cut. I was isolated.' He called in his wife, daughter and son-in-law. 'I knew there was about to be an attempt to intimidate me, or an attempt to arrest me and take me away somewhere. Anything was possible ... they could have tried anything, even with my family.' By now, the dacha was surrounded by KGB troops and Soviet border guards loyal to the coup plotters. Thirty of Gorbachev's own bodyguards were inside the house and declared that they would defend him to the end. An armed confrontation was in the offing. Convinced that her husband was facing imminent death, Raisa collapsed; the children were hurriedly taken upstairs.

When the plotters' delegation was shown in, they announced, falsely, that Yeltsin had been arrested. They said a state of emergency was the only way to rescue the country from disaster and they gave Gorbachev an ultimatum: either sign the state of emergency declaration himself, in which case he could stay on as president but would have to remain under guard in the Crimea, or sign over his powers to the new, self-declared president

Gennady Yanayev. According to Gorbachev's own account of his response, he used language so full of expletives that even the hardened politicians who had come to depose him were shocked. 'I told them that they and the people who had sent them were nothing but irresponsible gamblers and criminals … Their actions would mean their own doom and the doom of the whole country … only someone bent on suicide would propose the introduction of such a totalitarian regime in our country …'

Gorbachev refused to sign anything. His position seemed desperate, but he stood firm, telling the plotters their actions would unleash a civil war, with inevitable bloodshed and death. The Soviet people, he said, would prove they were no longer downtrodden slaves: *glasnost* and freedom had changed all that. '"You are wrong to think that the people will just do every-thing you order them to do," I told them. "You are wrong to count on the people being ready to submit to the first dictator who comes along …"'

For the next three days, Gorbachev and his family were in limbo. His demands to be flown to Moscow were ignored. Fearing that the plotters intended to poison him, he refused the food they brought him. His only contact with the outside world – and one that he later credited with bolster-ing his resolve in the darkest hours – was a short-wave radio his bodyguards had rigged up. He used it to listen to the BBC's reports of events in Moscow and was heartened to hear that the plotters were not having things all their own way.

On the morning of 19 August, after I had driven into central Moscow and discovered the columns of tanks descending on the Kremlin, I toured the key sites that anyone seeking to control the country would need to seize. At the headquarters of Soviet radio and television in the suburb of Ostankino, armoured cars had surrounded the main buildings; but the Russian White House, the seat of Boris Yeltsin's Russian parliament, seemed unaffected – military convoys were driving past on their way into the city centre. The greatest concentration of troops was around the Kremlin. Outside the Hotel National, under the Kremlin wall, a ring of tanks and armoured personnel carriers had cordoned off the approaches to Red Square. With some trepi-dation, I walked up to the soldiers who were milling around between the vehicles, showed my press pass and asked politely if I might go through. The young officer who spoke to me was apologetic, but explained that he had orders not to let anyone past. I asked if he had been told why his unit had been deployed, and he replied, 'Not really.' He did, though, confirm that his men had live ammunition in their weapons and that if the military command ordered them to shoot, they would do so.

At 11 a.m. a new radio broadcast by the State Emergency Committee announced that the state of emergency would last for six months. 'Our motherland is in mortal danger. The policy of reform begun by M.S. Gorbachev has run into a dead end ... The existing authorities have lost the trust of the people. Political manoeuvring has replaced any concern about the fate of the motherland. Institutions of the state are openly mocked and the country has become ungovernable.' The purpose of the State Committee was 'to overcome the profound and comprehensive crisis, political, ethnic and civil strife, chaos and anarchy that threaten the lives and security of the citizens of the Soviet Union'.

When I spoke to Muscovites on the streets of the capital, I found some who agreed with the aims of the coup leaders: people were attracted by their promises to revive the economy, end the shortages and re-establish the USSR as a world superpower. But I also came across growing instances of defiance. Some civilians were haranguing the troops or standing in the way of the advancing tanks. In one incident, demonstrators clambered onto an armoured personnel carrier and began to drag the driver out of his port-hole. The look of terror on the face of the teenage conscript suggested that some troops might not be spoiling for a fight.

By mid afternoon, the army was everywhere. Now a phalanx of heavy armour roared up to the White House, belching acrid fumes and smoke, thundering along the embankment of the Moskva River, leaving the imprint of their tracks in the tarmac. Rumours began to circulate that Boris Yeltsin had evaded the forces sent by the plotters to detain him and managed to take refuge inside the building. As I watched the line of tanks form up at the base of the parliament steps, I was convinced they were here to seize the parliament, to arrest Yeltsin and all those who opposed their masters in the Kremlin.

But the order to attack did not come. At the crucial moment it was Yeltsin himself who seized the initiative. Emerging dramatically from the parliament's main entrance, he descended the steps and strode towards the leading tank in the column. For a moment, we held our breath. Yeltsin was vulnerable, unprotected from a sniper's bullet or from a concerted attempt to arrest him. He heaved his burly frame firmly onto the back of the tank and then onto the turret itself. Panting from the effort, he leaned down and shook hands with the startled tank crew who were peering from inside the vehicle. With a trace of a smile, he rose to his full height and in a resolute voice urged the Russian people to unite against the coup:

> Citizens of Russia! The legal president has been removed from power. We are dealing with a right-wing, reactionary, anti-constitutional coup. The Union Treaty, due to be signed tomorrow … has angered the reactionary forces and pushed them into an irresponsible, criminal act. This is a *coup d'état* that discredits the Soviet Union in the eyes of the world. It returns us to the Cold War era. The assumption of power by the so-called Emergency Committee is unlawful. Gorbachev has been isolated; I have been denied the right to communicate with him. We appeal to citizens of Russia to rebuff the putsch. We appeal to all soldiers and servicemen to carry out their civic duty and refuse to take part in this reactionary coup. Until all our demands are met, we appeal for a general strike throughout the nation.

The cogency of Yeltsin's appeal for restraint, at a moment when bloodshed looked inevitable, was remarkable. It was a bravura performance and it galvanised the resistance campaign that would prove decisive over the next few days. The forces of the opposition had no access to the media – their communications were limited to intermittent radio transmissions from inside the White House – but Yeltsin's words spread like a jolt of electricity through the city. As soon as he finished speaking, the tanks turned around and left, sparking rumours that they had been persuaded to defect to the opposition. Within an hour, crowds had begun to gather around the building, and for the next three days they grew and grew. The White House had become the Alamo of democracy and the Russian people were determined to defend it.

On the other side of town, the coup plotters were about to give their side of the story. In the conference hall of the Soviet Foreign Ministry, the new 'president', Gennady Yanayev, and four of his fellow conspirators sat stony faced before the world's media. When I had interviewed Yanayev just a couple of weeks earlier, he had smiled and professed his loyalty to Mikhail Gorbachev and the ideals of *perestroika*. He had struck me then as an archetypal Communist forced to pay lip service to the politics of liberal reform, and now that he had usurped his master's throne, his contempt for Gorbachev was given full rein.* 'This country is disintegrating,' he told his audience. 'We are determined to take the most serious measures to reimpose the rule of law and order, to wipe the criminals from our streets ... We state firmly that we will not allow foreign powers to infringe the national sovereignty and territorial integrity of the Soviet Union. We are not afraid to assert our pride and patriotism, and we are determined that the coming generations will be brought up in this same spirit.'

As he called for the Soviet people to support the Emergency Committee, Yanayev seemed confident and in control. But when questioning turned to Boris Yeltsin's demands for opposition to the coup, his face began to twitch and his fingers twisted nervously on the desk in front of him. 'If Yeltsin is calling for strikes,' he said, 'he is acting irresponsibly. And that is something we cannot allow. Yeltsin and the Russian leadership are playing a very dangerous game that could lead to armed provocation. It is the duty of the State Emergency Committee to warn all Soviet people about the dangers of such actions ...'

With the State Committee in charge, Yanayev promised, there would be immediate improvements in the economy – more apartments, better food supplies, cheaper prices and a twofold increase in wages, pensions and benefits. Bribery had worked well for the men who overthrew Nikita Khrushchev

---

* Yanayev's last words to me were, in retrospect, something of a warning: 'I joined the Communist Party 30 years ago,' he told me, 'and I continue to believe that I made the right choice. I am and shall remain a Communist. Communism in the Soviet Union is not dead ... Let me tell you: you would be premature in saying that the Communist ideal is dead here.'

in 1964, and it did seem to soften some people's attitude towards Yanayev and his cronies.

But tough curfew measures were also announced, banning all movement between 11 p.m. and 5 a.m. Moscow would be divided into 33 military districts and put under the control of a military commander, who had carte blanche to crush opposition to the coup. The soldiers would have the right to seize any factory that threatened to strike, to run all public transport and to patrol all aspects of public life. Vehicles from outside the city would be prevented from entering Moscow, and the army would be deployed to search apartments, cars and pedestrians. The discovery of any weapons or 'printed or handwritten materials calling for the violation of public order' would result in 'severe legal measures' being taken. Demonstrations, rallies, meetings, marches and strikes had, of course, already been banned. Now even sports events and public entertainment, including theatres and cinemas, would need the permission of the military district commander. Political parties or groupings deemed hostile to the 'normalisation' process were suspended with immediate effect.

As evening fell, I returned to Yeltsin's White House. I found it surrounded by thousands, possibly tens of thousands, of civilians. Men and women, young schoolboys, gnarled workers, elderly pensioners and invalids had come to stand up for their rights: the defenders of democracy were living evidence that the years of reform had not been in vain. Before 1985 this could not have happened. But the experience of *glasnost* had shown people that life could be different, that *they* could make a difference, and they were not prepared to let the fruits of freedom be snatched away from them.

Now the people were building makeshift barricades and tank traps to ward off the attack all believed was imminent. Everything from park benches, concrete slabs and steel water pipes to the contents of entire construction sites was pressed into service; by midnight, every approach road to the parliament had some form of defensive barrier across it. They would have done little to delay a concerted assault, but they were good for morale; all felt safer to have them between us and the tanks we feared were on their way.

Camp fires were beginning to spring up among the crowds; people were roasting sausages and sharing food and drink. Huge Russian tricolours, the pre-revolutionary flag that had become the symbol of the opposition, rose from the ranks of the White House's defenders and hung from its windows and balconies. Mobile field hospitals were being set up in anticipation of casualties from the impending violence, but spirits were high. Above us, the White House itself was a pale ghost in the darkness.

Late that night, the poet Yevgeny Yevtushenko came to the BBC office from the White House, where he had just appeared on the balcony with Yeltsin as he encouraged the crowds and appealed for the Russian people to defend freedom and democracy. Yevtushenko had brought with him a poem, scribbled on the back of a leaflet carrying Yeltsin's decree declaring the putsch illegal, and asked for help with some points of the English translation. An hour later, he was broadcasting to the world:

This day will be glorified
in songs and ballads.
Today we are the people,
no longer fools
happy to be fooled.
And Sakharov, alive
again, with us
on the barricades,
shyly rubbing over his glasses
cracked by the crowd.
Conscience awakens even in the tanks.
Yeltsin rises on the turret,
and behind him
are not ghosts of the Kremlin,
but our simple people,
deceptively simple –
not yet vanished –
and weary Russian women –
victims of the endless lines.

No,

never again shall Russia be on its knees!

With us are Pushkin, Tolstoy;

With us are the people,

forever awakened.

And the Russian parliament,

Like a wounded marble swan of freedom,

defended by our people,

swims into eternity.

Remembering the moment 15 years later, Yevtushenko smiled and told me that those lines were his 'best worst poem'. He had been carried away by the emotion of the August days, he said, led into a false grandiloquence. But in 1991 they were the right words at the right time. Everyone present in Moscow that night felt Russia was embarking on an unprecedented new course of liberty, tolerance and democracy. If those hopes have been dashed in the years since then – and we both agreed they had been – the moment still shines in the people's memory and the poet's words. Yevtushenko told me he was proud and ashamed at the same time. 'Yes. And when I compare very romantically, a little bit stupidly, Russian parliament with a white swan – wounded white swan – you could kill me! Today it sounds very stupidly [sic], but in that times it sounded perfect. It was a poem like a spark, you know, like one bright star for one moment; then it fell down and touched the earth and it was dead ...'

Boris Yeltsin's moment of drama signalled the beginning of a decisive shift in the balance of power. The Gorbachev era of reform within the Communist Party and restructuring within the Soviet Union was coming to an end, and the Yeltsin era beginning. From 1991 onwards, the process would no longer be one of reform; it would be one of radical change that would sweep away the party, the system and the Union itself.

For the next two days, the stand-off between the coup plotters and the people of Moscow held the country and the world in thrall. Yanayev, Yazov, Pugo and Pavlov ordered more tanks onto the streets. An armoured unit advancing around the Moscow ring road was presumed to be heading for the White House and the news was quickly relayed to the crowds defending the building. But the tanks were intercepted by a group of civilians at an underpass near the US embassy. In the clash that followed, three young men were shot or crushed to death.

Blood had been shed now. At the White House, Boris Yeltsin and his fellow opposition leaders came out onto the balcony to address the 50,000 who had gathered to defend them. Eduard Shevardnadze was there with him, along with Alexander Yakovlev, Gavriil Popov and Sergei Stankevich. Stankevich expressed the anger of the crowd. 'I'm glad this coup has happened,' he said. 'I'm glad, because now we know who our enemies are; now we've seen the true colours of those bastards who want to destroy democracy! And when we beat this coup, believe me, we're going to put them all away!' The applause was tumultuous.

Boris Yeltsin began on a more sombre note; the crowd fell silent.

> The shadows of darkness have descended on our country, on Europe and on the world. But I can tell you one thing. I have resolved to resist these men! I have resolved to defeat these usurpers in the Kremlin!* I have resolved to do this and I call on you all to do the same! Without your help, I can do nothing … but together with you, together with the Russian people, we are capable of the greatest feats of heroism! Together we can defeat these traitors! Together we can ensure the triumph of democracy!

That evening, Yeltsin's staff invited foreign journalists inside the White House. The BBC and CNN were still broadcasting from Moscow, and our reports were being beamed by satellite back into the Soviet Union. We were taken around offices that had been fortified against attack. Yeltsin appeared only as a presence flitting between one corridor and another: we were told that he and his closest aides had an inner sanctum, a fortified bunker that

---

* Yeltsin used the word *samozvantsy*, redolent with overtones of impostors or pretenders from Russian history who dared to usurp the power of legitimate rulers and reaped the bloody consequences of their treachery.

would serve as a final refuge in case of a military assault. A few parliamentarians were there carrying machine guns, but most of them looked scared and out of their depth. Yeltsin's vice-president, Alexander Rutskoi, a former Soviet air force lieutenant, seemed calmer. His bravery during those August days was unquestionable – he organised the defences inside the White House and he instructed the demonstrators how to maintain the human shield around the building – but such was the speed at which Russian politics was evolving that two years later he would be numbered among Boris Yeltsin's fiercest enemies.

Outside the White House, stewards were advising people how to react if the tanks came, telling them they should form a series of human chains, link arms and stand firm. Unbeknown to the crowd, Yeltsin had spoken to the Russian defence chief, Pavel Grachev, and secured the cooperation of at least some of the Russian military. Half a dozen armoured vehicles arrived to great cheers from the crowds, and took up position in the defensive wall.

For another 24 hours, the crowd waited. By Wednesday 21 August, a cautious optimism was beginning to build. The coup plotters had had their chance to send in the troops, but they had failed to do so. Now it seemed they had seen the tens of thousands gathered at the White House, the splits in the military and the fierce resistance they would have to overcome, and their resolve was beginning to crumble. Rumours were circulating that the plotters were divided and squabbling among themselves; that Pavlov had had a heart attack, that Yanayev and Pugo were drunk and incapable, that Yazov had resigned.

At two o'clock in the afternoon, tanks were sighted on Leningradsky Prospekt, the continuation of Gorky Street where it leaves the Moscow city boundary, and this time they were heading away from the Kremlin. An hour later, armoured columns were seen driving out of town on the Vnukovo road. An hour after that, Radio Moscow confirmed that a general withdrawal was taking place. Marshal Yazov had seemingly weighed the consequences of an assault on the White House and recoiled before the inevitable bloodshed. He had ordered the tanks back into their barracks.

In the barricaded chamber of the Russian parliament, Yeltsin called together the loyal liberal deputies and made an announcement that caused pandemonium. 'A group of tourists,' he said, 'have been spotted on their way to the airport.' The coup plotters, said Yeltsin, were fleeing for their lives, their motorcade weaving in and out of the columns of tanks they themselves had ordered onto the streets. It would later transpire that they were flying to Foros to try to do a deal with the still-imprisoned Mikhail Gorbachev. Once there, they apologised and pleaded for their lives, but Gorbachev treated them with disdain, ordering his guards to place them under arrest. Most of the members of the State Emergency Committee, as well as Anatoly Lukyanov and several dozen others, were rounded up and thrown in jail. Boris Pugo, expecting terrible retribution for his treachery, shot his wife and then shot himself. Marshal Sergei Akhromeyev, who had supported the coup but taken no overt part in it, hanged himself in his office.

In the early hours of Thursday 22 August, Mikhail Gorbachev descended the steps of a Soviet air force jet at an airfield outside Moscow. In an open-necked shirt, dishevelled and exhausted, he seemed barely able to take in the magnitude of the changes that had taken place. The Soviet people had resisted the coup, he said, because the years of *glasnost* and *perestroika* had taught them to think for themselves. 'All the work we have done since 1985 has borne fruit. People and society have changed, and that is what provided the main obstacle to the victory of the putsch ... I congratulate the Soviet people. This is the great victory of *perestroika*.' His diagnosis was correct; but Gorbachev seemed too anxious to claim the credit for himself, too slow to acknowledge the pivotal role of his rival, Boris Yeltsin. It was as if he were expecting political life simply to resume its old course.

At a press conference later that day, Gorbachev appeared emotional, halting in his speech and visibly choking back tears. He seemed genuinely surprised that the coup against him had been led by men he had never suspected of disloyalty. 'They turned out to be men in the very centre of the leadership, close to the president himself,' he said. 'These were men I had personally promoted, believed and trusted.' But a moment later he was continuing to defend the Communist Party, seemingly unable to accept that it was the party itself that was the coup's organising force. 'I cannot agree with people who condemn the party as a whole, who call it a reactionary force. There are thousands of Communists who are true democrats ... I believe that on the basis of the party's new programme, it is possible to unite all the best and most progressive elements in society.'

Gorbachev rejected criticisms of the Central Committee, which later turned out to have instructed party branches around the USSR to support the coup. He refused to condemn party bosses, even when there was evidence they had been part of the plot. As a lifelong Communist, he said he remained committed to the ideals of the party and its founder, Vladimir Lenin. Gorbachev had failed to realise that Communism's day was over.

Yeltsin seized his moment in a series of triumphal appearances on the streets of Moscow. His heroics during the coup brought him a tidal wave of gratitude and adulation, and he exploited it to the full. While Gorbachev was warning against anti-Communist 'witch-hunts', Yeltsin was celebrating the triumph of democracy and responding to demands for vengeance. 'All those involved in the coup,' he promised, 'will face the full weight of the law. There will be no mercy for any official who supported the coup, or failed to oppose it!' He ordered the sacking of scores of party functionaries and announced that Soviet television, which had broadcast the coup plotters' propaganda, would be purged and brought under his direct control. All Communist cells in the army and KGB would be disbanded, because they had urged cooperation with the putsch; an independent Russian national guard would be created to 'protect Russia against dictatorship'. Yeltsin declared 22 August a national holiday, and announced that the Soviet flag with the Communist hammer and sickle would be replaced by the old Russian tricolour of white, blue and red horizontal bars.

That evening, outside the KGB headquarters on Lubyanka Square, the towering bronze statue of the organisation's hated founder Felix Dzerzhinsky was attacked by crowds wielding hammers and pickaxes. When they failed to topple him, the Moscow mayor Gavriil Popov sent a professional wrecking crew to tie a hawser around his neck and drag him to the ground. The Lubyanka itself, the symbol of decades of repression, torture and murder, had its windows smashed and walls daubed with graffiti. The momentum of anti-Communist rage was reaching the same high tide that had swept away the regimes of Eastern Europe.

The end of the week brought the political showdown that would determine the country's future. On the afternoon of Friday 23 August, Yeltsin invited Gorbachev to appear before a plenary session of the Russian parliament. It was a trap: Yeltsin had his long-time rival on the ropes and he humiliated the Soviet leader in a confrontation seen live on national television. When Gorbachev repeated his stubborn defence of the CPSU, Yeltsin strolled across the stage and thrust a sheaf of papers under his nose. 'You should read what is contained in these documents, Mikhail Sergeevich,' he said brusquely. A nonplussed Gorbachev looked at the papers and saw they were the minutes of a cabinet meeting held on the first day of the coup. They showed that every member of the government, all of them Gorbachev appointees, had supported the demands of the coup plotters. Gorbachev was mortified. 'Having read this,' he said quietly, 'I agree that the entire government must be made to resign; we must choose a new one ...' But still Yeltsin would not let him off the hook. All the disgraced ministers, he said, had been personally appointed by the Soviet president himself: would he now accept that the Communist party as a whole was culpable? Still Gorbachev would not abandon the party. 'No, I cannot agree that the CPSU is a criminal party. It has some reactionaries in it and they must be thrown out. But I will never accept that millions of workers, good Communists, are criminals. I won't!'

Yeltsin moved in for the kill. 'On that note,' he said, looking down at a piece of paper on the table in front of him, 'I am now going to sign a decree banning the Communist Party of the Russian Republic from any further activity in the political life of the country.' Gorbachev tried to protest – 'I am sure the Supreme Soviet will not agree to that,' he stammered, barely audible above the wave of applause that had filled the chamber. 'I think that banning the Russian Communist Party would be a major mistake ...' But it was too late. The idea of banning the Communist Party (albeit just the Russian branch of it, not the CPSU) had been uttered in public; it had been greeted with applause; and, most important of all, it had been heard on television by millions of ordinary people, most of whom welcomed the proposal.

Within hours of the drama at the Russian parliament, Yeltsin's allies were making his decree a reality. Mayor Gavriil Popov ordered militia units to enter party branches throughout Moscow and evict the occupants. The reaction of the Communist officials was incredulous: these were men who had ruled Russia for 70 years, whose right to rule had been enshrined in law as recently as six months ago. Now party offices were confiscated, doors sealed, drawers and safes searched for incriminating documents. At the Central Committee building, where the Moscow party had its headquarters, crowds had gathered to see the hated apparatchiks driven from the premises. Before being allowed to walk out of their own front door, yesterday's rulers were made to open their briefcases and empty their pockets to prove they were not removing any evidence of past misdeeds; then Boris Yeltsin's representatives moved in to occupy their desks.

The next morning, Saturday 24 August, both Yeltsin and Gorbachev attended the funeral of the three young men who had been killed trying to stop the tanks advancing on the Russian White House. Thousands lined the route and Yeltsin made an emotional speech asking forgiveness from the three sets of parents for having been unable to save their sons' lives. It seemed like a moment of spiritual rebirth: a man who had nothing to apologise for was accepting the burden of responsibility, in contrast to the decades of Communist misrule when few could be found to take responsibility for the darkest of crimes.

As Yeltsin was elevated to the role of popular hero, Gorbachev returned to the Kremlin to wrestle with his thoughts. Late on Saturday afternoon, he recorded a short address to be broadcast to the nation. In light of the events of the past week, Gorbachev announced, he felt he could no longer remain as General Secretary of the Soviet Communist Party; he was recommending that the CPSU Central Committee should take the decision to dissolve the party. For Soviet Communism, 74 years of political domination had come undone in a mere six days.

In my study, I have two front pages from the newspaper *Pravda* framed on the wall. The first, from 20 August 1991, carries the announcements of the State Committee declaring the state of emergency, installing military rule, appealing to world governments and the United Nations to recognise their authority. It is topped by the traditional *Pravda* masthead that had graced the paper for decades: '*Pravda*,' it proclaims, 'Organ of the Central Committee of the Communist Party of the Soviet Union; Workers of the world unite!' and – at the side, over a line drawing of the great man's face in profile – 'Founded by V.I. Lenin on 5 May 1912'.

The second is from two days later. Now the masthead announces that this is a 'General Political Newspaper'; the top story carries photographs of a smiling Mikhail Gorbachev and a serious-looking Boris Yeltsin. And in the right-hand corner is one of the great journalistic apologies of all time. 'An Announcement by the Editorial Staff of *Pravda*', it says. 'In recent days, a group of men attempted to carry out an illegal, anti-constitutional *coup d'état* in our country. Like other newspapers, *Pravda* showed a lack of objectivity in its reports [which supported the coup]. We admit frankly that a long history of relying on orders from above about what we print is behind the reasons for this. Much of the blame for the lack of integrity shown by this newspaper lies with the senior editorial team. In the coming days, the editorial team will be replaced.'

In that short time, things had changed irrevocably. In the days following the collapse of the coup, every one of the 15 Soviet republics declared its intention to leave the Union. Gorbachev's last three months in office – if not in power – were a desperate scramble to salvage at least something of the once mighty USSR. In October, he signed an economic cooperation agreement with eight republican leaders, but on 1 December his remaining hopes of keeping the Soviet Empire together were dashed when the people of Ukraine voted overwhelmingly to secede. (As Gorbachev himself admitted, 'There can be no Union without Ukraine.') Without consulting the Soviet president, Boris Yeltsin met Ukrainian and Belorussian leaders near Minsk and agreed that their countries would form a confederation to be known as the Commonwealth of Independent States (CIS). In his communiqué, Yeltsin invited other republics to join the CIS. 'The USSR as a subject of international law, and of geopolitical reality,' he declared, 'has ceased to exist.' Gorbachev argued that Yeltsin's manoeuvrings were illegal, but on 17 December he accepted the inevitable – the state he had fought to preserve and strengthen was no more. In an emotional television address on 25 December, Gorbachev announced the dissolution of the Soviet Union and his resignation as Soviet president. 'I leave my post with trepidation,' he told the millions of viewers. 'But also with hope, with faith in you, in your wisdom and force of spirit. We are the inheritors of a great civilisation, and now the burden falls on each and every one of us that it may be resurrected to a new, modern and worthy life.'

At midnight on 31 December 1991, the Soviet hammer and sickle was taken down from the Kremlin towers and replaced with the Russian flag. Boris Yeltsin was already sitting in Mikhail Gorbachev's old office, ready to guide Russia into his new era of democracy, freedom and liberal market economics. He was Russia's future, but his chance to reshape the country was the result of the actions of his predecessor.

Gorbachev had been – and remained – a committed Communist; he had tried to reform and revivify the party in order to strengthen its position as the wielder of autocratic power; but his plan for limited reforms had unleashed a tidal wave of popular demand for political transformation that had escalated out of his control. As the Russian army general and historian Dmitry Volkogonov wrote, the paradox of Gorbachev's historical role was to be 'an orthodox Communist who, despite his own intentions, emerged as the gravedigger of the Communist system'.

CHAPTER FORTY

Soon after Mikhail Gorbachev made his final televised address on Christmas Day of 1991, President George Bush spoke to the American nation. Bush's Christmas message had none of the sadness and trepidation that permeated Gorbachev's; instead, it had the elation of a baseball coach whose team has just won the World Series:

> Good evening, and Merry Christmas to all Americans across our great country! During these last few months, we have witnessed one of the greatest dramas of the twentieth century – the historic transformation of a totalitarian dictatorship, the Soviet Union, and the liberation of its peoples … For over forty years, the United States has led the West in the struggle against Communism and the threat it posed to our most precious values. This struggle shaped the lives of all Americans … But the confrontation is now over! The nuclear threat is receding. Eastern Europe is free. The Soviet Union itself is no more. This is a victory for democracy and freedom! It is a victory for the moral force of our values! Every American can take pride in this victory, from the millions of men and women who have served our country in uniform to the millions of Americans who supported their country and a strong defence under nine presidents!

It was as if the United States had singlehandedly wiped out autocracy in Russia. The implication was that 'American values' had triumphed, and Russia would henceforth adopt them too. A blinkered confidence that its leaders could simply be instructed in the art of becoming good capitalists 'like us' would be a hallmark of how the West would treat Russia for the next ten years.

Many Russians had heard about the freedoms and prosperity of the West, and they not unnaturally wanted the same. There was a rush to slough off the remaining trappings of Communism to make way for the new capitalist society: a new national anthem was commissioned, a new flag, and old names became new again – Leningrad became St Petersburg, Gorky Street in Moscow reverted to its old name of Tverskaya, Marx Prospekt became Okhotny Ryad, and so on across the country. I attended a bizarre event in Gorky Park, where Moscow's Communist-era statues – all the Lenins and Brezhnevs, and the towering Dzerzhinsky that the crowds had toppled in Lubyanka Square – were dumped unceremoniously on a plot of scrubby grass. The Moscow mayor, Gavriil Popov, declared that this would be an 'open-air museum of social history'. 'One era of history has ended,' he told the crowds. 'Now we must build the new one.'

But the exorcism of Communism from Russian society would not be so easy. The CPSU was far more than just a political party; over the course of 70 years it had virtually become the state. Gorbachev's spokesman, Vitaly Ignatenko spoke of the 'void' its abolition left in the running of the country and in the minds of its citizens.

This was a society whose resources had been allocated and whose needs had been supplied for decades by the party. Everything was done by and through the party. I even remember a poem by a young girl in the Communist youth newspaper. It said, 'Winter has gone; summer has come – thanks be to the party.' It sounds naive and funny today. But in those days we had the party to thank for everything. And all of a sudden to realise that the party is no longer there to tell you how to live your life, how to build your future …

For every Russian who welcomed the prospect of a new society built on democracy and capitalism, there were others – mainly, but not entirely, of the older generation – who pined for the Communist past. Eduard Shevardnadze warned that the Communists would not go easily, that revanchist forces were still active. 'In August 1991 we defeated fools,' he said. 'But now they are finding smarter leaders. The Communists are still strong, and we would be naive to think they have been swept from the historical arena. If we allow ourselves to be divided, they will be stronger than us.'

The collapse of the Soviet Union, 1991

territory controlled by USSR in 1945

Russian Federation from 1991

That lurking sense of the new regime's fragility, of its vulnerability to powerful Communist forces that might at any moment stage a comeback underpinned Boris Yeltsin's efforts to entrench himself in power and the values he represented in the fabric of Russian society. It meant he was happy to listen when Washington offered advice about how to lay the foundations of market democracy in the shortest possible time.

In the months after the collapse of the Soviet Union, much was made of the so-called Washington Consensus: that capitalist economic models had triumphed and were now the only way forward for the world's emerging economies. Learned theoreticians were dispatched to Eastern Europe to preach the gospel of freed prices, reduced government deficits, deregulated trade, export-led growth and integration into the world economy. A team of Western economists led by Harvard University's Jeffrey Sachs had already been at work in Poland with generally encouraging results. Now they came to Moscow, and under their influence Yeltsin committed himself to a programme of 'economic shock therapy'.

The rationale behind the policy was to shift Russia from the stagnation of Communist central planning to an economy where competition and private enterprise would breathe new vigour into the state. The Harvard economists, with the backing of economic liberals in the Russian government, notably the prime minister Yegor Gaidar and the economic guru Anatoly Chubais, convinced Yeltsin that delay would increase the scale of the task, and that the transformation had to be completed before the Communists could regroup and turn back the clock. Only by creating a new business elite and a middle class with a stake in the system could they be sure the Communists would never regain power. The reformers acknowledged that the speed of the change – the biggest and fastest privatisation exercise ever undertaken – would cause short-term pain, but argued that the long-term gain would make it worthwhile.

The pain was not long in coming. In January 1992, the Kremlin announced that prices for all but the most essential goods and services were being freed. After decades of strict state controls backed by billions of roubles of subsidies, the abrupt lifting of the lid sent prices rocketing. In the first month, inflation hit 400 per cent; some people's savings were spent on the purchase of just a few days' worth of food. It was not long before the sight of beggars on the street became commonplace and people were forced to sell possessions to feed their families. In an attempt to balance the national budget, state spending was slashed and taxes raised. When entitlement to free health care was reduced, few could afford the paid services that replaced it. Illnesses and infant mortality increased, along with alcoholism and suicide; by the mid 1990s, male life expectancy had fallen to 57 years.

Yeltsin's popularity, which had been high after his heroism of August 1991, began to slide. The effects of the 'shock therapy' were widely resented and the government did a poor job of explaining why it was needed – that in the last days of Communism the country had been close to bankruptcy; that Russia's national debt was so big that the world was no longer prepared to lend to it; that bitter medicine had to be taken. Much of the opprobrium was directed at Gaidar, Chubais and their team of young economists. Yeltsin's vice-president, Alexander Rutskoi, who had shown such bravery during the siege of the Russian White House, joined the critics, describing the reformers as 'young boys in pink shorts and yellow boots'. Yeltsin viewed the privatisation of state property as a priority, the key to unleashing enterprise and energy, and embedding the values of market democracy. He was determined that state assets should not be sold to foreign buyers; but homegrown investors with enough capital to purchase the colossal state industries he was selling off were rare. So the first attempt at privatisation in late 1992, masterminded by Gaidar and Chubais, was a voucher scheme that aimed to 'give away' Russia's state industries to the people. Every citizen was given a voucher worth 10,000 roubles (approximately $60), each one representing a very small stake in the country's economy. It was a quixotic attempt to create a shareholding middle class overnight. But it failed, because the people who *did* have money, and who had the inside knowledge that the vouchers were the key to untold future wealth – entrepreneurs such as Boris Berezovsky, Roman Abramovich and Mikhail Khodorkovsky – bought up the vouchers by the hundreds of thousands. Every street corner had hawkers with billboards advertising 'Vouchers bought – good prices paid'; the idealism of the operation had evaporated. Even the mathematics seemed perversely illogical. The population of Russia was nearly 150 million, so 150 million vouchers were issued... meaning that the greater part of the Russian economy was apparently being valued at a mere $9 billion. No wonder the future oligarchs were determined to buy it up.

Privatisation left most worse off; a handful became wealthy beyond imagination. Berezovsky would later brazenly boast that Russia's top seven businessmen controlled 50 per cent of Russia's economy. The oligarchs were widely despised by ordinary Russians, who accused them of 'robbing the state of its assets'; and the fact that most of them were Jewish added to the popular anger.

The Yeltsin era, begun with such high hopes, was turning sour. Food production in 1992 dropped by 9 per cent; industrial production was down by 18 per cent. The majority of Russians were experiencing their worst living conditions since the Second World War. Wages went unpaid and inflation ran out of control; homelessness and poverty rose to unprecedented levels. Vice-President Alexander Rutskoi, who had become the leading voice of opposition to Yeltsin, described his policies as 'economic genocide'. But a small minority were accumulating fabulous levels of wealth. The *novye Russkie* – 'new Russians' – in their Gucci and Prada, with their bodyguards, blacked-out Mercedes and Rolls-Royces, stood out on the poverty-stricken streets of Moscow, a tacit indictment of the new liberalism. With vast wealth up for grabs, gangsterism, corruption and violence flourished.

If economic liberalisation was failing to deliver, the other promise of the new era – democratisation – was also in trouble. The naked exploitation of Yeltsin's privatisation scheme had placed vast financial power in the hands of the oligarchs, and it was not long before they began to aspire to political power too. Several of them demanded and were given government posts. Boris Berezovsky became an intimate of the Kremlin, directing policy decisions from the shadows, reputedly the power behind Yeltsin's throne. A plutocratic new order was emerging in which business and political elites were closely intertwined. It would mutate into a Faustian bargain, with each side believing it had a hold over the other.

The years from 1991 were one of Russia's 'moments of destiny', when she threw off the shackles of autocracy and experimented with the values of liberal democracy. But after their initial enthusiasm, people were becoming disenchanted. The economy was crumbling, Russia had lost its superpower status and ethnic violence was brewing in the national enclaves within the Russian Federation. Yeltsin seemed to have no answer. When opposition to his policies reached boiling point in late 1992, he demanded to extend his right to issue presidential decrees, bypassing the scrutiny of parliament and allowing him to rule as a virtual dictator. The prophet of democracy was reaching for the methods of the autocratic system he had fought to overthrow. The irony did not pass unremarked; the ingrained tradition of autocratic rule was not an easy one to throw off.

But the Russian parliament, the Congress of People's Deputies, and its standing legislature, the Supreme Soviet, refused to extend Yeltsin's powers and refused to reappoint Yegor Gaidar as prime minister. Both refusals were a protest against the economic policies that had brought the country so much suffering with little sign of long-term reward. Yeltsin called a national referendum, asking the Russian people to choose between him and the parliament, between further economic liberalisation and a return to the old ways of doing things. When the referendum was held in April 1993, its questions were phrased in such a way that the alternative to Yeltsin's policies seemed to entail certain disaster. He won the backing of most voters; but the parliamentarians, under the leadership of Rutskoi and the chairman of the Supreme Soviet, Ruslan Khasbulatov, continued to block his reforms. Yeltsin threatened to disband the parliament. The stand-off between president and legislature was paralysing the workings of government. The newspaper *Izvestiya* commented acidly, 'The president issues decrees as if there were no Supreme Soviet, while the Supreme Soviet suspends decrees as if there were no president.' In late September, Yeltsin announced he was suspending negotiations on a new constitution, calling another referendum and dissolving the Supreme Soviet. Parliament responded by impeaching him and declaring that Alexander Rutskoi was now the president. Dual power was back, and Russia's future hung in the balance.

By early October, demonstrators were marching in support of the parliamentarians, wooed by their promises to halt the economic reforms, restore state controls and stabilise prices. Armed clashes broke out on the streets of Moscow; the police and army split between those loyal to the president and those supporting the rebels. A vicious battle was fought for control of the Russian Television headquarters at Ostankino, in which 62 people were killed.*

By now the parliamentarians had fortified the parliament building, the same Russian White House that Yeltsin had successfully defended against the hardline Communists in August 1991, and were appealing for Muscovites to come to their aid. In 1991, Yeltsin had been protected by 50,000 civilians, but significantly fewer turned out to help Rutskoi and Khasbulatov. In 1991, the hardliners had hesitated to attack the White House, but Yeltsin had no such scruples. In the early hours of 4 October 1993, tanks of the Russian army launched a sustained bombardment of the building and by mid morning the upper storeys were on fire. At midday, elite soldiers of the Vympel and Alpha Spetsnaz units entered the parliament and began to clear it floor by floor. Hundreds of heavily armed rebels were inside, but they were no match for the troops. Within hours, the dead were laid out in the corridors and the besieged parliamentarians were debating their next move with increasing desperation inside the barricaded assembly chamber. When they emerged in late afternoon waving white flags, over 200 people were dead and many more wounded. It had been the worst violence on the streets of Moscow since 1917.

Boris Yeltsin denounced the rebellion of the parliamentarians as a plot 'hatched by Communist revanchists, fascists and former deputies acting in the name of the Soviets'. 'The organisers are criminals and bandits,' he announced, 'a petty band of politicians recruiting mercenaries who are used to violence and murder, attempting by armed force to impose their will on the whole country … The men who wave red flags have once again stained Russia with blood.' But the rebel parliamentarians were neither revanchists nor fascists. They were not the Communist dinosaurs who led the August 1991 coup. These were politicians who opposed the liberal reforms Yeltsin

---

* The dead included the freelance television cameraman Rory Peck, who had previously been working for the BBC.

was introducing in Russia, and whose views, expressed in a democratic parliamentary forum, had been ignored. Boris Yeltsin may have championed freedom and democracy, but he had stooped to coercion to impose them; he may have fought against the old autocracy, but he was now using its methods. The Russian White House, the building that in 1991 had been the symbol of Russian democracy – Yevtushenko's 'white swan' – had been blown to pieces.

In the aftermath of the October events, Rutskoi and Khasbulatov were sent to jail. Yeltsin pushed through his plans for a new constitution and instituted a bicameral legislature to be known as the State Duma and the Federation Council. Its powers were significantly weaker than those of the old parliament: the president retained the right to rule by decree, to appoint the prime minister and to dissolve the Duma; he could no longer be impeached and he had the right to veto the parliament's legislation by a simple majority in the lower house. Concentrating so much power in the hands of the president, and the neutering of parliament, left Russia with only a truncated version of the democracy Boris Yeltsin had once advocated. Like Catherine the Great, he had found that democratic ideals are all very well, until they necessitate the sharing of power. The experiment with Western-style liberal values was being watered down, and worse was to follow.

Elections to the new Duma in December 1993 saw Yeltsin and Gaidar's party beaten into third place by the ultra-nationalist, anti-Western 'Liberal Democratic' Party of Vladimir Zhirinovsky, a populist rabble-rouser who pledged to send the Russian army marching through Afghanistan and Persia until its men could 'wash their boots in the Indian Ocean'. Two years later, in the 1995 Duma elections, the big winner was the reconstituted and resurgent Communist Party, in a landslide that said much about the people's disenchantment with the government and the president. The combination of the irresponsible, Western-sponsored 'shock therapy' and Boris Yeltsin's disastrous management of the economy had resulted in an onerous budget deficit. The state was collecting only a fraction of the taxes it needed to remain solvent; schoolteachers, civil servants and police were going unpaid; pensioners were not getting their pensions; industry was grinding to a halt.

At a nuclear submarine base in the northwestern port of Murmansk, the navy found its electricity cut off after failing to pay six months' fuel bills, leaving the vessels' reactors in imminent danger of meltdown. Russia was in chaos. To make things worse, presidential elections were due the following year, and the Communists, under their new leader Gennady Zyuganov, were threatening to make a sensational return to power – this time via the ballot box.

Yeltsin and his allies panicked. They needed a massive injection of cash to keep the economy going if their election campaign were to have any chance of success; and they needed the oligarchs, who by now controlled much of the country's media, to come to their aid in beating off the Communist challenge. For the oligarchs, too, the prospect of a Communist victory, with the promised horrors of re-nationalisation, corruption trials and political revenge, was not a happy one. Two leading oligarchs, Vladimir Potanin and Mikhail Khodorkovsky, proposed that Russia's tycoons would lend the president the equivalent of $1.8 billion. It would allow the Kremlin to reduce the backlog of salaries and pensions and to offer a few economic sweeteners to the electorate. The oligarchs would also undertake to swing the media behind the Yeltsin campaign. But Potanin and Khodorkovsky wanted much in return. As surety for their money, they would require the government to put up the deeds to Russia's remaining state industries, including the key sectors of iron, steel, gas and oil. The scheme would become known as 'loans for shares', and since there was very little chance of the bankrupt government ever repaying the loans, it was always clear that the oligarchs would get their hands on the key prizes of the Russian economy. But first they would have to use their money and influence to get Yeltsin re-elected: if the Communists came back, so would the old order. There would be no more private property, no more oligarchs and no more Yeltsin.

The infusion of cash and the blanket support of the media helped Yeltsin surge from disastrous poll numbers to beat the Communist Zyuganov in the second round of elections in July 1996. The oligarchs then claimed their prize. In September, the state organised a series of very unusual auctions for the nationalised firms that had been offered to the oligarchs as collateral for their loans. In each case, the only bidder for the assets in question was the oligarch who had made the loan to Yeltsin before the election. Potanin picked up the country's leading nickel and aluminium company for kopecks; Berezovsky, with his partner and protégé Roman Abramovich, got the Sibneft oil company; and Khodorkovsky got a majority stake in the massive Yukos oil conglomerate, then Russia's second largest producer, for the knockdown price of $309 million.

His pact with the oligarchs discredited Yeltsin. Corruption allegations surrounding his advisers and his family began to take their toll. He appeared as a politician who acted on impulse, whose behaviour – like that of Nikita Khrushchev – was unpredictable. The CIA's assessment that he was 'flaky' seemed to be borne out: as with Lech Walesa in Poland, Yeltsin had been the man for the dramatic moment, but was decidedly unsuited to the long haul of day-to-day politics. A long history of heavy drinking had resulted in embarrassing moments, including an alcohol-fuelled attempt to conduct a military band on a visit to Germany, a tottering performance at a press conference with world leaders, and a speech in which he read the same passage three times before being halted by his aides. (When I spoke to him before the 1996 presidential election, his face was puffy, he slurred his words and seemed uncertain of what he had and had not promised the electorate; immediately afterwards he disappeared from public view.)

Rumours that Yeltsin was seriously ill were strenuously denied by the Kremlin, but for the first weeks of the 1996 presidential campaign the president was absent from the scene. Then suddenly he was back, appearing at an election concert in his native Sverdlovsk, where he jumped up on stage to dance the rumba with a manic energy and an impressive sense of rhythm. It was only years later that we discovered the truth: Yeltsin had suffered a serious heart attack, one of several that would strike him in the next four years, and had been advised by his doctors to take a lengthy break from politics; but at the insistence of his election team he had been given adrenalin injections that shot him back into action. The long-term effects of such treatment were potentially disastrous, and for the rest of his time in office it was never clear how much he was in charge of events and how much he was being manipulated by the powerful 'advisers' he had acquired from the ranks of the oligarchs.

Yeltsin's commitment to liberal democracy had been undermined by the deterioration in the economic and political climate, and his previously stated support for the freedom of Russia's national minorities was also coming under strain. His advice to the nationalities to 'take as much sovereignty as you can swallow' had come back to haunt him; ethnic unrest had been growing since 1991, as different national regions attempted to take him at his word. Chechnya had elected a new president, the former Soviet air force general Dzhokhar Dudayev, who declared independence from Moscow; subsequent discrimination against Russians living in the republic had led to violent clashes. For three years, Yeltsin avoided the use of force, engaging in proxy negotiations with the separatists, but in December 1994 Chechnya was close to civil war. The Kremlin announced that the Russian army was being deployed to 'restore order'. The defence minister, Pavel Grachev, boasted that the fighting would be over in days, if not hours, but his ground forces suffered a series of embarrassing setbacks. As casualties mounted and Russian conscript prisoners were reportedly tortured and executed by their captors, Moscow retaliated with a campaign of carpet bombing, the heaviest of its kind since the allied destruction of Dresden in the Second World War. By the time Russian troops captured the Chechen capital a month later, little of the city was still standing; the presidential palace was in ruins and tens of thousands of civilians had been killed.

Russia had learned from centuries of experience that subduing the mountainous territories of the north Caucasus is not an easy task, and sporadic fighting continued for much of the next two years. The mullahs proclaimed Chechen resistance a *jihad* – a holy war with heavenly rewards for those who fell in it – and Islamic fighters from the Middle East flooded in. Guerrilla forces continued to harry Moscow's army, inflicting heavy casualties. Atrocities were widespread on both sides; prisoners could expect little mercy, and civilians suffered almost as much as the troops. Chechen detachments would regularly take hostages, most spectacularly when they seized a hospital at Budyonnovsk in southern Russia in June 1995. Dudayev was assassinated by a Russian guided missile in April 1996, but fighting continued until August when a ceasefire was signed. The First Chechen War (1994–6) would result in the deaths of 100,000 Chechens, mostly civilians, and between 5,000 and 10,000 Russian soldiers. Yeltsin's image as a democrat was in tatters; the viability of liberal government as a means of ruling Russia was looking distinctly questionable.

For most of the 1990s it seemed to be in the interest of the West to support Russia's experiment with democracy. It had, after all, brought an end to the Cold War, halted the ruinously expensive arms race and transformed Moscow from a feared opponent to a willing ally. Decades of Western demands for an end to totalitarian rule and political repression had been answered; Yeltsin's bold reforms had been praised by Washington and London, so now that he was in trouble there was an expectation that the West would help shore up his fortunes. But George Bush's Christmas message of 1991, and similar declarations by other leaders, had promised an end to worry about Russia, not an expensive campaign to support its government, however pro-Western it might be.

Russia had been accepted as a member of the G7, now G8, and the International Monetary Fund (IMF) had granted it an economic stimulus package worth around $10 billion. But further aid was slow to come. As early as October 1992, Yeltsin had begun to express Moscow's frustration at the lack of Western support. 'Russia is not a country that can be kept waiting in the ante-room,' he said, as the Kremlin expressed a desire for quick integration into the Western system. At various times, Yeltsin suggested that Russia could become a member of the European Union, the World Trade Organisation and even of NATO. But all his suggestions were rebuffed. NATO continued its expansion into the former Soviet satellites in Eastern Europe, signing up Poland, Hungary and the Czech Republic while leaving Russia with little more than a cooperation agreement. Moscow became alarmed at suggestions that former Soviet republics, including Ukraine, Georgia and the Baltic states, might also be recruited.

By the end of the 1990s, relations were frosty. Yeltsin denounced NATO's intervention in Serbia and Kosovo without a UN mandate; and Bill Clinton responded by attacking the Kremlin's renewed military activity in Chechnya. At a meeting of the Organisation for Security and Cooperation in Europe, President Clinton jabbed his finger at the Russian president and demanded he halt the bombing of Grozny; Yeltsin stormed out of the conference. Shortly afterwards he gave vent to his frustration. 'Yesterday,' he said, 'President Clinton sought to put pressure on Russia. He forgot for a moment, for a second, that Russia has a full arsenal of nuclear weapons. He has forgotten about that.' It was an echo of the disquieting rhetoric of Khrushchev and Kennedy.

The world economic crisis of 1998 cast harsh light on Russia's economic imbalance. The collapse in the price of oil, gas, metals and timber meant Moscow could no longer rely on the unbridled export of natural resources to finance its escalating budget deficit. In August, the Kremlin announced that it was devaluing the rouble and suspending the repayment of its foreign debts. The financial markets, panicked at the prospect of a Russian default, sent share prices tumbling. By the end of the year, thousands of people had lost their life savings as a series of banks collapsed; hundreds of firms and businesses went under; inflation hit 88 per cent and shops were again left with empty shelves. Demonstrators took to the streets of Moscow and other big cities, demanding an end to the liberal economic reforms. Yeltsin responded by firing his prime minister and the government. He announced that the reforms were being suspended, and Russia's experiment with Western-style liberal democracy ground to a halt.

In August 1999, with no sign of the crisis abating, Yeltsin appointed yet another new prime minister. He was a little-known bureaucrat named Vladimir Putin, who had been installed the previous year as head of the FSB, the successor to the KGB. Few expected him to last long in the job. But he brought a new ruthlessness to the Kremlin, a bullyboy swagger on the continuing unrest in Chechnya, and – behind his professions of support for Yeltsin's reforms – a belief that Russia needed strength and stability more than it needed democracy.

For most of the 1990s the Kremlin had loosened the reins of autocratic power, allowing political participation and economic freedom. The Yeltsin years had raised the prospect that Russia might turn away from her 'Asiatic' past and join the camp of 'European' nations. But it had come to nothing. On New Year's Eve 1999, Boris Yeltsin welcomed the new millennium with a dramatic speech on television. The old, sick president announced that he was stepping down six months early.

'Dear friends, my dears,' he began. 'Today I am offering you New Year greetings for the last time. Today, on the last day of the outgoing century, I am retiring.' Yeltsin's speech was emotional; at times he gasped to catch his breath. And though he spoke of hope for the future, his overriding message was one of failure – the failure of the experiment he had embarked upon in the heady days of August 1991, when it appeared that Russia was throwing off her thousand-year mantle of autocracy and embarking on a new course of freedom and democracy. 'Today, on this incredibly important day for me,' he said, 'I want to ask you for forgiveness. I ask your forgiveness because many of the hopes we had have not come true; because what we thought would be easy turned out to be terribly difficult. I ask you to forgive me for not fulfilling the hopes of those who believed we could jump from the grey, stagnating, totalitarian past into a bright, rich and civilised future. I myself believed we could do this. But it could not be done as simply as that ... and in my heart I have experienced the pain that each of you experienced ... As I go into retirement, I have signed a decree entrusting the duties of President of Russia to Vladimir Vladimirovich Putin ...'

A bloated old man squinting at the autocue, his speech slurred and his eyelids drooping: it was a sorry epitaph for twentieth-century Russia's last great 'moment of destiny'. Reform was once more giving way to the resurgent tradition of autocracy.

CHAPTER FORTY-ONE

Television showed the handover: a low-key, gauche little ceremony, in which the old king – already in his gabardine mac and in a hurry to leave the stage – waved the young pretender into his new office, muttering 'This is your desk.' Under the watchful eye of the patriarch of the Russian Church, the nuclear briefcase was handed over and Boris Yeltsin shuffled out to his car, struggling with his fur hat and subsiding into the back seat.

In his New Year message to the nation, Putin asked all Russians to raise their glasses to a 'new era' for their country. 'There will be no power vacuum,' he said, 'and anyone who tries to act outside the constitution will be crushed … the important thing is for the Russian state to be great and independent …' The tone was new, harsh where Yeltsin had been avuncular; Russians already understood their acting president was a hard man.

Vladimir Vladimirovich Putin was born in Leningrad in 1952. His grandfather had been Stalin's cook, his father was decorated for bravery during the Great Patriotic War, and his mother had terrible memories of suffering during the German blockade of Leningrad. Putin says he was raised in a cramped communal apartment where he had to fight off the rats. After a youthful dalliance with delinquency ('I was a hooligan, not a Pioneer') he decided he would devote his life to the defence of the motherland. At the age of 16, he walked into the Leningrad KGB headquarters and announced he was ready for service. In a brief autobiography that was distributed during the 2000 presidential elections, Putin claimed his decision was based on his passion for martial arts, which had taught him the need for discipline and hard work, and on his love of a popular TV drama series, *The Sword and the Shield*, in which brave KGB men risked their lives to protect the Soviet Union against the Nazis. Unfortunately for Putin, the KGB told him he was too young; he should go to university and wait for their call. He completed his law studies and the KGB took him on in 1975, but his career was far from stellar. His only foreign posting was to the less than glamorous KGB station in Dresden, East Germany. He was there when the Berlin wall fell in 1989, burning sensitive documents until the incinerator broke. The humiliation soured his view of Soviet Communism and convinced him that Russia must be made strong again. He left the KGB in 1991, but the values he had learned remained with him. 'A KGB officer never resigns,' he would say later. 'You can join but you can never leave.'

In the economic and political uncertainty of the 1990s, Putin worked for the mayor of St Petersburg, gaining a reputation as someone who could get things done. It persuaded Yeltsin to appoint him head of the FSB in 1998, and prime minister in 1999. Most of the previous incumbents had not lasted more than a few months, and Putin was determined to make an impression. A series of bombings in September 1999 that killed hundreds of people in apartment blocks in Moscow and southern Russia gave him his chance.

The Kremlin immediately attributed the apartment bombings to Chechen terrorists. Yeltsin's war in Chechnya between 1994 and 1996 had not crushed the republic's drive for independence; nor had it stamped out the region's endemic lawlessness. Money promised for the rebuilding of Grozny had been siphoned off by corrupt officials and organised crime groups; thousands of kidnappings had made Chechnya a centre of extortion and murder. Russians regarded it as the source of violent criminality.

On 17 September, Putin convened an emergency session of the Federation Council. He proposed decisive action to 'protect Russia', including a defensive cordon along the Chechen border and aerial bombardments of Chechen territory. He appeared on television to announce that 'action of the most uncompromising character' would be taken to deal with 'bandit bases' in Chechnya. 'The bandits must be exterminated,' he said. 'No other action is possible here.' No suspects had been arrested for the apartment bombs, and the Chechen guerrilla groups, who usually claimed responsibility for their actions, remained silent. But Putin's certainty that the Chechens were to blame impressed the electorate: his poll ratings, which had been languishing at 2 per cent, rose in step with the harshness of his rhetoric. In carefully rehearsed remarks that sounded like a parody of

Winston Churchill's 'fight them on the beaches' speech of 1940, Putin pledged to 'pursue the terrorists wherever they go; if they are at the airports, we will strike them there; and if – pardon my language – we catch up with them when they are sitting on the toilet, we will wipe them out in the lavatories. That's all there is to it; the problem is over.'

On 4 October 1999, the Russian army launched its second invasion of Chechnya. By December, Grozny was besieged, the separatists were on the defensive and there had been no more apartment bombs. Putin's ratings soared to over 60 per cent, and when presidential elections were held in March 2000 he won a handsome victory. Voters saw him as the antithesis of the shambling, alcoholic Yeltsin, a young, tough teetotaller and a firm hand to restore order after the chaos of Russia's failed liberal experiment.

Putin's trump card had been the vigorous prosecution of the Chechen War. But some in the Russian media were asking if the apartment bombings that sparked the renewed conflict had been just a little *too* convenient. When a journalist from the investigative newspaper *Novaya Gazeta* tackled Putin directly, asking if the apartments were deliberately blown up to justify the invasion, his response was emphatic: 'What! You're saying we blew up our own apartment blocks?' Putin shot back. 'Nonsense! Total rubbish! There's no one in the secret services who would commit such a crime. The suggestion is offensive; it's a slur against us.'

But the charges would not go away. It emerged that three FSB men had been intercepted planting explosives in another apartment block, this time in Ryazan, southeast of Moscow. The neighbourhood had been evacuated and 30,000 people spent the night in the open air. After being confronted with the Ryazan discovery, FSB director Nikolai Patrushev stated that the bomb was a dummy, part of a 'test' by the security forces, and he congratulated the residents on their vigilance in exposing the 'exercise'. But the Kremlin's claims were ridiculed by its political opponents, including a former security agent, Alexander Litvinenko. 'The FSB intended to blow up residential buildings in Ryazan, Tula, Pskov and Samara,' Litvinenko alleged. 'It was important for the FSB to drag Russia into a war in Chechnya as quickly as possible so that the presidential elections could be held against the background of a major armed conflict. It was a conspiracy with the goal of allowing the former KGB to seize power … and the FSB succeeded in getting its own candidate elected president. Putin is perfectly described by the definition of a "tyrant" given by *The Great Soviet Encyclopaedia*: "a ruler whose power is founded on arbitrary decision and violence". Litvinenko was the most strident of the conspiracy theorists and his accusations earned him the new president's undying hatred.

Putin boasted that he had grown up with a picture of Felix Dzerzhinsky on his bedroom wall and that he never forgot his roots in the KGB. At a gathering of FSB officers to celebrate his rise to power, he joked that 'the agent group charged with taking the government under its control has achieved the first step of its assignment'.

A vision of what Putin believed that 'assignment' to be came in a document he wrote in 2000. 'Russia at the Turn of the Millennium' made clear that he believed liberal democracy had failed in Russia and that the country needed strong state rule to prosper. 'Russia cannot become a version of, say, the US or Britain,' he wrote, 'where liberal values have deep historic traditions. Our state and its institutions and structures have always played an exceptionally important role in the life of the country and its people. For Russians, a strong state is not an anomaly to be got rid of. Quite the contrary, it is the source of order …'

The message was clear: the Yeltsin years had been an unwelcome aberration and the experiment with Western-style government, like all those before it, was proof of Russia's unsuitability to such a system; Russia needed a powerful state to impose order on a nation that had shown how unruly it could be when the restraints of autocracy were lifted. Putin's words could have been those of Konstantin Pobedonostsev, or the early Slavs appealing to Rurik the Viking to rule over them. But he added an important caveat, that 'modern Russia does not identify a strong and effective state with a totalitarian state'. Russia might be returning to its underlying tradition of autocratic rule, but it did not need to return to the horrors of the past.

Putin's immediate aims were to rescue the nation from the economic meltdown of the Yeltsin years; to restore order in society, halt the violence and crime on the streets and return Russia to her former standing as a world power. (Where Boris Yeltsin viewed the end of the Soviet Empire as his life's great achievement, Putin described the demise of the USSR as 'the biggest geo-political tragedy of the century'.) He would achieve all those goals and win the gratitude of the vast majority of Russian people. But Putin's critics complained that his successes came at the expense of democracy. During his time in office, the powers of parliament would be weakened and those of the president enhanced; the leaders of Russia's 89 federal regions would no longer be elected, but appointed by the Kremlin. National elections to the Duma and for the presidency would still be held, but opposition parties would suffer discrimination, harassment and exclusion from the media; political rallies would be broken up and protestors jailed. Freedom of the press would be restricted. Television news would be controlled by the Kremlin.

The description Putin adopted for his style of government was 'managed democracy'. Critics like Lilia Shevtsova of the Moscow Carnegie Institute had a different description: 'Our country is building an *imitation* democracy,' she wrote.

> The external wrappings of democracy are present: elections, parliament and so on, but the essence is absolutely different. In the Russian case, we are dealing with ... the deliberate use of democratic institutions as Potemkin villages [see p. 99] in order to conceal traditional power arrangements ... The political regime that has consolidated itself resembles the 'bureaucratic authoritarianism' of Latin American regimes in the 1960s and 1970s. It has all the characteristics: personalised power, bureaucratisation of society, political exclusion of the populace ... and an active role for the secret services (in Latin America it was the military).

Putin himself was ambivalent about such descriptions. He continued to describe himself as a democrat, but made no secret of his belief that only a strong state could return Russia to its lost greatness. If some civil liberties were lost in the process, that was a price to be paid. 'Russia is in the midst of one of the most difficult periods in its history,' he wrote.

For the first time in the past two or three hundred years, it is facing the real danger of sliding to the second, if not third, echelon of world states. We are running out of time to avoid this. We must strain all intellectual, physical and moral forces of the nation. We need coordinated, creative work. Nobody will do it for us. Everything depends on us and us alone – on our ability to see the size of the threat, to consolidate all our forces, and to set our minds to prolonged and difficult work.

By the time of his 2001 New Year message, he was able to point to the first successes of the new 'statist' policies. 'There have been hard times and hard decisions,' he said, 'but something that seemed impossible just a year ago has happened: now there are signs of stability in our country, in politics and in the economy, and that is an invaluable thing. We have learned to respect the dignity and value of our country ...'

Putin's international swagger met with the approval of patriotic Russians, pleased to have a strong leader after a decade of economic and military weakness. He revived many of the trappings of the Soviet era, including the old Soviet national anthem (albeit with new words), and the military parades through Red Square, with convoys of missiles, tanks and marching regiments shouting 'Ourah!' to their president. Putin's picture was hung in schoolrooms and public buildings; and he acquired a taste for pomp and ceremony, making regal entrances along red carpets with trumpets blaring. He reacted angrily to media criticism. When a popular TV satire show – the equivalent of the British *Spitting Image* – portrayed him as a rat, Putin banned it.

His personality cult did not attain the dimensions of Stalin's, but he was happy to appear in military uniform at army and naval bases, co-piloting a fighter plane or standing beside a tank. An official photo shoot of the president naked from the waist up, fishing in a sunlit river and riding a horse across mountainous terrain, elicited a gasp of excitement from female voters and, perhaps unintentionally, from Russia's gay websites. One newspaper, *Komsomolskaya Pravda*, splashed the photos on its front page under the headline 'Be Like Putin!' and a pop song titled 'Putin Is a Man of Strength' shot up the charts. A fanzine even called for Petersburg to be renamed Putinburg.

Putin's image as a 'strong tsar' helped him survive public relations disasters that would have undermined other leaders. In the summer of 2000, he was on holiday in the southern resort of Sochi when the *Kursk* nuclear submarine sank in the Barents Sea with 118 sailors on board. The British and Norwegian navies offered to stage a rescue mission but were turned down, most probably because Moscow did not want Western countries to gain access to the submarine's nuclear technology. For five days, Putin remained on holiday and made no public comment; when the vessel was finally lifted, all its crew were dead. The Russian media, privatised under Boris Yeltsin and enjoying a rare period of independence, criticised Putin for putting political interests before men's lives. When the mother of a young sailor tried to speak out about her son's death at a televised briefing, an official forcibly injected her with a hypodermic syringe, causing her to lose consciousness. Footage of the incident was shown around the world; Putin was accused of intolerance and repression.

The *Kursk* debacle prompted a crackdown on the Russian media. The most vocal critic of the Kremlin's handling of the tragedy had been a television channel owned by the oligarch Vladimir Gusinsky. Putin had seen how adverse coverage of the First Chechen War had damaged Boris Yeltsin and was determined to stop it happening again. Gusinsky was put under pressure to hand over his media interests to the state, then arrested and held in jail until he signed on the dotted line. Shortly afterwards, he emigrated to Israel.

Putin's willingness to take on the oligarchs also boosted his approval ratings. The tycoons who had gained control of Russia's industry and were perceived to be exerting covert influence over the government were despised by the majority of Russians. So when Putin announced, in a deliberate echo of Stalin's threat against the *kulaks*, that he intended to 'liquidate the oligarchs as a class', he was widely applauded. At first he had had to move cautiously: the leading oligarchs had helped to fund his election campaign, and Boris Berezovsky had acted as the main sponsor of his political party, Yedinstvo (United Russia). Berezovsky expected to become Putin's grey cardinal, the power behind the throne, just as he had been for Yeltsin; the others expected gratitude and respect for their support during the elections. Their expectations were to be dashed.

In July 2000, Putin called the leading oligarchs into the Kremlin to explain the rules of the game under which they would be expected to operate. He said he would not interfere with their business activities and would not reverse the privatisation process that had made them all rich, as long as they agreed to stay out of politics. They must not fund political parties; they must not seek personal political power; and, above all, they must not challenge or criticise the president.

The reaction of some of the oligarchs was scathing. Berezovsky felt personally insulted by the upstart Putin, whom he claimed to have brought to power, and pledged himself to enduring opposition. In 2001, he followed Gusinsky into exile and set up camp in London, from where he continued to rail at the master of the Kremlin. Roman Abramovich agreed to Putin's terms, remaining *persona grata* in Moscow while buying respectability in the UK by running a middle-ranking football team. The biggest thorn in Putin's side, however, the one man who thought he could take on the president and win, was Mikhail Khodorkovsky.

In the years after he acquired the Yukos Oil Company in Boris Yeltsin's rigged privatisations of 1996, Khodorkovsky had built it into the most powerful player in the Russian oil sector and one of the biggest in the world. He deployed his fabulous wealth to finance several parties in the Russian parliament and spoke openly of using them to lever himself into the Kremlin. He angered Putin by inviting the Americans – now regarded as global rivals, even enemies – to buy into Yukos's oil. And he began preparations to run for the Russian presidency. In a bitter showdown in Putin's offices, the two men traded insults, angrily accusing each other of corruption.

Putin knew that crushing Khodorkovsky and confiscating Yukos would make him the bogeyman of liberals and the West; it would make him look a capricious tyrant and scare away investors. But he also knew that oil was the key to the country's future. In October 2003, he dispatched machine gun-carrying troops to intercept Khodorkovsky's plane on the runway of a Siberian airfield. The richest man in Russia was hauled back to Moscow in handcuffs and a black canvas hood over his head. The Kremlin used bogus tax charges to bankrupt Yukos and seize its assets for the state, and Khodorkovsky himself was sentenced to eight years in a labour camp. The aim was to keep him out of politics and out of Putin's way.

The abuse of the judicial system brought much criticism from the West and from Russia's liberal opposition. But in purely pragmatic terms, Putin needed to reclaim Russia's oil resources for the state. Rocketing energy prices did much to bolster his authority: Russia's economy went from basket case to cash cow; Moscow could again punch its weight on the international stage and resume its seat at the world's top table.

The Yukos confrontation had important political consequences. When Putin first came to power, he had inherited Boris Yeltsin's team of ministers and officials. They were overwhelmingly reformers. Putin's own first government, led by the pro-Western prime minister Mikhail Kasyanov, had had the same liberal character. But soon Putin began to fill the Kremlin with his own people, allies who had worked with him in St Petersburg, and many of them were former KGB men. Headed by the presidential aides Viktor Ivanov and Igor Sechin and the new defence minister Sergei Ivanov, they formed a powerful clique known as the Siloviki or 'strongmen'.* They soon came into conflict with the Kremlin liberals.

The Siloviki were first and foremost 'statists' – they regarded the national interest as the main, perhaps the only, guiding principle for policy-making. They believed Yeltsin's privatisation programme had been a disaster for Russia, and they had an inborn hatred for the oligarchs who had profited from his 'sale of the century'. Putin put his friend Igor Sechin in charge of sorting out the oil barons. He was appointed to the board of the state oil company, Rosneft, with the brief of bringing the nation's supplies back under state control.

The Kremlin liberals, led by Kasyanov, continued to fight for a free market and economic integration with the West; they argued that wealthy business-men were a natural part of a properly functioning economy. But by 2003 their opponents had the upper hand. The decision to crush Khodorkovsky was taken by Sechin and Putin together, and it sealed the triumph of the Siloviki. From now on, strategic industries would be controlled by the government

---

* By 2002, former KGB and FSB agents were estimated to occupy more than half the positions in the higher echelons of the federal structure.

and used to challenge the West rather than cosy up to it. Putin's mission to 'make Russia great' led to a new toughness in international relations: Moscow's rhetoric became more strident and Russia's neighbours were held to ransom by cutting off – or threatening to cut off – oil and gas supplies.

The public applauded the Yukos arrests; the remaining Kremlin liberals, including Kasyanov, resigned in protest. In the years following the Yukos affair, the Kremlin became noticeably tougher in its attitude towards domestic opposition – the fate of Mikhail Khodorkovsky deterred prominent individuals from entering the political arena, and ordinary citizens who tried to protest or organise found themselves on the wrong end of police batons.

Putin's invasion of Chechnya in 1999 had drawn Russia into another long and brutal war. Russian missiles had again reduced Grozny to rubble, killing men, women and children. Hundreds of thousands of civilians fled to neighbouring Ingushetia; those who remained were deemed to be terrorists. Arkady Babchenko, a Russian soldier who served in both Chechen wars, told me in 2007 that Chechnya had turned him, and many young men like him, into inhuman agents of death; three years after he left the army, he still could not sleep. In his diaries, which would be published to equal measures of acclaim and abuse, he described the maelstrom of killing his unit discovered in the Chechen capital:

> Fighting rages on in Grozny. No one collects the bodies any more. They lie on the asphalt, on the pavements, between the smashed trees, as if they are part of the city. Armoured personnel carriers rumble over them at high speed; they get tossed around by explosions. Blackened bones are scattered around the burnt-out vehicles … Our whole generation died in Chechnya, a whole generation of Russians. Even those of us who stayed alive, can they really be those same laughing boys who once got sent off to the army? No, we died. We all died in that war.

The hellish conditions fostered despair and corruption. Drunkenness and suffering fostered cynicism. Torture, rape and looting were viewed as normal; few were brought to justice. When one colonel, Yuri Budanov, was charged with the rape and murder of a Chechen teenager, Elza Kungaeva, he claimed she was an enemy sniper. Unusually, his case went to trial, but the outcry from ex-servicemen and right-wing politicians made it a cause célèbre. Budanov's lawyer complained that 'we send our officers into Chechnya to clean a sewer; after they've cleaned it with their bare hands, people have no right to say they smell bad'. Budanov was released before the end of his sentence.

Kidnappings were common on both sides, with the victims being sold back to their families or, if no ransom was forthcoming, tortured and executed. One Russian officer estimated that 20 per cent of 'disappearances' were the work of Chechen guerrillas, 30 per cent criminals and 50 per cent Russian forces. Chechen males taken by the Russians rarely returned alive.

Despite the brutality, there was little public opposition to the war. It seems that the few journalists who tried to report the suffering caused by the Russian military were silenced. Andrei Babitsky, who contradicted Moscow's claim that only guerrillas were being killed in Grozny, was denounced by Putin as a 'traitor to Russia' and 'no longer a Russian journalist'. Anna Politkovskaya, who famously exposed the corruption and violence in Chechnya in her articles for *Novaya Gazeta*, was murdered on Putin's birthday in 2006.*

In response to the Russian occupation, Chechen extremists targeted Russian cities. In 2002, a group of 40 terrorists, including a number of women, took hostage 850 people at the Dubrovka Theatre in Moscow. After two days of fruitless negotiations, Russian Special Forces pumped toxic gas into the theatre and stormed the building. All the terrorists were killed, but 130 hostages also died from the effects of the gas.**

---

* The fate of journalists like Politkovskaya became frighteningly common. The Committee to Protect Journalists says 25 reporters and correspondents were killed in Russia in the decade since Putin came to power. Half of them were nowhere near a war zone. Many more were beaten or threatened.

** The casualties were partly the result of the Russian military's refusal to tell doctors the nature of the gas they used – it was, they claimed, a military secret.

In 2003, Moscow installed Akhmad Kadyrov as its puppet ruler in the republic and gave him carte blanche to impose order. When he was assassinated a year later, his son took over. Ramzan Kadyrov became known for the ferocity with which he crushed opposition to his rule, with allegations of government death squads, torture and murder. According to Movladi Baisarov, one of his former commanders, Kadyrov acted 'like a medieval tyrant. He can do whatever he likes. He can take any woman and do with her as he pleases ... He acts with total impunity. I know of many who were executed on his orders and I know where they are buried ... If anyone tells the truth about his activities, it is like signing your own death warrant.' In November 2006, Baisarov was assassinated in Moscow, less than a mile from the Kremlin.

Kadyrov continued to enjoy Putin's backing. The brutality of his regime was accepted as a necessary evil to ensure Russian security. Kadyrov told a British journalist that his job was to 'protect the whole of Russia so that people in Moscow and St Petersburg can live in peace'. 'Putin is a beauty,' he said. 'He should be made president for life. What we need is strong rule. Democracy is just an American fantasy.'

But Kadyrov could not protect Russia for ever. In 2004, Chechen 'black widows', women whose husbands had been killed by Russian forces, detonated bombs on the Moscow metro, on a train and on two aeroplanes, killing several hundred people. Shortly afterwards, guerrillas seized a school in Beslan, a town in the north Caucasus region of Northern Ossetia. For three days, the terrorists held a thousand pupils and teachers in the school gymnasium, while anxious parents, some of them armed, waited with the Special Forces troops surrounding the building. On the afternoon of 3 September, the Russian army stormed the school, using tanks, rockets and heavy weapons. During the gun battle that ensued, the gymnasium was engulfed by fire. More than 300 hostages, the majority of them children, lost their lives.

Vladimir Putin blamed the local authorities for the Beslan tragedy and called for increased security measures. 'We have shown weakness,' he said, 'and the weak get beaten.' He claimed that a number of the hostage-takers were Arabs, evidence – he said – that Russia was fighting the same war on international terror as the West. It allowed him to give short shrift to Western criticisms of Russian brutality in Chechnya. At a press conference in 2006, when George W. Bush urged Moscow to emulate 'institutional change … like in Iraq, where there's now a free press and free religion', Putin replied dismissively, 'We certainly would not want to have the same kind of democracy they have in Iraq, quite honestly.'

Chechnya, though, remained Putin's biggest challenge. Attacks on Russian civilian targets, including more bombs on the Moscow metro, continued. But Putin ruled out negotiations on autonomy for the region. His efforts to convince the West that his campaign against Chechen 'terrorists' was the moral equivalent of US and British intervention in Afghanistan and Iraq were equally unsuccessful.

Perceived Western interference in the former Soviet republics and satellite states in Eastern Europe – Russia's 'near-abroad' – added to Moscow's grievances. NATO's expansion into the Baltic states in 2004 was swiftly followed by the triumph of US-backed candidates in presidential elections in Ukraine and Georgia. Russia blamed Washington for meddling in its traditional 'sphere of influence'. After a heated debate about the Pentagon's plans to deploy US missile defence systems in Poland and the Czech Republic, Putin told an international security conference in Munich:

> The United States has overstepped its national borders in every way. It imposes economic, political, cultural and educational policies on other nations. Who likes this? Who is happy about this? It is extremely dangerous. It means no one can feel safe. I want to emphasise this – no one feels safe! Because no one can feel that international law will protect them. Such a policy stimulates an arms race.

After the acquiescence of the Yeltsin years, Russia under Putin had regained its former self-confidence. When the pro-American government of Georgia asserted its control of the disputed territories of Abkhazia and South Ossetia in the summer of 2008, the Kremlin sent in the army, pushing deep into Georgia itself and shelling the capital Tbilisi. It responded to Ukraine's 'defection' (to NATO and the West) by ramping up the prices of Russian oil and gas supplies. Ukraine's pro-Western president, Viktor Yushchenko, had been poisoned during the election campaign of 2004, leaving his health weakened and his face badly scarred. There were persistent, if unproven, allegations of Kremlin involvement in the affair, and a growing belief that Moscow was returning to the Soviet practice of eliminating its enemies abroad.

In November 2006, Alexander Litvinenko was murdered in London. After his accusations that Putin had staged the 1999 Moscow apartment bombs, Litvinenko had fled to the UK, where he was initially employed by the exiled oligarch Boris Berezovsky. Both men continued to denounce Putin in the most ferocious terms, and broadcast calls for a revolution on an independent Russian radio station. A British police inquiry established that Litvinenko had been killed by ingesting liquid polonium, and radioactive traces of the element were found in London locations visited by two former FSB agents, Andrei Lugovoy and Dmitry Kovtun. When Scotland Yard issued an extradition warrant for Lugovoy, Moscow refused. Putin declared that Britain was acting like a colonial power. 'They tell us we should change our constitution [to allow extradition]. I view that as an insult to our country and our people. They are the ones who need to change their thinking, not tell us to change our constitution!' Soon afterwards Lugovoy was elected as a pro-government member of the Russian parliament, giving him immunity from extradition.*

Commentators on Russian state television compared the Litvinenko murder to Stalin ordering the elimination of Trotsky. The remarks were intended to blacken those who oppose the Kremlin, but they also reflected a new willingness in the Putin years to rehabilitate the dictator's memory.

---

* When I visited the Kremlin in February 2007, I asked Putin's aide, Dmitry Peskov, if the Russian president had personally ordered Litvinenko's murder. He ridiculed the suggestion, but did not conceal that his boss had nursed a very personal hatred of the man. 'The president was very upset [by Litvinenko's allegations],' he told me. 'He was upset by these allegations made personally against him. He simply couldn't believe that people were saying these things about him *as a person* … He never tried to camouflage or to hide the fact that he was far from fond of Mr Litvinenko.'

In December 1999, soon after becoming prime minister, Putin had cele-brated his victory with a toast to Stalin; and in March 2003 he had allowed the fiftieth anniversary of the former leader's death to be commemorated in Red Square. Thousands of people came to pay their respects. School history books no longer dwelled on the violence and suffering of the Stalin era, preferring instead to highlight its achievements.*

Western unease at Moscow's hardening stance on human rights was tempered by Europe's dependence on Russian energy supplies. Germany, Greece, Finland, Italy, Austria and France, as well as all the former East European states, consumed large amounts of Russian gas, so few were willing to be overtly critical. The rise in international energy prices, and Russia's vast supplies, also strengthened Putin's hand in dealing with the Americans. After the collapse of the 1990s, he presided over an economic revival that gave Russia real clout on the international stage. The crash of 1998 had sent GDP plummeting, but Putin had arrested the decline and returned living standards to the relatively high levels of 1990. Salaries rose and inflation remained within manageable limits. A low flat rate tax of 13 per cent encouraged people to pay up rather than operate in the black economy, and state revenues increased. Problems remained, however. Although average wealth levels were higher, the disparity between rich and poor continued to widen. The economy remained stubbornly dependent on the export of raw materials, and little effort was made to diversify or improve productivity in other sectors. Agriculture in particular continued to be chronically inefficient. By 2008, oil and gas accounted for half of Russia's budget revenues, more than double the level of 1999.

Economic success maintained Putin's impressive approval ratings, which habitually hovered around 80 per cent and never fell below 65 per cent. In the 2007 parliamentary elections, his party, Yedinstvo, won an impressive two-thirds of the vote. There were clear indications of electoral irregularities

---

* Organisations such as Memorial, which campaigns for human rights and to ensure that the atrocities of the Soviet era are not forgotten or repeated, faced growing harassment. In 2008, Memorial had its entire database, containing the names of all who suffered during Stalin's purges, confiscated by the police.

(including a 99 per cent win in Chechnya), but Putin was genuinely popular. Few would have been surprised if the constitution had been altered to allow him a third term as president. Instead he chose to name a crown prince, the relatively unknown Dmitry Medvedev. It was announced that should Medvedev win, Putin would become prime minister; a campaign poster depicting the two standing side by side proclaimed, 'Together, we will triumph'. The succession was being deftly managed and it was no surprise when Medvedev won 70 per cent of the vote in the March 2008 election. He became the third president of the Russian Federation and, at 42, Russia's youngest leader since Nicholas II.

Like Putin, Medvedev was a lawyer from St Petersburg, and he too had worked in the office of the city's mayor before becoming Putin's deputy prime minister in 2005. He was undoubtedly a Putin crony, and at 5 feet 2 inches he was gratifyingly shorter than his patron (5 feet 6). But he lacked Putin's KGB background, and that seemed to influence the style, if not the substance, of his presidency. The newly installed Medvedev named among his most pressing policy objectives the establishment of the 'rule of the law'. 'I believe my most important aims will be to protect civil and economic freedoms,' he announced. 'We must fight for a true respect of the law and overcome legal nihilism, which seriously hampers modern development.'

It appeared on the face of it to be a return to the 'civic society' rhetoric of more liberal times. 'Legal nihilism' was a reference to the age-old tradition of courts doing the bidding of officials and politicians. The Kremlin had always had the final say in cases that affected the state or the national economy; the practice was known popularly as 'telephone justice' because judges waited by the phone to learn what verdict they should bring in. Now Medvedev appeared willing to cede some of the Kremlin's autocratic power and allow a more independent judiciary.

A high-profile test of his sincerity came with the second trial of Mikhail Khodorkovsky in 2009. With presidential elections due in 2012, the Kremlin had little interest in seeing a potential political opponent released from jail. New charges were brought against Khodorkovsky – that he had physically stolen millions of tons of oil from his own company – and they carried a much longer sentence. The accusations were so far-fetched that even the Russian media seemed aware this was a political prosecution. If Medvedev were serious about judicial freedom and the judges permitted to make an unbiased decision, there would undoubtedly be a not guilty verdict. But the charges were upheld. The judge's ruling quoted the prosecutors' submissions verbatim, and the court granted the 14-year sentence – to run concurrently with the original eight-year term – that the prosecution had demanded. Medvedev had been unwilling or, perhaps, unable to change the old ways of doing things.

Official corruption was not confined to the judicial system. The new 'statist' model of government in Russia had seen the Kremlin's Silovik officials appointed to run the key sectors of the economy. Igor Sechin remained at the head of the oil giant Rosneft after it took over the assets of Mikhail Khodorkovsky's Yukos; Sergei Ivanov ran the country's biggest arms manufacturer; Dmitry Patrushev (son of the FSB director) headed up the state export bank; Vladimir Yakunin the railways; and Medvedev himself was a former chairman of the state gas monopoly, Gazprom. The finances of all these enterprises remained distinctly opaque, as billions of dollars went through their books every day. The opportunity for personal enrichment was ever present, and Russian commentators accused the Kremlin's men of taking advantage. Vladimir Putin in particular was widely believed to have put aside more than adequate funds for his eventual retirement.*

The relationship between President Medvedev and Prime Minister Putin was the subject of much speculation. Medvedev's rhetoric suggested

---

* The former Kremlin insider Stanislav Belkovsky, who had parted ways with his Siloviki friends, claimed that despite officially receiving only a modest salary, Putin's bank account stood at $40 billion. 'I have been dealing with this question for two and a half years,' he told me in January 2008. 'So it is not a new topic for me. I estimate the assets controlled effectively by Vladimir Putin at the level of at least $40 billion. That includes 37.5 per cent of Surgutneftegaz oil company, 4.5 per cent of Gazprom and also the oil trader Gunvor, an offshore trader of oil and metals. It was unknown just nine years ago, and is connected with one of Putin's closest friends and business partners, Gennady Timchenko. So I can imagine the assets under Putin's control might be larger than I know, but they are at least $40 billion ... There are hundreds of people inside the Russian elite who can confirm these figures ...'

that he leaned towards the liberal values of democracy and free-market economics, while Putin remained a hardline statist. But there was little way of verifying such an assertion, and the broad direction of Kremlin policy did not change significantly after Medvedev's arrival. It may have been that Medvedev's 'liberalism' was exaggerated by political commentators, or it may have been that Putin retained the final say on key decisions. The fact that he addressed Medvedev using the familiar '*ty*', while Medvedev responded with the more deferential '*vy*', suggested Putin remained the senior partner. Nina Khrushchev, the granddaughter of Nikita, called Medvedev 'the First Lady … just there to keep up appearances'.

The slogan Medvedev adopted to characterise his presidency was 'modernisation'. He lamented Russia's continued reliance on the export of oil and gas and called for greater diversification, especially into the new high-tech industries. After travelling to California, he returned with Khrushchev-like enthusiasm and decreed that Russia must build its own version of Silicon Valley. At times, he suggested that economic modernisation would be accompanied by political liberalisation and democratic reform. 'Instead of the primitive raw material economy, we must create a smart new economy generating unique knowledge, new useful things and technologies,' he said in November 2009. 'Instead of the archaic society, in which the leaders think and make decisions for everyone, we will become a country of intelligent, free and responsible people.' The new rhetoric was welcomed in Washington: President Obama called for a 'reset' to improve relations with Moscow, and scrapped the much-resented US missile shield programme. But there were few perceptible improvements in Russia's human rights record under Medvedev, and no lessening in the pressure exerted by the Kremlin against its domestic political opponents. 'Legal nihilism' retained its hold on Russian society, economic performance was slow to improve and the unrest in the north Caucasus continued to claim its victims, including the 35 Russians and foreigners who died in the suicide bombing of Moscow's main international airport in January 2011.

A historian is not in the business of predicting the future. But these pages have traced underlying patterns in Russian history, and I think it is legitimate to ask if they will continue.

Russians have characterised the split in their national identity as a vacillation between the pull of Europe and the grip of Asia. Each enshrines a matrix of societal values – 'Europe' as participatory government, a civic society with personal and economic freedoms; 'Asia' as centralised, authoritarian rule, with a corresponding discount on individual liberty.

Why has 'Asiatic tyranny' proved so tenacious in Russia? Kievan Rus enjoyed the embryonic elements of participatory government, a startling glimpse of 'European' civic values. But it failed. Kiev fell because power devolved to the princes in the city states, and through them to the people, left no strong authority to secure national unity and national self-defence. The Mongols brought with them a different notion of statehood, one that recognised no rights other than the right of the state. And when the Mongols departed, Moscow prospered because it adopted a similar model. The eagerness with which Russians have embraced strong rulers stems from those years.

When autocracy became Russia's default form of governance, the absence of a developed civic society prevented the initiation of change 'from below'. Barring a revolution, the people did not have the means to make change happen. So nearly every attempt at reform has come 'from above' (from Russia's rulers), and all have been motivated by the compelling reason that the autocracy was under threat.

When a real revolution 'from below' did happen, in February 1917, it promised to make colossal changes, to shift Russia's historical paradigm to a liberal parliamentary system. But it was hijacked by another form of autocracy in the shape of the idealist despots of Leninist socialism. Lenin and Stalin revived the myth of Russia's messianic mission; Moscow the Third Rome became Moscow the Third International, destined to redeem the world through the new religion of Communism.

Gorbachev's reforms were also forced upon him. Just as Peter's and Catherine's changes were intended to shore up tsarist autocracy, Gorbachev's aim was to maintain and reinvigorate that of the Communist Party. But something was different now. The Russian people were no longer content to follow directives from above; they had learned to have their own opinions. The long-held conviction that change from below was impossible had evaporated, and in August 1991 it was the people who demanded freedom and democracy. It was a tectonic shift that suggested things might be different in the future.

It was globalisation, the information revolution and Gorbachev's recognition of it through *glasnost* that allowed change to happen. When I first worked in Moscow, I was not permitted to bring in a photocopier for my office lest unsavoury elements gain access to it to copy their anti-Soviet propaganda. I could listen to my own reports on the BBC World Service only if I leaned out of the window of my sixth-floor flat with a short-wave radio in my hand – otherwise Soviet jamming made Western broadcasts inaudible. The Kremlin kept its people in ignorance of the outside world so they would continue to believe the USSR was a paradise and the capitalist world a hellhole. But technology broke the party's monopoly on information. Gorbachev was forced to allow the use of computers to prevent Russia sinking into economic backwardness. The walls were starting to come down. Soon Russians had access to satellite television and then the internet; they began to travel to the West, and the success of democracy and free markets could no longer be hidden. Russians saw the former Communist states of Eastern Europe looking westwards, increasing their levels of prosperity. In the 1990s Russia seemed to be taking the same route.

But instead of prosperity and freedom, Russia got economic meltdown, crime and ethnic strife. The result was a hasty return to the methods that had worked in the past. Russians wanted order, and they didn't care if Putin suspended a few civil rights and undid Yeltsin's laissez-faire economics to provide it. The *silnaya ruka* – the strong ruler – was back, and Russians were happy about it.

The ending of the liberal experiment of the 1990s posed new questions. On this occasion, the reassertion of autocracy was carried out with the approval of the people, not imposed on them. The governments of Putin and of Putin–Medvedev remained genuinely popular. No one in Russia was hurrying to return to the Yeltsin era; Russia's liberal opposition enjoyed little influence or following. So did liberalism fail in the 1990s simply because it was introduced in an inept manner, because it was hamstrung by the old system and because the West failed to support it? Or was its failure the result of deeper factors? Could it be that centripetal Russia really can be ruled only by the *silnaya ruka*?

Western optimists say Russia's reliance on US and European investment and technology will bind her into Western political and cultural values – if

Russia wants our money, she will have to conform to our standards of legal and civil rights. It is a beguiling thought, but not supported by the facts.

When Vladimir Putin chose to seize the assets of the Yukos Oil Company and throw its owner in jail, there was criticism from London, Berlin and Washington. Commentators predicted that Western capital would flee a country where the rule of law is arbitrary and private businesses are confiscated with impunity. Even Dmitry Medvedev seemed to acknowledge the argument. Then Yukos was bankrupted and Khodorkovsky tried and convicted, not once but twice. It was a deliberate rebuff to 'Western values', but Western investors still came to Russia in search of a quick profit. BP signed a multibillion-dollar deal with Rosneft, the state oil company that was the main beneficiary of the sale of Yukos's assets. International trade links seemed not to have persuaded Russia to act like a European country, but to have convinced her that she can act as she likes.

For nearly a millennium, Russia had been an expanding empire ruled first by autocratic monarchs, then by an autocratic party. Its size and power were a challenge and a warning to its neighbours. Its rulers demanded, and received, obedience from its people, who, in turn, took solace from the vastness of their land and the richness of their culture. Then the empire collapsed, Russia was left shrunken and broken, its leaders exposed as weak men unable to understand, let alone dominate events.

The popular revolution of 1991 did not lead to liberty. Latter-day economic *boyars* stole the country's riches and used them to prop up a buffoon president. It was a new Time of Troubles, ended by a small but terrifying man. Vladimir Putin offered his country not the restoration of great power status, but the illusion of that restoration; not the restoration of peace and security at home, but the illusion of that security, periodically ripped apart by bombs and Islamic hit squads. The Kremlin was as powerful, as distant and as corrupt as under the Romanovs, and, knowing no other form of rule, Russians in the first decade of the twenty-first century bowed willingly to its command. George Bush's suggestion at Christmas 1991 that Russia will now be 'like us' seemed misguided at the time and seems so today.

TIMELINE

862	Rurik the Rus becomes first Rus-ian Prince of Novgorod
882	Oleg the Wise, son of Rurik, seizes Kiev and makes it the capital of the Rus-ian lands
911	Oleg secures first trade treaty with Constantinople
10th century	Adoption of the Cyrillic alphabet (created *c*.860 by Cyril and Methodius)
988	Vladimir converts Rus to Orthodox Christianity
1019	Martyrdom of Boris and Gleb at the hands of their brother Svyatopolk
1054	Schism between Eastern and Western Christianity
c.1110	Nestor completes the *Primary Chronicle*
1156	Founding of Moscow
1185	Prince Igor Sviatoslavich battles the Polovtsians, inspiring 'The Song of Igor's Campaign'
1240	Khan Batu's Tartars sack Kiev, beginning the Mongol yoke that will last for over 200 years
1242	Alexander Nevsky defeats the Teutonic Knights at Chudskoe Lake
1325	Ivan Kalita becomes the sole grand prince; persuades Metropolitan Pyotr to move his seat to Moscow
1380	Dmitry Donskoy leads union of princedoms to victory at Battle of Kulikovo Polye
1471	Grand Prince Ivan III brings Novgorod under Moscow's control
1480	Mongol yoke ends
1533	Ivan IV ('the Terrible') becomes Grand Prince of Moscow at the age of three
1547	Ivan IV becomes the first 'Tsar of all the Russias'

1555–61	St Basil's Cathedral built in Moscow to commemorate the conquest of the Tartar khanates of Kazan and Astrakhan
1564	Ivan IV creates the Oprichniki, first Russian secret police, in order to crush the *boyars* and his rivals
1570	Oprichniki sack Novgorod
1571	Crimean Tartars sack Moscow
1582	Yermak Timofeyevich leads the conquest of Siberia
1584	Death of Ivan IV, accession of Fyodor I
1598	Death of Fyodor, end of Rurik dynasty; Boris Godunov becomes tsar
1601–3	Famine; Time of Troubles begins
1604	False Dmitry marches on Moscow
1605	Death of Boris Godunov; false Dmitry becomes tsar
1606	Death of false Dmitry
1610	Poles occupy Moscow
1612	Kuzma Minin and Dmitry Pozharsky force Poles out of Moscow
1613	Mikhail Romanov elected tsar, beginning the Romanov dynasty that will rule Russia until 1917
1650s	Schism in the Russian Orthodox Church over Patriarch Nikon's reforms; Old Believers excommunicated and persecuted
1654	Council of Pereyaslav unites Russia and Ukraine
1670	Stenka Razin rebellion
1682	Avvakum Petrov burned at the stake
1696	Peter the Great becomes sole tsar; begins modernisation of Russia
1696–8	Peter visits Holland and England
1698	Streltsy uprising crushed
1703	Founding of St Petersburg
1708	Bulavin rebellion
1712	Seat of government transferred to St Petersburg
1721	Peter becomes the first Emperor of Russia
1722	Creation of the Table of Ranks

1725	Death of Peter the Great; Academy of Sciences set up in St Petersburg
1730	Anna becomes tsarina; failed attempt to reform autocracy
1741	Elizabeth claims throne
1754	Foundation of Moscow University; Rastrelli's Winter Palace built in St Petersburg
1755	Beginning of Seven Years War with Prussia
1762	Peter III becomes tsar, ends Russia's involvement in Seven Years War; Catherine II ('the Great') seizes power from her husband in a palace coup
1764	Hermitage Museum founded
1767	Catherine convenes the Legislative Commission and issues her *Nakaz*
1774–5	Pugachev rebellion, largest of the peasant revolts
1783	Annexation of Crimea
1785	Charter of the Nobility
1790	Radishchev's *Journey from Petersburg to Moscow*
1795	Partition of Poland; Imperial Library built in St Petersburg
1796	Death of Catherine the Great; accession of Paul I
1801	Murder of Paul I; accession of Alexander I
1800s	Alexander declines to introduce Speransky's suggested reforms
1807	Treaty of Tilsit signed with Napoleon
1812	Napoleon invades Russia; Battle of Borodino turns the tide; Napoleon defeated but Moscow burns
1814	Russian troops enter Paris
1816–18	Yermolov's campaign in the Caucasus; foundation of Grozny
1816–26	Karamzin's *History of the Russian State*
1825	Death of Alexander I and accession of Nicholas I; Decembrist revolt put down, with leaders executed or exiled
1826	Foundation of the Third Department (secret police)
1831	Pushkin's *Yevgeny Onegin* marks beginning of the golden age of Russian literature

1836	Chaadaev's *First Philosophical Letter*; Glinka's *A Life for the Tsar*
1840	Lermontov's *A Hero of Our Time*
1842	Gogol's *Dead Souls*
1848	Marx and Engel's *Communist Manifesto*
1854	French and British land troops in Crimea
1855	Death of Nicholas I and accession of Alexander II
1856	Treaty of Paris ends Crimean War
1861	Alexander II issues the 'Manifesto on the Emancipation of the Serfs'
1862	Turgenev's *Fathers and Children*
1863	Chernyshevsky's *What Is to Be Done?*
1864–9	Tolstoy's *War and Peace* published
1866	Dostoevsky's *Crime and Punishment*
1867	Alaska sold to USA
1872	Dostoevsky's *The Devils*
1881	Narodnaya Volya assassinate Alexander II in St Petersburg; accession of Alexander III, issues the 'Manifesto on Unshakable Autocracy'
1883	Repin's *Religious Procession in Kursk*
1889	Introduction of Land Captains
1891	Construction of the Trans-Siberian Railway begins
1894	Death of Alexander III and accession of Nicholas II
1896	Khodynka disaster
1898	Russian Social Democratic Labour Party formed, splitting into Bolshevik and Menshevik factions in 1903
1904–5	War with Japan
1905	Bloody Sunday leads to revolution on the streets of Moscow and St Petersburg; 'October Manifesto' promises a constitutional democracy
1906	First Duma meets but is soon dissolved; Stolypin becomes prime minister
1911	Stolypin assassinated in Kiev
1912	First issue of *Pravda*
1914	Outbreak of First World War

1917	February Revolution sees the toppling of the monarchy, Romanov rule ended after over 300 years; October Revolution ends Provisional Government; Lenin's Bolsheviks seize the initiative, dismiss the Constituent Assembly and take power for themselves; creation of the Cheka
1918	Treaty of Brest-Litovsk ends Russian participation in the war, with considerable loss of land; Nicholas II and his family murdered
1918–20	Civil war between Bolsheviks and Whites; Red Terror; peasant uprisings in the countryside
1919–20	Polish–Soviet War
1921	Kronstadt Revolt suppressed; factions banned within the party, and New Economic Policy (NEP) introduced at the Tenth Party Congress
1922	Union of Soviet Socialist Republics (USSR) officially formed, with Lenin as its leader; Stalin becomes general secretary of the Communist Party (Bolshevik) Central Committee
1924	Death of Lenin; constitution of the USSR ratified
1925	Trotsky replaced as commissar for war; Eisenstein's *Battleship Potemkin*
1928	End of NEP; beginning of first Five Year Plan; Shakhty trial; collectivisation of agriculture begins
1929	Trotsky expelled from the Soviet Union
1930	Mayakovsky commits suicide
1932	Stalin's wife, Nadezhda Alliluyeva, commits suicide
1932–3	Famine (*Holodomor*) in Ukraine and southern Russia
1933	Metropolitan-Vickers trial
1934	Seventeenth Party Congress ('Congress of the Victors'); Kirov assassinated; First Congress of Soviet Writers' Union adopts Socialist Realism as official doctrine
1936	Beginning of the purges; first of the Moscow show trials, Zinoviev and Kamenev convicted and shot; 'Stalin' constitution adopted; *Pravda* article, 'Muddle instead of music', heavily criticises Shostakovich

1937	Second Moscow show trial; 'Yezhovshchina' (terror) reaches its peak
1938	Trial of the Twenty-One, Bukharin and Yagoda amongst those shot; Beria replaces Yezhov as head of the NKVD; Russian made compulsory in all schools, including non-Russian-speaking republics; Eisenstein's *Alexander Nevsky*
1939	Nazi–Soviet Non-Aggression Pact signed; Soviet forces invade eastern Poland
1939–40	Winter War with Finland
1940	Lithuania, Latvia and Estonia forced to join USSR; Katyn Forest massacre; Trotsky assassinated
1941	Hitler launches Operation Barbarossa, sparking Great Patriotic War; 900-day siege of Leningrad begins
1941–2	Battle of Moscow
1942–3	Battle of Stalingrad; Order Number 227, 'Not a single step back!'
1943	Battle of Kursk; Tehran conference; deportations of nationalities begins
1944	New 'National Anthem of the Soviet Union' replaces the 'Internationale'
1945	Yalta conference; Soviet troops take Berlin, ending war in Europe; Potsdam conference, Baltic states internationally recognised as part of USSR; creation of United Nations
1946	Beginning of 'Zhdanovshchina' (crackdown on artistic freedom); Akhmatova among those expelled from the Union of Writers
1947	Cominform founded; beginning of Cold War
1948	Break with Tito's Yugoslavia; Mikhoels murdered
1948–9	Berlin blockade
1949	USSR explodes its first nuclear bomb; 'Leningrad Affair'; People's Republic of China founded
1950	Outbreak of the Korean War
1953	'Doctors' Plot' announced in *Pravda*; Stalin dies; Beria executed; Khrushchev becomes first secretary

1955	Warsaw Pact created
1956	Khrushchev's 'secret speech' at Twentieth Party Congress; Hungarian uprising quelled
1957	*Sputnik* launched; 'Anti-Party Group' defeated; Pasternak's *Doctor Zhivago*
1959	Khrushchev becomes first Soviet leader to visit America; Grossman's *Life and Fate*
1960	American U-2 spy plane shot down
1961	Yuri Gagarin becomes the first man in space; Berlin wall erected
1962	Cuban missile crisis; Novocherkassk unrest; Solzhenitsyn's *One Day in the Life of Ivan Denisovich*
1964	Coup removes Khrushchev as party leader; Brezhnev becomes first secretary
1966	Trial of Sinyavsky and Daniel
1968	'Prague spring' ends with invasion of Czechoslovakia by Warsaw Pact forces
1972	SALT I ushers in period of détente with the USA; 'era of stagnation' (latter years of Brezhnev's rule)
1974	Solzhenitsyn exiled
1975	Signing of the Helsinki Accords; Sakharov wins Nobel Peace Prize
1979	Soviet invasion of Afghanistan
1982	Brezhnev dies, succeeded by Andropov
1984	Andropov dies, succeeded by Chernenko
1985	Chernenko dies, succeeded by Gorbachev
1986	Chernobyl nuclear disaster; period of *glasnost* and *perestroika* begins
1989	Fall of Berlin wall; pro-independence demonstrators killed by Soviet troops in Tbilisi; end of war in Afghanistan
1990	Gorbachev wins Nobel Peace Prize; Soviet troops clash violently with protesters in Azerbaijan; Lithuania declares its independence from the USSR, Latvia and Estonia follow suit

1991	Troops kill demonstrators in Latvia and Lithuania; Yeltsin elected President of the Russian Republic; failed hardline coup against Gorbachev; Soviet Union dissolved
1992	'Economic shock therapy' launched in the Russian Federation
1993	Yeltsin dissolves the Supreme Soviet; violence on the streets of Moscow as Yeltsin orders the shelling of the White House; new constitution adopted
1994	Russian troops invade Chechnya
1995	'Loans for shares'; rise of the oligarchs
1996	Yeltsin re-elected president; end of First Chechen War
1998	'Rouble crisis' as economy collapses and Russia defaults on foreign debts
1999	Yeltsin resigns, Putin becomes acting president; terrorist attacks trigger Second Chechen War
2000	Putin wins election to remain president; *Kursk* submarine disaster
2002	Nord-Ost hostage crisis
2003	Khodorkovsky tried and imprisoned
2004	Putin re-elected president; Beslan school hostage crisis
2006	Alexander Litvinenko murdered in London
2008	Medvedev wins presidential election, appoints Putin as prime minister; Russo–Georgian war
2009–10	Second trial extends Khodorkovsky's sentence
2011	Terrorist attack at Domodedovo airport kills 37

NOTES

Note: Unless otherwise stated, translations of references given in Russian and French are by the author.

Introduction

p. vii 'Bless'd is he who visited this world ...', Fedor Tyutchev (1803–73), 'Tsitseron' [Cicero] (1830), Tyutchev, F.I., *Stikhotvoreniya* (Moscow: Khudozhestvennaya Literatura, 1972), 76.

p. vii 'Interests hostile to the Soviet people ...', Soviet radio and television (ORT) broadcast, 19 August 1991. TASS dispatch of same date; quoted verbatim on front page of *Pravda*, 20 August 1991.

p. ix 'If proof were needed ...', Levada Analytical Center, *Russian Public Opinion 2009* (Moscow, 2010), www.levada.ru

p. x 'Oh, yes – we are Scythians ...', Alexander Blok (1880–1921), 'Skify' [Scythians] (1918), A.A. Blok, *Izbrannye Proizvedeniya* (Moscow: Biblioteka Klassiki, 1988).

PART ONE

Chapter One

p. 3 'There was no law among them ...', *Povest' Vremennykh Let* (St Petersburg: Biblioteka Literatury Drevnei Rusi, 1997). English translation of passages from *The Russian Primary Chronicle* in Serge A. Zenkovsky (ed.), *Medieval Russia's Epics, Chronicles and Tales* (New York: Dutton, 1963), 49–50.

p. 4 'So they went overseas ...', ibid., 51.

p. 5 'I think that Rurik ...', interviews recorded in September 2010.

p. 6 'Upon arriving in the Bosporus strait ...', *Novgorodskaya Pervaya Letopis*, ed. B.M. Kloss (Moscow, 2000). English translation of passages from *The Novgorod Chronicle* in Zenkovsky, op.cit., 52.

p. 6 'Of the prisoners they captured ...', ibid., 52.

p. 6 'For lo, the Byzantine Emperor prayed ...', ibid., 51.

p. 7 'They sailed along the Dnieper river ...', ibid., 50–1.

p. 8 'So then did Oleg the Wise ride out ...', Alexander Pushkin (1799–1837), 'Pesn' o Veshchem Olege' [Song of Oleg the Wise] (1822), A.S. Pushkin, *Sochineniya v 3-kh tomakh* (Moscow: Izd. Khudozhestvennaya Lit., 1987).

p. 8 'Then in 911 Oleg set off ...', G. Vernadsky, *Kievan Rus* (New Haven: Yale, 1973), 26.

p. 9 'In the month of June …', Constantine Porphyrogenitus, 'Of the coming of the Russians in monoxyla from Russia to Constantinople', *De Administrando Imperio*, trans. and ed. Gyula Moravcsik and R.J.H. Jenkins (Washington, DC: Harvard, 1966), 57–63.

Chapter Two

p. 11 'This is the tale of bygone years …', *Povest' Vremennykh Let* (St Petersburg: Biblioteka Literatury Drevnei Rusi, 1997). English translation of passages from *The Russian Primary Chronicle* in Serge A. Zenkovsky (ed.), *Medieval Russia's Epics, Chronicles and Tales* (New York: Dutton, 1963), *Prolegomenon*, 44.

p. 14 'When the envoys returned …', ibid., 67–8.

p. 14 'Drinking is the joy of the Russians …', quoted in Walter G. Moss, *A History of Russia*, i: *To 1917* (London: Anthem, 2002), 64.

p. 15 'All I possess are eight slim tomes …', Vladislav Khodasevich, 'Ya rodilsya v Moskve' [In Moscow I was born], from *Egipetskaya Noch* [The Egyptian Night], in *Stikhotvoreniya* (Leningrad: Sovetsky Pisatel', 1989), 294–5.

p. 16 'So Vladimir did ordain …', *Primary Chronicle*, op. cit., 70.

p. 16 'For Vladimir now dwelled in the fear of God …', ibid., 71.

p. 17 'Svyatopolk secretly summoned his men …', attrib. Nestor, *Skazanie o Borise I Glebe* [The Tale of Boris and Gleb] (St Petersburg: Biblioteka Literatury Drevnei Rusi, 1997). Partial English translation in Zenkovsky, op. cit., 87–91.

Chapter Three

p. 20 'If you look at the records …', author's interview, Novgorod, September 2010.

p. 21 'I love you and you love me …', birch-bark documents on display at the Novgorod State Museum. Museum website carries facsimiles of the birch barks: http://gramoty.ru/index.php?key=bb&date[]=all&city[]=all&excav[]=all&safety[]=all&cath[]=all

p. 23 'And Prince Alexander's men were filled …', *Povest' Vremennykh Let* (St Petersburg: Biblioteka Literatury Drevnei Rusi, 1997). English translation of passages from *The Russian Primary Chronicle* in Serge A. Zenkovsky (ed.), *Medieval Russia's Epics, Chronicles and Tales* (New York: Dutton, 1963), 162–4.

p. 24 'Then Igor gazed upon the sun …', *Slovo o Polku Igoreve* ['The Song of Igor's Campaign'] (Moscow: Narodnaya Biblioteka). Partial English translation in Zenkovsky, op. cit., 54.

p. 25 'And, brethren, Kiev began to groan from grief …', ibid., 58.

Chapter Four

p. 27 'The accursed Batu …', *Povest' o Razorenii Ryazani Batyem* [The Tale of the Destruction of Ryazan by Baty] (St Petersburg: Biblioteka Literatury Drevnei Rusi, 1997). Partial English translation in *Medieval Russia's Epics, Chronicles and Tales*, ed. Serge Zenkovsky (New York: Dutton, 1963), 175–85.

p. 28 'When we passed through this region …', Giovanni de Plano Carpini, envoy of Pope Innocent IV, *Ystoria Mongalorum*, ed. E. Hildinger (Boston: Branden Books, 1996), 48.

p. 29   'In former times …', N.M. Karamzin, *Istoria Gosudarstva Rossiiskogo* [History of the Russian State] (Rostov: Rostovskoe Knizhnoe Izdatelstvo, 1990), v: ch. 4, 178.

p. 30   'Our history began in barbarity …', *Lettres philosophiques addressées à une dame* [Philosophical Letters Addressed to a Lady], in P. Ya. Chaadayev, *Polnoe Sobranie Sochinenii* (Moscow: Nauka, 1991), 121.

p. 30   'The princes crawled on their knees …', Karamzin, op. cit., 179.

p. 31   'Batu's invasion brought destruction …', ibid., 180.

p. 32   'But Prince Dmitry said, 'Fight on! …', *Zadonshchina* [Beyond the Don] (St Petersburg: Biblioteka Literatury Drevnei Rusi, 1997). Partial English translation in Zenkovsky, op. cit., 191–2.

p. 33   'O my Rus! My wife! …', A. Blok, *Na Pole Kulikovom* [On Kulikovo Field] (1908), in *Izbrannye Proizvedeniya* (Moscow: Biblioteka Klassiki, 1988).

Chapter Five

p. 36   'For Kalita won the favour of …', cited in S.M. Soloviev, *Istoria Rossii s Drevneishikh Vremen* (Moscow: Golos, 1993). Partial English translation in *Medieval Russia's Epics, Chronicles and Tales*, ed. Serge Zenkovsky (New York: Dutton, 1963), 213.

p. 37   'For the ancient city of Rome …', *Povest' o Belom Klobuke* [The Legend of the White Cowl] (St Petersburg: Biblioteka Literatury Drevnei Rusi, 1997). Partial English translation in Zenkovsky, op. cit., 270–1.

p. 39   'AD 1471. The Grand Prince Ivan Vasilievich …', *The Novgorod Chronicles*, R. Mitchell and N. Forbes (trans.), *The Chronicle of Novgorod, 1016–1471* (Camden, London: 1914), cited in W. Walsh, *Readings in Russian History* (New York: Syracuse University Press, 1948), 241.

p. 40   'Thus did Great Prince Ivan advance …', ibid., 242.

PART TWO

Chapter Six

p. 44   'Stalin: Have you studied history? …', J.V. Stalin, *Collected Works*, cited in G. Maryamov, *Kremlevskii Tsenzor* [The Kremlin Censor] (Moscow, 1992), 84–91.

p. 46   'For the first time …', Ivan's dialogue from the film *Ivan Grozny* [Ivan the Terrible] (1943–4), dir. S. Eisenstein.

p. 46   'For what is our country now?', ibid.

p. 47   'The form of their government …', Giles Fletcher, *Of the Russe Commonwealth* (1591), reprinted in facsimile (Cambridge: Harvard University Press, 1966), 20.

p. 47   'In the power which he holds …', Baron von Herberstein, *Rerum Muscoviticarum Comentarii* [Notes on Muscovite Affairs], trans. R.H. Major, as *Notes on Russia* (London: 1851).

p. 47   'We shall cut off heads without mercy …', Eisenstein film, op. cit.

p. 48   'Under orders from Ivan …', G. Hosking, *Russia and the Russians: A History* (London: Penguin, 2001), 124.

p. 48   'In his Kremlin interrogation of Eisenstein …', Maryamov, op. cit., 87.

p. 48   'To the Tsar, exalted by God …', J.L. Fennell (ed.), *The Correspondence between A.M. Kurbsky and Ivan IV, 1564–1579* (Cambridge: 1955), 2.

p. 48   'To him who is a criminal …', ibid., 180.

p. 49   'I spit on you and on your palace …', Ivan to Elizabeth. *Poslanie Angliiskoi Koroleve Elizavete* [Missive to the English Queen Elizabeth] (1570), quoted in *Ivan IV Sochineniya* (St Petersburg: Azbuka Klassiki, 2000), 101 et seq.

p. 50   'The Muscovite state …', V. Kliuchevsky, *Kurs Russkoi Istorii* (Moscow: 1937), iv: 352.

p. 50   'Russia owes her salvation …', N.M. Karamzin, *Istoria Gosudarstva Rossiiskogo* [History of the Russian State] (Rostov: Rostovskoe Knizhnoe Izdatelstvo, 1990), v: ch. 4, 182.

p. 51   'To despotism Russia owes her greatness …', G. Macartney, *An Account of Russia MDCCLXVII*, reprinted in facsimile (Elibron Classics, 2005), 63.

Chapter Seven

p. 53   'Here is conspiracy, sedition …', M. Mussorgsky, libretto to his opera *Boris Godunov*, after Pushkin. From the aria: *Dostig ya vysshei vlasti* … [I have attained the highest power …].

p. 54   'What if the murdered …', ibid.

p. 55   'Let us act together of one …', cited in S.M. Soloviev, *Istoria Rossii s Drevneishikh Vremen* (Moscow: Golos, 1993), viii: ch. 8, 143.

p. 58   'Glory to you, my native Russian land …', Glinka, *Zhizn' za Tsarya* [A Life (laid down) for the Tsar). Chorus: *Slavsya, slavsya, svyataya Rus!*

p. 58   'In 1612,' it announced, 'our enemies were the Poles and Lithuanians …' Radio Liberty report, by Viktor Yasmann, 4 November 2005: 'New Russian holiday has more behind it than National Unity'.

Chapter Eight

p. 60   'On the Volga, on the Kama …', *Kak prokhodit, bratsy, leto teploe* … [As summer goes, my brothers…], Don Cossack song, collected by Pyotr Krasnov, *Kartiny Bylogo Tikhogo Dona* [Scenes from the past times of the quiet Don] (1909).

p. 61   'It was at the little stream …', ibid.

p. 61   'The native commodities of the countrie …', Giles Fletcher, *Of the Russe Commonwealth* (1591), reprinted in facsimile (Cambridge: Harvard University Press, 1966), 7.

p. 63   'Mile after mile creeps by …', Shostakovich, libretto to his opera *Lady Macbeth of the Mtsensk District*, based on the novella by Nikolai Leskov.

p. 64   'At least 7,000 men and 600 women were imprisoned here …', archive file of the Soviet Interior Ministry, ref. Pr.0361MVD, dated 25.5.50, stored on the database of the Memorial organisation, www.memo.ru

p. 64   'Bazhenov was finally closed …', archive file of the Soviet Security Service, ref. Pr. 00329MGB, dated 23.5.52, stored on the database of the Memorial organisation, www.memo.ru

p. 65   'These involuntary peasant settlers …', Ye. Yevtushenko, *Stantsiya Zima* [Zima Junction], in *Izbrannoe: Stikhotvoreniya i Poemy* (Rostov: Vsemirnaya Biblioteka Poeta, 1997).

p. 67   'What we need to do is spit …', Avvakum Petrov, *Zhitie Protopopa Avvakum Im Samim Napisannoe* [The Life of the Archpriest Avvakum, Written by Himself] (Moscow: Khudozhestvennaya Literatura, 1960), 173.

p. 67   'As they were beating me, I felt no pain …', ibid., 185.

Chapter Nine

p. 69   '… with one mighty blow …', from the poem 'Volga, Volga, Mat' Rodnaya' [Mother Volga] by Dmitry Sadovnikov (1883).

p. 69   'By the autumn, his army was nearly 200,000 strong …', N. Riasanovsky, *A History of Russia* (New York: Oxford University Press, 1963), 197.

p. 70   'Why, good folk, are you not celebrating …', Ye. Yevtushenko, 'Kazn' Sten'ki Razina' [The Execution of Stenka Razin], in *Izbrannoe: Stikhotvoreniya i Poemy* (Rostov: Vsemirnaya Biblioteka Poeta, 1997).

p. 71   '… had a great regard for learning …', P. Gordon, *Passages from the Diary of General Patrick Gordon of Auchleuchries* (Aberdeen: 1859), 168.

p. 72   'No one who was acquainted …', A. Gordon, *The History of Peter the Great, Emperor of Russia* (Aberdeen: 1755), i: xxiii.

p. 72   'Soon after his arrival …' ibid., vii–viii.

p. 74   '… conversed with our English builders …', John Perry, *The State of Russia under the Present Czar* (London: 1716), 164.

p. 74   '… the Tsar of Muscovy worked with his own hands …', cited in I. Grey, 'Peter the Great in England', in *History Today*, 6 (1956), 229.

p. 75   'He spent most of his time …', Perry, op. cit., 166.

p. 75   'He now made those Englishmen …', ibid., 186.

p. 75   '… sold to America – for the derisory sum of $7 million …' Riasanovsky, op. cit., 431.

p. 76   'His epic poem "The Bronze" …', A.S. Pushkin, 'Mednyi Vsadnik' [The Bronze Horseman], in *Polnoe Sobranie Sochinenii. v 10 tomakh* (Leningrad: 1979), 372–3.

p. 78   'He, who our city by the sea …', ibid., 382.

p. 78   'About the statue, at its base …', ibid., 383.

p. 79   'Not only that, each rank …', Waliszewski, *Peter the Great: His Life and Work* (London: 1898), 454.

p. 82   'The Russians had always worn …', Jean Rousset de Missy, quoted in *Readings in Modern European History*, ed. J. Robinson and C. Beard (Boston: Ginn and Co, 1908), 61–3.

p. 84   'The argument, says Feofan …', Feofan Prokopovich, *The Spiritual Regulation*, quoted in T. Szamuely, *The Russian Tradition* (London: McGraw Hill, 1974), 106.

p. 84   'Vasily Tatishchev, concurs. He advances the contention ...', ibid.

Chapter Ten

p. 85   'The story has it that she turned up at the headquarters …', B. Antonov, *Russian Tsars: The Rurikids, the Romanovs* (Moscow: Fedorov, 2005), 106.

p. 86 'The woman history would know as Catherine the Great ...', S. Dixon, *Catherine the Great* (London: Profile, 2010), 4–6.

p. 87 'Anything that was necessary ...', *Zapiski Imperatritsy Yekateriny II* [The Writings of the Empress Catherine II], ed. A.S. Suvorin (St Petersburg: 1907), 57.

p. 87 'I understood very clearly that the Grand Duke did not love me ...', *The memoirs of Catherine the Great*, eds. M. Cruse and H. Hoogenboom (New York: 2006), 36.

p. 88 'In government by women ...', Frederick II, quoted in S. Sebag-Montefiore, *Potemkin, Prince of Princes* (London: Phoenix, 2000), 118.

p. 88 'I never saw in my life ...', George Macartney, quoted in S. Dixon, *The Modernisation of Russia, 1676–1825* (Cambridge: 1999), 45.

p. 90 'By chance your works fell into my hands ...', letter to Voltaire, included in Cruse and Hoogenboom, op. cit., 48.

p. 91 'You are greater than the Aurora Borealis ...', letter from Voltaire to Catherine, quoted in W. Reddaway, *Documents of Catherine the Great* (New York: 1971).

p. 91 A '*philosophe* on the throne', N. Pushkareva, *Women in Russian History*, trans. E. Levin (New York: Sharpe, 1997), 142.

p. 91 'For it is the wish of all worthy members ...', *Nakaz Yekateriny II*, full text included in *Imperatritsa Yekaterina II, 'O Velichii Rossii'* (Moscow, EKsmo: 2003).

p. 92 'There is no true sovereign except the nation ...', D. Diderot, quoted in *The Enlightenment: A Source Book and Reader*, ed. Paul Hyland (London: Routledge, 2003), 153.

p. 93 'At first you doubt ...', G. Derzhavin, *Opisanie Torzhestva* ... [A Description of the Celebration at the House of Field Marshal Potemkin in the Presence of Her Majesty the Empress Catherine II] (St Petersburg: 1808).

p. 93 'My dear friend, I love you ...', Catherine to Potemkin, quoted in Sebag-Montefiore, op. cit., 102.

p. 93 'Oh, Monsieur Potemkin, what sorcery have you used ...', ibid., 127.

p. 94 'A new scene has just opened ...', Robert Gunning dispatch, quoted in ibid., 117–22.

p. 95 'At that moment great crowds ...', A.S. Pushkin, *Kapitanskaya Dochka i Drugie Rasskazy* [The Captain's Daughter and Other Tales] (Moscow: AsT, 2007), 63.

p. 96 'Those who rally to me ...', manifesto of Yemilian Pugachev. Original in History Museum, Yekaterinburg.

p. 97 'The possessions of the Russian Empire ...', *Nakaz Yekateriny II*, op. cit., 77.

p. 98 'In the very nature of things ...', ibid., 80.

p. 98 'Since the honourable title ...', Charter of the Nobility, ibid., 127.

Chapter Eleven

p. 102 'Paul I's years in power ...', For Paul I, see N. Riasanovsky, *A History of Russia* (New York: Oxford University Press, 1963), 302 et seq.

p. 103 'The fundamental principle ...', M.M. Speransky, *Proekty i Zapiski* [Projects and Notes] (Moscow-Leningrad: 1961), 43–4.

p. 103 'Under Catherine, the government wished ...', ibid., 65.

p. 104 'Under autocratic rule there can be ...', ibid., 118.

p. 104 'What is the use of laws ...', ibid., 140–2.

p. 105 'I would then happily retire ...', G. Hosking, *Russia and the Russians: A History* (London: Penguin, 2001), 247.

p. 106 'A shell tore up the earth ...', L. Tolstoy, *War and Peace*, trans. R. Edmonds (London: Penguin, 1957), 943–7.

p. 107 'For Napoleon's generals ...', ibid., 977.

p. 108 'So the French army flows on to Moscow ...', Comte de Ségur, *Histoire de Napoléon et de la Grande Armée pendant l'année 1812* [History of Napoleon and of the Grand Army during the Year 1812] (Paris: 1839), 47–8.

p. 108 'According to the eyewitness testimony ...', ibid., 48–9. For French casualty figures, see Riasanovsky, op. cit., 345 et seq.

p. 111 'He consulted oracles ...', F. Gribble, *Emperor and Mystic: The Life of Alexander I of Russia* (Montana: Kessinger, 2007).

p. 112 'See the crowds are running ...', N. Nekrasov, *Russkie Zhenshchiny* [Russian Wives] (Russian Women) (Moscow: Russkaya Klassika, 2009), 28.

p. 113 'Crowds of civilians gathered around them ...', A. Mazour, *Russia's First Revolution, 1825* (Stanford: 1937), 67.

p. 114 'Oh unhappy country ...', C. de Grunwald, *Tsar Nicholas I* (New York: Macmillan, 1955), 69.

p. 114 'In far Siberia's deepest land ...', A.S. Pushkin, *Sochineniya, v 3-kh tomakh* (Moscow: Khudozhestvennaya Literatura, 1987), 178.

p. 115 'A desert landscape with a jail ...', Saltykov-Shchedrin, quoted in T. Szamuely, *The Russian Tradition* (London: McGraw Hill, 1974), 134.

p. 115 'Never to stir ... never to show ...', Uspensky, quoted in ibid.

p. 116 'Experience teaches us that ...', A. de Tocqueville, *L'Ancien Régime et la Révolution* [The Old Regime and the French Revolution] Paris: Adamant, 2002), 259.

PART THREE
Chapter Twelve

p. 120 'The bodies of Russian servicemen ...', author's reports for BBC News, 1995–7.

p. 122 'So shall I sing that glorious hour ...', A. Pushkin, *Kavkazskii Plennik* [A Captive of the Caucasus], op. cit. 109.

p. 123 'Yermolov said his aim ...', G. Hosking, *Russia and the Russians: A History* (London: Penguin, 2001), 239.

p. 123 '... destroy their towns, hang hostages and slaughter their women and children ...', ibid.

p. 123 'Awake, you braves ...', Chechen folk song, quoted in M. Gammer, *The Lone Wolf and the Bear: Three Centuries of Chechen Defiance of Russian Rule* (London, 2006), 36–7.

p. 125 'Yesterday, I arrived in Pyatigorsk ...', M. Lermontov, *A Hero of Our Time*, trans. P. Longworth (New York: Signet, 1962), 85.

p. 125 'No one spoke of hatred ...', Tolstoy, *Hadji Murat* (Moscow: Khudozhestvennaya Literatura, 1969), 89.

p. 126 'This flood [of revolutionary pressure] ...', S. Witte, *The Memoirs of Count Witte*, trans. A. Yarmolinsky (New York: Doubleday, 1921), 210.

Chapter Thirteen

p. 128 'So tell me, madam ...', N. Gogol, *Mertvye Dushi* [Dead Souls] (Moscow: Khudozhestvennaya Literatura, 1972), 92.

p. 129 'One may buy a slave ...', *Russkaya Pravda*. Full text in A.M. Kamchatnov, *Khrestomatiya po Istorii Russkogo Yazyka (Pamyatniki X–XIV vekov)* (Moscow, 2009).

p. 130 'The figures involved were stupendous ...' For the figures of bonded serfs in Russia, see T. Szamuely, *The Russian Tradition* (London: McGraw Hill, 1974), 116 et seq.

p. 131 'The setting was idyllic ...', ibid., 118.

p. 132 'Today I read in the newspaper ...', Tolstoy, *Ne Mogu Molchat'* [I Cannot Remain Silent], in *Sobranie Sochinenii v 20 tomakh, tom. 14* (Moscow: 1960).

p. 133 'By the Grace of God ...', 'Manifesto on the Emancipation of the Serfs'. Full text available online at http://schoolart.narod.ru/1861.html

p. 134 '... better to liberate the peasants from above ...', quoted in N. Riasanovsky, *A History of Russia* (New York: Oxford University Press, 1963), 411.

p. 134 'We count on the nobles to reach ...', See 'Manifesto on the Emancipation of the Serfs', op. cit.

p. 135 'I was still in bed ...', Kropotkin, *Memoirs of a Revolutionist* (Boston, New York: Houghton Mifflin, 1899), part 2, ch. 8, 142.

p. 135 'We ran, rather than marched ...', ibid., 143.

p. 137 'I was deafened by the blast ...' quoted in E. Radzinsky, *Alexander II: The Last Great Czar* (New York: Freepress, 2006), 415.

p. 138 '... spoke of "inviting society" ...', ibid., 374 et seq.

p. 138 'The policies of Count Loris-Melikov ...', diary of V. Figner, quoted in *Five Sisters: Women against the Tsar*, ed. Alpern Engel (New York: B. Knopf, 1975), 50–1.

Chapter Fourteen

p. 139 'Zhelyabov died smiling ...', A. Camus, *L'Homme révolté* [The Rebel] (Paris: Gallimard, 1951), 86.

p. 139 '... just another year of life'. Police records of Rysakov's interrogation in online database: http://www.hrono.ru/biograf/bio_r/rysakov.php

p. 139 'Don't cry over the corpses ...', 'Hymn of the Revolutionary' (1865). An early recorded performance and lyrics available at http://www.sovmusic.ru/text.php?fname=ne_plach

p. 140 'Our history began in ...', *Lettres philosophiques addressées à une dame* [Philosophical Letters Addressed to a Lady], in P. Ya. Chaadayev, *Polnoe Sobranie Sochinenii* (Moscow: Nauka, 1991), 121.

p. 141 'All classes and groups ...', K. Aksakov, *On the Internal State of Russia* (1855), quoted in N. Riasanovsky, *Russia and the West in the Teaching of the Slavophiles* (Cambridge: Harvard University Press, 1952).

p. 142 'Our land may be destitute ...', F. Dostoevsky, *The Diary of a Writer*, trans. B. Brasol (New York: Scribner, 1954), 980.

p. 142 'Suffering land of the Russian people ...', F.I. Tyutchev, *Stikhotvoreniya* (Moscow: Khudozhestvennaya Literatura, 1972), 208.

p. 142 'With the mind alone ...', ibid., 259.

p. 143 'A storm is approaching ...', A. Herzen, 'The Russian People and Socialism: A Letter to Michelet' (1851), in *The Memoirs of Alexander Herzen* (London: Chatto & Windus, 1968), iv: 1649.

p. 144 'I shall speak frankly with you ...', N. Chernyshevsky, *Chto Delat'?* [What Is to Be Done?], *Klassiki Mirovoi Literatury* (Moscow: Feniks, 2002), 287.

p. 145 'All these sores and foul contagion ...', F. Dostoevsky, *Besy* [The Possessed], trans. Constance Garnett (New York: Heritage Press, 1959), 563. Also S. Nechaev, *Catechism of a Revolutionist* (1869). Quoted in T. Szamuely, *The Russian Tradition* (London: McGraw Hill, 1974), 252. Full text available in archives of Marxist.org: http://www.marxists.org/subject/anarchism/nechayev/catechism.htm

p. 146 'In 1878, one of its members ...', diary of Vera Zasulich, reproduced in *Five Sisters: Women against the Tsar*, ed. Alpern Engel (New York: B. Knopf, 1975), 61–94.

Chapter Fifteen

p. 148 'The times are terrible ...', letter from Konstantin Pobedonostsev to Alexander III, in K.P. Pobedonostsev, *Pis'ma Pobedonostseva k Aleksandru III* (Moscow: 1925–6), i: 331.

p. 148 'Your Majesty, if you ...', ibid., 332.

p. 149 'Yes... Today's meeting ...', letter from Alexander III to Pobedonostsev, in *K.P. Pobedonostsev i ego korrespondenty: Pis'ma i zapiski* (Moscow: 1923), i: part 1, 49.

p. 149 'Thank God this over-hasty ...', ibid., 92.

p. 149 'A proclamation to all Our ...', Alexander III, 'The Tsar's Manifesto on Unshakable Autocracy'. Full text (in Russian) available online at http://www.hist.msu.ru/ER/Etext/1881.htm

p. 149 'From this day I shall be ...', Coronation speech of Ivan IV (1547). See Chapter Six, p. 46 note (p. 541).

p. 150 'It is a gross delusion to regard ...', Pobedonostsev, *Reflections of a Russian Statesman by K.P. Pobyedonostseff*, trans. C.R. Long (London: Grant Richards, 1898), 53.

p. 151 'These deplorable results ...', ibid., 48.

p. 151 'The so-called May Laws ...', quoted in L. Errera, *The Russian Jews: Extermination or Emancipation?*, trans. B. Loewy (London: 1894), 18; and in S. Dubnow, *History of the Jews in Russia and Poland*, trans. I. Friedlaender (Philadelphia: 1916–20), iii: 10.

p. 153 'I left college with my instruction ...', A. Mikhailov, diaries of student volunteers recorded in *Arkhiv 'Zemli i Voli'* [Archive of *Land and Freedom*] (Moscow: 1932). Available online at http://narovol.narod.ru/origin.htm

p. 153 'Of course the peasants hated ...', S. Lion, ibid.

p. 153 'The peasants reacted to all ...', P. Ivanovskaya, ibid.

p. 154 'The people are incapable ...', Lion, ibid.

p. 154 'The concept of the "invisible dictatorship" ...' Pyotr Tkachev, *Zadachi Revolyutsionnoi Propagandy v Rossii* [The Tasks of Revolutionary Propaganda in Russia], April 1874. Full text archived at http://az.lib.ru/t/tkachew_p_n/text_0060oldorfo.shtml

p. 155 'The belief that a party …', Pyotr Lavrov, 'To the Russian Social Revolutionary Youth', in *Izbrannye Sochineniya* (Moscow: 1934), iii: 360–1.

Chapter Sixteen

p. 156 'The crowd was pushing …', V. Gilyarovsky, *Sochineniya v 4-kh tomakh* (Moscow: Biblioteka Shkolnika, 1999), iii: 24 et seq. Full text available at http://tululu.ru/read74996/24/

p. 157 'no good will come from the reign of this tsar …', ibid., 27.

p. 157 'What shall become of me …', quoted in E. Feinstein, *Anna of All the Russias* (London: Weidenfeld, 2005), 3.

p. 157 'I understand that some people …', A. Mosolov, *At the Court of the Last Tsar: Being the Memoirs of A.A. Mosolov, the Head of the Court Chancellery, 1900–1916* (London: Methuen, 1935), *Part One – The Tsar*, 25.

p. 158 'I fear the Tsar's speech …', Robert F. Byrnes, *Pobedonostsev: His Life and Thought* (Bloomington: Indiana University Press, 1968).

p. 158 'When he called our hopes …', V. Obninsky, *Poslednii Samoderzhets, ocherk zhizni Nikolaya II* [The Last Autocrat: An Outline of the Life of Nicholas II] (Moscow: Respublika, 1992), 142.

p. 159 'Von Plehve was the pillar …', leaflet issued by the Central Committee of the Socialist Revolutionary Party, July 1904. Full text available (in English) at http://www.uea.ac.uk/his/webcours/russia/documents/plehve1.shtml

p. 159 'The most infamous of them …' For details of the Evno Azef affair, see R. Rubenstein, *Comrade Valentine: The True Story of Azef the Spy* (London: Harcourt Brace, 1994).

p. 160 'Sire! We the workers …' Full text of workers' petition to the tsar available at http://www.hrono.info/dokum/190_dok/19050109petic.php

p. 160 'From my balcony…', S. Witte, *The Memoirs of Count Witte*, trans. A. Yarmolinsky (New York: Doubleday, 1921), 252.

p. 161 'He pretended to be the people's …', recorded performance and lyrics available at http://www.sovmusic.ru/text.php?fname=peterbrg

p. 161 'The government began to …', Witte, op. cit., 251.

p. 162 'Early in 1906, he returned to Russia and approached …', R. Massie, *Nicholas and Alexandra* (New York: Tess Press, 2004), 107–11.

p. 162 'Before the uprising …', V.I. Lenin, 'The Beginning of Revolution in Russia', in *Lenin: Collected Works* (Moscow: Progress Publishers, 1997), viii: 98.

p. 163 'At heart, His Majesty …', Witte, op. cit., 186. See also von Plehve's alleged remark: 'We need a victorious little war to stem the tide of revolution,' quoted by Witte, op. cit., 250.

p. 163 'Their commander mistook …', *Report of the International Commission of Inquiry: Incident in the North Sea (The Dogger Bank Case)*, 22 February 1905.

p. 164 'Our ships were crowded together …', V. Kostenko, *Na Orle v Tsushime* [On Board the Orel at Tsushima: Memoirs of a Participant in the Russo–Japanese War of 1904–5] (Leningrad: Sudpromgiz, 1955), 423.

p. 164 'While there is no …', ibid., 538.

p. 165 'Our Tsar is Tsushima …', K. Balmont, in *Polnoe Sobranie Sochinenii* (Moscow: 1976), ii: 97.

Chapter Seventeen

p. 167 'Citizens! We've got the ruling clique …', L. Trotsky, *1905*, trans. A. Bostock (London: Allen Lane 1972), 116.

p. 167 'Citizens! If anyone among you believes …', ibid., 116.

p. 168 'As the October strike …', ibid., 110–11.

p. 170 'I have asked you here …', Nicholas's speech to workers delegation published in *Pravitel'stvennyi Vestnik* [Government Gazette], no. 15, on 20 January 1905, 1. See also S. Witte, *The Memoirs of Count Witte*, trans. A. Yarmolinsky (New York: Doubleday, 1921), 252–3.

p. 170 '… a good, religious, simple Russian …', quoted in R. Massie, *Nicholas and Alexandra* (New York: Tess Press, 2004), 214–15.

p. 170 'When in trouble or assailed …', ibid.

p. 170 'When in the course of my official …', Witte, op. cit., 246.

p. 171 'Such a contrivance was typical …', ibid., 230.

p. 171 'We, Nicholas the Second …', 'October Manifesto'. Full text (in Russian) available at http://www.hist.msu.ru/ER/Etext/oct1905.htm. Quoted in full (in English) in Witte, op. cit., 232–3.

p. 172 'In the years 1903–1904 …', Witte, op. cit., 217.

p. 172 'The onslaught of the revolutionary …', Trotsky, op. cit., 96–7.

p. 173 'His Majesty is afflicted …', Witte, op. cit., 224.

p. 173 'A stupid delegation is coming …', Nicholas's letter to his mother, quoted in Massie, op. cit., 238.

Chapter Eighteen

p. 177 'Information arrived that …', A. Solzhenitsyn, *August 1914*, trans. H. Willetts, (London: Penguin, 1990), 335–6.

p. 177 'Only now did Vorotyntsev notice …', ibid., 336.

p. 180 'I shall never forget …', General A.I. Denikin, *The Russian Turmoil: Memoirs, Military, Social, and Political* (London: Hutchinson & Co., 1922), 30.

p. 181 'This regime does not have the wisdom …', *Khrestomatiya po otechestvennoy istorii, 1914–45* [Textbook on National History], ed. A.F. Kiselev and E.M. Shchagin (Moscow: Vlados, 1996).

p. 182 'The craze of occultism …', *The Memoirs of Count Witte*, trans. A. Yarmolinsky (Garden City, NY: Doubleday, Page & Co., 1921), 195.

p. 182 'Rasputin stood before me motionless …', F. Yusupov, *Lost Splendor: The Amazing Memoirs of the Man Who Killed Rasputin*, trans. A. Green and N. Katkov (New York: Helen Marx Books, 2003), ch. 23.

Chapter Nineteen

p. 184 'A revolution in Russia?', A. Solzhenitsyn, *Lenin in Zurich*, trans. H. T. Willetts (New York: Farrar, Straus & Giroux, 1976), 201.

p. 185 'As the masses approached …', Osip Yermansky, quoted in E. Burdzhalov, *Vtoraya russkaya revolyutsiya: vosstanie v Petrograde* [Russia's Second Revolution: Uprising in Petrograd] (Moscow: Nauka, 1967), 138.

p. 185 'The working women took the initiative …', Gordienko, quoted in ibid., 124.

p. 186 'Military Headquarters, 24 February …', N. Romanov, *Dnevniki Nikolaya II, 1913–1918* [The Diaries of Nicholas II] (Moscow: Zakharov, 2007), 199.

p. 186 'The monarchist system is tottering …', Burdzhalov, op. cit., 276–7.

p. 186 'My information is completely different …', R. Massie, *Nicholas and Alexandra* (New York: Tess Press, 2004), 425.

p. 187 'The situation is growing worse …', Burdzhalov, op. cit., 289.

p. 187 'Not to sign any paper or constitution …', ibid., 293.

p. 187 'There is no sacrifice I would not bear …', ibid.

p. 188 'In the days of the great struggle …', ibid., 296–7.

p. 188 'Mikhail stressed his resentment …', *The Memoirs of Vladimir D. Nabokov: V.D. Nabokov and the Provisional Government, 1917*, ed. V.D. Medlin and S.L. Parsons (New Haven: Yale University Press, 1976), 49.

p. 189 'Nicholas the Second has abdicated …', Burdzhalov, op. cit., 304.

p. 189 'Guchkov had been addressing …', Account by Shul'gin in his memoirs, *Dni* (Belgrade, 1925), quoted in Burdzhalov, op. cit., 302.

p. 190 'As long as it didn't hinder …', Burdzhalov, op. cit. 239–40; N. Riasanovsky, *A History of Russia* (New York: Oxford University Press, 1963), 506.

Chapter Twenty

p. 192 'Bern, 23 March 1917', W. Hahlweg, 'Lenins Reise durch Deutschland im April 1917', in *Vierteljahrshefte für Zeitgeschichte* (Munich: 1957), 315.

p. 192 '… Send Lenin into Russia …', Churchill to the House of Commons, 5 November 1919, *Hansard*, Fifth Series (Commons), vol. 120, col. 1633.

p. 194 'The Russian revolution created by you …' quoted in *Pravda*, no. 24, 5 April 1917; included in *Lenin: Collected Works* (Moscow: Progress Publishers, 1997), xli: 399.

p. 195 'The first stage of the revolution …', *Vladimir Ilyich Lenin, Biograficheskaya Khronika*, tom 4, Mart–Oktyabr 1917 (Moscow: Izdatelstvo Politicheskoy Literatury, 1973), 60–1.

p. 196 '*Yest takaya partiya!*' Lenin speech to First All Russian Congress of Workers' and Soldiers' Deputies.

p. 197 'The man was gifted …', *The Memoirs of Vladimir D. Nabokov: V.D. Nabokov and the Provisional Government, 1917*, ed. V.D. Medlin and S.L. Parsons (New Haven: Yale University Press, 1976), 75.

p. 197 'I expressed my opinion …', ibid., 87.

p. 197 'Armoured cars and vehicles …', ibid., 148.

p. 198 'He would be gripped by a state of rage …', N. Valentinov, *Encounters with Lenin*, trans. P. Rosta and B. Pearce (London: Oxford University Press, 1968), 149–50.

p. 199 'Lenin and Co are spies!', Nabokov, op. cit., 137.

p. 199 'The Provisional Government could have ...', Nabokov, op. cit., 83.

Chapter Twenty-one

p. 201 'The whole world is turning to revolutionary struggle ...', the Third Communist International, 4 March 1919, in *Lenin: Collected Works*, (Moscow: Progress Publishers, 1997), xxix: 240–1.

p. 201 'I unreservedly recommend ...', introduction by V.I. Lenin to J. Reed, *Ten Days That Shook the World* (London: Penguin, 1977), 7.

p. 204 'On both sides of the main gateway ...', Reed, op. cit., 108–11.

p. 205 'Even to the very end ...', *The Memoirs of Vladimir D. Nabokov: V.D. Nabokov and the Provisional Government, 1917*, ed. V.D. Medlin and S.L. Parsons (New Haven: Yale University Press, 1976), 78.

p. 206 'And there was Lenin ...', *Reminiscences of V.I. Lenin, in 5 Volumes*, ii: 457.

p. 206 'Comrades! The revolution of workers ...', ibid.

p. 206 'There was a tremendous tension of course ...', BBC Radio archive recording, no date given.

p. 207 'You're finished ...', I. Thatcher, *Trotsky* (London: Routledge, 2002), 92.

p. 208 'The Bolsheviks make no fetish of democracy ..., speech, 23 December 1918, in *Lenin: Collected Works*, op. cit. xxviii: 368–72.

p. 208 '... ruthless contempt, worthy of an aristocrat ...', quoted in O. Figes, *A People's Tragedy: The Russian Revolution 1891–1924* (London: Jonathan Cape, 1996), 386.

p. 208 'She did not like the Russian Communist Party ...', M. Philips Price, *My Three Revolutions* (London: George Allen & Unwin Ltd., 1969), 160.

p. 209 'Dozens, perhaps hundreds ...', V. Grossman, *Everything Flows*, trans. R. and E. Chandler (New York: New York Review Books, 2009), 177–82.

PART FOUR

Chapter Twenty-two

p. 212 'Everything was fermenting, growing, rising ...', B. Pasternak, *Doctor Zhivago*, trans. M. Hayward and M. Harari (London: Collins Harvill, 1988), 132.

p. 212 'It just seems to me that ...', ibid., 151.

p. 213 'Everyone expected the Bolsheviks ...', *The Memoirs of Vladimir D. Nabokov: V.D. Nabokov and the Provisional Government, 1917*, ed. V.D. Medlin and S.L. Parsons (New Haven: Yale University Press, 1976), 166.

p. 214 'To relinquish the Soviet Republic won by the people ...', V. I. Lenin, 'Draft Decree on the Dissolution of the Constituent Assembly', 6 January 1918, in *Lenin: Collected Works* (Moscow: Progress Publishers, 1997), xxvi: 434.

p. 215 'The Right Socialist Revolutionary ...', ibid., 435.

p. 215 'For almost a hundred years ...', M. Gorky, articles from *Novaya Zhizn'*, 9 and 11 Jan 1918, in *Sobranie Sochinenii v 30 tomakh* (Moscow, 1956), xxvii: 98.

p. 215 'Everything has turned out for the best ...', H. Shukman, *The Russian Revolution*

(Stroud: Sutton, 1998), 67. See also L. Trotsky, in *Lenin, Notes for a Biographer* (New York: Putnam, 1971), ch. 8 ('Breaking up the Constituent Assembly'), who reports Lenin as saying, 'The breaking up of the Constituent Assembly by the Soviet power is the complete and public liquidation of formal democracy in the name of the revolutionary dictatorship. It will be a good lesson.'

p. 216 'Lenin and Trotsky do not have ...', M. Gorky, 'Untimely Thoughts', in *Novaya Zhizn*, no. 177, 7 November 1917. In English in *Untimely Thoughts: Essays on Revolution, Culture and the Bolsheviks, 1917–18*, trans. H. Ermolaev (New York: Paul Eriksson, Inc., 1968), 85–6.

p. 216 'Lenin's intolerance, his contempt for freedom ...', V. Grossman, *Everything Flows*, trans. R. and E. Chandler (New York: New York Review Books, 2009), 177–83.

p. 217 'We cannot, will not and must not ...', L. Trotsky, 'Announcement of Russian Withdrawal from Brest-Litovsk Peace Negotiations, 10 February 1918', in *Source Records of the Great War*, vol. VI, ed. C. Horne (New York: National Alumni, 1923). Full text reproduced (in English) at http://www.marxists.org/archive/trotsky/1918/commissar/ gov.htm

p. 218 'Either we sign the peace terms ...', ibid.

Chapter Twenty-three

p. 219 'But Nicholas's cousin, George V, refused ...', *The Memoirs of Vladimir D. Nabokov: V.D. Nabokov and the Provisional Government, 1917*, ed. V.D. Medlin and S.L. Parsons (New Haven: Yale University Press, 1976), 71–2.

p. 219 'Where they would be safer ...', extracts from statement of Ya. Yurovsky to Soviet commission of inquiry, quoted in R. Massie, *Nicholas and Alexandra* (New York: Tess Press, 2004), 554–6. See also E. Radzinsky, *The Last Tsar: The Life and Death of Nicholas II*, trans. Marian Schwartz (London: Arrow, 1993), 8–9: Radzinsky fails to find Yurovsky's statement in the Central State Archives of Moscow. The text of it is reproduced at http://www.alexanderpalace.org/palace/YurovskynoteRussian.html

p. 219 'The Tsar was carrying his young son ...', statement by Medvedev to Soviet commission of inquiry, quoted in R. Wilton, *The Last Days of the Romanovs* (London: Legion, 1920), 171 et seq.

p. 220 'Nicholas had put Alexei on a chair ...', Yurovsky statement, op. cit.

p. 221 'The field sways ...', M. Tsvetaeva, 'The Swans' Encampment', trans. Elaine Feinstein, in *Marina Tsvetaeva: Selected Poems* (London: Penguin, 1994), 34.

p. 222 'Comrade soldiers of the Red Army!' *Lenin: Collected Works* (Moscow: Progress Publishers, 1997), xxix: 244–5.

p. 223 'Our former masters ...', recorded performance and lyrics available at http://www.sovmusic.ru/text.php?fname=dubina

p. 223 'One division sent to ...', J. Silverlight, *The Victors' Dilemma: Allied Intervention in the Russian Civil War* (London: Barrie & Jenkins Ltd, 1970), 171.

p. 223 'While I was there I met ...', Miles Hudson, *Intervention in Russia, 1918–1920: A Cautionary Tale* (Barnsley: Leo Cooper, 2004), 79.

p. 223 'Other British troops spent …', Silverlight, op. cit., 185.

p. 224 'Red Warriors! On all …', L. Trotsky, *My Life: An Attempt at an Autobiography* (London: Penguin, 1979), 449.

p. 224 The Allies supplied …' O. Figes, *A People's Tragedy: The Russian Revolution 1891–1924* (London: Jonathan Cape, 1996), 652.

p. 225 'By early 1919…', ibid., 596–7.

p. 225 'The Red Army has united …', Lenin's speech in *Lenin: Collected Works*, op. cit., xxix: 244–5.

p. 226 'On that day, 22 July 1920 …', I. Babel, from *Konarmiya* (Moscow: Pravda, 1990), 119. 'Red Cavalry' in *Isaac Babel: Collected Stories* (London Penguin, 1961), 135–6.

p. 227 'Over the corpse of White Poland …', quoted in N. Davies, *God's Playground: A History of Poland* (Oxford: Oxford University Press, 1981), ii: 396.

p. 227 'Gaping mouths, torn open …', K. Paustovsky, *Story of a Life: In That Dawn*, trans. M. Harari and M. Duncan (London: Harvill Press, 1967), 218–19.

p. 228 'What do you see out there …', M. Bulgakov, *Flight* (London: Nick Hern Books, 1998), 49–51.

Chapter Twenty-four

p. 230 'My term of imprisonment …', R. Bruce Lockhart, *Memoirs of a British Agent: Being an Account of the Author's Early Life and of His Official Mission to Moscow in 1918* (London: Putnam, 1932), 326.

p. 231 'Lenin, shot twice …', *Pravda*, 3 September 1918, quoted in L. Kirschenbaum, 'Scripting Revolution: Regicide in Russia', in *Left History*, 7, no. 2 (2001), 50.

p. 231 'At six in the morning a woman was …', Bruce Lockhart, op. cit., 320.

p. 232 'Merciless mass terror …', decree on Red Terror published in *Krasnaya Gazeta*, 1 September 1918, and *Izvestiya*, 3 September 1918.

p. 232 'I shall never forget …', M. Philips Price, *My Three Revolutions* (London: George Allen & Unwin Ltd., 1969), 136.

p. 232 'Don't go looking …', cited in Ye. Albats, *KGB: State Within a State, The Secret Police and its Hold on Russia's Past, Present and Future*, trans. C. Fitzpatrick (London: I.B.Tauris, 1995), 93.

p. 233 'We stand for organised terror …', interview with Dzerzhinsky in *Novaya Zhizn*, 14 July 1918.

p. 233 'A city of icebergs …', G. Hosking, *Russia and the Russians: A History* (London: Penguin, 2001), 409.

p. 233 'With a clank, a squeal and a groan …', V. Rozanov, *Izbrannoe* (Selected Works) (Munich: Neimanis, 1970), 494. Also quoted in M. Heller and A. Nekrich, *Utopia in Power: The History of the Soviet Union from 1917 to the Present*, trans. M. Carlos (New York: Summit Books, 1986), 255.

p. 233 'Down with Lenin …', M. McAuley, *Bread and Justice: State and Society in Petrograd, 1917–22* (Oxford: Clarendon Press, 1991), 280.

p. 234 'Once their power is consolidated …', *Golos Truda*, November 1917.

p. 235 'Lenin's "purpose was to save ...", N. Riasanovsky, *A History of Russia* (New York: Oxford University Press, 1963), 527.

p. 235 'The only work done by the Soviet ...', report by Colonel Kimens, acting British vice-consul in Petrograd, 12 November 1918, reproduced in *The Russian Revolution, 1917* (London: The Stationery Office, 2001), 83.

p. 236 'A wave of *kulak* revolts ...', *Lenin: Collected Works* (Moscow: Progress Publishers, 1997), xxviii: 53–7, trans. J. Riordan.

p. 237 'The harvest had been annihilated ...', BBC archive interview with Sir Philip Gibbs, no date given.

p. 238 'The insurrection of the kulaks ...', quoted in Robert Service, *Lenin: A Biography* (London: Macmillan, 2000), 365.

p. 238 'We must put down all resistance ...', O. Figes, *A People's Tragedy: The Russian Revolution 1891–1924* (London: Jonathan Cape, 1996), 749.

Chapter Twenty-five

p. 240 'I can't listen to music ...', in a personal conversation with Maxim Gorky. quoted in Gorky, *Lenin the Man* (Berlin: Neue Rundschau, 1924).

p. 240 'We, the representatives ...', G. Hosking, *Russia and the Russians: A History* (London: Penguin, 2001), 414.

p. 241 'Since you are from Kronstadt ...', I. Getzler, *Kronstadt, 1917–1921: The Fate of a Soviet Democracy* (Cambridge: Cambridge University Press, 1983), 212–13.

p. 242 'The working class expected the Revolution ...', O. Figes, *A People's Tragedy: The Russian Revolution 1891–1924* (London: Jonathan Cape, 1996), 763–4.

p. 243 '... far more dangerous than ...', ibid., 758.

p. 243 'The New Economic Policy we are introducing ...', Lenin speech to the Tenth Congress of The Russian Communist Party (Bolshevik) in March 1921, in *Lenin: Collected Works* (Moscow: Progress Publishers, 1997), 93–5.

p. 244 'They asked me if I love ...', V.I. Mayakovsky, *Vy lyubite li NEP?* [Do You Love the NEP?] (1922). In Mayakovsky, *Sobranie Sochinenii v 13 tomakh* (Moscow: Khudozhestvennaya Literatura, 1961), iii: 29–30.

p. 245 'There must be an immediate dissolution ...', Hosking, op. cit., 415–16.

Chapter Twenty-six

p. 248 'Comrade Stalin, having ...', 'Zavet Lenina' [Lenin's Testament] in *Lenin: Collected Works (Moscow: Progress Publishers, 1997)*, xxxvi: 593–611.

p. 249 'When the Congress met ...', Arthur Ransome, article in *Manchester Guardian*, 23 January 1924.

p. 250 'The body of Lenin ...', ibid.

p. 251 '... sitting on the steps ...', B. Haugen, *Joseph Stalin: Dictator of the Soviet Union* (Minneapolis, MN: Compass Point Books, 2006), 49.

p. 251 '... the Russian people's worst ...', *Life Magazine*, 3 February 1958, 81.

p. 252 'The word Soviet has become known ...', Lenin speech, 'What is Soviet Power?', 30 March 1919, in *Lenin: Collected Works*, xxix: 248–9.

p. 253 'We had a great big banner ...', Harry Young, BBC Radio archive interview, no date given.

Chapter Twenty-seven

p. 256 'Oh yes, dear. It happened ...', recording of Masha Alekseevna, survivor of collectivisation in Tambov region.

p. 256 'The solution to our problems lies ...', Stalin speech, 27 December 1929, in J.V. Stalin, *Problems of Leninism* (Peking: Foreign Languages Press, 1976), 451–2.

p. 257 'We are turning the main mass ...', *Pravda*, no. 259, 7 November 1929, in J.V. Stalin, *Works* (Moscow: Foreign Languages Publishing House, 1954), xii: 124–41.

p. 257 'The peasants are joining the collective farms ...', ibid.

p. 259 'The collective-farm movement is ...', Stalin speech, 'On Agrarian Policy', 27 December 1929, in Stalin, *Works*, op. cit., xii: 147–8.

p. 260 'The exact number ...', see, *inter alia*, L. Hubbard, *The Economics of Soviet Agriculture* (London: Macmillan, 1939), 117–18.

p. 260 'We went into the house ...', BBC Radio archive recording, no date given.

p. 261 'Stalin had said, "The struggle for grain" ...', G. Hosking, *Russia and the Russians: A History* (London: Penguin, 2001), 453.

p. 261 'Akh, brethren ...', quoted in L. Viola, *Peasant Rebels under Stalin* (Oxford: Oxford University Press, 1996), 57–63.

p. 262 'In the kolkhoz they will ...', ibid.

p. 262 'Down with the Soviet commune ...', I.V. Klimkin, *Nachalo Kollectivizatsii, 1929–1930* [The Beginnings of Collectivisation, 1929–1930], in the local history section of the Pitelinsky District municipal website.

p. 263 'Many elected to slaughter their ...', M. Heller and A. Nekrich, Utopia in Power: The History of the Soviet Union from 1917 to the Present, trans. M. Carlos (New York: Summit Books, 1986), 238.

p. 263 'It was the big story ...', interview, BBC Radio archive recording, no date given.

p. 263 'Between two and four ...', *Famine in the Soviet Ukraine 1932–3: A Memorial Exhibition*, catalogue (Harvard University, 1986), 31.

p. 263 'This ruin I saw ...', Gareth Jones, *Manchester Guardian*, 29 March 1933. All Gareth Jones's articles are available at http://www.garethjones.org/

p. 264 'After Stalin, the most hated man in Russia ...', ibid.

p. 265 'I see you are a good ...', Heller and Nekrich, op. cit., 238.

p. 265 'In 1932 Mikhail Khataevich ...', R. Conquest, 'Comment on Wheatcroft', *Europe–Asia Studies*, University of Glasgow, 1999, vol. 51, no. 8, 1479.

p. 265 '... for Stalin, the peasants ...', Heller and Nekrich, op. cit., 238.

p. 265 'Unless we begin to straighten ...', *The Stalin–Kaganovich Correspondence 1931–1936* ed. R. W. Davies, O. V. Khlevniuk and E. A. Rees (New Haven & London: Yale University Press, 2003), 179–81.

Chapter Twenty-eight

p. 268 'The history of Russia is …', R. Daniels, *A Documentary History of Communism in Russia: From Lenin to Gorbachev* (Hanover, New Hampshire: University of Vermont, University Press of New England, 1993), 181–2.

p. 269 '… we have destroyed the country to defeat the Whites …', M. Heller and A. Nekrich, *Utopia in Power: The History of the Soviet Union from 1917 to the Present*, trans. M. Carlos (New York: Summit Books, 1986), 118.

p. 270 'All our spying operations …', M. Sayers and A. Khan, *The Great Conspiracy against Soviet Russia* (New York: Boni & Gaer, 1946), 60.

p. 270 'This is an ordeal …', ibid., 60.

p. 271 'They were extraordinarily …', ibid.

p. 271 'We live in an era of great fear …', A. Afinogenov, 'Strakh' [Fear] (1930), in *P'esy* (Moscow: Izd. Iskusstvo, 1947), 72–3.

p. 272 '… class enemies inside the USSR …', from J.V. Stalin, *Works* (Moscow: Foreign Languages Publishing House, 1954), vol. 1138.

p. 272 'The underlying causes …', from J.V. Stalin, *Problems of Leninism* (Peking: Foreign Languages Press, 1976), 526.

p. 273 'Trotsky boasted …', G. Hosking, *Russia and the Russians: A History* (London: Penguin, 2001), 434–5.

p. 273 'Ships sail and bridges rise …', 'Rabochii Chelovek' [The Working Man], song by Yu. Levitin and M. Matusovsky, text and performance available at http://www.sovmusic. ru/text.php?fname=rabochiy

p. 273 'Onwards, shock brigades …', V.I. Mayakovsky, 'Marsh Udarnykh Brigad' [March of the Shock Brigades] (1930), *Polnoe Sobrenie Sochinenii v 13 tomakh* (Moscow: Khudozhestvennaya Literatura, 1961), x: 162.

p. 274 'Here, sitting at this table …', J.V. Stalin, *Works*, op. cit., xiv: 174–5.

p. 275 'We live so well …', archive recording of Tatiana Fyodorova in PBS Radio documentary, *People's Century.* Available at http://www.pbs.org/wgbh/peoplescentury/about/ index.html

p. 277 'A few days ago …', Gareth Jones in *Evening Standard*, Friday, 31 March 1933.

Chapter Twenty-nine

p. 279 'Russia is the place where poetry …', O. Mandelstam, quoted in O. Lekmanov, *Osip Mandelshtam* (Moscow: Molodaya Gvardiya, 2009), 97.

p. 279 'We are living, but the ground …', Mandelstam, 'My zhivem, pod soboyu ne chuya… ' (1933), *Mandelshtam, Stikhotvorenia* (Tbilisi: Merani, 1990), 196.

p. 280 'Not a word …', Mandelstam in conversation with Emma Gerstein, quoted in E. Gerstein, *Moscow Memoirs*, trans. J. Crowfoot (London: Harvill, 2004), 61.

p. 280 'Stalin wanted to know if my father …', author's interview with Yevgeny Pasternak, 2006.

p. 281 'I am practising a new genre …', I. Babel, speech to First Congress of Soviet Writers' Union, quoted in H. Rappaport, *Josef Stalin: A Biographical Companion* (London: ABC-CLIO, 2000), 16.

p. 281 'In the car, one of the policemen …', Antonina N. Pirozhkova, *At His Side: The Last Years of Isaac Babel*, trans. A. Frydman and R. Busch (South Royalton, Vermont: Steerforth Press, 1996), 113.

p. 282 '… died of cardiac arrest …', V. Shentalinsky, *The KGB's Literary Archive*, trans. J. Crowfoot (London: Harvill Press, 1995), 71.

p. 282 'A typed submission …', ibid., 67–71.

p. 282 'The knowledge of free poetry …', author's interview with Yevgeny Pasternak, 2006.

p. 283 'Leave that cloud-dweller …', quoted in R. Tucker, *Stalin in Power* (New York: Norton, 1990), 445. Stalin was showing his knowledge of Pasternak's work: his remark is a reference to Pasternak's collection of poems *The Twins in the Clouds*.

p. 283 'Muddle instead of Music', *Pravda*, 28 January 1936.

p. 284 'It's terrible when an artist is persecuted …', author's interview with Irina Shostakovich, 2006.

p. 285 'Are we entitled …', M. Heller and A. Nekrich, *Utopia in Power: The History of the Soviet Union from 1917 to the Present*, trans. M. Carlos (New York: Summit Books, 1986), 139.

p. 286 'Not under foreign skies …', Anna Akhmatova, *Rekviem* [Requiem], in *Anna Akhmatova: Sochineniya v dvukh tomakh* (Moscow: Khudozhestvennaya Literatura, 1991), i: 107.

p. 286 'We will preserve you …', ibid., 109.

p. 287 'Opening before me …', Akhmatova, *Poema Bez Geroya* [Poem Without a Hero], ibid., i: 273–98.

p. 288 'He was delighted and happy …', author's interview with Yevgeny Pasternak, 2006.

p. 290 'What tears in eyes now … measure of death', M. Tsvetaeva, *Poems to Czechia, No. 8*, 'O Slezy na glazakh …', in *Marina Tsvetaeva: Stikhotvoreniya* (Moscow: Khudozhestvennaya Literatura, 1989), 127.

p. 290 'When I left Russia …', S. Rakhmaninov, quoted in A. Wehrmeyer, *Rakhmaninov* (London: Haus Publishing, 2004), 102.

p. 291 'Imitated in foreign cities…', V. Nabokov, *Speak Memory* (London: Penguin, 2009), 223.

p. 291 'The revolution was blood …', Nabokov, BBC Radio archive interview, no date given.

p. 291 'At first, the quiet and the snowy coolness …', Nabokov, 'A Visit to the Museum', in *The Stories of Vladimir Nabokov* (London: Penguin, 1995), 284–5.

p. 292 'He blamed the vandalism …', author's interview with Sviatoslav Prokofiev, 2006.

p. 293 'In the beginning he was just very happy …', ibid.

p. 293 'They are torturing me …', Shentalinsky, op. cit., 27.

p. 294 'People like to say …', author's interview with Sviatoslav Prokofiev, 2006.

p. 294 'Something very bad …', ibid.

p. 296 'Listen. I love …', author's interview with Yevgeny Pasternak, 2006.

p. 297 'People who had voices had their tongues cut out …', N. Mandelstam, *Hope against Hope* (New York: Modern Library, 1999), 204.

p. 297 'So, it seems Alexander Alexandrovich …', author's interview with Yevgeny Pasternak, 2006.

p. 297 'Well yes, we had the decree …', author's interview with Tikhon Khrennikov, 2006.

p. 298 'My word was law …', ibid.

p. 298 'Khrennikov's defence evokes …', author's interview with Irina Shostakovich, 2006.

p. 299 'The song and the verse …', V.I. Mayakovsky, *Razgovor s fininspektorom o poezii* [A conversation with the tax inspector about poetry] (1926), in Mayakovsky, *Polnoe Sobranie Sochinenii v13 tomakh* (Moscow: Khudozhestvennaya Literatura, 1961), iii: 141–9.

p. 299 'It is time for bullets …', G. Suny, *The Soviet Experiment: Russia, the USSR and the Successor States* (Oxford: Oxford University Press, 1998), 203–4.

p. 299 'Nonsense, stupidity …', ibid., 205.

p. 300 'It's past one o'clock …', V.I. Mayakovsky, *Lyubovnaya lodka razbilas' o byt* [The boat of love has smashed on the rocks of life], in Mayakovsky, op. cit., viii: 237.

p. 300 'I want to be a poet …', S. Yesenin, *Rus' Ukhodyashchaya* [Russia Departing], in Yesenin, *Sobranie Sochinenii v 7 tomakh* (Moscow: 1988), ii: 158.

p. 301 'I am not your tame canary!', Yesenin, [Stanzas], ibid., iii: 25.

p. 301 'Art must move organically …', Heller and Nekrich, op. cit., 194.

p. 301 'I'm no good at art …', V.I. Lenin, *Conversation with Yuri Annenkov*, quoted in I. McGilchrist, *The Master and His Emissary* (New Haven: Yale, 2009), 412.

Chapter Thirty

p. 303 'There is a danger…', Stalin report to Seventeeth Party Congress ('Congress of the Victors'), 26 Jan 1934, in J.V. Stalin, *Works* (Moscow: Foreign Languages Publishing House, 1954), xiii: 203.

p. 304 'In all areas of …', Kirov speech at 'Congress of the Victors', in *Stenograficheskii Otchet, zasedanie 10-oe, utrom, 31 January, 1934* (Moscow: Izd. Partizdat, 1934).

p. 306 'The foul murder …', Stalin speech on death of Kirov, in pamphet *The Defects in Party Work and Measures for Liquidating Trotskyite and Other Double Dealers*, report to the Plenum of the Central Committee of the RKP(b), 3 March 1937 (parts 1–3 of 5), published by the Cooperative Publishing Society of Foreign Workers in the USSR, Moscow, 1937.

p. 308 'The enemy is cunning …', A. Vaksberg, *Vishinski: Le Procureur de Staline, les grands procès de Moscou* (Paris: Albin Michel, 1991), 83.

p. 310 'Overcoming blood …', M. Heller and A. Nekrich, *Utopia in Power: The History of the Soviet Union from 1917 to the Present*, trans. M. Carlos (New York: Summit Books, 1986), 286.

p. 311 'Numbers were fixed for arrests …', R. Service, *A History of Twentieth-Century Russia* (London: Penguin, 1997), 221.

p. 312 'The weed and thistle …', quoted in Vaksberg, op. cit., 127.

p. 312 'This murderer of millions …', A. Solzhenitsyn, *The Gulag Archipelago, 1918–1956: An Experiment in Literary Investigation, Part I*, trans. T. Whitney (London: Collins & Harvill Press, 1974), 411.

p. 312 'At one stage …', F. MacLean, *Eastern Approaches* (London: Penguin, 1991), 120.

p. 313 'If one were to die …', N. Bukharin, *Last Plea – Evening Session*, 12 March 1938, quoted in Zh. and R. Medvedev, *The Unknown Stalin*, trans. E. Dahrendorf (London: I.B.Tauris, 2006), 294.

p. 314 '... become a slaughterer ...', A. Koestler, *Darkness at Noon*, trans. D. Hardy (London: Penguin, 1983), 122.

p. 314 '... one reason for his preposterous confession ...', A. Larina, *This I Cannot Forget: The Memoirs of Anna Larina, Nikolai Bukharin's Wife* (Pandora, 1994), 72.

p. 314 'Know comrades, that the banner you bear ...', S. Cohen, *Bukharin and the Bolshevik Revolution: A Political Biography, 1888–1938* (London: Wildwood House, 1974), 371.

p. 314 'I address this appeal ...', Larina, op. cit., 344–5.

p. 316 'Stalin's trial against me ...', L. Trotsky, television interview, recorded in Mexico, 1938, for broadcast on US television.

p. 316 'I know I shall not survive this ...', Trotsky's dying words, quoted in J. Gorkin, *L'Assassinat de Trotsky* (Paris: Julliard, 1970), 141.

p. 317 'According to the NKVD ...', R. Pipes, *Communism: A History of the Intellectual and Political Movement* (London: Phoenix Press, 2001), 66–7.

p. 317 'The hungrier we were...', G. Hosking, *Russia and the Russians: A History* (London: Penguin, 2001),468.

p. 317 'All were convicted ...', D. Volkogonov, *The Rise and Fall of the Soviet Empire: Political Leaders from Lenin to Gorbachev*, trans. H. Shukman (London: Harper Collins, 1998), 109.

p. 318 'God disturbed him ...', Service, op. cit., 226–7.

p. 318 'The deaths of the vanquished ...', ibid., 226.

Chapter Thirty-one

p. 320 'Of the areas belonging to the Polish state ...', W. Shirer, *The Rise and Fall of the Third Reich: A History of Nazi Germany* (USA: Nationwide Book Service, 1960), 541.

p. 321 'The sinister news ...', G. Roberts, *Stalin's Wars: From World War to Cold War, 1939–1953* (New Haven: Yale University Press, 2006), 30.

p. 321 'In view of the changed...', Shirer, op. cit., 541–2.

p. 322 'Hitler wanted to trick us ...', R. Service, *A History of Twentieth-Century Russia* (London: Penguin, 1997), 257.

p. 322 '... in order to aid and protect the Ukrainians ...', Roberts, op. cit., 37.

p. 322 'I cannot forecast ...', ibid., 38.

p. 323 'The head of the NKVD ...', Beria report to Stalin, 5 March 1940, marked 'top secret', among documents released by Russian government in April 2010. Facsimile of original Beria report available at http://news.bbc.co.uk/1/hi/world/europe/8649435.stm

p. 324 'We have conquered ...', A. Bullock, *Hitler and Stalin: Parallel Lives* (London: Harper Collins, 1991), 730.

p. 325 'Stalin confided to Molotov that they would "not be ready" ...', R. Service, *Stalin: A Biography* (London: Macmillan, 2004), 406.

p. 325 'This is all a panic ...', M. Heller and A. Nekrich, *Utopia in Power: The History of the Soviet Union from 1917 to the Present*, trans. M. Carlos (New York: Summit Books, 1986), 361.

p. 325 'The sparrows were chirping ...', *Khrushchev Remembers: The Glasnost Tapes*, trans. J. L. Schecter and V. V. Luchkov (Boston: Little, Brown and Co, 1990), 50.

p. 326 'On the very eve of the invasion ...', R. Braithwaite, *Moscow 1941: A City and Its People at War* (London: Profile Books, 2006), 67; and Service, *Russia*, op. cit., 260.

p. 326 'With 4 million men ...' Service, *Russia*, op. cit., 261.

p. 326 'Hitler described the Soviet Union as a rotten building ...', Roberts, op. cit., 85.

p. 326 'Do not give in to any provocations ...', Heller and Nekrich, op. cit., 371.

p. 326 'Citizens of the Soviet ...', Braithwaite, op. cit., 75.

p. 327 'Heavy counterattacks ...', Heller and Nekrich, op. cit., 371.

p. 327 'Everywhere the Russians ...', Service, *Russia, op. cit.*, 264.

p. 327 'Comrades! Citizens ...', Stalin speech, 3 July 1941, from *The World's Great Speeches: 292 Speeches from Pericles to Nelson Mandela*, ed. L. Copeland, L. Lamm and S. McKenna (New York: Dover Publications, 1999), 495–6.

p. 328 'Conditions in the ...', Braithwaite, op. cit., 310.

p. 329 'Hey comrades ...', quoted in P. Lidov, *Geroi Sovetskogo Soyuza Zoya Anatolevna Kosmodemyanskaya* (Moscow, 1942), 14–15. But M. Gorinov, in 'Zoya Kosmodemyanskaya, 1923–1941' in *Otechestvennaya Istoriya*, no. 1 (Moscow, 2003), reproduces the transcript of the Nazi interrogation of Zoya and suggests that her 'last words' might be the subsequent invention of Soviet propaganda.

p. 329 '... pikes, swords ...', Heller and Nekrich, op. cit., 375.

p. 329 '... the war with Russia ...', Roberts, op. cit., 84.

p. 329 '... no Soviet prisoners ...', quoted in R. Brakman, *Sekretnaya Papka Iosifa Stalina* [Stalin's Secret File] (Moscow: Ves' Mir, 2004), 297. Discussed by Yu. Teplyakov in 'Stalin's war against his own troops: The tragic fate of Soviet prisoners of war in German captivity', in slightly amended form in *The Journal of Historical Review*, Jul–Aug 1994, xiv, no. 4, 4–10.

p. 329 'Of the 3 million ...', Roberts, op. cit., 85.

p. 330 'A Jew is a Bolshevik ...', ibid., 87.

p. 331 'Yids of the city ...' Photograph of original newspaper cutting at http://www.archives. gov.ua/Sections/B-Yar/?88

p. 331 'We had expected only five to six thousand ...', Nuremberg Military Tribunal, *Einsatzgruppen Trial* judgment; transcript quoting exhibit NO-3157, 426.

p. 331 'It was all done so quickly ...', M. Berenbaum, *The World Must Know; the History of the Holocaust as Told in the United States Holocaust Museum* (Baltimore: Johns Hopkins University Press, 2006), 97–8.

p. 333 'The whole situation makes it ...', Braithwaite, op. cit., 180.

p. 333 'The Führer has decided ...', Roberts, op. cit. 104.

p. 334 'By the end of the operation ...', Braithwaite, op. cit., 276.

p. 335 'Borodino! Your ground stands firm ...', *Moskva za nami!* [Moscow stands behind us], words and music by B. Vasilev (1942), quoted in G. Alferova, *Borodino, pole russkoi slavy* [Borodino, the field of Russian glory] (State Museum of Borodino, 2002).

p. 335 'The villages were small …', Braithwaite, op. cit., 102.

p. 336 'All the peoples …', Stalin speech, 7 Nov 1941. Full text available at http://cccp.narod.ru/ work/book/stal_parad.html

p. 337 'Russia is a country …', C. Ailsby, *Images of Barbarossa: The German Invasion of Russia, 1941* (London: Ian Allan Publishing, 2001), 50.

Chapter Thirty-two

p. 338 'The German army is …', G. Roberts, *Stalin's Wars: From World War to Cold War, 1939–1953* (New Haven: Yale University Press, 2006), 114.

p. 338 'The Soviet forces …', G. Hosking, *Russia and the Russians: A History* (London: Penguin, 2001), 495.

p. 339 'Wait for me …', K. Simonov, 'Zhdi menya i ya vernus', tol'ko ochen' zhdi …', in Simonov, *Polnoe Sobranie Sochinenii* (Moscow: Khudozhestvennaya Literatura, 1987), ii: 90.

p. 339 'By mid 1943 …', Heller and Nekrich, op. cit., 376

p. 340 'They dragged out …', Hosking, op. cit., 502.

p. 340 'Praising American … far north and east.', M. Heller and A. Nekrich, *Utopia in Power: The History of the Soviet Union from 1917 to the Present*, trans. M. Carlos (New York: Summit Books, 1986), 376–81.

p. 341 'The Wehrmacht had ventured …', Roberts, op. cit., 126.

p. 341 'For all the love …', *Ni shagu nazad* [Not one step backwards], Order No. 227 of the People's Commissar for Defence (J.V. Stalin), 28 July 1942. Full text available at http://postrana.narod.ru/PR_227.HTM

p. 342 'Those who have been …', ibid.

p. 342 'More than 150,000 …', D. Volkogonov, *The Rise and Fall of the Soviet Empire: Political Leaders from Lenin to Gorbachev*, trans. H. Shukman (London: Harper Collins, 1998), 118.

p. 342 'If you leave …', R. Service, *Stalin: A Biography* (London: Macmillan, 2004), 453.

p. 344 'The home of the Russian is also your home …', R. Service, *A History of Twentieth-Century Russia* (London: Penguin, 1997), 283.

p. 344 'An indestructible union …', new Soviet anthem (1944), words by A. Alexandrov, music by S. Mikhalkov. Performance and full text available at http://www.sovmusic.ru/text.php?fname=ussr44

p. 345 'All of us are soldiers …', A. Axell, *Russia's Heroes, 1941–45* (London: Constable, 2001), 93–4.

p. 345 'Our common father …', Hosking, op. cit., 503.

p. 346 'For us, the war …', ibid., 505.

p. 346 'The defence of Stalingrad …', Roberts, op. cit., 134.

p. 346 'The battle had been …', pencil-written notes by W. Churchill and A. Harriman. Original document facsimile available at http://www.loc.gov/exhibits/churchill/interactive /_html/wc0176.html

p. 346 'We will save this …', V. Chuikov, *Srazhenie Veka* [The Battle of the Century], (Moscow: Izd. Sov. Rossiya, 1975), 48.

p. 347 'A voice boomed …', J. Bastable, *Voices from Stalingrad* (London: David & Charles, 2006), 41–2.

p. 348 'Stalingrad is no longer …', ibid., 136.

p. 348 'Mila Pavlichenko …', Axell, op. cit., 110.

p. 349 'A German carrying …', V. Grossman, 'An Everyday Stalingrad Story', in *Krasnaya Zvezda*, 20 November 1942.

p. 349 'The Soviets suffered …', Roberts, op. cit., 147.

p. 349 'At the end of the attack …', Axell, op. cit., 172.

p. 350 'Two great hammers …', Bastable, op. cit., 152.

p. 350 'By 23 November …' The figure is approximate and impossible to verify accurately. Antony Beevor suggests 290,000 in *Stalingrad* (London: Penguin, 2007), 281.

p. 351 'Army starving and frozen …', ibid., 320.

p. 351 'By 2 February 1943 …', William Craig, *Enemy at the Gates: The Battle for Stalingrad* (New York: Penguin, 1973), 369.

p. 351 'Of the approximately 2.5 million residents …', Heller and Nekrich, op. cit., 401–2.

p. 352 'On 4 July 1943, some 900,000 German soldiers …', D. Glantz and J. House, *The Battle of Kursk* (London: Ian Allan Publishing, 1999), 64–5.

p. 353 'Fifty-seven thousand captured Germans …', Roberts, op. cit., 202.

p. 354 'Know this, you cannot harm us …', quoted by Andrzej Wajda as inspiration for his film *Kanal*. Wajda carries the English translation of Szczepanski's poem on his website: http://www.wajda.pl/en/filmy/film02.html

p. 355 'By February 1945 it was …' Again the figures are of necessity approximate. In the final assault on Berlin, an estimated 80,000 Red Army men died and 300,000 were wounded. Roberts, op. cit., 262.

p. 355 'I take it you have read Dostoevsky …', ibid., 264.

p. 356 'The Germans are not human …', Bastable, op. cit., 64–5.

p. 357 '… pounding the Nazi capital …', A. Beevor, *Berlin: The Downfall, 1945* (London: Viking, 2002), 217.

p. 357 'The famous photo …', Roberts, op. cit., 263.

p. 357 'Comrades, I would …', D. Brandenberger, *National Bolshevism: Stalinist Mass Culture and the Formation of Modern Russian National Identity* (Cambridge, Massachusetts: Harvard University Press, 2002), 131.

p. 358 'Stalin had been …', Service, *Stalin*, op. cit., 480.

Chapter Thirty-three

p. 359 'The Soviet Union lost …', M. Heller and A. Nekrich, *Utopia in Power: The History of the Soviet Union from 1917 to the Present*, trans. M. Carlos (New York: Summit Books, 1986), 443.

p. 360 'The Soviet Union has proved …', speech by Stalin at a meeting of voters of the Stalin electoral district of Moscow on 11 December 1937, reported in *Pravda*, 12 December 1937; quoted in R. McNeal, *Stalin: Man and Ruler* (New York: New York University Press, 1988), 208.

p. 361 'Approximately 400,000 people ...', R. Conquest, *The Nation Killers* (London: Macmillan, 1970), 60.

p. 361 'Typical is Stalin's confidential ...', D. Koenker and R. Bachman (eds), *Revelation from the Russian Archives* (Washington: Library of Congress, 1997), 205–7. Also W. Fuller, 'The Great Fatherland War and Late Stalinism, 1941–1953', in G. Freeze (ed.), *Russia: A History*, (Oxford: Oxford University Press, 2002), 337.

p. 362 'The chairman of one of ...', A. Nekrich, *The Punished Peoples: The Deportations and Fate of Soviet Minorities at the End of the Second World War*, trans. G. Saunders (New York: Norton & Company, 1978), 59.

p. 363 'The journey eastwards ...', Heller and Nekrich, op. cit., 379–80.

p. 363 'Point five: "nationality" ...', V. Grossman, *Life and Fate* (Moscow: Knizhnaya Palata, 1998), 577.

p. 364 'In 1943, Jews were ...', Heller and Nekrich, op. cit., 486.

p. 364 'Approximately half of the ...', G. Hosking, *Rulers and Victims: The Russians in the Soviet Union* (Cambridge, MA: The Belknap Press of Harvard University Press, 2006), 265.

p. 365 'The ties its members...', J. Rubenstein and V. P. Naumov (eds), *Stalin's Secret Pogrom: The Post-War Inquisition of the Jewish Anti-Fascist Committee*, trans. L. E. Wolfson (London: Yale University Press, 2001), 2–10.

p. 365 'The Jews are foul, dirty...', J. Rubenstein, 'The Night of the Murdered Poets', in *New Republic*, 25 August 1997.

p. 366 'All the peoples ...', D. Brandenberger, *National Bolshevism: Stalinist Mass Culture and the Formation of Modern Russian National Identity* (Cambridge, Massachusetts: Harvard University Press, 2002), 43.

p. 366 'He was certain that ...', Grossman, op. cit., 316.

p. 366 'Stalin feared a new Decembrist movement ...', R. Conquest, *Stalin, Breaker of Nations* (London: Weidenfeld & Nicolson, 1991), 271.

p. 367 'Vlasor said his aim ...', G. Hosking, *Russia and the Russians: A History* (London: Penguin, 2001), 499.

p. 368 'No one was trusted ...', D. Volkogonov, *The Rise and Fall of the Soviet Empire: Political Leaders from Lenin to Gorbachev*, trans. H. Shukman (London: Harper Collins, 1998), 123.

p. 368 'France, for instance ...', P. Polian, 'Le Rapatriement des citoyens soviétiques depuis la France et les zones françaises d'occupation en Allemagne et en Autriche', in *Cahiers du Monde Russe*, Editions de l'Ecole des Hautes Etudes en Sciences Sociales, Paris, 41/1, janvier–mars 2000, 176.

p. 369 'The NKVD was allowed ...', S. Courtois and J.-L. Panne, 'The Comintern in Action', in M. Kramer (ed.), *The Black Book of Communism: Crimes, Terror, Repression* (Cambridge, MA: Harvard University Press, 1999), 320.

p. 370 'For the civilian population too ...', Hosking, *Rulers and Victims*, op. cit., 222.

p. 370 'Instead of making proper ...', ibid., 239.

p. 370 'In 1946 ...', ibid., 241.

Chapter Thirty-four

p. 372 'On 22 May ... not been consulted.' Documents from UK Public Records Office: CAB 120/691/109040 /002. Photographic facsimile available at http://www.history. neu.edu/PRO2/pages/002.htm and see J. Lewis, *Changing Direction: British Military Planning for Post-War Strategic Defence* (London: Routledge, 2008), xxix-xxxix.

p. 373 'From Stettin ...', *Churchill's 'Iron Curtain' Speech Fifty Years Later*, ed. J. Muller (Columbia, Missouri: University of Missouri Press, 1999), 9–10.

p. 373 'Mr Churchill and his allies ...', Robert McNeal (ed.), *Lenin, Stalin, Khrushchev: Voices of Bolshevism* (Englewood Cliffs, New Jersey: Prentice Hall Inc., 1963), 120.

p. 374 'Mr Churchill speaks ...', ibid., 121–3. Full text available at http://www.marxists. org/reference/archive/stalin/works/1946/03/x01.htm

p. 374 'The news [of Hiroshima and Nagasaki] ...', T. B. Cochran, R. S. Norris and O. A. Bukharin, *Making the Russian Bomb: From Stalin to Yeltsin* (Oxford: Westview Press, 1985), 24.

p. 375 'Werth was permitted ...', D. Holloway, *Stalin and the Bomb: The Soviet Union and Atomic Energy, 1939–1956* (London: Yale University Press, 1994), 171.

p. 375 'The total eventually provided ...', A. Milward, *The Reconstruction of Western Europe, 1945–51* (London: Methuen, 1984), 46.

p. 375 'Stalin was always suspicious ...', V. Yerofeev, interview for PBS radio documentary, no date given.

p. 376 'The governments of the United States ...', R. Bideleux and I. Jeffries, *A History of Eastern Europe: Crisis and Change* (London: Routledge, 1998), 528.

p. 377 'I have only one demand ...', Cochran, Norris and Bukharin, op. cit., 10.

p. 377 'Trofim Lysenko, largely because ...', M. Heller and A. Nekrich, *Utopia in Power: The History of the Soviet Union from 1917 to the Present*, trans. M. Carlos (New York: Summit Books, 1986), 482.

p. 377 'They were shielded ...', ibid., 440.

p. 378 'An exclusion zone ...', Holloway, op. cit., 201–2.

p. 378 'There are secrets ...', ibid., 202.

p. 378 'We believed that our work ...', ibid., 204; also G. Hosking, *Russia and the Russians: A History* (London: Penguin, 2001), 522.

p. 379 'I regard myself ...', Holloway, op. cit., 207.

p. 379 'You remember that Peter...', ibid., 186.

p. 379 'In 1950 a report...', ibid., 194.

p. 380 'All this remained...', Hosking, *Russia*, op. cit., 513.

p. 380 'On top of the tower...', Holloway, op. cit., 217.

p. 381 'We felt relief ...', ibid., 216.

p. 382 'We wanted to exert ...', ibid., 259.

p. 382 'At the same time, the British and US ...', R. Miller, *To Save a City: The Berlin Airlift, 1948–1949* (College Station: Texas A&M University Press, 2000), 201.

p. 383 'I will shake my little finger ...', S. Sebag-Montefiore, *Stalin: The Court of the Red Tsar* (London: Weidenfeld & Nicolson, 2003), 511.

p. 383 'According to the Soviet ...', article in the *Independent*, Saturday, 12 June 1993: http://www.independent.co.uk/news/world/europe/stalin-planned-to-kill-tito-by-infecting-him-with-the-plague-1491079.html

p. 384 'While we study ...', article in *Time* magazine, Monday, 23 August 1948: http://www.time.com/time/magazine/article/0, 9171, 799003-3,00.html

p. 384 'As early as 1945...', S. Ramet, *The Three Yugoslavias: State Building and Legitimation, 1918–2005* (Bloomington, Indiana: Indiana University Press, 2006), 176.

p. 384 'In Prague ...', A. London, *On Trial*, trans. A. Hamilton (London: Macdonald, 1968), 315–16.

p. 385 'Khrushchev recalled ...', D. Halberstam, *The Coldest Winter: America and the Korean War* (New York: Hyperion, 2007), 352.

p. 385 'I have come here ...', ibid., 352–3.

p. 385 'What of it ...', Holloway, op. cit., 280.

p. 386 'The Americans are not ...', G. Roberts, *Stalin's Wars: From World War to Cold War, 1939–1953* (New Haven: Yale University Press, 2006), 370.

p. 386 'I'm finished ...', Holloway, op. cit., 273.

p. 387 'They perish one after another ...', Sebag-Montefiore, op. cit., 515.

p. 387 'During the investigation ...', K. Gottwald, *Selected Speeches and Articles, 1929–1953* (Prague: Orbis, 1954), 230–1.

p. 388 'This terrorist group ...', *Pravda*, 13 January 1953, cited in Ya. Rapoport, *The Doctors' Plot of 1953*, trans. N. Perova and R. Bobrova (Cambridge MA: Harvard University Press, 1991).

p. 388 'Stalin called the judge ...', Sebag-Montefiore, op. cit., 558.

p. 388 'See! You are like blind ...', Holloway, op. cit., 292.

p. 389 '... go and get some sleep ...', S. Devyatov and V. Zhilyayev, *Blizhnyaya Dacha Stalina* [Stalin's Near Dacha] (Moscow: 2008), 42 et seq.

p. 390 'What are you looking at ...', ibid.

p. 391 'For the last twelve hours ...', R. Conquest, *Stalin, Breaker of Nations* (London: Weidenfeld & Nicolson, 1991), 312.

p. 391 'Dear Comrades ...', Soviet radio announcement, 6 March 1953. For a contemporary Western account by the *Guardian*'s correspondent Victor Zorza, see http://century.guardian.co.uk/1950-1959/Story/0, , 105154,00.html

p. 391 'Leader and Teacher ...', Heller and Nekrich, op. cit., 507.

p. 392 'Only a kindly neighbour ...', S. Morrison, *The People's Artist: Prokofiev's Soviet Years* (Oxford: Oxford University Press, 2009), 388.

p. 392 'The Soviet people ...', A. de Jonge, *Stalin and the Shaping of the Soviet Union* (London: Collins, 1986), 508.

p. 393 'The breath of tens ...', Y. Yevtushenko, *A Precocious Autobiography* (New York: Dutton, 1963), 85–6.

Chapter Thirty-five

p. 396 'He warned Malenkov ...', N. Khrushchev, *Memoirs of Nikita Khrushchev, Volume 2:*

Reformer, ed. Sergei Khrushchev (University Park, Pennsylvania: Pennsylvania State University Press, 2006), 186.

p. 396 'What's going on …', C. Andrew and O. Gordievsky, *KGB: The Inside Story of Its Foreign Operations from Lenin to Gorbachev* (London: Sceptre, 1991), 423–4.

p. 396 'Beria was killed …', N. Riasanovsky, A History of Russia (New York: Oxford University Press, 1963), 598

p. 397 'They had no idea …', A. L. Solzhenitsyn, *The Gulag Archipelago, Part V*, trans. H. T. Willetts (London: Collins & Harvill, 1978), 289.

p. 397 'After 42 days …', M. Heller and A. Nekrich, *Utopia in Power: The History of the Soviet Union from 1917 to the Present*, trans. M. Carlos (New York: Summit Books, 1986), 520.

p. 398 'He had begun life …', R. Service, *A History of Twentieth-Century Russia* (London: Penguin, 1997), 348.

p. 398 'In his memoirs …', W. Taubman, *Khrushchev: The Man and His Era* (London: Free Press, 2003), 334–5. Also V. Molotov, *Molotov Remembers: Inside Kremlin Politics – Conversations with Felix Chuev* (Chicago: Ivan R. Dee, 1993), 161.

p. 399 'If we don't tell…', G. Hosking, *Russia and the Russians: A History* (London: Penguin, 2001), 529.

p. 399 'Comrades, it is foreign …', M. Charlton, *Footsteps from the Finland Station: Five Landmarks in the Collapse of Communism* (New Brunswick: Transaction Publ., 1992), 35 et seq. Full text of the speech in an English translation available at http://www.marxists.org/archive/khrushchev/1956/02/24.htm

p. 400 'Comrades! Stalin was …', ibid.

p. 400 'He was a coward …' Taubman, op. cit., 273.

p. 400 'The foreign communists …', Hosking, *Russia*, op. cit., 530.

p. 401 'Years of propaganda …', Taubman, op. cit., 287.

p. 401 'He praised Khrushchev's …', ibid., 282.

p. 402 'In East Germany …', Heller and Nekrich, op. cit., 538.

p. 402 'Perhaps mindful of Stalin's acerbic conclusion …', S. White, *Communism and Its Collapse* (London: Routledge, 2001), 36.

p. 402 'On 23 October …', Hosking, op. cit., 531.

p. 403 'What option do we have?', Taubman, op. cit., 297.

p. 403 'On 4 November …', Heller and Nekrich, op. cit., 542.

p. 403 'Pockets of resistance …', Service, op. cit., 343.

p. 404 'Treacherous revisionist …', L. Luthi, *The Sino-Soviet Split: Cold War in the Communist World* (Princeton: Princeton University Press, 2008), 219 et seq.

p. 404 'Granddad, are you …', Service, op. cit., 349.

p. 405 '… the impending vote …', Hosking, op. cit., 531.

p. 405 'Your words yet…', Service, op. cit., 345.

PART FIVE
Chapter Thirty-six
p. 408 'I heard a whistle …', J. Doran and P. Bizony, *Starman: The Truth Behind the Legend of Yuri Gagarin* (London: Bloomsbury), 103

p. 408 'Before the launch …', ibid., 110.

p. 409 'Arrogant commentators …', W. Taubman, *Khrushchev: The Man and His Era* (London: Free Press, 2003) 492.

p. 409 'When he met Queen …', Doran and Bizony, op. cit., 139.

p. 410 'His identity, and that …', F. French, *Into That Silent Sea: Trailblazers of the Space Era, 1961–65* (Lincoln: University of Nebraska Press, 2007), 26.

p. 410 'There is no record …', S. Gerovitch, '"New Soviet Man" Inside Machine: Human Engineering, Spacecraft Design, and the Construction of Communism', from *OSIRIS*, vol. 22, no. 1 (University of Chicago Press, 2007), 141. Also French, op. cit., 370.

p. 411 'As [Komarov] was seeing …', Doran and Bizony, op. cit., 196.

p. 411 'This devil ship …', ibid., 199.

p. 412 'They knew they had …', ibid., 200.

p. 413 'Now the arrested …', Akhmatova, quoted in Taubman, op. cit., 285.

p. 413 'In the course of the 1970s …', W. Tompson, *Khrushchev: A Political Life* (New York: St Martin's Press, 1997), 238.

p. 414 'The party solemnly …', R. Service, *A History of Twentieth-Century Russia* (London: Penguin, 1997), 363.

p. 414 'Much has changed in …', M. Gorbachev, *Report to the Twenty-Seventh Party Congress of the CPSU*, 1986.

p. 414 'As a result, Khrushchev …', M. Heller and A. Nekrich, *Utopia in Power: The History of the Soviet Union from 1917 to the Present*, trans. M. Carlos (New York: Summit Books, 1986), 590.

p. 415 '… a dead herring …' Service, op. cit., 356.

p. 415 'catch up and overtake …', S. Khrushchev, 'The Cold War through the Looking Glass', in *American Heritage Magazine*, October 1999, vol. 50, no. 6.

p. 415 'To use the words …', N. Khrushchev, *Khrushchev Remembers: The Last Testament*, trans. S. Talbott (London: André Deutsch, 1974), 423.

p. 415 '… Soviet city dweller …', J. Sillince, *Housing Policies in Eastern Europe and the Soviet Union* (London: Routledge, 1990), 16.

p. 416 'Moral Code of the Communist Worker …', N. Khrushchev, *Report to the Twenty-Second Congress of the CPSU* (1961).

p. 416 'The local party boss …', R. and Zh. Medvedev, *Khrushchev: The Years in Power*, trans. A. Durkin (New York: W.W. Norton & Co., 1978), 97–101.

p. 417 'By 1960 …', Service, op. cit., 350.

p. 418 'Bad weather in the spring …', G. Hosking, *Russia and the Russians: A History* (London: Penguin, 2001),539.

p. 418 'Garst was invited to …', S. Khrushchev, 'The Cold War …' op. cit.,

p. 419 'At the Novocherkassk …', S. Baron, *Bloody Saturday in the Soviet Union: Novocherkassk, 1962* (Stanford: Stanford University Press, 2001), 66–7.

p. 419 'Father didn't understand …', Taubman, op. cit., 608

p. 420 'Like it or not …', S. Khrushchev, *Nikita Khrushchev and the Creation of a Superpower* (University Park, Pennsylvania: Pennsylvania State University Press, 2001), 242.

p. 420 'Sergei Khrushchev recalls …', S. Khrushchev, 'The Cold War …' op. cit.

p. 421 'Who would have guessed ...', Taubman, op. cit., 420–3.

p. 422 'I think this slogan ...', N. Khrushchev, *Memoirs* (University Park, Pennsylvania: Pennsylvania State University Press, 2006), ii: 101.

p. 422 'Washington declared that ...', F.G. Powers, *Operation Overflight: The U-2 Spy Pilot Tells His Story for the First Time* (London: Hodder & Stoughton Ltd, 1970), 132–3.

p. 423 'Things were going well ...', Taubman, op. cit., 447.

p. 423 'He seemed pleased ...', ibid., 466–7.

p. 424 'I remember President ...', N. Khrushchev, *Khrushchev Remembers*, op. cit., 530.

p. 425 'We had to have a commitment ...', Heller and Nekrich, op. cit., 577.

p. 425 'Khrushchev's aim ...', ibid., 575.

p. 426 'How can I deal ...', Taubman, op. cit., 566.

p. 427 'Comrades, forgive me ...', Service, *Russia*, op. cit., 377.

p. 427 'The *Pravda* editorial ...', Taubman, op. cit., 620.

p. 428 'I am old and tired ...', ibid., 13.

Chapter Thirty-seven

p. 430 'At a modern art exhibition ...', M. Heller and A. Nekrich, *Utopia in Power: The History of the Soviet Union from 1917 to the Present*, trans. M. Carlos (New York: Summit Books, 1986), 589.

p. 430 'I write myself ...', G. Hosking, *Russia and the Russians: A History* (London: Penguin, 2001),556.

p. 431 'When the Leningrad poet ...', Brodsky obituary in the *New York Times*, 29 January 1996.

p. 431 'I am different ...', in *On Trial: The Soviet State versus 'Abram Tertz' and 'Nikolai Arzhak'*, trans. Max Hayward (London: Harper & Row, 1966), 182.

p. 432 'As if to prove ...', Hosking, op. cit., 557.

p. 432 'In the early hours ...' The figures for troops and tanks deployed are the subject of debate. It is clear that the numbers of both rose quickly. K. Williams, *The Prague Spring and Its Aftermath: Czechoslovak Politics, 1968–1970* (Cambridge: Cambridge University Press, 1997), 112, gives figures of 165,000 troops and 4,600 tanks, rising to 500,000 and 6,000 within the week.

p. 433 'I believed you ...', D. Volkogonov, *The Rise and Fall of the Soviet Empire: Political Leaders from Lenin to Gorbachev*, trans. H. Shukman (London: Harper Collins, 1998), 291.

p. 433 'A *Pravda* editorial ...', Hosking, op. cit., 547.

p. 434 'Since taking office ...', M. Sandle and E. Bacon (eds), *Brezhnev Reconsidered* (Basingstoke: Palgrave Macmillan, 2002), 90.

p. 435 'Nobody lives on ...', R. Service, *A History of Twentieth-Century Russia* (London: Penguin, 1997), 384.

p. 435 'When Brezhnev hailed ...', Heller and Nekrich, op. cit., 644–5.

p. 436 'Collectivised agriculture ...', Service, op. cit., 401.

p. 436 'As living standards ...', Heller and Nekrich, op. cit., 664.

p. 436 'In 1959 ethnic …', Service, op. cit., 422.

p. 437 'A Permanent Commission …', Heller and Nekrich, op. cit., 670.

p. 437 'A Jew approaches …', N. Sharansky, *Fear No Evil: A Memoir*, trans. Stefani Hoffman (London: Weidenfeld & Nicolson, 1988), 61.

p. 438 'The name they adopted …', R. Boobyer, *Conscience, Dissent and Reform in Soviet Russia* (London: Routledge, 2005), 75.

p. 438 'All Soviet citizens …', Heller and Nekrich, op. cit., 662.

p. 438 'In 1973 he wrote …', A. Solzhenitsyn, *Letter to Soviet Leaders*, trans. H. Sternberg (London: Collins & Harvill, 1974), 28, 31, 47.

p. 439 'For an unprepared …', Heller and Nekrich, op. cit., 684.

p. 439 'The anti-democratic traditions …', Boobyer, op. cit., 91, 223.

p. 440 'Brezhnev would later dismiss …', Heller and Nekrich, op. cit., 651.

p. 440 'Western technology and foreign expertise …', ibid., 649.

p. 441 'People are writing to me …', Volkogonov, op. cit., 303.

p. 442 … 'by the early 1980s …' Hosking, op. cit., 542.

p. 443 'How am I supposed to get anyplace …', M. Dowd, 'Where's the Rest of Him?', in the *New York Times*, 18 November 1990.

Chapter Thirty-eight

p. 444 'Raisa Gorbachev was…', M. Thatcher, *The Downing Street Years* (London: Harper Collins, 1993), 460–1.

p. 445 'Mr Gorbachev insisted…', ibid., 462.

p. 445 'We both believe in…', ibid.

p. 446 'We cannot go on…', A. Brown, *The Gorbachev Factor* (Oxford: Oxford University Press, 1997), 336; D. Volkogonov, *The Rise and Fall of the Soviet Empire: Political Leaders from Lenin to Gorbachev*, trans. H. Shukman (London: Harper Collins, 1998), 445. Gorbachev repeated the remark in public interviews, including *Der Spiegel*, reprinted in *Izvestiya*, 25 March 1991.

p. 446 'Our party has…', Volkogonov, op. cit., 438.

p. 448 'Three weeks after the new…', J. Matlock, 'Washington's view of Gorbachev's Perestroika', speech to ICCEES, Stockholm, 26 July 2010.

p. 448 'Mikhail Gorbachev had been born…', Volkogonov, op. cit., *passim*, and Brown, *passim*; also M. Gorbachev, *Memoirs* (New York: Random House, 1997), *passim*.

p. 449 'In April 1985 he…', Volkogonov, op. cit., 450.

p. 450 'Many of you see the solution…', S. Bialer and J. Afferica, 'The Genesis of Gorbachev's World', in *Foreign Affairs*, 64, no. 3 (1985), 605–44.

p. 453 'A new clan of people…', Volkogonov, op. cit., 455.

p. 453 'The widening of glasnost…', M. Gorbachev, report to Twenty-Seventh Party Congress of the CPSU, 1986.

p. 453 'Chernobyl, he said…', R. Service, *A History of Twentieth-Century Russia* (London: Penguin, 1997), 447

p. 454 'How could you fail to…', Volkogonov, op. cit., 521; Brown, op. cit., 409–500.

p. 455 'Public ownership unites…', Ye. Ligachev, speech to Twenty-Eighth Party Congress, July 1990. See also Ligachev, *Inside Gorbachev's Kremlin* (New York: Pantheon, 1993), 321, for Ligachev's views on private ownership.

p. 455 'Dr Sakharov has…' article in *L'Humanité*, Paris, 7 February 1986; M. Sixsmith, *Moscow Coup: The Death of the Soviet System* (London: Simon & Schuster, 1991), 66.

p. 456 '"Recently", he said…', Sixsmith, op. cit.,104–5; see also Volkogonov, op. cit., 471–2, 505.

p. 457 'In March 1988…', Sixsmith, op. cit., 68; Brown, op. cit., 504–5. Full text of Nina Andreeva letter available at http://www.revolucia.ru/nmppr.htm

p. 459 'By the way, comrades…', Brown, op. cit., 515; Sixsmith, op. cit., 69.

p. 459 'I am doomed to go…', A. Chernyayev, *My Six Years with Gorbachev*, trans. R. English and E. Tucker (University Park Pennsylvania: Pennsylvania State University Press, 2000), 272. See also Service, *Russia*, op. cit., 486.

p. 460 'Followers of the Lithuanian…', Sixsmith, op. cit., 71–2.

p. 460 'A multiparty system…', ibid., 72.

p. 461 'Eighty-six per cent…', ibid.

p. 462 'Their statements, he said…' ibid., 75.

p. 462 'Some people say…', author's interview with Boris Yeltsin, 1989.

p. 462 'Multiparty democracy…', ibid.

p. 463 'The leading and guiding…', text taken from Soviet constitution of 1977; Article Six 'on the leading role of the party'.

p. 463 'The Soviet Union must decide…', D. Murray, *A Democracy of Despots* (Oxford: Westview, 1995), 71–80; Sixsmith, op. cit. 75.

p. 463 'If necessary we shall…', Sakharov on perestroika; Murray, op. cit.

p. 464 '"He was," he said…', Yevtushenko on Sakharov in Paul Quinn-Judge, *Boston Globe*, 19 December 1989.

p. 464 'The Communist Party of the Soviet Union…', report from RIA Novosti, 14 March 1990.

p. 466 'Having been elected…', Yeltsin speech to Twenty-Eighth Congress of the CPSU, July 1990; Sixsmith, op. cit., 77.

p. 468 'The conservative and …', Alexander Yakovlev article in *Moskovsky Komsomolets*, 14 December 1990; Sixsmith, op. cit., 79.

p. 468 'The reformers have gone into hiding …', Sixsmith, op. cit., 79.

p. 468 'We need a new Hitler …', author's interview with Alexander Yakovlev, December 1990; Sixsmith, op. cit., 88.

p. 468 'Surrounding the president with …' Sixsmith, op. cit., 80.

p. 469 'To act to protect the unity …', ibid., 97.

p. 469 'I warned in 1987 that …', ibid., 99.

p. 469 'We never wanted this to …', ibid.

Chapter Thirty-nine

p. 471 'Our information …', Popov press conference, 28 September 1990; cited in M. Sixsmith, *Moscow Coup: The Death of the Soviet System* (London: Simon & Schuster, 1991), 90.

p. 472 'As early as June 1988, he told …', Sixsmith, ibid., 68.

p. 472 'Twenty pro-independence …', A. Brown, *The Gorbachev Factor* (Oxford: Oxford University Press, 1997), 560–1.

p. 474 'The people are full of gratitude …', Sixsmith, op. cit., 104.

p. 475 'I have felt a discernible …', ibid., 104–5.

p. 475 'After the humiliation he suffered …', ibid., 106.

p. 475 'I was thinking to myself …', ibid., 107.

p. 476 'But we have the strength …', ibid., 109.

p. 478 'I had a whole series of …', ibid., 122–3. See also M. Ebon, *KGB: Death and Rebirth* (Westport, Connecticut: Praeger, 1994), 3 et seq. for details of events in Foros.

p. 479 'I told them that they and the …', Sixsmith, op. cit., 123.

p. 479 'You are wrong to think …', ibid.

p. 480 'Our motherland is in …', ibid., 11.

p. 481 'Citizens of Russia …', ibid., 15.

p. 482 'I joined the Communist …', author's interview with Gennady Yanayev, July 1991.

p. 482 'This country is disintegrating …', Yanayev press conference, 19 August 1991; Sixsmith, op. cit., 23.

p. 482 'If Yeltsin is calling …', ibid., 24.

p. 484 'This day will be glorified …', Yevtushenko poem; cited in Sixsmith, op. cit., 16–17; also in author's interview with Yevtushenko, August 1991.

p. 485 'Yes. And when I compare …', author's interview with Yevtushenko, July 2008.

p. 486 'I'm glad this coup …', Sixsmith, op. cit., 34.

p. 486 'The shadows of darkness …', ibid., 36.

p. 488 'A group of tourists …', ibid., 118–19.

p. 488 'All the work we have …', ibid., 121.

p. 488 'They turned out to be men …', ibid., 122–5.

p. 489 'All those involved in the coup …', ibid., 126.

p. 490 'You should read what …', ibid., 130–1.

p. 492 'There can be no …', G. Hosking, *Russia and the Russians: A History* (London: Penguin, 2001), 589.

p. 492 'The USSR as a subject of international …', ibid.

p. 493 'I leave my post with trepidation …', R. Service, *A History of Twentieth-Century Russia* (London: Penguin, 1997), 507.

p. 493 'An orthodox communist who …', D. Volkogonov, *The Rise and Fall of the Soviet Empire: Political Leaders from Lenin to Gorbachev*, trans. H. Shukman (London: Harper Collins, 1998), 474.

Chapter Forty

p. 494 'Good evening, and Merry Christmas …', full text of George Bush speech available at G. Bush Presidential Library: http://bushlibrary.tamu.edu/research/public_papers.php?id=3791&year=1991&month=12

p. 495 'One era of history …', M. Sixsmith, *Moscow Coup: The Death of the Soviet System* (London: Simon & Schuster, 1991), 165.

p. 495 'This was a society …', ibid.

p. 495 'In August 1991…', ibid., 166.

p. 498 'In the first month inflation …', G. Hosking, *Russia and the Russians: A History* (London: Penguin, 2001),589.

p. 499 'Alexander Rutskoi, who had shown …', R. Service, *A History of Twentieth-Century Russia* (London: Penguin, 1997), 512.

p. 500 'Boris Berezovsky would later …', M. Sixsmith, *Putin's Oil: The Yukos Affair and the Struggle for Russia* (New York: Continuum, 2010), 30–1.

p. 500 'Food production in …', Service, *Russia*, op. cit., 517.

p. 501 'The President issues decrees …', *Izvestiya*, 13 August 1993. See also J. Carey and M. Shugart, *Executive Decree Authority* (Cambridge: Cambridge University Press, 1998), 76.

p. 502 'Boris Yeltsin denounced …', presidential press statement, 4 October 1993.

p. 503 '… wash their boots …', speech by Zhirinovsky during the campaign for the Russian parliamentary election in December 1993.

p. 504 'Two leading oligarchs …', Sixsmith, *Putin's Oil*, op. cit., 34.

p. 505 'Potanin picked up the country's leading nickel and aluminium company …', ibid., 35.

p. 505 'Yeltsin had suffered …', author's report for BBC News, June 1993.

p. 506 'As casualties mounted …', author's reports for BBC News, *passim*.

p. 507 'Russia is not a country …', Yeltsin, remarks at meeting with officials at Russian Foreign Ministry, 27 October 1992. cited in *International Affairs*, Moscow, no. 11, vol. 38 (1992), 1–2. See also Hosking, *Russia*, op. cit., 609.

p. 508 '"Yesterday," he said …', M. Laris, 'Yeltsin Lashes Out at Clinton: Criticisms of Chechen War Are Met with Blunt Reminder of Russian Nuclear Power', *Washington Post*, 10 December 1999.

p. 508 'Inflation hit 88 per cent …', *Moscow Times*, September 1998.

p. 509 'Dear friends, my dears …', Yeltsin speech on Russian television, 31 December 1999.

Chapter Forty-one

p. 510 'There will be no power …', V. Putin, New Year's message, broadcast on Russian television, 1 January 2000.

p. 510 'I was a hooligan …', V. *First Person: An Astonishingly Frank Self-Portrait by Russia's President Vladimir Putin*, with N. Gevorkyan, N. Timakova and A. Kolesnikov, trans. C. Fitzpatrick (London: Hutchinson, 2000), 18.

p. 511 'A KGB officer never …', A. Jack, *Inside Putin's Russia* (London: Granta, 2005), 67.

p. 511 'On 17 September …', M. Sixsmith, *The Litvinenko File: Politics, Polonium and Russia's War with Itself* (London: Macmillan, 2007), 152.

p. 512 '… pursue the terrorists …', ibid.

p. 512 'Putin's ratings soared to …', ibid., 153.

p. 512 'When a journalist from the …', ibid., 153–4.

p. 512 'The neighbourhood had …', ibid., 155.

p. 513 'At a gathering of FSB …', Jack, op. cit., 14.

p. 513 'Russia cannot become a version …', Putin, *First Person*, op. cit., 214.

p. 513 … 'modern Russia does not identify …', ibid.

p. 514 … 'the biggest geo-political …', BBC News report, Monday, 25 April 2005.

p. 514 'Our country is building an …', Jack, op. cit., 157.

p. 514 'Russia is in the midst of …', Putin, *First Person*, op. cit., 219.

p. 515 'There have been hard times …', Putin, New Year's message, broadcast on Russian television on 1 January 2001.

p. 515 'One newspaper, *Komsomolskaya* …', *Komsomolskaya Pravda*, 22 August 2007.

p. 516 'The most vocal critic of the Kremlin's …', M. Sixsmith, *Putin's Oil: The Yukos Affair and the Struggle for Russia* (New York: Continuum, 2010), 46–7 and 106.

p. 516 … 'liquidate the oligarchs as a class', ibid., 45. See also R. Sakwa, *Putin: Russia's Choice*, (Oxford: Routledge, 2008), 143.

p. 517 'In a bitter showdown …', Sixsmith, *Putin's Oil*, op. cit., 59–63.

p. 518 'Putin put his friend Igor Sechin …', Jack, op. cit., 314.

p. 518 'By 2002, former KGB …', Sixsmith, *Putin's Oil*, op. cit., 115.

p. 519 'Our whole generation died …', A. Babchenko, *One Soldier's War in Chechnya*, trans. N. Allen, proof copy (London: Portobello Books, 2007), 143, 162.

p. 519 'Fighting rages on in Grozny …', ibid., 143.

p. 519 'Torture, rape and looting …', ibid., 305.

p. 520 'Budanov's lawyer complained that …', G. Chazan, 'Russian Colonel Hailed as Hero for Killing of Chechen Woman', in *Daily Telegraph*, 15 April 2001.

p. 520 'One Russian officer estimated …', Jack, op. cit., 121.

p. 520 'Andrei Babitsky, who contradicted …', Putin, *First Person*, op. cit., 172.

p. 520 'The Committee to Protect …' Figures for journalist deaths available at http://cpj.org/killed/europe/russia/

p. 520 'In 2002, around 40 terrorists …', Jack, op. cit., 88.

p. 521 'According to Movladi Baisarov …', the *Independent*, 4 January 2007; also interview in Russian *GQ*, October 2005.

p. 521 'We have shown weakness …', J. McAllister and P. Quinn-Judge, 'Defenseless Targets', *Time* magazine, Sunday, 5 September 2004.

p. 522 'At a press conference in 2006 …', joint US–Russian news conference, 15 July 2006, at G8 summit in St Petersburg.

p. 522 'The United States has overstepped …', Putin speech at conference on security policy, Munich, 10 February 2007.

p. 523 'They tell us we should change our constitution …', D. Nowak, 'Putin Lashes out at Nashi Gathering', *St Petersburg Times*, Friday, 27 July 2007.

p. 523 'He ridiculed the suggestion …', author's interview with Dmitry Peskov, February 2007.

p. 524 'In 2008 Memorial had its entire…', C. Bass and T. Halpin, 'Gulag Files Seized during Police Raid on Rights Group', *The Times*, 13 December 2008.

p. 524 'A low flat tax …', 'Trouble in the Pipeline', *The Economist*, 8 May 2008.

p. 524 'Economic success maintained ...', Putin poll ratings available at the Levada Opinion Research Center, http://www.levada.ru/prezident.html

p. 525 'I believe my most...', M. Stott and O. Shchedrov, 'Russia's Medvedev Takes Power and Pledges Freedom', Reuters, Wednesday, 7 May 2008.

p. 526 'The former Kremlin insider, Stanislav ...', author's interview with Belkovsky in January 2008

p. 527 'The fact that he addressed ...', A. Osborn, 'Dmitry Medvedev's Russia Still Feels the Cold Hand of Vladimir Putin', *Sunday Telegraph*, 7 March 2010.

p. 527 'Instead of the primitive raw material ...', M. Tkachenko, 'Medvedev Wants Russia to Go Hi-Tech', CNN, 12 November 2009.

BIBLIOGRAPHY

Key:
Sochineniya – Writings
(Polnoe) Sobranie Sochinenii – (Complete) Writings
v xx tomakh – in xx volumes
(Izbrannye) Proizvedeniya – (Selected) Works

Afinogenov, A., 'Strakh' [Fear] (1930), in *P'esy* [Plays] (Moscow: Izd. Iskusstvo, 1947)

Ailsby, C., *Images of Barbarossa: The German Invasion of Russia, 1941* (London: Ian Allan Publishing, 2001)

Akhmatova, A., *Selected Poems*, trans. D. Thomas (London: Penguin, 1988)
  Sochineniya v dvukh tomakh [Works in 2 Volumes] (Moscow: Izd. Khudozhestvennaya Literatura, 1986)

Albats, Y., *KGB: State Within a State: The Secret Police and Its Hold on Russia's Past, Present and Future*, trans. C. Fitzpatrick (London: I.B.Tauris, 1995)

Alferova, G., *Borodino, Pole Russkoi Slavy* [Borodino, the Field of Russian Glory] (State Museum of Borodino, 2002)

Alliluyeva, S., *Dvadtsat' Pisem k Drugu* [Twenty Letters to a Friend] (London: Hutchinson, 1967)

Amalrik, A., *Will the Soviet Union Survive until 1984?* (London: Penguin, 1970)

Andrew, C. and Gordievsky, O., *KGB: The Inside Story of Its Foreign Operations from Lenin to Gorbachev* (London: Sceptre, 1991)

Antonov, B., *Russian Tsars: The Rurikids, the Romanovs* (Moscow: Fedorov, 2005)

Aron, L., *Yeltsin: A Revolutionary Life* (London: HarperCollins, 2000)

Axell, A., *Russia's Heroes, 1941–45* (London: Constable, 2001)

Babchenko, A., *One Soldier's War in Chechnya*, trans. N. Allen (London: Portobello Books, 2007)

Babel, I., *Collected Stories* (London: Penguin, 1961)

Bakunin, M., *Selected Writings*, ed. A. Lehning (London: Jonathan Cape, 1973)

Balmont, K., *Polnoe Sobranie Sochinenii* (Moscow: Izd. Khud. Lit., 1976)

Barna, Y., *Eisenstein* (Boston: Little, Brown & Co., 1973)

Baron, S., *Bloody Saturday in the Soviet Union: Novocherkassk, 1962* (Stanford: Stanford University Press, 2001)

Baron von Herberstein, *Rerum Muscoviticarum Comentarii* [Notes on Muscovite Affairs], trans. R.H. Major as *Notes on Russia* (London: 1851)

Bastable, J., *Voices from Stalingrad* (London: David & Charles, 2006)

Beevor, A., *Berlin: The Downfall, 1945* (London: Viking, 2002)

 Stalingrad (London: Penguin, 2007)

Berenbaum, M., *The World Must Know: The History of the Holocaust as Told in the United States Holocaust Museum*, 2nd edition (Baltimore: Johns Hopkins University Press, 2006)

Berlin, I., *The Hedgehog and the Fox: An Essay on Tolstoy's View of History* (London: Weidenfeld & Nicolson, 1967)

 The Soviet Mind: Russian Culture under Communism, ed. H. Hardy (Washington: Brookings Institution Press, 2004)

Bialer, S. and Afferica, J., 'The Genesis of Gorbachev's World', in *Foreign Affairs*, 64, no. 3 (1985)

Bideleux, R. and Jeffries, I., *A History of Eastern Europe: Crisis and Change* (London: Routledge, 1998)

Binyon, T., *Pushkin: A Biography* (London: HarperCollins, 2002)

Bloch, S. and Reddaway, P., *Russia's Political Hospitals: The Abuse of Psychiatry in the Soviet Union* (London: Futura Books, 1978)

Blok, A.A., *Izbrannye Proizvedeniya* (Moscow: Biblioteka Klassiki, 1988)

Boobyer, P., *Conscience, Dissent and Reform in Soviet Russia* (London: Routledge, 2005)

Borovik, A., *The Hidden War: A Russian Journalist's Account of the Soviet War in Afghanistan* (New York: Grove Press, 1990)

Braithwaite, R., *Moscow 1941: A City and Its People at War* (London: Profile Books, 2006)

Brakman, R., *Sekretnaya Papka Iosifa Stalina* [Stalin's Secret File] (Moscow: Ves' Mir, 2004)

Brandenberger, D., *National Bolshevism: Stalinist Mass Culture and the Formation of Modern Russian National Identity* (Cambridge, Massachusetts: Harvard University Press, 2002)

Briggs, A., *Brief Lives: Leo Tolstoy* (London: Hesperus, 2010)

Brown, A., *The Gorbachev Factor* (Oxford: Oxford University Press, 1997)

 The Rise and Fall of Communism (London: Vintage Books, 2010)

 Seven Years That Changed the World: Perestroika in Perspective (Oxford: Oxford University Press, 2007)

 (ed.), *The Demise of Marxism–Leninism in Russia* (London: Palgrave Macmillan, 2004)

 (ed.), *The Soviet Union: A Biographical Dictionary* (London: Weidenfeld & Nicolson, 1990)

Brown, M., *Art Under Stalin* (Oxford: Phaidon, 1991)

Bruce Lockhart, R., *Memoirs of a British Agent: Being an Account of the Author's Early Life and of His Official Mission to Moscow in 1918* (London: Putnam, 1932)

Bulgakov, M., *Flight* (London: Nick Hern Books, 1998)

 The White Guard (London: Flamingo, 1973)

Bullock, A., *Hitler and Stalin: Parallel Lives* (London: HarperCollins, 1991)

Burdzhalov, E., *Vtoraya Russkaya Revolyutsiya: Vosstanie v Petrograde* [Russia's Second Revolution: Uprising in Petrograd] (Moscow: Nauka, 1967)

Byrnes, Robert F., *Pobedonostsev: His Life and Thought* (Bloomington: Indiana University Press, 1968)

Camus, A., *L'Homme révolté* [The Rebel] (Paris: Gallimard, 1951)

Carey, J. and Shugart, M., *Executive Decree Authority* (Cambridge: Cambridge University Press, 1998)

Chaadayev, P. Ya., *Polnoe Sobranie Sochinenii* (Moscow: Nauka, 1991)

Charlton, M., *Footsteps from the Finland Station: Five Landmarks in the Collapse of Communism* (New Brunswick: Transaction Publishers, 1992)

Chernyayev, A., *My Six Years with Gorbachev*, trans. R. English and E. Tucker (University Park, Pennsylvania: Pennsylvania State University Press, 2000)

Chernyshevsky, N., *Chto Delat'?* [What Is to Be Done?] (Moscow: Klassiki Mirovoi Literatury, Feniks, 2002)

The Chronicle of Novgorod, 1016–1471, trans. R. Mitchell and N. Forbes (London: Camden Society, 1914)

Chuikov, V., *Srazhenie Veka* [The Battle of the Century] (Moscow: Izd. Sov. Rossiya, 1975)

Churchill, W., To the House of Commons, 5 November 1919, *Hansard*, Fifth Series (Commons), Volume 120

Coates, T., *The Russian Revolution, 1917* (London: The Stationery Office, 2000)

Cochran, T.B., Norris, R.S. and Bukharin, O.A., *Making the Russian Bomb: From Stalin to Yeltsin* (Oxford: Westview Press, 1985)

Cohen, A., 'Europe's Strategic Dependence on Russian Gas', *Heritage Foundation Bulletin*, 5 November 2007

Cohen, S., *Bukharin and the Bolshevik Revolution: A Political Biography, 1888–1938* (London: Wildwood House, 1974)

Conquest, R., 'Comment on Wheatcroft', *Europe–Asia Studies*, University of Glasgow, 1999, vol. 51, no. 8

Lenin (London: Fontana, 1972)

The Nation Killers (London: Macmillan, 1970)

Present Danger: Towards a Foreign Policy (Oxford: Basil Blackwell, 1979)

Stalin, Breaker of Nations (London: Weidenfeld & Nicolson, 1991)

Copeland, L., Lamm, L. and McKenna, S. (eds), *The World's Great Speeches: 292 Speeches from Pericles to Nelson Mandela*, 4th enlarged edition (New York: Dover Publications, 1999)

Courtois, S. and Panne, J.-L. 'The Comintern in Action', in M. Kramer (ed.), *The Black Book of Communism: Crimes, Terror, Repression* (Cambridge, Massachusetts: Harvard University Press, 1999)

Craig, W., *Enemy at the Gates: The Battle for Stalingrad* (New York: Penguin, 1973)

Cruse, M. and Hoogenboom, H. (trans. and eds), *The Memoirs of Catherine the Great* (New York: Modern Library, 2006)

Daniels, R. (ed.), *A Documentary History of Communism in Russia: From Lenin to Gorbachev* (Hanover, New Hampshire: University of Vermont, University Press of New England, 1993)

Davies, N., *Europe: A History* (London: Pimlico, 1997)

God's Playground: A History of Poland, Vols. 1 and 2 (Oxford: Oxford University Press, 1981)

White Eagle, Red Star: The Polish–Soviet War, 1919–1920 (London: Orbis Books, 1983)

Dawisha, K., *The Kremlin and the Prague Spring* (Berkeley: University of California Press, 1984)

Defects in Party Work and Measures for Liquidating Trotskyite and Other Double Dealers, Report to the Plenum of the Central Committee of the RKP(b), 3 March 1937 (parts 1–3 of 5), pamphlet published by the Cooperative Publishing Society of Foreign Workers in the USSR (Moscow: 1937)

de Grunwald, C., *Tsar Nicholas I* (New York: Macmillan, 1955)

de Jonge, A., *Stalin and the Shaping of the Soviet Union* (London: Collins, 1986)

Denikin, General A.I., *The Russian Turmoil: Memoirs: Military, Social and Political* (London: Hutchinson & Co., 1922)

de Plano Carpini, G., *Ystoria Mongalorum*, ed. E. Hildinger (Boston: Branden Books, 1996)

de Ségur, Comte, *Histoire de Napoléon et de la grande armée pendant l'année 1812* [History of Napoleon and of the Grand Army during the year 1812] (Brussels: Arnold Lacrosse, 1839)

de Tocqueville, A., *L'Ancien Régime et la révolution* [The Old Regime and the French Revolution] (Paris: Adamant, 2002)

Devyatov, S. and Zhilyayev, V., *Blizhnyaya Dacha Stalina* [Stalin's Near Dacha] (Moscow: 2008)

Dixon, S., *Catherine the Great* (London: Profile Books, 2010)

The Modernisation of Russia, 1676–1825 (Cambridge: Cambridge University Press 1999)

Doran, J. and Bizony, P., *Starman: The Truth behind the Legend of Yuri Gagarin* (London: Bloomsbury, 1998)

Dostoevsky, F., *Besy* [The Possessed], trans. C. Garnett (New York: The Heritage Press, 1959)

The Diary of a Writer, trans. B. Brasol (New York: Scribner, 1954)

Dubnow, S., *History of the Jews in Russia and Poland: From the Earliest Times until the Present Day*, trans. I. Friedlaender (Philadelphia: The Jewish Publication Society of America, 1916–1920)

Ebon, M., *KGB: Death and Rebirth* (Westport, Connecticut: Praeger, 1994)

Svetlana: The Story of Stalin's Daughter (New York: New American Library, 1967)

Ehrenburg, I., *Memoirs, 1921–1941* (New York: World Publishing Company, 1964)

and Grossman, V. (eds.), *The Black Book: The Ruthless Murder of Jews by German–Fascist Invaders throughout the Temporarily Occupied Regions of the Soviet Union and in the Death Camps of Poland during the War of 1941–1945*, trans. J. Glad and J. Levine (New York: Holocaust Library, 1980)

Engel, B. and Rosenthal, C. (eds.), *Five Sisters: Women Against the Tsar* (New York: Knopf, 1975)

Errera, L., *The Russian Jews: Extermination or Emancipation?*, trans. B. Loewy (London: D. Nutt, 1894)

Famine in the Soviet Ukraine, 1932–1933: A Memorial Exhibition (Cambridge, Massachusetts: Harvard University Press, 1986)

Feinstein, E., *Anna of All the Russias: The Life of Anna Akhmatova* (London: Weidenfeld & Nicolson, 2005)

Fennell, J.L.I. (ed. and trans.), *The Correspondence between A.M. Kurbsky and Ivan IV, 1564–1579* (Cambridge: Cambridge University Press, 1955)

Figes, O., *A People's Tragedy: The Russian Revolution, 1891–1924* (London: Jonathan Cape, 1996)

Fleming, P., *The Fate of Admiral Kolchak* (Edinburgh: Birlinn, 2001)

Fletcher, G., *Of the Russe Commonwealth* (1591), reprinted in facsimile (Cambridge, Massachusetts: Harvard University Press, 1966)

French, F., *Into that Silent Sea: Trailblazers of the Space Era, 1961–1965* (Lincoln: University of Nebraska Press, 2007)

Fuller, W., 'The Great Fatherland War and Late Stalinism, 1941–1953', in G. Freeze (ed.), *Russia: A History*, 2nd edition (Oxford: Oxford University Press, 2002)

Gammer, M., *The Lone Wolf and the Bear: Three Centuries of Chechen Defiance of Russian Rule* (London: C. Hurst and Co., 2006)

Garrard, J. and C., *The Bones of Berdichev: The Life and Fate of Vasily Grossman* (New York: The Free Press, 1996)

Gerovitch, S., '"New Soviet Man" Inside Machine: Human Engineering, Spacecraft Design, and the Construction of Communism', in *OSIRIS*, vol. 22, no. 1 (University of Chicago Press, 2007)

Gerstein, E., *Moscow Memoirs*, trans. J. Crowfoot (London: Harvill, 2004)

Getzler, I., *Kronstadt, 1917–1921: The Fate of a Soviet Democracy* (Cambridge: Cambridge University Press, 1983)

Gilyarovsky, V., *Sochineniya v 4-kh tomakh* (Moscow: Biblioteka Shkolnika, 1999)

Glantz, D. and House, J., *The Battle of Kursk* (London: Ian Allan Publishing, 1999)

 When Titans Clashed: How the Red Army Stopped Hitler (Lawrence, Kansas: University Press of Kansas, 1995)

Gogol, N., *Mertvye Dushi* [Dead Souls] (Moscow: Khudozhestvennaya Literatura, 1972)

Goldman, M., *Petrostate: Putin, Power and the New Russia* (Oxford: Oxford University Press, 2008)

Gorbachev, M., *The August Coup: The Truth and the Lessons* (London: HarperCollins, 1991)

 Memoirs (New York: Random House, 1997)

Gordon, A., *The History of Peter the Great, Emperor of Russia* (Aberdeen: 1755)

Gordon, P., *Passages from the Diary of General Patrick Gordon of Auchleuchries* (Aberdeen: 1859)

Gorkin, J., *L'Assassinat de Trotsky* [The Assassination of Trotsky] (Paris: Julliard, 1970)

Gorky, M., *Days with Lenin* (London: Martin Lawrence Ltd, 1952)

 Lenin the Man (Berlin: Neue Rundschau, 1924)

 Untimely Thoughts: Essays on Revolution, Culture and the Bolsheviks, 1917–1918, trans. H. Ermolaev (New York: Paul Eriksson Inc., 1968)

Gottwald, K., *Selected Speeches and Articles, 1929–1953* (Prague: Orbis, 1954)

Gribble, F., *Emperor and Mystic: The Life of Alexander I of Russia* (Montana: Kessinger, 2007)

Grossman V., 'An Everyday Stalingrad Story', in *Krasnaya Zvezda*, 20 November 1942

 'Everything Flows', trans. R. and E. Chandler, in *New York Review Books*, New York, 2009

Vasily Grossman with the Red Army, 1941–1945, ed. and trans. A. Beevor and L. Vinogradova (London: Harvill Press, 2005)

Zhizn I Sudba [Life and Fate] (Moscow: Knizhnaya Palata, 1988)

Hahlweg, W., 'Lenins Reise durch Deutschland im April 1917' [Lenin's Journey Through Germany in April 1917], in *Vierteljahrshefte für Zeitgeschichte* (Munich: 1957)

Halberstam, D., *The Coldest Winter: America and the Korean War* (New York: Hyperion, 2007)

Haugen, B., *Joseph Stalin: Dictator of the Soviet Union* (Minneapolis, Minnesota: Compass Point Books, 2006)

Heller, M., and Nekrich, A., *Utopia in Power: The History of the Soviet Union from 1917 to the Present*, trans. N. Carlos (New York: Summit Books, 1986)

Herzen, A., 'The Russian people and Socialism: A Letter to Michelet' (1851), in *The Memoirs of Alexander Herzen*, vol. IV (London: Chatto and Windus, 1968)

Kto Vinovat? [Who is to blame?] (Moscow: Khudozhestvennaya Literatura, 1969)

Sochineniya v dvukh tomakh [Works in 2 Parts] (Moscow: Izd. Khud. Lit., 1986)

Holloway, D., *Stalin and the Bomb: The Soviet Union and Atomic Energy, 1939–1956*, 2nd edn. (London: Yale University Press, 1996)

Horne, C. (ed.), *Source Records of the Great War*, vol. VI (New York: National Alumni, 1923)

Hosking, G., *Rulers and Victims: The Russians in the Soviet Union* (Cambridge, Massachusetts: The Belknap Press of Harvard University Press, 2006)

Russia: People and Empire, 1552–1917 (London: Fontana, 1997)

Russia and the Russians: A History (London: Penguin, 2001)

Hubbard, L., *The Economics of Soviet Agriculture* (London: Macmillan, 1939)

Hudson, M., *Intervention in Russia, 1918–1920: A Cautionary Tale* (Barnsley: Leo Cooper, 2004)

Hyland, P. (ed.), *The Enlightenment: A Source Book and Reader* (London: Routledge, 2003)

Ignatieff, M., *Isaiah Berlin: A Life* (New York: Metropolitan Books, 1998)

Ivan IV Sochineniya (St Petersburg: Azbuka Klassiki, 2000)

Jack, A., *Inside Putin's Russia*, revised edition (London: Granta, 2005)

Kamchatnov, A.M., *Khrestomatiya po Istorii Russkogo Yazyka (Pamyatniki X–XIV vekov)* [Sourcebook for the History of the Russian Language (Documents of the X–XIV Centuries)], (Moscow: Biblioteka Literatury Drevnei Rusi, 2009)

Karamzin, N., *Istoria Gosudarstva Rossiiskogo* [History of the Russian State] (Rostov: Rostovskoe Knizhnoe Izdatelstvo, 1990)

Karamzin's Memoir on Ancient and Modern Russia, trans. R. Pipes (New York: Atheneum, 1974)

Keenan, E., *The Kurbskii–Groznyi Apocrypha: The Seventeenth Century Genesis of the "Correspondence" Attributed to Prince A.M. Kurbskii and Tsar Ivan IV* (Cambridge, Massachusetts: Harvard University Press, 1971)

Kelly, C., *Comrade Pavlik: The Rise and Fall of a Soviet Boy Hero* (London: Granta, 2005)

Kennan, G., *The Marquis de Custine and His Russia in 1839* (New Jersey: Princeton University Press, 1971)

Khodasevich, V., *Stikhotvoreniya* [Poems] (Leningrad: Sovetsky Pisatel', 1989)

Khrushchev, N.S., *Khrushchev Remembers: The Glasnost Tapes*, trans. J.L. Schecter and V.V. Luchkov (Boston: Little, Brown and Co., 1990)

Khrushchev Remembers: The Last Testament, trans. S. Talbott (London: André Deutsch, 1974)

Memoirs of Nikita Khrushchev, Vols. 1 and 2, ed. Sergei Khrushchev (University Park, Pennsylvania: The Pennsylvania State University Press, 2006)

Khrushchev, S.N., 'The Cold War through the Looking Glass', in *American Heritage Magazine*, vol. 50, no. 6 (October 1999)

Khrushchev on Khrushchev: An Inside Account of the Man and His Era (Boston: Little, Brown and Co., 1990)

Nikita Khrushchev and the Creation of a Superpower (University Park, Pennsylvania, Pennsylvania State University, 2001)

Kiaer, C. and Naiman, E. (eds.), *Everyday Life in Early Soviet Russia: Taking the Revolution Inside* (Bloomington, Indiana: Indiana University Press, 2006)

Kirschenbaum, L., 'Scripting Revolution: Regicide in Russia', in *Left History*, 7, no. 2 (2001)

Kiselev, A.F. and Shchagin, E.M. (eds.), *Khrestomatiya po otechestvennoy istorii (1914–1945)* [Textbook on national history] (Moscow: Vlados, 1996)

Klebnikov, P., *Godfather of the Kremlin: Boris Berezovsky and the Looting of Russia* (Orlando: Harcourt, 2000)

Kleveman, L., *The New Great Game: Blood and Oil in Central Asia* (London: Atlantic Books, 2003)

Kliuchevsky, V., *Kurs Russkoi Istorii* [Course in Russian History] (Moscow: Mysl', 1995)

Kloss, B.M. (ed.), *Novgorodskaya Pervaya Letopis'* [The Novgorod Primary Chronicle] (Moscow: Biblioteka Literatury Drevnei Rusi, 2000)

Koenker, D. and Bachman, R. (eds.), *Revelations from the Russian Archives* (Washington: Library of Congress, 1997)

Koestler, A., *Darkness at Noon*, trans. D. Hardy (London: Penguin, 1983)

Kopelev, L., *The Education of a True Believer* (New York: Harper & Row, 1978)

Kostenko, V., *Na Orle v Tsushime* [On Board the Orel at Tsushima: The Memoirs of a Participant in the Russo–Japanese War of 1904–1905] (Leningrad: Sudpromgiz, 1955)

Krasnov, P., *Kartiny Bylogo Tikhogo Dona* [Scenes from the Past Times of the Quiet Don] (Moscow: 1909)

Kropotkin, P., *Memoirs of a Revolutionist* (Boston: Houghton Mifflin, 1899)

Laqueur, W., *The Long Road to Freedom: Russia and Glasnost* (New York: Collier Books, 1989)

Larina, A., *This I Cannot Forget: The Memoirs of Anna Larina, Nikolai Bukharin's Wife* (London: Pandora, 1994)

Lavrov, P., 'To the Russian Social-Revolutionary Youth', in *Izbrannye Sochineniya* (Moscow: Izd-vovses ob-va politkatorzhan, 1934)

Lekmanov, O., *Osip Mandelstam* (Moscow: Molodaya Gvardiya, 2009)

Lenin, V.I., *Biograficheskaya Khronika* [A Biographical Chronicle] (Moscow: Izd. Polit. Lit., 1973)

Collected Works, 4th English edition (Moscow: Progress Publishers, 1997)

Lermontov, M., *A Hero of Our Time*, trans. P. Longworth (New York: Signet, 1962)

Lewis, J., *Changing Direction: British Military Planning for Post-War Strategic Defence*, 2nd edition (London: Routledge, 2008)

Lidov, P., *Geroi Sovetskogo Soyuza: Zoya Anatolevna Kosmodemyanskaya* [Heroes of the Soviet Union: Zoya Anatolevna Kosmodemyanskaya] (Moscow: 1942)

Lieven, D., *The Cambridge History of Russia, Volume II: Imperial Russia, 1689–1917* (Cambridge: Cambridge University Press, 2006)

Ligachev, Y., *Inside Gorbachev's Kremlin: The Memoirs of Yegor Ligachev* (New York: Pantheon Books, 1993)

Lipkine, S., *Le Destin de Vassili Grossman* (Paris: L'Age d'Homme, 1990)

Litvinenko, A. and Felshtinsky, Y., *Blowing Up Russia: Terror from Within* (London: Gibson Square, 2007)

London, A., *On Trial*, trans. A. Hamilton (London: Macdonald, 1968)

Luthi, L., *The Sino–Soviet Split: Cold War in the Communist World* (Princeton: Princeton University Press, 2008)

Macartney, G., *An Account of Russia MDCCLXVII*, reprinted in facsimile (New York: Elibron Classics, 2005)

McAuley, M., *Bread and Justice: State and Society in Petrograd, 1917–1922* (Oxford: Clarendon Press, 1991)

McGilchrist, I., *The Master and His Emissary: The Divided Brain and the Making of the Western World* (New Haven: Yale University Press, 2009)

MacLean, F., *Eastern Approaches* (London: Penguin, 1991)

McMahon, J., *The Cold War: A Very Short Introduction* (Oxford: Oxford University Press, 2003)

McNeal, R.H., *Stalin: Man and Ruler* (New York: New York University Press, 1988)

  (ed.), *Lenin, Stalin, Khrushchev: Voices of Bolshevism* (Englewood Cliffs, New Jersey: Prentice Hall Inc., 1963)

Mandelstam, N., *Hope Abandoned: A Memoir*, trans. M. Hayward (London: Penguin, 1976)
  Hope Against Hope (New York: Modern Library, 1999)

Mandelstam, O., *Stikhotvoreniya* [Poems] (Tbilisi: Merani, 1990)

Markish, S., *Le Cas Grossman* [The Grossman Case] (Paris: Julliard, 1983)

Maryamov, G., *Kremlevskii Tsenzor* [The Kremlin Censor] (Moscow: Kinotsentr, 1992)

Maslov, Y., *The Russian Federation* (Moscow: Foreign Languages Publishing House, 1960)

Massie, R., *Nicholas and Alexandra* (New York: Tess Press, 1967)

Mayakovsky, V., *Sobranie Sochinenii 13 tomakh* (Moscow: Izd. Khudozhestvennaya Literatura, 1961)

Mazour, A., *Russia's First Revolution, 1825* (Berkeley: University of California Press, 1937)

Medvedev, R. and Medvedev, Z., *Khrushchev: The Years in Power*, trans. A. Durkin (New York: W.W. Norton & Co., 1978)

  The Unknown Stalin, trans. E. Dahrendorf (London: I.B.Tauris, 2006)

Medvedev, Z., *The Rise and Fall of T.D. Lysenko* (New York: Columbia University Press, 1969)

Medvedkov, O., *Soviet Urbanization* (London: Routledge, 1990)

Miller, R., *To Save a City: The Berlin Airlift, 1948–1949* (College Station, Texas: Texas A&M University Press, 2000)

Milward, A., *The Reconstruction of Western Europe, 1945–1951* (London: Methuen, 1984)

Molotov, V., *Molotov Remembers: Inside Kremlin Politics – Conversations with Felix Chuev* (Chicago: Ivan R. Dee, 1993)

Morrison, S., *The People's Artist: Prokofiev's Soviet Years* (Oxford: Oxford University Press, 2009)

Mosolov, A., *At the Court of the Last Tsar: Being the Memoirs of A.A. Mosolov, the Head of the Court Chancellery, 1900–1916* (London: Methuen, 1935)

Moss, W., *A History of Russia, Volume I: To 1917* (London: Anthem, 2002)

Moynahan, B., *The Russian Century: A History of the Last Hundred Years* (London: Pimlico, 1997)

Muller, J. (ed.), *Churchill's 'Iron Curtain' Speech Fifty Years Later* (Columbia, Missouri: University of Missouri Press, 1999)

Murray, D., *A Democracy of Despots* (Oxford: Westview Press, 1995)

Musmanno, M., *The Eichmann Kommandos* (London: Peter Davies, 1962)

Nabokov, V.D., 'The Memoirs of Vladimir D. Nabokov', in *V.D. Nabokov and the Provisional Government, 1917*, ed. V.D. Medlin and S.L. Parsons (New Haven: Yale University Press, 1976)

Nabokov, V.V., *Speak Memory: An Autobiography Revisited* (London: Penguin, 2000)

'A Visit to the Museum', in *The Stories of Vladimir Nabokov* (London: Penguin, 1995)

Nakaz Yekateriny II, full text included in *Imperatritsa Yekaterina II, 'O Velichii Rossii'* [The Empress Catherine II, 'On the Greatness of Russia'], (Moscow: EKsmo, 2003)

Nekrasov, N., *Komu Na Russi Zhit' Khorosho* [Who Lives Well in Russia] (Moscow: Dyetskaya Literatura, 1966)

Russkie Zhenshchiny [Russian Wives/Russian Women] (Moscow: Russkaya Klassika, 2009)

Nekrich, A., *The Punished Peoples: The Deportations and Fate of Soviet Minorities at the End of the Second World War*, trans. G. Saunders (New York: Norton & Company, 1978)

Nestor (attrib.), *Skazanie o Borise I Glebe* [The Tale of Boris and Gleb] (St Petersburg: Biblioteka Literatury Drevnei Rusi, 1997)

Obninsky, V., *Poslednii Samoderzhets, ocherk zhizni Nikolaya II* [The Last Autocrat, an outline of the life of Nicholas II] (Moscow: Respublika, 1992)

O'Clery, C., *Melting Snow: An Irishman in Moscow* (Belfast: Appletree Press, 1991)

On Trial: The Soviet State versus 'Abram Tertz' and 'Nikolai Arzhak', trans. M. Hayward (London: Harper & Row, 1966)

Pasternak, B., *Doctor Zhivago*, trans. M. Hayward and M. Harari (London: Collins Harvill, 1988)

Paustovsky, K., *Story of a Life: In That Dawn*, trans. M. Harari and M. Duncan (London: Harvill Press, 1967)

Perekrest, V., *Za chto sidit Mikhail Khodorkovsky?* [Why is Mikhail Khodorkovsky in jail?] (Moscow: Izvestiya, 2008)

Perrie, M. (ed.), *The Cambridge History of Russia, Volume I: From Early Rus' to 1689* (Cambridge: Cambridge University Press, 2006)

Perry, J., *The State of Russia under the Present Czar* (London: 1716)

Petrov, A., *Zhitie Protopopa Avvakum Im Samim Napisannoe* [The Life of the Archpriest Avvakum, Written by Himself] (Moscow: Gos. Iz. Khud. Lit., 1960)

Philips Price, M., *My Three Revolutions* (London: George Allen & Unwin Ltd., 1969)

Pipes, R., *Communism: A History of the Intellectual and Political Movement* (London: Phoenix Press, 2001)

Russia Under the Old Regime (London: Penguin, 1995)

Russian Conservatism and Its Critics: A Study in Political Culture (New Haven: Yale University Press, 2005)

Pirozhkova, A., *At His Side: The Last Years of Isaac Babel*, trans. A. Frydman and R. Busch (South Royalton, Vermont: Steerforth Press, 1996)

Pobedonostsev, K.P., *Pis'ma Pobedonostseva k Aleksandru III* [Pobedonostsev's Letters to Alexander III], 2 vols. (Moscow: Novaya Moskva, 1925–1926)

Reflections of a Russian Statesman by K.P Pobyedonostseff, trans. C.R. Long (London: Grant Richards, 1898)

Polian, P., 'Le Rapatriement des citoyens sovietiques depuis la France et les zones françaises d'occupation en Allemagne et en Autriche' [The Repatriation of Soviet Citizens from France and the French-occupied Zones in Germany and Austria'], in *Cahiers du Monde Russe*, Editions de l'Ecole des Hautes Etudes en Sciences Sociales, Paris, 41/1, janvier–mars 2000

Politkovskaya, A., *Putin's Russia*, trans. A. Tait (London: Harvill, 2004)

Popov, G., *Summoning the Spirit of General Vlasov*, trans. L. Tretyakov (New York: Vantage Press, 2009)

Porphyrogenitus, Constantine, 'Of the coming of the Russians in monoxyla from Russia to Constantinople', in *De Administrando Imperio*, ed. G. Moravcsik (Washington, DC: Dumbarton Oaks, 1966)

Povest' o Belom Klobuke [The Legend of the White Cowl] (St Petersburg: Biblioteka Literatury Drevnei Rusi, 1997)

Povest' o Razorenii Ryazani Batyem [The Tale of the Destruction of Ryazan by Baty] (St Petersburg: Biblioteka Literatury Drevnei Rusi, 1997)

Povest' Vremennykh Let [The Tale of Bygone Years] (St Petersburg: Biblioteka Literatury Drevnei Rusi, 1997)

Powers, F.G., *Operation Overflight: The U-2 Spy Pilot Tells his Story for the First Time* (London: Hodder & Stoughton Ltd, 1970)

Pushkareva, N., *Women in Russian History*, trans. E. Levin (New York: Sharpe, 1997)

Pushkin, A., *Kapitanskaya Dochka i Drugie Rasskazy* [The Captain's Daughter and other tales] (Moscow: AsT, 2007)

'Mednyi Vsadnik' [The Bronze Horseman], in *Pol. Sob. Soch. v 10 tomakh* (Leningrad: Izd. Khud. Lit., 1979)

Selected Verse (London: Penguin, 1964)

Sochineniya v 3-kh tomakh (Moscow: Khudozhestvennaya Lit., 1987)

Putin, V., *First Person: An Astonishingly Frank Self-Portrait by Russia's President Vladimir Putin*, with N. Gevorkyan, N. Timakova and A. Kolesnikov, trans. C. Fitzpatrick (London: Hutchinson, 2000)

Radzinsky, E., *Alexander II: The Last Great Czar*, trans. A Boius (New York: Freepress, 2006)

Ramet, S., *The Three Yugoslavias: State Building and Legitimation, 1918–2005* (Bloomington, Indiana: Indiana University Press, 2006)

Rapoport, Ya., *The Doctors' Plot of 1953*, trans. N. Perova and R. Bobrova (Cambridge Massachusetts: Harvard University Press, 1991)

Rappaport, H., *Josef Stalin: A Biographical Companion* (London: ABC-CLIO, 2000)

Rayfield, D. (ed.), *The Garnett Book of Russian Verse: A Treasury of Russian Poets from 1730 to 1996* (London: The Garnett Press, 2000)

Read, A., and Fisher, D., *The Deadly Embrace: Hitler, Stalin and the Nazi-Soviet Pact, 1939–1941* (London: Michael Joseph, 1988)

Reddaway W.F. (ed.), *Documents of Catherine the Great: The Correspondence with Voltaire and the Instruction of 1767* (Cambridge: Cambridge University Press, 1971)

Reed, J., *Ten Days that Shook the World* (London: Penguin, 1977)

Report of the International Commission of Inquiry: Incident in the North Sea (The Dogger Bank Case), 22 February 1905

Riasanovsky, N.V., *A History of Russia* (Oxford: Oxford University Press, 1963)

Russia and the West in the Teaching of the Slavophiles (Cambridge, Massachusetts: Harvard University Press, 1952)

Roberts, G., *Stalin's Wars: From World War to Cold War, 1939–1953* (New Haven: Yale University Press, 2006)

Robinson, J., and Beard, C. (ed.), *Readings in Modern European History* (Boston: Ginn and Co, 1908)

Romanov, N., *Dnevniki Nikolaya II, 1913–1918* [The Diaries of Nicholas II] (Moscow: Zakharov, 2007)

Rozanov, V., *Izbrannoe* [Selected Works] (Munich: Neimanis, 1970)

Rubenstein, J., 'The Night of the Murdered Poets', in *New Republic*, 25 August 1997

and Naumov, V.P. (eds.), *Stalin's Secret Pogrom: The Post-War Inquisition of the Jewish Anti-Fascist Committee*, trans. L.E. Wolfson (New Haven and London: Yale University Press, 2001)

Rubenstein, R., *Comrade Valentine: The True Story of Evno Azef the Spy – the Most Dangerous Man in Russia at the Time of the Last Czars* (New York: Harcourt, Brace & Co., 1994)

Russkiye Poeti: Antologia v 4 tomakh [Russian Poets: An Anthology in 4 volumes] (Moscow: Dyetskaya Literatura, 1968)

Sakharov, A., *Memoirs*, trans. R. Lourie (London: Hutchinson, 1990)

Sakwa, R., *Putin: Russia's Choice*, 2nd edition (Oxford: Routledge, 2008)

Sandle, M. and Bacon, E. (eds.), *Brezhnev Reconsidered* (Basingstoke: Palgrave Macmillan, 2002)

Sayers, M. and Khan, A., *The Great Conspiracy Against Soviet Russia* (New York: Boni & Gaer, 1946)

Sebag-Montefiore, S., *Potemkin: Prince of Princes* (London: Phoenix, 2004)

  Stalin: The Court of the Red Tsar (London: Weidenfeld & Nicolson, 2003)

Service, R. *Comrades: A World History of Communism* (London: Macmillan, 2007)

  A History of Twentieth-Century Russia (London: Penguin, 1997)

  Lenin: A Biography (London: Macmillan, 2000)

  Stalin: A Biography (London: Macmillan, 2004)

  Trotsky: A Biography (London: Macmillan, 2009)

Sharansky, N., *Fear No Evil: A Memoir*, trans. S. Hoffman (London: Weidenfeld & Nicolson, 1988)

Shentalinsky, V., *The KGB's Literary Archive*, trans. J. Crowfoot (London: Harvill Press, 1995)

Sheridan, C., *Russian Portraits* (Cambridge: Ian Faulkner Publishing, 1992)

Shirer, W., *The Rise and Fall of the Third Reich: A History of Nazi Germany* (New York: Simon & Schuster, 1990)

Shukman, H., *The Russian Revolution* (Stroud: Sutton, 1998)

Sillince, J., *Housing Policies in Eastern Europe and the Soviet Union* (London: Routledge, 1990)

Silverlight, J., *The Victors' Dilemma: Allied Intervention in the Russian Civil War* (London: Barrie & Jenkins Ltd, 1970)

Simonov, K., *Polnoe Sobranie Sochinenii* (Moscow: Izd. Khud Lit., 1987)

Sixsmith, M., *The Litvinenko File: Politics, Polonium and Russia's War with Itself* (London: Macmillan, 2007)

  Moscow Coup: The Death of the Soviet System (London: Simon & Schuster, 1991)

  Putin's Oil: The Yukos Affair and the Struggle for Russia (New York: Continuum, 2010)

  Slovo o Polku Igoreve [The Song of Igor's Campaign] (Moscow: Narodnaya Biblioteka, 1964)

Smith, H., *The Russians* (London: Times Books, 1976)

Smith, M., *Property of Communists: The Urban Housing Program from Stalin to Khrushchev* (Chicago: Northern Illinois University Press, 2010)

Soldatov, A. and Borogan, I., *The New Nobility: The Restoration of Russia's Security State and the Enduring Legacy of the KGB* (New York: Perseus, 2010)

Soloviev, S.M., *Istoria Rossii s Drevneishikh Vremen* (Moscow: Golos, 1993)

Solzhenitsyn, A., *August 1914*, trans. H. Willetts (London: Penguin, 1990)

  Gulag Archipelago, 1918–1956: An Experiment in Literary Investigation, Part I, trans. T. Whitney (London: Collins Harvill, 1974, and New York: Harper & Row, 1975)

  Gulag Archipelago, 1918–1956: An Experiment in Literary Investigation, Part V, trans. H.T. Willetts (London: Collins Harvill, 1978)

  Lenin in Zurich, trans. H.T. Willetts (New York: Farrar, Straus & Giroux, 1976)

  Letter to Soviet Leaders, trans. H. Sternberg (London: Collins Harvill, 1974)

Speransky, M.M., *Proekty i Zapiski* [Projects and Notes] (Moscow– Leningrad: Izd. Akademiya Nauk SSSR, 1961)

Stalin, J., *O Velikoi Otechestvennoi Voine Sovetskogo Soyuza* [On the Great Patriotic War of the Soviet Union] (Moscow: Gospolitizdat, 1950)

  Problems of Leninism (Peking: Foreign Languages Press, 1976)

  Works (Moscow: Foreign Languages Publishing House, 1954)

The Stalin–Kaganovich Correspondence, 1931–1936, ed. R.W. Davies, O.V. Khlevniuk and E.A. Rees (New Haven & London: Yale University Press, 2003)

Stettinius Jr., E., *Roosevelt and the Russians: The Yalta Conference* (New York: Doubleday, 1949)

Suny, G., *The Soviet Experiment: Russia, the USSR and the Successor States* (Oxford: Oxford University Press, 1998)

Suny, G. (ed.), *The Cambridge History of Russia, Volume III: The Twentieth Century* (Cambridge: Cambridge University Press, 2006)

Suvorin, A.S. (ed.), *Zapiski Imperatritsy Yekateriny II* [The Writings of the Empress Catherine II] (St Petersburg: 1907)

Szamuely, T., *The Russian Tradition* (London: McGraw-Hill, 1974)

Taubman, W., *Khrushchev: The Man and His Era* (London: Free Press, 2003)

Taylor, S., *Stalin's Apologist: Walter Duranty, the New York Times' Man in Moscow* (Oxford: Oxford University Press, 1990)

Teplyakov, Yu., 'Stalin's war against his own troops: The tragic fate of Soviet prisoners of war in German captivity', in *The Journal of Historical Review*, vol. 14, no. 4, July–August 1994

Thatcher, I., *Trotsky* (London: Routledge, 2002)

Thatcher, M., *The Downing Street Years* (London: HarperCollins, 1993)

Tkachev, P., *Zadachi Revolutsionnoi Propagandy v Rossii* [The Tasks of Revolutionary Propaganda in Russia], April 1874

Tolstoy, L.N., *A Confession*, trans. A. Briggs (London: Hesperus, 2010)

Hadji Murat (Moscow: Khudozhestvennaya Literatura, 1969)

'Ne Mogu Molchat' [I Cannot Remain Silent], in *Sobranie Sochinenii v 20 tomakh*, vol. 14 (Moscow: 1960)

War and Peace, trans. R. Edmonds (London: Penguin, 1957)

Tompson, W., *Khrushchev: A Political Life* (New York: St Martin's Press, 1997)

Trotsky, L., *1905*, trans. A. Bostock (London: Penguin, 1972)

My Life: An Attempt at an Autobiography (London: Penguin, 1979)

Truscott, P., *Putin's Progress: A Biography of Russia's Enigmatic President* (London: Simon & Schuster, 2004)

Tsvetaeva, M., *Selected Poems*, trans. E. Feinstein (London: Carcanet, 1999)

Selected Poems, trans. D. McDuff (Newcastle: Bloodaxe Books, 1987)

Stikhotvoreniya [Poems] (Moscow: Khudozhestvennaya Literatura, 1989)

Tucker, R., *Stalin in Power* (New York: Norton, 1990)

Tyutchev, F.I., *Stikhotvoreniya* [Poems] (Moscow: Khudozhestvennaya Literatura, 1972)

Vaksberg, A., *Vishinski: Le Procureur de Staline, les grands procès de Moscou* [Vyshinsky, Stalin's Prosecutor: the Great Moscow Trials] (Paris: Albin Michel, 1991)

Valentinov, N., *Encounters with Lenin*, trans. P. Rosta and B. Pearce (London: Oxford University Press, 1968)

Vernadsky, G., *Kievan Rus* (New Haven: Yale University Press, 1973)

Viola, L., *Peasant Rebels under Stalin* (Oxford: Oxford University Press, 1996)

Volkogonov, D., *The Rise and Fall of the Soviet Empire: Political Leaders from Lenin to Gorbachev*, trans. H. Shukman (London: HarperCollins, 1998)

Stalin: Triumph and Tragedy, trans. H. Shukman (London: Weidenfeld & Nicolson, 1991)

Trotsky: The Eternal Revolutionary, trans. H. Shukman (London: HarperCollins, 1996)

Volkov, S. (ed.), *Testimony: The Memoirs of Dmitri Shostakovich*, trans. A. Bouis (New York: Harper & Row, 1979)

Waliszewski, K., *Peter the Great: His Life and Work* (London: Forgotten Books, 2010)

Walsh, W., *Readings in Russian History* (Syracuse: Syracuse University Press, 1948)

Wehrmeyer, A., *Rakhmaninov* (London: Haus Publishing, 2004)

Wilton, R., *The Last Days of the Romanovs* (London: Legion, 1920)

Witte, S., *The Memoirs of Count Witte*, trans. A. Yarmolinsky (Garden City, New York: Doubleday, Page & Co., 1921)

Wrangel, A., *General Wrangel, 1878–1929: Russia's White Crusader* (London: Leo Cooper, 1990)

Yeltsin, B., *Against the Grain: An Autobiography*, trans. M. Glenny (London: Jonathan Cape, 1990)

Midnight Diaries (London: Weidenfeld & Nicolson, 2000)

Yesenin, C., *Sochineniya* [Works] (Moscow: Khudozhestvennaya Literatura, 1988)

Yevtushenko, Y., *Don't Die Before You're Dead*, trans. A. Bouis (New York: Random House, 1995)

'Kazn' Sten'ki Razina' [The Execution of Stenka Razin], in *Izbrannoe: Stikhotvoreniya i Poemy* (Rostov: Vsemirnaya Biblioteka Poeta, 1997)

A Precocious Autobiography (New York: Dutton, 1963)

'Stantsiya Zima' [Zima Junction], in *Izbrannoe: Stikhotvoreniya i Poemy* (Rostov: Vsemirnaya Biblioteka Poeta, 1997)

Yusupov, F., *Lost Splendor: The Amazing Memoirs of the Man Who Killed Rasputin*, trans. A. Green and N. Katkov (New York: Helen Marx Books, 2003)

Zadonshchina [Beyond the Don] (St Petersburg: Biblioteka Literatury Drevnei Rusi, 1997)

Zamyatin, Y., *We*, trans. B.G. Guerney (London: Penguin, 1972)

Zenkovsky, S. (ed. and trans.), *Medieval Russia's Epics, Chronicles and Tales* (New York: Dutton, 1963)

INTERVIEWS AND ARCHIVE RECORDINGS

Author's interviews with: Boris Yeltsin (1989), Mikhail Gorbachev (1989 and 1992), Alexander Yakovlev (1990), Gennady Yanayev (1991), Eduard Shevardnadze (1991), Vladimir Zhirinovsky (1990), Sergei Stankevich (1988), Gavriil Popov (1988), Bill Clinton (1992), George Bush Senior (1994), George Bush Junior (1994), Henry Kissinger (1993), Margaret Thatcher (1987 and 1989), John Major (1992), Sergei Khrushchev (1990), Yevgeny Pasternak, Irina Shostakovich, Sviatoslav Prokofiev, Tikhon Khrennikov (all 2006), Dmitry Peskov (2007), Stanislav Belkovsky and Yevgeny Yevtushenko (2008)

BBC archive interviews with: Sir Philip Gibbs, Dr E.M. Herbert, Malcolm Muggeridge, Vladimir Nabokov, Harry Young

PBS radio recordings: Vladimir Yerofeyev; Tatiana Fyodorova interviewed for *People's Century*

INDEX

Entries in *italics* denote maps.

PICTURE CREDITS

BBC Books would like to thank the following individuals and organisations for providing photographs and for permission to reproduce copyright material. While every effort has been made to trace and acknowledge copyright holders, we would like to apologise should there be any errors or omissions.

Abbreviations: *t* top, b bottom, *l* left, *r* right, *c* centre, *bl* bottom left, *br* bottom right, *tl* top left, *tr* top right.

Plate 1: 1*b* MOSFILM/The Kobal Collection; 2*b* State Russian Museum, St. Petersburg, Russia/The Bridgeman Art Library; 3*t* Tretyakov Gallery, Moscow, Russia/The Bridgeman Art Library; 3*c* Clive Barda/ArenaPAL; 4*tl* Hamburger Kunsthalle, Hamburg, Germany/The Bridgeman Art Library; 4*tr* Hermitage, St. Petersburg, Russia/The Bridgeman Art Library; 4*b* Borodino, Mozhaysky, Moscow Oblast, Russia/The Bridgeman Art Library; 5*t* Private Collection/Archives Charmet/The Bridgeman Art Library; 5*b* Tretyakov Gallery, Moscow, Russia/ The Bridgeman Art Library; 6*tl* Tretyakov Gallery, Moscow, Russia/The Bridgeman Art Library; 7*t* Topfoto; 7*c* Getty Images; 7*b* Private Collection/The Bridgeman Art Library; 8*tl* Topfoto; 8*tr* Topfoto.

Plate 2: 1*t* RIA Novosti; 1*b* The Print Collector/Alamy; 2*t* Mary Evans Picture Library/Alamy; 2*c* Pictorial Press Ltd/Alamy; 2*b* The Gallery Collection/Corbis; 3*tl* Mary Evans Picture Library / Alamy; 3*b* Hulton-Deutsch Collection/CORBIS; 4*tl* World History Archive/Alamy; 4*tr* RIA Novosti/Alamy; 4*b* RIA Novosti; 5*tl* Photos 12/Alamy; 5*tc* Mary Evans Picture Library/Alamy; 5*tr* Lebrecht Music and Arts Photo Library/Alamy; 5*cl* ITAR-TASS Photo Agency/Alamy; 5*c* Archive Pics/Alamy; 5*cr* Lebrecht Music and Arts Photo Library/Alamy; 5*bl* INTERFOTO/Alamy; 5*bc* Lebrecht Music and Arts Photo Library/Alamy; 5*br* ITAR-TASS Photo Agency/ Alamy; 6*t* Getty Images; 6*b* Gamma-Keystone/Getty Images; 7*t* Corbis; 7*c* Bettmann/Corbis; 7*b* Yevgeny Khaldei/Corbis; 8*t* Pictorial Press Ltd/Alamy; 8*b* ITAR-TASS Photo Agency.

Plate 3: 1*t* Topfoto; 1*b* Topfoto; 2*t* RIA Novosti/Alamy; 2*b* AF archive/Alamy; 3*t* Tim Graham/Alamy; 3*b* RIA Novosti; 4*t* RIA Novosti; 4*b* ITAR-TASS Photo Agency/Alamy; 5*t* RIA Novosti; 6*t* RIA Novosti; 6*c* RIA Novosti; 6*b* ITAR-TASS Photo Agency/Alamy; 7*t* Alexander Zemlianichenko/AP/PA; 7*c* Getty Images; 7*b* vario images GmbH & Co.KG/Alamy; 8*t* P-59 Photos/Alamy.